CONSUMER BEHAVIOR

CONSUMER BEHAVIOR

Fourth Edition

James F. Engel
Wheaton College

Roger D. Blackwell
The Ohio State University

The Dryden Press
Chicago   New York   Philadelphia   San Francisco   Montreal   Toronto
London   Sydney   Tokyo   Mexico City   Rio de Janeiro   Madrid

Acquisitions Editor: Anne Elizabeth Smith
Project Editor: Kathy Richmond
Design Director: Alan Wendt
Production Manager: Mary Jarvis
Cover and text design by Alan Wendt
Copy editing by Ruth Henoch
Index by Wanda Giles, Naples Editing Services
Permissions by Nel Stryk, Naples Editing Services

Address orders to:
383 Madison Avenue
New York, New York 10017

Address editorial correspondence to:
901 North Elm Street
Hinsdale, Illinois 60521

Library of Congress Catalog Number 81-67232
ISBN: 0-03-059242-9
Printed in the United States of America
234-144-987654321

CBS College Publishing
The Dryden Press
Holt, Rinehart and Winston
Saunders College Publishing

PREFACE

In 1965, Roger Blackwell and David Kollat joined James Engel at The Ohio State University in developing an academic program in a field that soon became very popular—consumer behavior. At that time, there were no texts on the subject, and existing writings dealt only with isolated topics. It soon became apparent that a textbook was needed to give this field shape and direction. Some of those who helped the most to develop our original text now are productive contributors to the field of consumer behavior. A review of the footnotes and references of this text will reveal the impact of Larry Light, Brian Sternthal, Orville Walker, Samuel Craig, Beverlee Anderson, and Philip Kuehl, among others.

The Dryden Press published the first edition in 1968. Subsequent editions appeared in 1973 and 1978, which included the rapid changes that were appearing in the field.

Probably because we were the first to publish, *Consumer Behavior* is regarded as the standard against which others are measured.[1] In one sense, we are humbled and gratified by this, because it makes the year of hard work worthwhile. But, in another sense, we are intimidated, because it is a tall order even to keep up with this changing field today, let alone achieve any kind of leadership. Leadership demands frequent revision accompanied by concentrated effort to stay on top of what is happening simultaneously in many arenas. All kinds of specializations have emerged—information processing, multi-attribute models, involvement theory, and others—and as a result, each successive revision becomes more difficult to write.

When planning this edition, we reluctantly faced the fact that the EKB team could not stay together forever. Two of us left Ohio State in 1972, but we tried our best to meet the constant pressure for revision. Inevitably, the old gang broke up. David Kollat dropped out because of job responsibilities and professional interests, but our close friendship and

[1]See Carol A. Scott's review of six texts in *Journal of Marketing,* vol. 45 (Winter 1981), 160-161 and Harold H. Kassarjian, "Presentation of the ACR Award: 'Fellow in Consumer Behavior' to John A. Howard and James F. Engel," in Kent B. Monroe (ed.), *Advances in Consumer Research,* vol. 8 (Ann Arbor, Mich.: Association for Consumer Research, 1981); 7-8.

partnership always will be intact. EKB now has become EB, although much of David's work still remains in this book.

Given the plethora of books on consumer behavior, we have done our best to stick with the purposes that guided the three previous editions:

1. To explore and evaluate a growing body of published and unpublished research.

2. To advance generalizations and propositions from this evidence when possible.

3. To assess the practical implications of what has been learned.

4. To pinpoint areas where research is lacking.

Because of our backgrounds and interests, our primary perspective is marketing. This is also true of the great majority of published literature in the field. Students of consumer behavior who have differing perspectives, however, will find much of value here because we have attempted to assume a broader viewpoint whenever possible.

Besides updating and refining the text, the fourth edition has incorporated several changes in structure and content.

1. The writing is much easier to read and teach.

2. There are more examples of managerial application in each of the six parts.

3. This edition restores the emphasis on learning by adding a new chapter on consumer learning, Chapter 8. It also includes new information on consumer behavior modifications.

4. While other consumer education literature only mentions the low-involvement model, we've taken a major step by adding a low-involvement model to the text.

5. Marketing examples and statistics from other countries have been added where appropriate so that students are given a more global view of the field.

6. This edition is more future-oriented in terms of demographics and social trends than the previous editions.

We have always used a model of consumer behavior as our basic method of exposition. This has come to be known as the EKB model. We think a model is important because it provides a structure for learning and research. While the basic model in this edition bears only a scant resemblance to its 1968 version, it has only minor changes from the 1978 version. What is new is the distinction between high-involvement behavior and low-involvement behavior. They are radically different. We are using these two models for the first time. The earlier EKB model emphasized high-involvement behavior, and that limitation had to be remedied. Now those who refer to this book may have to designate between EKB$_1$ and EKB$_2$. Students who are interested in model development, quantification, and the ways in which various conceptualizations are similar and different can refer to the appendix at the end of the book for a brief technical discussion.

Many people helped with this edition, but two deserve special mention. We are especially grateful to Paul W. Miniard of The Ohio State University, who meticulously examined all the last edition and provided detailed suggestions. The senior author's colleague at Wheaton Graduate School, Laura K. Horton, has helped significantly by providing much encouragement and support. She also has aided in revising the *Instructor's Manual.*

We gratefully acknowledge the comments and suggestions of those who have used the first three editions. While we have not always made the suggested changes, we have always taken seriously what they've told us. Our thanks to Rohit Deshpande, University of Texas; David Gardner, University of Illinois; Paul Green, University of Pennsylvania; Harold Kassarjian, University of California, Los Angeles; and Robert Woodruff, University of Tennessee; for their help. Others who have helped in various ways include Tom Murnane, Jeanne Sheppard, Theresa Woodward, Reginald Monah, students at Ohio State, and our colleagues J. Paul Peter, W. Wayne Talarzyk, and Wesley Johnston from Ohio State. We also want to express special appreciation to the Management Horizons staff for use of its excellent library facilities and the staff's overall cooperation. Special appreciation goes to William R. Davidson, Cyrus Wilson, and Dan Sweeney, all from Management Horizons, for all they have done. Finally, Wayne Stayskal of the *Chicago Tribune* contributed much with his delightful cartoons, and Katey Downs typed accurately and rapidly for us.

We know that writers traditionally acknowledge their families in the preface. But our acknowledgement goes far beyond writers' tradition and reflects truly what our wives, Sharon and Ann, and our children mean to us.

James F. Engel   Wheaton, Illinois
Roger D. Blackwell   Columbus, Ohio

CONTENTS

APPENDIX   MODELS OF CONSUMER BEHAVIOR: FORMALIZATION AND QUANTIFICATION

PART ONE

INTRODUCTION AND OVERVIEW

What is consumer behavior all about? Is it a legitimate subject of inquiry? Why should it receive emphasis as a separate area of study within the general field of marketing? These and many other questions are considered in this introduction, which serves as a framework of concepts around which subsequent parts of the text are built.

Of particular significance is Chapter 2, which presents diagrammatic models of consumer motivation and behavior. Models of this type are indispensable for showing how various elements fit together to shape behavior. Each model begins with inputs of various types from the environment and ends with the consequences of a terminal act such as a purchase. All intervening steps and processes are clearly designated so that the relation of each to the whole becomes apparent. It is important that the chapter be given considerable critical emphasis, since the models presented here are followed step by step in subsequent chapters of the book.

CHAPTER 1

UNDERSTANDING THE CONSUMER

Picture yourself in the boardroom of one of the "big three" automobile manufacturers on a cold wintry day in Detroit late in 1974.[1] Among those present to plan future strategy were: the Chairman of the Board; the Vice-presidents of Finance, Production, and Marketing; and a senior representative of the company's primary advertising agency. Also present but almost overlooked was the company's Director of Marketing Research (Figure 1.1).

The Chairman began, "Gentlemen, these are the best of times. This has been one of our greatest years. We have successfully introduced the *Flipper* (a small, inexpensive subcompact), and sales and profits from our full-size and intermediate lines have never been better."

Al Knudsen, Vice-President of marketing, added, "The imports' current share is holding under 20 percent, and I don't expect it to increase. We're outdoing the imports all down the line now."

"You bet," echoed George Latta, Vice-President of Production. "Anyone buying one of those tinny junkers now will come back to American quality soon enough."

"I wonder about that quality bit, George," Al Knudsen said. "We're getting lots of dealer complaints. Cars are coming back for repair while they're still under warranty. Some of the owners seem to be pretty mad."

"Let them be mad," Latta replied. "Our production lines have to run at more than 100 cars per hour if we are to make the budget. Do you know how much it costs to stop the line and fix something? Also, the union has my hands tied. Those guys don't seem to care what they produce."

"Do what you can, George," the Chairman said, moving on to the real issue of the day. "Gentlemen, all signs point to what we knew all along—the American buyer is returning to the big car. We are going to

---

[1]While this scenario is fictitious, it reflects the insights of many who analyzed the industry during this period. See Jack Givens, "Automobile Industry, Heal Thyself," *Advertising Age* (September 29, 1980), S-32 and S-33; "U.S. Autos Losing a Big Segment of the Market—Forever?" *Business Week* (March 24, 1980), 78 +; "Detroit's New Sales Pitch. Is it on the Right Road?" *Business Week* (September 22, 1980), 78 +; and Jack Honomichl, "Consumer Signals: Why U.S. Auto Makers Ignored Them," *Advertising Age* (August 4, 1980), 43–48.

**Figure 1.1
Detroit's
Marketing
Concept: A
Lesson in How *Not*
To Do It**

Source: Courtesy of Wayne
Stayskal.

increase production of the full-size and intermediates for the next few years. We'll have the Z-car coming on line about 1980 if we need a front-wheel drive model, but I say let's make hay while the sun shines."

Tom England, Vice-President of Finance, agreed. "We will average $1000 profit on each large car, compared with just $250 for each *Flipper* we sell. We'd be crazy not to push the big cars, and the dealers sure agree. Last year they averaged 25 percent markup on the big cars and only 15 percent on the *Flipper.*"

"Johnson, can the agency deliver the goods if we up our advertising for the intermediates and full-size models?" The agency rep's reply was quick and positive. "Of course, Mr. Chairman, the more you want to spend the more we can do."

"Then it's agreed that we accept the marketing plan," stated the Chairman. To his surprise, Dr. Burton Thorne, Director of Marketing Research, disagreed. "Maybe we should rethink this a bit. Our surveys show that only 15 percent of those customers now buying *Flippers* say they will buy another one. Most say they will turn to an import next time. Also, a growing number of people in our target market are saying the imports are beating us and others in Detroit in overall quality, attention to detail, maneuverability, operating economy and overall performance. I guess what disturbs me most is that 43 percent of those living in Marin County, California, are now planning to buy an import. We have always found that to be a bellwether county for predicting future sales."

"Marin County?" George Latta laughed. "Isn't that where a bunch of wierdos live across the bay from San Francisco? What else would you expect from them? Come on, Thorne, pull your head out of your printouts and face reality. All the imports offer is small size and low price, and the *Flipper* will beat them on all counts. I say, let's go ahead." Everyone agreed, and the meeting ended.

When the same group met again in early 1979, there was just one change. Dr. Thorne had been "retired" to a business school. His successor, Carol Martin, took her place at the table, prepared to "do battle."

The Chairman opened the meeting with his usual remarks. "Gentlemen and lady," bowing to Carol, "our predictions have been on the money. The American love affair with the large car has not ended. In fact, it may be in its heyday."

"Agreed," added Al Knudsen. "We've been too afraid of the imports. Their share has only grown to 22 percent, and none of their lines is selling well now. In fact, the *Flipper* isn't moving much either. Our biggest problem is that we can't get full-sized and intermediates to the dealers as fast as the buyers want them. What's wrong with production, Latta?"

Latta replied defensively. "Lay off, Buster. The problem is that Z-car we're supposed to introduce next year. How can I get more V-8 engines when the East Overshoe plant is gearing up for that four-cylinder job no one will want, anyway? Why don't we just hold that thing off for awhile?"

Before anyone could reply, Carol Martin asked, "Gentlemen, may I have a turn?" For the next 30 minutes she reviewed the results of a study done in 1978 and 1979 by the Motor and Equipment Manufacturers Association based on 10,000 consumer interviews. The results showed widespread agreement that the imports were perceived to lead in fuel economy, engineering, styling, and durability. All of these factors were stated to be important in a purchase decision. "I would say that the upswing in demand for the larger models is only temporary. We are seeing clear signs of a growing desire for better quality products that can match what the imports are giving. It wouldn't surprise me if their share is 30 percent or more by 1981. The best thing we can do now is to step up the production schedule for the Z-car so we can stay competitive."

There was a momentary pause and then a sarcastic response from Tom England. "So you would like us to spend even more cash tooling up for something that may never be needed? That makes no financial sense at all. I say let's delay the introduction date of the Z-car and cut initial production levels from 200,000 to 100,000 units. What George says about making V-8s is right on target."

"Then it's agreed," concluded the Chairman. "Let's get back to doing what we understand best and not worry about those imports. We will push back the Z-car as recommended and switch East Overshoe back to V-8s. Also, we'll put more heat on Washington to call off those stupid gas mileage requirements."

The Resulting Automobile Market Debacle

If the same group had met again in December, 1980, there would have been many new faces. Only Carol Martin and Dr. Thorne (now a consultant) deserved to appear. Their clear research-based warnings went unheeded.

In just one year, the American automobile industry had faced its greatest catastrophe. Over 200,000 workers were unemployed at the peak. Plants were closed, corporate losses hit an all-time high, and, most important, the market share of imports approached the 30 percent level. Quite predictably, some managements blamed these troubles on continuing world crises, competition by foreign companies, poor worker productivity, and unreasonable government safety and mileage requirements. Few administrators faced the obvious root cause as clearly as did Jack Givens, Director of Sales Operations at Chrysler:

. . . what the Japanese do is find out what we Americans want. And then they build those features and value into their cars. And then they price them wherever they have to be priced. . . Today, the import cars provide the primary source of individual expression and the primary success symbol among a broad spectrum of car owners . . . Their cars offer the ambiance, the practicality and the operating economy that Americans want. People are buying imports today because they like them, because they're right for the times. And any other excuse we use for their success just isn't worth a damn.[2]

Givens went on to state that all of this was clearly evident to any sensitive observer. *All of the cataclysmic consequences could have been prevented had the consumer been taken seriously.*

A Defective Understanding of the Consumer

The executives in the scenario described above made a dangerous assumption—*they believed that the consumer will respond to the product or service offered as long as it is backed with sufficient selling firepower.* That assumption can be false.

For example, the Polaroid Corporation recently took a $68-million write-down on a new product, *Pola-Vision.*[3] In the past, chief executive Dr. Edwin Land relied solely on his inventive genius to build a $1.2-billion business. Most of the time, his intuition paid off handsomely, but this time market research could have discovered the reason for consumer disinterest. Home movies never have attained the popularity levels of still photography because the benefits offered in no way compensated for the cost of equipment and film. Nonetheless, Polaroid introduced an instant movie camera complete with a small viewer for $675 and accompanying two-minute film cartridges costing $9.95. The home-movie product never attracted consumers, despite heavy promotion.

Similarly, the Amstar Corporation introduced *Domino Liquid Brown Sugar* in 1978. The company spent over $1 million in consumer advertising in confident expectation that the product would capture at least a 12 percent share of the total market.[4] This success never materialized, because most consumers considered the benefits of the liquid form (no lumps and lower cost per unit used) to be of little importance.

---

[2]Givens, "Automobile Industry, Heal Thyself," S-33.
[3]"Polaroid's Land Steps Down," *Time* (March 17, 1980), 68.
[4]Leah Rozen, "What Happened to Liquid Sugar?" *Advertising Age* (May 26, 1980), 3+.

Mennen E was another unsuccessful product.[5] It was launched with a $12 million advertising campaign, expected to become a leader in the $475 million deodorant product category. The substitution of Vitamin E for harsh germicides was lauded as the first deodorant breakthrough in 25 years. Nevertheless, the product failed miserably because most potential users believed Vitamin E was an unimportant addition.

These stories are all examples of the theory that the consumer is little more than a pawn to be moved by the manufacturer. In an extension of this theory, emphasis is placed on *production* with little regard for market forces. In reality, the consumer is sovereign, deciding whether to accept or reject a product on the basis of whether or not it meets perceived needs and desires. This simple and obvious point should be apparent to any observer. Unfortunately, the truth still has not fully penetrated the citadels of business. More than one-half of all new products introduced each year ultimately fail because of management's defective understanding of demand forces.

"Right Thinking" about the Consumer

The above examples illustrate the consequences of disregarding consumer demand, but notice the difference consumer research made in the following case histories.

Pantyhose sales boomed in the late 1960s and early 1970s because most young women were wearing miniskirts. During that period, Hanes Hosiery emerged as a market leader with its *L'eggs* brand. But before long women began wearing slacks and switched from pantyhose to knee-high stockings or no hosiery at all. When other manufacturers abandoned the slacks-wearing market, Hanes introduced an entirely new pantyhose concept, *Underalls.*[6]

In 1974, the company initiated market research to determine if slack wearers might use some type of pantyhose to improve their appearance. As yet, no such product had been produced. Various concepts were tested with small focus groups, each one offering a different potential benefit. The concept of a cooler, slim/smooth look in the form of built-in underpants generated great interest. Further research demonstrated the central importance of appearance—panty lines disappearing under slacks and dresses. Five months of test marketing in Orlando, Florida, generated a 24 percent share of the department-store market. Similar results were achieved when the product was introduced nationally, spawning a number of imitators—the ultimate evidence of true marketing success. The key? Consumer research.

Consumer research also opened the door to the mouth-care market which historically has been difficult to penetrate because of long domination by *Crest, Colgate,* and *Gleem.* Research indicated that not everyone was satisfied with these alternatives and that a niche could be

---

[5]Theodore G. N. Chin, "New Product Success and Failures—How to Detect Them in Advance," *Advertising Age* (September 24, 1973), 61.

[6]"Underalls' Success Due to 'Flanking Strategy,' Product Idea, Positioning," *Marketing News* (November 14, 1980), 11.

gained for a new product that offered better taste for children, a gel formula for fast spreading on the brush, bright color, and stannous fluoride.[7] *Aim* toothpaste was designed to meet these desires, and it has gained a profitable share of the market with its slogan "Take Aim against cavities."

Finally, a product that goes from nothing to $70 million in sales in one year is doing something right. General Mills' *Hamburger Helper* was perceived as a real timesaving boon by the busy homemaker. The benefits that generated such a response are: "Help for five. One pan, one pound of hamburger, and one package of Hamburger Helper change hamburger into a real dinner dish for a family of five."[8]

These product examples succeeded in the market because each offered attributes perceived by consumers as being pertinent to felt needs and desires. Furthermore, success was the outcome of "right thinking" about the consumer by members of management. The following three premises are foundational.

The Consumer Is Sovereign

The consumer, as a rule, is purposeful and goal-oriented. Behavior always has a reason, even though it may appear to be illogical or even irrational to an observer. The key to understanding is to avoid judgment and to accept these behavioral determinants as they are, attempting where possible to present realistic choice alternatives through the products and services which are offered.

Furthermore, each individual has full ability to "see and hear whatever he or she wants to see and hear." This basic premise will be amplified and defended in later chapters. It is important because information from advertising and selling is processed *selectively,* and that which is felt not to be pertinent is ignored, disregarded, or forgotten. In other words, the consumer is not an unthinking robot as some marketers apparently assume. Although most of those involved would emphatically deny it, faulty thinking on this sensitive point probably is the underlying reason for the types of managerial decisions leading to product failure.

Consumer Motivation and Behavior Can Be Understood through Research

Consumer behavior is a process, of which the purchase is only one stage. There are many underlying influences, both internal and external, from the social environment. The combination of these inputs and internal factors can be complex indeed. Yet, the tools of marketing research can assess motivation and behavior with considerable accuracy. Perfect prediction of behavior never is possible, but properly designed research efforts can significantly lower the risks of the types of product failure cited above.

---

[7]Kenneth Roman and Jane Maas, *How to Advertise* (New York: St. Martin's Press, 1976), 7.
[8]Chin, 62.

Consumer Motivation and Behavior Can Be Influenced

While the consumer cannot knowingly be induced to act in a way contradictory to his or her own goals or purposes, motivation and behavior can be influenced by outside sources. This influence is not successful, however, unless motivational factors are understood through research and correctly adapted to the product offered, price, distribution, and promotion. In other words, the total marketing offering must be designed so that the consumer perceives its features as providing an answer to a perceived problem and felt needs. The product successes cited above are good illustrations of the real meaning of creative adaptation to a rapidly changing consumer environment, whereas the failures demonstrate what can happen when this principle is disregarded for one reason or another.

Consumer influence and persuasion in the context discussed here is a socially legitimate activity. Note that the consumer, in effect, sets the agenda for the whole process. The influence process becomes unethical, however, if anything is done to interfere with free choice through intentional deception or distortion or through the exercise of monopoly power. Unfortunately, abuses are sufficiently common and flagrant that consumer protection legislation and education play an increasingly significant role. Much more is said on this point throughout the book.

THE ECONOMIC AND SOCIAL ROLE FOR CONSUMER RESEARCH

Any observer of the contemporary world scene very quickly will come to an obvious conclusion: selling, buying, and consuming lie at the very core of life in most developed countries. Over $30 billion is spent on advertising in the United States alone. The ultimate target of all this activity is a person known as a consumer, who must wade through the flood of competing products and the myriad of frequently contradictory advertising and selling claims. What kind of person is this consumer? What determines motivation and behavior in the marketplace? These questions and others define the subject matter of consumer behavior as viewed in this book—*those acts of individuals directly involved in obtaining and using economic goods and services, including the decision processes that precede and determine these acts.*

Why should the consumer be singled out as a topic for such intensive study? One answer might be simply to provide greater understanding about an important component of general human behavior. More direct reasons exist, however. The most obvious has already been demonstrated—consumer research is an indispensable input to marketing-management decisions. But, of equal importance, growing attention is now being paid to the important issue of consumer protection. This is the essential motivation for increased governmental regulation and for burgeoning interest in consumer education. Furthermore, consumer research serves as essential input for general public policy decisions.

Finally, this whole subject matter has grown into a noteworthy academic discipline.

Consumer Behavior and Marketing Management

Three major types of strategic issues present the greatest challenge to marketing management: (1) evaluating new market opportunities; (2) brand shifting; and (3) increasing the effectiveness of marketing strategy and tactics.

Evaluating New Market Opportunities

Free-enterprise Western economies are based on a pervasive and fundamental premise that *a high and rising standard of living is both necessary and desirable.* As we will stress later, this belief can have some decidedly unfortunate long-run social and economic consequences. Nonetheless, it prevails and shows no signs of diminishing. Therefore, continued new-product introduction and innovation are an absolute necessity if most firms are to survive. Success lies in management's ability to detect and respond to unmet consumer needs and to evaluate whether or not an economically viable opportunity exists.

The ability to succeed in a highly competitive market environment resides to a large degree in sensitive consumer research accompanied by sufficient ingenuity and marketing skill to capitalize upon the opportunities presented. For example, a recent survey conducted by the Benjamin Company on the subject of meal planning and cooking concluded that nutrition is the central factor. More specifically, there will be a growing demand for ". . . foods in their natural form without preservatives or other additives."[9] Seizing this opportunity, the Nestlé Company is introducing a line of 30 food items under the name *New Cookery*. They are deliberately positioned not to compete with the H. J. Heinz *Weight Watchers* line and others designed to attract dieters. Rather, these products all are low in fat, starch, and sugar; and they will be marketed to those who are trying to maintain and improve their health and nutrition.

In this example, the Nestlé Company is pursuing a strategy of market segmentation. The challenge of market segmentation is to uncover groups of people whose preferences are sufficiently similar to each other, yet different from others, so as to justify product introductions or modifications to meet the preferences of that group. Those concerned about health and nutrition constitute a large and growing segment and hence warrant the response of such giants as Nestlé. Notice that consumer wants and preferences are taken seriously as *the starting point* of all product and marketing decisions and not largely ignored as was the case in Detroit during the 1970s. The automobile manufacturers tended to disregard the clear signal that growing segments desired the high quality, durability, and performance features of the imports. This neglect permitted foreign manufacturers to deliberately pursue a strategy of market segmentation that virtually brought Detroit to its knees in 1980.

[9]"Nutrition Key Factor in Food Trends: Survey," *Advertising Age* (October 27, 1980), 98.

Brand Shifting Strategies

In some product categories extensive new product innovation is unlikely. Then, the strategy becomes one of attempting to shift consumers from one brand to another.

One approach, of course, is simply to copy the product of a competitor and then outspend with advertising and promotion. This appears to be the technique used in the 1970s. For example, General Foods introduced *Country Time* lemonade (a copy of Wyler's); Johnson and Johnson's *Stay Free* maxipads were virtually identical to a Kotex brand; and Lehn & Fink's *Love My Carpet* was a copy of Airwick's *Carpet Fresh* rug deodorizer. The rationale for this marketing philosophy according to Lehn & Fink is: "Be first to be second and you can expect to get between 30 and 40 percent of the market."[10] Of course you have to be fully prepared to outspend the competitor on advertising.

This follow-the-leader strategy has little to commend it. First, there are many instances when it simply does not work. Even more crucial, it is a deplorable waste of economic and social resources. A far more viable strategy is to monitor demand shifts, no matter how small or subtle, and to reposition existing products or introduce new options. In the $100 million shampoo market, for example, 40 percent of consumers were discovered to prefer a specialty shampoo designed to combat dandruff, grease or split ends; add fragrance and body; or simply revitalize a lackluster look.[11] Procter & Gamble capitalized by introducing *Pert,* a conditioning shampoo marketed as creating "bouncin' and behavin' hair." *Prell* liquid and concentrate, a long-established item, is now touted for cleansing benefits in contrast to its earlier appeals to appearance. Similarly, *Clairol* products have been repositioned by Bristol-Myers in terms of the benefit of hair body-building.[12]

Clearly the strategy of market segmentation also works in stimulating brand shifting. Once again careful research is the key to success.

Increasing the Effectiveness of Strategy and Tactics

Competition in a market economy is precarious, always subject to encroachment or outright assault by competitors. Effectiveness requires continual improvement in the efficiency of the strategy and tactics employed. Reliable analysis of consumer behavior is an essential input for this purpose.[13]

Once Detroit fought to recoup its lost market share, each "big three" member introduced fuel-efficient front-wheel drive models reflecting particular attention to quality and performance. Even so, some observers felt these cars were not fully competitive in terms of fuel efficiency and

---

[10]Rance Crain, "Product Innovation, Ad Daring Essential for Booming '80s," *Advertising Age* (November 13, 1980), 6.

[11]Tobie Sullivan, "Shampoo Marketing—Keeping Pace With Fickle Consumer," *Advertising Age* (February 25, 1980), S-10.

[12]Sullivan.

[13]For background material on marketing strategy, see David T. Kollat, Roger D. Blackwell, and James Robeson, *Strategic Marketing,* 2nd ed. (Hinsdale, Ill.: Dryden Press, 1981).

other important features. Yet Detroit gambled that consumers will buy in large numbers, even though *prices were deliberately set at high levels in a recession year.*[14] The assumption was that demand is price "inelastic"—i.e., price is not a determining criterion in the purchase decision. Detroit's need, of course, is to generate cash to recoup recent losses and to pay the high tool-up costs of new product introduction. If this assumption is wrong, competitors could flood the market with lower-priced imports and virtually doom Detroit's hopes. To a high degree, this type of assumption can be tested and verified by research and not left to the whims of market forces. In other words, properly done research can help reduce decision risk in similar situations. (By the way, this assumption *was* wrong, and Detroit was forced into price rebates.)

Price, of course, is just one area of market strategy in which research provides valuable input. It would be impossible to prepare a complete list of such issues, but here is just a sample of additional questions considered in this book:

1. What types of advertising appeals are most effective in different product categories?

2. How do buyers learn about new brands and products? Which information sources tend to be most effective?

3. Does advertising really change attitudes?

4. How many times should an ad be run?

5. Do black consumers respond to marketing strategies differently from their nonblack counterparts?

6. To what degree can marketing strategies proving effective in the United States be effective elsewhere in the world?

7. How can "impulse" purchasing be stimulated in a retail store?

8. Are some customers more loyal to one brand than another? If so, how can brand loyalty be undermined and shifted?

Improving Retail Performance

In 1976 AT&T opened 49 retail "phone stores," and now there are more than 2,000, mostly located in high-rent urban areas and high-traffic shopping malls. This decision was prompted by a court order specifying that customers are free to use Bell equipment, *or* equipment manufactured elsewhere, on Bell telephone lines entering the home.[15] Yet, only two million sets were sold in 1979 at the retail level, far below projected levels. A survey (*after* stores were opened and faltering) disclosed the reasons for disappointing sales. First, about one-third of phone nonowners (those renting their equipment and paying a monthly fee) fear that repair or service of phones purchased at a retail store could be a problem. Others are concerned about the negative reaction of "Ma Bell" if they

---

[14]"Detroit's High-Price Strategy Could Backfire," *Business Week* (November 24, 1980), 109-111.
[15]"Retail Phone Sales Suffer Due to Customer Satisfaction," *Marketing News* (March 21, 1980), 16.

would even consider buying a Bell phone or a competitor's. More than 40 percent did not even know they could install their own phones. Finally, the negative response was further complicated by the lack of advertising support for retail outlets by the manufacturer. These fears could have been anticipated by efficient consumer research. Careful advertising and promotion could have allayed the fears of potential buyers and overcome the awareness gap, for example. Or, if consumer barriers and resistance appeared to be too strong, $100 million or more of investment at the retail level could have been saved.

Retailing, of course, is the final link in the process of moving goods from producer to consumer. Regardless of how much value the manufacturer has built into the product, how well this value is communicated, and how smoothly the production and physical distribution systems function, it is the retailer who either consummates or obstructs the sale. Hence, the manufacturer stands to gain a great deal from consumer research focusing on where and how the product should be sold.

Most retailers are independent businesses, however, separate from the manufacturer. Thus, they can have a marketing problem of their own. There has been much progress in recent years in improvement of what might be called the cost-revenue approach to improved retailing performance, but there have been limited advances in what might be called the demand-analysis approach. Significant advances have been made in accounting control, computerized inventory systems, merchandise planning, location selection, physical layout, warehousing, and other operational aspects of retailing management. These technologies have been diffused so widely, however, that their potential for differentiating one retailing firm from another is approaching diminishing returns. The alternative is to increase the ability to understand, predict, and stimulate consumer response to a retailing firm's offering. Improved strategies to produce a more appealing offering provide an increasing potential as a basis for differentiating one retailing firm from another in profitability and consumer satisfaction.

Retailing performance is of critical concern in consumer behavior for another reason. The additional reason is the essential role retailing institutions play in total urban planning. The type of retailing institutions that will exist in cities of the next decade influence the kind of transportation cities will need, the kind of communication system (that is, the rise of telecommunications systems for transactions), the location and form of leisure activities, and the kind of integration with other time-consuming activities required for "new towns" and revitalization of existing cities. Thus the strategies of many types of business firms will be affected profoundly by the *form* and *place* of retailing transactions.

Consumer Protection

The cornerstone of a free enterprise economy is the right of the consumer to make an informed choice from an array of product alternatives, which is not restricted by exercise of monopoly power. The consumer cannot make a knowledgeable choice, of course, if inaccurate or incomplete information is provided through a deliberate effort to mislead and manipulate. Moreover, restricted choice is the inevitable consequence of monopoly power, in which case profit results from this fact alone and not from service to the consumer.

Outright deception is regulated by governmental agencies and by voluntary business organizations such as the Advertising Review Board. Nevertheless, every consumer can point to examples where he or she has been deceived by less than full disclosure. Unfortunately the incidence of this type of abuse does not seem to be declining. Monopoly power also is regulated to a degree by antitrust legislation, and some of its more blatant forms are not observed today. Monopoly gain can result, however, when an economy shifts from one of abundance to one characterized by scarcity. This was certainly the case in many industries during the energy crisis of the middle 1970s in the United States. The producer now was in a position to shift limited resources to the most profitable products, regardless of consumer desires. The consumer really had no option whatsoever, and short-run financial considerations frequently took the place of service to the consumer. Finally this situation was reversed by the recession that followed, but it does illustrate the degree to which consumer orientation can disintegrate into a mere platitude rather than a central aspect of business life.

In a market economy governmental regulation always will be required to curb these abuses, and consumer protection legislation has expanded remarkably at all levels of government. All too frequently such legislation is based on the opinions of a small group of people rather than on consumer research focusing on the consequences of these abuses of consumer behavior. The outcome tends to be ineffective and, in some instances, counterproductive consumer legislation. There now is a growing awareness that greater reliance must be placed on research if consumer protection is to function as intended.

Consumer education is the most productive long-range strategy. The consumer can be taught how to detect the presence of deception and other abuses and made aware of the remedies that exist and the opportunities for redress. Also, everyone can benefit from insight into money-saving buying strategies. These programs also must be based on research into consumer motivation and behavior. Otherwise, educational programs can be totally irrelevant for the real world of consumer life.

The consumer can be both purposeful and sovereign but still behave unwisely in the sense of not making the "best buy." Outcomes might be quite different if the individual had more insight on ways to evaluate products and their selling claims. There is a famous case history that illustrates this point. A manufacturer put out a new ceiling tile without holes or perforations of any kind, and it could be demonstrated that sound absorption capability was markedly improved. Yet, consumers rejected the product on the basis that an effective ceiling tile must have holes. After a period of unsuccessfully fighting this misbelief through advertising, the manufacturer inserted the holes and thereby reduced the performance of the product. Sales then responded positively. A more knowledgeable consumer would have reacted quite differently to this manufacturer's initial efforts.

The seller is placed in a dilemma in this kind of circumstance. Efforts at reeducation often are disregarded totally. Fortunately, consumer education is now becoming common in secondary schools and through community organizations of various types. In so doing, the consumer is taught to evaluate product offerings and appeals in a much more sophisticated manner. The sensitive marketer, in turn, has nothing to fear if product claims are truthful.

Essential Input for Public Policy

The principle of individual choice permeates the economic theories and practices of many societies in the world. No disciplined determination of public policy can exist, therefore, without assumptions—correct or incorrect—about how consumers as individuals will choose to spend their money, time, energy, and votes. To design public policy that will be accepted by consumers and will be efficient as a solution to societal problems requires thorough understanding of the needs, desires, and aversions of the consumers for whom the policies are developed.

Kotler and Zaltman have commented that even products with obvious value to a society, such as free medical care, pollution control, or public transportation, must be presented with understanding of consumer behavior and sophistication in marketing programs if the products are to be accepted by the society's consumers.[16] A good example of the need for consumer analysis as an input in public policy might be in the area of urban transportation. It is apparent from the failures of many United States urban transportation systems that there is an enormous need to design urban transit systems to appeal to individual consumers' tastes if high usage is to be attained. In an industrialized society, the practical alternative to designing public policy with analysis of consumer behavior is forceful coercion to gain acceptance.

In the communal society that is becoming common worldwide, more and more *individual* consumption decisions affect other individuals, especially in the tightly interwoven fabric of consumption.[17] The individual choices of consumers concerning automobiles, for example, affect immensely the air breathed by all other consumers. The choices of consumers about detergents, in another example, affect the water quality for many other consumers. When public policy is enacted without adequate understanding of why and how consumers are going to make their individual decisions, chaos in public policy may ensue to the detriment of those whom policy makers had hoped to help. It is increasingly difficult

[16]Philip Kotler and Gerald Zaltman, "Social Marketing: An Approach to Planned Social Change," *Journal of Marketing,* vol. 35 (July 1971), 3-12.

[17]Daniel Bell, "The Post-Industrial Society: A Speculative View," in Edward and Elizabeth Hutchings, eds., *Scientific Progress and Human Values* (New York: Elsevier, 1967), 154-170.

to consider consumer decisions "private" because of their impact on many "public" areas. This interlocking of interests is described by Laurence Feldman:

. . . there are signs that the marketing system's ability to promote consumption and to provide consumers with a growing range of choice is increasingly inconsistent with the needs of the larger society. One reason for this is that marketing decisions have been made which expanded the range of consumer product choice but disregarded their environmental impact. There has been a failure to recognize that these products, which are marketing outputs designed for individual satisfaction, are simultaneously inputs to a larger environmental system and as such the well-being of society.[18]

As an Emerging Academic Discipline

For most of this century, economists and marketers were the only ones who worried much about consumer behavior. Many theories were developed, usually reflecting little more than armchair analysis. There was no concentrated study of the consumer undertaken with the intent of building a consistent field of knowledge.

Matters began to change after World War II when marketers suddenly discovered that they possessed vastly more productive capacity than the market could absorb. The interests of firms shifted from production to marketing—to adaptation of output to the needs and desires of the consumer. This, in turn, gave rise to a strong demand for greater knowledge about consumer behavior.

Trained psychologists found their way into the business world and launched an era of inquiry known as "motivation research." While the outcome of this invasion was not especially notable (it generated more heat than light), it did serve to stimulate awareness that the behavioral sciences have much to contribute both to marketing and to consumer education.

Consumer behavior emerged as a legitimate field of academic study during the 1960s as marketers and economists began to develop expertise in the behavioral sciences. Suddenly, the behavioral sciences became the "in" thing. Marketers, in particular, borrowed rather indiscriminately from social psychology, sociology, anthropology, or any other field of study that might relate to consumer behavior in some way, no matter how remote. Yet, in retrospect, this sense of indirection characterizes any field in its immaturity. Soon this unfocused inquiry began to assume maturity.

While a more definitive historical overview is provided later, it should be noted that a major step forward occurred after the publication of three pioneering books in the middle 1960s.[19] These books defined important

---

[18]Laurence P. Feldman, "Societal Adaptation: A New Challenge for Marketing," *Journal of Marketing,* vol. 35 (July 1971), 54-60.

[19]See Francesco M. Nicosia, *Consumer Decision Processes: Marketing and Advertising Implications* (Englewood Cliffs, N.J.: Prentice-Hall, 1966); John A. Howard and Jagdish N. Sheth, *The Theory of Buyer Behavior* (New York: John Wiley & Sons, 1969); and James F. Engel, David T. Kollat, and Roger D. Blackwell, *Consumer Behavior,* 1st ed. (New York: Holt, Rinehart and Winston, 1968).

variables, specified functional relationships between them, and clarified the practical implications for marketers and, to a much lesser degree, for consumer education. Soon courses on consumer behavior became commonplace, and scientists from various behavioral sciences began to view the consumer as a legitimate focus of inquiry. Researchers from these diverse backgrounds were united through the formation of the Association for Consumer Research following a conference sponsored by the authors at Ohio State University in 1969. As of this writing, membership is nearing 750.

The outcome is that consumer behavior is now an important field of study in its own right. The literature has grown sharply,[20] and the *Journal of Consumer Research* was first published in 1975. Research contributions also are increasingly appearing in the literature of related behavioral sciences. In other words, research in consumer behavior is now making important contributions to knowledge of human behavior in general. The field has grown from infancy to a healthy state of adolescence.

PLACING CONSUMER RESEARCH IN PROPER PERSPECTIVE

Research now seems to indicate that many potential buyers of the newer generation of stereo equipment desire more adjustments and features previously thought to be the sole concern of the stereo enthusiast.[21] Figure 1.2 shows what the outcome might be if this finding is not interpreted with a bit of common sense. Naive reliance on research, in other words, can have some unfortunate consequences. Another example comes from a series of life-style studies conducted from 1975 to 1979 by Needham, Harper & Steers, a Chicago-based advertising agency.[22] There was a sharp increase in expressed consumer concern about the amount of sugar consumed. This led to a prediction that sales of such sugared snack items as *Twinkies* and *Ding-Dongs* would decline, whereas the opposite occured. This result was interpreted by Dr. William Wells, research director, as meaning that concern over consumption of sugar *in general* may have little to do with purchase of a specific product. Much more needs to be known before jumping to that conclusion. Again, judgment and common sense are needed.

In reality, any decision with respect to the consumer, whether by a marketer, educator, or legislator, must be made on three bases: (1) experience; (2) intuition and creative ability; and (3) research. This might

[20]Here is a partial list of available books. David L. Loudon and Albert J. Della Bitta, *Consumer Behavior: Concepts and Applications* (New York: McGraw-Hill, 1979); Fred D. Reynolds and William D. Wells, *Consumer Behavior* (New York: McGraw-Hill, 1977); Gerald Zaltman and Melanie Wallendorf, *Consumer Behavior: Basic Findings and Management Implications* (New York: John Wiley & Sons, 1979); Leon G. Schiffman and Leslie L. Kanuk, *Consumer Behavior* (Englewood Cliffs, N.J.: Prentice-Hall, Inc., 1978); Kenneth E. Runyon, *Consumer Behavior,* 2nd ed. (Columbus, Ohio: Charles E. Merrill, 1980); Carl E. Block and Kenneth J. Roering, *Essentials of Consumer Behavior,* 2nd ed. (Hinsdale, Ill.: Dryden Press, 1979); and James R. Bettman, *An Information Processing Theory of Consumer Choice* (Reading, Mass.: Addison-Wesley, 1979).

[21]Donald Fuller, "Stereo System Marketers Let Those Doodads Do the Work," *Advertising Age* (June 2, 1980), S-20.

[22]"Broad Attitude Trends Don't Always Predict Specific Consumer Behavior," *Marketing News* (May 16, 1980), 8.

**Figure 1.2
Marketing
Madness**

Source: Courtesy of Wayne
Stayskal.

be visualized best as a three-legged stool. Pull away one leg and the stool will not stand. Apparently Detroit executives ignored the research leg with disastrous consequences. Experience and intuition simply did not suffice in a complex and changing environment. But it is equally dangerous to remove any of the other legs as well (see Figure 1.2, where a product decision is made with one leg only). The obvious point, then, is that research input is vital and necessary, but it is just one component, albeit a major one, in the managerial decision process.

Summary

This chapter has one primary purpose—to establish three essential foundational premises about consumer motivation and behavior through use of numerous examples and illustrations:

1. The consumer is sovereign.

2. Consumer motivation and behavior can be understood through research.

3. Consumer motivation and behavior can be influenced through persuasive activity which takes the individual seriously.

When these premises are disregarded or abused, the consequences are almost inevitably negative. It was further demonstrated that consumer research, properly conceived and interpreted, serves as essential input to the policies of a business firm, helps to improve retailing performance, serves as the basis for consumer protection and education, and provides important information for public policy decisions.

Review and Discussion Questions

1. Which of the following decisions should be considered legitimate topics of concern in the study of consumer behavior? (a) selection of a college by a student, (b) purchase of a life insurance policy, (c) smoking a cigarette, (d) selecting a church to join, (e) selecting a dentist, (f) visiting an auto showroom to see new models, and (g) purchasing a college textbook.

2. Examine current advertisements for consumer products and select one for a new product. Will this product succeed in the long run in the consumer market place? What factors determine success?

3. A family has just come into the local office of a lending agency asking for a bill consolidation loan. Payments for a new car, television, stereo, bedroom set, and central air conditioning have become excessive. The head of the family does not have a steady source of income, and real help is now needed. Is this an example of purposeful consumer behavior, or has this family been manipulated into making unwise purchases?

4. If it is true that motivations and behavior can be understood through research, is it also true that the marketer now has greater ability to influence the consumer adversely than would have been true in an earlier era?

5. What contributions does the analysis of consumer behavior make to the field of finance? of production? of real estate? of insurance? of top management administration?

6. Would it be equally necessary to understand consumer behavior if the economic system were not one of free enterprise? In other words, is the subject matter of this book only of interest to those in capitalistic systems, or does it also have relevance for socialism and communism?

7. What differences in perspective on consumer behavior would you expect to find among the following types of researchers? (a) experimental psychologist, (b) social psychologist, (c) clinical psychologist, (d) anthropologist, (e) sociologist, and (f) economist?

8. Consumer protection is an important issue. What areas of consumer behavior appear to be most in need of increased regulation and/or consumer education?

CHAPTER 2

CONSUMER DECISION PROCESSES: AN OVERVIEW

Here are two product lists. The items within each list have something in common, and this common feature sharply separates the two.

List 1	List 2
Automobile	Toilet tissue
Coffee	Frozen orange juice
Extra strength pain remedy, over-the-counter	Unleaded gasoline
Designer jeans	Crackers
A component stereo set	A ball point pen
King-size mattress and box spring	Light bulbs
	Aluminum foil

What is it that differentiates the items on one list from those on the other list? Price is the most obvious answer, but another quality is far more basic.

Each product on List 1 has *personal relevance* to the consumer for one reason or another and is designated a *high-involvement* product.

It is probably obvious that purchase of an automobile, a stereo, and the mattress and box spring set have high relevance because of high price, complex features, large differences between alternatives, and high perceived risks of making a wrong decision. Designer jeans also would have relevance because of the extent to which they are seen as conveying a message about the wearer to the world. But what about coffee and the pain reliever? There is a temptation to say that just about any alternative is as good as any other, but this is not the case. With many people, the quality of coffee served is perceived as one important measure of ability as a homemaker; hence strong brand preference and loyalty. On the other hand, many people place great reliance on the quality of pain relievers conveyed by brand name, and fear the risks of purchasing something that might be inappropriate or even dangerous. Hence this product category, too, generates a measure of involvement and pertinence.

The products on List 2 tend to be *low involvement* for most consumers. First, the product category itself does not reflect one's ego or self-worth. Also, the alternatives within the product class are largely similar. Thus, there is not much risk if one brand is used rather than another. The buying decision, in turn, is much simpler and less demanding, and brand shifts are commonplace.

The nature of the decision process and resulting marketing strategy vary strongly between high- and low-involvement situations. Therefore, each must be elaborated and discussed separately. It is our purpose in this chapter to present simplified models or depictions of both high- and low-involvement product decision making. Only an abbreviated version of each model is presented here, following a general discussion of the nature of consumer behavior models. Details are added in Parts 4 and 5 of the book.

MODELS OF CONSUMER BEHAVIOR

Every decision maker or observer of consumer behavior has some idea or conceptualization of the variables and factors underlying both motivation and action. In other words, everyone has a *model* of the process. The problem enters, however, when the model being used is either incomplete or inaccurate. In one example, it is common to view the central role of advertising only as a trigger to immediate buying action. Advertising that does not generate this outcome thus will be classed as a failure. However, it might have had a major effect in stimulating initial awareness which will result in a purchase at a later time. It is necessary to specify the conditions under which advertising can perform a triggering function and when it cannot. Otherwise, marketing strategy is likely to misfire.

A model is nothing more than a replica of the phenomenon it is intended to designate. In effect, it specifies the underlying variables, the nature of the relationships between them, and the manner in which behavior is shaped and affected.

As consumer behavior emerged as a subject for intensive study in its own right, confusion developed with respect to these variables. A real step forward occurred with the publication of three models of consumer behavior in the 1960s,[1] two of which have been substantially revised over the years.[2] These are discussed in detail in the Appendix to this book.

Models of consumer behavior usually are elaborate flow charts explaining the process. Some variables and the relationships between them can only be hypothesized at this time. No model can be considered definitive or final, because revision is necessary as new research becomes

---

[1]See Francesco M. Nicosia, *Consumer Decision Processes: Marketing and Advertising Implications* (Englewood Cliffs, N.J.: Prentice-Hall, 1966); John A. Howard and Jagdish N. Sheth, *The Theory of Buyer Behavior* (New York: John Wiley & Sons, 1969); and the first edition of this text which articulated what came to be known as the Engel, Kollat, Blackwell model. The first edition was published in 1968 by Holt, Rinehart & Winston, Inc.

[2]The Howard and Sheth model was revised in John U. Farley, John A. Howard, and L. Winston Ring, *Consumer Behavior Theory and Application* (Boston: Allyn & Bacon, Inc., 1974). Howard has published subsequent revisions as well. The Engel, Kollat, and Blackwell model has been revised in each edition of this book.

available. Models offer these advantages to the student and to the researcher:

1. *A frame of reference is provided for research.* Through descriptions of the variables and relationships, gaps in information and knowledge are clearly identified.

2. *Research findings can be integrated into a meaningful whole.* When a model of the entire process of consumer behavior in both high-involvement and low-involvement decisions is available, it becomes feasible to utilize research findings from a variety of behavioral sciences with greater sophistication and precision. In other words, a perspective is provided for assessing the significance of and assimilating new research data.

3. *Models become useful in theory construction.* Researchable hypotheses flow readily from a carefully designed model, and a basis thus is provided for extending knowledge.

4. *Explanations are provided for behavior itself.* A mere description of the motivational determinants of consumer action is of little use; it is necessary to explain relations and thus gain an ability to predict outcomes under varying sets of circumstances. This is nearly impossible to do without a model of some type, no matter how crude.

THE HIGH-INVOLVEMENT DECISION PROCESS

More than 70 years ago, John Dewey itemized what he termed the steps in problem solving to explain the process an individual goes through in arriving at a decision.[3] Dewey's theory has stood the test of time and offers the distinct advantage of viewing behavior as a *process* rather than a discrete act and is as concerned with how a decision is reached as it is with the decision itself. There are five important phases of consumer decision-making behavior:

1. *Problem recognition.* What happens to initiate the process?

2. *Search.* What sources of information are used to help arrive at a decision and what is the relative influence of each?

3. *Alternative evaluation.* What criteria are used by the consumer to assess alternatives? What are the resulting beliefs and attitudes about the alternative? What is the status of purchase intention?

4. *Choice.* What selection is made from among the available alternatives?

5. *Outcomes.* Is choice followed by satisfaction or by doubt that a correct decision was made?

This type of process is often referred to as *extended problem solving.*

[3]John Dewey, *How We Think* (New York: Heath, 1910).

Extended problem solving occurs only under high-involvement conditions.[4] When low involvement is present, there will be no search, and alternative evaluation itself is markedly different. Because involvement is such an important issue, it is necessary to probe more deeply into its determinants before proceeding further.

The Characteristics of High Involvement

Following Petty and Capicoppo and others,[5] involvement is defined here as *the activation of extended problem-solving behavior when the act of purchase or consumption is seen by the decision maker as having high personal importance or relevance.* This can take place when the product itself is perceived as reflecting on one's self image, as might be the case with some clothing, jewelry, or cosmetic items.[6] At other times, involvement is activated when the product being considered is costly and the risks of a wrong decision are high.[7] It also is seen when there is strong outside reference-group influence and motivation to comply with these pressures.[8]

Because it is extended problem solving, there is active search and use of information.[9] This information is then carefully processed and stored in memory in such a form that it may readily be recalled for use in later purchasing action.[10] In the decision process itself, many product attributes are weighed and evaluated in a complex manner.[11] The outcome is the development of beliefs about the various alternatives, an evaluation pro or con (referred to as attitude) toward the act of purchasing and using each option, and purchase intentions.[12] In other words, thinking leads to feeling which leads to action.

This, then, is the picture of the rational, problem-solving consumer. This occurs, however, only with a minority of product purchases. Most

[4]This has been stressed most clearly by Richard Vaughn, "The Consumer Mind: How to Tailor Ad Strategies," *Advertising Age* (June 9, 1980), 45-46; Michael J. Houston and Michael L. Rothschild, "Conceptual and Methodological Perspectives on Involvement," in S. C. Jain, ed. *Research Frontiers in Marketing: Dialogues and Directions* (Chicago: American Marketing Association, 1978), 184-187.

[5]Richard E. Petty and John T. Capicoppo, "Issue Involvement as a Moderator of the Effects on Attitude of Advertising Content and Context," in Kent B. Monroe, ed., *Advances in Consumer Research,* vol. 8 (Ann Arbor, Mich.: Association for Consumer Research, 1981), 20-24; and Clark Leavitt, Anthony G. Greenwald, and Carl Obermiller, "What is Low Involvement Low in?" in Monroe, 15-19.

[6]Vaughn; John L. Lastovicka and David M. Gardner, "Components of Involvement," in John C. Maloney and Bernard Silverman, eds., *Attitude Research Plays for High Stakes* (Chicago: American Marketing Association, 1979), 53-73; and Houston and Rothschild.

[7]Vaughn; and Michael L. Rothschild, "Advertising Strategies for High and Low Involvement Situations," in Maloney and Silverman, 74-93.

[8]Houston and Rothschild.

[9]Vaughn; and Houston and Rothschild.

[10]See especially Herbert E. Krugman, "Low Involvement Theory in Light of New Brain Research," in Maloney and Silverman, 16-22.

[11]Rothschild, "Advertising Strategies;" and Houston and Rothschild, "Conceptual and Methodological Perspectives."

[12]Vaughn, "The Consumer Mind;" Petty and Capicoppo, "Issue Involvement;" and Bobby J. Calder, "When Attitudes Follow Behavior—A Self-Perception/Dissonance Interpretation of Low Involvement," in Maloney and Silverman, 25-36.

items, quite frankly, are not sufficiently important to justify this kind of activity. Such involvement probably is best detected by the number of product attributes actually weighed and evaluated in the decision process. To the extent that the consumer makes use of many evaluative criteria (i.e., low price, durability, etc.) and has a narrow range of acceptable values along each dimension, such activity appears to be a valid indicator that high involvement is present.[13]

High-Involvement Decision Making in Action: The Case of What Happens When Detroit Fights Back

Let's return now to the beleagured American automobile industry and the kind of buying behavior that might be expected now that it has begun to "fight back." Certainly this provides a good illustration of high involvement.

The Chrysler Corporation has pinned its survival on the sale of 600,000 of its compact K-cars, the Dodge *Aries* and the Plymouth *Reliant.* Ford, in turn, is hoping to sell a half-million of its new Ford *Escort* and Mercury *Lynx* subcompacts. Later, General Motors will introduce its subcompact J-car. Because the J-car has not appeared as of this writing, discussion is confined to the Aries/*Reliant* and *Escort/Lynx.*

Bear in mind that these new entries offer good fuel economy, although many imports still are superior. Perhaps more important, however, every effort will be made to convince prospects that quality and performance will match or even exceed that offered by the imports. This is quite a challenge indeed, given the generally poor marks assigned to American cars by the public on these dimensions.

Problem Recognition

The first step in any type of consumer decision process is problem recognition. This occurs when an individual perceives a difference between an ideal and the actual state of affairs at any given point in time. It can be activated by arousal of motives—enduring predispositions to strive to attain specified goals. When activated, motives can both arouse and direct behavior. Examples in this situation might be motives to "have the very latest," patriotism expressed in a desire to "buy American," and avoidance of discomfort and uncertainty caused by mechanical unreliability.

Problem recognition also can be stimulated by some sort of outside stimulus, perhaps even an ad. The perceived fact that the Chrysler K-car, for example, can match the imports might serve to establish a new concept of the ideal, thereby enhancing a gap between actual and ideal.

Not every perceived discrepancy between ideal and actual will result in problem recognition. There is a minimum level of perceived difference which must be surpassed before decision making is activated. This threshhold is learned and will vary with circumstances.

[13]See Michael L. Rothschild and Michael J. Houston, "The Consumer Involvement Matrix: Some Preliminary Findings," in Barnett A. Greenberg and Danny N. Bellenger, eds., *Contemporary Marketing Thought* (Chicago: American Marketing Association, 1977), 95-98.

Search

Once a problem is recognized, the consumer then must decide what to do. The initial step is an internal search within memory to determine whether or not enough is known about alternatives to permit some kind of choice. Often one brand will be strongly preferred over others based on past experience, and a decision will then be made on the spot to make a purchase as soon as possible. This is an example of routinized consumer behavior which is discussed in more detail later. Because of the length of time between purchases and the rapid changes within the industry, this is not likely to be the case with the automobile purchaser. It is more probable that it will be necessary to turn to *external search,* making use of a variety of information sources.

There always will be individual differences in the propensity to engage in search. First, because of perceived risk of making a wrong choice, some consumers are known to be cautious and unwilling to act even when alternatives are known. Hence, further information is sought as additional justification. Others are more willing to act on hunch and intuition. The extent of search always is governed by the balance between expected gains and the costs of time, energy, and financial outlay that must be expended.

In all probability, consumer advertising will play a major role. When the Volkswagen *Dasher* was introduced, initial awareness was stimulated most frequently by television commercials.[14] This often is the case, but note that extended problem solving tends to be an activity of the left part of the brain, and it is likely that consumers will make considerable use of print ads which are processed in this sector. Through print it is possible to elaborate on essential brand differences and selling points which cannot be done as thoroughly through the electronic media. Chrysler especially has made heavy use of long-copy newspaper and magazine ads, but Ford also has followed suit (see Figure 2.2).

It also is probable that those who buy at a later time will pay considerable attention to the counsel of those who made an earlier purchase. Among the first buyers of the *Escort,* 62 percent stated that they thought the *Escort* (or *Lynx*) *would* match the imports in terms of benefits offered.[15] The term *would* was interpreted by Joseph Cappy, General Marketing Manager of the Lincoln-Mercury Division, as meaning that, "People liked the fit and finish of the *Escort/Lynx,* but are waiting to see if it holds up."[16] This only underscores the prevalence of skepticism regarding the quality and workmanship offered by Detroit, and it is to be expected that recent buyers will be actively consulted as "opinion leaders."

Dealer visits and test drives usually are a part of the search process in automobile buying. Front-wheel drive is new to many potential pur-

[14]See the Volkswagen *Dasher* case in Roger D. Blackwell, James F. Engel, and W. Wayne Talarzyk, *Contemporary Cases in Consumer* Behavior (Hinsdale, Ill.: Dryden Press, 1977), 360-374.

[15]Dan Jedlicka, "Ford Studies California *Escort* Sales for Clues to New Buying Patterns," Chicago *Sun-Times* (November 6, 1980), 75.

[16]Jedlicka.

chasers, and some form of product trial probably will be necessary for most. This trial also is a chance to examine quality of finishing and workmanship. Skillful personal selling can be a real consumer aid, but this does not always prove to be the case. Dealer salesmen for the Volkswagen *Dasher* tended to ignore the product benefits desired by potential buyers and stressed other features.[17] Quality of workmanship, reputation of manufacturer, and previous positive experience with a VW were rarely stressed, even though these attributes were of central importance to the buyer.

Alternative Evaluation

Once search has been completed, the buyer must evaluate competing alternatives and arrive at a purchase intention. This involves the interaction of several different types of variables.

1. Formation of a Purchase Intention   Alternative evaluation begins with *evaluative criteria.* These are the specifications and standards used by the consumer to evaluate products and brands. In other words, they are the desired outcomes from choice and use expressed in the form of preferred product benefits.

Of the October, 1980, *Escort/Lynx* purchasers who were surveyed, 14 percent traded in an import, and nearly 40 percent considered buying an import this time as well.[18] This implies that high fuel economy, quality of workmanship, handling ease, and overall quality were important evaluative criteria. When they were specifically queried on this point, more than half mentioned high fuel economy, and 27 percent mentioned the importance of the front-wheel drive option.

Low price does not appear to be a determining criterion. This may provide at least an initial verification of Detroit's assumption that automobile demand is price inelastic (recall the discussion in Chapter 1).[19] The *Escort* and *Lynx* were introduced at prices just slightly under those of the closest intermediate or full-sized alternatives. The one danger sign here is that the Chrysler K-cars did not sell well initially because they were loaded with high-priced options. Once these were removed, sales seemed to pick up, although all Detroit manufacturers later introduced price rebates. Whether or not Detroit is vulnerable to price competition from government-subsidized foreign imports would seem to depend on whether comparable benefits are offered by the imports at a lower initial price.

In high-involvement decision making, the consumer next compares the information gained through the search process against these evaluative criteria. The outcome is formation of *beliefs*—whatever the individual believes to be true about the various alternatives in terms of the stan-

---

[17]See the Volkswagen *Dasher* case in Blackwell, Engel, and Talarzyk.

[18]Jedlicka.

[19]"Detroit's High-Price Strategy Could Backfire,"*Business Week* (November 24, 1980), 109-111.

**Figure 2.1
Problem
Recognition,
Search, and
Alternative
Evaluation**

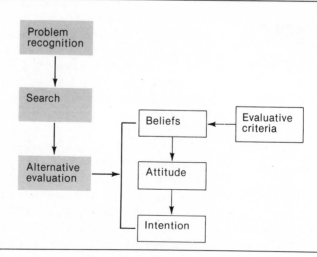

dards being utilized. In the case of the *Escort* and *Lynx,* 62 percent of early purchasers felt quality would match the imports and 75 percent also felt this would be true with respect to fuel economy.[20] Ford apparently had done a good job in convincing most that these new offerings could measure up on important evaluative criteria.

Once beliefs have been formed or changed, *attitudes toward the act of purchasing a given alternative* also will change, all things being equal. An attitude is a positive or negative evaluation of the consequences of buying and using a particular product or brand. If the attitude is favorable, it then is followed by formation of a *purchase intention*—the subjective probability that a given product or brand will be purchased. Once again it is necessary to qualify with an "all things being equal" clause, because intentions as well as attitudes can be affected by a host of outside social and environmental influences.

2. A Partial Model of the Decision Process It may prove helpful now to visualize the discussion of high-involvement decision making to this point (problem recognition, search, and alternative evaluation) through use of a diagrammatic model of the process. This appears in Figure 2.1.

This model shows the flow of the decision process from one stage to the next. As yet, however, nothing explicit has been said about the effects of search on beliefs, attitude, and intention. This is added in the following section.

3. The Effects of Search Detroit made a determined effort with its 1981 advertising to erase the image that U.S. cars, and small cars in particular, are poorly made. Ford went to great lengths to position the

[20]Jedlicka.

**Figure 2.2
The Ford Escort as
a "World Car"**

Source: Ford Division, Ford Motor Company. Reprinted by permission.

Escort as a "world car," hoping to profit from the belief that foreign cars are superior (Figure 2.2). Ford was not held back by a finding that 87 percent of the U.S. public never had heard of a world car.[21] The company chose instead to create its own definition. It positioned Ford as a world competitor, absorbing the best technology from all over to make the best car in America. The first ads depicted the *Escort* covered by a drapecloth of flags of major car-producing nations. Later Ford was forced to downplay the Union Jack when it discovered that British cars have a poor quality reputation.[22]

Chrysler, on the other hand, positioned the *Reliant-K* by an appeal to patriotism. The consumer is urged to buy a K-car as a means of reducing oil imports form OPEC countries. "The U.S. is not going to be

[21]"Detroit's New Sales Pitch. Is it on the Right Road?" *Business Week* (September 22, 1980), 78+.
[22]"Detroit's New Sales Pitch," 84-85.

pushed around any more!" Ads are replete with red, white, and blue colors and the stars and stripes. The front-wheel drive has even been named the "Yankee Doodle." The goal is not so much to attract the import customer but rather the so-called "silent majority" who "want to fight back."[23]

Both of these cars have been designed and marketed through a strategy of market segmentation discussed in Chapter 1. Sometimes referred to as *benefit segmentation,* the approach was to discover the evaluative criteria used by those not currently buying an existing American make and produce a car meeting these desires. Presumably both the *Escort/Lynx* and the *Reliant/Aries* have succeeded in this respect. Now, what is the probable impact of the differing promotional appeals each has chosen to use? This question can only be answered by considering the way individuals process incoming information, and this can be understood by further use of a diagrammatic model appearing in Figure 2.3.

This model is not as complex as it may appear. Let's begin in the upper-left-hand corner with incoming stimuli. These can either be initiated by the marketer in the form of advertising, displays, sales pitches, and so on; or they can represent a host of other messages from sources beyond the control of the business firm. Comment from recent purchasers would be an example.

Assume for the moment that the stimuli are the two ads shown earlier. It is possible that one or the other could be encountered *voluntarily* by the consumer in the process of active search for information. Or exposure could have occurred *involuntarily* as the individual was watching a TV program or reading a magazine for entirely different purposes.

Before anything can happen, the message must be gotten to the consumer where he or she happens to be. This is depicted here as *exposure,* the first step in information processing. This activates one or more of the senses, and preliminary information processing takes place. It may or may not attract *attention,* which is defined as allocation of information-processing capacity to the incoming stimulus. If exposure is voluntary, it is much more likely that attention will be attracted. It is then further processed in short-term memory in order to clarify the meaning of its content. This stage is referred to here as *comprehension.* Short-term memory, by the way, is the component of total memory in which this preliminary processing takes place. It is distinctly limited in capacity, with the result that information processing is highly selective. By no means all that reaches the consumer is processed and stored as intended.

In the case of information processing under conditions of high involvement, incoming information may never move from short-term into long-term memory. Obviously, it will have no effect whatsoever on the decision process. Once the stimulus is comprehended and given meaning (this may turn out to be something quite different than what the mar-

---

[23]"Detroit's New Sales Pitch, 88.

**Figure 2.3
Consumer
Information
Processing**

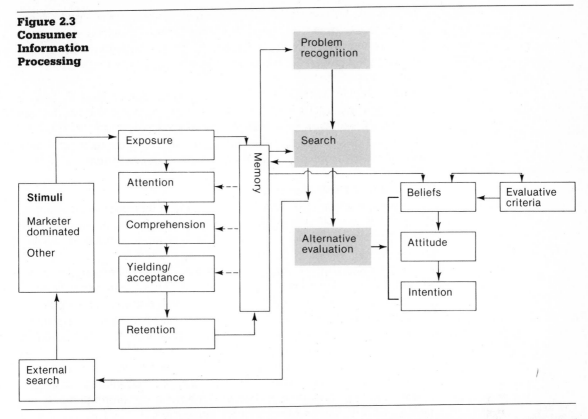

keter actually said), it is compared against existing evaluative criteria and beliefs which are stored in long-term memory. Unless there is compatibility with these beliefs (shown here as *yielding/acceptance*), information processing terminates. If there is compatibility, existing beliefs will either be reinforced or changed, and the message thus is *retained* in long-term memory.

This stimulus, now in long-term memory, can have several effects, as the arrows extending out from memory in Figure 2.3 show. First of all, new information can affect problem recognition. Or, it may modify existing evaluative criteria in some way. Consumer education is particularly likely to have this effect, whereas advertising and selling will have greatest effect on beliefs about the product or brand. Hopefully these beliefs will be modified or changed in the way the manufacturer desires. If so, the persuasive communication has had a positive influence on the decision process.

Both auto companies are taking a risk in this situation with their present advertising campaigns. First, patriotism has never been known to work as a stimulus to automobile purchases.[24] But it also could be argued that times have changed as has been demonstrated by the success

[24]"Detroit's New Sales Pitch," 88.

of recent conservative, patriotism-oriented political campaigns. Then, Chrysler could emerge as a winner. Ford, on the other hand, is pitted directly against the imports. If its world car appeal is seen as lacking credibility, the company could be in danger.

What this discussion illustrates, of course, is that information processing is highly selective. Under high-involvement conditions, people see and hear what they want to see and hear. The rationale behind this proposition is complex and finds its roots in the very nature of memory and information processing. The discussion here is only preliminary, and these issues are considered again in greater depth in Chapter 9.

Choice and its Outcomes

Figure 2.4 completes the model of high-involvement decision making in two ways. It will be elaborated and expanded later (see Figure 17.2). First, it depicts *choice.* Usually this will take place in some kind of retail setting, although mail order purchasing and other forms of nonstore choice are becoming increasingly common in some product categories. Second, the model shows a major outcome of choice—*satisfaction* (or dissatisfaction) from actual product use. This information can exercise a strong effect on beliefs, attitudes, and future intentions. Favorable experience, of course, strengthens future intentions and dissatisfaction will have the opposite effect.

One dimension of choice often is selection of a dealer or retail outlet. This, in itself, can be a high-involvement decision process and is especially important when purchasing a car. Traditionally, the dealer has been selected on the basis of proximity to the customer, but there is every reason to believe that this criterion now is less important than quality of after-sale service. Here, too, the automobile industry has had a serious black eye, and the consumer is wise to make after-sale service a determining factor in the dealer-selection decision.

What about post-sale satisfaction as "Detroit fights back?" This looms large as a major issue in future survival of the industry, because Detroit cannot afford more problems on this dimension. Determined efforts have been made to improve quality and workmanship,[25] and the study of initial *Escort/Lynx* purchasers gives cause for encouragements.[26] Of those surveyed, about 75 percent reported quality of their car to be excellent or very good. Moreover, 80 percent claimed to be "very" or "completely" satisfied. Both of these figures proved to be substantially higher than the responses given by buyers of the 1978 *Fairmont,* Ford's first "downsized" car.

Additional Comments

Figure 2.4 represents a simplified version of the model of high-involvement decision process behavior known for many years as the EKB model. It does not depict, for example, the role and influence of cultural norms and values, reference group and family, anticipated circum-

[25]Ernest E. Hickman, "Keeping the Customer Satisfied," *Advertising Age (September 29, 1980),* S-28-30.

[26]Jedlicka.

**Figure 2.4
An Abbreviated
Model of the High-
Involvement
Decision Process
Showing Choice
and One Outcome**

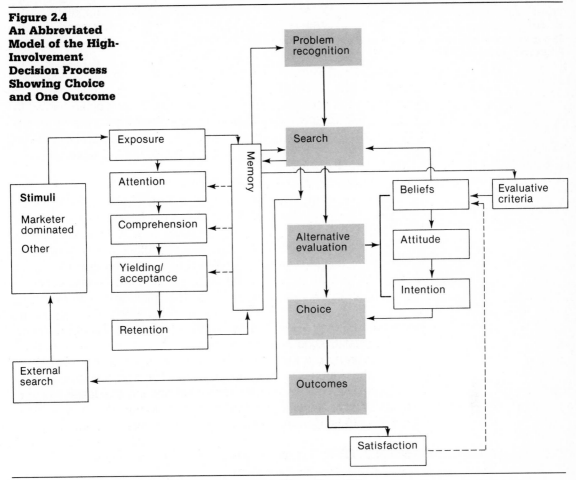

For the complete elaborated model, see Figure 17.2.

stances, unanticipated circumstances, motives, life-style, and normative compliance (i.e., a tendency to yield to social influence). The more complete model is fully developed in Part 4 (see especially Figure 17.2).

One more variation of high-involvement decision process behavior should be mentioned before the discussion proceeds further. This might be termed *routine decision making based on high involvement*. In the event that satisfaction from product use reinforces future buying intentions, the decision process will be much simpler. This time problem recognition is followed by an internal search which immediately reveals a well-formed purchase intention. The intention, in turn, leads directly to choice. This is represented in Figure 2.5.

Under these conditions high brand loyalty develops and is further reinforced by continued satisfaction. Brand shifting is not likely unless other alternatives are developed which clearly are superior. It will be difficult to convince the consumer of this fact, however; beliefs and attitudes

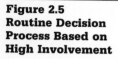

Figure 2.5
Routine Decision
Process Based on
High Involvement

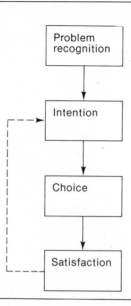

toward the brand stored in long-term memory will be resistant to change. It is a long-established principle of persuasion that beliefs and attitudes which have *centrality* (based on involvement as we have discussed it) resist change. Persuasion designed to achieve change may never attract attention in the first place, be miscomprehended, and fail to achieve yielding and acceptance. Therefore it never enters long-term memory in such a way that cognitive structures give way to modification.

THE LOW-INVOLVEMENT DECISION PROCESS

Figures 2.6–2.8 are ads for four different brands in the same product category. Examine them closely before proceeding further.

Notice that all of these brands *(Perk, Mop & Glo,* and *Solar Bright)* offer identical benefits. Each of them even claims to be "new" and presumably different. The consumer probably could purchase any one of them and not find making the purchase to be a matter of great personal importance. To begin with, the product category itself is distinctly low involvement in that it is unlikely to involve the ego as the floor is cleaned. While mopping is not a pleasant thing to do, it probably does not cause much anxiety about the outcome. Therefore, the decision process will be much simpler and quite different from that used in the high-involvement situation. The essence of the low-involvement type of process is shown in Figure 2.9, and its stages are described below.

Problem
Recognition

Problem recognition is likely to be quite noncomplex. It may be as simple as desiring an easy way to clean a no-wax floor and retain its original appearance. Product advertising could be helpful in at least establishing

**Figure 2.6
New Perk**

Perk™– It's specially formulated to keep a good thing glowing!

Perk beauty freshener is specially formulated to freshen the look of your no-wax floor as it gently cleans. On no-wax floors, detergents can leave a dulling film. And water alone won't really clean.

But Perk is specially formulated to gently clean as it brings out the highlights you paid all that money for in the first place! If you love the beauty and convenience of your no-wax floor, get new Perk, and keep a good thing glowing. **No wax, no detergent works like new Perk!**

Source: Lehn & Fink Products Co. Reprinted by permission.

the fact that there is something else to use beside a mop and scrub bucket.

**Alternative
Evaluation**

Notice that there is no motivated search for information. Under low involvement, the costs of such activity are likely to outweigh the benefits. Rather, internal search will suffice. In effect, the consumer proceeds on the basis of what he or she already knows.

Only a limited number of evaluative criteria will be used, and the individual will not demand that all alternatives meet tight specifications. In a sense, any acceptable brand will do.

In high-involvement decisions, choice is the result of a process consisting of changes in beliefs, attitudes, and intentions. That is not the case here, because a choice is made only on the basis of already existing information. In effect, fully formed beliefs, attitudes, and intentions are the *outcomes* of purchase, not the *cause*.

Figure 2.7
Mop & Glo

No-Wax Floor   Regular Floor

"When my
    no-wax floor
started to
    look dull...
Mop & Glo
    brought it
back to beautiful."

"Mop & Glo
    cleans and
shines my
    regular floor...
It's as easy
    as damp
        mopping."

Source: Lehn & Fink Products Co. Reprinted by permission.

All of this implies that various forms of information, especially advertising, play a role, and this indeed seems to be the case. Figure 2.10 expands the model of low-involvement decision making to encompass information processing. In most ways, it looks very similar to Figure 2.3, but there is an essential difference—the yielding/acceptance stage is missing. Information can be received and processed in such a way that it is stored without making much of an impact on the existing cognitive structure. Processing when involvement is low takes place in the right part of the brain and information is stored in the form of an image without words.[27] In other words, it is retained merely as information, which is stored without much impact until a behavior trigger of some type occurs.

In the case of no-wax floor cleaners, the consumer might readily no-

[27]Krugman, "Low Involvement Theory."

**Figure 2.8
Solar Bright**

Source: Courtesy of Lundmark Wax Company, Chicago, Illinois.

tice ads for such brands as *Perk* and *Mop & Glow,* especially if they appear on television (which is processed in the right sector of the brain.) There would be little resistance to these inputs, because the product class is of relatively low centrality or personal importance. Therefore, there could be some impact on problem recognition (as the arrow shows) or in the form of new information. Again, not much change will occur until a later point. This represents strictly passive learning and information processing.

**Choice and its
Outcomes**

Assume that a potential buyer for the product discussed here encounters a large display with a clearly marked price reduction. This information will be readily processed, and it is likely to serve as a purchase trigger. In

**Figure 2.9
The Low-
Involvement
Decision Process**

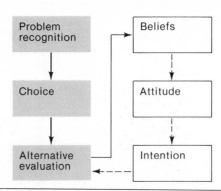

effect, he or she simply says, "Why not?" The cost is low and the risks of a bad choice are minimal.

Once the brand is tried, then there can be quite an effect on cognitive structure. The individual now has important information upon which to decide whether or not the brand is any good. Does it clean as it says it does? If so, this becomes stored as a belief which, all things being equal, leads to a positive attitude toward the act of purchasing that brand next time around, and an intention to do so. In this situation, action *precedes* formation of belief and attitude.

**Repeat-Purchase
Behavior**

One could argue that satisfaction leads to a form of brand loyalty and routinized behavior of the type described in Figure 2.5. The difference here is that loyalty is likely to be low and propensity for brand switching high. Remember that the choice of brand is of low personal relevance, and the differences between alternatives are not great. Assuming that each has about an equal level of awareness, a brand switch could be stimulated by a free trial, coupon, or other direct-action incentive. This is not nearly so likely when brand loyalty is based on high involvement.

**Figure 2.10
Information
Processing under
Low Involvement**

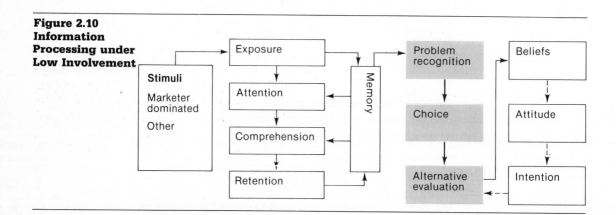

Summary

This chapter has provided the conceptual framework for the remainder of the book by differentiating between high- and low-involvement behavior. Involvement was defined as the extent to which a purchase decision has high personal relevance. When it does (high involvement), the decision process will take the form of extended problem solving, complete with information search and complex alternative evaluation. When this is not the case, decisions are made quite differently; without problem solving. A model of each form of decision-process behavior depicted the variables involved, the linkages between variables, and the manner in which marketing decisions can affect choice behavior.

First of all, the social and cultural environment profoundly affects all forms of consumer behavior. Therefore, chapters in Part 2 cover the topics of economic and demographic influences, cross-cultural and sub-cultural influences, social stratification, reference group and family, and life-style research. Then the two chapters in Part 3 cover the important foundational subjects of information processing and learning.

Part 4 of the book elaborates on the whole process of high-involvement decision processes, and Part 5 focuses on low involvement. Before this more extended discussion can be undertaken effectively, however, the reader must have some additional background.

While much of the content is managerial in nature, there are many issues of consumer welfare which must be addressed. While this is done to some extent in all chapters, Part 6 is specifically devoted to consumerism and the regulation and ethics of consumer influence.

There are some who have a special interest in this field from a more conceptual and historical perspective. Therefore, an appendix is included on "the status of consumer research: problems and prospects."

Review and Discussion Questions

1. What is meant by involvement? How would you classify the following types of purchases? Toothpaste, flour, men's cologne, carpeting, toilet tissue, bread, light bulbs, a 35mm camera. What factors did you use in making your assessment? Is it possible that there can be real variations between individuals for the same product class?

2. What is a model? What role do models play in understanding consumer behavior?

3. In speaking of the problems that might result from psychological analysis of consumer behavior, Vance Packard stated, "Much of it seems to represent regress rather than progress for man in his struggle to become a rational and self-guiding being."[28] The main point is that marketing persuaders now have new tools that enable them to manipulate the consumer and circumvent processes of reasoning. Comment.

4. How might a large manufacturer of automatic washers and dryers use a decision-process approach to better understand how consumers purchase his product?

[28]Vance Packard, *Hidden Persuaders,* (New York: McKay, 1957), 6.

5. Mrs. Jones is watching her favorite afternoon television program, which is on the air from 2:30 to 3:00 P.M. There are seven commercials in 30 minutes, and she does not leave the room. Yet she cannot recall a single commercial after the show has ended, whereas she can recount the plot of the story in detail. What explanations can be given?

6. Much buying supposedly occurs on impulse; that is, a person sees a display or other stimulus and buys with little or no forethought. Can impulse behavior be accounted for in the models? How?

7. Latin American culture differs in major ways from the North American culture. For example, people tend to be more important than things. Materialism, while significant, does not dominate this concern with the feelings of others. Time tends to be of little consequence. "If it doesn't get done today, there is always tomorrow" is not an unusual sentiment. Finally, "machismo" or assertion of manly superiority is a powerful male motivation in all phases of life. While there is much more to be said about the Latin culture, how would these three factors affect consumer behavior in that setting as compared with the North American environment?

8. Indicate which type of decision making would be most likely in each of the following situations (assume all things are equal): (a) past experience with the product has been unsatisfactory, (b) the product is purchased each week, (c) a new home has been purchased, (d) the consumer earns less than $3,000 per year, (e) the product is needed immediately.

9. What is meant by perceived risk? What is the relevance of this concept?

10. Charles Terwilliger is a high school senior and faces the dilemma of choosing a college. He is a good student and has made all-state mention as defensive end in football. His father is a graduate of a well-known eastern school and would like to see Charles go there. Two schools in his home state have offered him football scholarships, and one has twice been national champion in the past five years. Charles's three best friends, however, are going to live at home and go to the local university, whereas the girl he has dated for three years will be attending a university on the West Coast, 2,000 miles away. He has applied to all of these schools and has been accepted. He needs financial aid and plans to become a consulting engineer. Finally he accepts the football tender at the school in his state, which has been national champion. In addition, this university has a good engineering curriculum. The problem, though, is that he has no friends there and has no real desire to join a fraternity, the apparent key to popularity. To test your grasp of the model presented in this chapter, explain what must have happened during and after this decision. Make any assumptions that are necessary.

PART TWO

THE SOCIAL AND CULTURAL ENVIRONMENT

The preceding two chapters have presented an overview of the decision process of consumers. Now the task is to begin to examine the determinants of behavior in more detail.

The question can be asked: Where should one begin in the effort to understand why people do the things they do and make the choices they make? Although a variety of beginnings is possible, one logical starting place is with the broad environmental variables that shape and constrain consumer choices.

Environmental influences such as cultural, economic, and demographic realities are lifetime experiences. That is, they not only influence specific consumer choices but they are operative from birth to determine and shape the nature of a person in ways that influence all his or her decisions. Because of the generic nature of environmental influences, they become especially important when large segments of the population experience the same environmental influences. When social and cultural influences are operative for a large group of persons, that group may be identified as a market segment for which specific communication or marketing strategies are appropriate.

Four chapters are presented in this part of the textbook, analyzing environmental influences on consumer behavior. They present some of the most important and most interesting, yet often neglected and misunderstood, aspects of the study of consumer behavior.

Chapter 3 analyzes the broadest category of environmental influences, the economic structure variables that provide the economic context of consumer behavior. The economic and demographic structures of markets in the United States are described, but many of the trends discussed here are also occurring in other industrially advanced countries.

The topic of cultural norms and values is introduced in Chapter 4. In this chapter, the emphasis is upon values in a cross-cultural setting, both in various nations and in various subcultures such as ethnic, racial and religious groups. A subsection of the chapter discusses black consumer behavior as compared with white consumer behavior. This chapter also contains a description of formal methods of studying cultural norms and values, especially from a cross-cultural approach.

Is social class becoming more or less important as a phenomenon in the American culture? Chapter 5 analyzes this issue and the process of stratification. This chapter describes the factors that determine a person's social class, some methods of measuring social class, and some of the empirical research which indicates differential consumer behavior between social classes.

Chapter 6 describes reference group and family influences on consumer decisions. Reference groups play an important role in determining individual decisions and functions in society as conformity-enforcing devices. Family influences are of great importance in consumer behavior as reference group influences on individual decisions. In addition, there is much to be learned from studying the decisions of families considered as buying units. This chapter describes the basic terminology involved in analysis of family buying, as well as the empirical research that is emerging concerning family structure and decision making.

The final chapter in the part concerns life-styles and their role in developing marketing strategy. In many ways, this chapter is built upon the previous four chapters because life-styles encompass all of the other economic and sociopsychological chapters described in this part, in a manner that is particularly useful in the development of marketing strategy.

CHAPTER 3

ECONOMIC DEMOGRAPHICS: THE FOUNDATION OF CONSUMPTION

A student of consumer behavior, after considering that automobiles are high-involvement goods and understanding something of the decision process described in Chapter 2, decided to search aggressively to find the car that would best express his self-concept life-style preference. After thorough analysis of the market offerings, the student came to the conclusion that there existed a car that precisely matched his preferences. The car: A Porsche *Turbo Carerra*!

When checking the price of the Porsche, however, the young consumer sadly concluded that the car did not meet the realities of his economic circumstances even though it satisfied his attitude and belief structure quite nicely. It matters little what a consumer's preferences may be if the consumer lacks the income to express those preferences. The economic and demographic structure of the marketplace is the subject of this chapter.

THREE BUYING DECISIONS

The study of buyer behavior focuses on three major types of buying decisions:

1. Deciding which *products* will be purchased with available resources.

2. Deciding which *brands* will be purchased among competing products.

3. Deciding which *supplier* will be patronized among competing brands.

Economic and demographic factors may have their greatest influence in determining the *types of products* people need and can purchase but have important influences on brand choice and supplier patronage as well. A market is usually defined as *people,* with *ability to buy* and the *willingness to do so.* As a first area for in-depth study of consumer behavior, therefore, it is appropriate to talk about people in quantitative terms—how many, how old, where they live, and their ability to buy or income. Then, in later chapters, we will look also at some of the influences on their willingness to buy one kind of product or one brand rather than another—influences such as cultural norms, social and family influences and so forth.

**Figure 3.1
Influences of
Anticipated and
Unanticipated
Circumstances on
Intention and
Choice**

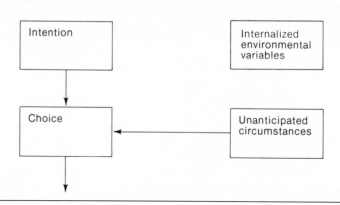

**Internalized
Environmental
Variables**

Demographic and economic variables are internalized into a consumer's decision making and thus influence intentions and choices of that consumer. The circumstances that make up a consumer's environment may be *anticipated*—knowledge of one's income and demographic situation—resulting in intentions to purchase a product or brand. Circumstances may operate either as a positive (inducing) variable or as a negative (inhibiting) constraint. Such variables are described as environmental variables that exist external to the consumer but which have been internalized into the consumer's decision making.

Intentions to purchase may be modified by *unanticipated circumstances* during the choice process. Unanticipated circumstances might include sudden changes in income (such as those caused by unemployment or even losing the cash with which one intended to make a purchase), changes in residence or physical circumstances (such as low temperatures in a home caused by an energy shortage), changes in income taxes, or other variables which become internalized in the consumer's mind and affect the choice process. Other unanticipated variables may include marketing-dominated variables such as price deals, coupons, stock-outs, salesperson influences and so forth. This latter type of influence will be discussed in Chapters 10 and 11 and again in Chapters 19 and 20. The process of influence on intentions and choices by internalized environmental variables is shown in Figure 3.1.

The market potential for a new or existing product is often assessed in a market research report. The starting point in such a report would be a demographic and economic analysis of the potential market. This structural analysis of consumption usually must be completed before more in-depth studies of behavioral variables are begun. Often the sampling plan for other studies must be based upon an understanding of the demographic and economic structure of the market. An important part of the knowledge base and a typical activity of consumer analysts, therefore, is the compilation of detailed information about numbers of consumers, age structure, geographic characteristics and other demographic variables.

In the following pages, some of the important demographic and economic trends are described as they occur in the United States, Canada

Table 3.1
Projected U.S. Population to 2000

	Millions				Percent Change		
	1970	1980*	1990	2000	1970-80	1980-90	1990-2000
Under 5 years	17,158	16,020	19,437	17,852	−6.4%	21.3%	−8.2%
5–14	40,734	33,896	35,758	39,153	−16.7	5.6	9.5
15–19	19,315	20,609	16,777	19,727	6.7	−18.4	17.6
20–29	30,901	39,848	38,122	33,367	28.8	−4.3	−12.5
30–39	22,727	31,275	40,178	38,416	37.9	28.4	−4.4
40–49	24,138	22,817	31,220	39,899	−5.8	37.4	27.8
50–59	21,162	23,069	21,838	29,991	9.0	−5.6	37.3
60–64	8,667	9,797	10,360	10,151	12.6	6.1	−2.0
65+	20,086	24,927	29,824	31,822	23.9	19.7	6.7
Total	204,878	222,159	243,513	260,378	8.5%	9.6%	6.9%

Source: U.S. Census of Population, P-25, #704.

and other industrialized societies. There are numerous examples of how organizations must respond to changes in economic and demographic resources, including the important consumer resource—time. At the end of the chapter, there is a discussion of the major sources of data for these variables and some ways to analyze demographic data for marketing purposes.

PEOPLE: FIRST REQUIREMENT FOR MARKETS

People—how many and what types? That is the first question in the study of markets. This type of analysis is called *economic demographics,* defined as the *study of the economic consequences of changes in the characteristics of a nation's population.*

The populations of the United States, Canada and most industrialized societies are still expanding, but at a decreasing rate. Table 3.1 shows that the U.S. population is expected to increase from 222 million in 1980 to about 243 million in 1990 and 260 million in the year 2000. Table 3.2 shows that the Canadian population is projected to grow from

Table 3.2
Projected Canadian Population to 2001

Year	Population as of June 1 2000	Annual Rate of Population Growth (Percent)	Distribution by Age (Percent)			
			0-19	20-44	45-64	65+
1971	21,568.3	...	39.4	33.9	18.6	8.1
1976	22,772.4	1.1	35.7	36.5	19.1	8.7
1981	24,041.4	1.1	32.0	39.6	19.0	9.4
1986	25,382.9	1.1	29.3	41.9	18.7	10.1
1991	26,591.4	0.9	28.4	41.5	19.1	11.0
1996	27,569.7	0.7	27.8	39.8	20.9	11.5
2001	28,369.7	0.6	26.7	37.9	23.6	11.8

Source: Series C Projections, Statistics Canada.
(Series C assumes total fertility will change to 1.80 by 1985 and remain constant through 2001, net migration gain of 60,000 per year and expectation of life at birth will increase gradually to 70.2 years for males and 78.4 for females by 1986 and then remain constant through 2001.)

the present 24 million to over 26 million by 1990 and over 28 million by 2000.

At some point in the future—the exact year is not yet projectable—population growth in the U.S. and Canada will probably hit ZPG (zero population growth). This situation will dramatically affect marketing strategies that historically have been built upon the assumption of increasing *quantities* of consumers and must shift to emphasis upon development in the *quality* of consumption rather than quantity.

Changing Age Structure

Markets in North America are still increasing but the increases are not uniform by age group. Particularly important is the decline in the importance of young markets in the time period of 1980 to 1990, a trend adversely affecting organizations such as Coca-Cola, Levi-Strauss, the Army and most universities and colleges!

The Older-Youth Market

The population explosion during the decade of the 1980s is among consumers ages 25 to 44, the "youth market" of the seventies. This group of post-World War II babies moves through the decades like a python swallowing a pig and becomes the "mature" market of the 1990s and beyond.

Marketing opportunities arise from understanding the products and marketing programs that will satisfy the 25 to 44 age group; many in this group will be two-earner families with substantial affluence compared to the same group in past decades. The firms that will emerge as big winners will be those with products appealing to these sophisticated time-conscious consumers. They will expect quality and convenience and be able to evaluate whether the marketing offer provides good value. They will buy homes and everything to go in them, high-technology leisure and communications equipment, quality apparel, and convenient, but pleasing, dining experiences.

How should marketing organizations respond to shifts in population? One large organization—U.S. Shoe—benefited greatly during the seventies by appealing to the true "youth market," consumers under 25. U.S. Shoe's strategy consisted of opening specialty apparel stores, *Casual Corner* for women and *J. Riggins* for men. These stores are carefully positioned for a young market target. The eighties, however, brought older but still youthful consumers in the 25 to 34 age group. They want more quality and more sophistication in both product lines and store atmospherics. They are able also to afford higher price points. Thus, U.S. Shoe started two new specialty chains appealing to the 25 to 34 age group—*August Max* for women and *Outrigger* for men.

The *Limited*, also a successful specialty apparel store, adapted to the same changes in the demographics but with a different strategy than that used by U.S. Shoe. The *Limited* remained a single chain but adapted the offerings and atmospherics of the store to the changes in the population. Notice in Figure 3.3 the picture of a 1973 *Limited* store and contrast it with the increased sophistication of a *Limited* store in

**Figure 3.2
Strategies for
Divisions of U.S.
Shoe in Adapting
to the Changing
Age Structure of
Population**

**Youth
Market**

**Older-Youth
Market**

Source: Courtesy of Management Horizons, Inc.

1980, which has been redesigned in atmosphere and reprogrammed in product offering to match the slightly older quality-oriented, fashion-conscious and rapidly expanding market target of the 1980s.

The Middle-Aged Affluent Market   The over-45 market is sometimes neglected because of its slow growth or decline compared to the older-youth market, but the middle-aged market may be more important to many marketers because of its affluence.

**Figure 3.3
Positioning
Strategy of The
Limited to Adapt
to Changing Age
Structure of
Population**

Source: Courtesy of Management Horizons Inc.

This group can be divided into the following market segments:[1]

40 percent active affluents

22 percent homemakers

15 percent active retired

17 percent disadvantaged

1 percent in poor health

6 percent other

The first three categories provide significant market opportunities, principally because they have more money than other families and more discretion in how they spend it. The 45 to 54 age-bracket consumers have a *per capita* income approximately 12 percent above the country's norm and consumers in the 55 to 64 bracket run 30 percent above the average.[2] They have money to spend on luxury goods and services, especially top-of-the-price-line merchandise. In fact, they may be the only consumers able to afford many products of that type. For example, the older consumers buy automobiles that average 20 percent higher than the average spent by consumers in the 25 to 44 group.

Many middle-aged affluents are at the height of their careers, have reduced family responsibilities, have low or no mortgages to pay, are in relatively good health, have limited free time, and have more descretionary money than at any time in their family life. They indulge in luxury travel, restaurants and the theatre—which often means they need more fashionable clothing, jewelry and department stores. They watch their waistlines and diets, are good prospects for spas, health clubs, cosmetics and beauty parlors. When they retire, their money budgets shrink, but they have more time to spend on frequent, but less-expensive vacations. Retired people also may become more concerned shoppers, using coupons and "shopping around" more for good value.

[1]Rena Bartos, "Over 49: The Invisible Consumer Market," *Harvard Business Review* (January-February 1980), 140-148.
[2]Stephen O. Frankfurt, *Middle Age: A State of Affluence* (New York: Kenyond & Eckhardt, Inc., 1979).

Advertising to the middle-aged or older markets is usually more oriented to "reason-why" advertisements or demonstrations. Older consumers are less gullible—they have been round the track before. They may be more aware of word-of-mouth. They like to understand the benefits of a product and probably have the ability to postpone purchases until they find just what they want—but are able to afford it when the right value arises. And they know how to complain when things don't perform right.[3]

Households or Population?

An important distinction must be made by marketers between population and households. A "household" comprises all persons who occupy a "housing unit;" that is, a house, an apartment or other group of rooms, or a room that constitutes "separate living quarters." A household includes the related family members and all the unrelated persons, if any, who share the housing unit. The percentage of nonfamily households has risen from 18.8 percent in 1970 to 26.2 percent in 1980 and is projected to be 29 percent in 1990.

The traditional household was usually defined as having a gainfully employed father, a mother as a housewife and children present. Today only about 19 percent fit those criteria. This is due to the emergence of the single life-style, a rising divorce rate, childless couples and working women. The percentage of single households in the United States has risen from about 13 percent in 1960 to over 22 percent in 1980.

Analyzing the nature of households is essential to marketers. For example, a prominent tile-manufacturing company found that no matter how much advertising and sales support it poured into Manhattan, sales of ceramic tile were below expectations. In San Diego County, however, with fewer households, sales were excellent. Management failed to realize that the number of people in the area did not define the market: The number of owner-occupied households determined the market. Ceramic tile is so expensive that only people who live in their own homes would invest in it. Of the 670,000 households in Manhattan, only 46,000 were owner-occupied, but San Diego had 534,000 households of which 302,000 were owner-occupied.[4] Careful market studies should look at statistics about households as well as population.

THE GEOGRAPHY OF DEMAND

Where are the people? Where do they live? Where are they moving? Those are the next questions a market researcher faces in understanding the structure of consumption. The discipline of geography is important in studying the spatial aspects of the market.

---

[3]Betsy D. Gelb, "Gray Power: Next Challenge to Business?" *Business Horizons* (April 1977), 38-45. Compliant behavior may increase with age, however. See Gerald Zaltman, R. K. Srivastava and Rohit Deshpande, "Perceptions of Unfair Marketing Practices: Consumerism Implications," in Keith Hunt, ed., *Advances in Consumer Research,* vol. 5 (Ann Arbor: Association for Consumer Research, 1978), 247-253.

[4]Taken from Mike Horen, "Small Can Be Beautiful," *American Demographics* (May 1979), 21.

Mobility

People move most when they are young. The following statistics indicate the proportion of the population moving each year, classified by length of the move.[5]

Age	Within County	Between Counties
15–19	11.0%	9.5%
20–24	20.8	22.0
25–29	20.1	21.4
30–34	13.4	13.7
35–44	13.5	13.6
45–54	8.9	8.3

This would lead to less brand loyalty in the younger age groups for geographically specific market offerings—such as banks, grocery stores, medical services and so forth, requiring aggressive advertising strategies to reach the mobile market. Mobility may be an advantage, however, to firms with a national reputation serving young markets such as McDonald's, Wendy's and T.G.I. Friday's. Firms serving ages 35 and above, however, must "go for the long run" providing good offerings and personalized service that will cause customers to return rather than depending upon attracting new residents. As the population matures, lower overall mobility in the nation will occur.

Suburbanization and Gentrification

A long-term population concentration has occurred in metropolitan areas of North America. Suburbs have been the real winners in population growth. Since World War II, the population of the suburbs has been increasing more than twice as fast as the total population and over five times as fast as central cities. People fled the sidewalks of the cities for the trees and grass of the suburbs. Soon the shopping centers and the department stores—and also the crime and other problems of the cities—followed them.[6]

Gentrification Now Seems to be Occurring.

Gentrification is the process of people moving back to the city in a renaissance of neighborhoods—often displacing low-income families who had occupied the neighborhood. Usually, gentrification includes growth in industry and retail trade, housing improvement and change in the number (more) and composition (younger, more affluent) of residents. In spite of well-publicized examples of such rejuvenated neighborhoods, however, the numbers—which must be the basis for market analysis—are overwhelmingly in the direction of the suburbs. For every person who

[5]U.S. Bureau of the Census, P-20, #331.

[6]William Kowinski, "Suburbia: End of the Golden Age," *New York Times Magazine* (March 16, 1980), 16 ff.

moved into a central city during the 1970s, nearly two left. The average population of central cities declined substantially even in recent years.[7]

The energy shortage, the scarcity and expense of capital to build new housing, slower population growth and other reasons argue persuasively for the need to remain in the city[8] but it appears that consumers still prefer the grass of the suburbs. Nonmetropolitan areas, especially those adjacent to metropolitan areas, are experiencing the fastest growth of all. Marketers may find slower growth of regional shopping malls and similar phenomena but no major rush back to cities. More than families moving back from the suburbs, at best it appears that younger people without children are remaining in the city longer and perhaps older retirement-aged consumers are finding more hope of remaining or even returning to a more energy-efficient urban neighborhood.

The Rising Sunbelt

The big news in consumer mobility is the movement to the "Sunbelt" states in the United States. In Canada, the major movement is to the Western Provinces. Today, about 50 percent of the U.S. population lives in the South, up from 45 percent in 1960 but on its way to 55 percent by 1990. Many retailers and their suppliers are finding that areas of the Northeast are "overstored" while the opportunities for growth are in the new shopping centers of the West and South. Some people who move are, of course, retired. The other type of consumer likely to move, however, is a young well-educated, two-earner family with no children—an excellent prospect for many marketing organizations.

The big increases in markets are in California and Texas. This is shown in Table 3.3, which also shows that the big losers are New York, Washington, D.C., Pennsylvania, and Rhode Island.[9] The fastest-growing states are Nevada, Arizona, Wyoming and the other states shown in Table 3.3. These are all small states, however, with the exception of Florida. In the last decade, three states—California, Texas and Florida—accounted for 42 percent of the total U.S. net population change.

The significance of understanding mobility is demonstrated by William R. Davidson, who states, "Today, real fortunes can be made in consumer goods merchandising simply through the *pursuit of the significant minority*—especially one that tends to be swiftly increasing in numbers."

THE EDUCATION EXPLOSION

Consumers in much of the world are becoming more educated. In 1960, there were only 8.2 million college graduates in the United States, but by 1985 the number is projected to about 25 million. These figures are shown in Table 3.4.

---

[7]John Goodman, Jr., "People of the City," *American Demographics* (September 1980), 14-17.

[8]Andrew Hamer, "The Back-to-the-City Movement," *Atlantic Economic Review* (March- April 1978), 4-6.

[9]Also see Peter A. Morrison, "The Shifting Regional Balance," *Amercian Demographics* (May 1979), 9-15.

Table 3.3
Population Change
of States

Gained Most Population	1970 Population	1980 Population	Population Gain 1970-1980
California	19,970,000	22,950,000	2,980,000
Texas	11,200,000	13,600,000	2,400,000
Florida	6,790,000	9,080,000	2,290,000
Arizona	1,780,000	2,530,000	750,000
Colorado	2,210,000	2,830,000	620,000
Virginia	4,650,000	5,250,000	600,000
Georgia	4,590,000	5,170,000	580,000
North Carolina	5,080,000	5,650,000	570,000
Washington	3,410,000	3,970,000	560,000
Tennessee	3,930,000	4,430,000	500,000

Lost Population	1970 Population	1980 Population	Population Loss 1970-80
New York	18,240,000	17,600,000	−640,000
Washington, D.C.	760,000	650,000	−110,000
Pennsylvania	11,800,000	11,720,000	−80,000
Rhode Island	950,000	930,000	−20,000

Fastest Growing	1970 Population	1980 Population	Percent Increase In Population 1970-1980
Nevada	490,000	730,000	50.1
Arizona	1,780,000	2,530,000	42.1
Wyoming	330,000	460,000	39.4
Florida	6,790,000	9,080,000	33.7
Alaska	300,000	400,000	33.3
Utah	1,060,000	1,400,000	32.1
Idaho	710,000	920,000	29.6
Colorado	2,210,000	2,830,000	28.1
New Mexico	1,020,000	1,260,000	23.5
Oregon	2,090,000	2,570,000	23.0

Source: David Kaplan and Cheryl Russell, "What the 1980 Census Will Show," *American Demographics* (April 1980), 13. Reprinted by permission.

The effects of college education are shown in Figure 3.4 for both product categories and retail patronage. This chart displays a consumption index, the percentage a market segment purchases of a product category compared to the average for all households. College graduates, Figure 3.4 shows, consume above-average amounts of furniture and floor coverings, housewares, and apparel but below-average amounts of tobacco, appliances and personal-care items. College graduates are especially likely to be patrons of camera stores, garden center/florists, and some other stores but unlikely to purchase from door-to-door or party-sales representatives.

The most significant effects of education are found among the 25 to 34 age group of consumers. Now almost half of this group have been to college and one-fourth of them have degrees. Jones explains the effects of college education on this important type of consumer that emerged from the post-war baby boom:

Trained in rational decision making—to compare, question, and analyze—baby boomers as a group are far less likely to blindly follow brand loyalties. Goods must prove themselves. On the other hand,

Table 3.4
Estimates and Projections of Persons by Highest
Level of Educational Achievement,
United States 1975–1985 (selected years)

Educational Level	Persons 25 Years and Over (In Millions of Persons)						Change: 1980-1985	
	1975		1980		1985			
	Number	Percent	Number	Percent	Number	Percent	Number	Percent
Elementary school or less	27.0	22.8	23.5	18.3	20.1	14.4	(3.4)	(14.5)
Some high school	19.9	16.8	20.9	16.3	21.6	15.4	.7	3.3
High school graduate	42.8	36.3	48.7	37.9	54.4	39.0	5.7	11.7
Some college	13.3	11.3	16.1	12.5	19.2	13.7	3.1	19.3
College graduate or more	15.1	12.8	19.3	15.0	24.5	17.5	5.2	26.9
Total	118.2	100.0	128.5	100.0	139.9	100.0	11.4	8.9

Source: U.S. Department of Commerce and authors' calculations.

baby boomers are more likely to appreciate the difference that quality can make. They do not buy just any stereo set; they buy the best stereo set. They do not buy any tennis racquet, they buy the best tennis racquet. The transformation of the 25 to 34 age group into an educated class powered the cultural boom of the seventies. More people went to museums and ballets and theaters in that decade simply because there were far more people who had been exposed to the arts by college . . .[10]

INCREASING EMPLOYMENT OF WOMEN

Women generally have been recognized by marketers as the primary purchasing agents for many consumer products. Special attention is demanded, therefore, when those same women are also employed outside the home. Today, over half of all adult women have such a job and so do most married women (see Table 3.5). During the last decade, women left hearth and home to bring home some of the bacon. This trend has been attributed to women's rights, higher education and inflation. Regardless of the reasons, large numbers of women consumers are employed in the labor force and it is likely that more will be there in the future. During the last decade, the 25 to 34 age group of women increased their labor force participation from 45 to 60 percent and the forecast for this segment is nearly an 80 percent participation rate by 1990.

The emergence of more and more women working outside the home creates marketing opportunities for numerous products and services, including apparel, cosmetics, day-care centers and convenience foods. Working women are receptive to time- and labor-saving devices, home maintenance items, and sports equipment to help them keep fit and trim.

There is evidence that the typical working woman of the sixties was

[10]Landon Y. Jones, "The Baby-Boom Consumer," *American Demographics* (February 1981), 28-35.

Figure 3.4a
Product
Consumption
Profile—A College
Graduate**

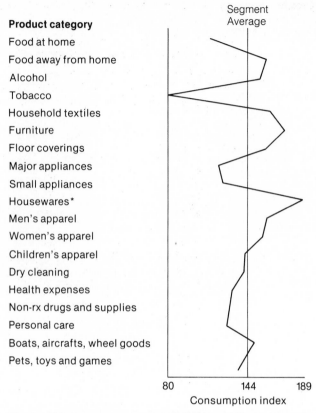

Product category
Food at home
Food away from home
Alcohol
Tobacco
Household textiles
Furniture
Floor coverings
Major appliances
Small appliances
Housewares*
Men's apparel
Women's apparel
Children's apparel
Dry cleaning
Health expenses
Non-rx drugs and supplies
Personal care
Boats, aircrafts, wheel goods
Pets, toys and games

Segment
Average

80   144   189
Consumption index

*Read as: This consumer segment spends 89% more dollars on housewares
compared to the all household average (100%).

**Growth rate (1980-1990) 67.9%

Source: Management Horizons, Inc. Reprinted by permission.

Table 3.5
Labor Force Participation and Unemployment Rates,
Teens, Women, Men, 1950-80

	Total Population		Teens 16-19		Men 20+		Women 20+	
	Partici-pation	Unemploy-ment	Partici-pation	Unemploy-ment	Partici-pation	Unemploy-ment	Partici-pation	Unemploy-ment
1950	59.2%	5.3%	51.8%	12.2%	88.4%	4.7%	33.3%	5.1%
1960	59.4	5.5	48.9	14.7	86.0	4.7	37.6	5.1
1965	58.9	4.5	47.5	14.8	83.9	3.2	39.4	4.5
1970	60.4	4.9	45.7	15.2	82.6	3.5	43.3	4.8
1975	61.2	8.5	49.9	19.9	80.3	6.7	46.0	8.0
1979	65.8	5.8	58.1	16.1	79.8	4.1	50.6	5.7
1980	63.8	7.5	56.7	17.5	79.5	6.7	51.2	6.1

Source: Bureau of Labor Statistics.

Figure 3.4b Retail Patronage Profile A—College Graduate**

Store type | Segment Average

HIC/lumber yard
Department store
Variety store
Discount store
Catalog showroom
Apparel store
Shoe store
Fabric store
Furniture store
Appliance/tv store
Drug store
Jewelry store
Sporting goods store
Camera store*
Garden center/florist
Optical goods stores
Music stores
Toy stores
Mail order
Door to door/party

87   116   141
Patronage index

*Read as: This consumer segment is 41% more likely to shop at camera stores compared to the all household average (100%).

**Growth rate (1980-1990) 67.9%

Source: Management Horizons, Inc. Reprinted by permission.

very different from the typical working woman of the eighties. Previously, women who worked, particularly those with children, were often apologetic about their employment. Increasingly during the last decade, non-working women found themselves explaining their housewife status. In addition, women began describing their jobs as careers. They may step out for a short time to have children but many return almost immediately. Perhaps no marketer has benefitted so much from incorporating these changes into its advertising as the most successful cigarette brand of the most successful cigarette company (see Figure 3.5).

The Proliferation of Affluence

Willie Sutton, the noted bankrobber, said, "I go where the money is . . . and I go there often."

So should marketers.

**Figure 3.5
Advertisement
Showing the
Changing Role of
Women**

Source: Phillip Morris Company. Reprinted by permission.

For decades, millions of consumers have enjoyed steadily increasing earnings. Even with setbacks during recessions, the overall trend has been a shift of millions of families from lower earning levels to the middle-income brackets. A projection of increased median income for U.S. families is shown in Figure 3.6. In Canada, income has grown rapidly but has been affected significantly by inflation. Disposable income on a *per capita* basis is still growing, however.[11]

Analyzing income data is a difficult process because of the effects of inflation and the differential abilities of families to compete for inflationary dollars. Changes in family size also complicate the income issue. Between 1970 and 1980, for example, real median income increased very

[11]For an excellent summary of Canadian income and other statistics, see *Tomorrow's Customers 1980* (Toronto: Woods Gordon, 1980).

Figure 3.6
United States Families By Age and Money Income

1990–$22,500

Income	18-24	25-34	35-44	45-54	55-64	65 +	Total
Under $10,000	5	11	8	5	6	19	54
$10,000–15,000	4	11	8	5	6	11	45
$15,000–25,000	7	34	25	14	12	10	102
$25,000–35,000	2	23	22	13	10	4	74
$35,000–50,000	1	11	16	12	7	2	49
$50,000 or more		4	9	8	5	1	27
Total	19	94	88	57	46	47	**351 Dots**

1977–$16,300

Income	18-24	25-34	35-44	45-54	55-64	65 +	Total
Under $10,000	11	16	11	9	12	23	82
$10,000–15,000	5	14	8	7	6	8	48
$15,000–25,000	4	28	24	23	17	6	102
$25,000–35,000		5	6	10	6	2	29
$35,000–50,000		2	5	5	4	2	18
$50,000 or more			1	2	1	1	5
Total	20	65	55	56	46	42	**284 Dots**

Each dot represents 200,000 households

Source: Census Bureau P-60 #108, #109, #114, #116, P-23 #47 and Management Horizon's Retail Intelligence System. Reprinted by permission of Management Horizons, Inc.

little but on a *per capita* basis—because of smaller families—income increased by over 18 percent. Black income did not increase at all on a real family basis but increased even more than among whites—26.5 percent—on a *per capita* basis because of the rapid decrease in black family size.[12]

The proliferation of income can be seen in Figure 3.6, especially for some market segments. The 25 to 34 age group with $15,000 to $35,000 income is projected, by 1990, to account for more than 25 percent of all households versus only about 17 percent at the end of the last decade. The proliferation of income, at least for some segments, creates consumers who *can buy most anything they want but they cannot buy everything they want.* Life, for large numbers of affluent consumers, is a continual process of choices among a huge array of goods and services from which some, or even many, but almost never all can be chosen. It is the great increase in choice possibilities and the complexity of decision influences that has in part stimulated consumer research and given rise to so many courses in the discipline of consumer behavior.

The other side of the coin, however, is that inflation has taken a heavier impact on down-scale households than on up-scale households. This is primarily due to the fact that the prices of many necessities, such as utilities and gasoline, have risen faster than the general consumer price index. Since a greater proportion of down-scale households' disposable income is devoted to necessities, their descretionary income is shrinking at a faster rate than that of up-scale households.

CONSUMER TIME BUDGETS

In recent years, it has been recognized that consumer resources consist of two budget constraints—a *money budget* and a *time budget.* Although rising incomes mean that consumers conceivably can *buy* more of everything, they cannot conceivably *do* more of everything. Doing more things, as opposed to buying more things, requires an additional resource—time. Understanding the circumstances that affect consumer intentions must include, therefore, time budgets.[13]

The value of time increases relative to money as money budgets increase. Whereas money budgets have no theoretical expansion limits, time has an ultimate restraint. It can readily be seen that as discretionary income continues to increase in a society, markets for time-related goods or services become more important. The consumer implications are described by Garretson and Mauser:

---

[12]David Kaplan and Cheryl Russell, "What the 1980 Census Will Show," *American Demographics* (April 1980), 11-17.

[13]This section is drawn from Justin Voss and Roger Blackwell, "Markets for Leisure Time," in Mary Jane Slinger (ed.), *Advances in Consumer Research* (Chicago: Association for Consumer Research, 1975), 837-45 and Justin Voss and Roger Blackwell, "The Role of Time Resources in Consumer Behavior," in O. C. Ferrell, Stephen Brown and Charles Lamb, (eds.), *Conceptual and Theoretical Developments in Marketing* (Chicago: American Marketing Association, 1979), 296-311.

**Figure 3.7
Conceptualizations
of Consumer Time
Budgets and
Leisure**

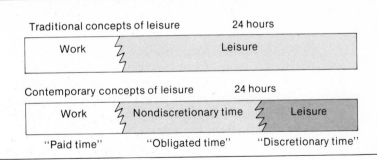

The affluent citizen . . . will be oriented to buying time rather than product. His chief concern will be to provide himself with free time in which he can conveniently use products that function to conserve time for leisure and pleasure. It is scarcity which creates value. Hence, as scarcity of product disappears, the scarcity of time ascends the value scale.[14]

For the consumer, time must be consumed both in learning about consumption choices and in consuming products and services.[15] Traditionally, however, these activities were not treated in a framework that recognized their costs from the consumer's time budget. Frequently, the 24-hour budget of consumers was naively regarded as a two-component budget—work and leisure. This conceptualization is shown in the upper portion of Figure 3.7.

A contemporary conceptualization of consumer time budgets is shown in the lower portion of Figure 3.7, in which consumer time budgets are divided into three blocks of time—work (paid time), nondiscretionary time and discretionary time.[16] It is only this latter block of time that can be truly regarded as leisure time. Voss concludes:

Leisure . . . may be defined as follows: Leisure is a period of time referred to as discretionary time. It is that period when an individual feels no sense of economic, legal, moral, or social compulsion or obligation, nor of physiological necessity. The choice of how to utilize this time period is solely his.[17]

Time Goods

A contemporary conceptualization of consumer time budgets leads to the recognition that goods and services have important time properties. Products and services classified by their time properties may be called

[14]Robert C. Garretson and Ferdinand F. Mauser, "The Future Challenges Marketing," *Harvard Business Review,* vol. 41 (November-December 1963), 168 ff.

[15]Philip B. Schary, "Consumption and the Problem of Time," *Journal of Marketing,* vol. 35 (April 1971), 50-55.

[16]Voss and Blackwell, "Markets."

[17]Justin Voss, "The Definition of Leisure," *Journal of Economic Issues,* vol. 1 (June 1967), 91-106. Voss analyzes conceptions of leisure for analytical purposes. For other conceptions of leisure, see Douglass Hawes, "Time and Behavior," in Ferrell et al, 1979, 281-295.

time goods and the time properties of goods have important marketing implications.

Time-Using Goods

One category of products and services is that which requires the use of time with the product. Examples would be watching television, skiing, fishing, golfing, tennis and many other activities usually classified as leisure time activities. They would normally fall in the portion of time called discretionary time or leisure in Figure 3.7.

To understand the nature of time-using goods of the discretionary type that would be purchased, it is necessary to understand what is happening to the other categories of time usage in a typical 24-hour day. Contrary to popular opinion, perhaps, there has been no significant decline in the workweek since the end of World War II.[18] The only increases in leisure time, from reduced paid time, have been associated with an increased number of holidays, length of vacations, and earlier retirement.

Nondiscretionary time, or obligated time, includes physical obligations (sleeping, commuting, personal care, and so forth), social obligations (which seem to increase with urbanization and the rising proportion of professional and white collar occupations) and moral obligations. It appears that nondiscretionary activities also are not declining and, at least in consumer perceptions, are increasing. Thus, the net effect of trends in time usage leads to a feeling by many consumers of less leisure rather than more.

When the effect of increased money budgets is considered, the conclusion must be that consumers will be willing to pay more money to enjoy their limited leisure time. In such an economy, it would be predicted that consumers would be willing to pay more and more dollars to enjoy their leisure time (such as is required in travel, skiing, expensive sports equipment, and so forth) and would be likely to switch from less intense leisure activities such as golf to more intense leisure activities such as tennis. This was shown in a study of leisure-time satisfactions in which highly educated and high income men (presumably busier) were more likely to derive satisfaction from tennis than from golf.[19]

Time-Saving Goods

One way for consumers to obtain increased discretionary time (leisure), is to decrease nondiscretionary time. That frequently may be achieved through the purchase of goods and services.

---

[18]Geoffrey H. Moore, "Measuring Leisure Time," *The Conference Board Record* (July 1971), 53-54. Belief in a reduced workweek may be due to confusion in statistics, which as typically reported are usually based upon manufacturers' payrolls. As such, they usually include both full-time and part-time workers, which distorts the averages for all workers in decades of increasing proportions of part-time workers. Also, manufacturers' payroll records do not include second jobs, which are part of the workweek from the consumer's perspective. It is also misleading to consider only manufacturing statistics in an era when a rising proportion of workers are technical, professional and managerial—and may have longer workweeks than manufacturing employees.

[19]Douglass K. Hawes, W. Wayne Talarzyk, and Roger D. Blackwell, "Consumer Satisfactions from Leisure Time Pursuits," in Mary J. Slinger, *Advances,* 822.

Services represent the obvious marketing offering that provides additional discretionary time. The purchase of a lawn-mowing or lawn-fertilizing service (such as *Chem-lawn)* may free the consumer for true leisure activities. Similarly, much of the restaurant and frozen food industry can be considered to be selling time. Convenience goods and disposable products of many types are ways in which the consumer can buy time. Jet airplanes may cost more money but whisk a consumer away to Florida in order to have more leisure compared to driving there in an auto. Finally, many so-called labor saving devices or consumer durable goods are actually time-saving products.

There is an increasing recognition by marketing organizations that the desire to save time is an important marketing element. This may lead to new products (pouches for quick cooking, microwave ovens, dishwashers, and so forth) or may lead to "positioning" strategies in which time properties are featured in communications about the product. Some advertisers are now featuring the "time price" of the product—such as "only two hours to install" or "save time with new 'dry' deodorant."

Measuring Time Expenditures

The methodology for measuring time is embryonic. Jacoby has provided a comprehensive review of the concept of time as it is used in consumer behavior.[20] Fox suggests that important attributes of time include *performance time* (actual and perceived), *flexibility* or *fixity* of carrying out activities, *frequency* (how often activity is conducted), *regularity, duration, disruption/simultaneity,* and *monitoring time* (how much effort is required to remember to carry out the activity).[21]

A simple way of measuring time is to ask consumers to recall the amounts of time spent in various activities. But this is subject to considerable bias. A diary is probably more accurate although the additional complexity and nonresponse bias may offset this accuracy for many marketing research studies.[22] Hawes used the diary approach in his landmark study as did Robinson in the description of American time budgets[23] shown in Table 3.6.

There is a great amount of research conducted currently on the nature of time and its relationship to leisure.[24] The attempt is to relate time to other variables of interest—media patterns, income, activities that involve the marketing of products and services, and, of course, to shopping patterns. Statistics Canada collects data of the type shown in Figure 3.8.

[20]J. Jacoby, G. J. Szybillo, and C. K. Berning, "Time and Consumer Behavior: An Interdisciplinary Overview," *The Journal of Consumer Research* (March 1976), 320-339.

[21]Karen Fox, "Time as a Component of Price in Social Marketing," in R. P. Bogozzi (ed.), *Marketing in the 80's* (Chicago: American Marketing Association, 1980) 464-467.

[22]Doyle Bishop, Claudine Jeanrenaud, and Kenneth Lawson, "Comparison of a Time Diary and Recall Questionnaire for Surveying Leisure Activities," *Journal of Leisure Research,* vol. 7 (1975), 73-80.

[23]J. P. Robinson, *Changes in American's Use of Time: 1965-1975* (Cleveland: Communication Research Center, Cleveland State University, 1977).

[24]B. Linder, *The Harried Leisure Class* (New York: Columbia University Press, 1970); J. F. Murphy, *Concepts of Leisure* (Englewood Cliffs: Prentice-Hall, 1974); J. Neulinger, *The Psychology of Leisure* (Springfield, Illinois: Charles C. Thomas, 1974); M. Kaplan, *Leisure: Theory and Policy* (New York: John Wiley & Sons, 1975).

Table 3.6
Time Budgets of
U.S. Consumers

Activity*	Employed Men		Employed Women		Housewives Married (N = 141)
	Married (N = 245)	Single (N = 87)	Married (N = 117)	Single (N = 108)	
Sleep	53.4	54.1	55.1	54.3	56.8
Work for pay	47.4	40.0	30.1	38.8	1.1
Family care	9.7	9.0	24.9	16.6	44.3
Personal care	21.4	20.0	26.2	21.9	21.4
Free time	36.1	44.9	31.7	36.4	44.4
Organizations	3.7	4.8	2.2	4.4	4.8
Media	18.9	18.5	15.6	14.5	20.4
Social life	6.4	8.9	6.6	8.9	10.1
Recreation	1.3	4.1	0.8	0.5	0.7
Other leisure	5.8	8.6	6.5	8.1	8.4

*Average hours per week.

Source: Derived from J.P. Robinson, *Changes in American's Use of Time: 1965-1975* (Cleveland: Communication Research Center, Cleveland State University, 1977), Table 4. Used with permission.

This figure relates leisure activities to education. Study Figure 3.8 and you will see that some activities such as TV viewing decrease with increasing education while other activities such as reading increase with education. Participation in most types of cultural activities increases with education.

COLLECTING AND ANALYZING DEMOGRAPHIC DATA

The final section of this chapter describes sources of economic and demographic data and some of the techniques for applying them to marketing problems. At this point, you may be getting tired of studying so many tables and charts. Be assured that you won't have to do so much of this in the rest of the book. Demographic analysis, however, usually involves poring over numbers—questioning how they were collected and what they mean.

Hopefully, you will have spent adequate time on each figure and have thought about what the data might mean for marketing programs. You will have learned many (hopefully) interesting and useful things about consumers. More importantly, you will have gained an appreciation for the type of data that are available when you begin your own analysis of a problem in consumer behavior. You will have also noted some of the sources of data, just by giving attention to the references provided for each figure. It is usually safe to assume that data exist somewhere on the topic in which you are interested—if only you can figure out where!

Census Data

The first nationwide population census in the United States was conducted in 1770. It took 18 months to complete and was an enumeration of "free and slave" persons in each state. In 1820, questions on citizenship and industry were added and in 1850, questions pertaining to marital status, place of birth, occupation, and value of real estate were added. In 1950, the Census Bureau introduced several sampling techniques as

**Figure 3.8
Leisure Habits in
Canada**

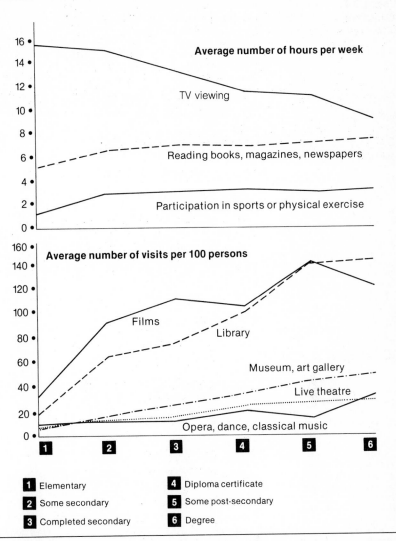

Source: Statistics Canada

alternative methods to collecting census-required information and today many questions that are described as census data are really sampling data based on interviews of 5 to 20 percent of the population. Only a few basic questions needed for sensitive government allocation of funds are asked of 100 percent of the population queried.

Sources of Data

The most important source of demographic data in Canada is Statistics Canada. In the United States, it is the Bureau of the Census of the U.S. Department of Commerce. The data collected in a decennial census changes somewhat from decade to decade, as shown in Table 3.7,

Table 3.7
Comparison of Population Questions in the
1970 and 1980 Censuses[a]

Population Question	1980 100 Percent Questionnaire	1980 Sample Questionnaire Only	1970 100 Percent Questionnaire	1970 Sample Questionnaire Only
Age	X		X	
Sex	X		X	
Race	Modified		X	
Household relationship	Modified		X	
Marital status	X		X	
Spanish origin	Modified			X
Place of birth		X		X
Citizenship		X		X
If foreign born, year of immigration		X		X
Place of birth of parents		Omitted		X
Ancestry		New item	—	—
Language used as a child		Omitted		X
Language used at home		New item	—	—
Ability to speak English		New item	—	—
Year moved to present residence		Modified		X
Place of residence 5 years ago		X		X
Major activity 5 years ago		Modified		X
School enrollment		X		X
Public or private school		X		X
Educational attainment		X		X
Industry and occupation 5 years ago		Omitted		X
Veteran status		Modified		X
Disability		Modified		X
Children ever born		X		X
Marital history		X		X
Work status last week		X		X
Hours worked		X		X
Place of work		X		X
Usual travel time to work		New item	—	—
Means of transportation to work		Modified		X
Carpooling		New item	—	—
Temporarily absent from work		X		X
Looking for work last week		X		X
Year last worked		X		X
Industry of current job		X		X
Occupation of current job		X		X
Class of worker of current job		X		X
Work in previous year		X		X
Weeks worked		X		X
Usual hours worked per week last year		New item	—	—
Weeks looking for work or on layoff from a job in 1979		New item	—	—
Amount of income by source		Modified		X
Total income		New item	—	—
Vocational training		Omitted		X

[a]Excludes screening questions and other information collected, but not intended for tabulation. "X" means included.

Source: Mark Littman, "The 1980 Census of Population: Content and Coverage Improvement Plans," *Journal of Consumer Research* (September 1979), 204-212. Reprinted by permission.

which compares the 1970 census with the 1980. New questions were added in 1980 about commuting time, language spoken and employment. Of course some questions therefore must be dropped. Some idea of what questions may be added in a future census is also provided in cartoon form in Figure 3.9. The Bureau of Economic Analysis of the De-

**Figure 3.9
Census Questions
of the Future**

"*Have there been any recent births, deaths or clonings in your family?*"

Source: Cheney ©, 1979, *AMERICAN DEMOGRAPHICS*.

partment of Commerce also provides valuable information by making midyear projections, estimates of per capita income, and other projections into the future.

**Private Data
Firms**

There has been an explosive growth in recent years of private firms providing analyses of government data for marketers. One of these, American Research Bureau, compiles data on the basis of area of dominant influence or ADI, a geographical market area of contiguous counties defined by television viewing. For each ADI, information is available concerning the estimated number of television households by county, number of adult women and number of adult men, and number of teenagers and children.

Another widely used source of demographic data is Sales Management's "Survey of Buying Power" (SBP). Published in July each year, the SBP contains data on population; effective buying income; and retail sales for all standard metropolitan statistical areas (SMSAs), states, counties and cities in the United States and for most metropolitan areas, provinces, counties, and cities in Canada.

In recent years, many other firms have emerged that purchase computer tapes of census data and provide their own analyses of the data, either on a syndicated basis with standard reports for each of their clients or on a customized basis. Firms such as Donnelly Marketing, Claritas, Compusearch and many others provide valuable data for marketing planners. American Demographics, itself a most useful publication for consumer analysts and marketing researchers, provides a description of the names, addresses, and typical services of the major demographic analysis firms.[25] Many of these provide data classified by ZIP code with detailed information about each of the over 38,000 residential ZIP codes in the United States. These allow marketers to target direct mail, broadcasts, and magazines to consumers closely matched to the firm's market targets.

Demographic Analysis and Marketing Programs

A demographic and economic analysis of circumstances affecting consumer intentions and choices is important in the planning of marketing strategy. An example of how an analysis might be made of trends such as those discussed in this chapter is shown in Figure 3.10. In this matrix, Management Horizons, a consulting firm, prepared a systematic analysis of demographic trends for its client firms in retailing organizations. Each of these trends is analyzed in terms of probable positive or negative effects on sales of products by merchandise line.

Finally, we can summarize how to use this chapter by looking at a detailed example of how demographic analysis can be applied to a specific product, such as sheets and pillowcases. Read through this example in Exhibit 3.1, and you should understand how to bring economic demographic data together in a meaningful analysis providing the basis for marketing plans. This example shows how demographic analysis can be used for establishing quotas in one city. In the future, such information and methods of analysis will be computerized so that sales plans for the entire country can be quickly calculated and the effects of changes in assumptions can be analyzed through simulation models. Often, demographic analysis will be displayed with easy-to-use computer-generated graphics.[26]

---

[25]Martha Riche, "Demographic Supermarkets of the Eighties," *American Demographics* (February 1981), 15-21.

[26]Constance Bart, "Seeing May Be Believing," *American Demographics* (March 1979), 24-27.

**Figure 3.10
Demographic
Impact on
Marketing
Strategy**

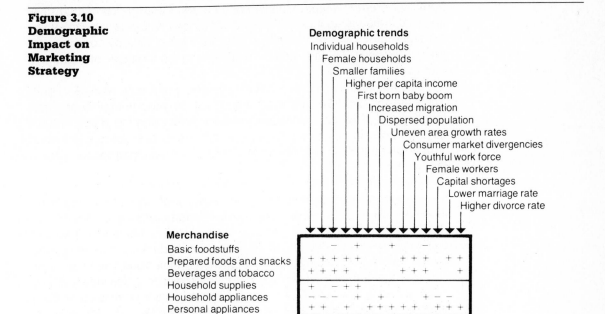

Source: Reprinted by permission of Management Horizons, Inc.

**Exhibit 3.1
The Demographics
of Selling Sheets
and Pillowcases**

To see how demographic analysis works, let's construct an example and follow it to its logical conclusion. We are going to be manufacturers of sheets and pillowcases. As a general rule, about 30 million dozen of these items are produced and sold each year in every type of outlet in the United States.

The example we are constructing will be for a portion of this output: a brand-name product that is sold only in conventional department stores (as opposed to national chains such as Sears, J.C. Penney and Wards, or discounters and mass merchandisers such as K-Mart). The department stores have about a 40 percent market share of the total output, so we will be working with 12 million dozen of the product. Within this total we should also know that our company has a 20 percent market share, or a total of 2.4 million dozen.

The easiest thing for management to do is to decide to increase production to achieve an additional 3 percent market share. While a 3 percent increase seems achievable, once translated to the actual units involved it means an increase of 360,000 dozen. The first thing the sales manager must know is where to sell the additional 360,000 dozen sheets and pillowcases. To understand the answer to the problem, let's examine it at the level of a single SMSA, Cleveland, Ohio.

According to 1976 data, Cleveland has a population of 1.95 million. There are 671,000 households, with a total disposable income of $11.9 billion. Total retail sales in 1976 were $6 billion, and the market had a buying power in excess of 1.1547 (which means that we would expect 1.1547 percent of all retail sales in the country to be made in the Cleveland metropolitan area).

These are the market's dry statistics, which if carried on indefinitely are guaranteed to lose the audience, who cannot see the relationship those figures have to the particular products the company is selling.

To understand the market potential for the sheet and pillowcase company it is necessary to use weighted demographic data such as the age of population, the kinds of households, their incomes, total retail sales, and other relevant factors. For various reasons, Clevelanders buy more goods in the city's 17 national chains and in its 46 mass-merchandiser outlets than in its four department stores with their 22 separate units. These four department stores can be expected to sell 111,192 dozen sheets and pillowcases per year, our statistics tell us. Remember, our company is striving for a 23 percent market share, which in Cleveland would represent 25,574 dozen units.

But the 25,574 figure is for the entire year. Our figures show that 46.6 percent of the total sales in Cleveland take place in the first half of the year. Further, in the first quarter we can expect 20.5 percent and the second quarter 26.1 percent of the year's sales. In the second half of the year the 53.4 percent of sales breaks out as 22.3 percent in the third quarter and 31.1 percent in the fourth quarter.

To achieve the goal of selling 25,574 dozen units, therefore, we can set four separate quotas. The first quarter quota is 5,243 dozen, the second quarter is 6,675 dozen, the third quarter quota is 5,703 dozen, and the last quarter quota is 7,954 dozen.

Moreover, our corporation has to break down the figures further to shipments we expect to make each month, since that is part of our shipping budget. For example, of the 6,675 dozen sheets and pillowcases to be sold in the second quarter, we expect to ship 7.1 percent in April, 7.7 percent in May, and 11.3 percent in June. Thus, we are now looking at 1,816 dozen for April, 1,969 dozen for May, and 2,890 dozen for June. We can also examine the potential of each department store in Cleveland, based on its size and environment, so that we can develop our quota by store or by units.

Source: Mike Horen, "Small Can Be Beautiful," *American Demographics* (May 1979), 21-23. Reprinted by permission.

Summary

A good starting place in the analysis of consumer behavior is the economic and demographic context of consumption. These variables become internalized within the consumer. There they influence intentions and choices of the consumers about products, brands, and suppliers. Economic, demographic, and other variables affect consumer decisions either as *anticipated* or *unanticipated* circumstances.

Key changes in the North American economies include an "older" youth group (the rise in economic power of the 25 to 44 age group) and an affluent mature market, mobility among the young but declining for the nation as a whole, continuing suburbanization with some counter-trend of gentrification, the rise of the *Sunbelt,* an education explosion, increasing employment of women, and a proliferation of affluence for some—but not all—families.

Consumer behavior is affected by *time budgets* as well as by money budgets. Products may therefore be analyzed in terms of their *time-using* properties as well as their *time-saving* properties. A useful method of analyzing such properties is by classifying consumer time expenditures into work (paid time), nondiscretionary time activities, and leisure (discretionary time activities.)

The Census of Population provides a wealth of information, changed each ten years to reflect new concerns of government leaders and marketers. Most of the value of these data is achieved through sophisticated computer analysis of the data on a ZIP code or other basis.

Review and Discussion Questions

1. Why is economic demographics a logical starting place for the in-depth analysis of consumer behavior?

2. Assume that you are a marketing officer for a large furniture retailer. Prepare a marketing program that would be successful in reaching consumers in the 25 to 34 age group.

3. How would the marketing program differ for the above furniture retailer if the market target were the 49 to 65 group?

4. Research the marketing strategies of U.S. Shoe and The *Limited* described in this chapter. What are the strengths and weaknesses of each approach? What have been the financial results of each firm?

5. Why is it important to distinguish between population and households? How has the structure of households in the United States changed in recent years?

6. What are the major effects on marketing of increasing education?

7. Describe the relationship that rearranged work weeks (flex-time, reduced-day workweeks) might have on consumption patterns, using the analysis of time budgets presented in this chapter.

8. Find a description in a newspaper of the "renewal" of a neighborhood in a nearby city. Compare any descriptions you may find of "return to the city" opinions with statistical data for that city. Analyze the effects of your conclusions on marketing programs for that city.

9. Find and interview a firm that specializes in the analysis of economic demographic data. How are such analyses used by marketing organizations? What does the firm provide that is not available from public sources?

Ego, a new deodorant brand, was advertised in an African country with a television commercial showing a short, fumbling man failing to be sexually successful, in a harem full of women. But after he applied *Ego* deodorant, the women pulled him inside the tent and overpowered him. This ad apparently was successful with white consumers in that country but was totally rejected by black consumers. Do you know the reason for this difference in reaction?

In Europe, McCain Foods distributes a highly successful brand of frozen french fried potatoes. Television commercials seen in Germany show the potatoes served at the dinner table with a glass of beer nearby. If the same ad were shown in France, consumers would probably find it offensive and ineffective. Why?

In Montreal, Bay department store features an in-store display with prices described in French. In order to inform its English-speaking customers of a special offer, the store manager also includes signs showing the price in English. The store manager receives complaints about the display from some of the store's customers and may even be charged with a legal offense because of the sign. Why would this happen?

In New York City, Ford Motors undertakes an advertising campaign as aggressive and well-designed as that of General Motors, featuring cars that are competitive in function and price with GM. Yet GM outsells Ford by a far greater margin than in other markets. What is the explanation?

All of the above scenarios have the same explanation. They differ only in specifics. In each case, marketers were unaware of or failed to overcome the effects of culture.

In the African culture, deodorant did not have the same sexual connotation for blacks as for whites. Within the black population, however, there is a strong cultural belief that men who are weak are not respected. Blacks who saw the ad featuring a man being overpowered by women interpreted it to mean that using *Ego* deodorant made a person weak; not a very good sales appeal!

In the case of McCain Foods, an ad for food in Germany would properly include a glass of beer, but this ad would be considered ineffective in France where wine is the usual drink with meals. In Montreal, the problem for the store manager is created by a fear that the French culture is being subverted by Anglo culture and that English should not be perpetuated alongside French culture. This has resulted in a law, surprising in a nation that is officially bilingual, prohibiting the use of English in Montreal stores.

In New York, it is nearly impossible to practice marketing effectively without considering the city's ethnic groups and their cultures. Over the years, General Motors carefully put together a network of dealers sensitive to and often personally a part of the Jewish, black, Puerto Rican, or other cultures. This ethnically based distribution network provides a major obstacle for competitors to overcome.

In this chapter, you will learn how a consumer's cultural background shapes and influences the kind of products that people value most, their media exposure, brand preferences and patterns of shopping. These determinants of consumer behavior reflect the *core values* of the nation in which a consumer lives. Values also vary by subculture. Subcultures of interest to consumer analysts include ethnic, religious, and racial groups as well as less-defined groups such as the "campus" subculture. The chapter concludes with an introduction to marketing research methods that are particularly appropriate to cross-cultural analysis on a global or subcultural basis. First, a look at background material on the concept of culture and its importance in shaping human behavior.

WHAT IS CULTURE?

The term *culture* can be used in varied ways but in consumer behavior it usually means the *complex of values, ideas, attitudes, and other meaningful symbols created by people to shape human behavior and the artifacts of that behavior, transmitted from one generation to the next*. Culture does not refer to the instinctive response tendencies of people nor does it include the inventive innovations occurring within an individual's lifetime that take place as one-time solutions to unique problem situations.

A culture includes both abstract and material elements. Abstract elements include values, attitudes, ideas, personality types, and summary constructs such as religion. These are learned patterns of behavior, feeling, and reaction that are transmitted from a generation to succeeding ones. Material elements of the culture include items as diverse as a stone wheel or a *Space Invaders* game. Material components include television and other forms of transmitting advertisements, as well as books, computers, tools, buildings, and many other artifacts of a society. And most importantly, the material aspects of a culture include the products offered by marketing organizations.

Abstract elements of culture affect consumer preferences for material elements of culture (including products). Thus the focus in our study of consumer behavior needs to be upon abstract elements—the norms and shared beliefs that create the underlying drives of consumer behavior and conform those drives into behavior acceptable within the culture.

Where Do Consumers Get Their Values?

No human exists without values. Yet babies are not born with values. So, where do people develop their values? The processes by which people develop their values are called socialization and acculturation. *Socialization* is the process of absorbing a culture in which one is raised. *Acculturation* is the process of learning a new culture—as when a consumer moves to a new country or changes group identification by marrying someone of a different culture, entering the university, or making a major career change.

Values are group norms which have been internalized by individuals, often with some modification by the individual. Values can be measured on an individual basis, but that is usually not as productive for marketing practitioners as trying to understand the values of a group. Groups make larger market targets than individuals. The most basic group in which a person exists is the family—the topic discussed in Chapter 6. Other groups such as work groups, social classes, nationalities, racial groups, and so forth also provide the norms that guide consumer behavior. Norms are *quantitative statements or beliefs held by a consensus of a group concerning the behavior rules for individual members*. The source of a culture's norms is the culture itself. Several assumptions about this process are widely accepted.[1]

Culture is a set of learned responses. Humans are not born with their norms of behavior in the way that animals are born with instincts. Instead, norms and values must be learned from the environment through a process of reward and punishment by a society of its members who adhere to or deviate from the group's norms.

Cultural items learned early in life tend to resist changes more strongly than those learned late in life. This fact has important implications for marketing strategy, since those cultural elements learned early in life are likely to be highly resistant to promotional effort of marketers. When an advertiser is dealing with deeply ingrained, culturally defined behavior, it is usually easier to conform to the cultural values than attempt to change them through advertising. While advertisers usually cannot change cultural values for the benefit of specific products, it should be recognized that the content or themes of advertising may in themselves be transmitters and reinforcers of cultural values.[2]

Culture is inculcated from one generation to another. Primarily, culture is passed on from parents to children and by institutions such as schools. Religious groups are also important to the process, as Chapter 7 describes. While the institutions of one generation are heavily involved

---

[1]This discussion is based upon G. P. Murdock, "Uniformities in Culture," *American Sociological Review*, vol. 5 (1940), 361-369; Omar K. Moore and Donald Lewis, "Learning Theory and Culture," *Psychological Review*, vol. 59 (1952), 380-388.

[2]Jules Henry, *Pathways to Madness* (New York: Random House, 1971).

in the inculcation process, individuals may accept all or some portion of these inculcated values depending upon the individual's own makeup, reference group influences, and movement between groups with differing norms of behavior.

Cultural values are social phenomena in that they refer to group habits or norms rather than an individual's way of behaving. This is of particular importance to marketing strategists since most marketing programs must be designed for groups of persons (market segments) rather than individual preferences or behavior.

People belong to many groups, however, and sometimes the various groups to which they belong will have norms or values that conflict with each other. A person may find the business organization has norms of behavior that conflict with his or her religious, racial, or other cultural norms. Even within the organization, norms of behavior exist for marketing people that are different from financial, personnel, production, or research and development executives.[3]

Cultural norms reward socially gratifying responses. Culture develops and exists, almost as if it were an entity in itself, to meet the basic biological and secondary needs of a society. When norms are no longer gratifying to the existence of that society, they become extinguished because individual members are no longer rewarded for adhering to them.

An example of this can be observed in the development of individuals to fill occupations needed by a society to perpetuate itself. Physicians and scientists must engage in many years of difficult, relatively nonproductive labor before they are able to perform the services a society regards as essential for survival. To induce individuals to enter these strenuous positions, a society organizes itself in such a way that material and social rewards are given to people who enter these positions.

In an era when national defense is a great need of the society, for example, esteem and other rewards are given to military strategists or defense-related scientists. As a society changes from strong national defense needs to a need for solution to ecological or energy problems, the society will evolve in such a way that greater rewards are provided to scientists working on these problems than to military leaders.

The principle of gratification of cultural norms is of considerable significance to marketing organizations. This is because of the insight that can be gained into the types of products and marketing practices that will be permitted and rewarded in a society and those that will be unrewarded or eliminated. Only products and marketing practices that gratify the current needs of a society will, in the long run, be permitted or retained by the society.

Finally, culture is adaptive, either through a dialectical or evolutionary process. Culture responds to the physical and social environment in which it operates and has contact. Dialectical or sharply discontinuous

---

[3]Robert C. Shirley, "Values in Decision Making: Their Origin and Effects," *Managerial Planning* (January/February 1975), 1-5.

cultural change, associated with persons such as Hegel and Marx, occurs when the value system of a culture becomes associated with the gratification of only one class or group. In such instances, other classes of the society reject the logic of the value system and replace it (perhaps suddenly, in a revolution) with a new value system. In an evolutionary process, change occurs but is a process of modification rather than revolution.[4]

The adaptive nature of culture is important in developing an understanding of consumer behavior. In the past, cultural change was usually slow and gradual. It appears, however, that the vastly accelerated technological change that characterizes contemporary societies is also reflected in the values and ideas of the society. The effect of such changes, together with the rapid changes in institutions described in the preceding chapter, is creating an environment in which strategies based upon assumptions about values must be more closely monitored and evaluated than in the past.

ANALYZING THE NATIONAL CULTURE

The broadest understanding of cultural impact upon consumer behavior is at the national level; cultural values that are widely shared throughout a nation that affirm the goals of people within that nation and that have an impact on behavior of the "normal" (used in a quantitative sense) residents of that nation.

Marketing programs appealing to mass markets must consider the values of the nation which may be classified under the categories of *control, direction* and *feeling*.[5] *Control* refers to the impact of cultural norms felt by consumers. *Direction* refers to basic motivations or life goals, and *feeling* refers to the pleasure perceived by consumers from a situation or activity.[6] More understanding of these terms is provided by looking at Table 4.1, a checklist of the types of questions that a marketing manager should ask about cultural values before developing a marketing or communications program.

Core Values

The core values of a nation are important to marketing strategists in two ways. Core values provide positive valences toward products and activities portrayed in advertising. For the creative marketer, positive valences suggest headlines, themes, illustrations, and so forth to assist in the development of the creative strategy. Core values also suggest new prod-

---

[4]A lucid discussion of the contrasting philosophies of dialectical and evolutionary change in the values of a society is provided by an economist who has influenced marketing thought considerably. See Kenneth Boulding, *A Primer on Social Dynamics* (New York: Free Press, 1970), esp. Chap. 2, "Organizers of Social Evolution."

[5]Mechranian and J. A. Russell, *An Approach to Environmental Psychology* (Boston: M.I.T. Press, 1974).

[6]A thorough discussion of the marketing implications of each of these terms is found in Del Hawkins, Kenneth Coney, and Roger Best, *Consumer Behavior: Implications for Marketing Strategy,* (Dallas: Business Publication, Inc., 1980), Chapter 4.

**Table 4.1
Cultural Values of
Relevance to
Consumer Behavior**

Control

Individual—Collective   Are individual activity and initiative valued more highly than collective activity and conformity?
Performance—Status   Is the culture's reward system based on performance or on inherited factors such as family or class?
Tradition—Change   Are existing patterns of behavior considered to be inherently superior to new patterns of behavior?
Masculine—Feminine   To what extent does social power automatically go to males?
Competition—Cooperation   Does one obtain success by excelling over others or by cooperating with them?
Youth—Age   Are wisdom and prestige assigned to the younger or older members of a culture?

Direction

Active—Passive   Is a physically active approach to life valued more highly than a less active orientation?
Material—Nonmaterial   How much importance is attached to the acquisition of material wealth?
Hardwork—Leisure   Is a person who works harder than economically necessary admired more than one who does not?
Risk taking—Security   Are those who risk their established positions to overcome obstacles or achieve high goals admired more than those who do not?
Problem-solving—Fatalistic   Are people encouraged to overcome all problems or do they take a "what will be, will be" attitude?
Nature   Is nature regarded as something to be admired or overcome?

Feeling

Adult—Child   Is family life organized to meet the needs of the children or the adults?
Postponed gratification—Immediate gratification   Are people encouraged to "save for a rainy day" or to "live for today"?
Sensual gratification—Abstinence   To what extent is it acceptable to enjoy sensual pleasures such as food, drink, and sex?
Humor—Serious   Is life to be regarded as a strictly serious affair or is it to be treated lightly?
Romantic orientation   Does the culture believe that "love conquers all"?
Cleanliness   To what extent is cleanliness pursued beyond the minimum needed for health?

Source: Del Hawkins, Kenneth Coney, and Roger Best, *Consumer Behavior: Implications for Marketing Strategy.* (Dallas: Business Publications, Inc., 1980), 71. Reprinted by permission.

ucts that are likely to be attractive to consumers. They suggest policies of retailers that are likely to be acceptable to consumers.

You can see some of America's core values in Table 4.2. They include achievement and success, activity, efficiency and practicality, progress, material comfort, individualism, freedom, external conformity, humanitarianism, and youthfulness.[7] You can also see their relevance to consumer behavior in Table 4.2 and think of ways communication and marketing strategies might take these core values into consideration.

Core values also provide *negative valences* to marketing programs by suggesting activities, colors, situations, and so forth to be avoided. Failure to recognize such realities can lead to serious marketing blunders. Colgate-Palmolive introduced a brand of toothpaste called *Cue* into French-speaking countries, not knowing that "cue" was a pornographic

[7]Leon Schiffman and Leslie Kanuk, *Consumer Behavior* (Englewood Cliffs, N.J.: Prentice-Hall, Inc., 1978), 342-360. Also see the 1968 Edition of Engel, Kollat, and Blackwell, *Consumer Behavior*, 240-252 for discussion of American core values.

**Table 4.2
American Core
Values**

Value	General features	Relevance to consumer behavior
Achievement and success	Hard work is good; success flows from hard work	Acts as a justification for acquisition of goods ("You deserve it")
Activity	Keeping busy is healthy and natural	Stimulates interest in products that save time and enhance leisure-time activities
Efficiency and practicality	Admiration of things that solve problems (e.g., save time and effort)	Stimulates purchase of products that function well and save time
Progress	People can improve themselves; tomorrow should be better	Stimulates desire for new products that fulfill unsatisfied needs; acceptance of products that claim to be "new" or "improved"
Material comfort	"The good life"	Fosters acceptance of convenience and luxury products that make life more enjoyable
Individualism	Being one's self (e.g., self-reliance, self-interest, and self-esteem)	Stimulates acceptance of customized or unique products that enable a person to "express his own personality"
Freedom	Freedom of choice	Fosters interest in wide product lines and differentiated products
External conformity	Uniformity of observable behavior; desire to be accepted	Stimulates interest in products that are used or owned by others in the same social group
Humanitarianism	Caring for others, particularly the underdog	Stimulates patronage of firms that compete with market leaders.
Youthfulness	A state of mind that stresses being young at heart or appearing young	Stimulates acceptance of products that provide the illusion of maintaining or fostering youth

Source: From *Consumer Behavior,* by Leon Schiffman and Leslie Kanuk, © 1978, p. 359. Reprinted by permission of Prentice-Hall, Inc., Englewood Cliffs, New Jersey 07632.

word in French. General Mills attempted to enter the British cereal market with a package showing an "all-American" youngster. This did not appeal to a culture that possesses a more formal view of the role of children. Goodyear Tire and Rubber demonstrated the strength of its *3 T* tire cord in the United States by showing a steel chain breaking. When this demonstration was to be included in German advertising, however, it was perceived as uncomplimentary to steel chain manufacturers and regarded as improper.

In Quebec, a canned fish manufacturer attempted to market that product through an advertising program that showed a woman in shorts, golfing with her husband, and intending to serve canned fish for the evening meal. The program was a failure because, as studies by an anthropologist revealed, all three of these activities violate the norms of that culture.[8]

Another marketing blunder is illustrated by the following case of a western-oriented tobacco company attempting to enter a new market.

[8]These and other examples are contained in David A. Ricks, Jeffrey S. Arpan and Marilyn Y. Fu, *International Business Blunders* (Columbus: Grid Publishing, 1975).

The managers of a joint-venture tobacco company in an Asian country were warned that their proposed new locally named (a token adaptation) and manufactured filtered cigarettes would fail because filters had not yet been introduced there. Nevertheless, the resident Western managers, along with their local executives whose SRC (self-reference criterion) was predominantly Western because of their social class and education, puffed smugly on their own U.S. filtered cigarettes. Meanwhile the product flopped, leaving the company with idle equipment and uncovered setup and launch costs.

The basic reason for the prediction of failure was a difference in fear of death—especially from lung cancer. A life expectancy of 29 years in that Asian country does not place many people in the lung-cancer bracket. Moreover, for those in this age bracket, there is not the general cultural value of sanitation, the literacy rate, or a *Reader's Digest* type of magazine to motivate them to give up unfiltered cigarettes.[9]

The concepts of family and social class are interrelated to core values of a nation. For instance, women in many Moslem countries play little role in purchasing decisions. American and African children have more importance in purchasing decisions than in many other cultures. Showing pairs of anything carries a negative connotation in the Gold Coast of Africa. Selling door to door—a strategy used successfully by Avon and other companies—is taboo in many societies. Cultural norms found in some countries that strictly separate business and social activities may prevent the use of strategies for selling to housewives through parties—a technique used effectively by Tupperware in the U.S. Older members of the family may have the most influence on purchasing in Asian and other countries but be ignored in America.

Cultural values of a society are clearly an important determinant of consumer behavior. Henry has demonstrated this in the choice of automotives[10] but it can be observed in both high-involvement and low-involvement products.

Needed: Cultural Competence

Consumer analysts and marketing practitioners need awareness of core values of a culture and insights of their meaning for marketing programs. Such awareness may come from formal study of anthropology and from formal marketing research about a culture using the techniques described later in this chapter. Often, though, marketing decisions must be made quickly with no time for research or more formal analysis.

The need for cultural understanding is particularly important in the development of communications programs in a culture in which the marketing manager has not been socialized. An American executive may develop a communications theme, for example, without realizing that core values of American culture, such as individualism, youthfulness, in-

---

[9]Charles Winick, "Anthropology's Contributions to Marketing," *Journal of Marketing* (July 1961), 53.
[10]Walter A. Henry, "Cultural Values Do Correlate with Consumer Behavior," *Journal of Marketing Research*, vol. 13 (May 1976), 121-127.

formality, respect for hard work and so forth, may be alien to the cognitive structure of the host country.[11]

For international executives to have cultural competence in dealing with the realities of a global marketplace, they should, among other things, have:

1. Sensitivity to cultural differences.

2. Cultural empathy, or the ability to understand the inner logic and coherence of other ways of life, plus the restraint not to judge them as bad because they are different from one's own ways.

3. Ability to withstand the initial cultural shock, or the sum of sudden jolts that awaits the unwary American abroad.

4. Ability to cope with and to adapt to foreign environments without going native.[12]

SUBCULTURAL INFLUENCES ON CONSUMER BEHAVIOR

Subcultural influences refer to the norms and values of subgroups within the larger or national culture. Individual consumers may be influenced only slightly by membership in specific subgroups or the subgroups may be a dominant force on the life-style or behavior of the consumer.

Four types of subcultures are described below. They are nationality groups, religious groups, geographic areas, and racial groups. The first and last types, because of their importance in contemporary American culture, are given a more extended analysis.

Nationality Groups

Many large cities contain relatively homogeneous groups within the city composed of nationality groups. These include Puerto Rican communities in New York, Cuban communities in Florida, and areas in many cities composed of first- and second-generation Scandinavians, Germans, Italians, Polish, Irish, Mexican-Americans, and so forth. Some consumers in these communities become acculturated to the surrounding environment and lose much of their ethnic identity as a nationality group. Others retain their original language, interact primarily with other members of the nationality, expose themselves mostly to ethnic media and sometimes even search for products similar to those in the old country.

Retailers are particularly affected by ethnic influences on a community basis. They need to be sensitive to purchasing patterns of each nationality group and may need to locate wholesalers who are able to supply ethnic products. Staff may need to be bilingual. Management must

---

[11]James A. Lee, "Cultural Analysis in Overseas Operations," *Harvard Business Review*, vol. 44 (March-April, 1966), 106-114, at 107. Copyright 1966 by the President and Fellows of Harvard College; all rights reserved. Theodore O. Wallin, "The International Executive's Baggage: Cultural Values of the American Frontier," MSU *Business Topics*, vol. 24 (Spring 1976), 49-58.

[12]Y. Hugh Furuhashi and Harry F. Evarts, "Educating Men for International Marketing," *Journal of Marketing*, vol. 31 (January 1967), 51-53.

make the special effort to understand ethnic media—which often provide excellent cost per thousand figures for relevant market segments.

Funeral firms, physicians and dentists as well as many other service organizations are often oriented toward the language and values of nationality groups. The Bank of America, for example, is designed to be a part of the Chinese culture in its location in the Chinese community of San Francisco. Other locations reflect Hispanic or other ethnic orientations.

Hispanic Markets

Hispanics have become the fastest growing minority group in America. There is some controversy whether it is proper to group all Hispanics— Spanish-Americans, Cubans, and Puerto Ricans—as a market, but the similarities among these groups are sufficient to do so for some products. Spanish, if basic language is used rather than slang or idioms, is similar across all three groups. Culturally unaware marketers may assume that since most Latinos are bilingual, it is adequate to communicate with them in English. Yet about 94 percent speak Spanish in the home and studies show that Hispanics *think* in Spanish—creating the need for marketers to communicate in Spanish-based forms to be most effective.[13]

Language is not the only element of culture of importance in understanding the Hispanic market. Anglo consumers may be impressed by the health claims of *Colgate* toothpaste but the Hispanic consumer is more interested in what toothpaste does for personal appearance. Best Foods promotes *Mazola* corn oil with a health claim but Hispanics are more interested in how the oil tastes rather than in the Anglo-oriented feature of low cholesterol.

Many Hispanics have emigrated from poorer countries and in their drive for a better life seek status symbols that demonstrate that they've "arrived." For example, Bulova watches had an image of a "cheap American product" and to counter this image in the Hispanic market, Hispanic media were used to position Bulova as an expensive, but affordable piece of jewelry. Emphasis was placed upon the fact that Bulova had an extensive line of 18-karat gold watches because Hispanics view 14-karat as synonymous with gold-plated. These efforts achieved for Bulova a 40 percent share in the Spanish-speaking market.

Coupons generally are not as effective with Hispanics as with Anglos because of the stigma they have for people who came to this country poor and now are proud that they are making a better living and do not want to use coupons which are "for people who can't afford to pay the full price."[14]

By 1990, the Hispanic population is projected to be about 17 million or about 7 percent of the total population of the United States in contrast

[13]Jim Sondheim, Rodd Rodriguez, Richard Dillon, Richard Paredes, "Hispanic Market—the Invisible Giant," *Advertising Age* (April 16, 1979), S-20.

[14]These examples are provided by Luiz Diaz-Albertini, "Brand-Loyal Hispanics Need Good Reason for Switching," *Advertising Age* (April 16, 1979), S-22, S-23.

to only about 4 percent at the beginning of the seventies. The growth is a result of both higher fertility levels and immigration. On a regional basis, Hispanic markets are often even more significant. More than one-third of New Mexico's population is Hispanic and more than one in five Texans and almost one in five Californians is Hispanic. Hispanics outnumber blacks in 18 states, including the nation's most populous state, California.[15]

Some products have made successful adaptations to the Hispanic market. Cudahy established a premium bacon called *Rex* based on the strategy that a lean, premium bacon could sell in a 12-ounce size for prices comparable to the biggest competitor's (*Farmer John*) 16-ounce package. The package shouts the message, "*Valo Su Peso En Carne*." Beers such as *Budweiser* and *Miller* have battled to sponsor community celebrations such as *Cinco de Mayo* and the *Independence Day Fair* because of their importance in the Spanish culture. *Gillette* razors are promoted with Spanish models in Hispanic environments. Usually the messages are educational, involve a hard sell, and are always simple and direct.[16]

How should media adapt to be effective in reaching the Hispanic market? Some examples are provided in the advertisement of the Gannett group of communication outlets. Read the copy of that ad in Figure 4.1 and you will see some of the possibilities for communicating effectively in the Hispanic culture.

Religious Subcultures

Religious groups may provide important subcultures. Mormons, for example, may refrain from purchasing tobacco, liquor, and certain stimulants—but be prime prospects for fruit juices endorsed by Marie and Donnie Osmond. Christian Scientists are not prime prospects for *Anacin* or *Tylenol*. Seventh Day Adventists limit their purchases of meat but may be prime targets for vegetable-based foods. Evangelical Christians may avoid conspicuous consumption or ostentatious jewelry but be the primary audience for Christian televison and radio stations.

The Jewish subculture provides an attractive market for many organizations. Food products provide specific identification with the kosher certification but other brands may also make special appeals. *Maxwell House* and *Tetley* feature bagels in ads; *Star-Kist* says, "Beautify a bialy with *Star-Kist* tuna salad surprise;" and *Chef Boy-Ar-Dee* promotes its macaroni shells with the line, "Treat your macaroni mayvin to real Italian taste." Jewish culture is sometimes used for a wider appeal as when *Alka-Seltzer* made famous the slogan, "Try it, you'll like it."

[15]Reid T. Reynolds, Bryant Robey and Cheryl Russell, "Demographics of the 1980s," *American Demographics* (January 1980), 11-19 and Supplement to *American Demographics* (April 1981), 2. For additional demographic materials see Roberto Anson, "Hispanics in the United States: Yesterday, Today, and Tomorrow," *The Futurist* (August 1980), 25-31 and Stephanie Ventura and Robert Heuser, "Births of Hispanic Parentage," *Monthly Vital Statistics Report* (March 20, 1981).

[16]These examples are drawn from various articles in "Hispanic Marketing" (a special section of) *Advertising Age* (April 16, 1981) S-1 to S-24.

**Figure 4.1
Adapting
Communications
Media to the
Hispanic Market**

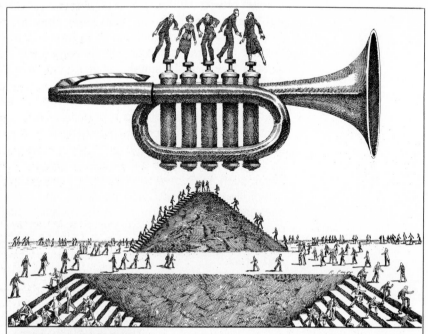

SOUNDING HISPANIC FREEDOM

Hispanics in the United States number 18 million or more, 1 in 12 of all Americans. In some communities they are the majority.

Yet these numbers have not translated into proportionate civic and community participation. The result is inequity in job opportunities, education, fair treatment under the law and sharing of public funds.

This deprives the individuals of their full measure of freedom and the communities of their fullness of life.

Gannett newspapers and broadcast stations are working hard to do something about that.

The Nevada State Journal and Reno Evening Gazette described abuses in jobs, education and housing suffered by Northern Nevada's large but largely ignored Hispanic population. By focusing on the struggles of individual Hispanics pursuing their American dream, the series of articles clarified needed community remedies.

An El Paso Times series offered readers a close inspection of the problems Mexican-Americans face in their daily lives within the unique border community.

KBTV in Denver scheduled public-service spot announcements in all parts of its broadcast day, urging Hispanics to cooperate fully with the 1980 census. Hispanics make up an estimated one-fourth of the Colorado population.

In San Bernardino, California, The Sun opened a news bureau in the heart of the Hispanic and Black West Side. A vibrant, active community is now better known to all area residents. The Sun also added a columnist who writes exclusively about Hispanic political activities.

KPNX-TV in Phoenix airs a weekly public-affairs program concentrating on Hispanic needs and events.

To better serve the entire community, the Tucson Citizen in Arizona offers free Spanish lessons to every staff member.

And Gannett and Michigan State University have launched a large-scale study of communication behavior and attitudes of Hispanic-Americans. The study will help newspaper and broadcast professionals serve the audience according to its needs and preferences.

In these ways and others, Gannett members strive to serve all segments of their communities, each according to its own special needs.

At Gannett, we have a commitment to freedom in every business we are in, whether it is newspaper, TV, radio, outdoor advertising, film production, magazine or public opinion research.

That freedom rings throughout Gannett, from Tucson to Tarrytown, from Salinas to Santa Fe, from Visalia to the Virgin Islands, in news coverage, in editorial opinions, in community service, each member serving its own audience in its own way.

For more information, write: Gannett, Lincoln Tower, Rochester, N.Y. 14604. Or call (716) 546-8600.

**GANNETT
A WORLD OF DIFFERENT VOICES
WHERE FREEDOM SPEAKS**

Source: The Gannett Co. Inc. Reprinted by permission.

**Geographic
Areas**

Geographic areas in a nation sometimes develop their own culture. The southwest area of the United States is known for casual life-styles featuring comfortable dress, outdoor entertaining, and active sports. The Southwest may also appear to be more innovative toward new products and programs when compared to the conservative, inhibited attitudes that characterize some areas of the nation. Climate, religious affiliations of the population, nationality influences, and other variables are interrelated to produce a core of cultural values in a geographic area.

French-Canadian Markets

One of the largest and most distinct subcultures in North America is the French-Canadian area of Canada, mostly in Quebec. This might be considered either a nationality group or a geographic subculture. The Province of Quebec accounts for over 27 percent of the Canadian population and about 25 percent of income and retail sales.[17] For years, the French culture was somewhat ignored by English-oriented advertisers, thereby creating a social problem as well as limiting the potential effectiveness of communications to the French market. Some of the differential treatment may have been due to different social class groupings compared to Anglo markets.[18]

Marketing strategists need to be concerned with the question of whether advertising is transferable between the French Canadian (FC) culture and English Canadian (EC) or Anglophone culture. Some observers believe that separate advertising material must be developed to be effective in the FC subculture.[19] Research has begun to focus on similarities as well as differences between FC and EC consumers[20] although it tends to focus on limited aspects of consumer behavior and lacks the kind of framework needed to evaluate cross-cultural communications.[21] Figure 4.2, however, shows how DuPont of Canada appeals to both cultures by relying on graphics rather than on copy for most of the message presentation.

Tamilia's research comparing communications with FC and EC consumers on a cross-cultural basis indicates the potential for increasing effectiveness in advertising communications by the use of a communications model that identifies the perceptual process of each subculture. Previous research comparing ethnic personality and communications led Tamilia

[17]Detailed estimates of market statistics for each province are available in "Canadian Survey of Buying Power," *Sales and Marketing Management* 2nd. ed. (July 26, 1976). Also see projections of Canadian markets in Edward B. Harvey, "Demographics and Future Marketing: Implications in Canada," *The Business Quarterly* (Summer 1976), 61–65, which is based upon Statistics Canada, *Population Projections for Canada and the Provinces, 1972–2001* (Catalogue No. 91-514).

[18]Pierre C. Lefrancois and Giles Chatel, "The French-Canadian Consumer: Fact and Fancy," in J. S. Wright and J. L. Goldstucker, (eds.), *New Ideas for Successful Marketing* (Chicago: American Marketing Association, 1966), 705–717; Bernard Blishen, "Social Class and Opportunity in Canada," *Canadian Review of Sociology and Anthropology*, vol. 7 (May 1970), 110–127.

[19]R. Gelfand, "French-Canadian is More Purposive to Ads than English Counterpart," *Advertising Age* (November 16, 1964), 124; R. Gelfand, "It's Much More than Language," *Marketing* (June 9, 1969), 18 ff; R. Gelfand, "French Canada as a Minority Market," in Ronald C. Curhan, (ed.), *1974 Combined Proceedings* (Chicago: American Marketing Association, 1975), 680–682; Maurice Watier, "Pris dans le Moule American," *Culture Vivante*, no. 16 (February 1970), 8–12.

[20]Lefrancois and Chatel, "The French Consumer"; Richard W. Crosby, "Attitude Measurement in a Bilingual Culture," *Journal of Marketing Research*, vol. 6 (November 1969), 421–426; Doug Tigert, "Can a Separate Marketing Strategy for French Canada Be Justified: Profiling English-French Markets through Life Style Analysts," in D. Thompson and D. Leighton, (eds.), *Canadian Marketing: Problems and Prospects* (Toronto: John Wiley & Sons, Canada, Ltd., 1973), 113–142.

[21]Robert Tamilia, "Cross-Cultural Advertising Research: A Review and Suggested Framework," in Ronald C. Curhan, (ed.), *1974 Combined Proceedings*, "French Canada," 131–134.

**Figure 4.2
Example of a
Cross-Cultural
Advertisement in
Canada**

Source: Reprinted by permission of DuPont Canada Inc., Montreal, Quebec.

to conclude that the French would evaluate objects more along concrete, objective, direct, and sensual or sensorial dimensions. Therefore, in communications that emphasized the source more than the message, the French would exhibit a greater affinity with the source of the communication and how the source is positioned in the consumer's effective-meaning system rather than with the message, which presumes a more cognitive orientation. This is also compatible with some life-style research by Tigert indicating that the French seem to be more responsive to people-oriented advertisements than to message-oriented advertisements.

Tamilia conducted his study in Montreal and Quebec City and concluded that French Canadians do react more to the source of the advertisements than do English Canadians who are more message-oriented.[22] This type of research, while only investigating part of the marketing program needed to reach a subculture effectively, indicates the potential for future advances. In addition to obtaining the objective of increased effectiveness of communication, the Quebec government has issued a statement, following a study by 17 offices, *de la Langue Francaise*, encouraging advertisers to improve the quality of French advertising and linguistics.[23]

Because of the size of the French-Canadian market, the world attention Quebec is receiving, and the distinctiveness of the FC market, a great deal of interest is being generated in the cross-cultural aspects of FC and EC consumers. However, the research that occurs here is also of interest in understanding other market situations such as Spanish-speaking Mexican-Americans, and bilingual markets in Belgium, as well as black and white markets in the United States.

[22]Tamilia, 1977, "Cross-Cultural Advertising."
[23]Brian Heath, "The French Language Market," *Marketing* (June 5, 1972), 19–46.

Black Cultural Influences on Consumption

Racial groups constitute another important subculture. Oriental groups have importance in San Francisco, Vancouver, and some other cities. The three-quarter million American Indians are found in every state but constitute substantial groups mostly in western states.[24] The most significant racial group in the United States, other than whites, is the black subculture.

Black culture refers to a common heritage rather than skin color. In the United States, the black heritage is conditioned by an American beginning in slavery, a shared history of discrimination and suffering, confined housing opportunities, and denial of participation in many aspects of the majority culture. This core of values and economic realities still permits substantial variation just as there is among white markets. Greater homogeneity in black markets than among white markets has historically been a valid assumption, although that may be changing.

The black market is worthy of marketing attention. With over $90 billion in buying power and a population of 25,000,000 and growing faster than whites, the black market makes up about 11 percent of the national marketplace. If the U.S. black consumer market were considered a separate country, it would rank as eleventh largest in the free world.[25] Currently, the black middle class is emerging as a dominant consumer and social influence; and with this emergence comes an evolution in many black perceptions and values. Blacks are becoming more venturesome and independent with less interest in impressing whites.[26]

Structural influences shape black subculture and also inhibit some of its manifestations. These structural influences include low income, educational deprivation, different family characteristics, and of course, discrimination.

Income Deprivation

The black culture is frequently confused with the low-income culture. There is good reason for this confusion to exist because black consumers average much less income than white consumers. Even Hispanics are earning more on the average than black families, as Table 4.3 shows. About 30 percent of all black families are below the poverty level, as defined by the U.S. Department of Commerce, compared to only about 10 percent of white families. Of course, there are more white families below the poverty level in absolute terms than black families.[27]

Two effects of low income among black families are significant in the study of consumer behavior. First, there is the direct effect on the subculture derived from so many people being poor. Consumers must buy from stores that accept food stamps; many products are not within the

[24]Laurence S. Rosen and Kurt Gorwitz, "New Attention to American Indians," *American Demographics* (April 1980), 18–25.

[25]Clarence O. Smith, "Black Market? It's Virtually Untapped," *Advertising Age* (April 16, 1979), S-14.

[26]D. Parke Gibson, "Black Middle Class Emerges as Dominant Consumer Force," *Advertising Age* (April 16, 1979), S-27.

[27]U.S. Department of Commerce, Current Population Reports, Series P-20.

Table 4.3 Comparison of White, Black, and Spanish Income in the United States	Median Family Income		
	White	Black	Spanish
1970	10,236	6,279	NA
1971	10,672	6,440	NA
1972	11,549	6,864	8,183
1973	12,595	7,269	8,715
1974	13,456	7,943	9,540
1975	14,320	8,723	9,551
1976	15,571	9,264	10,259
1977	16,782	9,485	11,421
1978	18,432	10,820	12,566
1979	20,524	11,648	14,315

Source: U.S. Department of Commerce.

possible reach of poor consumers; income must be spent on basics of life to a large degree. The second effect is the methodological complexity of separating effects due to lack of income from effects due to being black. Some studies attempt to correct for the income differences when reporting black-white differences, but many do not focus on this distinction.

There are many black families of middle and higher income, of course, and marketers must be aware of their preferences and sensitivities. There is considerable question whether middle-income blacks are more like low-income blacks or more like middle-income whites. In either case, middle-income blacks constitute an important and growing market for contemporary organizations.

Educational Deprivation

Inadequate education places black consumers at a disadvantage not only in earning income but in acquiring consumer skills; skills that must be learned "on the street" if not at school. In other instances schools have often been ineffective, because of inadequate resources or by design, at helping black consumers master educational skills needed for full participation in the market system.[28]

Family Characteristics

The black culture is affected by unique family characteristics, primarily a highly mobile family structure and a high proportion of families headed by females, perhaps twice as high as for whites. This gives more importance to females in the purchasing influence as well as providing subtleties of relationships which an advertiser must understand and consider in the execution of creative strategy. The black family is much younger than the typical white family. By 1985 the median age for blacks is expected to be five to seven years younger, a factor accounting for considerable difference in preferences for clothing, music, shelter, cars, and many other products and activities.

[28]For additional discussion and documentation of this section of the chapter, see the 1978 edition of this text.

Discrimination

The effects of discrimination on the black subculture are so massive and enduring that they cannot be ignored in the analysis of consumer behavior, even though serious consideration of the topic is beyond the scope of this book. Discrimination has been particularly restrictive on black-consumption decisions in the area of housing.

For decades, black consumers who wished to move to middle- and upper-class areas of the city have been prevented from doing so by restrictive financing agreements, restrictive policies of real estate brokers, and by social pressure from potential neighbors. Many black families may have been discouraged from the pride of ownership in housing found among majority markets. One result is more emphasis on consumption of other status goods such as automobiles, clothing, and entertainment outside of the home.

The black subculture should, as a result of years of discrimination, provide substantial skepticism toward the white businesses which have contributed to segregated residential patterns and limited employment opportunities and that have supported invisibility of blacks in the media. Advertising by such firms may receive limited response. Firms that make the special effort to show sensitivity to the black culture, use black media wisely, and stand against discrimination and similar abuses may be able to turn a problem into an opportunity.

Notice how the Eastern Airlines advertisement shown in Figure 4.3 attempts to build rapport with black consumers. The black airline captain is in a position superior to the white co-pilot. Anyone who understands seniority at an airline must understand that Eastern has not merely recently hired a black pilot—and the ad states that the pilot came to Eastern 14 years ago. All readers would want assurance of the pilot's competency and that Eastern was not hiring just anyone in order to meet affirmative action goals. The statement in the ad concerning the pilot's military experience with fighter jets provides that reassurance. This ad was in *Ebony* magazine.

Black Consumption Patterns

How are the effects of the black subculture manifested in consumption? In what ways do blacks and whites differ? Actually, they are much more similar than different, especially among middle-income groups. Some differences in leisure activities are shown in Table 4.4. On some items there is little difference (tennis, for example) but on others (camping or using city parks) the differences are substantial. Careful analysis of Table 4.4 leads to the conclusion that some differences are the result of differences in income and resource availability while others represent differences in values and interests.

Many factors must be considered in developing marketing programs directed toward the black market.[29] Some of these are cultural and some are structural. A fast-food chain, for example, completed a mar-

[29]D. Parke Gibson, $70 *Billion in the Black* (New York: Macmillan, 1978).

Figure 4.3
Example Designed
to Build Credibility
among Black
Consumers

At Eastern Airlines, we want to give you the best service we can. The kind that makes you want to fly with us again and again.

To do that, we hire people like Captain Leslie Morris.

Captain Morris came to Eastern 14 years ago as a second officer. Fresh from the National Guard where he flew F86's and T33's.

Today, he's flying bigger jets. And last year alone, he and his fellow pilots flew over 41 million Eastern passengers. Surely and expertly.

It's people like Captain Morris who give you the kind of service you want from an airline. And it's this kind of commitment all of us try to have that keeps Eastern flying in the right direction.

And that's just where we want to be going.

EASTERN
WE HAVE TO EARN OUR WINGS EVERY DAY.

IT'S PEOPLE LIKE CAPTAIN LESLIE MORRIS WHO KEEP EASTERN FLYING IN THE RIGHT DIRECTION.

LESLIE MORRIS
CAPTAIN, EASTERN AIRLINES.

Source: Eastern Airlines. Reprinted by permission.

ket research project among black consumers and found significantly fewer *per capita* purchases of hamburgers among blacks than among white consumers. The chain's stores located in black, inner-city areas, however, had the highest volume of any stores in the nation—apparently a conflict with the market research reports. At first, executives were bewildered by the research findings. The answer, however, lies in the population-density ratios of the areas surrounding the store. While the

Table 4.4	Percentage Involved in Activity	
Black and White	White	Black
Leisure Activities		
I jog regularly	11.7	8.1
I usually go boating in the summer	24.6	6.8
I often play tennis/racquetball	21.9	21.6
I often play golf	13.3	5.4
I often go disco dancing	14.8	39.2
I often go camping	31.9	12.2
Last summer I used the city parks fairly often	31.3	47.3
I bought several music albums and tapes last year	40.0	54.1
I often eat out at a good restaurant	41.2	31.1
I often do art work or crafts	29.4	42.5

Source: Roger D. Blackwell, H. Lee Mathews, and Carolyn E. Randolph, *Living in Columbus* (Columbus, Ohio: Nationwide Communications, Inc., 1979). Reprinted by permission.

average *per capita* consumption was lower, so many people living in the neighborhood bought hamburgers that the store's total volume was high.

Considerable consumer research has focused on similarities and differences between whites and blacks in the United States. Such studies have been reviewed by Bauer and Cunningham[30] and by Alexis and Smith;[31] thus, only the highlights are presented below. As you read these findings, remember that some were conducted in a single city, often several years in the past. They should be studied as hypotheses that may be helpful in the design of marketing programs but when you are in the position of responsibility for marketing programs, you will want to repeat and extend the studies to your specific product or situation before investing large amounts of resources.

Search Processes and Interpersonal Communications

Considerable research has focused on communications in black communites and search processes of black consumers. Major findings are reported below with attention given to mass-media influences and to interpersonal communications.

1. Black consumers appear to be reached more effectively by general media for advertisers appearing in both black and white media and by black-oriented media for products specifically directed to black consumers.[32]

2. The use of black models in advertising did not increase in the period of 1946 to 1965 (although the social status of blacks in ads had in-

[30]Raymond A. Bauer and Scott M. Cunningham, *Studies in the Negro Market* (Cambridge, Mass.: Marketing Science Institute, 1970). Also, a similar synthesis is available in Donald Sexton, "Black Buyer Behavior," *Journal of Marketing*, vol. 36 (October 1972), 36-39.

[31]Marcus Alexis and Clyde M. Smith, "Marketing and the Inner-City Consumer," *Journal of Contemporary Business*, vol. 2 (Autumn 1973), 45-80.

[32]John V. Petrof, "Reaching the Negro Market: A Segregated vs. a General Newspaper," *Journal of Advertising Research*, vol. 8 (April 1968), 40-43.

creased) but the proportion of blacks in ads did increase (from 4 percent to 13 percent) from 1967 to 1974.[33]

3. Black consumers react more favorably to advertisements with all black models or to integrated groups of models than to advertisements with all white models.[34] Whites in these same studies appear to react to black models as favorably or more so than white models, although this varies by product category[35] and by amount of prejudice.[36] Black consumers under the age of 30 appear to react unfavorably to advertisements with integrated settings.[37]

4. Black consumers appear to respond (in recall and attitude shift) more positively to advertisements than do white consumers.[38]

5. Black consumers listen to radio more than whites, particularly in the evenings and on weekends.[39]

6. Black television viewers dislike programs emphasizing subjects such as families and organizations and watch more on the weekends in contrast to whites' higher viewing through the week.[40]

7. Participation by blacks in social organizations is higher than by whites with comparable socioeconomic characteristics, especially in the lowest income groups. Blacks are more likely than whites to belong to church and political groups and equally likely to belong to civic groups.[41]

[33]Harold H. Kassarjian, "The Negro and American Advertising, 1946-1965," *Journal of Marketing Research,* vol. 6 (February 1969), 29-39; also William H. Boyenton, "The Negro Turns to Advertising," *Journalism Quarterly,* vol. 42 (Spring 1965), 227-235. Motivations of advertisers for using black models are reported in Taylor W. Meloan, "Afro-American Advertising Policy and Strategy," in Bernard A. Morin, (ed.), *Marketing in a Changing World* (Chicago: American Marketing Association, 1969), 20-23. More recent increases are reported in Ronald Bush, Paul Solomon, and J.F. Hair, Jr., "There Are More Blacks in Commercials," *Journal of Advertising Research.* vol. 17 (February 1977), 21-30.

[34]Arnold M. Barban, "The Dilemma of 'Integrated' Advertising," *Journal of Business,* vol. 42 (October 1969), 477-496; B. Stuart Tolley and John J. Goett, "Reactions to Blacks in Newspapers," *Journal of Advertising Research,* vol. 11 (April 1971), 11-17; John W. Gould, Normal B. Sigband, and Cyril E. Zoerner, Jr., "Black Consumer Reactions to 'Integrated' Advertising; An Exploratory Study," *Journal of Marketing,* vol. 34 (July 1970), 20-26; Pravat K. Choudhury and Lawrence S. Schmid, "Black Models in Advertising to Blacks," *Journal of Advertising Research,* vol. 14 (June 1974), 19-22.

[35]William V. Muse, "Product-Related Response to Use of Black Models in Advertising," *Journal of Marketing Research,* vol. 8 (February 1971), 107-109; James E. Stafford and Al E. Birdwell, "Verbal versus Non-Verbal Measures of Attitudes: The Pupilometer," paper presented at the Consumer Behavior Workshop, American Marketing Association, Columbus, Ohio (August 1969); Mary Jane Schlinger and Joseph T. Plummer, "Advertising in Black and White," *Journal of Marketing Research,* vol. 9 (May 1972), 149-153; Ronald Bush, Robert Gwinner, and Paul Solomon, "White Consumer Sales Response to Black Models," *Journal of Marketing,* vol. 38 (April 1974), 25-29.

[36]James W. Cagley and Richard N. Cardozo, "Racial Prejudice and Integrated Advertising: An Experimental Study," in McDonald, *op. cit.,* 52-56; Carl E. Black, "White Backlash to Negro Ads: Fact or Fantasy," *Journalism Quarterly,* vol. 49 (Summer 1972), 258-262.

[37]Gould et al., "Black Consumer," 25; Michael K. Chapko, "Black Ads Are Getting Blacker," *Journal of Communication* (Autumn 1976), 175-178.

[38]Tolley and Goett, "Reactions," 13-14; Petrof, "Reaching the Negro Market," 42.

[39]Gerald J. Glasser and Gale D. Metzger, "Radio Usage by Blacks," *Journal of Advertising Research,* vol. 15 (October 1975), 39-45.

[40]James W. Carey, "Variations in Negro-White Television Preference," *Journal of Broadcasting,* vol. 10 (1966), 199-211.

[41]These findings are in contrast with previously held beliefs about black social interaction, but the evidence is reasonably convincing for the more recent conclusions. See Anthony M. Orum, "A Reappraisal of the Social and Political Participation of Negros." *American Journal of Sociology,* vol. 72 (July 1966), 32-46; Marvin E. Olsen, "Social and Political Participation of Blacks," *American Sociological Review,* vol. 35 (1970), 682-696.

8. Black opinion leadership and community control appears currently to be in a period of conflict between "old line" upper-class black leaders who were acceptable to white power holders, and upwardly mobile, usually young, aggressive blacks willing to tap latent aggressions toward "uppity niggers," "Jew merchants," and "crackers."[42]

Alternative Evaluation

The process of evaluating alternative offerings in the marketplace appears to be influenced by a number of experience and environmental variables, which, in turn, affect the beliefs, attitudes, and intentions of black consumers. A number of studies have disclosed some generalizations that may be true about black consumers, although considerable caution is necessary in interpreting such findings because of the danger of ignoring variations that occur between market segments within the black market. Barry and Harvey, after surveying many of the studies of black consumer behavior, concluded the heterogeneous elements of the black market consist of four distinct market subsections, which they describe as (1) "Negroes," (2) "blacks," (3) "Afro-Americans," and (4) "recent foreign black immigrants."[43] Although segments exist within the black market, most research has not made such delineations. The following generalizations are typical of the research based upon the less refined classification of black-white consumer behavior.

1. Blacks save more out of a given income than do whites with the same incomes.[44] Blacks use fewer savings and insurance services, however, and end up with less total financial resources than white families of equivalent income and tend to use the less advantageous types of financial services with the end result that the savings approach of blacks tends to widen the gap of well-being between black and white households.[45] The usage of checking accounts by blacks is almost half the rate among white families.[46]

2. Blacks spend more for clothing and nonautomobile transportation; less for food, housing, medical care, and automobile transportation; and equivalent amounts for recreation and leisure, home furnishings, and equipment than comparable levels of whites.[47]

[42]These terms and research are from Seymour Leventman, "Class and Ethnic Tensions: Minority Group Leadership in Transition," *Sociology and Social Research,* vol. 50 (April 1966), 371-376; also Frank A. Petroni, "Uncle Toms: White Stereotypes in the Black Movement," *Human Organization,* vol. 29 (Winter 1970), 260-266.

[43]Thomas E. Barry and Michael G. Harvey, "Marketing to Heterogeneous Black Consumers," *California Management Review,* vol. 17 (Winter 1974), 50-57.

[44]Marcus Alexis, "Some Negro-White Differences in Consumption," *American Journal of Economics and Sociology,* vol. 21 (January 1962).

[45]Roxanne Hiltz, "Black and White in the Consumer Financial System," *American Journal of Sociology,* vol. 76 (1971), 987-999. For changes, see Charles Van Jassel, "The Negro as a Consumer—What We Know and What We Ought to Know," in M. S. Moyer and R. E. Vosburgh, (eds.), *Marketing for Tomorrow . . . Today* (Chicago: American Marketing Association, 1967), 166-168.

[46]Edward B. Selby, Jr., and James T. Lindley, "Black Consumers—Hidden Market Potential," *The Bankers Magazine,* vol. 156 (Summer 1973), 84-87.

[47]Alexis, "Some Negro-White Differences"; also James Stafford, Keith Cox, and James Higginbotham, "Some Consumption Pattern Differences between Urban Whites and Negroes," *Social Science Quarterly,* (December 1968), 619-630.

3. Blacks tend to own more larger, and perhaps more luxury, cars and fewer foreign cars. Ownership of large cars may be required because of the larger size among black families and the need for more pooled transportation.[48]

4. Blacks appear to be more brand loyal than equivalent whites.[49]

5. Black families purchase more milk and soft drinks, less tea and coffee, and more liquor than white families. Blacks accounted for almost one-half of all rum consumption in the United States, 41 percent of all gin, over 50 percent of all Scotch whiskies, and over 77 percent of the Canadian whiskies.[50]

6. Blacks spend more time in commuting to work, travel longer distances, and have lower per capita consumption of automobiles than whites.[51]

Choice Processes

Choice processes of blacks and whites do not show dramatic differences except where circumstances (such as nonavailability of quality retail offerings) create or cause differences. Basically, the black consumer is a practical and economical shopper first and foremost and "black" second.[52] Some distinctions that have been disclosed in black choice processes, however, are reported in the following studies.

1. Black consumers appear to have more awareness of both private and national brands than do white consumers and to be better informed about prices than white counterparts.[53]

2. Black consumers appear to respond as well to package design (for beer) designed for white consumers as for packages designed specifically for black consumers.[54]

3. Black consumers tend not to shop by phone or mail order as much as white consumers.[55]

4. Black grocery consumers tend to make frequent trips to neighborhood

---

[48]Fred C. Akers, "Negro and White Automobile-Buying Behavior: New Evidence," *Journal of Marketing Research,* vol. 5 (August 1968), 283-290; Carl M. Larson and Hugh G. Wales, "Brand Preferences of Chicago Blacks," *Journal of Advertising Research,* vol. 13 (August 1973), 15-21.

[49]Frank G. Davis, "Differential Factors in the Negro Market," (Chicago: National Association of Market Developers, 1959), 6; privately published report based upon data collected by *Ebony* magazine.

[50]Data from Bernard Howard and Co., Inc., and *Ebony,* reported in Oladipupo, *How Distinct?,* 30-34.

[51]James O. Wheeler, "Transportation Problems in Negro Ghettos," *Sociology and Social Research,* vol. 53 (January 1969), 171-179.

[52]W. Leonard Evans, Jr., *"Ghetto Marketing: What Now?"* in Robert L. King, (ed.), *Marketing and the New Science of Planning* (Chicago: American Marketing Association, 1968), 528-531.

[53]Robert L. King and Earl Robert DeManche, "Comparative Acceptance of Selected Private-Branded Food Products by Low-Income Negro and White Families," in McDonald *op. cit.,* 63-69. The sample size in this study is very small, however. Feldman and Starr also found that black consumers were more concerned wtih price than white consumers who were more concerned with value.

[54]Herbert E. Krugman, "White and Negro Responses to Package Design," *Journal of Marketing Research,* vol. 3 (May 1966), 199-200.

[55]Laurence P. Feldman and Alvin D. Star, "Racial Factors in Shopping Behavior," Keith Cox and Ben Enis, (eds.), *A New Measure of Responsibility for Marketing* (Chicago: American Marketing Association 1968), 216-226; Keith K. Cox, James B. Higginbotham, and James E. Stafford, "Negro Retail Shopping and Credit Behavior," *Journal of Retailing,* vol. 48 (Spring 1972), 54-66.

stores. This may be due to inadequate refrigeration and storage and lack of transportation that would allow carrying large amounts of groceries.[56]

5. Black consumers tend to shop at discount stores compared to department stores more than do comparable white consumers.[57]

6. Black consumers tend to be unhappier with supermarket facilities and functions than do white consumers (with complaints including poor prices, poor cleanliness, crowded conditions, poor displays, and unfriendly employees.)[58]

7. Black consumers place more emphasis upon convenience, shopping location, price, quality, and service than upon the appeal of buying black; although younger segments of the black community place more appeal on buying from black-owned firms.[59]

8. Black consumers tend to "shop around" less than do white consumers.[60]

Pepsi-Cola Hits the Spot!

An example of how a firm can make a major commitment to the black market and be successful is provided by Pepsi-Cola.[61] The black market is important in the soft-drink business because blacks consume 10 percent more soft drinks than the general population, constituting 17 percent of the soft-drink market and 15 percent of the cola market. In addition, *Pepsi* brand-loyal blacks have a considerably higher consumption rate than white *Pepsi* users.

To coordinate its marketing approach, Pepsi-Cola appointed a black vice-president who conducted extensive research and developed an extensive promotion and distribution program. Using black-oriented media, Pepsi-Cola created ads featuring black community life-styles. Blacks are several years younger than whites on the average so Pepsi-Cola used the theme, "Now It's Pepsi—For Those Who Think Young." Local bottlers, at Pepsi's encouragement, used local black media and nationally Pepsi-Cola used *Ebony* extensively as well as national black newspapers.

Pepsi-Cola annually attends over 30 national black conventions where *Pepsi* is distributed for sampling. The company co-sponsored the International Golf Tournament, a black golfers' meet, and provides rec-

---

[56]Donald F. Dixon and Daniel J. McLaughlin, Jr., "Shopping Behavior, Expenditure Patterns, and Inner City Food Prices," *Journal of Marketing Research*, vol. 8 (February 1971), 960-999; Feldman and Star present data to show that blacks do not shop more frequently than whites, however.

[57]Feldman and Star, "Racial Factors," similarity between blacks and whites was found, however, in Cox, et al., "Negro Retail Shopping," 60.

[58]John V. Petrof, "Attitudes of the Urban Poor toward Their Neighborhood Supermarkets," *Journal of Retailing*, vol. 47 (Spring 1971), 3-17.

[59]Deniis H. Gensch and Richard Staelin, "The Appeal of Buying Black," *Journal of Marketing Research*, vol. 9 (May 1972), 141-148; Dennis Gensch and Richard Staelin, "Making Black Retail Outlets Work," *California Management Review*, vol. 15 (Fall 1972), 52-62.

[60]Donald E. Sexton, Jr., "Differences in Food Shopping Habits by Area of Residence, Race, and Income," *Journal of Retailing*, vol. 50 (Spring 1974), 37-48.

[61]Summarized from Gibson, *$70 Billion in the Black*, 134-146.

ognition medallions to national organizations such as the National Medical Association. Pepsi-Cola began a joint venture with the Distributive Education Clubs of America (DECA) allowing young people to learn management by selling refreshments, with an emphasis on black students. The company sponsored free tennis lessons in the inner city, sponsored *Hotshot*, a cooperative program co-sponsored by the National Basketball Association, and "The Black Journal" on television.

The net effect of this black-oriented program was a massive increase in sales. From 1961 when it was begun until the 1980's, substantial increases in both sales and market share were gained. In one four-year period, sales jumped nearly $100 million and sales to black markets contributed a significant proportion of the increase.

CROSS-CULTURAL ANALYSIS OF CONSUMER BEHAVIOR

One of the most important job skills that consumer analysts and marketing practitioners need today is the ability to function globally. The multinational corporation (MNC) is the wave of the future. Firms whose success was once determined domestically increasingly are affected by markets, suppliers, and competitors from other countries. It is essential that a consumer analyst be competent to think globally about markets.

Cross-cultural analysis provides an approach to understanding consumer behavior that can be helpful for analyzing subcultures or groups within a nation. In Africa, for example, tribal cultures *within* countries such as Zambia, Nigeria, Zimbabwe, and South Africa may be far more influential than differences that exist *between* countries. In fact, many of the tribal influences cut across national boundaries that were established by white colonists with little regard to cultural or tribal boundaries. In Europe, also, people in the south of Switzerland may have more cultural similarity to France than to the north of Switzerland. In North America, people in the western provinces of Canada may be more similar to people in the western states of the USA than to eastern provinces. Cross-cultural analysis provides an approach for understanding such situations.

What Is Cross-Cultural Analysis?

Cross-cultural analysis is the *systematic comparison of similarities and differences in the material and behavioral aspects of cultures.* Anthropologists developed techniques to be able to catalogue similarities and contrasts among peoples of various cultures. Among societies so remotely located that they could not possibly have come into contact with each other, remarkable similarities are found in the methods they use to handle common problems. Some of the similarities among cultures, defined as items prohibited or compelled by the culture, are described in Table 4.5.

Cross-cultural research methodology involves the research techniques described in the final part of this chapter adapted to the special requirements of different languages, structural characteristics of the so-

**Table 4.5
Behaviors
Prohibited and
Compelled in 25
Primitive Cultures**

Behavior items both prohibited and compelled in the 25 cultures

Eating, drinking, vocalizing, talking, defecating, urinating, playing, marrying, working, harming others, harming self.

Behavior items prohibited

Sucking, cannibalism, biting, crying, . . . incest, adultery, . . . murdering, stealing, assuming another's prerogatives, harming food, hindering manufacturing, hindering course of war, inviting bad luck, . . . being angry, . . . deceiving others, angering others, committing suicide, destroying goods, committing treason, being jealous, being irresponsible, hating, playing, being lazy.

Behavior Items Compelled

Wailing, weeping, sleeping, giving, entering, being formal, . . . mourning, naming others, respecting others, cleansing self, protecting others, obeying others, purifying self, being secluded, helping others, learning, avoiding retaliation, . . . avenging, being hospitable, concealing parts of body, . . . expressing grief, fighting outgroup, pacifying others, being friendly, thanking others, being fertile, participating in food quest, . . . being brave, avoiding bad luck, ensuring good luck, aiding food quest, being generous, being kind, manufacturing, being industrious.

Source: From C. S. Ford, "Society, Culture, and the Human Organism," *Journal of General Psychology.* 1939, vol. 20, 135-179; reprinted in Frank W. Moore, (ed.), *Readings in Cross-Cultural Methodology* (New Haven, Conn.: Human Relations Area Files Press, 1961), 158. Reprinted by permission of Journal Press.

cieties, and values of the investigator that may differ from the society studied.[62]

Cross-cultural studies may be *statistical* in nature, describing the *structure of the culture or specific components.* A statistical study might compare the distribution structure of the United States with that of Russia, for example, to be used by the marketing manager of Levi Strauss or Pepsi-Cola, companies which recently began marketing in Russia. Such a study could compare the highly dependent relationship between suppliers and retailers in Russia compared to the more independent manufacturer-wholesaler-retailer structure typical of the United States. The structure of government specialty and department stores would be compared to the competitive chains of the United States and the uniquely Russian "kassa" system in which customers view merchandise from one salesperson (after waiting in line) and then go to the cashier (after waiting in line again) to pay for the merchandise before returning to the original point to obtain the merchandise.[63] Even though Levi Strauss jeans might be the same product in both countries, successful marketing would require considerable adaptation in Russia and a cross-cultural analysis would provide useful information for the design of the marketing program.

Cross-cultural studies may be *functional* and *analytical* in nature, focusing upon comparisons of that culture. A functional study would focus

[62]An introduction to cross-cultural methods in Frank W. Moore, (ed.), *Readings in Cross-Cultural Methodology* (New Haven, Conn.: Human Relations Area Files Press, 1961); Oscar Lewis, "Comparisons in Cultural Anthropology," in William L. Thomas, Jr., (ed.), *Current Anthropology: A Supplement to Anthropology Today* (Chicago: University of Chicago Press, 1956), 259-292; R. W. Bristin, W. J. Lonner and R. M. Thorndike, *Cross-Cultural Research Methods* (New York: John Wiley & Sons, 1973).

[63]Thomas Greer, *Marketing in the Soviet Union* (New York: Praeger, 1973); Coskun Samli, *Marketing and Distribution Systems in Eastern Europe* (New York: Praeger, 1978).

upon the reasons activities are performed in the ways observed and why behaviors have developed. A statistical approach may be used as an aid to functional analysis, of course, as Plummer has done in a study which considered the role of hygiene across cultures. Functionally, the role of cleanliness varied considerably across cultures and it appears consumers in the United States might be paranoid about cleanliness. Plummer found the following percentages in each nation to agree with the statement, "Everyone should use a deodorant."[64]

United States	89 percent
French Canada	81
English Canada	77
United Kingdom	71
Italy	69
France	59
Australia	53

A functional cross-cultural study provides insights for marketers by linking cultural materials and behaviors to consumer purchasing and usage. An outline for conducting a cross-cultural analysis of consumer behavior is provided in Table 4.6.

Can Marketing Be Standardized?

Must marketing programs be modified for each culture or is it possible to be successful with standardized marketing programs used in all or at least many different cultures? This question is enormously important because if programs must be modified to each culture, many firms will fail when they omit such modifications or fail to do them well. But if marketing programs are modified for each culture, the production and other expenses will be prohibitive compared to the efficiency possible if one program can be used in many cultures.

Erik Elinder advanced the position that consumer behavior is subject to cultural universals and that advertising can be standardized.[65] Fatt amplifies this position by stating "that even different peoples are *basically* the same, and that an international advertising campaign with a truly universal appeal can be effective in any market."[66] He illustrates his position with these examples:

The desire to be beautiful is universal. Such appeals as mother and child, freedom from pain, glow of health, know no boundaries.

In a sense, the young women in Tokyo and the young women in Berlin are sisters not only "under the skin," but on their skin and on their lips and fingernails, and even in their hair styles. If they could, the girls of Moscow would follow suit; and some of them do.[67]

[64]Reprinted by permission from Joseph Plummer, "Consumer Focus in Cross-National Research," *Journal of Marketing* (November 1977), 5-15, published by the American Marketing Association.

[65]Erik Elinder, "How International Can European Advertising Be?" *Journal of Marketing,* vol. 29 (April 1965), 7-11.

[66]Arthur C. Fatt, "The Danger of 'Local' International Advertising," *Journal of Marketing,* vol. 31 (January 1967), 60-62.

[67]Fatt, "Dangers," 61; also Arthur C. Fatt, "A Multi-National Approach to International Advertising," *International Executive,* vol. 7 (Winter 1965), 5-6.

**Table 4.6
Outline of Cross-Cultural Analysis of Consumer Behavior**

Determine Relevant Motivations in the Culture:

What needs are fulfilled with this product in the minds of members of the culture? How are these needs presently fulfilled? Do members of this culture readily recognize these needs?

Determine Characteristic Behavior Patterns:

What patterns are characteristic of purchasing behavior? What forms of division of labor exist within the family structure? How frequently are products of this type purchased? What size packages are normally purchased? Do any of these characteristic behaviors conflict with behavior expected for this product? How strongly ingrained are the behavior patterns that conflict with those needed for distribution of this product?

Determine What Broad Cultural Values are Relevant to This Product:

Are there strong values about work, morality, religion, family relations, and so on, that relate to this product? Does this product connote attributes that are in conflict with these cultural values? Can conflicts with values be avoided by changing the product? Are there positive values in this culture with which the product might be identified?

Determine Characteristic Forms of Decision Making:

Do members of the culture display a studied approach to decisions concerning innovations or an impulsive approach? What is the form of the decision process? Upon what information sources do members of the culture rely? Do members of the culture tend to be rigid or flexible in the acceptance of new ideas? What criteria do they use in evaluating alternatives?

Evaluate Promotion Methods Appropriate to the Culture:

What roles does advertising occupy in the culture? What themes, words, or illustrations are taboo? What language problems exist in present markets that cannot be translated into this culture? What types of salesmen are accepted by members of the culture? Are such salesmen available?

Determine Appropriate Institutions for This Product in the Minds of Consumers:

What types of retailers and intermediary institutions are available? What services do these institutions offer that are expected by the consumer? What alternatives are available for obtaining services needed for the product but not offered by existing institutions? How are various types of retailers regarded by consumers? Will changes in the distribution structure be readily accepted?

There are many obstacles, but a trend does appear to be developing toward greater standardization.[68] In a study of 27 multi-national companies operating in the United States and Europe, including companies such as General Foods, Nestlé, Coca-Cola, Procter & Gamble, Unilever, and Revlon, Sorenson and Wiechmann found that 63 percent of the total marketing programs were rated as "highly standardized."[69] These authors concluded by describing the importance of cross-cultural (or "cross-border") analysis:

. . . managements of multi-nationals should give high priority to developing their ability to conduct systematic cross-border analysis, if they are not already doing so. Such analysis can help management

[68]Robert D. Buzzell, "Can You Standardize Multinational Marketing?" *Harvard Business Review,* vol. 46 (November-December 1968), 102-113.

[69]Ralph Z. Sorenson and Ulrich E. Wiechmann, "How Multinationals View Marketing Standardization," *Harvard Business Review,* vol. 53 (May-June 1975), 38-56.

avoid the mistake of standardizing when markets are significantly different. At the same time, systematic cross-border analysis can help avoid the mistake of excessive custom-tailoring when markets are sufficiently similar to make standardized programs feasible.[70]

A realistic assessment of the standardization-localization controversy is that the management of a firm must be adaptive to some elements of the marketing program that are localized and others that are standardized. Marketing strategy that is not built upon an understanding of cultural realities will have unpredictable success patterns.[71] Yet, there is ample evidence to show that marketing strategies can be developed that are applicable worldwide.[72] Marketing research studies of a wide variety have been completed which indicate the feasibility of standardization and at the same time provide the kind of cross-cultural data needed for successful implementation of multi-national marketing.[73]

Overcoming Language Problems

Language problems often seem difficult for marketers to overcome but a number of techniques borrowed from cross-cultural analysis are helpful with such problems.

Serious mistakes often occur when literal translations are made of brand names or advertisements by people who know a language but not a culture. An example occurred in Canada when Hunt-Wesson attempted to use the *Big John* family brand name by translating it into French as *"Gros Jos,"* which is a colloquial French expression denoting a woman with big breasts. The incident caused *Playboy* magazine to award its annual "Booby Boo Boo Award" to the company.

General Motors uses the phrase, "Body by Fisher" in its marketing. Some problems occurred, however, when it was translated into Flemish and took on the meaning of "Corpse by Fisher." When General Motors introduced a car called the *Nova* in Puerto Rico, sales were poor until the company discovered the word *Nova* was pronounced as *no va* — with the literal Spanish meaning of "doesn't go." Sales went better when the name was changed to *Caribe.* The phrase, "Come alive with *Pepsi"* experienced problems when it was translated in German ads as, "Come alive out of the grave," and in Chinese as, *"Pepsi* brings your ancestors back from the grave."[74]

The Standard Oil Company reportedly spent millions on a world-wide

[70]Ibid, 48.

[71]Montrose Sommers and Jerome Kernan, "Why Products Flourish Here, Fizzle There," *Columbia Journal of World Business,* vol. 2 (March-April 1967), 89-97.

[72]Dean Peebles, "Goodyear's Worldwide Advertising," *The International Advertiser,* vol. 8 (January 1967), 19-22 (both good and weak examples are cited in this article); Walter P. Margulies, "Why Global Marketing Requires a Global Focus on Product Design," *Business Abroad,* (August 22, 1966), 22-23; Norman Heller, "How Pepsi-Cola Does It in 110 Countries," in John S. Wright and Jac L. Goldstrucker, (eds.), *New Ideas for Successful Marketing* (Chicago: American Marketing Association, 1966), 700-715.

[73]Space does not allow a description of this research but if you are interested in such studies, see the Third Edition of *Consumer Behavior,* 86-87.

[74]Kevin Lynch, "Adplomacy Faux Pas Can Ruin Sales," *Advertising Age* (January 15, 1979), S-2ff.

basis when changing its name to *Exxon*. It was necessary to research the legal problems that might be encountered in each country, to determine a name unused by any other firm in the world but also to research the possible meanings the name *Exxon* might have in every language. The steps that a company should use in finding a name acceptable on a cross-cultural basis are described below:

1. Does the English name of the product have another meaning, perhaps unfavorable in one or more of the countries where it is to be marketed?

2. Can the English name be pronounced everywhere? For example, Spanish and some other languages lack a *k* in their alphabets, an initial letter in many popular U.S. brand names.

3. Is the name close to that of a foreign brand or does it duplicate another product sold in English-speaking countries?

4. If the product is distinctly American, will national pride and prejudice work against the acceptance of the product?[75]

Back-Translation

The most useful and straightforward technique for overcoming language problems is *back-translation*. In the back-translation procedure, a message (word or a series of words) is translated from its original language to the translated language and back to its original language by a number of translators. This process may be repeated several times with the translated versions being interchanged with the original among the translators. The purpose of the iterations is an attempt to achieve conceptual equivalency in meaning by controlling the various translation biases of the translators.[76]

An example of a research instrument involving verbal and quantitative responses is shown in Figure 4.4, a questionnaire given to airline passengers. Sometimes it is desirable to use scales other than verbal or quantitative scales. Figure 4.5 shows an example from *Holiday Inn* in which questions are given in English and Afrikans but responses are given with smiling or unhappy faces.

RESEARCH METHODOLOGY FOR CULTURAL ANALYSIS

Consumer behavior and marketing have borrowed from many other disciplines to obtain research methods. Anthropology, linguistics and sociology have been the primary sources of methodology for studying cul-

---

[75]Walter P. Margulies, "Why Global Marketing Requires a Global Focus on Product Design," *Business Abroad,* vol. 94 (January 1969), 22.

[76]Richard W. Brislin, "Black-Translation for Cross-Cultural Research," *Journal of Cross-Cultural Psychology*, vol. 1 (September 1970), 185-216; and Osward Werner and Donald T. Campbell, "Translating, Working through Interpreters, and the Problems of Decentering," in Raoul Naroll and Ronald Cohen, (eds.), *A Handbook of Method in Cultural Anthropology* (Garden City, N.J.: The Natural History Press, 1970), 398-420.

Figure 4.4
Would You Like to
Help Us Help You?
(Part of a Canadian
Pacific Airline
Questionnaire)

Pouvons-nous Compter sur Votre Collaboration?

Pour pouvoir vous offrir un service aussi parfait que possible, nous aimerions connaître plus de détails sur vous-même, votre voyage et vos opinions.
Nous vous serions reconnaissants de bien vouloir remplir le questionnaire ci-joint durant ce voyage.
Au cas où vous voyagez en groupe, chaque participant de plus de onze ans est invité à remplir également ce questionnaire.

Vos réponses nous aideront à améliorer notre service et à rendre vos voyages subséquents encore plus agréables.
Nous vous remercions et vous souhaitons de passer un bon voyage.
Remarque: Les employés de la compagnie aérienne et leurs dépendants ne sont pas supposés remplir ce formulaire.

SONDAGE AUPRES DES PASSAGERS DES VOLS DOMESTIQUES

CP Air vous remercie de bien vouloir remplir ce questionnaire et apprécie votre collaboration à ce sujet. Vos réponses seront employées à des fins statistiques seulement et seront considérées strictement confidentielles.   1

No. de vol _____   2 Mois   Jour   5
Date

1. a) Veuillez inscrire le nom de la compagnie aérienne qui a émis votre billet.   11

    b) Veuillez maintenant inscrire le numéro qui figure à l'angle droit supérieur de votre coupon de billet, même s'il n'a pas été émis par CP Air. (Les informations notées sur votre coupon-billet seront employées à des fins statistiques seulement et son strictement confidentielles.)

       Numéro du billet _____

2. Dans quelle ville êtes-vous monté(e) a bord de cet avion?   24
       Ville   Province

3. Où se trouve votre domicile actuel?   27
       Ville   Province/Etat   Pays

4. Quel est ou, si vous rentrez chez vous, quel a été le lieu de destination principal de votre voyage?   31
       Ville   Province/Etat   Pays

Would you like to help us help you?

In order to give you the best possible service, we need to know more about you, your journey and your opinions.
We would like you to complete, the following questionnaire at your convenience during this flight.
If you are travelling with a group, we would like each person over the age of 11 to complete a questionnaire.

The answers to these questions will be of great help to us in planning to meet your future travel requirements.
Thank you—and enjoy a pleasant journey.
Note: Airline employees and their dependents should not complete this questionnaire.

DOMESTIC

We at CP Air would like to thank you for your cooperation in answering this questionnaire. The information received will remain strictly confidential and will only be used for statistical purposes.   1

Flight No. _____   2 Month   Day   5
Date

1. a) Will you please write in the name of the airline that issued your ticket?   11

    b) And now, will you please write in your ticket number (top right hand corner of your ticket coupon) even if it was not issued by CP Air. (The information provided on your ticket coupon will be used for statistical purposes only and will be treated in strict confidence.)

       Ticket Number _____

2. In which city did you board this particular flight?   24
       City   Province

3. In what city are you now living?   27
       City/Town   Province/Centre   Country

4. What is the main destination of your journey, or if you are now returning home, what was your main destination away from home?   31
       City/Town   Province/State   Country

Source: Reprinted by permission of the Marketing Planning Department, CP Air, Vancouver, Canada.

ture.[77] In recent years, however, consumer behavior has begun to develop its own approaches for cultural and cross-cultural analysis.[78]

Field studies are conducted by sending a trained observer to the culture of interest for intensive collection of data about that culture. Field studies may be either the mass-observation type or the participant-observer study.

Mass Observations

Mass observations refer to the process of a researcher interacting with members of a culture who appear to understand the culture of the group, listening to conversations and attempting to synthesize these experi-

[77]Introductions to methodology for cultural research and descriptions of specific technique can be found in B. K. Stravianis, "Research Methods in Cultural Anthropology," *Psychological Review*, vol. 57 (1950), 334-344; Gardner Lindsey, *Projective Techniques and Cross-Cultural Research* (New York: Appleton, 1961); Charles E. Osgood and Thomas A. Sebeck, "Psycholinguistics: A Survey of Theory and Research Problems," a Morton Prince Memorial Supplement to *Journal of Abnormal and Social Psychology*, vol. 49 (1954); Francis L. K. Hsu, (ed.), *Psychological Anthropology: Approaches to Culture and Personality* (Homewood, Ill.: Dorsey Press, 1961); Bert Kaplan, (ed.), *Studying Personality Cross-Culturally* (New York: Harper & Row, 1961); R. L. Carneiro and S. F. Tobias, "The Application of Scale Analysis to the study of Cultural Evolution," transcript, New York Academy of Science, ser. 2, vol. 26 (1963), 196-207; Allen D. Grimshaw, "Sociolinguistics," in I. de Sola Pool and Wilbur Schramm, (eds.), *Handbook of Communication* (Chicago: Rand McNally, 1973), 47-92.

[78]Peter Cooke, "Market Analysis Utilizing Cultural Anthropological Indicators," *European Journal of Marketing*, vol. 6 (1972), 26-34; Yoram Wind and Susan Douglas, "Some Issues in International Consumer Research," *European Journal of Marketing*, vol. 8 (1974), 204-217; Charles Lamb, "Domestic Applications of Comparative Marketing Analysis," *European Journal of Marketing*, vol. 9 (1975), 167-172.

**Figure 4.5
Cross-Cultural
Research
Instrument**

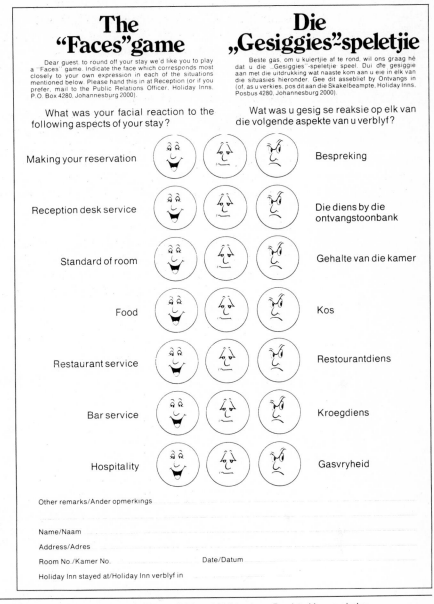

The "Faces" game

Dear guest, to round off your stay we'd like you to play a "Faces" game. Indicate the face which corresponds most closely to your own expression in each of the situations mentioned below. Please hand this in at Reception (or if you prefer, mail to the Public Relations Officer, Holiday Inns, P.O. Box 4280, Johannesburg 2000).

What was your facial reaction to the following aspects of your stay?

Making your reservation

Reception desk service

Standard of room

Food

Restaurant service

Bar service

Hospitality

Die „Gesiggies"speletjie

Beste gas, om u kuiertjie af te rond, wil ons graag hê dat u die „Gesiggies"-speletjie speel. Dui die gesiggie aan met die uitdrukking wat naaste kom aan u eie in elk van die situasies hieronder. Gee dit asseblief by Ontvangs in (of, as u verkies, pos dit aan die Skakelbeampte, Holiday Inns, Posbus 4280, Johannesburg 2000).

Wat was u gesig se reaksie op elk van die volgende aspekte van u verblyf?

Bespreking

Die diens by die ontvangstoonbank

Gehalte van die kamer

Kos

Restourantdiens

Kroegdiens

Gasvryheid

Other remarks/Ander opmerkings

Name/Naam

Address/Adres

Room No./Kamer No.   Date/Datum

Holiday Inn stayed at/Holiday Inn verblyf in

Source: Courtesy of the South African division of Holiday Inns. Reprinted by permission.

ences into conclusions about the culture. The difficulty with such studies is that there is usually no systematic sampling. Also, they rely upon the observer's ability to be objective and comprehensive as well as his or her ability to select the proper people or activities to be included in the study.

Because of the subjective nature of mass observations, their primary value is mostly for preliminary investigation of market potential and for developing hypotheses to be investigated with more systematic studies.

Participant-Observer Studies.
Participant-observer studies involve an investigator or team of investigators living in intimate contact with a culture, making careful and comprehensive notes of observations about the culture. They are only "one step up" in rigor of respondent selection compared to mass observations but may be quite rigorous in the depth of inquiry. The data collection may include records of what is observed, interviews with "key" informants, and structured methods such as attitude scales, projective tests, and so forth administered by the researcher. Using a comprehensive model of consumer behavior such as the one introduced in Chapter 2 can also be helpful in guiding the decisions about data to be collected in a participant-observer study.

Content Analysis

Content analysis is a technique for determining the values, themes, role prescriptions, norms of behavior, and other elements of culture from objective materials produced by the people of a culture in the ordinary course of events.[79] Usually, the content studied is verbal in nature such as newspaper or magazine stories although it could be advertisements or any other objective material such as art, products or even the garbage discarded by consumers.[80]

Content analysis has been used in marketing studies, mostly in the measurement of advertising themes. In a carefully executed study, Kassarjian analyzed occupational roles of Negroes in America, discovering some changes in occupational roles but the continuation of many stereotypes.[81] Other content analyses have focused upon the roles of women in advertisements.[82]

Cross-Sectional Studies

Cross-sectional studies of culture are similar to cross-sectional studies of any other area of consumer and marketing research. They are more refined in their sampling procedures than intensive field studies although they may lack the depth of understanding those methodologies reveal. The challenge is to formulate questions that reveal values or behavioral norms of the culture or subculture studied. Large-scale cross-sectional

[79]For details of the method, see Bernard Berelson, *Content Analysis in Communication Research* (New York: Free Press, 1952). See also various readings in I. Pool, (ed.), *Trends in Content Analysis* (Urbana, Ill.: University of Illinois Press, 1959); R. C. North et al., *Content Analysis: A Handbook with Applications for the Study of International Crisis* (Evanston, Ill.: Northwestern University Press, 1963).

[80]Eugene J. Webb et al., *Unobtrusive Measures* (Chicago: Rand McNally, 1966).

[81]Harold H. Kassarjian, "The Negro and American Advertising, 1946-1965," *Journal of Marketing Research,* vol. 6 (February 1969), 29-39.

[82] Alice E. Courtney and Sarah W. Locker et al., "A Woman's Place: An Analysis of the Roles Portrayed by Women in Magazine Advertisements," *Journal of Marketing Research,* vol. 8 (February 1971), 92-95, and Louis C. Wagner and Janis B. Banos, "A Woman's Place: A Follow-up Analysis of the Roles Portrayed by Women in Magazine Advertisements," *Journal of Marketing Research,* vol. 10 (May 1973), 213-214.

Table 4.7
Cross-Sectional Study of Values in Representative Campuses (selected questions and responses)

Indicate your views on the following twenty political proposals for the United States by writing in a number signifying the following:

(1) Definitely in favor
(2) Somewhat in favor
(3) Indifferent or no opinion
(4) Somewhat opposed
(5) Definitely opposed

Full socialization of all industries

	SL %	Wms %	Yale %	Marq %	BU %	Ind %	SC %	Hwd %	Reed %	Dav %	Bran %	Stan %
(1)	11	2	8	2	9	4	—	10	11	4	7	3
(2)	34	13	17	9	29	14	8	26	27	11	30	17
(3)	9	7	11	11	11	9	11	18	16	8	8	7
(4)	21	28	25	21	20	20	18	16	14	25	26	23
(5)	24	49	40	56	29	51	61	25	29	51	23	48

Socialization of basic industries

	SL	Wms	Yale	Marq	BU	Ind	SC	Hwd	Reed	Dav	Bran	Stan
(1)	34	10	21	9	26	13	4	31	29	12	25	15
(2)	41	29	34	23	34	20	24	27	28	23	34	29
(3)	8	8	6	10	9	8	12	13	11	5	8	8
(4)	5	28	22	26	15	22	20	15	13	31	17	22
(5)	9	26	17	32	13	34	40	9	16	28	11	24

National Health Insurance

	SL	Wms	Yale	Marq	BU	Ind	SC	Hwd	Reed	Dav	Bran	Stan
(1)	63	39	54	28	56	30	31	54	58	27	61	32
(2)	18	35	28	35	27	28	34	15	18	46	22	38
(3)	14	14	13	15	11	20	15	14	10	11	9	15
(4)	3	6	3	13	3	10	12	3	8	9	1	7
(5)	—	5	2	8	1	8	7	—	3	5	2	4

Have you ever smoked marijuana?
(1) Yes   (2) No

	SL %	Wms %	Yale %	Marq %	BU %	Ind %	SC %	Hwd %	Reed %	Dav %	Bran %	Stan %
(1)	82	75	65	33	74	42	34	40	76	33	65	66
(2)	18	24	34	67	25	58	65	56	22	66	33	33

All things considered, do you think more lenient college administrations standards for black applicants should be adopted?
(1) Yes   (2) No   (3) Unsure or no opinion

	SL %	Wms %	Yale %	Marq %	BU %	Ind %	SC %	Hwd %	Reed %	Dav %	Bran %	Stan %
(1)	59	61	55	36	42	38	24	63	50	54	62	63
(2)	26	24	25	48	38	45	65	24	22	35	22	20
(3)	11	11	17	15	15	12	9	9	23	9	13	17

**Table 4.7
(continued)**

Would you say that at the present time

(1) I am in substantial agreement with the religious tradition in which I was raised.
(2) I partially agree with the religious tradition in which I was raised but have important reservations.
(3) I wholly reject the religious tradition in which I was raised.

	SL %	Wms %	Yale %	Marq %	BU %	Ind %	SC %	Hwd %	Reed %	Dav %	Bran %	Stan %
(1)	13	8	11	17	9	17	18	11	10	10	20	9
(2)	65	71	54	74	56	52	62	63	47	74	61	61
(3)	22	20	33	6	32	27	19	24	40	16	19	27

Below are several very brief, rough statements of various conceptions of the Deity. Check the one that most nearly approximates your views.

(1) There is an immensely wise, omnipotent, three-person God Who created the universe and Who maintains an active concern for human affairs.
(2) There is a God precisely as described in (1) except that He is absolutely One and in no sense possesses trinitarian nature.
(3) I believe in a God about Whom nothing definite can be affirmed except that I sometimes sense Him as a mighty "spiritual presence" permeating all mankind and nature.
(4) There is a vast, impersonal principle of order or natural uniformity working throughout the whole universe and which, though not conscious of mere human life, I choose to call "God."
(5) Because of our ignorance in this matter, I see no adequate grounds for either affirming or denying the existence of God.
(6) I reject all belief in anything that could reasonably be called "God" and regard every such notion as a fiction unworthy of worship.
(7) Other

	SL %	Wms %	Yale %	Marq %	BU %	Ind %	SC %	Hwd %	Reed %	Dav %	Bran %	Stan %
(1)	3	5	14	45	9	24	39	21	5	23	2	15
(2)	3	3	2	3	2	4	1	3	2	1	3	1
(3)	22	28	26	29	30	29	25	23	8	35	20	25
(4)	22	21	20	6	22	16	10	21	17	13	28	24
(5)	22	18	16	4	18	13	11	16	29	11	23	15
(6)	9	4	8	2	6	4	3	4	16	6	8	9
(7)	11	17	7	8	6	6	5	6	16	8	9	7

Notes: Question numbers correspond to source.

The schools included were Sarah Lawrence College (SL), a small, private, nonsectarian women's school; Williams College (Wms), a small, private nonsectarian men's liberal arts college in New England; Yale University (Yale), a large, private nonsectarian school in Connecticut; Marquette University (Marq), a large, Milwaukee-based coeducational Catholic school; Boston University (BU), a large, private coeducational school with many commuter students; Indiana University, (Ind), a giant Midwestern land-grant institution dominating the small city of Bloomington; the University of South Carolina (SC), a recently integrated state-supported school of the South; Howard University (Hwd), a private, nondenominational, predominantly black university in Washington, D.C.; Reed College (Reed), a small, private coeducational school in Portland, Ore., noted for educational and political progressivism; Davisons College (Dav), a small, private Presbyterian men's school in rural North Carolina; Brandeis University (Bran), a medium-sized school in Boston with a predominantly Jewish student body and a reputation for political liberalism; and Stanford University (Stan), a large, private California university traditionally catering to the upper middle and upper classes.

Source: Philip P. Ardery, "Opinion on the Campus," *National Review*, vol. 23 (June 15, 1971), 635-650. Reprinted with permission from *National Review Magazine*, 150 E. 35th St., New York, New York 10016.

studies have the advantage of revealing data about the subcultures that may exist in a larger culture. Careful analysis may reveal that some subcultures—youth or blacks, for example—are forerunners for broader acceptance in the culture, a finding of great usefulness in monitoring new product or creative strategy opportunities.

An example of how large-scale cross-sectional studies reveal differences between subcultures is shown in Table 4.7 and you will note major differences on some cultural values between schools like Sarah Lawrence College and Marquette University for example. You may want to study Table 4.7 and indicate how you would personally rate each questionnaire item and then see how well you could predict the responses of your school or a school listed in the chart with a cultural background similar to your school.

Longitudinal Studies

Longitudinal research involves studies of specified phenomena over an extended period of time. Longitudinal studies are useful in many areas of consumer research including the study of values, especially for monitoring and predicting changes in values. Longitudinal studies involve "panels" or groups of people who agree to report their beliefs over an extended time period. Since panels are expensive to recruit and maintain and may introduce some biases from questioning the same people, marketing researchers often use repeated measures.

Repeated Measures.

A practical method of measuring shifts in values is through repeated measures of representative samples of the culture. The selection of respondents is generally done using probability samples to achieve projectability.

Some of the more commonly reported polls or surveys in the United States include the Gallup Poll, the Harris Poll, the Yanklelovich "Monitor" and Stanford Research Institute (SRI) VALS. An example of repeated measures about values toward marijuana legalization is indicated by the following data from the Gallup Poll.[83]

Should Marijuana Be Legalized?	Yes	No	No Opinion
National	25%	70%	5%
1979	25	70	5
1977	28	66	6
1973	16	78	6
1972	15	81	4
1969	12	84	4

In ending our discussion of cultural-research methodology, it is useful to note that many hybrid research approaches exist. Many of the research

[83]George Gallup, "Opposition to Legalization of Marijuana Remains Unchanged," *The Gallup Poll* (September 14, 1980). Reprinted by permission.

approaches used for other purposes in consumer research are appropriate for studying values, even on a cross-cultural basis. There is plenty of room for innovation in this area in the future. It will be needed as market segmentation becomes even more important in advanced, industrialized nations. More and more consumer researchers need to think globally in the development of marketing strategy and programming.

Summary

This chapter defines culture as a learned set of responses inculcated in a society, retained so long as they are gratifying to the society.

Culture can be analyzed by consumer researchers on a national basis or on a subcultural basis. Sub-cultural values are based upon nationality groups—of which Hispanics are the largest in the United States—religious and geographic groups, and racial groups—of which blacks are the largest and most studied by marketing researchers. In Canada, the French-Canadian culture provides a large and culturally rich market.

The black subculture has been shaped by a variety of factors such as income deprivation, inadequate educational institutions, differential family characteristics, and discrimination. There is no "black " market any more than a "white" market. Rather, a heterogeneous group of segments within the black population possesses, to varying degrees, some core values and consumption patterns. These patterns can be described in terms of the environmental influences on consumer behavior, search processes, alternative evaluation and choice processes.

Cross-cultural analysis is the systematic comparison of similarities and differences in the behavioral and physical aspects of cultures. Cross-cultural analysis provides an approach to understanding market segments both across national boundaries and between groups within a society. The process of analyzing markets on a cross-cultural basis is particularly helpful in deciding which elements of a marketing program can be standardized in multiple nations and which elements must be localized.

Various research methodologies are available for cross-cultural analysis of consumer behavior. These include intensive field studies, content analysis, cross-sectional studies, and longitudinal studies.

Review and Discussion Questions

1. What is meant by the term culture? Why does the term create confusion about its meaning?

2. Where do consumers get their values?

3. Examine the "American core values" of Table 4.2. Consider how they might impact a marketer of consumer electronics products.

4. Assume that a soft-drink marketer wanted to increase penetration in the Hispanic market. Prepare a set of recommendations for doing so.

5. Prepare a report that documents the effects of religious subcultures on consumer behavior.

6. Assume that a French manufacturer of women's apparel is seeking to expand markets by exporting to Canada. What marketing program should be recommended for maximum effectiveness?

7. Assume that a manufacturer of shoes receives a report of low-market share among black consumers. What questions would you raise about the report?

8. What is meant by the term cross-cultural analysis? Why is it important for marketers?

"Consumers are like chickens. They are much more comfortable with a pecking order that everybody knows about and accepts."[1] Because consumers so consistently display such behavior, brands and retail outlets also have a pecking order or cognitive consistency in the minds of customers. The simple word for this consistency or mental stratification is frequently called *position* and marketing strategies designed to influence the location of a brand or store in the minds of potential customers are called *positioning strategies*.

Positioning strategies involve many variables. Advertising is usually primary as the communication vehicle for establishing a set of attributes in the mind of the consumer. The product itself must possess or at least be consistent with those attributes, of course, but the retail outlet must also possess a location in the consumer's mind that is consistent with the positioning efforts of the firm. Positioning or the stratification of brands is a topic of great concern in marketing today but the fundamental concept of positioning or dividing into groups with which one feels most comfortable is not new.

All living creatures divide themselves into stratified societies. Even among animals this is true and has been observed in studies of insects, deer, mice, wolves, birds, and other creatures. One famous study concerned barnyard society in which it was found that each hen tends to maintain a definite position in the peck order of the group. Thus, the term used so frequently in contemporary society, the pecking order.[2]

SYSTEMS OF EQUALITY AND INEQUALITY

In some ways you are probably high in a pecking order but in other ways you may feel low in the pecking order. Inequality exists in many variables: intelligence, power, income, wealth, physical appearance, family

[1]Al Ries and Jack Trout, *Positioning: The Battle for Your Mind* (New York; McGraw-Hill Book Company, 1981), 53.
[2]T. Schjelderup-Ebbe, "Social Behavior of Birds," in C. Murchison, (ed.), *A Handbook of Social Psychology* (Worchester, Mass.: Clark University Press, 1935).

reputation, occupation, and so forth. But in some way, not always apparent, we tend to feel more comfortable with people on our own level. Although the bases for the stratification may result in a person being higher in some variables and lower in other variables, there is some overall way that people in all societies sense rank or order between the various groups of people in society.[3] The major forms of stratification include castes, estates, and social class.

The *caste* system places great emphasis upon hereditary status with large differences in the power and status of the highest and lowest castes. To a large degree, the basis for the traditional Indian caste system is religious. Only relatively controlled interaction is generally found or permitted between castes and mobility between groups is especially limited.

The *estate* system, prevalent in medieval Europe, presented clear boundaries about the rights and obligations of each group. The system was founded upon power and alliances—mainly the power of the lords and their warriors to offer protection from violence. Force was the basis of power, status, the right to vassalage, and a share of the land's produce.

A new version of the estate system may be establishing itself in the American economy. Justin Davidson describes this new feudalism:

As is characteristic of a feudal society, we have the fiefdoms of trade unionism. Yesterday it was Jimmy Hoffa and the Teamsters; today it is Douglas Fraser and the United Auto Workers. In the world of government and commerce, the United States has developed a new kind of fiefdom—the joint realm of regulators and clients. Yesterday it was the Department of Agriculture and the farmers; today it is the Department of Treasury and Chrysler. Feudalism is not a monopoly of professions, labor unions and government; it is growing in business. The competitive market economy that has produced much of the wealth of the United States is unstable. To reduce the uncertainty of the market, the tendency of corporate management is to move toward monopoly, mercantilism, protectionism, and finally, feudalism . . . In all aspects of U. S. life, collective and feudal tendencies are producing a new kind of class society.[4]

The *class system* is the predominant system found today in industrialized societies. The class system is of particular importance in marketing because classes form the basis for social interaction and therefore influence consumption. Relations existing between people of different

---

[3]The fact that stratification is ubiquitous is recognized by nearly all sociologists, although there is considerable question whether stratification is inevitable. The classic article delineating why stratification has arisen in all societies is that by Kingley Davis and Wilbert E. Moore, "Some Principles of Stratification," *American Sociological Review,* vol. 5 (1945), 242-249. For an opposing view, see Melvin M. Tumin, "Some Principles of Stratification: A Critical Analysis" *American Sociological Review,* vol. 13 (1953), 387-393.

[4]Justin Davidson, "Management in the 1980s," presented to Young Presidents Organizations, Columbus, Ohio, February 1981. Reprinted by permission.

classes tend to be specialized rather than the general interactions in which people share meals, leisure activities, neighborhoods, and so forth—the activities that affect the buying and consumption of products and services. So, let us take a close look at this concept of social class.

SOCIAL CLASS DEFINED

Social classes may be defined as *relatively permanent and homogeneous* divisions in a society in which individuals or families sharing similar values, life styles, interests, and behavior can be categorized. Little agreement exists about the nature of these divisions or the criteria for defining them[5] but one attempt to model how social classes can be studied in America is shown in Figure 5.1.

Beeghley's model for studying stratification in America forces us to see how many variables are involved. Observers can examine the model vertically or horizontally. By looking down on the top of the model, the social institutions may be identified that are related to social interactions designed to achieve the goal-oriented activities of the society. The vertical dimension of the model can be seen by looking at its sides where various levels of inequality called strata or classes are. Individual consumers would be studied by examining their economic, political, legal, religious, familiar, and educational characteristics. Social mobility, however, can be studied by examining rates of intra- and inter-generational mobility in the population or market segments. Related to this issue is the issue of status attainment or how individuals come to occupy various statuses.

Four occupational statuses are shown in Figure 5.1, but more detailed levels could also be defined. Social status is not limited to these variables, however, because hereditary variables such as sex and race may also be analyzed to understand the socioeconomic characteristics of a consumer.[6]

Some of the essential realities of social classes are that they restrict behavior and are hierarchical, multidimensional, and dynamic.

Behavior Restriction

Social classes tend to *restrict behavior between individuals of different classes* except for specialized activities. People have their close social relationships with people who like to do the same things they do, in the same ways, and with whom they can feel comfortable. This also restricts interpersonal communications about products, stores, and similar topics. There may be a great exchange of information, for example, among the upper social classes about the *Clenet,* considered by many to be the finest American-made car, while lower social classes may not even know

---

[5]An excellent discussion of the problems in defining social class, stratification, and status and of the theoretical perspectives that exist in status research is found in Thomas E. Lasswell, *Class and Stratum; An Introduction to Concepts and Research* (Boston: Houghton Mifflin Co., 1965), Chaps. 1-4.

[6]For additional details of this model, see Leonard Beeghley, *Social Stratification in America* (Santa Monica, Calif.: Goodyear Publishing Company, Inc., 1978), 99-103.

**Figure 5.1
Social Institutions
and Social Strata
in American
Society**

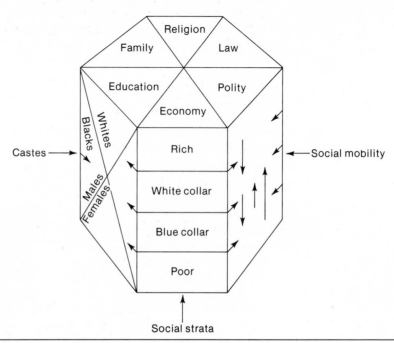

Source: Leonard Beeghley, *Social Stratification in America* (Santa Monica, Calif: Goodyear Publishing Company, Inc., 1978), 102. Reprinted by permission.

the car exists. Lower social classes may have a great deal of interaction and communication concerning the merits of *Thunderbird* or *Annie Greensprings* while upper social classes may not even know whether the customers for these products are speaking of wines or an automobile.

**Hierarchical
Positions**

Just as there is a Hertz and an Avis, so among people some are classed as number one and others as number two. People may not know the basis of the ranking, but they do know that ranking exists in their own minds and in the minds of other people. Social class exists as a *position* in these rankings without reference to a specific person. A person can be defined as a member of a social class even if that member does not uphold all of the norms of the class.

Multidimensional

Social class is *based upon many dimensions* as you saw in Figure 5.1. When people think of social class they actually think of a combination of variables that typically are possessed by a group. These variables include prestige, income, influence, and good manners which are associated with occupation, education, and heredity.

It is worth emphasizing that *social class is not the same as income*. Truck drivers, in spite of their higher incomes and superior Willie Nelson record collections, do not score as well on social class as bank tellers and school teachers. The multidimensional nature of social class also creates measurement problems in marketing research. Usually, though, *proxy variables* are used to measure consumers' social class—such as occupation, place of residence, education, and so forth.

Dynamic

Classes are not static; they *change some over time*, although usually not a lot and not rapidly. Truck drivers (perhaps because of their superior Willie Nelson collections) may be improving over time in their status relative to bankers and teachers. As society changes in the behavior and skills it values, some change will occur in social classes. Individuals may also experience some social class mobility, especially on the fringes of a class.

WHAT DETERMINES SOCIAL CLASS?

What causes your social class? The answer is that the family in which you were raised has a large effect. Your father's occupation probably had a significant effect upon your social class, since a man's occupation is the most important determinant, followed closely by the wife's occupation in contemporary society.[7] But what besides your family occupation determines social class? The answer, according to sociologist Kahl, includes in addition to occupation, personal performance, interactions, possessions, value orientations, and class consciousness.[8]

A more theoretical question can also be asked concerning why social classes even exist in a society. These answers are of two basic types: conflict theories (often Marxian) and nonconflict theories.[9] Some have even suggested that contemporary stratification is actually a civil war within the ruling class with the cultural bourgeoisie based upon the professions and education rather than the old moneyed class.[10] Issues such as these are beyond the scope of our study of consumer behavior, however.[11] The focus here is upon understanding the variables identified by Kahl as determinants of an individual's social class.

Occupation

When strangers meet, a question often asked is, "What kind of work do you do?" This question provides a good clue to the social class of the

[7]Stephen L. Nock, "Social Origins as Determinants of Family Social Status," Paper presented to Mid-South Sociological Association, 1980. Also, see Steven L. Nock and Peter H. Rossi, "Ascription versus Achievement in the Attribution of Family Social Status," *American Journal of Sociology,* vol. 84 (1978), 565-590.

[8]Joseph A. Kahl, *The American Class Structure* (New York: Holt, Rinehart and Winston, 1957), 8-10.

[9]Tommy Garnett, "A Critical Appraisal: Theories of Industrialization and Social Stratification with Implication for Social Change," Paper presented to Mid-South Sociological Association, 1980.

[10]Alvin W. Gouldner, "The New Class Project, II," *Theory and Society,* vol. 6 (1978), 343-389.

[11]The reader who is interested in general sociological theory of stratification, see Talcott Parsons, *The Social System* (New York: Free Press, 1955); Bernard Barber, *Social Stratification: A Comparative Analysis of Structure and Process* (New York: Harcourt, 1957); Robert K. Merton, *Social Theory and Social Structure* (New York: Free Press, 1949); Gerhard E. Lenski, *Power and Privilege: A Theory of Social Stratification* (New York: McGraw-Hill, 1966).

individual. Consumer analysts consider *occupation the best single indicator of social class.* Hewitt explains:

A feature of industrial society is that occupations are the social positions most important for differential evaluation, perhaps because the work that men do intimately affects their life chance and life styles. Even though prestige ideologies often stress the intrinsic worth of all men, occupation status is the single most important basis for according prestige, honor and respect.[12]

People can rate the prestige of an occupation even if they do not know who fills the position. When they have little information about the occupation, people rely on stereotypes concerning the extent of educational investment and monetary payoff. Rankings of prestige tend to coincide with control over means of production.[13] Professions may derive their prestige, however, from arrangements of power and the social meaning of the profession in a society.[14] The stability in occupation ratings exists on a cross-national basis. Various studies have indicated that physicians rate very high in almost all societies, for example. The correlations for ranks of all occupations tend to exhibit very high correlations (usually above 0.9) among nations in a cross-cultural sample.[15]

A person's social class can also be influenced by the success relative to other persons in the same occupation; by an individual's personal performance. Statements such as, "She is the finest trial lawyer in town," or "Frank is the only programmer that I trust to do it right," or "That professor is doing the most significant research in the field," are examples of evaluations of personal performance. Even though income is not a good indicator of overall social class, it may be a good indicator of personal performance *within* an occupation. The top 25 percent of income producers in any occupation probably are also likely to be the most highly respected as personally competent in an occupation.

Personal performance can relate to activities other than job performance. Perhaps your father has an occupation of low status but your family may still be perceived higher than others if your father is perceived as one who helps others in need, is usually kind and interested in fellow workers, or is a faithful worker in civic or religious organizations. The president of a corporation who serves as chairman of the United Way or a trustee of a university may achieve higher social status than the president of a similar corporation not involved in such activities. A Jim Plunkett may have more prestige than a Dan Pastorini even though both are professional quarterbacks under contract for similar amounts of money.

[12]John P. Hewitt, *Social Stratification and Deviant Behavior* (New York: Random House, 1970), 25.

[13]Marie R. Haug, "Occupational Differences and Social Stratification," Paper presented to International Sociological Association, 1978.

[14]Douglas Klegon, "The Sociology of Professions: An Emerging Perspective," *Sociology of Work and Occupations,* vol. 5 (August 1978), 259-283.

[15]Alex Inkeles and Peter H. Rossi, "National Comparisons of Occupational Prestige," *American Journal of Sociology,* vol. 61 (1956), 329-339; Robert W. Hodge, Donald J. Treiman, and Peter H. Rossi, "A Comparative Study of Occupational Prestige," in Bendix and Lipset, *Class, Status and Power,* 309-321.

Even a reputation as a good mother or a good father may contribute to one's status.

Interactions

People seem to feel most comfortable when they are with people of similar values and behavior. Sociologists who place a great deal of emphasis on analyses of social interactions are sometimes called the who-invited-whom-to-dinner school. In such an approach, group membership and interactions are considered a primary determinant of a person's social class.

Frequent and intimate association with other occupants of a social class is essential to the maintenance of one's social class. The "unsinkable Molly Brown," for example, could not enter the elite classes of Denver without the proper friends, in spite of her wealth, luxurious residence, and European education.

Interactions are probably the most important determinant of social class although not as useful as a variable for consumer behavior researchers as occupation because of the difficulty in measuring social interactions. The essence of social class, however, is the way a person is treated by others and, reciprocally, the way that person treats others. Barber explains the role of social intimacy:

The assumption underlying the use of the interactional indicator of social class position is that social intimacy is expressive of social equality. The assumption rests on the fact that the kind of interchange of sentiments and ideas that goes on in intimate association is possible only among people who know each other well and who value each other equally. It is, in other words, possible only among social class equals, and therefore it is an indicator of social class equality.[16]

Social interactions are limited by social class. Hollingshead found that most marriages—83 percent—occur within the same or adjacent social classes.[17] In public schools, children reveal definite patterns of restricted association and have names for each group—the "straights," the "grubbies," the "cheerleaders," and so forth.[18] Perhaps the most obvious example of restricted social interaction is the *Social Register* in twelve United States cities, with its rigid criteria for gaining admission.[19]

Possessions

Possessions are symbols of class membership. Not only the amount of possessions, but the nature of the choices that are characteristic of one social class or another. Thus, a middle-class family may choose wall-to-

[16]Barber, *Social Stratification*, 122.

[17]A. B. Hollingshead, "Cultural Factors in the Selection of Marriage Mates," *American Sociological Review*, vol. 15 (1950), 619-627.

[18]The classic study on this topic and one that makes fascinating reading is A. B. Hollingshead, *Elmstown's Youth* (New York: John Wiley & Sons, 1949).

[19]For a description of the *Social Register* and an analysis of the criteria for gaining admission to it, see E. Digby Baltzell, "Who's Who in America and the Social Register," in Bendix and Lipset, *Class, Status, and Power* (New York: Free Press, 1966), 266-275.

wall carpeting while an upper-class family is more likely to choose oriental rugs, even when the prices are equal.

Probably the most important possession that reflects a family's social class is the decision about where to live, both type of residence and neighborhood. Another very important possession decision that reflects one's social class is the college one attends. One of the best predictors of admission to college is class background. Upper-class individuals usually select the "best" schools which in turn reinforces class consciousness and cohesion.[20] Other possessions which serve as indicators of social status include club memberships (which also reflect interactions), preferred furniture styles, clothing, appliances, type of vacations chosen, and many others. As possessions become diffused more widely between social classes, changes may occur over time. This has happened in housework for example, as patterns of housework once associated with upper classes have filtered down to lower classes as conditions and ideologies have diffused more widely between the social strata.[21]

Consumer analysts need to study social class manifestations through possessions because of the high impact upon buying decisions.

Value Orientations

Values—shared beliefs about how people ought to behave—indicate the social class to which one belongs.[22] When a group of people tend to share a common set of abstract convictions that organize and relate a large number of specific attitudes, it is possible to categorize an individual by the degree to which the person possesses these values.

Consumer analysts must ask the question, "What values characterize specific market segments?" These beliefs may refer to general values about political ideals, religious practices, work motivation, the capitalistic economic system, and so forth; and more specific activities such as child rearing, family structure, sexual behavior, abortion, impulsiveness in decision making, and so forth. Some of the values that significantly impact consumer behavior will be examined later in this chapter.

Class Consciousness

A person's social class is indicated to some extent by how conscious that person is of social class in a society. Individuals who are relatively conscious of class differences in society are more likely to be from higher classes. This suggests that marketing organizations with market targets in the upper classes need to study social class and build marketing strategies on such knowledge more than companies appealing to lower social classes.

A firm that has displayed a consistent marketing program reflecting Kahl's determinants of social class is the New York department store,

[20]Michael Useem and S. M. Miller, "The Upper Class in Higher Education," *Social Policy,* vol. 7 (January-February 1977), 28-31.

[21]Joann Vanek, "Household Technology and Social Status: Rising Living Standards and Status and Residence Differences in Housework," *Technology and Culture,* vol. 19 (July 1978), 362-375.

[22]Donna Darden, William Darden and Michael Carlson, "Social Class and Values," Paper presented to Mid-South Sociological Association, 1980.

**Figure 5.2
Department Store
Advertisement
Appealing to
Upper Social
Classes**

Source: Bloomingdale's. Reprinted by permission.

Bloomingdale's. The store carries merchandise appealing to persons in high status occupations, who interact with other people who shop at Bloomingdale's, and who have values, high performance, and status awareness. The store presents a consistency of status appeal in its total marketing offering. Notice in Figure 5.2 the image portrayed by the store with the posture of the models, the mood of the background, the fashion orientation of designer (*Calvin Klein*) apparel and the sleek, contemporary overall effect of New York upper class (which might be quite different than upper classes in other cities, especially in the South where tradition would be emphasized.) Normally, an upper-class ad featuring a car would include a *Porsche*, *Imperial*, or other expensive car, but Bloomingdale's has included a Chrysler *K*-car. At the time of the advertisement the *K*-car had been designed to save Chrysler. While it is perhaps not immediately apparent that a moderately priced car would be consistent with the upper-class image, the car probably does so because it appeals to a sense of patriotism, an attempt to save a major capitalistic firm, energy conservation, and to innovators who are more likely to be from upper-middle classes, as we shall observe in Chapter 12. Figure 5.2 also illustrates a marketing technique called associative advertising—the inclusion of products offered by more than one advertiser.[23]

[23]Associative marketing is defined as "the simultaneous integration of two or more noncompetitive products in a specific marketing program for the mutual benefit of each product involved." For greater detail on this concept, see W. Wayne Talarzyk and Robert A. Drevs, "Structure and Use of Associative Marketing," Working Paper, Ohio State University, 1972.

HOW TO MEASURE SOCIAL CLASSES

Many methods have been developed to measure and describe social class. For consumer analysts, the challenge is to use such measures for the purpose of *defining market segments* and to *understand the consumption patterns of those segments.* Four principal types of methods are used for establishing the social class of an individual. These types are usually described as:

1. reputational,

2. sociometric,

3. subjective, or

4. objective.[24]

Reputational Methods

Reputational methods of measuring social class involve asking people to rank the social position of other persons. Usually, respondents are asked to rank people they know in the particular community in which they live. Even people who say they are not class conscious almost always can divide the community into social groups and tell in which group the people they know belong. The following is an example of a typical interview asking for a description of the social-class structure to which residents of the community belong. This interview is with George Green, long-time resident of the town and a member of the city government.

You'll find there's a definite division between the men and the women in the upper strata in this town. The men are common like us. They'll talk to you at any time. But the women draw the class line, and no one gets over or around it. I can see this just as clearly as I can see you.

We're in a unique position here because of my relation to a couple of families in this group. A cousin of mine married Jim Radcliffe. This relates us to several other people. We've been invited over to their house to parties a few times, and I'm disturbed at how these people look down at others in town. They have several cliques within the larger stratum. Below this stratum is the one composed of prominent business and professional families. Some of those who have money and family are rated in the top group. However, if they have only family and not much money, they rank in the upper-middle class.

The small-businessmen and the foremen out at the mill are in the lower- but middle-strata. I mean a lower strata than the one we have been talking about. I don't know much about their social life, but I know just about where they fit in here in town. The sub-foremen, machinists, several stationary operators, and people like that are in the lowest middle-strata. The ordinary workmen in the

---

[24]David Krech, Richard S. Crutchfield, and Egerton L. Ballachey, *Individual in Society* (New York: McGraw-Hill, 1962), 313-319.

foundry and the mill are mostly ranked as lower-class around here. But they're not as low as the older Poles, the canal renters, and the people back of the tannery.

The Poles and the poor Americans who work in the mill are on the bottom. These poor Americans and Poles may be working side by side on the same job and getting the same income, but socially they're miles apart. You might say they're each an exclusive group. The several social strata in town are segregated into definite areas, and in each you generally find a class distinction.

Now, that's about the way that the town is divided. That's the way it looks to me, and I am pretty sure that's the way it is.[25]

The reputational method was developed in the United States by Warner and is the basis of much of the most important empirical research on social classes in America. A comprehensive set of instructions for interpreting the interviews and for collaborating social-class ratings has been devised and is called the *evaluative participation method* of establishing the social class of a person.[26]

Jain's Conjoint Analysis

A variation of the reputational method of measuring social class was developed by Jain to understand the structure of social class as perceived by the average person. Jain employs conjoint analysis, a technique for analyzing the contribution of variables to total preferences or results (and used in many other consumer research applications).[27]

Conjoint analysis is used to understand both the relative importance of various levels of socioeconomic characteristics in judgments about social class and to predict the responses of consumers to various product and service attributes. The technique is used by giving each respondent a vignette that contains core social class variables. Three levels of the following variables are used: occupation, education, family income, and ethnic background. The value of this technique is in its ability to disclose the implicit value system manifest in the choice behavior of decision makers. This might be used in choosing alternative features to be developed in a new product, understanding the importance of multiple attributes in selecting a product, or understanding what kinds of persons would be effective in testimonial or other types of advertising.[28]

Sociometric Methods

Sociometric studies involve observing or asking people about their intimate associations with other people. The reports and observations can

---

[25]From pp. 56-57 in *Social Class in America: A Manual of Procedure for the Measurement of Social Status* by W. Lloyd Warner, Marchia Meeker, and Kenneth Eels. Copyright © 1949 by Science Research Associates. By permission of Harper Torchbooks, Harper & Row, Publishers, Inc.

[26]Warner et al., *Social Class,* 47-120.

[27]An easy-to-understand description of this technique is found in Joseph F. Hair, Jr., Rolph E. Anderson, Ronald L. Tetham and Bernie J. Grablowsky, *Multivariate Data Analysis* (Tulsa: Petroleum Publishing Company, 1979), 284-340.

[28]Arun K. Jain, "A Method for Investigating and Representing Implicit Social Class Theory," *Journal of Consumer Research,* vol. 2 (June 1975), 53-59.

be analyzed with standard sociometric techniques to determine the cliques and social classes. Hollingshead used this technique in his famous study of *Elmstown's Youth*.[29] Sociometric methods are useful in theoretical social-class research but are usually too expensive for most consumer research.

Subjective Methods

Subjective methods of determining social classes ask respondents to rate themselves on social class. Such methods have been used on occasion but are of limited use for consumer analysts for two reasons: (1) respondents tend to overrate their own class position (often by one class rank),[30] and (2) respondents avoid the connotative terms upper and lower classes and thus exaggerate the size of the middle classes.

In marketing studies, what is needed is a self-administered rating scale to identify consumer social classes on a subjective basis without actually asking the respondent his or her social class. Such a scale would ask the consumer to choose attitudinal-value statements relating indirectly to social class that characterize the respondent.

Objective Methods

Objective methods of determining social classes rely upon the assigning of status on the basis of respondents possessing some value of a stratified variable. The most often used variables are occupation, income, education, size and type of residence, ownership of possessions, and organizational affiliations. Objective methods can be divided into those that involve single indexes and those that use multiple indexes.

Single-Item Indexes

Occupation is generally accepted as the single best proxy indicator of social class. Occupational position and individual life-styles have demonstrated high correlations for two reasons. People who share similarly ranked occupational levels often share roughly similar access to the means of achieving a particular life-style. Leisure time, income independence, knowledge, and power are often common to specific or occupational categories. Second, people in similar occupations are likely to interact with one another. Of particular interest to consumer analysts is the explanation of Barth and Watson:

> The products of such occupational interaction are likely to be an increased concensus concerning the types of activities, interests, and possessions that are important; some agreement as to how, in general, family resources should be allocated in order to implement the achievement of these goals; and the development of a shared set of norms of evaluation.[31]

[29]Hollingshead, *Elmstown's Youth*.

[30]John C. Coyder and Peter Pineo, "The Accuracy of Self-Assessments of Social Status," *La Revue Canadienne de Sociologie et d'Anthropologie*, vol. 14 (May 1977), 235–246.

[31]Ernest A. T. Barth and Walter B. Watson, "Social Stratification and the Family in Mass Society," *Social Forces*, vol. 45 (March 1967), 394.

Table 5.1
Occupational Titles and Occupational Status Scores for Seven Major Occupational Groups

Occupational Group and Title	Occupational Status (Treiman's Scale)	Occupational Group and Title	Occupational Status (Treiman's Scale)
Day Labor:		Mechanic	42.9
		Painter	31.0
Day laborer	18.1	Carpenter	37.2
Farm worker	18.1	Mason, bricklayer	34.1
Farm hand	22.9	Miller	32.9
		Woodworker	34.4
Agriculture:		Radio operator	49.2
		Baker	33.2
Farmer*	37.7	Printer	40.6
Farm foreman	40.8	Aviation mechanic	49.6
Coffee picker	36.7	Craftsman	34.4
Ranch worker	25.6	Shoemaker	28.1
		Electronics worker	40.9
Unskilled:		Watchmaker	39.7
		Machine operator	38.3
Launderer	22.1	Plumber	33.9
Milkman	30.7	Aqueduct, sewer installer	37.6
Fruit seller	24.4	Barber	30.4
Construction worker	30.0	Radio technician	49.2
Carpenter's apprentice	22.6	Draftsman	54.9
Building caretaker	25.0	Jeweler	43.0
Tractor driver	28.6	Blacksmith	32.2
Processing-plant worker	36.7		
Trashman	12.7	*Semiprofessional:*	
Wood seller	24.4		
Egg seller	24.4	Businessman	50.0
Ticket puncher	35.8	Accountant	54.6
Coal man	29.3	Merchant	49.3
Ox driver	25.6	Engineer	45.5
Coal seller	21.9	Traveling salesman	31.9
		Sales agent	31.9
Semiskilled:		Tavern owner	48.0
		Nurse	53.6
Chauffeur	31.5	Property owner (real estate)	63.4
Postman	32.8	Contractor	59.4
Janitor	32.7	Secretary	53.0
Policeman	30.2	Municipal worker	55.3
Factory worker	40.6	Inspector	34.7
Lumberjack	19.2	Money lender	15.3
Seamstress	39.3	Civil clerk	36.8
Worker foreman	39.3	Sailor	29.0
Sales clerk	33.6		
Guard	30.6	*Professional:*	
Office worker	37.5		
Promoter	50.0	Schoolteacher	57.0
Sewer worker	39.5	Doctor	77.9
Store attendant	23.2	Schoolmaster	57.0
Head maid	37.2	Professional (unspecified)	57.0
Municipal foreman	62.8	Lawyer	70.6
Presidential guard	34.7	Journalist	54.9
Cook	30.9	Administrator	59.4
Soldier	38.7	Health officer	47.6
Knitter	30.4	Priest	59.7
Miner	31.5	Mathematician	66.9
Agent	39.4	Economist	60.5
		Veterinarian	47.8
Skilled:		Architect	71.8
		Customs official	44.4
Electrician	44.5	Tax collector	51.6
Butcher	31.5		

*Farmers are different from the day laborers in that at least one member of the household owns land.

Source: Maciarlane Smith, *Interviewing in Market and Social Research* (London and Boston: Routledge and Kegan Paul, 1972), 61-63 and App. A. Reprinted by permission.

An example of an occupation scale, the Treiman scale[32] is shown in Table 5.1. It can be used in consumer studies by asking respondents to write in their exact occupation, which can later be coded numerically according to the scale value of occupational status listed in Table 5.1. A scale such as this provides a precise, numerical estimate of occupational status of each respondent, convenient for statistical analysis.

Other measures of occupational status include the Edwards scale defining the status value of a few basic categories of occupations,[33] the Duncan scale which contains ratings of 425 occupations[34] and has successfully been used for profiling innovators,[35] and the social grading scale widely used in Great Britain.[36] Generally scales of occupation status are more suitable than direct prestige ratings and of value for analysis of special groups such as college seniors as well as the general public.[37]

Consumer analysts may be able to devise single-item indexes of social class that are product specific or relevant to a company's marketing program. With furniture, for example, a famous study revealed that social class could be accurately determined by observing the type of floor in the living room, the presence of draperies, the number of armchairs, the number of bookcases, the presence of a sewing machine, the number and type of periodicals displayed, and so forth.[38] A more recent European study also found class differences among social strata with the general finding that the higher the status, the higher the quality of furniture.[39]

Multiple-Item Indexes

Multiple-item indexes combine several indicators of social class into one index, hopefully a richer measure of social status than single-item indexes. These scales are operational measures of the concept of social status and are validated by reputational or sociometric methods.

[32]D. J. Treiman, *Occupational Prestige in Comparative Perspective* (New York: Academic Press, 1977).

[33]Alba M. Edwards, *A Social Economic Grouping of the Gainful Workers of the United States* (Washington, D. C.: U. S. Government Printing Office, 1939); U. S. Bureau of the Census, *1960 Census of Population Classified Index of Occupations and Industries* (Washington, D. C.: U. S. Government Printing Office, 1960); American Marketing Association, "Occupation and Educational Scales," *Journal of Marketing*, vol. 15 (April 1951). See comments about this scale in Theodore Caplow, *The Sociology of Work* (Minneapolis, Minn.: University of Minnesota Press, 1954), esp. 42-48.

[34]Albert J. Reiss, Jr. et al., *Occupations and Social Status* (New York: Free Press, 1961).

[35]Robert J. Kegerreis, James F. Engel, and Roger D. Blackwell, "Innovativeness and Diffusiveness: A Marketing View of the Characteristics of Earliest Adopters," in David T. Kollat, Roger D. Blackwell, and James F. Engel, (eds.), *Research in Consumer Behavior* (New York: Holt, Rinehart and Winston, 1970), 671-689, esp. 677-678.

[36]Marciarlane Smith, *Interviewing in Market and Social Research* (London and Boston: Routledge and Kegan Paul, 1972), 61-63 and App. A.

[37]Joe L. Spaeth, "Measures of Occupational Status in a Special Population," *Social Science Research* (March 1978), 7, 48-60.

[38]F. Stuart Chapin, *Contemporary American Institutions* (New York: Harper & Row, 1935), Chap. 19; Dennis Chapman, *The Home and Social Status* (London: Routledge, 1955).

[39]Urban Franz Pappi and Ingeborg Pappi, "Social Status and Consumption Style: A Case Study of Living Room Furniture (tr)," *Kölner Zeitschrift für Soziologie und Sozialpsychologie*, vol. 30 (March 1978), 87-115.

Warner's ISC   A frequently used multiple-item index is Warner's Index of Status Characteristics (ISC). It has been validated with reputational methods and other scales, has considerable theoretical support, and can be used under a wide variety of circumstances.[40]

A respondent's rating on each objective variable is multiplied by a weight which was determined by regression analysis and the scores are totaled to indicate the status of a respondent. The weight for each variable is as follows:

Occupation	x4
Source of income	x3
House type	x3
Dwelling area	x2

Other Multiple-Item Indexes   A number of other multiple-item indexes can be used to measure the social status of consumers. Richard Coleman's *Index of Urban Status* (IUS) is similar to Warner's ISC but it includes two additional variables, education and associational behavior, and includes ratings for both husband and wife.[41] Carman's *Index of Cultural Classes* measures occupation, education of household, and expenditures for housing as proxy variables for *culture,* a variable that creates ownership of products interesting to marketing managers.[42] Hollingshead's *Index of Social Position* (ISP) is a three-variable index similar to Warner's ISC with ratings for area of residence, occupation, and education.[43] The *Index of Class Position* is also similar to Warner and Hollingshead scales except that young respondents (college students) are asked to report their *father's* occupation and to evaluate subjectively their father's position in the class structure.[44]

A number of scales are currently being developed which measure social status by assigning a status value to the ZIP code or other geographic designation of a respondent's residence. Several of the research firms specializing in ZIP code marketing (strategies based upon reaching people in areas defined by US postal ZIP codes) have developed their own systems involving the ratio of certain occupations in a ZIP code, the distribution of educational characteristics, income, condition of housing, and so forth. These offer great potential because of the ability to measure social status without the need to collect additional data from respon-

[40]For additional documentation, see previous editions of this book.

[41]Lee Rainwater, Richard P. Coleman and Gerald Hanel, *Workingman's Wife* (New York: Oceana, 1959) and R. P. Coleman and Lee Rainwater, *Social Standing in America: New Dimensions of Class* (New York: Basic Books, 1979).

[42]James M. Carman, *The Application of Social Class in Market Segmentation* (Berkeley: Institute of Business and Economic Research, University of California Graduate School of Business Administration, 1965).

[43]A. B. Hollingshead and F. C. Redlish, *Social Class and Mental Illness* (New York: John Wiley & Sons, 1958).

[44]Robert A. Ellis, Clayton Lane, and Virginia Olesen, "The Index of Class Position: An Improved Intercommunity Measure of Stratification," *American Sociological Review*, vol. 28 (April 1963), 271-277.

dents beyond their address and ZIP code; as well as the ability to design media strategies efficient in reaching designated ZIP codes.

Why should you as a reader be interested in all of these measures of social status? Why not settle on one and just use that? The reason is that the concept of social class is a rich, multidimensional variable. Social status has so many subtle nuances that studies could easily reveal little of value to marketers unless the right measure is used. When you are faced with a marketing problem in which you believe social status is likely to play an important role, you should review the various measures and ask, "What about this measure seems particularly appropriate to our situation? How might results vary if one measure were used rather than another?" At a more basic research level, there is much to be discovered about these scales and their relationships to each other and to consumption of products and services offering substantial opportunities for theory construction and conceptual development.

Status Inconsistency

One further complexity in measuring social class, as if any more were needed, is the problem of status inconsistency or consideration of people who rate high on one variable but low on another. Status inconsistencies are logical consequences of the normal growth processes in status hierarchies.[45] Lenski developed an index of status crystallization and as a result of his studies concluded that people with a low degree of status crystallization—people such as a black physician, a poorly educated but rich business person, or a lowly-paid professor—are subject to pressures from the social order likely to make them more liberal and willing to support programs of social change.[46] The consequences will be greatest when the status inconsistency has high social visibility.[47]

SOCIAL CLASSES IN INDUSTRIALIZED SOCIETIES

Some people question the prevalence of social classes. Maybe they are vanishing among working- and middle-class people. This theory is sometimes called the embourgeoisment of society or the *massification theory*. Perhaps the widespread mass media and increasing incomes as well as dissemination of economic and political power on a wider basis have eliminated many of the differences between working- and middle-class people.[48] Measures of stratification over time must unfortunately center upon financial data—income, wealth, and so forth. It is not that they are the best indicators of social status; it is merely that only for such variables as wealth and income do reasonably good data exist over long

[45]Volker Bornschier and Peter Heintz, "Status Inconsistency and Stratification: An Extension of Status Inconsistency Theory," (tr) *Zeitschrift für Soziologie,* vol. 6 (January 1977), 29-48.

[46]Gerhard E. Lenski, "Status Crystallization: A Non-Vertical Dimension of Social Status," *American Sociological Review,* vol. 21 (August 1956), 458–464.

[47]Ekkart Zimmerman, "Bringing Common Sense Back In: Some Neglected Assumptions in Status Inconsistency Theory and Research," (tr) *Archives Europeennes de Sociologie,* vol. 19, 53-73.

[48]R. A. Nisbet, "The Decline and Fall of Social Class," in R. A. Nisbet, (ed.), *Tradition and Revolt* (New York: Random House, 1968); Gerhard Lensky, *Power and Privilege* (New York: McGraw-Hill, 1969).

Table 5-2
Share of Aggregate Income Received by Each Fifth and Top Five Percent of Families and Unrelated Individuals 1947–1975

	Percentage of Aggregate Income					
Year	Lowest Fifth	Second Fifth	Middle Fifth	Fourth Fifth	Highest Fifth	Top 5 Percent
1947	3.4	10.6	16.8	23.6	45.5	18.7
1950	3.1	10.6	17.3	24.1	44.9	18.2
1955	3.3	10.6	17.6	24.6	43.9	17.5
1960	3.2	10.6	17.6	24.7	44.0	17.0
1965	3.6	10.6	17.5	24.8	43.6	16.6
1970	3.6	10.3	17.2	24.7	44.1	16.9
1975	3.9	9.9	16.7	24.4	44.5	17.0

Source: U.S. Bureau of the Census 1977, Table 13, 57.

periods of time. Table 5.2, for example, shows the distribution of income received by each quintile and the top five percent of the population since 1947. There has been only a very minor change. An extensive review of such factors as power, income, wealth, status, and participation in the political process lead Kriesberg to conclude:

Although the information on inequality is limited . . . these data show the proportion of the population in poverty increased during the depression, decreased during World War II, increased after the war, and then was stable until a small decline began in the 1960s . . . . . . income was probably even more unequally distributed before World War II but it has not materially changed since then. . . . Personal wealth has probably become more equally distributed in the past fifty years but wealth in the form of corporate shares has not; concentration in ownership of the means of production has increased, as is reflected in the decline in self-employment.[49]

When Does Social Status Begin?

Are young children aware of the social status of some occupations? That question was conclusively answered in a study by Simmons and Rosenberg who studied nearly 2,000 black and white children of varying social backgrounds in grades 3 to 12 and their parents. The children perceived occupational prestige and inequality of opportunity with dramatic awareness. As early as in elementary school, children rated 15 occupations in a prestige order almost identical to that of their parents and of the older high-school pupils. Both younger and older children learn quickly not to believe in equal opportunity in obtaining the good things in life.[50]

Can Social Class Be Changed?

Can you change your social class from that of your parents? How often and how likely is that to occur? These are issues of *intergenerational mobility* and the answers to the above questions seem to be that, while it is possible to climb upward (or downward) in the social order, the prob-

[49]Louis Kriesberg, *Social Inequality* (Englewood Cliffs, N. J.: Prentice-Hall, Inc., 1979), 77-78.
[50]Robert G. Simmons and Morris Rosenberg, "Functions of Children's Perceptions of the Stratification System," *American Sociological Review*, vol. 36 (April 1971), 235-249.

abilities are not very high of it actually happening.[51] Furthermore, the chances are not increasing. One of the most distinguished researchers in this field concludes:

> To put the matter crudely, but correctly, there has been no change in the odds that a man of high status origin will achieve higher rather than lower occupational standing.[52]

Both men and women are affected by the low probability of change in social class although women may have a bit more mobility through marriage than do men through occupations, since men are more likely to inherit their fathers' statuses.[53]

How to Change Your Social Class

If you want to battle the odds and change your social status regardless of what the textbooks say about the feasibility of it happening, what is the key to doing so? Very simply, intergenerational mobility is achieved by occupational achievement which is, in turn, heavily influenced by educational achievement and the willingness (ability) to be geographically mobile.[54]

A model of how intergenerational mobility occurs is shown in Figure 5.3 based freely upon what is known as the Wisconsin model of mobility.[55]

A family produces an individual with genes and environmental influences—personality, a self-concept and so forth—which combine to produce educational ability. Parental status effects suggest that the social-psychological benefits of higher socioeconomic origins are most important at the highest schooling levels.[56] The model in Figure 5.3 shows educational achievement to be influenced by two variables—the individual's actual ability and the evaluation of that ability by educational institutions, since educational outcomes depend more on the criteria of selection than on the process within schools.[57] Educational ability is heavily influenced by the self-concept of a person, transmitted from the family.[58]

---

[51]For an overall review of mobility studies, see Andrea Tyree and Robert W. Hodge, "Five Empirical Landmarks," *Social Forces,* vol. 56 (March 1978), 761-769.

[52]Robert Hauser et al., "Structural Changes in Occupational Mobility among Men in the United States," *American Sociological* Review, vol. 40 (October 1975), 585-598.

[53]Ivan D. Chase, "A Comparison of Men's and Women's Intergenerational Mobility in the United States," *American Sociological Review,* vol. 40 (August 1975), 483-505.

[54]Aage B. Sorensen, "The Structure of Intragenerational Mobility," *American Sociological Review,* vol. 40 (August 1975), 456-471.

[55]W. H. Sewell and R. M. Hauser, *Education, Occupation and Earnings* (New York: Academic Press, 1975); and Karl L. Alexander, B. K. Eckland and L. J. Griffin, "The Wisconsin Model of Socioeconomic Achievement: A Replication," *American Journal of Sociology,* vol. 81 (1976), 324-341.

[56]Robert D. Mare, "Social Background and School Continuation Decisions," *Journal of the American Statistical Association,* vol. 75 (June 1980), 295-304.

[57]Barbara Heyns, "Social Selection and Stratification within Schools," *American Journal of Sociology,* vol. 79 (1974), 1434-1451; and K. L. Wilson and A. Portes, "The Educational Attainment Process: Results from a National Sample," *American Journal of Sociology,* vol. 81 (1976), 343-362.

[58]Angela Lane, "The Occupational Achievement Process, 1940-1949: A Cohort Analysis," *American Sociological Review,* vol. 40 (August 1975), 472-482, and Thomas W. Miller, "Effects of Maternal Age, Education, and Employment Status on the Self-Esteem of the Child," *The Journal of Social Psychology,* vol. 95 (1975), 141-142.

**Figure 5.3
Selected Influences
on Intergenerational
Social Mobility**

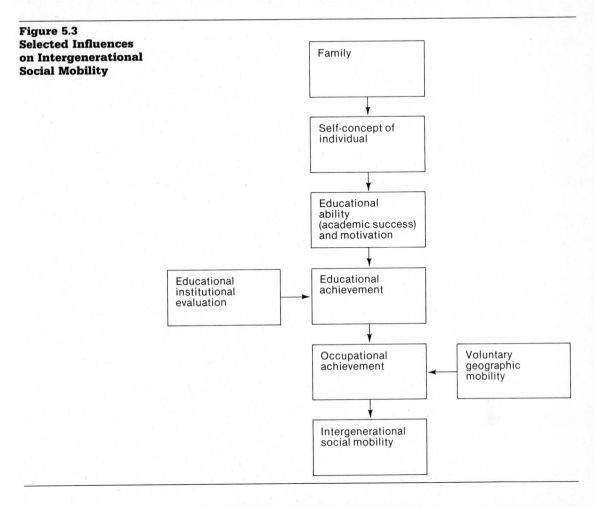

Getting ahead through educational attainment is fundamentally the same in the United States and Great Britain although the British stratification system is somewhat more closed than that of the United States.[59]

Educational achievement leads to occupational opportunity but in the final analysis social mobility is not likely to occur unless a person is willing to move on geographically. The proportion of the population changing social status is small—but often these people are of high interest to marketers. As a badge of their upward mobility—or maybe just because they can finally express their repressed wishes—they are likely to be visible spenders and consumers. They may be more affluent, more innovative and more quality oriented; in short, socially mobile consumers are outstanding prospects for most marketing organizations.

In an inflationary economy, one other aspect of social mobility is of interest to marketers. Inflation provides a means by which dominant

[59]Donald J. Treiman and Kermit Terrell, "The Process of Status Attainment in the United States and Great Britain," *American Journal of Sociology*, vol. 81 (1976), 563-581.

**Figure 5.4
Social Classes in
the United States**

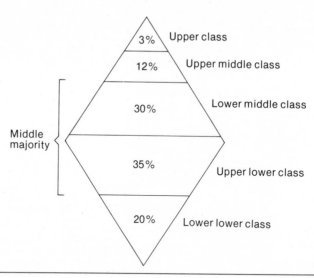

3% Upper class

12% Upper middle class

30% Lower middle class

Middle majority

35% Upper lower class

20% Lower lower class

Source; Charles B. McCann. *Women and Department Store Newspaper Advertising* (Chicago: Social Research. 1957), 94. Reprinted by permission of the publisher.

groups or social classes maintain the economic and political equilibrium needed to maintain profits when faced by the demands of organized social movements that may be in conflict with the upper classes.[60]

How Large Are Social Classes?

There is no unqualified answer to the question of how large are specific social classes. A number of studies report sizes of each class but their definitions of each class do not permit comparison.[61] The most commonly accepted view by marketing practitioners is that the social class structure looks something like the diamond in Figure 5.4, even though the exact proportions may have changed slightly over the years. Somewhat similar proportions were reported by Carman's study of cultural classes, except for a smaller percentage in the lower class. Carman found .038 percent in upper, 10.82 percent in upper-middle, 30.82 percent in lower-middle, 49.96 percent in upper-lower, and 8.02 percent in the lower-lower class.[62]

Social Class Behavior

How do people in each social class typically behave? This will vary somewhat between countries and between areas within a country. But some core behavior is found that typifies each social class. A summary of some of the more important elements of these behaviors is presented in Table 5.3. Read through Table 5.3 and you will have a description of

[61]W. L. Warner et al., *Yankee City* (New Haven, Conn.: Yale University Press, 1963), 43; Richard Centers, *Psychology of Social Class,* 77; August B. Hollingshead and Frederick C. Redich, "Social Stratification and Psychiatric Disorders," *American Sociological Review,* vol. 18 (1953), 163-167, Arthur J. Vidich and Joseph Bensman, *Small Town in Mass Society; Class, Power, and Religion in a Rural Community,* Princeton, N.J.: Princeton University Press, 1968, 52.
[62]Carman, *Application of Social Class,* 53.

**Table 5.3
Social Class
Behavior in
America**

Upper Upper

Upper uppers are the social elite of society. Inherited wealth from socially prominent families is the key to admission. Children attend private preparatory schools and graduate from the best colleges.

    Consumers in the upper-upper class spend money as if it were unimportant, not tightly but not with display either, for that would imply that money is important. For some products a trickle-down influence may exist between social classes. The social position of these individuals is so secure that they can deviate from class norms if they choose to without losing status.

Lower Upper

Lower uppers include the very high-income professional people who have earned their position rather than inherited it. They are the *nouveaux riches,* active people with many material symbols of their status. They buy the largest homes in the best suburbs, the most expensive automobiles, swimming pools and other symbols of conspicuous consumption, making them innovators and good markets for luxury marketing offerings.

Upper Middle

The key word for upper middles is career. Careers are based on successful professional or graduate degrees for a specific profession or the skill of business administration. Members of this class are demanding of their children in educational attainment.

    The *quality* market for many products is the upper-middle class and gracious living in a conspicuous but careful manner characterizes the family's life-style. The home is of high importance and an important symbol of the family's success and competence.

Lower Middle

Lower-middle class families are typical Americans, exemplifying the core of respectability, conscientious work habits, and adherence to culturally defined norms and standards. They believe in attending church and obeying the law and are upset when their children are arrested for law violations. They are not innovators.

    The *home* is very important to the lower-middle family and they want it to be neat, well-painted, and in a respected neighborhood. They may have little confidence in their own tastes and adopt standardized home furnishings—perhaps from Levitz or Wickes. This is in contrast to the upper-middle consumer who feels freer to experiment with new styles and new arrangements and with the upper-lower consumer who is not very concerned about the overall plan for furnishing the home. The lower-middle consumer reads and follows the advice of the medium-level shelter and service magazines in an attempt to make the house pretty.

    The lower-middle class consumer works more at shopping than others and considers purchase decisions demanding and tedious. He/She may have a high degree of price sensitivity.

Upper Lower

Upper-lower social classes—the largest segment of society—exhibit a routine life, characterized by a day-to-day existence of unchanging activities. They live in dull areas of the city, in small houses or apartments. The hard hats are included in this class, with many members working at uncreative jobs requiring manual activity or only moderate skills and education. Because of unions and security, many may earn incomes that give them considerable discretionary income.

    The purchase decisions of the working-class are often impulsive but at the same time may show high brand loyalty to national brands. Buying them is one way to prove knowledge as a buyer, a role in which he/she feels (probably correctly) that he/she has little skill. This consumer has little social contact outside the home and does not like to attend civic organizations or church activities. Social interaction is limited to close neighbors and relatives. If he/she takes a vacation, it will probably be a visit to relatives in another city. Upper lowers are concerned that they not be confused with the lower lowers.

Lower Lower

The lower-lower social class contains the so-called disreputable people of the society who may try to rise above their class on some occasions but usually fail to do so and become reconciled to their position in society. An individual in the lower-lower class often rejects middle class morality and gets his kicks wherever he can—and this includes buying impulsively. This lack of planning causes purchases that cost too much and may result in inferior goods. This person pays too much for products, buys on credit at a high interest rate and has difficulty evaluating the quality or value of a product.

what may be expected in the behavior of consumers in each social class.[63]

Social class behavior exhibits dynamism which can be characterized as new patterns overlying old patterns. Some types of status related behavior become more subtle or more complicated but do not usually disappear. Old norms are not discarded; rather new ones are added to the old ones to make an even more complicated pattern to confront the consumer analyst attempting to understand the behavior of stratified market segments.

MARKETING TO SOCIAL CLASS CONSUMER SEGMENTS

After you have read through the preceding pages, you should have a good grasp of what is meant by social stratification, how it is measured, how it is changing—both for individual consumers and in the society as a whole—and some reasonably specific descriptive ideas of how people in one social strata differ in their behavior from people in higher or lower strata. Now it is time to bring this all together and ask, "How are buying decisions affected by social class? What does this mean for a marketing organization?" Fortunately, there has been quite a bit of research about the specific decisions of consumers that are influenced by social class.

Most of the stratification studies in consumer behavior have concerned the influence of social class on product choice rather than brand choice. There have been brand choice studies but often they were proprietary in nature, concerned with the specific social class connotations of one brand compared to another. Consequently, those studies are not as available in the published literature as more general studies.

Market Segmentation

Social class has been most directly applied in marketing to the problem of market segmentation—the process of defining homogeneous customer groups and making an especially strong offering to them. Social class is a useful concept for understanding market segments in a wide variety of products and services.[64]

The procedures for market segmentation include the following steps:

1. Identification of social class usage of product.

2. Comparison of social class variables for segmentation with other variables (income, life cycle, etc.).

---

[63]For a more extensive description and documentation of these social classes, see the 1973 edition of this book.

[64]Pierre Martineau, "Social Classes and Spending Behavior," *Journal of Marketing,* vol. 23 (October 1958), 121-130; Sidney Levy, "Social Class and Consumer Behavior," in Joseph W. Newman, (ed.), *On Knowing the Consumer* (New York: John Wiley & Sons, 1966), 146-160; Phillip Kotler, "Behavioral Model for Analyzing Buyers," *Journal of Marketing,* vol. 29 (October 1965); Richard P. Coleman and Bernice L. Newgarten, *Social Status in the City* (San Francisco: Jossey-Bass, 1971).

**Table 5.4
Identifying
Socioeconomic
Market Segments**

Socioeconomic/Life-Cycle Grid

Population _____ Characteristic _____

		Socioeconomic Class				Life-Cycle Totals
		Lower	Lower-middle	Upper-middle	Upper	
Life-Cycle Category	Younger Households — No Children	1.5	5.7	6.8	2.9	16.9
	Younger Children	0.9	6.2	8.1	4.3	19.5
	Older Children	1.4	8.7	10.8	4.8	25.7
	Older Households	12.5	13.5	8.8	3.1	37.9
	SES class totals	16.3	34.1	34.5	15.1	100.0

Composite Totals

SES	Life-Cycle		Total
Middle-class*	Family Households[+]	Younger Households	Middle-class Family Households
68.6	45.2	62.1	33.8

*Lower-middle and upper-middle classes

[+]Younger households-younger and older children

Source: R. B. Ellis, "Composite Population Descriptors: The Socio-Economic/Life Cycle Grid," in *Advances in Consumer Research II,* ed. M. J. Schlinger (Association for Consumer Research, 1975), 490. Reprinted with permission.

3. Description of social class characteristics identified in market target.

4. Development of marketing program to maximize effectiveness of marketing mix based upon consistency with social class attributes.

An example of this process is illustrated by AT&T marketing of telephones. Table 5.4 shows the socioeconomic/life-cycle grid used to identify market targets. In this instance, another variable was found useful in conjunction with social class. The other variable was life-cycle—a topic we will look at in some depth in the next chapter. Notice how AT&T has identified in quantitative terms the number of families in each cell, con-

Table 5.5
Descriptions of Socioeconomic Market Segments

A General Psychographic Profile of Customer's Socioeconomic Status

Style/Color Statements	Lower Class Agreement (%) ($n = 25$)	Lower-Middle Class Agreement (%) ($n = 108$)	Upper-Middle Class Agreement (%) ($n = 202$)	Upper Class Agreement (%) ($n = 105$)
I am generally willing to try even the most radical fashion at least once	32	25	42	37
When I must choose between the two, I usually dress for fashion not for comfort	9	15	24	29
Our home is furnished for comfort, not style	96	87	79	79
I have more modern appliances in my home than most people	17	23	41	48
I prefer colored appliances	57	73	87	92
I enjoy the better things in life and am willing to pay for them	36	70	70	82

Note: All significant levels are based on X^2 with $p < .05$, 3 d. f.

A Product-Specific Psychographic Profile of Customer's Socioeconomic Status

Style/Color Statements	Lower Class Agreement (%) ($n = 25$)	Lower-Middle Class Agreement (%) ($n = 108$)	Upper-Middle Class Agreement (%) ($n = 202$)	Upper Class Agreement (%) ($n = 105$)
Phones should come in patterns and designs as well as colors	60	80	63	58
A telephone should improve the decorative style of a room	47	82	73	77
Telephones should be modern in design	58	85	83	89
A home should have a variety of telephone styles	8	46	39	51
You can keep all those special phones. All I want is a phone that works	83	67	68	56
The style of a telephone is unimportant to me	86	54	58	51

Source: A. Marvin Roscoe, Jr., Arthur LeClaire, Jr., and Leon G. Schiffman, "Theory and Management Applications of Demographics in Buyer Behavior," in Arch G. Woodside, Jagdish N. Sheth, and Peter D. Bennett, (eds.), *Consumer and Industrial Buying Behavior* (Amsterdam: North-Holland, 1977), 74-75. Reprinted by permission.

sidered on the axes of life-cycle and socioeconomic class. The next stage in this strategy is describing the social class characteristics of each cell. From another study by AT&T, some indication of how this is done can be observed in Table 5.5.

Notice that social class segments can be described with two types of variables:

1. General profile information.

2. Product-specific information.

Table 5.5 contains both types of information. Other types of marketing research can be conducted to build a comprehensive understanding of each segment. Generalized information from the literature will be helpful for the general profile but product-specific information must usually be collected by an individual company.

From an analysis of market segments by socioeconomic profile, the company is prepared to develop a comprehensive marketing program to match the socioeconomic characteristics of the market target. This would include product attributes, media strategy, creative strategy, channels of distribution, pricing, and so forth.

Income or Social Class?

Some controversy exists about the efficacy of social class as a segmentation variable compared to income. This controversy was initiated by Wasson whose findings indicated that occupational class was a more important determinant of spending allocations than income.[65] When Myers, Stanton, and Haug compared social class to income, however, they found income to be a better indicator of buying behavior except for some categories such as dry instant milk, instant coffee, variety bread, powdered detergent, facial tissues, paper towels, and cottage cheese.[66] Later the product categories of black and white TV, commercial air travel and possession of a passport were added to the list.[67] To some degree, the issue was resolved by Hisrich and Peters who indicated that additional variables such as nature of product or more sensitive variables such as frequency of usage were included.[68]

Much of the problem in using social class as a marketing segmentation variable may stem from failure to use multiple-item indexes of social class.[69] A European study of 58 consumer products concluded that major differences between social classes were not so likely to be expected as more subtle differences. What counts is not so much large

[65]Chester R. Wasson, "Is it Time to Quit Thinking of Income Classes?" *Journal of Marketing,* vol. 33 (April 1969), 54-56.

[66]James H. Myers, Roger R. Stanton, and Arne F. Haug, "Correlates of Buying Behavior: Social Class vs. Income," *Journal of Marketing,* vol. 35 (October 1971), 8-15.

[67]James H. Myers and John F. Mount, "More on Social Class vs. Income as Correlates of Buying Behavior," *Journal of Marketing,* vol. 33 (April 1973), 71-73.

[68]R. D. Hisrich and Michael Peters, "Selecting the Superior Segmentation Correlate," *Journal of Marketing,* vol. 38 (July 1974), 60-63.

[69]Ronald E. Frank, William F. Massy, and Yoram Wind, *Market Segmentation* (Englewood Cliffs, N.J.: Prentice-Hall 1972), 47-49.

contrasts between social classes as the small nuances that give products higher appeal—and higher profit margins—than others.[70]

Problem Recognition and Evaluative Criteria

Social class research reveals many insights into the basic use patterns of consumers which may create problem recognition leading to decision making and provide criteria for evaluating the product or services that meet consumer needs. The final portion of this chapter describes some of these findings.

Clothing

The kind, quality, and style of clothing people wear is closely linked to that person's social class. Clothing furnishes a quick, visual cue to the class culture of the wearer,[71] just as was observed in the Bloomingdale's advertisement earlier in this chapter. When adolescent girls were asked to describe the characteristics of the popular girls, "dressed well" was the response most frequently given linked to social class characteristics.[72] Clothing serves as a symbol of social differentiation because of its high visibility.[73] In another study, Rich and Jain found high interest in clothing fashions among all social classes, but greatest attention to fashion information among upper social classes.[74]

Home Furnishings

Criteria used by families to furnish a home appear to be closely related to social class.[75] In a very interesting study by Laumann and House, the contents and characteristics of the living room were carefully observed using a 53-item checklist inventory. Using a cluster technique called Smallest Space Analysis (SSA), the researchers were able to arrange the 53 variables into the two-dimensional space shown in Figure 5.5 on the axes of social status and modern-traditionalism. Interestingly, the modern respondents were generally upwardly mobile within this generation; they were frequently *nouveau riches.*

The *nouveau riches* may have a strong need to validate their newly found status. Yet they may not have been accepted socially by the traditional upper classes so they turn to conspicuous consumption. The turn is done with taste in order to validate their claim to high status rather

[70]Q. J. Munters, "Social Stratification and Consumer Behavior," *The Netherlands Journal of Sociology,* vol. 13 (December 1977), 153-173.

[71]Thomas Ford Hoult, "Experimental American Measurement of Clothing as a Factor in Some Social Rating of Selected American Men," *American Sociological Review,* vol. 19 (June 1954), 324-325.

[72]Arlene Bjorngoard Ostermeier and Joanne Bubolz Eicher, "Clothing and Appearance as Related to Social Class and Social Acceptance of Adolescent Girls," *Michigan State University Quarterly Bulletin,* vol. 48 (February 1966), 431-436.

[73]C. Wayne Gordon, *The Social System of the High School* (New York: Free Press, 1957), 114.

[74]Stuart U. Rich and Subhash C. Jain, "Social Class and Life Cycle as Predictors of Shopping Behavior," *Journal of Marketing Research,* vol. 5 (February 1968), 41-49.

[75]Edward O. Laumann and James S. House, "Living Room Styles and Social Attributes: The Patterning of Material Artifacts in a Modern Urban Community," *Sociology and Social Research,* vol. 54 (April 1970), 321-324.

**Figure 5.5
Social Status
Attributes of
Living-Room
Objects**

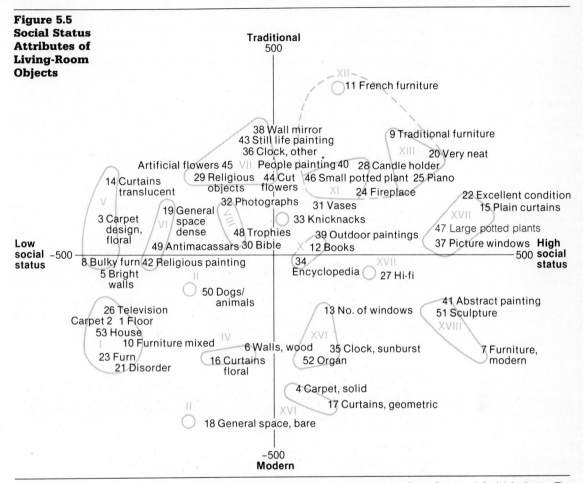

Source: Edward O. Laumann and James S. House, "Living Room Styles and Social Attributes: The Patterning of Material Artifacts in a Modern Urban Community," *Sociology and Social Research,* vol. 54 (April 1970), 326. Reprinted by permission of *Sociology and Social Research: An International Journal.* (University of Southern California, Los Angeles, California 90007.)

than merely possessing money. The researchers conclude that the evaluative criteria used by this mobile class reflect the *chic* norms of tastemakers:

Discovery of such norms is easy in a society that possesses a class of professional tastemakers (e.g., architects, interior decorators, fashion designers) and taste-setting media (ranging from *Better Homes and Gardens* through *The New Yorker*). Normative consumption trends are evident in styles of decor adopted by business and government for their new offices and stores. In all cases, the norms today favor modern decor.[76]

[76]Laumann and House, "Living Room Styles,", 337.

Leisure

Leisure is affected by social class in a variety of ways. The proportion of the family income may not vary a great deal between social classes[77] but the evaluative criteria used in selecting type of recreation is heavily influenced by social class. Bridge is an upper-class game, while bingo is lower class. Tennis is an upper-class sport, boxing is predominately lower class. Opera is upper class, roller derby is lower class.[78]

Leisure activities have a prestige hierarchy associated with occupational status. In a random sample of males and females, Bishop and Ikeda examined leisure patterns and status (using the North-Hatt occupational scale and Warner's ISC). A multiple discriminant analysis produced three discriminant functions accounting for 53.1 percent of variance. Social status accounted for the most variance in leisure patterns—27.9 percent.[79]

Prestige activities such as ice skating, bicycling, swimming, basketball, and tennis involve fairly rapid movement with extreme use of arms and legs, possibly suggesting a compensatory form of leisure for the otherwise sedentary life of many prestige occupations. Most of these pursuits do not require a lot of time to the degree that activities such as hunting, fishing, or boating would. Time may be a critical element in the prestige classes' use of leisure (see, also, Chapter 3). Members of lower social classes tend to participate in team sports while people of higher socioeconomic status tend to participate in individual or dual sports.[80]

Choice of leisure activities is also affected by social class-family interaction. There is a linear association between occupational stratum and couple participation in commercial leisure pursuits, with the exception that couples of the very highest occupational stratum reflect a slight decrease in recreation interaction compared to the upper middle class.[81] Rainwater, Coleman, and Handel have characterized the working-class wife as not sharing in her husband's recreational activities because her husband has no desire for her to participate.[82] Other investigators, however, report an increasing importance of commercial recreation in the lives of lower-status persons.[83]

The heaviest users of both commercial leisure facilities and public facilities (such as parks, museums, and swimming pools) are the middle classes, since upper classes frequently have their own facilities and the

---

[77]Carman, *Application of Social Class,* 31.

[78]Bert N. Adams and James E. Butler, "Occupation Status and Husband-Wife Social Participation," *Social Forces,* vol. 45 (June 1967), 501-507, at 506.

[79]Doyle W. Bishop and Masaru Ikeda, "Status and Role Factors in the Leisure Behavior of Different Occupations," *Sociology and Social Research,* vol. 54 (January 1970), 190-208.

[80]Susan L. Greendorfer, "Social Class Influence on Female Sport Involvement," *Sex Roles,* vol. 4 (August 1978), 619-625.

[81]Adams and Butler, "Occupational Status," 504.

[82]Rainwater et al., *Workingman's Wife,* 76.

[83]Alfred C. Clarke, "The Use of Leisure and Its Relation to Levels of Occupational Prestige," *American Sociological Review,* vol. 21 (June 1956), 304.

lower classes frequently cannot afford them or do not have the propensity to participate in them.[84]

Credit Cards

Credit-card acceptance and usage appear to be related to some extent to social class. Mathews and Slocum concluded that the lower classes preferred to use bank credit cards for durable and necessity goods (appliances, furniture, clothing) in contrast to the upper class desire to charge luxury items (gasoline, luggage, restaurants).[85] They also found more favorable attitudes toward credit usage among higher social classes. In a later study by the same investigators, however, they concluded that income was equally valuable as a basis for segmentation.[86]

In a study by Plummer, it was found that charge cards were widespread and cut across many demographic segments of the population. The most frequent users, however, were of higher income, better education, middle age, and professional occupation.[87] This same pattern of credit card usage was found in the studies of Hawes, Blackwell, and Talarzyk.[88]

Other Products

Evaluative criteria for other products have been found to be related to social class. For automobiles, Peters found his measure of relative occupational class income useful. He found that the average income group within each social class bought many more foreign, economy, intermediate-sized, and compact cars than would have been expected. The overprivileged groups within each social class owned more medium-sized and large cars and fewer foreign economy cars.[89] In another study using Q methodology, Sommers found that lower-class housewives felt appliances represented their self-concept in contrast to upper-class housewives who chose clothing as products most symbolic of themselves.[90]

Search Processes   The amount and type of search undertaken by an individual varies by social class as well as by product and situation category.[91] Unfortunately, the lowest social classes have limited information sources and are there-

[84]Lasswell, *Class and Stratum,* 258-264.

[85]H. Lee Mathews and John W. Slocum, Jr., "Social Class and Commercial Bank Credit Card Usage," *Journal of Marketing,* vol. 33 (January 1969), 71-78.

[86]John W. Slocum and H. Lee Mathews, "Social Class and Income as Indicators of Consumer Credit Behavior," *Journal of Marketing,* vol. 34 (April 1970), 69-74.

[87]Joseph T. Plummer, "Life Style Patterns and Commercial Bank Credit Card Usage," *Journal of Marketing,* vol. 35 (April 1971), 35-41.

[88]Douglass K. Hawes, Roger D. Blackwell, and W. Wayne Talarzyk, "Attitudes toward Use of Credit Cards: Do Men and Women Differ?" *Baylor Business Studies,* no. 110 (January 1977), 57-71.

[89]Peters, "Relative Occupational Class," 77.

[90]Montrose S. Sommers, "The Use of Product Symbolism to Differentiate Social Strata," University of Houston *Business Review,* vol. 11 (Fall 1964), 1-102.

[91]Gordon R. Foxall, "Social Factors in Consumer Choice: Replication and Extension," *Journal of Consumer Research,* vol. 2 (June 1975), 60-64.

fore at a disadvantage at filtering out misinformation and fraud in a complex, urbanized society.[92] To compensate, working-class consumers often rely on relatives or close friends for information about consumption decisions.[93] Middle-class consumers put more reliance upon media-acquired information and actively engage in external search from the media.[94] Upper-class individuals have far more access to media information than do lower-class individuals.[95]

Individuals also appear to be more responsive to information sources that they perceive to be compatible with their own social class, and there are good examples of marketers who have customized a basic promotional strategy to the requirements of specific classes.[96] It is clear that sharp differences exist in the class connotations of standard media sources such as newspapers and television, even though all classes have some exposure to them. One study in 15 major cities found, for example, that upper-middle-class people consistently preferred the NBC channel, while lower-middle class people preferred CBS, in keeping with the class images of the networks at that time.[97]

Interpersonal communications vary in other ways. In one study of blue-collar families, the researchers found significant differences between urban and suburban residents. Suburbanites indicated greater neighbor familiarity and displayed a greater sensitivity for their neighbor's work and church activities than did urban counterparts. Conversely, a higher proportion of city dwellers claimed virtually no knowledge of their neighbor's activities, income, or education.[98] The hypothesis generated from such a study would be that personal communications would be more important concerning consumption decisions than media for suburban consumers compared to city dwellers.

Social Language

The language patterns of an individual are closely correlated with that individual's social class. Ellis reported a revealing set of experiments on this topic. In one experiment he measured social class of respondents and had them make a 40-second recording of the fable, "The Tortoise and the Hare." These short recordings were played to groups of 15 to 30 regionally diverse college students who served as judges. The average ratings of social class by these judges correlated 0.80 with the speakers' social classes.[99] When the studies were conducted in such a way that speakers were asked through role playing to alter their voices to make

[92]Caplovitz, *Poor Pay More.*

[93]Rainwater et al., *Workingman's Wife,* 166.

[94]Rainwater et al., *Workingman's Wife.*

[95]Haer, "Predicting Utility."

[96]Mozell C. Hill, "Ice Cream in Contemporary Society," *New Sociology,* vol. 2 (1963), 23-24.

[97]Ira O. Glick and Sidney J. Levy, *Living with Television* (Chicago: Aldine, 1962).

[98]Irving Tallman and Romona Morgner, "Life-Style Differences Among Urban and Suburban Blue-Collar Families," *Social Forces,* vol. 48 (March 1970), 334-348; also Rita J. Simon, Gail Crotts, and Linda Mahan, "An Empirical Note about Married Women and Their Friends," *Social Forces,* vol. 48 (June 1970), 520-525.

[99]Dean S. Ellis, "Speech and Social Status in America," *Social Forces,* vol. 45 (March 1967), 431-437.

them sound upper class, the student judges' correlation with measured actual class was still 0.65.[100] All of the subjects used proper grammar, but their choice of vocabulary, sentence length, sentence structure, and fluency varied by social class. In still another approach, Ellis had the speakers count from 1 to 20 and even in this situation, college students' rankings correlated 0.65 with social class of the speakers.

An additional study by Harms found that the credibility of speakers is also associated with status. High-status persons are perceived as being more credible than low-status persons.[101]

The importance of language can be illustrated by looking at an ad featured in Chapter 11. The ad (Figure 11.3) is for a lower-priced car, the Honda. The appeal is to upper-middle class, however. The term well-off is used to express their own status by people who are in upper-middle class. Lower class people describe them as rich but the phrase used in the ad is positioned appropriately for the social class market target of middle- and upper-middle class, bothered by the energy shortage and inflation. Other consumers might be very interested in the physical attributes of the car but it is important that the communication about it be consistent with the social class associations of the market target.

Purchasing Processes

Social status influences where and how people feel they should shop. Lower-status people prefer local, face-to-face places where they get friendly service and easy credit.[102] Upper-middle consumers feel more confident in their shopping ability and will venture to new places to shop or will range throughout a store to find what they want. The discount store appeals to the middle classes because they are most careful and economy minded in their buying.[103] The lower classes may not have found what they wanted in the discount stores in the early years because of the initial failure of these stores to carry national brands. Lower-class consumers rely on national brands whenever possible to make sure they are getting a good buy.[104] It has also been found that working-class buyers are reluctant to try a new store. They limit their shopping to a few stores.[105]

Socioeconomic segments differ in their patronage of discount stores for some types of products but not for others. Specifically, Prasad found that products with high social, low economic risk and those of high social, high economic risk were products with which social classes differed significantly in their patronage attitudes toward discount stores.[106]

---

[100]Ellis, "Speech."

[101]L. S. Harms, "Listener Judgments of Status Cues in Speech," *Quarterly Journal of Speech,* vol. 47 (April 1961), 164-168.

[102]Levy, "Social Class," 153.

[103]Pierre Martineau, "The Pattern of the Social Classes," in Richard Clewett, (ed.), *Marketing's Role in Scientific Marketing* (Chicago: American Marketing Association, 1957), 233-249, at 248.

[104]M. Ross, "Uptown and Downtown," *American Sociological Review,* vol. 30, (1965), 255-259.

[105]Ross, "Uptown."

[106]V. Kanti Prasad, "Socioeconomic Product Risk and Patronage Preferences of Retail Shoppers," *Journal of Marketing,* vol. 39 (July 1975), 42-47.

**Figure 5.6
Housewife
Perceptions of
Department-Store
Status**

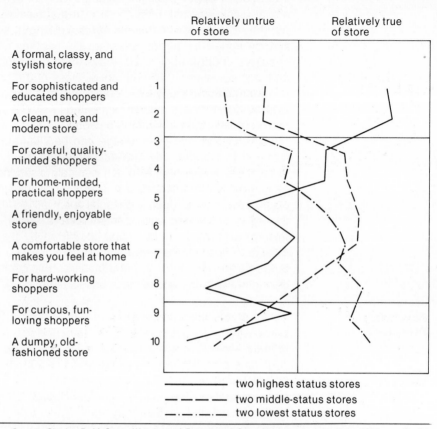

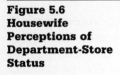

Source: Charles B. McCann, *Women and Department Store Newspaper Advertising* (Chicago: Social Research, 1957), 15-55. Reprinted by permission of the publisher.

Consumers have an image of what social class a store appeals to, even if a consumer has no shopping experience in that store. Figure 5.6 is a classic illustration of this phenomenon. Women were asked to evaluate a department store on various factors that would establish the status group the store served. Women were able to rate accurately a store they had never seen, merely by seeing its advertisements.[107] People in upper classes more frequently specify a pleasant store atmosphere and displays with excitement as enjoyable features, but lower classes emphasize acquiring household things or clothing as enjoyable. Upper classes shop more frequently than middle or lower classes.[108] Shopping by husband and wife together is more likely to occur among lower-middle-class families. Adams and Butler found the greatest propensity to shop together among lower, white-collar, skilled, and semiskilled

[107]Charles B. McCann, *Women and Department Store Newspaper Advertising* (Chicago: Social Research, 1957), 15-55.
[108]Rich and Jain, "Social Class."

classes.[109] Shopping, especially for the middle-class family, has taken on the characteristics of a form of recreation for many. It is they who are the most willing to experiment with store brands and who are the most price sensitive.[110]

A Concluding Note

Social class is essential to positioning—the creating of attributes about an organization or product in consumers' minds. Positioning is difficult, however, if those in charge of marketing strategies do not understand the class characteristics desired for the product or the class characteristics of the target market.

It is a fact that beer companies have not usually maintained long-term relationships with Madison Avenue ad agencies. The beer companies have often gone to agencies outside of Manhattan. The reason, some veteran advertising observers have commented, is that there are too many martini drinkers on Madison Avenue. Whether that is true or not may be questioned, but the conclusion to draw is that if you are selling to market targets of different social classes than your own, be sure you do your homework in order to understand well the social class characteristics of your market target.

Summary

Social classes are relatively permanent and homogeneous divisions in a society in which groups of people are compared with one another. These groups are recognized as having inferior or superior positions by the individuals who comprise the society, although the basis of superiority is not established.

Social classes are discrete groups in theory, but in practice they are treated as continuous. Some people, therefore, exhibit behavior that is partially aligned with one social class and partially aligned with another. One reason for this phenomenon is multidimensionality, which exists when people rank in different positions on the specific determinants of social class.

Occupation is the most important single measure of an individual's social class. Other important variables are the personal performance of an individual within his occupational group, the interactions he has with other individuals, his possessions, the value orientations of his group, and his class consciousness. Measurement of social class may involve any or all of these determinants.

Social classes in America are frequently divided into six groups: upper upper, lower upper, upper middle, lower middle, upper lower, and lower lower. Each of these groups displays characteristic values and behaviors that are useful in analyzing consumer decisions.

---

[109]Adams and Butler, "Occupation Status," 506.

[110]Patrick E. Murphy, "The Effect of Social Class on Brand and Price Consciousness for Supermarket Products," *Journal of Retailing*, vol. 54 (Summer 1978), 33-42 ff.

**Review and
Discussion
Questions**

1. What variables determine an individual's social class? In what order of importance should they be ranked?

2. In what way does income relate to social class? Why is it used so little as an indicator of social class? What should be its proper value as an indicator of social class?

3. Prepare an outline of the major problems involved in the measurement of social classes.

4. Some observers of contemporary America believe that social classes have declined in importance and presence, but others disagree. Outline your analysis of what has happened in recent years to social classes in America.

5. A marketing researcher is speculating on the influence of the upper classes on the consumption decisions of the lower classes for the following products: automobiles, food, clothing, baby care products. What conclusions would you expect for each of those products? Describe a research project that could be used to determine the answer to this question.

6. The leisure products group of a large conglomerate is constantly seeking additional products for expanding markets and additional penetration for existing products. What conclusions that would be helpful in the design of marketing strategy might be reached concerning social class and leisure?

7. The operator of a large discount chain is contemplating a new store in an area of upper-lower class families. He asks for a consulting report defining the precautions he should take to insure patronage among this group. What would you place in such a report? Assume that the area was mostly lower-lower class families. Would you recommend he enter this market?

8. Prepare a research report comparing the search processes of the major social classes of consumers in America.

Imagine, if you will, a hot summer evening. In a local mental hospital, a man is interviewed by a sociologist, who records the following dialogue:

Q. How did you happen to come here?
A. I don't know. I was just minding my own business.

Q. Who brought you here?
A. The police.

Q. What had you been doing?
A. Nothing. Just minding my own business.

Q. What were you doing at the time?
A. Just walking along the street.

Q. What street?
A. (He gave the name of one of the busiest streets in the city.)

Q. What had you done just before that?
A. It was hot, so I took my clothes off.

Q. All your clothes?
A. No. Not my shoes and stockings.

Q. Why not those too?
A. The sidewalk was too hot.[1]

This man acted totally rationally if judged from his own individual perspective. Other people in society disagreed. The man violated society's norms—either because he did not think of society's norms when he took his clothes off or maybe he knew the norms but went right ahead and violated them.

Or consider Mary's friend Nancy. Nancy was asked to attend a Tupperware party being given by Mary. Nancy declined, explaining she had no need for additional housewares. Mary said, "Oh, please come to the party. I will get a free gift just for having my friends come to the party.

[1]Quoted from James S. Slotkin, *Social Anthropology* (New York: Macmillan, 1950), 70-71.

You don't need to buy anything and we will have fun." Nancy went. She spent $17.60 on items she had not previously realized she needed.

It is obvious that some powerful forces are at work between individuals and the others around them. Those forces sometimes cause people to do something of interest to marketers—like buy Tupperware. Most of the time those forces cause people to wear clothes, unlike the gentleman described at the beginning of the chapter. If we are going to understand why consumers do the things they do, we had better take a close look at the influence of other people, especially in groups that are important. One of the most important group influences, of course, is the family and so we shall take an in-depth look at it in this chapter.

WHAT ARE REFERENCE GROUPS?

Groups are two or more individuals related to each other by shared norms of behavior or values. A consumer is a member of many groups, but *reference groups* are those which provide norms and values that become the *perspectives* that influence behavior. Sometimes a reference group affects behavior of a consumer because the consumer is making a conscious effort to emulate the behavior of others in the group or to be identified with the group's behavior. Sometimes the influence of the group is more subtle, occurring without conscious effort of the individual who is influenced. Often some individual will symbolize the values of a group to which one aspires—such as a champion athlete might for a young person. This may not seem like a group—and technically the individual is a *reference person*—but we will treat this dyad under the same topic as reference groups since the effects, and in some instances the process, are the same.

Consumers are members of many groups. Thus group influence can be analyzed in a variety of ways, often tied to the kind of group which is being analyzed.

Primary groups are collections of individuals small enough and intimate enough that all the members can communicate with each face to face. Primary groups include the family—the most important one in our analysis in this chapter. Other primary groups include playmates, co-workers on the job, friendship groups in the neighborhood, and other types of intimate groupings.

Secondary groups are social organizations, where less continuous, face-to-face interaction takes place. Secondary groups include professional associations, religious organizations, trade unions, and similar groups. For marketers, it is relatively easy to obtain lists of secondary groups—members of the American Marketing Association or students at a university, for example—but the groups that have the most direct influence on buying behavior are usually the primary groups. Primary groups often are subsets of the secondary group, however.

Reference groups may also be classified as *formal groups* (with a defined structure and usually specified membership requirements) or *in-*

formal groups. Informal groups occur on the basis of proximity, interests or other bases with less specified structure or membership. Formal groups are easier to study but, again, informal groups are likely to be of more influence on consumption decisions. Most of the sociological and social psychological research focuses on informal groups because they have such a strong influence on human behavior.[2]

Reference groups may also be categorized by the status of the individual in those groups. *Membership groups* are groups in which a person is recognized by others as belonging. An *aspirational group* is one to which an individual wishes or aspires to belong. A *dissociative group* is one with whose values or behavior an individual does not want to be associated; a motorcyclist not wanting to be thought of as a member of the Hell's Angels, for example, or a straight not wanting to be perceived as a gay.

All definitions of a group imply the existence of functional interdependence among people rather than a mere statistical summation of individuals. Greer states it this way, "A social group is an aggregate of individuals who exist in a state of functional interdependence from which evolves a flow of communication and a consequent ordering of behavior.[3]

HOW DO REFERENCE GROUPS INFLUENCE CONSUMERS?

Reference groups function in several ways of interest to consumer analysts. First, reference groups create *socialization of individuals*—the process by which individuals become aware of or learn behavior and lifestyles. Second, reference groups are important in the process of *developing and evaluating one's self-concept.* Third, reference groups are a *device for obtaining compliance* with norms in a society.

Socialization

Socialization, you will remember, is the process by which a member learns the value system, norms, and the required behavior patterns of the society, organizations, or groups in which a person becomes a member. Socialization occurs and is necessary because of the individual's need to participate in the social environment.

The process of socialization is accomplished through the influence of various reference groups. A company manual may explain to the new employee, for example, when coffee breaks are to be taken, but informal work groups teach the person when they are actually taken as well as where and how and perhaps whether doughnuts are normally consumed along with coffee. Should consumers believe Continental Airlines or American Airlines provides good service and Braniff or US Air provides bad? Social groups of businesspersons will develop norms about what

[2]Stephen Wilson, *Informal Groups* (New York: Prentice-Hall, 1978).

[3]Scott Greer, *Social Organization* (New York: Doubleday, 1955), 18. For amplification of the concept of a group see James W. Vander Zanden, *Sociology: A Systematic Approach* (New York: 1970), 174-195; and Jeffrey Ford and Elwood Ellis, "A Reexamination of Group Influence on Member Brand Preference," *Journal of Marketing Research* (February 1980), 125-132.

travelers should believe about each airline and will teach those norms to new members of the group.

The process of socialization and acculturation permits an individual to know what behavior is likely to result in stability both for the individual and for the group. Of particular interest in consumer behavior today is the socialization of children—how they learn about brands, whether or not to trust television advertising, whether to prefer products with sugar or with artificial coloring and so forth. That topic is important and we will consider it in more depth in Chapter 8 when we think together about how human learning occurs.

Development of Self-Concept

Reference groups fulfill a second important function by developing a person's concept of *self*—a variable of importance in several places in this book as we build our understanding of consumer behavior. As we saw in the last chapter, self-concept is important in social mobility and it is the family that develops an individual's self-concept during childhood. Other reference groups may become dominant in adult life causing the self-concept to be reinforced or changed over time, a process that may cause changes in consumer behavior.[4] The self is defined by Hewitt as having five components:

The first component is an organized set of motivations. . . . The second component of the self is a series of social roles to which the person is committed, along with a knowledge of how to play them. Social roles are clusters of norms that are related to particular positions that a person occupies. . . . The third component of the self is a more general set of commitments to social norms and their underlying values. . . . The fourth component of the self is a set of cognitive abilities, including the ability to create and understand symbols, which guide response to the intended meanings of others in social interaction and provide a "map" of the physical and social setting in which the person finds himself. . . . The fifth and final component of the self is a set of ideas about one's qualities, capabilities, commitments, and motives—a self-image—that is developed by the individual in the course of his socialization.[5]

People protect and modify their self-concept in their interactions with others in the reference group. What we think of ourselves is influenced in our social interactions by the reactions of others whose values we share and value. One form of social interaction is the consumption of products. We communicate meaning to others when we buy and use products.

Our clothing, our car, our career, all make a statement to those we care about. Goffman and Shibutani are behavioral scientists who identi-

[4]Terrence O'Brian, Humberto Tapia, and Thomas Brown, "The Self-Concept in Buyer Behavior," *Business Horizons* (October 1977), 65-71.

[5]John P. Hewitt, *Social Stratification and Deviant Behavior* (New York: Random House, 1970), 32-33.

fied most clearly that our behavior or life-style is the presentation of our self or an idealized self to our reference group.[6]

The products consumers buy and use are part of the symbols we present to others. This process is illustrated in Figure 6.1 based upon research by Grubb and Grathwohl. Assume that individual *A* perceives himself or herself as thrifty, economical, and practical. That person may purchase a Volkswagen partly because it is a symbol of these qualities, thereby achieving internal self-enhancement. The audience *B* may include peers, parents, and significant others. The double-headed arrows *B* and *C* in Figure 6.1 indicate that the Volkswagen is attributed meaning by *A* and that the audience *B* is also attributing meaning to it. If the Volkswagen has commonly understood meaning between *A* and the reference group *B*, communication of self has occurred and the reaction of *B* will provide self-enhancement to individual *A*.

Empirical evidence for this process has been provided by Grubb and Hupp[7] for automobiles, for beer, soap and cigarettes by Birdwell[8] and for toothpaste by Dolich[9] and some other brand store-selection situations by others.[10]

Testimonial advertising is a direct application of understanding the social consequences of the self-concept. A child looks at "Mean" Joe Green drinking a *Coca-Cola* and subconsciously (perhaps consciously in some instances) attributes the respect and strength that the child wants in the *Coke* being consumed by Mr. Green. The same is true with attributes projected by Joe Namath, O. J, Simpson, Cathy Rigby, Muhammed Ali, Jack Nicklaus, and others. Outside of sports, testimonials by Florence Henderson, Danny Thomas, Betty White or Cheryl Tiegs can be very effective *if*—and this is where careful research may be required—the self projected by the reference person in the testimonial is consistent with the idealized self of the consumer in the audience target (see Figure 6.2).

Roles

People also maintain their self-concept by conforming to roles they have learned. Roles are patterns of behavior expected of people who occupy a position in the group. Traditional roles of mothers may include cooking chicken soup when someone in the family is sick and thus advertising

---

[6]Erving Goffman, *The Presentation of Self in Everyday Life* (New York: Doubleday, 1959) and Tamtosu Shibutani, "Reference Groups as Perspectives," *American Journal of Sociology* (May 1955), 562-569.

[7]Edward L. Grubb and Gregg Hupp, "Perception of Self, Generalized Stereotypes, and Brand Selection," *Journal of Marketing Research,* vol. 5 (February 1968), 58-63.

[8]Al E. Birdwell, "A Study of the Influence of Image Congruence on Consumer Choice," Unpublished Ph.D. dissertation (Austin, Texas: University of Texas, 1964).

[9]Ira J. Dolich "Congruence Relationships between Self Images and Product Brands," *Journal of Marketing Research,* vol. 6 (February 1969), 80-84.

[10]The importance of self-concepts in retail store evaluation is presented in Joseph Barry Mason and Morris L. Baker, "The Problem of the Self-Concept in Store Image Studies," *Journal of Marketing,* vol. 34 (April 1970), 67-69. Significant methodological flaws in this study have been suggested, however, by Ira J. Dolich and Ned Shilling, "A Critical Evaluation of the Problem of Self-Concept in Store Image Studies," *Journal of Marketing,* vol. 35 (January 1971), 71-73.

**Figure 6.1
Relationship of the
Consumption of
Goods and
Symbols to Self-
Concept**

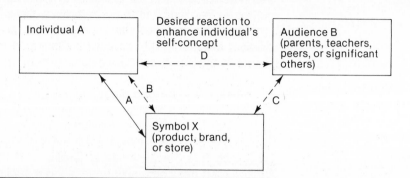

Source: Edward L. Grubb and Harrison L. Grathwohl, "Consumer Self-Concept. Symbolism and Market Behavior: A Theoretical Approach," *Journal of Marketing,* vol. 31 (October 1967), 25. Reprinted by permission from the *Journal of Marketing* published by the American Marketing Association.

**Figure 6.2
Testimonial by
Idealized Self—
"Mean" Joe Green**

Source: Courtesy of the Coca-Cola Company.

may be effective if such a situation is shown along with a cold remedy. Physicians are supposed to behave in prescribed ways in advertisements because of their position in society. Professors are expected to be analytical and erudite. The danger, though, is that these roles may not be shared by all of the audience or the roles or role stereotype may change. In the living of everyday life, it is not uncommon for individuals to experience *role conflict;* a parent expected to spend ample time with his/her family but also expected to spend long hours in his/her role as a successful executive. Role conflict, however, can generate problem recognition; problem recognition by consumers is the prerequisite for marketing opportunity and communications effectiveness.

Compliance with Group Norms

A third function of reference groups is to achieve individual compliance with group norms. *Norms* are stable expectations held by a consensus of the group concerning the behavior rules for individual members. Norms exist for both small groups and larger groups such as the social classes, subcultural groups, and society norms discussed in the last two chapters.

Do consumers comply with group norms by buying products in order to keep up with the Joneses? This is called the *normative function of reference groups*—a pressure for people to conform to similar patterns—in contrast with the *evaluative or informational function* of providing a reference point by which an individual evaluates the self-concept and other aspects of behavior.[11]

Most early marketing studies investigating reference group influence followed the normative approach. Compliance with group norms was thought of as depending on the ability of the group to allocate rewards to an individual (material, status or other rewards) as well as the attractiveness of the reference group (source) to the individual whose behavior is being influenced. In informal groups, Festinger hypothesized that the amount of influence on an individual depends upon the similarity or co-orientation of an individual with the group on various attributes.[12] Moschis supported Festinger's theory in a marketing study involving consumer decisions about cosmetics.[13]

A number of studies in marketing showed normative compliance and are usually described as the Asch or Sherif studies.[14] The most influential study in marketing was conducted by Stafford in which he introduced various "brands" of bread to groups of housewives. The "brands" of bread were all identical and had plain wrappers with no differences except identifying letters chosen from the middle of the alphabet. The subjects in the experiment tended to choose brands over time that were the choices of the leaders of the informal groups that developed. Thus, Stafford concluded that informal groups have a definite influence on their members toward conformity behavior with respect to choice of bread.[15]

[11]Harold H. Kelly, "Two Functions of Reference Groups," in C. W. Swanson, T. M. Newcomb, and E. L. Harley, (eds.), *Readings in Social Psychology* (New York: Holt, Rinehart and Winston, 1952).

[12]Leon Festinger, "A Theory of Social Comparison Processes," *Human Relations* (May 1954), 117-140.

[13]George P. Moschis, "Social Comparison and Informal Group Influence," *Journal of Marketing Research* (August 1976), 237-244.

[14]S. E. Asch, "Effects of Group Pressure upon the Modification and Distortion of Judgments," in H. Proshansky and B. Seidenberg, (eds.), *Basic Studies in Social Psychology* (New York: Holt, Rinehart and Winston, 1965), 393-401; and Muzafer Sherif, "Formation of Social Norms: The Experimental Paradigm," in Proshansky and Seidenberg, *Basic Studies,* 461-470.

[15]James E. Stafford, "Effects of Group Influence on Consumer Brand Preferences," *Journal of Marketing Research* (February 1966), 68-75.

The Stafford study conflicted with a theory about reference groups, however, that indicated that products that are most susceptible to group influences would be products high in visibility, complexity, and perceived risk and low in testability. Bread hardly fits that description. A direct replication of Stafford's study was conducted therefore and Ford and Ellis report results that refute the Stafford experiment.[16] This research makes more sense for a product with low involvement, as bread probably has little normative compliance.

For a high-involvement product, however, normative compliance should be considerably greater. An experimental study by Venkatesan for men's suits shows such influence, along the lines of the classic Asch studies. Venkatesan presented business students with three suits (A,B,C) of identical style, color and size and asked them to choose the best suit. Control groups, in which the choices of other members were unknown, were compared to conformity groups in which a naive subject was grouped with confederates who unanimously chose the same suit. In the absence of any group influence, each suit was equally likely to be selected but in the conformity condition, individuals significantly yielded to the group conformity, choosing the majority preference.[17]

Why Do People Adhere to Norms?

Sociologist George Homans provided a theory to explain why people conform to group norms. Homans' equation of human exchange is built upon the premise that interpersonal activities and sentiments (defined as symbols of approval or esteem for another person) emitted by one individual responding to another are more or less reinforcing or punishing to the behavior of the other individual. That is, they are more or less valuable to him. If someone is asked to join another person for a cup of coffee, for example, there will be rewards (companionship, coffee, esteem indicated by the invitation, etc.) but there may also be costs (time lost, perhaps association with a person of lower status, giving up association with other possibly more valuable persons, and other costs). The nature of interactions will be determined by an individual's perception of the profit of the interaction. Homans defines this in familiar economic terms:

$$profit = rewards - costs.$$

Individuals arrange their social relations in such a way as to maximize total profit. The groups a person chooses to belong to and the degree to which the individual adheres to the norms of that group are based upon the net profit figure, not rewards or costs alone.[18]

Pressure to conform to group norms is present in all aspects of life.

---

[16]Jeffrey Ford and Elwood Ellis, "A Reexamination of Group Influence on Member Brand Preference," *Journal of Marketing Research* (February 1980), 125-132.

[17]M. Venkatesan, "Experimental Study of Consumer Behavior Conformity and Independence," *Journal of Marketing Research* (November 1966), 384-387.

[18]George Homans, *Social Behavior: Its Elementary Forms* (New York: Harcourt, 1961). See Chapter 3 for an outline of Homans' theory.

Of particular interest to marketing strategists is the influence of group norms on conformity in household products and everyday behavior patterns. This is illustrated in a study of the new town, Levittown:

The culture of the block jelled quite rapidly too. Standards of lawn care were agreed upon as soon as it was time to do something about the lawn, and by unspoken agreement, the front lawn would be cared for conscientiously, but the backyard was of less importance. Those who deviated from this norm, either neglecting their lawn or working on it too industriously, were brought into line through wisecracks. When I, in a burst of compulsive concern, worked very hard on my lawn at the start, one of my neighbors laughed and said he would have to move out if I was going to have "that fancy a lawn." Since I was not interested in a "fancy lawn," I found it easy to take the hint but those who wanted a perfect lawn stayed away from the talkfests that usually developed evenings and on Saturday mornings when the men were ostensibly working on the lawns, so as not to be joked about and chastised as ratebusters.[19]

Anomie and Deviance

A different but related concept is *anomie,* originally translated from Durkheim to mean "normlessness."[20] The word has various meanings. Generally, a societal use of the term means a weakened respect for the norms of a society rather than complete absence of norms. (See Form's scale in Table 6.1.) In this sense, anomie means an ambivalence that causes people to conform grudgingly or to nonconform with misgivings or simply for a low consensus to exist in a society about its norms. Where two conflicting norms exist, one for public purposes but another for commonly accepted noncompliance to the public norms, *patterned evasion of norms* is said to exist and include examples such as the following:

. . . prohibition versus bootlegging; sexual chastity versus clandestine affairs and prostitution; classroom honesty versus established patterns of exam cribbing; impersonal, disinterested, honest government versus political graft, "fixing," and the like; professional codes versus fee splitting among doctors, ambulance chasing among lawyers, and so on; an income tax system versus cheating on tax returns; and concepts of truthful versus fraudulent advertising.[21]

[19]Herbert J. Gans, "The Levittowners: Ways of Life and Politics in a New Suburban Community," Frank Sweetser, (ed.), *Studies in American Urban Society* (New York: Crowell, 1970), 185-220.

[20]Emile Durkheim, *Suicide,* trans. by George Simpson, (New York: Free Press, 1951). For a cultural perspective on anomie, see Robert Merton, "Anomie, Anomia, and Social Interaction: Contexts of Deviate Behavior," in M. B. Clinard, (ed.), *Anomie and Deviate Behavior* (New York: Free Press, 1964).

[21]Vander Zanden, *Sociology,* 116. For an excellent discussion of the societal implications of anomie, see 115-131 of this source. Also, see Kenneth R. Schneider, *Destiny of Change* (New York: Holt, Rinehart and Winston, 1968), 81-104.

People who score high on anomie scales are poor and uneducated and do not participate in organizations controlled by people in higher strata. People who profit most in a society have low levels of anomie while the deprived have high levels.[22] Thus, theories of anomie are frequently related to social class or cultural alienation. Anomie is also seen then as *deviance* from norms.

The psychological meaning of *anomie* focuses upon the absence of norms or standards for behavior because the *individual* is alienated psychologically from the dominant normative order. This may occur for various reasons. Winch holds, though, that one of the core functions of religion is the prevention of a state of normlessness at the societal level and therefore the prevention of alienation at the individual level.[23] Religion provides guidelines for behavior and gives adherents a firm notion that there are right and wrong ways of thinking and acting as well as the specifics of those ways. It appears that religious variables are of greater importance than socioeconomic factors as sources of variance in personal normlessness.[24]

In spite of the large amount of research relating anomie to various aspects of behavior, this variable is just beginning to appear in consumer studies. Examples of anomie scales are shown in Table 6.1. Some of these items have been used in life-style studies as AIO (Activity, Interest, Opinion) statements but usually without the conceptual basis in other anomie studies. In one marketing study, however, Pruden and Longman included an anomie scale and found that as anomie increases, so does a tendency to have negative attitudes toward marketing and increased belief in government intervention in the marketplace.[25] Anomie may be a topic of increasing interest in consumer studies in the future.

Informational Conformity

In marketing, many people accepted the normative theory of compliance—keeping up with the Joneses—until the influential research of Burnkrant and Cousineau. They found that when people are unable to assess the characteristics of a product from direct observation and contact, they will accept views of others as evidence about the nature of the product. In a carefully constructed experiment, Burnkrant and Cousineau concluded that people use information or reactions about a product from other people in evaluating the characteristics of the product. People may frequently buy products that others in their groups buy, not to establish some self-fulfilling role relationship to the others nor to obtain some re-

[22]William H. Form, "The Social Construction of Anomie: A Four-Nation Study of Industrial Workers," *American Journal of Sociology,* vol. 80 (1975), 1165-1189.

[23]Robert F. Winch, *The Modern Family,* 3d ed. (New York: Holt, Rinehart and Winston, 1971), 7.

[24]Gary R. Lee and Robert W. Clyde, "Religion, Socioeconomic Stature, and Anomie," *Journal for the Scientific Study of Religion,* vol. 13 (March 1974), 35-47.

[25]Henry O. Pruden and Douglas S. Longman, "Race, Alienation and Consumerism," *Journal of Marketing,* vol. 36 (July 1972), 58-63.

**Table 6.1
Examples of
Anomie Scales**

Pruden and Longman*

Anomie items (based on Strole)
1. These days a person doesn't really know who he can count on.
2. Nowadays a person has to live pretty much for today and let tomorrow take care of itself.
3. It's hardly fair to bring children into the world with the way things look for the future.
4. In spite of what some people say, the lot of the average man is getting worse.
5. There's little use in writing to public officials because they aren't really interested in the problems of the average man.
   Anomie Index Construction: For each of the above anomie questions respondents check one of six categories from "strongly agree" to "strongly disagree." "Strongly agree" has an index of one and "strongly disagree" an index value of six. Each respondent's anomie index is the sum of the index value for the five anomie questions.

Form's Societal Anomie Scale†

1. In the everyday problems of life, it is easy to know which is the right path to choose.
2. It is hard to rear children nowadays because what is right today is wrong tomorrow.
3. It seems that nobody agrees on what is right and wrong because everyone is following his own ideas.
4. It is easy to find agreement on what is morally right.
5. There are so many organizations with different goals that it is impossible to trust any of them.
6. The world is changing so fast that it is difficult to be sure that we are making the right decisions in the problems we face daily.
7. The man with morals and scruples is better able to get ahead in this world than the immoral and unscrupulous person.
   (Different sets of the above 7 statements are used as Guttman scales, yielding scores of 0 to 5.)

Rushing's Anomie Scale‡

	Yes	No
Is a person justified in doing almost anything if the reward is high enough?	___	___
Some people say you have to do things that are wrong in order to get ahead in the world today. What do you think?	___	___
Would you say that the main reason people obey the law is the punishment that comes if they are caught?	___	___
Some people say that to be a success it is usually necessary to be dishonest. Do you think this is true?	___	___
In your opinion, is the honest life the best regardless of the hardships it may cause?*	___	___
In your opinion, should people obey the law no matter how much it interferes with their personal ambitions?*	___	___

(Total scores for an individual range from 0 to 6, based on the number of yes answers. Asterisked item is reverse scored.)

*Reprinted by permission from H. O. Pruden and D. S. Longman, "Race, Alienation and Consumerism," *Journal of Marketing* (July 1972), 60, published by the American Marketing Association. Based upon Leo Strole, "Social Integration and Certain Corollaries: An Exploratory Study," *American Sociological Review.* vol. 21 (December, 1956), 709-716.

†William H. Form, "The Social Construction of Anomie" *American Journal of Sociology,* vol. 80 (The University of Chicago Press, 1975), 1170. © 1975 The University of Chicago Press. Reprinted by permission.

‡William A. Rushing, "Class, Culture, and Social Structure and Anomie," *American Journal of Sociology.* vol. 76 (The University of Chicago Press, 1971), 861. © 1971 The University of Chicago Press. Reprinted by permission.

ward or avoid some punishment, but simply to acquire what they perceive to be a good product.[26]

Another direction in the understanding of social influences is *attribution theory.* Attribution refers to the cognitive processes through which

[26]Robert Burnkrant and Alain Cousineau, "Informational and Normative Social Influence in Buyer Behavior," *Journal of Consumer Research* (December 1975), 206-215. Also see H. C. Kelman, "Processes of Opinion Change," *Public Opinion Quarterly* (1961), 57-78.

**Table 6.2
Typical Reference
Group Influences
on Brand Decisions**

Informational Influence

1. The individual seeks information about various brands of the product from an association of professionals or independent group of experts.
2. The individual seeks information from those who work with the product as a profession.
3. The individual seeks brand-related knowledge and experience (such as how Brand A's performance compares to Brand B's) from those friends, neighbors, relatives, or work associates who have reliable information about the brands.
4. The brand which the individual selects is influenced by observing a seal of approval of an independent testing agency (such as Good Housekeeping).
5. The individual's observation of what experts do influences his choice of a brand (such as observing the type of car which police drive or the brand of TV which repairmen buy).

Utilitarian Influence

1. To satisfy the expectations of fellow work associates, the individual's decision to purchase a particular brand is influenced by their preferences.
2. The individual's decision to purchase a particular brand is influenced by the preferences of people with whom he has social interaction.
3. The individual's decision to purchase a particular brand is influenced by the preferences of family members.
4. The desire to satisfy the expectations which others have of him has an impact on the individual's brand choice.

Value-Expressive Influence

1. The individual feels that the purchase or use of a particular brand will enhance the image which others have of him.
2. The individual feels that those who purchase or use a particular brand possess the characteristics which he would like to have.
3. The individual sometimes feels that it would be nice to be like the type of person which advertisements show using a particular brand.
4. The individual feels that the people who purchase a particular brand are admired or respected by others.
5. The individual feels that the purchase of a particular brand helps him show others what he is, or would like to be (such as an athlete, successful businessman, good mother, etc.).

Source: C. Whan Park and V. Parker Lessig, "Students and Housewives: Differences in Susceptibility to Reference Group Influence," *Journal of Consumer Research,* (September 1977), 105. Reprinted by permission.

an individual infers the cause of an actor's behavior.[27] Many of these causes are internal to an individual but they can be affected, perhaps increased in effectiveness, by the actions of others. We will need to look at the topic of attribution theory more closely when we think about interpersonal influence in Chapter 12.

The effects reference groups have on consumer behavior can be varied but there is no question of their importance. Reference group influence can affect brand choice in a number of ways. One description of the various influences is provided by Park and Lessig in Table 6.2. In the model of consumer behavior, we will group all of these influences together and consider them under the term of conformity or social influence. This is shown in Figure 6.3.

**Reference Groups
and the Family**

In the preceding pages we discussed various types of reference groups, describing some basic terminology as well as the general functions of reference groups. The reference group of overriding importance for most

[27]Bobby Calder and Robert Burnkrant, "Interpersonal Influence on Consumer Behavior: An Attribution Theory Approach," *Journal of Consumer Research* (June 1977), 29-38.

**Figure 6.3
Reference Group
Influences on
Conformity**

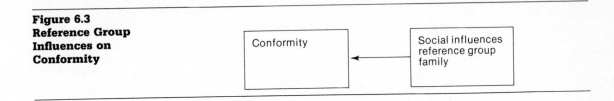

consumers, however, is the family. The remainder of the chapter, therefore, focuses specifically upon the topic of the family.

THE FAMILY

The term family is used in a wide variety of ways. For the purposes of this book, the following terminology is adequate. *Nuclear family* means the immediate group of father, mother and child(ren) living together. The *extended family* refers to the nuclear family and other relatives, including grandparents, uncles and aunts, cousins, and in-laws. The family one is born into is called the *family of orientation,* while the one established by marriage is the *family of procreation.* When conducting research, you often will encounter the term *household.* This is a term used to describe all the persons, both related and unrelated, who occupy a housing unit such as a house or apartment.

In contrast to larger social systems, the nuclear family is a *primary* group. As such, it is characterized by face-to-face intimacy and meaningfulness. This intimacy and association mean, among other things, that the family is often uniquely important in its influence, not merely on normative compliance, but also on personality, attitudes, and motives.

The family differs from other reference groups in that it is both an earning and a consuming unit. The consumption needs of each individual as well as family needs, such as a car and home, must be satisfied from a common pool of financial resources. This means that individual needs must sometimes be subordinated to those of other family members or to the needs of the family as a whole.

Because the family is a primary group that both earns and consumes, it differs from larger social systems in the sense that it performs what might be termed a mediating function. The norms of larger social systems—culture, subculture, reference groups, social class, and so on—are filtered through and interpreted by individuals in a family setting. This process of mediation may substantially alter the influences of larger social systems on individual consumption behavior and is shown in Figure 6.4.

There are, then, many ways in which the family differs from larger reference groups. While there are other unique aspects of the family, the above are most relevant for our purposes. You will get an opportunity to think in more depth about these relationships, however, when we examine family-role structure in the last section of this chapter. First, however,

Figure 6.4
Family Influences on Individual Information and Experiences

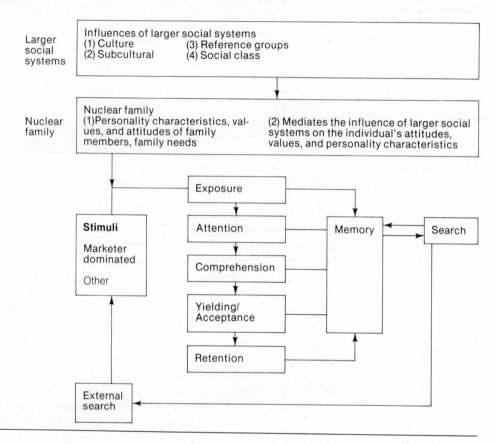

let's look at some of the most important structural characteristics of the family.

FAMILY STRUCTURE AND DYNAMICS

What is the structure of contemporary families? How is that structure changing? How does structure affect consumption? Are the developing realities of family structure a problem or an opportunity for marketing organizations? We looked at some of the basics concerning these questions in Chapter 3 but now we need to examine in more depth the structure and dynamics of families.

Marriages—To
Be or Not To Be?

Marriage is still in the cards for most consumers. Approximately 93 percent of American adults marry at some time in their lives.[28] However,

[28]A good review of this topic is found in William Lazer, "The 1980's and Beyond: A Perspective," MSU *Business Topics* (Spring 1977), 21-35.

Table 6.3
Distribution of Household Units by Type, 1940-1995

	Total Households (000s)	Family Households			Nonfamily HHs		Median Size of HHs (Persons)
		Total	Married Couples	Other Family	Total	Living Alone	
1940	34,949	90.1%	76.0%	14.1%	9.9%	7.7%	3.67
1950	43,554	89.2	78.2	11.0	10.8	9.1	3.37
1960	52,799	85.0	74.2	10.7	15.0	13.1	3.33
1970	63,401	81.2	70.5	10.7	18.8	17.1	3.14
1980	79,080	73.8	60.9	12.9	26.2	22.6	2.75
1985	88,565	72.6	58.9	13.7	27.4	23.6	2.58
1990	96,653	71.0	56.6	14.4	29.0	24.9	2.47
1995	103,856	69.6	54.5	15.1	30.4	26.0	2.39

Note: Based on Series II and Series B Census Projections.

Source: Commerce Department, Estimates from P-25, No. 805.

Americans are marrying at later ages and experiencing more divorces. Thus, at any point in time a higher proportion of households is composed of nonmarried individuals. Table 6.3 shows that the proportion of households composed of married couples was as high as 78.2 percent in 1950 but is projected to decline to 54.5 percent in 1995. In 1979, there were also 1.3 million households of two unrelated adults of the opposite sex, double the number at the beginning of the decade.

The median age at which people get married has increased substantially. Among males the median age at first marriage was 22.8 in 1960 but increased to 24.4 by 1980. For women, the median age increased from 20.3 to 22.1.[29] In spite of the increasing age, the number of marriages has increased in recent years—producing markets for housing, appliances, carpeting, furniture, and many other products. At current rates, however, 40 percent of all marriages will end in divorce and about 45 percent of the children born in the 1970s will spend part of their lives before 18 living in a one-parent home.[30] Marriage, while still the norm, has become somewhat more tenuous, as Figure 6.5 shows.

Do modern women want marriage, especially one with children? The Gallup Poll conducted a nationwide survey of women in the years 1975 and 1980 and found the opinions about the ideal life-style listed in Table 6.4.

How Many Babies?

Oscar Wilde once observed that "People who count their chickens before they are hatched act very wisely because chickens run around so absurdly that is is impossible to count them accurately." Perhaps that is true with children as well, although there are some difficulties in predict-

[29]U.S. Bureau of the Census, *Current Population Reports*, Series P-20, No. 349.
[30]Cheryl Russell, "Divorce and Other Facts of Life," *American Demographics* (December 1979), 40-41.

Figure 6.5
Modern Marriage

"I hope to."

Source: *The New Yorker* (February 1981), 101. Drawing by D. Reilly; © 1981 The New Yorker Magazine, Inc.

Table 6.4
Ideal Life-Style

	Ideal Life-style (Views of Women)	
	1975	1980
Married with children	76%	74%
With full-time job	32	33
With no full-time job	44	41
Married with no children	9	10
With full-time job	6	6
With no full-time job	3	4
Unmarried with full-time job	9	8
Not sure	6	8

Source: George Gallup, "Ideal Life-style for Women Is to Be Married, Have Children," (Chicago: Field Newspaper Syndicate, 1980). Reprinted by permission.

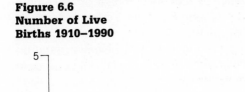

**Figure 6.6
Number of Live
Births 1910–1990**

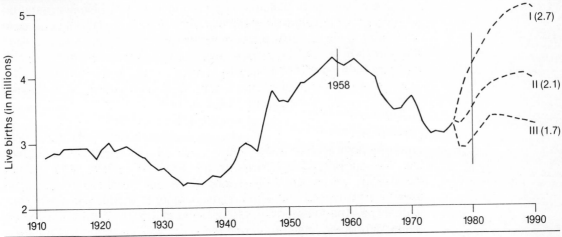

Source: Bureau of the Census, Statistical Abstract, No. 704, 25.

ing how many babies will be "hatched" and become the markets of the future.

You should carefully distinguish between fertility rate and birth rate when you are analyzing statistics concerning babies. The *fertility rate* is the number of *live* births per 1,000 population. The number of births in any year is determined by the fertility rate, which has' been *decreasing* dramatically in recent years, multiplied times the number cf women of child-bearing age, which is *increasing* dramatically during the 1980s.

It is easy to predict the number of women of child-bearing age but very difficult to predict the fertility rate. Thus, projections of births in the future—a critical statistic for planning purposes—are often made for different assumptions. The Census Bureau calls these Series I with an assumption of 2.7 children per woman, Series II with 2.1 children per women and Series III with 1.7 children per woman. You can see in Figure 6.6 what an enormous difference will occur in the number of births depending on what happens to future fertility.

Order Effects

One of the most significant aspects of births for marketers is the proportion of first-order (first-born) babies compared to higher-order (second, third, fourth, and so on) babies. Management Horizons estimates the first baby generates about $1,500 in retail sales but higher-order babies average only $600 in retail sales the first year. In 1960, only one child in four was first-born but in 1979 that figure was 43 percent and it is expected to be nearly 50 percent by 1990.

High-order effects increase the total economic impact of babies but some companies benefit more than others. Eastman Kodak benefits by first-order babies that cause happy parents to buy a camera and take massive quantities of pictures. Higher-order children, however, may be lucky to get one picture at graduation time. Families with only one child can afford to eat at better restaurants, buy wanted equipment (extension telephones in the children's room, expensive leisure equipment, new and better clothes instead of hand-me-downs).

The evidence suggests that birth rates of childbearing for young women and higher-order birth rates among older women will decline throughout the 1980s. To have one's first child at age 30 suggests fewer children per family but more dollars to spend on each child for a vast array of goods and services. It also suggests a slower-growing population, the possibility of ZPG, fewer people available to serve in the military in the future, less crime, fewer people to pay for social security benefits, lower unemployment rates, and a host of other economic and social consequences. The total fertility rate declined to 1.8 in 1978 from a record 3.8 in 1957. If the total fertility rate remains this low and there is no influx of immigrants, the US population will eventually begin to shrink.[31] In Canada, similar trends are occurring with Quebec experiencing the greatest decline in fertility of any province.

Another factor affecting births, of course, is abortions. The Alan Guttmacher Institute in New York reports that abortions increased from 744,000 in 1973 to 1,540,000 by 1979. The US rate of abortion—28.2 per 1,000 women—ranks about in the middle internationally. Canada's rate, 11.3 per 1,000 women is very low. Among the highest are Cuba with a rate of 52.1 and Bulgaria with a rate of 68.3.

Smaller Families

The net effect of these structural changes is to produce smaller families, requiring different sizes of food products, different sizes of homes, and many other changes in marketing programs. By 1990, more than 40 percent of American families will consist of only two persons. Another 22 percent will be three-person families.

The trend toward smaller families is a world-wide development. In a Gallup poll conducted in 23 countries, respondents in every country report they want small families (four or fewer children). Table 6.4 shows that the proportion wanting four or more is highest in the Phillipines. In the United States where data were collected over a longer period, the percentage wanting four or more children dropped from 41 percent in 1968 to only 11 percent in 1980, a plunge or 30 percentage points.[32] These attitudes have already led to declining birth rates in Western Europe. According to Common Market statistics, Europe had 20 percent of the world's people in 1800 but now has 9 percent and will have 4 percent

[31]Bryant Robey, "Fertility Fantasies, And a Few Facts," *American Demographics* (January 1981), 2.
[32]George Gallup, "Large Families Going Out of Style in U.S.," *The Gallup Poll* (Chicago: Field Enterprises, Inc., 1981).

**Table 6.5
Ideal Number of
Children**

| | (Percent Saying Four or More) | | |
	1975	1980	Change
Philippines	NA	25	−
Mexico	25	25	−
Brazil	44	21	−23
Venezuela	NA	21	−
Australia	29	18	−11
Great Britain	13	15	+2
Netherlands	*	14	−
Peru	NA	14	−
South Africa	NA	13	−
Finland	**	11	−
Norway	**	11	−
U.S.A.	18	11	−7
Japan	15	10	−5
Denmark	**	6	−
West Germany	5	6	+1
France	4	5	+1
Luxembourg	*	5	−
Sweden	**	5	−
Switzerland	NA	5	−
Austria	NA	4	−
Belgium	*	4	−
Italy	4	4	−
Portugal	NA	3	−

*The figure for the Benelux nations (Belgium, Netherlands, and Luxembourg) in the 1980 survey is 8 percent inclusive. The comparable figure in the 1975 survey is 5 percent.
**The figure for the Scandinavian nations (Denmark, Finland, Norway, and Sweden) in the 1980 survey is 8 percent. The comparable figure in the 1975 survey is 6 percent.

Source: George Gallup, "Large Families Going Out of Style in U.S.," The Gallup Poll (Chicago: Field Enterprises, Inc., 1981). Reprinted by permission.

in 2075, the year ZPG is expected in Europe. Of the 17 countries of Western Europe, only Ireland, Spain, Portugal and Greece have birth rates higher than the 2.1 required for replacement of a population.

It is no wonder that the Roman Meal Company recently introduced the *Roman Meal Half Loaf.* It contains only 10 to 12 slices of bread instead of 22 to 24 in a regular loaf. A marketing officer announced that, after demographic analysis, the company had concluded that a 20-ounce loaf contained too much bread for contemporary households.

Affluent Individuals

Individual households are worthy markets for many organizations even though their total household income is less than family households. In 1955, the average primary individual household had income only 28 percent of that of the typical family. In the 1970s, *per capita* income of the two types of households became equivalent and by 1985, the *per capita* income of individual households will be 60 percent *above* that of families. This means that marketing organizations that historically have been oriented toward a traditional family structure will have to be open to new requirements and potentials of the individual household.[33]

[33]John Smallwood and Ronald Ernst, *Distribution Demographics* (Columbus, Ohio: Management Horizons, 1975), 49.

Gray Power

Consumer analysts are paying increasing attention to older consumers—known variously as mature markets, senior citizens, or gray power. The demographic family trends described above will cause industrialized nations to become much older on average. You may want to look back to Chapter 3 to see the numbers of older consumers that can be expected in the future.

Older consumers tend to be careful shoppers. They have to be careful because inflation—the affliction of most industrialized societies—limits greatly the buying power of older consumers on fixed incomes. They also have the experience and ability to wait to find good value in their buying process. They may respond more to coupons and be willing to shift their buying to off-peak times for retailers if given an adequate incentive to do so.

Senior citizens use the mass media more than younger consumers and have less interpersonal contact. They may need special services such as delivery or telephone shopping but they are also more loyal to the firm that provides good service and value. Older consumers are more likely to be newspaper readers than are younger consumers.[34] Age-based conclusions about older consumers could change, however, if mandatory age retirement is abandoned in favor of health and competency standards, as many observers believe may happen.

Changing Roles of Women

Marketing managers have always been interested in women because of their importance in buying so many products. That interest has intensified in recent years because of greater numbers, improved purchasing and employment status, and changed roles.

The female population has been growing faster than the male population, primarily due to the higher survival rate of women. Life expectancy has been increasing faster for women than for men and women now live about eight years longer than men. It is expected that the total number of females will exceed the total number of males by 6.5 million in 1985 and 7.5 million in 2000.[35]

In 1960, there were only 1.232 million females enrolled in college but by 1980, the total was about five million, slightly more than the number of males in college. The principal reason the majority of college students is female is the greater number of women over 25 returning to campus compared to men over age 25.

The topic of feminine roles is one of great concern to consumer analysts and marketers. As you read this book, you might want to think how you as a dispassionate consumer analyst will approach this topic when you are asked to prepare such a report for use by an advertising

---

[34]L.W. Phillips and Brian Sternthal, "Age Differences in Information Processing: A Perspective on the Aged Consumer," *Journal of Marketing Research* (November 1977), 444-445.

[35]William Lazer and John Smallwood, "The Changing Demographics of Women," *Journal of Marketing* (July 1977), 14-22.

agency or some other organization. What roles are expected of contemporary women? How are those roles changing?

Feminine Research

The most significant development of recent years in the study of women is the recognition of *pluralism* as the reality of women's roles. At one time, market studies tended to classify consumer behavior as male or female but more often today the behavior of women will be further defined by subcategories. The most frequent classification of women is into working women (WW) defined as having a job for pay outside the home and nonworking women (NWW) or full-time housewife (FW) or homemaker. There are practical and philosophical problems with such labels and numerous variations are sometimes used.

Working or nonworking is not sufficiently detailed as a category for studying women's roles in the opinion of many consumer researchers. Further detail usually takes one of two forms. Either the categories of WW and NWW are subdivided or a scale is devised to measure a more basic attribute, such as feminism.

A typical scale used in consumer research is the Arnott scale of feminine autonomy. It contains ten items (such as the following) to which respondents indicate their agreement on a four-point scale:

1. The word "obey" should be removed from the marriage service. (+)

2. Girls should be trained to be homemakers, and boys for an occupation suited to their talents. (−)

3. Within their marriage, women should be free to withhold or initiate sexual intimacy as they choose. (+)

4. The husband should be regarded as the legal representative of the family group in matters of law. (−)[36]

Fortunately, there exists an excellent encyclopedia of tests and measures about feminism and related topics. This book by Beere provides many instruments of potential value to consumer researchers.[37]

Consumer research frequently focuses upon *working women* for more detailed classification. An example is the classification system used by Needham, Harper and Steers, a major advertising agency. Their studies classified women as "full-time homemaker"; but break working women into the further categories of "satisfaction-seeking" (SS) or women who work because they like to—career-oriented types who gain personal satisfaction from working, and "income seeking" (IS) or working women who work because they have to—women who are financially

---

[36]Catherine Arnott, "Husbands' Attitudes and Wives' Commitment to Employment," *Journal of Marriage and Family* (1972), 673-681; and Catherine Arnott, "Feminists and Antifeminists as 'True Believers'," *Sociology and Social Research* (1973), 300-306.

[37]Carole A. Beere, *Women and Women's Issues* (San Francisco: Jossey-Bass Publishers, 1979).

strapped. Other studies, such as the Yankelovich Monitor, indicate that about one out of three women is strongly committed to a career. They are more oriented toward working for self-realization, self-expression and personal fulfillment, and are more likely to be college educated.[38]

Feminine Roles

A *role* is what the typical occupant of a given position is expected to do in that position in a particular social context. A literature review of role theory by Wilson disclosed that much of the research on role theory deals with sex roles, often of women in the family and in their position as purchasing agents.[39]

The differences in feminine roles can be observed in a study by Venkatesh, who collected a large bank of life-style data about women, categorized on the basis of traditionalists, moderates, and feminists.[40] Feminists and moderates were younger than traditionalists and generally more educated and more likely to be employed full-time. More traditionalists labeled themselves as "housewives" and more feminists were likely to label themselves as "co-head of household."

From a large amount of data, Venkatesh was able to reduce the topics into ten factors. Space does not permit reproduction of all of them but two factors, "sex stereotyping" and "fashion and personal appearance" are displayed in Table 6.5. Look at the factor on sex stereotyping and you will see that responses to every statement are statistically significant between groups. Look at the fashion and appearance factor, however, and you will see that no statistically significant differences exist between groups of women in the study except one concerning beauty parlors.

This is important information for marketers because it indicates that on some topics, marketers must be very sensitive to different perceptions about what is bad or good that might be included in an advertisement. An ad appealing to feminists appearing in *Ms.* would properly show boys playing with dolls but the same illustration would have little appeal to traditionalists. Concerning fashion, however, about 90 percent of all types of women say, "I like to feel attractive." Ads with such an appeal are likely to cut across almost all types of women.

An advertisement for *the limited* is shown in Figure 6.7 appealing to women. Do women want to be thought of as career oriented or do they want to be sexually attractive? The copy and illustration of Figure 6.7 show how both appeals can be achieved. While the orientation is more to the WW, the appeal is universal.

If you were the account executive or creative director of an advertis-

---

[38]Rena Bartos, "What Every Marketer Should Know About Women," *Harvard Business Review* (May-June 1978), 73-85.

[39]David Wilson, "Role Theory and Buying-Selling Negotiations: A Critical Review," in Richard Bagozzi, (ed.), *Marketing in the 1980's* (Chicago: American Marketing Association, 1980), 118-121. Although Wilson's purpose in this review was not to focus upon women, his results serve nicely for the reader who wants a quick summary of consumer research about women's roles.

[40]Alladi Venkatesh, "Changing Roles of Women—A Life-Style Analysis," *Journal of Consumer Research* (September 1980), 189-197.

Table 6.6
Feminine Roles

Factor Analysis of Life-Style Variables

Extracted Factor	Percent in Each Group Who Agree with the Statements		
	Trad-tionalists	Moderates	Feminists
Sex stereotyping			
American advertisements picture a woman's place to be in the home.	38[a]	64	89[b]
American advertisements seem to have recognized the changes in women's roles.	48	33	22[b]
American advertisements depict women as sexual objects.	44	56	81[b]
American advertisements depict women as independent without needing the protection of men.	14	8	4[b]
I would like to see more and more young girls play with mechanical toys.	18	42	75[b]
I would like to see boys playing with dolls just the way girls do.	10	30	66[b]
Boys and girls should play with the same kind of toys.	30	64	80[b]
Fashion and personal appearance			
An important part of my life and activities is dressing smartly.	39	38	38
I like to feel attractive.	86	92	90
I would like to go to the beauty parlor as often as I can.	17	12	5[c]
I enjoy looking through fashion magazines to see what is new in fashions.	60	63	57
I like to do a lot of partying.	26	39	38
I love to shop for clothes	49	46	47

[a]Based on Chi-square tests results
[b]Significant at 0.01 level;
[c]Significant at 0.05 level.

Source: Alladi Venkatesh, "Changing Roles of Women—A Life-Style Analysis," *Journal of Consumer Research* (September 1980), 189–197. Reprinted by permission.

ing agency handling a household cleaning product, how would you prepare the ad? The advertising agency Needham, Harper and Steers did research to understand the role of the "diligent cleaner." What is he or she like? Exhibit 6.1 describes the results of their research. Perhaps this consumer has different role expectations than your own but if you were preparing the advertising campaign directed to this individual, how would you do it?

Women and Time
One of the most consistent findings about feminine roles is the time pressure which the working woman experiences. Working women have two jobs—household responsibilities plus their jobs in the marketplace. Studies show they have significantly less leisure time than either their husbands or than full-time homemakers.[41] This would suggest that working

[41]Marianne Ferber and Bonnie Birnbaum, "One Job or Two Jobs: The Implications for Young Wives," *Journal of Consumer Research* (December 1980), 263–271.

**Figure 6.7
Advertising to
Multiple Roles of
Women**

Source: Reprinted by permission of The Limited.

wives would buy more time-saving appliances, use more convenience foods, spend less time shopping and so forth. Actually, working wives and nonworking wives are similar in such behavior if income is the same, suggesting that widely held values and expectations—and perhaps guilts, traditions and so forth—affect women's behavior more than their employment status.

Exhibit 6.1 "The Diligent Cleaner"

The Diligent Cleaner's life is centered around her home and family. She has little involvement in community activities and has little interest in the world at large. The Women's Liberation Movement has passed her by and she firmly believes that a woman's place is in the home carrying out the traditional homemaking tasks.

She finds the complexities of today's world unsettling, and is conservative and authoritarian in her views. She feels powerless to control the events that shape her life and distrustful of those in power. She feels most secure within the confines of her home where she can maintain an orderly, if limited existence.

As one might expect, the Diligent Cleaner is not an easy going person. She is beset by many anxieties. She is very concerned about what other people think of her. Much of her behavior is aimed at pleasing others and avoiding their disapproval. Maintaining an attractive personal appearance, eliminating offensive body odor, and indulging her family are manifestations of this need for social approval, as is effective performance of housekeeping tasks. Maintaining a clean and spotless home is important to her as it serves as visible proof to herself and to others that she is a good wife and mother.

Another major source of anxiety is related to health. She is somewhat of a hypochondriac as evidenced by her concerns about food, air and water, her many physiological complaints and her heavy use of over-the-counter drugs. Dirt in her home is therefore perhaps feared not only as a cause for other's disapproval, but as a breeding ground for germs which could threaten her health and the health of her family. Germs can be particularly anxiety arousing because they are invisible. Even if the house looks clean, germs might still be present, and frequent cleaning is therefore required.

A heavy user of all types of cleaning products, she is likely to be attracted to those brands that promise to eliminate germs and odor as well as dirt, and is likely to be especially attracted to strong products that have a powerful odor or otherwise provide a visual or olfactory trace that indicates they have been used and are working.

Although she is having trouble making ends meet on her blue-collar husband's salary and constantly worries about money, she is unlikely to skimp when it comes to cleaning products, and is probably willing to pay more for any product that can better alleviate her anxieties.

Television is her primary source of entertainment and information and she can best be reached through this medium.

Source: "Life Style Profile of the Diligent Cleaner," reprinted by permission of Needham, Harper, and Steers Advertising, Inc.

Working women feel the pressure of too little discretionary time; but if they don't have more income, they find ways of coping with the problem which cause their behavior to be not too different from full-time homemakers.[42] As income of the two-earner family increases relative to the one-earner family, however, the husband and wife may purchase many things that increase convenience and time. Differences in store patronage and other buying decisions may be more meaningfully understood by looking at type of employment (professional versus nonprofessional, for example, or satisfaction seeking versus income seeking) to find the best explanations of behavior.[43]

Women and Advertising

For many years advertising portrayed women in limited, stereotyped roles. Generally, women were shown as purchasers of low unit-price items and as homemakers rather than career persons.[44]

How do women consumers react to ads which show mostly traditional roles? Wortzel and Frisbie investigated this topic and found only

---

[42]Myra Strober and Charles B. Weinberg, "Strategies Used by Working and Nonworking Wives to Reduce Time Pressures," *Journal of Consumer Research* (March 1979), 338-347.

[43]Suzanne McCall, "Meet the Workwife," *Journal of Marketing* (July 1977), 55-65; Mary Joyce and Joseph Guiltinan, "The Professional Woman: A Potential Market Segment for Retailers," *Journal of Retailing* (Summer 1978), 59-70; Rena Bartos, "The Moving Target: The Impact of Women's Employment on Consumer Behavior," *Journal of Marketing* (July 1977), 31-37.

limited differences in the preferred roles by consumers who were supporters of women's liberation movements and those who were not.[45] Duker and Tucker came to even stronger conclusions that advertisers who changed their appeals to be with it would, in fact, be appealing only to a small group of moderns rather than the larger group of consumers. They suggested, "Advertisers, especially those who look to the long run, should be cautious about confusing what might be considered alleged 'in vogue' attitudes with more deeply rooted value changes."[46]

Specific media choice can be influenced by feminist views however. Using the Arnott feminism scale described earlier, Venkatesh found that *Reader's Digest* is one of the most establishment-oriented magazines with high readership among traditionalists and moderates and much lower ranking among feminists. *Time* and *Newsweek* ranked highest among feminists along with the *New York Times*. The greatest difference was the case of *Ms.* with considerable readership among feminists, moderates exactly half-way in readership, and practically no readership among traditionalists.[47]

Changing Masculine Roles

The roles of men in families are also changing substantially. As women increasingly participate in the labor force and values shift in society, men are taking on new roles in consuming and purchasing products. In a survey of 1,000 American males reported in 1981 by Cunningham & Walsh, the New York advertising agency, more and more men could be observed as househusbands. The survey disclosed that 47 percent of men vacuum the house, 80 percent take out the garbage, 41 percent wash dishes, 37 percent make beds, 33 percent load the washing machine, 27 percent clean the bathroom, 23 percent dust, 23 percent dry dishes, 21 percent sort laundry, 16 percent clean the refrigerator and 14 percent the oven. Over half take part in regular shopping trips, suggesting that men are important targets for marketing activity for many types of household products. Even for a role so traditionally rooted in mother dominance, the feeding of a baby, it is possible to see recognition of the need for male roles. Figure 6.8 shows a creative effort of Gerber's baby food to involve Dad in the role of feeding the baby.

Family Life-Cycle

A summary construct for many variables of family structure is the *family life-cycle* (FLC). Although the concept has been used in the literature since 1931, it received its widest influence in marketing research as a

[44]Donald Sexton and Phyliss Habertman, "Women in Magazine Advertisements," *Journal of Advertising Research* (April 1974), 41-46; Ahmed Belkaoui and Janice Belkaoui, "A Comparative Analysis of the Roles Portrayed by Women in Print Advertisements: 1958, 1970, 1972," *Journal of Marketing Research* (May 1976).

[45]Larry Wortzel and J. M. Frisbie, "Women's Role Portrayal Preferences in Advertisements: An Empirical Study," *Journal of Marketing* (October 1974).

[46]Jacob M. Duker and Lewis Tucker, Jr., "Women's Libbers Versus Independent Women: A Study of Preferences for Women's Roles in Advertisements," *Journal of Marketing Research* (November 1977), 469-475.

[47]Alladi Venkatesh and Clint Tankersley, "Magazine Readership by Female Segments," *Journal of Advertising Research* (August 1979), 31-38.

**Figure 6.8
Advertising to
Multiple Roles
of Men**

We help Dad have a hand in Dale's feeding.

Dale is a breast feeding infant. But even though the breast milk of a well-nourished mother is normally a complete food, the adequacy of some of its nutrients, like vitamin C, is dependent on the mother's diet. To provide an extra margin of safety, the doctor has recommended the addition of vitamin C to Dale's diet. To get that added vitamin C, Dale's mother chose Gerber Apple Juice over vitamin drops. That way Dad could get involved in feeding. Like all Gerber Juices, Gerber Apple Juice is fortified with more than enough vitamin C to meet Dale's daily needs, and is full strength, 100% fruit juice with no sugar added.

At Gerber, we're proud to help Dad have a part in Dale's feeding, because we know that feeding Dale can be a rewarding part of being Dad.

Gerber
Babies are our business...
and have been for over 50 years.
Gerber Products Company, Fremont MI 49412

We've learned a lot about food because we care a lot about babies.

Source: Reprinted by permission of Gerber Products Company.

result of pioneering work by Wells and Gubar.[48] The most thorough study of how the concept affects consumer behavior is provided by Reynolds and Wells.[49]

[48]William D. Wells and George Gubar, "The Life Cycle Concept," *Journal of Marketing Research* (November 1966), 355-363.
[49]Fred D. Reynolds and William D. Wells, *Consumer Behavior* (New York: McGraw-Hill, 1977), Chaps. 3-7.

Over time, people pass through a series of stages in their lives. The behavior typically associated with each stage is described in Table 6.6, known as the family life-cycle. These stages are of the size described below (as of 1970) and are given the following labels:

1. Bachelor stage; young single males and females not living at home (8.2%).

2. Newly married couples; young, no children (2.9%).

3. Full nest I; young married couples with youngest child under six (24.2%).

4. Full nest II; young married couples with youngest child six or over (13.2%).

5. Full nest III; older married couples with dependent children (14.2%).

6. Empty nest I; older married couples, no children living with them, household head in labor force (5.5%).

7. Empty nest II; older married couples, no children living at home, household head retired (5.2%).

8. Solitary survivor in labor force (.02%)

9. Solitary survivor, retired (2.0%).

10. All other (23.3%).

These categories are evolving with the changing structure of the family. A modernized family life-cycle has been developed by Murphy and Staples which should be even more useful to consumer researchers in the future. The Murphy-Staples version of the FLC gives explicit condition to the rise in divorce, smaller size of families, and delayed age of marriage.[50]

The life-cycle affects consumer behavior in substantial ways. A simple and admittedly incomplete description of stages in the life-cycle is provided in Table 6.6. But it should provide an adequate background for understanding the kind of information that should be collected in a consumer analysis for a particular product or organization.

Life-cycle information is valuable for *market segmentation* strategies because of the variations in patterns of usage, amount of consumption, and media usage of the varying segments. FLC can also be *used to forecast demand* by combining expenditure levels by age group with estimates of future size and age structure of the family population. Bomball, Primeaux and Pursell have shown that the number of families in categories of life-cycle can be predicted accurately.[51]

The government collects extensive data on expenditures by age of family head. These data are shown in Table 6.7. Look at the families

[50]Patrick E. Murphy and William Staples, "A Modernized Family Life Cycle," *Journal of Consumer Research* (June 1979), 12-22.

[51]Mark Bomball, Walter Primeaux and Donald Pursell, "Forecasting Stage 2 of the Family Life Cycle," *Journal of Business*, vol. 48, 65-73.

**Table 6.7
Life-Cycle
Influences on
Buying Behavior**

Bachelor Stage

Although earnings are relatively low, they are subject to few rigid demands, so consumers in this stage typically have substantial discretionary income. Part of this income is used to purchase a car and basic equipment and furnishings for their first residence away from home—usually an apartment. They tend to be more fashion and recreation oriented, spending a substantial proportion of their income on clothing, alcoholic beverages, food away from home, vacations, leisure time pursuits, and other products and services involved in the mating game.

Newly Married Couples

Newly married couples without children are usually better off financially than they have been in the past and will be in the near future because the wife is usually employed. Families at this stage also spend a substantial amount of their income on cars, clothing, vacations, and other leisure time activities. They also have the highest purchase rate and highest average purchase of durable goods, particularly furniture and appliances, and other expensive items, and appear to be more susceptible to advertising in this stage.

Full Nest I

With the arrival of the first child, some wives stop working outside the home, and consequently family income declines. Simultaneously, the young child creates new problems that change the way the family spends its income. The couple is likely to move into their first home, purchase furniture and furnishings for the child, buy a washer, dryer, and home maintenance items, and purchase such products as baby food, chest rubs, cough medicine, vitamins, toys, wagons, sleds, and skates. These requirements reduce family savings and the husband and wife are often dissatisfied with their financial position.

Full Nest II

At this stage the youngest child is six or over, the husband's income has improved, and the wife often returns to work outside the home. Consequently, the family's financial position usually improves. Consumption patterns continue to be heavily influenced by the children as the family tends to buy food and cleaning supplies in larger sized packages, bicycles, pianos, and music lessons.

Full Nest III

As the family grows older, its financial position usually continues to improve because the husband's income rises, the wife returns to work or enjoys a higher salary, and the children earn money from occasional employment. The family typically replaces several pieces of furniture, purchases another automobile, buys several luxury appliances, and spends a considerable amount of money on dental services and education for the children.

Empty Nest I

At this stage the family is most satisfied with their financial position and the amount of money saved because income has continued to increase, and the children have left home and are no longer financially dependent on their parents. The couple often make home improvements, buy luxury items, and spend a greater proportion of their income on vacations, travel, and recreation.

Empty Nest II

By this time the household head has retired and so the couple usually suffers a noticeable reduction in income. Expenditures become more health oriented, centering on such items as medical appliances, medical care products that aid health, sleep, and digestion, and perhaps a smaller home, apartment, or condominium in a more agreeable climate.

The Solitary Survivor

If still in the labor force, solitary survivors still enjoy good income. They may sell their home and usually spend more money on vacations, recreation, and the types of health-oriented products and services mentioned above.

The Retired Solitary Survivor

The retired solitary survivor follows the same general consumption pattern except on a lower scale because of the reduction in income. In addition, these individuals have special needs for attention, affection, and security.

whose head is aged 65 or over, for example, compared to those under age 25. Their family income is approximately the same but the budget spent for food at home is 15.17 percent for the older families, compared to only 8.26 percent for younger families. Similarly, the proportion of budget spent for fuel and utilities is 5.28 percent for families over age 65 but only 2.83 percent for younger families. Younger families, however, spent 7.05 percent of their budget on clothing while older families spent only 4.57 percent. Finally, FLC information can be helpful to consumer analysts with a *social welfare concern* as a tool to understand needs of consumers as they change through life.[52]

Family Dynamics and Market Opportunity

A careful analysis of family structure and dynamics can lead to market opportunities for innovative marketing organizations. Such analysis might lead to smaller portions in packaged food products for either young markets or the rapidly expanding senior citizen market. Furniture and appliances might be designed for smaller living quarters and the need for smaller capacity. Baby boutiques—such as Mothercare, a British firm expanding on a worldwide basis—can merchandise high-quality products for the first-order baby boom. Stores may change their hours and perhaps delivery services for the increases in individual households and employed women. More exciting apparel and leisure facilities may be developed to fit the lifestyles of premarriage independent singles, single-again, or recycled families.

FAMILY DECISION MAKING AND ROLE STRUCTURE

Families are important in two basic ways. First, they *shape and influence* the individual consumer's self-concept, personality, evaluative criteria, attitudes and other behavioral patterns. Second, families *function as the decision-making unit* in the purchase of many goods. The first function is certainly important but will not be discussed now because when you look at individual behavior in depth in later chapters, you will be, in effect, studying the effects of family influences.[53]

We will focus in the remaining part of this chapter on how families make buying and consuming decisions as a unit. A lot of research on this topic has occurred in recent years and we will only be able to examine the most important findings. If you want to go into more depth, good guides to the literature are available by Jenkins[54] and Burns and Granbois.[55]

---

[52]Ronald W. Stampfl, "The Consumer Life Cycle," *Journal of Consumer Affairs* (Winter 1978), 209-219.

[53]For a discussion on the changing impact of the socialization process, see Barbara Laslett, "Family Membership, Past and Present," *Social Problems* (1978), 476-490.

[54]Roger Jenkins, "Contributions of Theory to the Study of Family Decision-Making," in Jerry Olson, (ed.), *Advances in Consumer Research*, VII (Ann Arbor: Association for Consumer Research, 1980), 207-211.

[55]Alvin Burns and Donald Granbois, "Advancing the Study of Family Purchase Decision Making," in Olson, Advances in Consumer Research, 221-226.

Table 6.8
Percentage of Family Budget Expended on Product
Categories by Age of Family Head

	Total	Under 25	25-34	35-44	45-54	55-64	65 & over
Family Income	11,802	6,855	12,044	14,515	15,645	13,080	6,841
1. *Food at Home*	11.68%	8.26%	9.61%	13.29%	11.70%	10.98%	15.17%
2. *Tobacco*	1.08	1.33	1.13	1.10	1.09	1.05	.90
3. *Fuel and Utilities*	3.63	2.83	3.22	3.62	3.36	3.66	5.28
Gas, Total	.80	.63	.70	.80	.72	.79	1.26
Gas, Piped	.66	.52	.60	.65	.61	.64	.97
Gas, Bottled	.14	.11	.10	.14	.11	.14	.28
Electricity	1.39	1.30	1.39	1.42	1.26	1.29	1.79
Gas and Electricity	.39	.31	.33	.39	.35	.50	.44
Fuel Oil	.47	.26	.32	.40	.46	.51	.92
Other Fuel	.04	.02	.02	.04	.04	.04	.10
Water/Trash	.54	.32	.46	.53	.53	.53	.78
4. *House Furnishings*	3.90	5.44	4.81	4.35	3.39	2.94	3.28
Textiles	.46	.46	.50	.50	.43	.41	.50
Furniture	1.24	1.98	1.69	1.52	1.02	.73	.82
Floor Coverings	.40	.28	.42	.45	.37	.36	.42
Major Appliances	.80	1.25	1.02	.87	.64	.61	.72
Televisions	.40	.80	.47	.36	.34	.32	.41
Small Appliances	.08	.10	.09	.08	.08	.08	.08
Housewares	.08	.14	.09	.09	.08	.07	.05
Miscellaneous	.43	.44	.53	.48	.43	.37	.28
5. *Clothing*	5.68	7.05	6.15	6.47	5.60	4.65	4.57
Male	1.88	2.22	2.14	2.33	1.92	1.44	1.05
Female	2.74	2.90	2.68	3.16	2.77	2.36	2.59
Children	.14	.42	.29	.12	.10	.05	.01
Dry Cleaning	.67	1.26	.80	.60	.55	.58	.69
Materials/Services	.24	.24	.24	.26	.25	.21	.22
6. *Vehicle Purchases*	6.22	11.15	6.64	5.98	6.48	5.78	3.86
7. *Vehicle Operation*	6.52	9.21	6.59	6.48	6.59	6.18	5.64
Gasoline	3.13	4.38	3.28	3.24	3.17	2.90	2.41
Other	3.38	4.83	3.31	3.23	3.42	3.29	3.22
8. *Reading*	.41	.44	.47	.42	.37	.37	.46
9. *Education*	.89	.50	.50	.87	1.68	.91	.14
Private	.53	.22	.34	.60	.94	.53	.06
Public	.36	.28	.17	.27	.73	.37	.08
10. *Gifts/Contributions*	3.66	1.59	2.11	3.13	3.47	4.56	7.38

Source: Authors' calculations based upon 1973 data from "Consumer Expenditure Survey Series; 1973," (Washington D.C.: U.S. Department of Labor, Bureau of Labor Statistics, Report 455-2, 1976), Table 4b.

Family decision-making and role-structure studies were initially conducted mostly by sociologists. In recent years, consumer researchers have added to this literature. Ordinarily such studies are directed to questions such as, What is the relative influence of various family members in the purchase process? Do husbands or wives exert more influence? How does this vary by product, life-cycle and decision style? How is decision making impacted by changing sex roles? How do families search for and process information? What is the role of children? What happens when the motives, attitudes and evaluative criteria of family members conflict? How are these conflicts resolved and what is the nature of the conflict process? What happens when they are not resolved? What research methods are appropriate for studying families? All of these questions are intriguing for consumer analysts.

It is difficult to overstate the importance of the family in understanding how people buy and use products. After reviewing the literature on this topic, Davis concluded:

Major items of consumer spending such as food, shelter, and transportation are often jointly "consumed." A husband may buy a station wagon, given the reality of having to transport four children, *despite* his strong preference for sports cars. Husbands wear ties, underwear, and socks, yet the purchase of these products is often made by wives. A housewife bases product and brand decisions to some extent on orders or requests from family members and on her judgment of what they like or dislike and what is "good for them." Even preferences for products individually consumed are likely to be influenced by feedback from members of the family—e.g., "Gee, Mom! That dress makes you look fat," or "I like the smell of that pipe tobacco." The number of products that an individual always buys for individual consumption must certainly represent a very small proportion of consumer expenditures.[56]

A problem exists for consumer researchers because although most purchase decisions are *family decisions*, most research about consumer behavior has been conducted with *individuals*. It hardly should be expected that an individual's attitudes, intentions, and other variables will always coincide or even be correlated very highly with those of the family. Yet most of the research literature implicitly makes such an assumption. Even the model in this book is a model of individual decision making, giving little more explicit recognition to the problem than that the family influences individual decisions. Sheth has attempted to resolve this problem with a model of family buying, shown in Figure 6.9. This model is gaining more use in consumer research and is valuable as an attempt to translate a model of individual buying behavior into a model of family buying behavior. You should look at Figure 6.9 care-

[56]Harry L. Davis, "Decision Making within the Household," *Journal of Consumer Research* (March 1976), 241-260, at 241. Reprinted by permission.

Figure 6.9
Sheth's Model of Family Buying

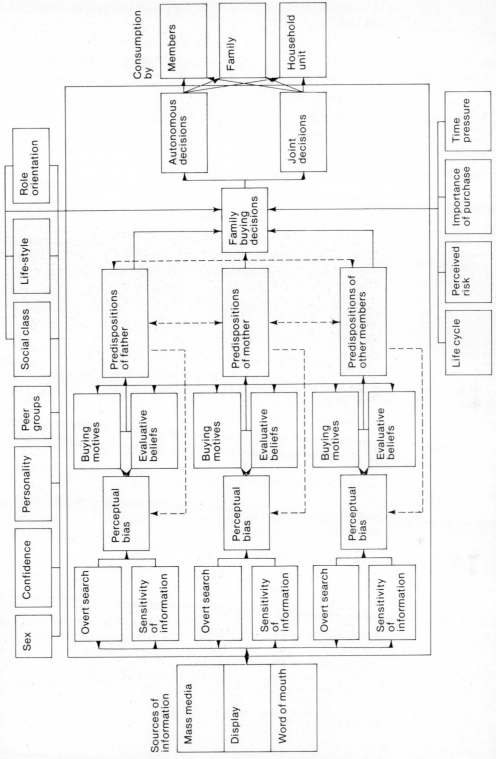

Source: "Sheth's model of family buying," pp. 22-23, in *Models of Buyer Behavior* by Jagdish N. Sheth. Copyright © 1974 by Jagdish N. Sheth. By permission of Harper & Row, Publisher, Inc.

fully and you may want to look at the supporting materials for the model as well.[57]

Types of Decision Making

The influence of family members on decisions of the family is a continuum. It is often convenient to use role-structure categories, however, such as the following:

1. *Autonomic*, when an equal number of decisions is made by each spouse, but each decision is individually made by one spouse or the other,

2. *Husband dominant*,

3. *Wife dominant*, and

4. *Syncratic*, when most decisions are made by both husband and wife.

In marketing research, simpler categories are often used such as "husband more than wife," "wife more than husband," "both husband and wife," or simply "husband only," "wife only," or "children only." The more complex role-structure categories are shown in Figure 6.10, based upon research by Davis and Rigaux.[58]

What Causes Influence in the Family?

Who has the influence or power in a family? A number of theories and empirical studies have attempted to answer this question. Some focus on *influence* in decision making and other focus on *power*. Power suggests that there is a *conflict* situation and power is needed to win out over another.

Conflict resolution involves three possible strategies; problem solving, bargaining and persuasion. *Problem solving* involves gathering more information before making a decision, family discussion of the problem, and having the family member most knowledgeable in the area make the decision. *Bargaining* involves the promise of future consideration to the family member agreeing to a choice or delaying of the decision. *Persuasion* strategies involve forming of a coalition by two or more family members in order to convince an individual to agree to a choice or exertion of authority by a family member.[59]

Sociocultural Influences

All societies have role specifications for men and women. Anthropological studies reveal differences between cultures of these role specifications and thus, within a society, male-female roles will vary by ethnic

[57]Jagdish N. Sheth, *Models of Buyer Behavior* (New York: Harper & Row, 1974), 17-33.

[58]Harry Davis and Benny Rigaux, "Perception of Marital Roles in Decision Processes," *Journal of Consumer Research* (June 1974), 51-61.

[59]Michael Belch, George Belch and Donald Sciplimpaglia, "Conflict in Family Decision Making: An Exploratory Investigation," in Olson, loc. cit., 475-479.

variables, as well as social class and other variables. Since sociocultural variables—such as employment of wives, income, location—change over time, the logical conclusion is that role structures of families will evolve in response to such changes. The Deacon and Firebaugh model is a systems framework for analyzing how a family manages itself to meet its internal needs in response to changing external requirements of the society in which the family operates.[60]

Hempel and Tucker found that family decision making regarding financial affairs is affected by changing sociocultural conditions. When changes occur in the external environment such as inflation, recession, or changing interest rates, previous specialized decision making becomes unstable and couples return to more joint decision making. When a family places more emphasis on socioeconomic status, financial decisions are more likely to be shared. Shared decision making also increases as the wife's commitment to a career increases.[61] Most studies found considerable variation in decision-making influence over the family life-cycle.

Resource Contribution

A popular explanation of influence or power in family decision making is the relative *resource-contribution* hypothesis. This theory suggests that the greater the relative contribution of an individual, the greater the influence in decision making. For example, the spouse who has higher income, higher occupational prestige, or higher social status, will have more decision-making authority or power in the household.

Least Interested Partner

A related explanation as to which member possesses the influence in family decisions is the *least-interested-partner* hypothesis. It focuses not on the value to each spouse of the resources contributed by the other, but on the value placed on these resources outside the marriage. The greater the difference between the value to the wife of the resources contributed by her husband and the value to the wife of the resources she might earn outside the existing marriage, the greater the influence of the husband in decision making.

Connectedness

The amount of family decision making may also be influenced by the connectedness of the social network of the family, the degree to which

[60]Ruth Deacon and Francile Firebaugh, *Home Management: Context and Concepts* (Boston: Houghton-Mifflin, 1975).

[61]Donald Hempel and Lewis Tucker, "Issues Concerning Family Decision Making and Financial Services," in Olson, 216-220. Also see Donald Hempel, "Family Role Structure and Housing Decisions, in M. J. Slinger, (ed.), *Advances in Consumer Research* (Association for Consumer Research, 1975), 71-80; Robert Ferber and Lucy Lee, "Husband-Wife Influence in Family Purchasing Behavior," *Journal of Consumer Research* (June 1974), 43-50, and John Scanzoni, "Changing Sex Roles and Emerging Decisions in Family Decision Making," *Journal of Consumer Research* (1977), 185-188.

the husband and wife have the same friends and interests. If a family has low mobilitiy, lives in a fairly homogeneous neighborhood and the husband is in the working class, the family will possess a high degree of connectedness. Such a family is likely to have less shared decision making.

Of these three hypotheses, the least-interested-partner hypothesis seems to be the most powerful. It explains as much variation in family role structures as the relative-contributions hypothesis and, in addition, it can accommodate the changing patterns of family-member interaction that occur over the life-cycle and in a changing sociocultural environment. However, all of these hypotheses are limited explanations.

Type of Product

The degree of joint decision making varies considerably from product to product. You probably noticed that when you examined Figure 6.10. The extent of joint decision making tends to increase as the price of the product increases. In the purchase of lower-price products, there is generally a tendency for purchase decisions to be delegated to the husband and wife according to their respective skills and knowledge about that product.

Role differentiation by product category has been clearly shown in numerous marketing studies. The husband was found to be definitely dominant in 69 percent of the decisions of when to buy an automobile, but decreased to 16 percent in considering when to buy furniture in a study by Shuptrine and Samuelson, replicating earlier research by Davis.[62] In another replication study, variations in role structure by product category were investigated over time. In this study it was found that between 1955 and 1973, family decision making for some products (groceries and life insurance) had become more specialized but that for other products (housing and vacation spots) the trend was toward egalitarianism between spouses.[63] Woodside found dominance in the marital decision-making process to vary significantly across eight product categories and found the concept of power, discussed above, useful in explaining differences. He found that decisions for lawnmowers and beer tend to be highly dominated by the husband; while automobiles, gardening supplies and television sets appear to be more moderately dominated by the husband. Wives tend to dominate the purchase decisions for cheese more than they do for rugs or washing machines.[64]

Wortzel mentions that whether a product is low involvement or high involvement is a factor to be considered in analyzing family decision

[62]F. K. Shuptrine and G. B. Samuelson, "Dimensions of Marital Roles in Consumer Decision Making: Revisited," *Journal of Marketing Research* (February 1976), 87-91; Harry L. Davis, "Dimensions of Marital Roles in Consumer Decision Making," *Journal of Marketing Research* (May 1970), 168-177. Also see F. K. Shuptrine and G. B. Samuelson, "Automobiles and Furniture: Who Decides?" *Business and Economic Review*, vol. 21 (June 1975), 23-27.

[63]Isabella Cunningham and Robert Green, "Purchasing Roles of the U.S. Family, 1955 and 1973," *Journal of Marketing* (October 1974), 61-81.

[64]Arch Woodside, "Dominance and Conflict in Family Purchasing Decisions," *Association for Consumer Research Proceedings* (1972), 650-659.

Figure 6.10
Marital Roles in 25
Decisions

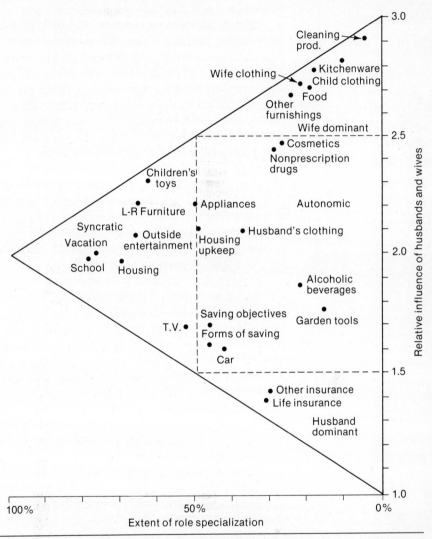

Source: Harry L. Davis and Benny P. Rigaux, "Perception of Marital Roles in Decision Processes," *Journal of Consumer Research*, vol. 1 (June 1974), 57. Reprinted by permission.

making.[65] It is probable that involvement will become more of an issue in such studies in the future.

Decision Stage Influences

The most valuable analysis of family influences for marketers may be on the basis of stages of the decision-making process. For example, the husband may recognize the problem while the wife engages in external

[65]Lawrence Wortzel, "Marital Roles & Typologies as Predictors of Purchase Decision Making for Everyday Household Products: Suggestions for Research," in Bagozzi, *Marketing in the 1980s*, 212-215.

search, with both the husband and the wife evaluating alternatives and the wife actually purchasing a specific brand.

One of the most thorough studies of role structure through the decision-making process is reported by Woodside. For various products, he included questions on who brought up the idea of purchasing the product; discussion of the purchase with friends, neighbors, relatives; obtaining information from mass media; obtaining information from stores (dealers); style or type decisions; who visited stores or dealer showrooms; who selected the specific retail outlet to purchase; who made the actual purchase; and who, if anyone, experienced dissatisfaction.[66]

For housing decisions, considerable variation has been found to exist in role structure and stages of the decision. Hempel found that husbands are more likely to be involved as the initiator of the home-buying process but the roles are reversed for the search task. Husbands were more involved in decisions concerning mortgage, price, and when to buy, while wives were more involved in decisions regarding neighborhood and house style.[67] Similar conclusions about housing decisions were reported by Munsinger, Weber, and Hansen.[68]

Variations in spouse influence across the stages of a decision may be most clearly seen by looking at Figure 6.11 and comparing it with Figure 6.10. Davis and Rigaux identified three stages or phases of the family decision-making process.[69] Phase I was problem recognition. Phase II was a search for information and Phase III was the final decision. Comparison of the two figures shows that marital roles vary throughout these three phases of the decision process. The authors suggest a number of marketing implications. For example, in the advertising of alcoholic beverages to autonomic decision makers, it would be more justifiable to develop two campaigns—one stressing husband-oriented appeals and the other wife-oriented appeals—rather than to use one campaign that tries to mix the two. Implications for the timing of messages would require additional information about the length of the decision span from problem recognition to final decision, but perhaps an airline attempting to encourage families to take winter vacations would find decision spans of several months. Such an organization might use a joint campaign during September stressing the idea of taking a vacation rather than consuming other forms of leisure, followed by individual campaigns (directed to husband and wives separately) during October which describe alternative vacation plans, and finally, a joint campaign during November and December which tries to convince couples that now is the time to make the final decision.[70]

Some recent work in analysis of family decisions involves an attempt

[66]Arch G. Woodside, "Effects of Prior Decision-Making, Demographics and Psychographics on Marital Roles for Purchasing Durables," in M. J. Slinger, *Advances*, 81-92.

[67]Hempel, "Family Buying."

[68]Gary M. Munsinger, Jean E. Weber and Richard W. Hansen, "Joint Home Purchasing Decisions by Husbands and Wives," *Journal of Consumer Research*, (March 1975), 60-66.

[69]Davis and Rigaux, *Perception of Marital Roles*.

[70]Ibid, p. 60.

**Figure 6.11
Changes in Marital
Roles between
Phase II and Phase
III**

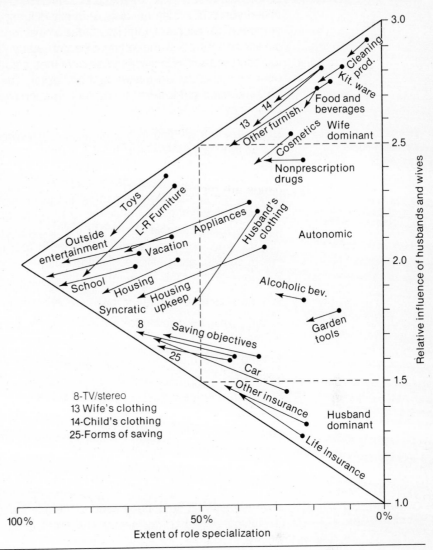

8-TV/stereo
13 Wife's clothing
14-Child's clothing
25-Forms of saving

Source: Harry L. Davis and Benny P. Rigaux, "Perception of Marital Roles in Decision Processes," *Journal of Consumer Research,* vol. 1 (June 1974), 54. Reprinted by permission.

to understand how couples agree about evaluative criteria. The work of Curry and Menasco develops methods for analyzing the importance of attributes of a product. They found that rank order of attribute importance is more important than any metric property. This is encouraging for advertisers because messages directed to couples that attempt to increase each individual's weight for a particular attribute can be effective without having to promote strong changes in weights.[71]

[71]David Curry and Michael Menasco, "Some Effects of Differing Information Processing Strategies on Husband-Wife Decisions," *Journal of Consumer Research* (September 1979), 192-203.

RESEARCH METHODOLOGY FOR FAMILY DECISION STUDIES

When you prepare an analysis of family influences on buying or the consumption decisions of families, most of the research techniques will be similar to any other marketing-research study. There are a few unique aspects of family-decisions research that should be considered, however, in these last few pages of the chapter. The following issues should present some guidelines for conducting such research.

Decision-Process Framework

Role-structure studies in the past usually viewed purchasing as an act rather than a process and based findings on questions such as, Who usually makes the decision to purchase? or Who influences the decision? Yet the evidence discussed above indicates that the role and influence of family members varies by stage in the decision process. Consequently, meaningless answers are likely to result from single-act questions. An example of process methodology is provided in a study by Wilkes, who measured family influence in four stages—problem recognition, search, alternative evaluation (intention), and purchase or choice. His decision-process measures of influence included the following:

1. Who was responsible for initial problem recognition?

2. Who was responsible for acquiring information about the purchase alternatives?

3. Who made the final decision as to which alternative should be purchased?

4. Who made the actual purchase of the product?[72]

The research using this methodology produced better results than more global measures of influence. Additionally, husbands and wives within families were found to hold similar perceptions about their relative influence for a given phase of the decision process.

Questioning Techniques

Several methods have been used to identify the roles of family members in making purchase decisions. The most common approaches are as follows:

1. General questions about influence of the respondent and other members of the family.

2. Direct questions about specific decisions and activities.

3. Questions concerning how conflicts are resolved in the family.

4. Where there is a disagreement among family members, a comparison of the brand purchased and the brand preferred by family members.

5. Given a fixed imaginary income, the proportion of purchases sug-

---

[72]Rober E. Wilkes, "Husband-Wife Influence in Purchase Decisions—A Confirmation and Extension," *Journal of Marketing Research*, vol. 12 (May 1975), 224-227.

gested by each family member and the amounts of money other family members agree to spend on the items suggested by that individual.

Role-Structure Categories

The relevant role-structure categories to be included in a research project depend on the specific product or service under consideration. In many product categories only the husband and wife are involved. In this case a defensible approach is to measure the relative influence for each specific decision at each stage in the decision process.

Children are involved in many types of purchase situations, but the nature of their influence has often been ignored. For example, while it is well known that children influence cereal and soft-drink purchases, other areas of influence are not so well recognized, dog food being an example. For other products, children exert a passive influence in the sense that one of the spouses continues to buy brands until finding one that the children will consume. Many role-structure studies probably grossly underestimate the influence of children.

Respondent Selection

In measuring role structures, it is necessary to decide which member(s) of the nuclear family should be asked about the influence of family members in purchasing decisions. The respondent decision is important since the reported influence of family members often varies considerably depending on which family members are interviewed.

The most common approach is to interview wives, yet there is a disagreement concerning the extent to which their reports accurately report purchase influence. Some researchers have found a substantial or acceptable similarity between husbands' and wives' responses. But others have found that the percentage of couples whose responses agree is unacceptable, perhaps averaging only slightly more than 50 percent.[73]

Granbois and Summers found husbands' responses concerning purchase intentions to be better than wives' as predictors of total planned cost and number of items planned from joint responses; although wives predicted better for certain products such as appliances, home furnishings, and entertainment-equipment plans. They concluded that joint responses may be more desirable since they uncover more plans of the family.[74] This suggests that decisions about whether only one spouse can be interviewed or whether both must be interviewed are determined by the circumstances of a specific research project.

Interviewing

The sex of the interviewer or observer may influence the roles husbands and wives say they play in a purchase situation.[75] To overcome this bias,

[73]Robert Ferber, "On the Reliability of Purchase Influence Studies," *Journal of Marketing*, vol. 19 (January 1955), 225-232; John Scanzoni, "A Note on the Sufficiency of Wife Responses In Family Research," *Pacific Sociological Review*, vol. 8 (Fall 1965), 109-115.

[74]Donald H. Granbois and John O. Summers, "Primary and Secondary Validity of Consumer Purchase Probabilities," *Journal of Consumer Research,* vol. 1 (March 1975), 31-38; Donald H. Granbois and Ronald P. Willet, "Equivalence of Family Role Measures Based on Husband and Wife Data," *Journal of Marriage and the Family*, vol. 3 (February 1970), 68-72.

[75]William F. Kenkel, Sex of Observer and Spousal Roles in Decision-Making," *Marriage and Family Living*, vol. 23 (May 1951), 185-186.

Table 6.9
Influence Structure in the Vacation and Lodging Decisions Process

Subdecision: In What Proportion Did the Husband/Wife/Children Influence Your Family's Decision	Influence as Perceived by	Influence of			A Statistical Significance of Differences in Influence of			B Statistical Significance of Differences in Perceptions of	Influence of		C Statistical Significance of Differences in Influence of	D Statistical Significance of Differences in Perceptions of
		(1) Husband (H)	(2) Wife (W)	(3) Children (C)	H-W (1-2)	H-C (1-3)	W-C (2-3)	H-W (4-5)	(7) Husband (H)	(8) Wife (W)	H-W (7-8)	H-W (4-5)
(1) ...to take a vacation this year	(4) Husband	42.1	40.8	17.1	0.63	—ᵃ	—ᵃ	0.18 (H)	51.6	48.4	0.23	0.79 (H)
	(5) Wife	45.4	35.8	18.8	—ᵃ	—ᵃ	—ᵃ	0.02 (W)	52.1	47.9	0.12	0.08 (W)
	(6) Both	43.7	38.3	18.0	—ᵃ	—ᵃ	—ᵃ	0.49 (C)	51.9	48.1	0.08	—
(2) ...to take a vacation this summer	(4) Husband	41.7	38.5	19.9	0.27	—ᵃ	—ᵃ	0.29 (H)	52.4	47.6	0.07	0.79 (H)
	(5) Wife	44.4	35.6	19.9	—ᵃ	—ᵃ	—ᵃ	0.18 (W)	52.9	47.1	0.02	0.80 (W)
	(6) Both	43.0	37.1	19.9	—ᵃ	—ᵃ	—ᵃ	0.94 (C)	52.6	47.4	0.01	—
(3) ...concerning exactly when you take this vacation	(4) Husband	59.5	28.4	11.6	—ᵃ	—ᵃ	—ᵃ	0.82 (H)	57.1	43.0	—ᵃ	0.55 (H)
	(5) Wife	58.8	27.1	14.1	—ᵃ	—ᵃ	—ᵃ	0.19 (W)	61.4	38.6	—ᵃ	0.38 (W)
	(6) Both	59.2	28.0	12.8	—ᵃ	—ᵃ	—ᵃ	0.36 (C)	60.2	39.8	—ᵃ	—
(4) ...concerning the length of this vacation	(4) Husband	61.6	30.2	8.1	—ᵃ	—ᵃ	—ᵃ	0.69 (H)	59.1	40.9	—ᵃ	0.38 (H)
	(5) Wife	63.0	26.4	10.6	—ᵃ	—ᵃ	—ᵃ	0.19 (W)	61.4	38.6	—ᵃ	0.38 (W)
	(6) Both	62.3	28.3	9.3	—ᵃ	—ᵃ	—ᵃ	0.30 (C)	60.2	39.8	—ᵃ	—
(5) ...concerning the amount of money to be allocated to your vacation budget	(4) Husband	64.0	33.0	2.2	—ᵃ	—ᵃ	—ᵃ	0.57 (H)	65.1	34.9	—ᵃ	0.26 (H)
	(5) Wife	65.9	31.8	2.4	—ᵃ	—ᵃ	—ᵃ	0.71 (W)	62.1	38.0	—ᵃ	0.21 (W)
	(6) Both	64.9	32.4	2.3	—ᵃ	—ᵃ	—ᵃ	0.78 (C)	63.6	36.4	—ᵃ	—
(16) ...concerning the particular hotel/motel in which you are staying	(4) Husband	49.1	39.9	11.0	—ᵃ	—ᵃ	—ᵃ	0.38 (H)	55.0	45.0	0.01	0.89 (H)
	(5) Wife	46.4	48.8	12.8	0.09	—ᵃ	—ᵃ	0.74 (W)	54.8	43.2	0.01	0.89 (W)
	(6) Both	47.8	40.3	11.9	0.01	—ᵃ	—ᵃ	0.51 (C)	54.9	45.1	—ᵃ	—
(17) ...concerning the choice of your particular hotel room	(4) Husband	47.5	41.4	11.4	0.17	—ᵃ	—ᵃ	0.65 (H)	53.8	47.4	0.01	0.53 (H)
	(5) Wife	49.0	39.8	11.2	0.01	—ᵃ	—ᵃ	0.68 (W)	55.4	41.8	—ᵃ	0.52 (W)
	(6) Both	48.2	40.5	11.3	0.01	—ᵃ	—ᵃ	0.89 (C)	54.6	44.6	—ᵃ	—

Family Respondents (*n* = 234) — Couple Respondents (*n* = 306)

ᵃIndicates level of significance less than 0.01.

Source: Excerpted from Pierre Filiatrault and J. R. Brent Ritchie, "Joint Purchasing Decisions: Comparison of Influence Structure in Family and Cope Decision-Making Units," *Journal of Consumer Research* (September 1980), 131–140.

either self-administered questionnaires should be used or the sex of the observer should be randomly assigned to respondents.

There are many other considerations that could be mentioned in discussing research methodology about family decisions and role structure.[76] Perhaps the best way to see how these considerations are implemented, however, is to look at the example in Table 6.8 that addresses most of the issues discussed above. It is a decision-process study of vacation decisions by Filiatrault and Ritchie which measures the influence of the children as well as each parent, includes a wider variety of decision-making units, contains validity checks on the responses of an individual by asking for similar information from other family members, and employs a 100-point constant-sum scale that permits more sophisticated analyses than Likert scales.[77]

[76]Michael Heffring, "Measuring Family Decision Making: Problems and Prospects," in Richard Bagozzi, ed., *Marketing in the 1980s* (Chicago: American Marketing Association, 1980), 492–496.

[77]Pierre Filiatrault and J. R. Brent Ritchie, "Joint Purchasing Decisions: A Comparison of Influence Structure in Family and Couple Decision-Making Units," *Journal of Consumer Research* (September 1980), 131–140.

Summary

As a primary group, the family is perhaps the ultimate in face-to-face interaction, and from the individual consumer's point of view, it differs from larger reference groups in that these family members must satisfy their unique and joint consumption needs from a common and relatively fixed amount of financial resources. As a consequence of these and other factors, family influences affect individual personality characteristics, attitudes, evaluative criteria and consumption patterns; and these influences change as the individual proceeds through the family life-cycle.

Family demographic structures are of high importance in understanding consumption choices, and panel data indicate substantially different proportions of the family budget spent on various product categories. Other important trends in marriage patterns are developing in US markets. These include a new type of baby boom which is founded on an increasing proportion of first-order babies, later marriages, more affluent individual households, and an increase in female head-of-households. All of these create exciting opportunities for marketing organizations that are sensitive and adaptive to changing demographic characteristics of families.

Family role structures—or the behavior of nuclear family members at each stage in the decision-making process—are of fundamental importance to marketers. Types of role structures, determinants of role structures, and methods of measuring role structures were analyzed, thereby laying the foundation for the discussion of role structure on consumer decision processes in the remainder of the book.

Review and Discussion Questions

1. Define the following terms and assess their importance in consumer analysis: (a) reference group, (b) membership group, (c) aspirational group, (d) dissociative group, and (e) primary group.

2. In what ways are reference groups associated with adult socialization? Describe some examples of this that might affect consumer decisions.

3. Why is the concept of group norms of relevance to marketing strategists? How does informational compliance differ from normative compliance?

4. Explain the Homans equation of human exchange and critically assess its importance in understanding the formation of reference groups.

5. Assume that a large manufacturer of living room furniture has asked for an analysis of the term self-concept as it relates to his marketing problems. Outline your analysis of the relevance of the term.

6. What is meant by the term family? What type of family is most relevant in the study of consumer behavior?

7. From an individual's point of view, how does the family differ from larger reference groups?

8. According to the text, a family is a mediating social system. What does this mean and of what importance is it?

9. Many students of consumer behavior maintain that the family rather than the individual should be the unit of analysis. What are the advantages and disadvantages of using the family as the unit of analysis?

10. In a given purchase situation, assuming that the motives of other family members are operative, how would marketing strategy differ, depending on whether the motives of other family members are compatible with an individual's motives? Using an actual product of your own choice, compare and contrast the types of marketing strategies that could be used when motive compatibility prevails as opposed to when it does not.

CHAPTER 7

LIFE–STYLE RESEARCH AND MARKETING STRATEGY

How would you respond to the following statements? Consider each and decide whether you would agree or disagree.

1. A woman's place is in the home.

2. Generally speaking, women should not have positions of authority over men.

3. Liquor is a curse on American life.

4. If it was good enough for my mother, it is good enough for me.

5. I usually stay at home on Saturday night.

6. Premarital sex is immoral.

7. Sex is more important to men than it is to women.

8. To buy anything, other than a house or car, on installment credit is unwise.

If you agree or agree strongly with most of the above statements, you probably would be classified by your life-style as Middle America. If you disagree with these statements more than most people who are Middle America, you would be in a different life-style segment. Consider further how you would respond to the following questions:

1. I get more satisfaction from my job or other outside activities than I do from being a housewife.

2. The use of marijuana should be made legal.

3. A husband and wife should not conceive more than two children.

4. My idea of housekeeping is once over lightly.

5. I like to go to parties where there is lots of music and talk.

6. I generally have sex three or more times per week.

7. I will probably have more money to spend next year than I have now.

8. I buy many things with a credit card or charge card.

If you agree or strongly agree with most of the above statements, however, you are more likely to be classified as a Younger Trendsetter.

In the study from which these statements are excerpted, about 44 percent of women were classified as Middle America and about 25 percent were classified as Younger Trendsetters. Another group of 20 percent were Middle-Age Affluents, and about 11 percent were Older Sophisticates.[1] This is an example of "life-style research." The theory and techniques involved in life-style research as well as their application to the development of marketing strategy are the concern of this chapter.

LIFE-STYLE CONCEPTS AND MEASURES

Life-styles can be defined as the *patterns in which people live and spend time and money.* The concept of life-style has become widely diffused in the marketing literature and among marketing practitioners even though its use was not common until about 1969 or 1970. To some degree, the term *life-style* is an outgrowth of the concept known as personality and also is related to research that was done in the 1950s called motivation research. Life-style research also yields many of the kind of insights described in Chapter 5 as social class and is especially similar to the social class studies of Pierre Martineau and Lloyd Warner.

The process of life-style influence on consumer decisions is shown in Figure 7.1. Life-styles are learned by individuals as the result of many influences such as culture, social class, reference groups, and the family. More specifically, however, life-styles are derivatives of a consumer's personal value system and personality. Thus, there is great overlap in meaning among the terms values, personality, and life-styles. Life-style can be considered a derivative concept combining the influences of personality and social values that have been internalized by an individual. The theory of life-styles is based upon a theory of human behavior proposed by George Kelly,[2] which states that people try to predict and control their lives. To do this, people form constructs or patterns to construe the events happening around them and use such constructs to interpret, conceptualize, and predict events. Some persons will have constructs or patterns for interpreting their universe different from other individuals—accounting for differences in life-styles. Kelly noted that this construct system is not only personal but it is also continually changing in response to a person's need to conceptualize cues from the changing environment to be consistent with one's personality.

People develop their set of constructs *to minimize incompatibilities or inconsistencies,* which is why a person who agrees with the statement "I buy many things with a credit card" is also likely to agree with the statement, "I will probably have more money to spend next year." Although less obvious, perhaps, this construct theory also explains why

---

[1]David T. Kollat, *Profile V Survey of American Households* (Columbus: Management Horizons, Inc., 1976).

[2]George A. Kelly, *The Psychology of Personal Constructs,* vol. 1 (New York: W.W. Norton & Co., 1955). The following discussion is drawn heavily from Fred Reynolds and William Darden, "Construing Life Style and Psychographics," in William D. Wells, (ed.), *Life Style and Psychographics* (Chicago: American Marketing Association, 1974), 71-96.

**Figure 7.1
Life-Style
Influences on
Consumer
Decisions**

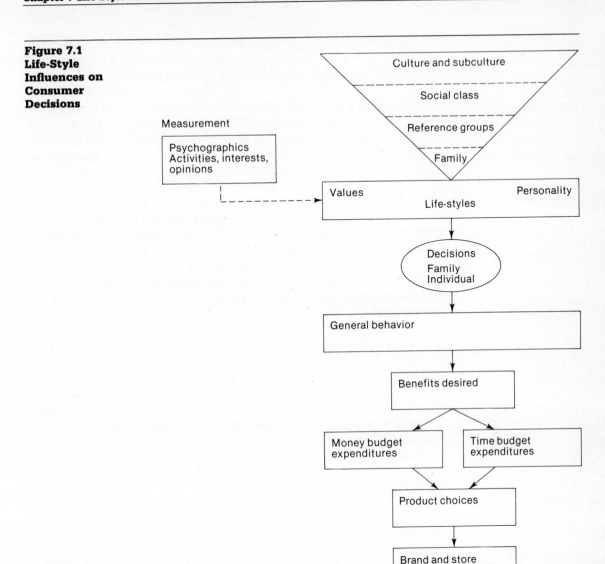

the same person is likely to agree with the statements, "A husband and wife should not conceive more than two children," and "The use of marijuana should be made legal." Only a limited part of a person's life-style is visible or measurable by the consumer researcher, but from that portion that is measured, conclusions are made about their type or overall pattern. The failure to comprehend fully or measure the whole life-style may account for apparent inconsistencies in a person's style of life or pervasiveness in the person's personality. This, of course, complicates prediction of consumer choices related solely to life-style measures.

Psychographics

Psychographics is the principal technique used by consumer researchers as an *operational measure of life-style* as shown in Figure 7.1. A function of psychographics is to provide *quantitative measures* of consumer life styles, in contrast to soft or qualitative research from focused group interviews, depth interviews, and similar techniques.

In reaction to the small samples of most qualitative research, consumer analysts previously tried to explain consumers' life patterns in terms of demographics—income, education, place of residence, and so forth. While demographics are very important in explaining consumer behavior—because they define and constrain the life patterns that are possible for most people—they do not go far enough. The concept and name of psychographics were originated by Demby to describe a technique that added the richness of the behavioral and social sciences to demographics.[3]

The term psychographics has come to mean about the same as AIO measures and will be used interchangeably in this discussion. AIOs refer to measurements of activities, interests, and opinions.[4] Keep in mind when reading the literature in this field that some people use the term *activities and attitudes*[5] rather than AIO measures and sometimes AIO is used to mean *attitudes,* interests, and opinions. In the rest of this book, however, the term AIO will be used to mean activities, interests, opinions, the same as the term psychographics. Definitions of the three components have been formulated by Reynolds and Darden as follows:

An *activity* is a manifest action such as viewing a medium, shopping in a store, or telling a neighbor about a new service. Although these acts are usually observable, the reasons for the actions are seldom subject to direct measurement.

An *interest* in some object, event, or topic is the degree of excitement that accompanies both special and continuing attention of it.

An *opinion* is a verbal or written "answer" that a person gives in response to stimulus situations in which some "question" is raised. It is used to describe interpretations, expectations, and evaluations—such as beliefs about the intentions of other people, anticipations concerning future events, and appraisals of the rewarding or punishing consequences of alternative courses of action.[6]

---

[3]Emanuel Demby, "Psychographics and from Whence It Came," in Wells, *Life Style,* 11-30.

[4]William Wells and Doug Tigert, "Activities, Interests and Opinions," *Journal of Advertising Research* vol. 11 (August 1971), 27-35; and Joseph T. Plummer, "Life Style Patterns and Commercial Bank Credit Card Usage," *Journal of Marketing,* vol. 35 (April 1971), 35-42.

[5]Thomas P. Hustad and Edgar A. Pessemier, "The Development and Application of Psychographic Life Style and Associated Activity and Attitude Measures," in Wells, *Life Style* (1974), 33-70.

[6]Reynolds and Darden, "Construing Life Style," 87.

When researchers use AIO measures, variables such as income, life-cycle, education and other demographics are also included. Plummer describes variables typically included in life-style research as:

. . .measures of people's activities in terms of (1) how they spend their time; (2) their interests, what they place importance on in their immediate surroundings; (3) their opinions in terms of their view of themselves and the world around them; and (4) some basic characteristics such as their stage in life cycle, income, education, and where they live.[7]

General and Specific AIOs

Two basic types of AIO statements are used in life-style research. One type—probably the most common—uses general life-style items that are intended to determine the overall patterns of living or basic constructs that affect a person's activities and perceptual processes. Examples of such statements would include those given in the opening paragraphs of this chapter. General statements allow the consumer researcher to define overall patterns such as satisfaction with life, family orientation, price consciousness, self-confidence, religious beliefs, and so forth.

The specific approach to life-style research includes items that measure product-related activities, interests and opinions. This approach may include such items as attitudes toward the product class or brands, frequency of use of a product or service, media in which information is sought, and so forth. Frequently, product-specific AIO statements relate to the *benefits desired* which result from more general behavior. (Refer to Figure 7.1.)

Current research practice often includes both general and specific AIO statements in the same study. In a survey of consumer attitudes toward health care issues, for example, the following general statements were included, accompanied by an agree-disagree scale:

1. I usually have a good tan each year.

2. It seems that I am sick a lot more than my friends are.

3. I generally approve of abortion if a woman wants one.

4. I generally do exercises at least twice a week.

Although these are related to health care, they are quite general and designed to discover the overall patterns that exist in reference to health care. This study also had as its purpose a very specific objective of predicting what types of consumers were likely to bring malpractice suits. Since attitude theory indicates that consumers will try to behave in such a way as to achieve consistency between their behavior and their attitudes, it was necessary to determine specific attitudes toward physicians

[7]Joseph T. Plummer, "The Concept and Application of Life Style Segmentation," *Journal of Marketing,* vol. 38 (January 1974), 33-37, at 33.

as well as specific attitudes toward malpractice. Thus, statements such as the following were included:

1. I have a great deal of confidence in my own doctor.

2. About half of the physicians are not really competent to practice medicine.

3. Most physicians are overpaid.

4. In most malpractice suits, the physician is not really to blame.

In this study, respondents who indicated that they have a great deal of confidence in their doctors also reported a much lower likelihood of bringing a malpractice suit. Respondents agreeing with the statements that physicians are not really competent and they are overpaid, and disagreeing with the statement that physicians are not really to blame in malpractice suits had a much greater likelihood of filing a malpractice suit. Thus, these specific AIO statements could be used to profile specific behaviors and opinions associated with malpractice suits. However, analysis of the general statements also revealed that persons who agree with the general statements "I generally do exercises" and "I am sick a lot more than my friends are" were found also to be more likely to bring malpractice suits—supporting the position that both general AIOs and specific AIOs can be used to profile consumers and relate their life-styles to behavior.[8]

There is considerable concern about the differences in usefulness between general and specific AIO statements. Some researchers believe that specific AIOs may be better for *predicting* actual consumer choices of products or brands but that general AIOs may yield better *understanding* of consumer behavior.[9] This suggests that the *use* of the research must influence whether general or specific AIOs will be best. Additional considerations in the measurement of life-styles will be discussed in the latter part of this chapter.

If life-styles were static phenomena, research would be greatly simplified. Under static conditions, once a research study was conducted it could be placed in the file and simply retrieved when additional decisions were to be made concerning marketing strategy and programming. Such a scenario does not describe reality, however, because American life-styles are changing substantially. Firms or other organizations that hope to survive must monitor closely changing life-styles and proportions of the population adopting specific life-styles.

Sources of Life-Styles

Life-styles result from the interaction of social and personal variables. Individuals are bombarded with influences from their environment. The

---

[8]The above research is summarized from Roger Blackwell and Wayne Talarzyk, *Consumer Attitudes toward Health Care and Malpractice* (Columbus: Grid Publishing, Inc., 1977), Chapter 5.

[9]This issue is investigated in Michel A. Zins, "An Exploration of the Relationship between General and Specific Psychographic Profiles," in Kenneth L. Bernhardt, (ed.), *Marketing 1776-1976 and Beyond* (Chicago: American Marketing Association, 1976), 507-511.

most important of these occur during childhood through the process of socialization, described in Chapter 6. Social influences continue to surround the individual throughout life, however, originating in the family, reference groups, social classes, important subcultures, and the overall culture. Economic influences also provide constraints and opportunities in the manifestation of one's life-style.

Values

Life-styles result, in a sense, from all the influences discussed in the previous four chapters in Part 2. These are represented as *values* in Figure 7.1. In the next section of this chapter, we will try to draw together some of the most important of these social influences that are forces for *changing* consumer life-styles. The purpose of this is two-dimensional. The first dimension is *descriptive*, describing the basic life forces that are likely to influence consumer decisions in the next decade. This is important as background for relating to much of the rest of the book. All of the research reported in the rest of the book has been done in the *past*. While the basic relationships and variables are likely to remain constant in the future, the *specific parameters are constantly changing*. Thus, while reading the rest of the book, you may want to keep in mind how some of the specifics that are reported in research studies may change over time, partly because of changes in the fundamental forces that create consumer life-styles.

The second dimension or reason for analyzing changes in life-style forces is *analytical*. That is, what are the structural elements common to all or most consumer behavior that can be applied to various circumstances? In the following section, a paradigm for sociocultural analysis will be presented that can be used to collect information on changes in the environment beyond the times described in the following pages.

Personality

Personality provides an explanation for why two individuals receiving the same social influences have different life-styles. This topic will be described and analyzed following the discussion of changing influences on values.

FUNDAMENTAL FORCES SHAPING AMERICAN LIFE-STYLES

From the time a baby looks up and begins cooing and smiling, the process of socialization begins. In this process, a person is being shaped and influenced into what is thought to be human behavior, or what will become an individual's personality. The influences continue throughout a lifetime, causing people to adopt general values that influence consumption—such as thrift, pleasure, honesty, and so forth. These life forces also produce specific preferences—such as color preferences, packaging and convenience preferences, preferred hours of shopping, characteristic interactions with sales persons, and so forth.

Values

Values are generalized beliefs or expectations about behavior, it will be remembered from Chapter 4. Values are important life-style determinants and are broader in scope than attitudes or the types of variables contained in AIO measures. Values serve as a basic, integrating framework for our attitudes.[10]

Individuals are not born with their values. Rather, values are learned or passed on from generation to generation in a society or from member to member in a subcultural group. Many values are relatively permanent from generation to generation but others are undergoing considerable change in the contemporary environment. The values most in transition frequently are of most interest to marketing strategists because they provide the *basis for differences among life-style market segments*. They may hold the key to growth for marketing strategists seeking to understand and predict future opportunities or challenges for a particular company or industry.

Two types of forces may be isolated and analyzed in understanding values in a society. The first type of values source is the *triad of institutions*: families, religious institutions, and schools. The second source of values is *early lifetime experiences* and includes a wide range of diversified experiences while a person is growing up and forming values. Such experiences include wars, civil rights movements, economic factors, and many other events. And of course diversified institutions such as government and the media are important in transmitting these influences on values.

The transmission of values from generation to generation is shown in Figure 7.2. The following pages describe some important trends in the family, religious institutions, and schools as well as some contrasts in the value influencing experiences of pre-World War II consumers and post-World War II consumers. This exhibit also shows that peers exhibit influence on an individual in the process of internalizing values of a group. These peer or reference group influences were discussed in Chapter 6.

Institutional Influences on Values

The triad of institutions shown in Figure 7.2 plays a key role in understanding the values of a society. As long as these institutions are stable, the values transmitted are likely to be relatively stable. When these institutions change rapidly, however, the values of consumers also change rapidly, causing serious discontinuity in the effectiveness of communication and marketing strategies.

Some of these dislocative changes are presented in the following paragraphs. While the changes are described in the context of the United States, many of them are also applicable in many other countries of the world.

---

[10]Milton Rokeach, "A Theory of Organization and Change within Value-Attitude Systems," *Journal of Social Issues* (January 1968), 13-33; Milton Rokeach, "The Role of Values in Public Opinion Research," *Public Opinion Quarterly* (Winter 1968-69), 547-549; Milton Rokeach, *The Nature of Human Values* (New York: The Free Press, 1973).

**Figure 7.2
Intergenerational
Value
Transmission**

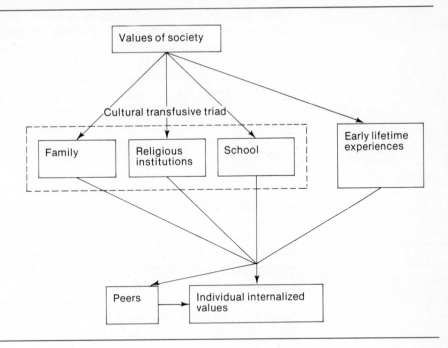

**Declining Family
Influences**

In most cultures, the family is the dominant transfusive agent of values. Several trends indicate a decline in this influence with the effect that values change toward more flexibility. Since the family was a major topic of discussion in Chapter 6, only a few additional trends that relate specifically to value transmission are discussed here.

A decreasing amount of time is available for in-home or parent-child influences among the very young. This is largely due to increased enrollments in pre-school or day-care facilities. Among three- to four-year olds, only 5.7 percent were enrolled in schools in 1965. Today that number is over 50 percent. In the past, children spent the formative years of zero to six with their parents. More recently, this parent-child interaction has decreased markedly, permitting values to be learned outside the family to an increasing extent.

Increasing *divorce rates* also contribute to decreased family influence and the socialization of children in a one-parent household. For every two marriages today, there is one divorce. The divorce rate was at a low 2.1 per 1,000 people in the 1960s but by 1978 was at a record high of 5.1 per 1,000 people. If this rate continues, almost 40 percent of all marriages will end in divorce.[11] About 45 percent of all children will spend some of their childhood in a one-parent household.

Weekend parents cause values to be transmitted to children by sub-

[11]Cheryl Russell, "Divorce And Other Facts of Life," *American Demographics* (December 1979), 40-41.

stitute parents such as babysitters, schools, and media. In an older, agrarian society and even in a blue-collar economy, children spent time with their fathers. This all changed in a post-World War II society with the enormous rise in white collar or professional occupations. The elite of white-collar fathers frequently have extensive travel as well as longer, irregular working hours leaving less opportunity to implant their values among children. The dramatic rise in working wives also leaves children open to value transmission by persons other than the family.

The *isolated nuclear family* or geographical separation of the immediate (nuclear) family from the grandparents and other relatives (extended family) also contributes to a substantial decline in family influences on value transmission. Massive increases in the proportion of young people attending college has created a condition where a much higher percentage of families take career positions geographically separated from where the family grew up and from the influence of the extended family. This removes an important stabilizing or traditionalizing influence on values and perhaps results in more basic conditions of lack of heritage identity or a yearning for roots.

How do companies respond to the diminished influence of family? Some companies are reviewing their policies about job interference with family life, providing quality day-care centers for employees, encouraging family to travel out-of-town with executives sometimes, involving spouses in company seminars and newsletters, providing scholarships for children of employees, providing marital counseling, and in other ways recognizing the role of the family. Long distance communications can also help, as Figure 7.3 shows, by being the next best thing to being there.

Changing Religious Influences

Judaic-Christian religious institutions have historically played an important role in transmitting values from one generation to another. In recent years, these institutions generally have declined in influence on values.

Church membership and religious attendance declined in recent years.[12] Gallup Poll statistics, shown in Table 7.1, indicate that the greatest decline has been among Catholics. The decline in religious attendance occurred in Europe after World War II then spread to England and finally to North America.

The role of religious institutions is further diminished by the *secularization of religious institutions*—or loss of function. Religion has become compartmentalized and lost its capacity to judge secular values and structure. This thesis is articulately presented by Francis Schaeffer[13] who describes how religion historically provided the values by which justice, science, the arts, and all other relevant dimensions of a culture were evaluated. In contemporary society this world-view has been replaced with a system in which religion is, at most, only relevant to a limited

[12]Jon P. Alston, "Social Variables Associated with Church Attendance, 1965 and 1969: Evidence from National Polls," *Journal for the Scientific Study of Religion*, vol. 10 (Fall 1971). 233-236.

[13]Francis A. Schaeffer, *How Should We Then Live?* (Old Tappan, New Jersey: Fleming H. Revel Company, 1976).

**Figure 7.3
Communication
Strategy Based on
the Emergence of
the Isolated
Nuclear Family**

Source: Courtesy of AT&T.

portion of life and, at least, not relevant to any of life. The view of Herzberg that traditional religion has lost its impact on the American way of life is summarized in the following passage:

Religiousness in America has become a "religiousness without religion," lacking real inner commitment and stressing social adjustment and legitimation of secular value orientations. Religion be-

**Table 7.1
Attendance at
Religious Services**

Year	Protestants	Catholics	Jews
1958	44%	74%	23
1968	38	65	20
1978	40	52	24
1980	39	53	24

Source: Gallup Poll (January 25, 1981). Copyright Field Enterprises, Inc. Reprinted by permission.

comes a reactive system; it is shaped by secular values rather than shaping them. It no longer exerts creative leverage for judging and influencing secular life.[14]

There is considerable empirical evidence of the secularization of society as perceived by consumers themselves. In a nationwide Gallup sample in 1957, 76 percent felt religion was increasing its influence in daily life, but more recently only 14 percent did so. While nearly every socioeconomic stratum changed to the same extent, young people changed more.[15] In a comprehensive study of college students from 1931 to 1968 using the Thurstone Attitude Scales, Jones concluded:

It would seem that whatever weakening in students' favorable attitudes toward religion that occurred in the last 37 years has not been so much a decrease in belief in the Deity—although there has been some of that—as a disillusionment with the church establishment and the use of its beliefs and preachments in the solution of current social, civic, and economic problems.[16]

Although religion as an institution appears to be declining in influence in American and other cultures, it is still possible for it to be very important for individuals and for subgroups in the culture. There have been many studies that attempt to relate socioeconomic and other variables to religious belief and involvement, although a review of such research is beyond the present discussion.[17] It also appears that a new sense of religious commitment and understanding may be emerging in the United States, Canada, and some other countries. The largest selling book dur-

---

[14]Judith R. Porter, "Secularization, Differentiation and the Function of Religious Value Orientation," *Sociological Inquiry,* vol. 43 (1973), 67-74, at 70.

[15]J. P. Alston and R. C. Hollinger, "Review of the Polls," *Journal for the Scientific Study of Religion,* vol. 11 (1972), 401-403.

[16]Vernon Jones, "Attitudes toward the Church," *Genetic Psychology Monographs* (1970), 5-53, at 52. Also see Angelo Danesion and William A. Layman, "Catholic Attitudes and Beliefs in Transition: A Decade Study of a Jesuit College," *Psychological Reports,* vol. 28 (1971), 247-250.

[17]Milton Rokeach, "Value Systems in Religion," *Review of Religious Research,* vol. 11 (Fall 1969) 3-23; Bruce L. Warren, "Socioeconomic Achievement and Religion: The American Case," *Sociological Inquiry,* vol. 40 (Spring 1970), 130-155; Waldo W. Burchard, "Denominational Correlates of Changing Religious Beliefs in College," *Sociological Analysis,* vol. 31 (Spring 1970), 36-45; Armand L. Mauss, "Dimensions of Religious Defection," *Review of Religious Research,* vol. 10 (Spring 1969), 128-135; John Photiadis and William Schweiker, "Attitudes toward Joining Authoritarian Organizations and Sectarian Churches," *Scientific Study of Religion,* vol. 9 (Fall 1970), 227-234; Harold E. Quineley, "The Dilemma of an Activist Church: Protestant Religion in the Sixties and Seventies," *Scientific Study of Religion,* vol. 13 (1974), 1-21; Ralph Van Roy, Frank Bean, and James Wood, "Social Mobility and Doctrinal Orthodoxy," *Scientific Study of Religion,* vol. 13 (1974), 427-439; Stephen M. Sales, "Economic Threat as Determinant of Conversion Rates in Authoritarian and Nonauthoritarian Churches," *Journal of Personality and Social Psychology,* vol. 23 (1972), 420-428.

Reactions to Various Sects	Taken Part	Interested	Neutral	Opposed	Never Heard of Group
TM	8	45	32	8	7
Hare Krishna	2	18	45	21	15
Scientology	2	12	33	20	33
Zen	4	36	41	8	12
Campus Crusade	4	17	37	26	17
Jews for Jesus	1	12	43	14	31
Children of God	1	9	37	21	31
Yoga	10	46	36	7	3
Satanism	1	2	31	58	7
Hassidism	1	6	26	7	60

**Table 7.2
Interest in New
Religious
Movements**

Source: Robert Wuthnow and Charles Y. Glock, "The Shifting Focus of Faith: A Survey Report," *Psychology Today* (November, 1974), 133. Reprinted by permission.

ing the past decade was Hal Lindsey's *The Late Great Planet Earth*, which accepts the Bible as true revelation from God. In addition, about one out of every three Americans now indicates that he is a born-again Christian.[18]

What are the specific effects of declining religious institutions for marketers? Values of consumers in coming years are likely to be more personal, more diversified and influenced less by traditional institutions. Retailers may have increased shoplifting problems because of a decreasing moral belief that stealing is wrong. This problem for retailers creates an opportunity for firms that produce security systems—such as electronic strips that can be sewn into apparel so that an alarm is triggered when someone leaves a store without paying for the garment and deactivating the electronic device.

The individual influence of managers on ethics in the firm should become more important as firms recognize that definitions of right and wrong are not so much based in societal values as individual values. Humans inherently seek values and if these are not supplied by mainstream organizations, people will seek them in other organizations—cults, for example, such as Jonestown, Guyana. New religions—such as Transcendental Meditation and other Eastern religions—can be expected to come and go as well as diverse forms of traditional religions. The level of interest in such religions is indicated in Table 7.2, based upon a youthful survey of *Psychology Today* readers.

Can religious institutions use marketing methods and a knowledge of consumer behavior to enhance their effectiveness, even in an unfavorable environment? The answer is clearly yes. Most of the theory presented in this text has been organized by Engel into a text specifically designed for religious organizations.[19] Even orthodox religious institutions can do consumer research and apply the results to marketing plans for the organization.[20]

[18]George Gallup and David Poling, *The Search for America's Faith* (Nashville: Abingdon, 1980).

[19]James Engel, *Contemporary Christian Communications* (Nashville: Thomas Nelson, 1979).

[20]James F. Engel and H. Wilbert Norton, *What's Gone Wrong with the Harvest?* (Grand Rapids: Zondervan Publishing House, 1975); Donald McGavran, *Understanding Church Growth* (Grand Rapids: William B. Eerdmans, 1970).

**Figure 7.4
Advertising Appeal
Based on the
Stresses of Modern
Families**

Source: Courtesy of Zondervan Corporation.

One successful application of consumer research by a religious organization is the Garden Grove Community Church in California. Started in a drive-in theatre only a little over 20 years ago, the church now has thousands of members attending consecutive services each week in the multimillion dollar Crystal Cathedral. More impressively, the church supports hospitals, senior citizen centers, and relief programs throughout the world and produces a television program that is top rated in many cities of Canada, Australia, and the United States. The basic approach of the church's minister is to do research to determine felt needs or areas of life where people need help and then develop "a shopping center for God—a part of the service industry to meet those needs."[21]

Another example of how changes in religious institutions produce market opportunities for adaptive organizations is provided in Figure 7.4 for Zondervan Publishing. This firm formerly distributed books through bookstores that served mostly the market segment who were evangelical Christians. Now the organization owns a chain called "Family Book Stores" located in regional shopping malls, attractively designed to serve a broader market target. Notice in Figure 7.4 that Zondervan is addressing the problems and stresses that occur in contemporary families. In the past, many people might have sought help from their minister or rabbi but with the secularization of society, many do not have those relationships and thus need an easy-to-understand Bible and other books such as those published by Zondervan to provide help.

Educational Institutions

The third major institution that transmits values to consumers is education. The influence of education appears to be increasing, partly due to increased participation of Americans in formal education and partly due to the vacuum left by families and religious institutions.

The dramatic rise in formal education has occurred at all levels. You will remember from Chapter 3 that over half of consumers in the 25 to 34 age group can be expected to have some college or university education. Most adults now have high school. Even the proportion of factory workers with some university education increased from 6 percent to 16 percent during the past decade. Dramatic increases are also occurring in continuing education with more and more persons, especially women 25 to 45, returning to college. Franklin University in Ohio pioneered with classes on Sunday afternoons, "Early Bird" classes at 7 a.m., and "Night Owl" courses at midnight. Many universities are adapting their MBA and other offerings to attract market segments back to the campus.[22]

Other factors change the influence of educational institutions on val-

---

[21]Robert H. Schuller, *Your Church Has Real Possibilities!* (Glendale, California: Regal Books, 1974). Also see "Possibility Thinking and Shrewd Marketing Pay Off for a Preacher," *The Wall Street Journal* (August 26, 1976), 1ff.

[22]See H. Lee Mathews and Roger Blackwell, "Implementing Marketing Planning in Higher Education;" Leonard Berry and William Kehoe, "Problems and Guidelines in University Education;" and Karen Fox and William Ihlanfeldt, "Determining Market Potential in Higher Education," all in Richard P. Bogozzi, (ed)., *Marketing in the 80s* (Chicago: American Marketing Association, 1980), 1-13. Also see "The Search for Students," *Futurist* (February 1981), 65-67.

ues and life-styles. Prior to World War II, teachers originated mostly from the middle class and taught middle-class values. During the 1950s a new breed of teachers emerged as college enrollments from all social classes soared. While the middle classes still dominated teaching, teachers now came to some extent from the entire spectrum of society. Students could reasonably expect to encounter teachers with values different from their own—and in some cases radically different.[23]

Another trend in education involved the emergence and proliferation of new teaching methods. Previously, teaching often emphasized description and memorization. This approach to learning implicitly, if not explicitly, says, "This is the way things are; just learn it," with no latitude for questioning. More recently, however, there has been a gradual but steady trend away from description and memorization in favor of analytical approaches emphasizing questioning of the old and the formulation of new approaches and solutions.

In many instances this approach concludes that there is no one correct answer; new horizons are encouraged. The case method in business school is an example of this analytical, questioning approach.

The reality of consumers socialized in the new teaching environment is the rejection of rigid definitions of right or wrong. The central reality is that individuals, particularly younger consumers, are no longer willing to lead unexamined lives. This leads to more aggressive consumerism, so much so that we will need to examine this topic in more depth in the last section of this book. Marketing organizations must develop sales programs and product-information formats that give answers when customers ask (or just think to themselves) why and why not to market offerings.The net effect of changed educational influences is often the rise of diverse life-styles for substantial portions of a society. Marketing organizations must adapt to the need for market segmentation and detailed positioning strategies as well as creative and adaptive communications programs.

These three institutions—family, religion, and school—all contribute to transmitting traditional values as well as creating receptivity for changed life-styles. In addition to these institutions, early lifetime experiences are also important in creating values among consumers.

Intergenerational Motivating Factors

People are products of their environment and they strive to achieve as adults what they feel they were deprived of in early stages of life. As a result, consumer analysts must pay attention to early lifetime influences. To understand such influences on individual consumer behavior would require more information than marketers can usually hope to obtain. Consequently, attention is usually focused upon large groups of people who experienced similar influences while growing up. The analysis of

[23]For expansion of these ideas, see Harvey C. Burke, "The University in Transition," *Business Horizons* (August 1969), 5-17.

influences of groups of the population born at the same time is called *cohort analysis.*

Pre-World War II Consumers

Over 80 percent of contemporary consumers were not yet born during the Great Depression of the 1930s. For the vast majority, even World War II predates them. Yet, the severity of these two events profoundly and indelibly affected the lives of the consumers who experienced them. The effects of these events were so pervasive that they left their impact on the national experience as well as individual behavior. Hence, there is a marked tendency for consumers who experienced the Depression and World War II—many who are in key positions of influence today—to hold values that emphasize *job security, patriotism,* and the *acquisition of material goods*. These things were the deprivations of the cohort that experienced the Depression and the War.

Interpersonal Generation

The consumers who were markets of the past decade experienced their childhood in the 1950s and 1960s—the greatest period of prolonged economic expansion in the history of the United States and most other industrialized countries. During the 1950s, the U.S. economy nearly doubled and repeated the growth again in the 60s. Not until the mid-70s did this expansion lose momentum. Even though a substantial amount of this growth represented inflation, there remained a tremendous proliferation of affluence among this cohort.

The critical experiences of the youth of the 70s and the older youth of the 80s vary greatly, but among the prominent influences are the following: the nuclear age, the civil rights movement, pockets of poverty amidst mass affluence, questionable space exploration, the Viet Nam War, concern about the economy, pervasive university experiences, campus disorders and protest, and a lack of communication—both in quantity and quality—with parents.

From the cohort who were children in the 50s and 60s—the Interpersonal Generation—came great awareness and concern for other people. This manifested itself in social concern on issues of civil rights and equal opportunity but, of special interest to marketers, made fashion more important. Not fashion in the sense of keeping up with the Joneses as had been true of their parents, but fashion that emerged because of so much social contact and interpersonal awareness. Not only was clothing a fashion industry, but also groceries, hardware, the media, and most other products. Vinson and Munson measured the values of students and compared them to similar measures of values of parents, particularly related to automobiles. The researchers concluded that parents emphasized attributes signifying utilitarian or functional characteristics associated with automobile ownership (e.g., quality of warranty, service required, handling) while students were more concerned with aesthetic and socially observable features (styling, prestige, luxury interior).[24]

The "Me Generation"

What of the new consumers of the future? What have been the critical influences of the new cohort of consumers? What will be their motivations and how will they influence older consumers as the values of the most recent cohort trickle up to older generations?

The critical influences of the most recent cohort to become consumers included energy crises, massive and continuing inflation, feminism, Watergate, and an expanding tax and social security burden. Where the concern of the previous cohort was how to *help others achieve the good life*, the concern of the most recent cohort—and much of the rest of the population—is with the problem of *maintaining the good life-style*.

The description of the emerging mainstream value might be *egoism* (not to be confused with egotism) or the moral philosophy that when people take care of themselves and leave others to do the same, the society is most likely to thrive. One of the firms doing considerable research in the area of life-styles is Yankelovich, Skelly & White. A paper from that firm reports their findings:

The cornerstone of the new values is a shift from the concept of self-denial to a new focus-on-self. . . . The new focus-on-self subsumes, "I have a duty to myself;" and more specifically: self-understanding, self-expression, self-fulfillment, concern with physical self, etc. It means putting yourself, either on par with, or a little above the others that perhaps you once considered before you yourself.[25]

The new self-orientation of the "Me Generation" manifests itself in many ways. It has brought about changes in government with the election of President Reagan and an emphasis on reduction in government spending, reductions in government regulation, and more of a belief in the role of business and the personal incentive economic system. On campus, more students are choosing majors in business and the pragmatic subjects likely to bring financial success. A survey of 190,000 entering freshmen conducted by UCLA's Laboratory for Research on Higher Education disclosed that in 1979 compared to 1969, 77 percent more women and 28 percent more men cited their important goal as "being very well-off financially." "Having administrative responsibility" was cited by 110 percent more women and 32 percent more men and "success" seems to be the current fad on campus. One sorority president stated it this way at her campus:

[24]Donald Vinson and J. M. Munson, "Personal Values: An Approach to Market Segmentation," in Kenneth Bernhardt, (ed.), *Marketing: 1776-1976 and Beyond* (Chicago: American Marketing Association, 1976), 313-317.

[25]Florence R. Skelly, "Emerging Attitudes and Life Styles," Paper presented to American Association of Advertising Agencies Annual Meeting, White Sulphur Springs, West Virginia (May 16-19, 1979).

On Friday nights I'm so lonely. I'd like to date more people, but it's not possible . . . How many girls can you point to that date anybody with any regularity? . . . A lot of them haven't been out once this entire quarter. The problem is everybody's so busy studying, they don't have *time* for a boyfriend or a girlfriend. You'd like to study less, but if you do, your grades are down."[26]

This is certainly not representative of all students but indicative of an underlying trend, which is experienced to different degrees depending on the reputation of the school and the norms of the campus.

For business firms, the "Me Generation" and emphasis on self creates many market opportunities to serve consumers seeking personal peace and affluence. Figures 7.5 and 7.6 illustrate two different approaches. In Figure 7.5, the Crown Center is seeking to attract people for today's pleasurable life-styles with an emphasis on a natural environment, good food, exciting aesthetics, and the other accoutrements of the good life. Figure 7.6 focuses on the self-orientation also but in a more personal, health oriented manner, with specific appeal to women for a successful new magazine.

Life-Styles and Marketing Strategy—A Case Example

After a marketing organization understands the nature and causes of changed life-styles, how can this information be used for developing marketing programs? Is life-style information most useful for advertising programs? Or for new product development? Or for programming channels of distribution? The answer, of course, is that life-styles are the beginning point for developing the total marketing strategy and thus affect all aspects of the marketing program.

It would be difficult to explain all the possible ways a life-style study might be used but a case example may help. The matrix in Table 7.3 shows such an example. You will need to spend some time looking at Table 7.3 to grasp its full significance. First, notice that some emerging life-styles are described. As a manager, you might be able to discern the changes occurring in society simply because you are a creative, insightful person. In this case, a research project was the basis for defining the emerging segments. The study involved a psychographic survey of 10,000 households as well as repeated measures of some variables by polling services.

This case was funded by the Home Furnishings Marketing Institute, whose members are interested in both manufacturing and retailing. Thus the trends or life-style segments are traced through the channel of distribution with implications for all components of the marketing program. Notice in the third and fourth columns the range of marketing decisions that may be affected by life-style data. These include product, price, and advertising elements as well as many distribution elements.

---

[26]Quoted from Colin Covert, "The Undergraduate," *Ambassador* (November 1980), 63-66ff, at 82.

**Figure 7.5
Crown Center:
Appeal to Today's
Life-Styles**

CROWN CENTER HOTEL BROUGHT A WATERFALL AND
TROPICAL GARDENS TO DOWNTOWN KANSAS CITY.

Imagine a sparkling city in the heart of Kansas City.

Where you walk to everything — restaurants, shops, and businesses.

And at the center of this city within a city, you'll find the finishing touch.

A magnificent hotel built around a natural limestone cliff, five-story waterfall and lush, green tropical gardens.

An attendant smiles and takes your bag. Your room is spacious — with a private balcony and lovely view.

And then, whatever suits your mood. Something exotic in Trader Vic's? A dance at the Top of the Crown restaurant? Or perhaps jogging, a sauna, or a refreshing dip in the pool?

It's the most comfort you could possibly imagine. But that's the best part. At the Crown Center Hotel, you don't have to leave anything to your imagination.

WESTERN INTERNATIONAL

Source: Courtesy of Westin Hotels.

**Figure 7.6
Advertising to the
"Me Generation"**

Source: Courtesy of *Self* Magazine.

Table 7.3
Case Example of Marketing Strategy and
Programming Based on Life-Style Trends

Trend	Description of Trend	Illustrative Product Implications for Manufacturers and Retailers	Illustrative Additional Manufacturer Strategy Implications	Illustrative Additional Retailer Strategy Implications
More Casual Life-Styles	Desire to live a less traditional, conservative, formalized life-style in terms of behavior, dress, eating, entertainment, and so on.	Potential increase in sales of furniture that is more comfortable. More casual, perhaps rugged, case goods. Potential long-term reduction in sales of formal living and dining room furniture. Good growth prospects for indoor/outdoor furniture.	Consider advertising featuring furniture and home furnishings in more realistic and casual life-style settings. Think about emphasizing comfort where appropriate.	Same as manufacturer.
Desire for Elegance and Personalization	Growing interest in a personalized life-style that is different from others and consistent with one's self-concept.	Growing market for uniquely designed furniture that is visibly different from what is widely available. Growing market for old, second-hand furniture including antiques. Increasing tendency to mix styles between and/or within rooms. Potential increase in sales of refinish-it-yourself furniture, including kits.	Consider advertising featuring unique furniture and furniture settings that mix styles and designs harmoniously. Evaluate distribution through retailers having a reputation for uniqueness; brochures and sales promotion pieces that recommend what goes with what.	Consider devoting some inventory dollars to unique and unusual merchandise that is not available elsewhere. Some room settings and advertising might mix styles and designs harmoniously.
Flexibility of Roles/ Women's Liberation	Men and women perform multiple roles—parent, host, spouse, servant. Greater exchange of many roles between sexes.	Growing market for interchangeable (room-to-room) furniture as well as furniture that can serve a variety of purposes (multiple purpose).	Consider advertising and sales promotion featuring the interchangeability and multiple purpose features of appropriate items.	Same as manufacturer. Add interchangeability and multiple purpose features to sales presentations where applicable. Avoid double standards (male, female) in extending credit.
Instant Gratification	Living more for today and planning and living less for the future. Desire for instant standard of living, instant career achievement. Interest in "solutions to problems" rather than parts of problems. Growing intolerance of incompetence— waiting in line, etc.	Enlarging market for low cost, reasonable quality, and well-designed furniture and home furnishings analogously, the Mustang (or fun watches). Greater interest in groupings (packages) of furniture that go together—not necessarily the same style.	Continue to reevaluate delivery time. Evaluate advertising and sales promotion for complete rooms using themes like "decorate your family room by bedtime."	Same as manufacturer. Also consider trying to speed up the time required to process a customer transaction. For regular customers, think about maintaining a file containing room layout, items purchased, including swatches, and so on.

Table 7.3 (Continued)
Case Example of Marketing Strategy and
Programming Based on Life-Style Trends

Trend	Description of Trend	Illustrative Product Implications for Manufacturers and Retailers	Illustrative Additional Manufacturer Strategy Implications	Illustrative Additional Retailer Strategy Implications
New Theology of Pleasure	Interested in having fun and in products, services, and other experiences that make life fun. This is a reaction to the boredom of life emanating partly from job tedium and dissatisfaction.	Favors unique, interesting furniture and furnishings that are conversation pieces. Also fun items like bean-bag chairs and water beds.	Consider advertising and promoting furniture and furnishings in unique, fun settings. Evaluate distribution through retailers having a unique fun image.	Create store excitement through unique displays. Reevaluate how frequently they are changed. Consider music and other techniques that are consistent with your market. Think about establishing a play area for children, refreshment center, etc. Advertise and promote furniture in unique, fun settings.
Life Simplification	Removing or reducing the time and/or energy required to perform what are perceived by some to be mundane, undesirable tasks. Examples include self-cleaning ovens, trash compactors, power lawnmowers, etc.	Furniture and home furnishings that are easy to care for, easy to repair, and require less frequent cleaning, dusting, and so on. Minimum maintenance wall coverings. Opportunity for services such as furniture and carpet cleaning and repair, complete interior cleaning, painting, refurbishing, and so on.	Consider advertising and promoting easy maintenance features.	Same as manufacturer.
Changing Morality	Growing tendency to believe that premarital sex, extramarital sex, homosexuality, etc., are not morally wrong. Increasing tendency to live together without being married.	Creates new needs for temporary furniture and home furnishings, including rental. Growing market for modular sofa and chair units that can be pushed together to create a large lounging area. Opportunity for unique beds, headboards, and bedroom furniture designs that create atmosphere and facilitate lounging as well as sleeping. Emphasis on products of minimum deterioration or obsolescense for rental programs.	Think about advertising and promoting the modular features of sofa and chairs, if applicable. Also emphasize the lounging features of beds and bedroom furniture. Feature bedroom and other furniture in tastefully sensual settings. Potential opportunity for diversification into furniture rental.	Same as manufacturer, depending upon local market characteristics and opportunities.

Table 7.3 (Continued)
Case Example of Marketing Strategy and
Programming Based on Life-Style Trends

Trend	Description of Trend	Illustrative Product Implications for Manufacturers and Retailers	Illustrative Additional Manufacturer Strategy Implications	Illustrative Additional Retailer Strategy Implications
Concern About Appearance and Health	Partial outgrowth of youth orientation. Concern about health, weight, physical appearance—often youthful appearance. Illustrations include wigs, hair dye, face lifts, vitamins, bust development, diet foods, etc.	Potential market for health and exercise equipment that has good design and is like furniture so that it looks well in bedrooms and/or other furnished areas, or which can be marketed as an accessory item, to be attached to or used with some item of furniture.		
Novelty, Change, and Escape	Reaction to the perceived boredom of life, resulting partly from the absence of meaningful work. Interest in products, services, and experiences that provide for novelty, change, and escape.	Potential market for less long-lasting, relatively low-priced, furniture and furnishings provided they are well-designed—i.e., the *Timex* concept. Growth potential for novelty items. Growing market for furniture and home furnishings for camping, camping vehicles and trucks, second homes, and so on. Potential opportunity for multiple coverings for upholstered goods.	Through advertising and promotion, evaluate positioning the home (apartment) as a place to get away from it all. Also show how furniture and furnishings can be rearranged to create a fresh change and new feeling.	Same as manufacturer. Also include in merchandise presentations and sales presentations.
Naturalism	Growing desire to have the best of both worlds—the advantages of technology and the standard of living that it makes possible on the one hand—and naturalism, return to nature on the other. Rejection of artificial forms of behavior and dress.	Continuing market for natural woods and other materials. Earth tones should be popular. Designs that facilitate openness and bring the outdoors inside should do well. Less demand for wall-to-wall carpeting; more for area and throw rugs. Potential growth of patterns and materials using natural scenes and outdoor living.	Through advertising and sales promotion, consider featuring the natural characteristics of the product—natural woods, natural wool, etc.	Same as manufacturer. Include naturalness in sales presentations. Consider expanding assortment of area rugs.

Table 7.3 (Continued)
Case Example of Marketing Strategy and
Programming Based on Life-Style Trends

Trend	Description of Trend	Illustrative Product Implications for Manufacturers and Retailers	Illustrative Additional Manufacturer Strategy Implications	Illustrative Additional Retailer Strategy Implications
Personal Creativity	For reasons of economy and/or self-expression, desire to make selected things and perform certain functions that have historically been purchased—i.e., crafts, home sewing, home repair and improvement, etc.	Growing market for products that allow final accessorization by the purchaser. Sales of unfinished furniture should increase, including higher quality furniture and knock-down pieces that require finishing as well as assembling. Growing market for used furniture that is unique. Opportunity for carpeting and floor covering products with do-it-yourself installation. Limited, but growing opportunity for high cost gourmet cookware. Opportunity for do-it-yourself wall covering kit.	Advertising and promotion that shows consumers how to finish, assemble, refinish, upholster, reupholster furniture, install carpeting, wall coverings, etc. Potential theme might be: "If we can do it, so can you."	Same as manufacturer. Consider offering refinishing, reupholstering, cleaning, and similar services to customers. Also consider conducting classes in things like finishing and upholstering and sell kits.
Changing Attitudes Toward Credit	Expectation that credit will be available to finance the good life.	Increasing stability of sales		Process credit applications quickly and politely. If third parties are involved, develop a mechanism to make the transition as smooth as possible.
New Work Ethic	Having fun is not bad and is not necessarily something to be minimized. Trend toward working to live rather than living to work.	More time at home to enjoy furniture. Growing market for indoor/outdoor casual furniture and furnishings.	Think about advertising and promotion emphasizing "You deserve to relax." Utilize background settings in which people are relaxing and having fun. Where possible, adjust personnel policies to changing work ethic—flexible work hours, limited night and weekend commitments, and so on.	Same as manufacturer.

Table 7.3 (Continued)
Case Example of Marketing Strategy and
Programming Based on Life-Style Trends

Trend	Description of Trend	Illustrative Product Implications for Manufacturers and Retailers	Illustrative Additional Manufacturer Strategy Implications	Illustrative Additional Retailer Strategy Implications
Institutional Reliance	Reliance on institutions—particularly government and business—to solve society's problems and a growing number of consumption needs.	Potential increase in the number of furniture and home furnishings items that are built in at the time of construction.	Consider developing working relationships with large builders, developers, architects, etc.	Same as manufacturer.
Eroding Confidence in Institutions	Dramatic reductions in the confidence people have in major institutions, particularly business.		Develop consumerism program.	Same as manufacturer.
Consumerism	Increasing concern over price/quality/quantity relationships. Increasing product and service expectations.	Growing need to tighten quality control. Guarantees and warranties will become more important.	Use guarantee/warranty cards to monitor who is buying your product(s) and where. Set up system to encourage customer complaints and to respond honestly and fairly. Periodically conduct studies of your customers and other people to measure your image.	Same as manufacturer. Also think about encouraging salespeople to talk in customer-oriented rather than technical terms. For example, "The difference between wool and nylon carpeting is ____. What this means to you, Ms. Consumer, is ____."
International Orientation	Gradual emergence of a one world orientation resulting from political and trade relationships and increasing travel, education, and communications. Early manifestations likely to be the gradual assimilation of selected Western European traditions and life-styles—particularly among younger, higher educated, more affluent segments.	Monitor trends in Europe to identify items that are popular there, particularly those that appeal to people under 35 years of age. Pay particular attention to furniture and home furnishings in countries having high density and smaller size (square footage) housing—such as Sweden and Holland.		

Table 7.3 (Continued)
Case Example of Marketing Strategy and
Programming Based on Life-Style Trends

Trend	Description of Trend	Illustrative Product Implications for Manufacturers and Retailers	Illustrative Additional Manufacturer Strategy Implications	Illustrative Additional Retailer Strategy Implications
Energy/Ecological/ Environmental Orientation	Gradual proliferation of energy conservation ethic, which in turn may be generalized into natural resources conservation, and then into anti-waste in general.		Consider publicizing how your company buys wood only from resources that have an acceptable restoration program. Follow same policy for other natural resources that you use—including energy.	Same as manufacturer.
Price/Value Orientation	Emanating from the loss of real income and rising prices, growing concern about the value received for the price.	Products should have visible price-quality relationships. Greater attention should be placed on engineering products that give good value for the price. Warranties and guarantees will become more important. Potential decline in middle price points compared to upper and lower.	Think about emphasizing that furniture and many other home furnishings are one of the best investments that can be made. Reevaluate pricing strategy in the context of achieving a visible price-quality relationship. If applicable to your company, develop a contingency strategy for the potential erosion of middle price points.	Same as manufacturer.
Eclecticism	Trend away from homogeneous fashion and life-styles toward the acceptance of a multiplicity of acceptable styles. Decline of fashion and life-style dictatorship toward more individualistic, often peer group influence.	Eclectic product line and assortment (that goes together) may become more effective. Comfort may become a more important criterion in selecting items. Growing market for accessories based on astrology, the occult, mysticism. Also accessory collections—medals, stamps, etc.	Through advertising and promotion, show eclectic furniture groupings, and dramatize comfort. Where appropriate, emphasize maintenance/durability aspects; for example, "(brand name) lets kids be kids."	Same as manufacturer.
Time Conservation	Growing recognition that time is a critical resource and constraint in many consumers' lives.	Furniture and home furnishings that are easy to care for, easy to repair, require less frequent cleaning, dusting, and so on.	Consider featuring ease of cleaning and maintenance in advertising and promotion.	Same as manufacturer. Also include in sales presentations. Also, improve ability of consumer to buy some items without visiting store.

Source: David T. Kollat, *Profile V Management Report* (Columbus: Management Horizons, Inc., 1976); David T. Kollat and Roger D. Blackwell, *Direction 1980* (Columbus: Management Horizons, Inc., 1970), and other related materials. Used by permission.

Up to this point, we have examined life-styles from a societal or cultural perspective—why and how things develop in the society. Now we must go further; we must begin to shift our focus to the individual consumer. To do that, a most useful concept is the one described next—personality.

PERSONALITY AND LIFE-STYLE

If all consumers in a society are exposed to the same basic life forces, would they all have the same life-styles? The answer is unmistakably no. It is unlikely that all consumers would be exposed to the same influences, of course, but even if they were, differences would exist among individual life-styles. The reason for the differences is called *personality*.

The definitions of personality vary greatly depending on the specific focus of the researcher using the term. The most general meaning of personality, however, is linked to the concept of *consistent responses to environmental stimuli*.[27] Personality is based on characteristics that determine general patterns of behavior. Major theories of personality that have influenced the study of consumer behavior include psychoanalytic, social-psychological and trait-factor theories. All three are discussed below.

Psychoanalytic Theory

The psychoanalytic theory[28] posits that the human personality system consists of the id, ego, and superego. The *id* is the source of psychic energy and seeks immediate gratification for biological and instinctual needs. The *superego* represents societal or personal norms and serves as an ethical constraint on behavior. The *ego* mediates the hedonistic demands of the id and the moralistic prohibitions of the superego. The dynamic interaction of these elements results in unconscious motivations that are manifested in observed human behavior.

The psychoanalytic theory served as the conceptual basis for the motivation-research movement that was the precursor to life-style studies. According to the philosophy of motivation researchers, consumer behavior was the result of unconscious consumer motives. These unconscious motives could be determined only through indirect assessment methods that included a wide assortment of projective and related psychological techniques.

The motivation research movement produced some extraordinary

---

[27]H. H. Kassarjian, "Personality and Consumer Behavior: A Review," *Journal of Marketing Research* (November 1971), 409-418, at 409.

[28]For a marketing level view of psychoanalytic theory, see W. D. Wells and A. D. Beard, "Personality and Consumer Behavior," in Scott Ward and T. S. Robertson, (eds.), *Consumer Behavior: Theoretical Sources* (Englewood Cliffs, N.J.: Prentice-Hall, 1973); C. S. Hall and G. Lindzey, *Theories of Personality;* 2d ed. (New York: John Wiley & Sons, 1970); R. J. Markin, *The Psychology of Consumer Behavior* (Englewood Cliffs, N.J.: Prentice-Hall, 1969).

findings.[29] Typical of the psychoanalytical explanations of consumer purchase motivations are these often related findings:

1. A man buys a convertible as a substitute mistress.

2. A woman is very serious when she bakes a cake because unconsciously she is going through the symbolic act of birth.

3. Men want their cigars to be odiferous in order to prove their masculinity.

These examples are interesting and perhaps even useful in obtaining a thorough, in-depth understanding of personality and consumer decision-making. There is a need to go further, however.

Social-Psychological Theory

Social-psychological theory[30] differs from psychoanalytic theory in two important respects. First, social variables[31] rather than biological instincts are considered to be the most important determinants in shaping personality. Second, behavioral motivation is conscious. People know their needs and wants and behavior is directed to meet those needs.

A representative example of social-psychological personality theory is the Horney paradigm. This model suggests that human behavior results from three predominant, interpersonal orientations—compliant, aggressive, and detached.[32] The Horney theory has been used in marketing research in a form developed by Cohen called the CAD scale.[33] This scale has substantial unresolved questions about its reliability, validity and internal structure[34], but is oriented in the right direction of attempting to relate general personality instruments to more specific consumer choices.

Trait-Factor Theory

Trait-factor theory represents a quantitative approach to the study of personality. This theory postulates that an individual's personality is com-

---

[29]The classic example of this literature is Ernest Dichter, *Handbook of Consumer Motivations* (New York: McGraw-Hill, 1964).

[30]Social-psychological personality theory specifically recognizes the interdependence of the individual and society. The individual strives to meet the needs of society, while society helps the individual to attain his goals. The theory is therefore not exclusively sociological or psychological, but rather a combination of the two (review Chapter 6). This theoretical orientation is most widely associated with Adler, Horney, Fromm, and Sullivan. For a more complete explanation of this approach, see Hall and Lindzey, *Theories of Personality*, Ch. 4, 117-159.

[31]There was no general agreement among the social theorists as to the relative importance of social variables. Fromm emphasized the importance of social context, while Sullivan and Horney stressed interpersonal behavior, and Adler eclectically employed many different variables. See Hall and Lindzey, *Theories of Personality*, 154-155.

[32]Compliant people are dependent on other people for love and affection, and are said to move toward others. Aggressive people are motivated by the need for power, and move against others. Detached people are self-sufficient and independent, and move away from others. For a marketing-level explanation of the Horney paridigm, see J. B. Cohen, "An Interpersonal Orientation to the Study of Consumer Behavior," *Journal of Marketing Research*, vol. 4 (August 1967), 270-278; J. B. Cohen, Toward an Interpersonal Theory of Consumer Behavior," *California Management Review*, vol. 10 (1968), 73-80.

[33]The CAD scale is a 35-item Likert scale developed by Cohen. The scale and scoring procedure appear in Cohen, "An Interpersonal Orientation," 277-278.

[34]Jon P. Noerager, "An Assessment of CAD—A Personality Instrument Developed Specifically for Marketing Research," *Journal of Marketing Research* (February 1979), 53-59.

posed of definite predispositional attributes called traits. A *trait* is more specifically defined as any distinguishable, relatively enduring way in which one individual differs from another.[35] Traits, therefore, can alternatively be considered individual difference variables.[36]

Three assumptions delineate this theory. It is assumed that traits are common to many individuals and vary in absolute amounts between individuals.[37] It is further assumed that these traits are relatively stable and exert fairly universal effects on behavior regardless of the environmental situation.[38] It follows directly from this assumption that a consistent functioning of personality variables is predictive of a wide variety of behavior. The final assumption asserts that traits can be inferred from the measurement of behavioral indicators.

The most commonly used measurement technique is the standard psychological inventory such as the California Psychological Inventory or the Edwards Personal Preference Scale (EPPS). Borrowing standard scales that were designed for clinical purposes may produce poor results for marketing purposes.[39] A better practice is to modify standard tests for marketing usage. An example of such a test is shown in Table 7.4 measuring the traits of "sociable, relaxed, and internal control." The research of Villani and Wind indicates that such tests are reliable measures of such traits.[40]

Trait-factor theory has been used almost exclusively as the conceptual basis of marketing personality research. In this research, the typical study attempts to find a relationship between a set of personality variables and assorted consumer behaviors such as purchases, media choice, innovation, fear and social influence, product choice, opinion leadership, risk taking, attitude change, and so forth.[41] Personality has been found to relate to specific *attributes* of product choice.[42] Research also indicates that people can make relatively good judgments about other people's traits and how they relate to such choices as automobile brands, occupations, and magazines.[43]

Predicting Buyer Behavior

Predicting consumer behavior has been the objective of most personality research. These studies generally fall into two classifications: (1) susceptibility to social influence, and (2) product and brand choice. The rich

[35]J. P. Guilford, *Personality*, (New York: McGraw-Hill, 1959), 6.

[36]A good introduction to the theory and techniques of this approach is found in A. R. Buss and W. Poley, *Individual Differences: Traits and Factors* (New York: Halsted Press, 1976).

[37]W. Mischel, *Personality and Assessment* (New York: John Wiley & Sons, 1968), 6.

[38]N. Sanford, *Issues in Personality Theory* (San Francisco: Josey-Bass, 1970), 8-9.

[39]Raymond L. Horton, "The Edwards Personal Preference Schedule and Consumer Personality Research," *Journal of Marketing Research*, vol. 11 (August 1974), 335-337.

[40]Kathryn E. A. Villani and Yoram Wind, "On the Usage of 'Modified' Personality Trait Measures in Consumer Research," *Journal of Consumer Research*, vol. 2 (December 1975), 223-228.

[41]Kassarjian, "Personality," 409.

[42]Mark I. Alpert, "Personality and the Determinants of Product Choice," *Journal of Marketing Research*, vol. 9 (February 1972), 89-92.

[43]Paul E. Green, Yoram Wind, and Arun K. Jain, "A Note on Measurement of Social-Psychological Belief Systems," *Journal of Marketing Research*, vol. 9 (May 1972), 204-208.

**Table 7.4
Test Items in the
Modified
Personality
Instrument**

Sociable

I am always glad to join a large gathering.
I consider myself a very sociable, outgoing person.
I find it easy to mingle among people at a social gathering.
When I am in a small group, I sit back and let others do most of the talking.
I have decidedly fewer friends than most people.
I am considered a very enthusiastic person.

Relaxed

I get tense as I think of all the things lying ahead of me.
Quite small setbacks occasionally irritate me too much.
I wish I knew how to relax.
I shrink from facing a crisis or a difficulty.

Internal Control

Sometimes I feel that I don't have enough control over the direction my life is taking.
Many times I feel that I have little influence over the things that happen to me.
What happens to me is my own doing.
Becoming a success is a matter of hard work; luck has nothing to do with it.
Getting a good job depends mainly on being in the right place at the right time.

Source: Kathryn E. A. Villani and Yoram Wind, "On the Usage of 'Modified' Personality Trait Measures in Consumer Research," *Journal of Consumer Research*, vol. 2 (December 1975), 223-228. Reprinted by permission.

literature on personality in psychology and other behavioral sciences has enticed many researchers to theorize that personality characteristics should predict brand or store preference and other types of buyer activity.

Much of the interest in personality by consumer researchers was stimulated by Evans, who attempted to test the assumption that automobile buyers differ in personality structure.[44] A standard personality inventory, the Edwards Personal Preference Schedule, was administered to owners of Chevrolets and Fords. There were only a few statistically significant differences between the two groups. Using a discriminant analysis, he was able to predict correctly a Ford or Chevrolet owner in only 63 percent of the cases, not much better than the 50 percent that would be expected by chance. Using 12 objective variables, such as age of car, income, and other demographics, a correct prediction was made in 70 percent of the cases. Evans concluded, therefore, that personality is of relatively little value in predicting automobile brand ownership.

A number of studies investigated the hypothesis that personality could be directly related to product choice. Some of these studies reported some relation between product use and personality traits.[45] Most other studies found only very small amounts of variance in product

[44]F. B. Evans, "Psychological Objective Factors in the Prediction of Brand Choice: Ford versus Chevrolet," *Journal of Business,* vol. 32 (1959), 340-369.

[45]M. J. Gottlieb, "Segmentation by Personality Types," in L. H. Stockman, (ed.), *Advancing Marketing Efficiency* (Chicago: American Marketing Association, 1959), 148-158; W. T. Tucker and J. J. Painter, "Personality and Product Use," *Journal of Applied Psychology,* vol. 45, (1961) 325-329; D. M. Ruch, "Limitations of Current Approaches to Understanding Brand Buying Behavior," in J. W. Newman, (ed.), *On Knowing the Consumer* (New York: John Wiley & Sons, 1966), 173-186.

choice explained by personality.[46] Looking back from today's vantage, it is not surprising that these studies found little relationship between personality and overall brand or product choice. After all, personality is but one variable even in the concept of life-style, and life-style is only one variable in the overall model of consumer decision making.

But even if personality traits were found to be valid predictors of buyer behavior, would they be useful as a means of market segmentation? In order for a positive answer to be given, the following circumstances must prevail:

1. People with common personality dimensions must be homogeneous in terms of demographic factors such as age, income, and location so that they can be reached economically through the mass media. This is necessary because data are available on media audiences mostly in terms of demographic characteristics. If they show no identifiable common characteristics of this type, there is no practical means of reaching them as a unique market segment.

2. Measures that isolate personality variables must be demonstrated to have adequate reliability and validity. The difficulties in this respect have already been pointed out.

3. Personality differences must reflect clear-cut variations in buyer activity and preferences that, in turn, can be capitalized upon meaningfully through modifications in the marketing mix. In other words, people can show different personality profiles yet still prefer essentially the same product attributes.

4. Market groups isolated by personality measures must be of a sufficient size to be reached economically. Knowledge that each person varies on a personality scale is interesting but impractical for a marketing firm, which, of necessity, must generally work with relatively large segments.

It seems that the evidence to date falls short of these criteria, and personality has not been demonstrated convincingly as a useful means of market segmentation. There is no reason to assume, for example, that individuals with a given personality profile are homogeneous in other respects; nor does it seem reasonable to expect that they have enough in common to be reached easily through the mass media without attracting a large number of nonprospects.

Therefore, it appears that future research that attempts to predict buyer behavior or identify market segments based on personality dimensions is destined to a low practical payout. There are, however, some significant applications of personality theory where the outlook is much brighter. These applications are described in the following sections.

[46]Ralph Westfall, "Psychological Factors in Predicting Product Choice," *Journal of Marketing*, vol. 26 (1962), 34-40; F. B. Evans, "Ford versus Chevrolet: Park Forest Revisited," *Journal of Business*, vol. 41 (1968), 445-459; A. Koponen, "Personality Characteristics of Purchasers," *Journal of Advertising Research*, vol. 1 (1960), 6-12; W. F. Massy, Ronald Frank, and T. Lodahl, *Personal Behavior and Personal Attributes* (Philadelphia: University of Pennsylvania Press, 1968); "Are There Consumer Types?" (New York: Advertising Research Foundation, 1964).

Personality as a Moderator Variable

Many theorists now believe that personality and the environment interact to shape behavior, as pointed out previously. An extension of this view leads to the prediction that a set of personality characteristics may be a better predictor of behavior in one situation than in another. In other words, it may be useful to distinguish situations in advance in which sample subgroups are differentially affected by specific personality traits. If these differentials are operative, then these personality traits are said to *moderate* the situation.[47] The resulting predictions from the use of personality inventories should then be more accurate.

Brody and Cunningham proposed a theoretical framework to predict the situational importance of consumer decision variables. In this conceptualization, the situational importance of any decision variable depends upon the choice situation.[48] Brody and Cunningham postulated that situational variables will moderate the choice situation when performance risk and specific self-confidence are perceived as being high. Thus, in *some* product buying situations and in *some* kinds of situations, personality will be an intervening variable. In other situations, it will not be. This hypothesis was tested with a reanalysis of Koponen's data on coffee purchases. Sample subgroups were isolated on the pertinent dimensions and regression equations were recomputed. The predictions obtained increased strikingly from virtually no variance accounted for by personality to as much as 32 percent.[49]

Fry cast self-confidence as a moderator variable in cigarette brand choice. He hypothesized greater explanation of cigarette brand choice among the subset of buyers high in self-confidence. Regression equations for a combination of socioeconomic and personality variables explained between 20 percent and 30 percent of the purchase variance.[50] This increase in predictive ability is equivalent to the Brody and Cunningham result.

Both of these studies demonstrate empirical advantages in utilizing personality as a moderator variable. This usage, however, raises three pertinent issues. First, the selection procedure for useful moderator variables is not intuitively clear. Several authors have noted this problem[51] and Brody and Cunningham readily admit the deficiency of their model in this area. Second, only a fraction of explained variance is accounted for in either study. Fry indicates refinements in measurement procedures

---

[47]For a more thorough discussion of the concept of moderator variables, see D. R. Saunders, "Moderator Variables in Prediction," *Educational and Psychological Measurement,* vol. 16 (1956), 209-222; E. E. Ghiselli, The Prediction of Predictability," *Educational and Psychological Measurement,* vol. 20 (1960), 308; E. E. Ghiselli, "Moderating Effects and Differential Reliability and Validity," *Journal of Applied Psychology,* vol. 47 (1963), 81-86.

[48]Specifically, situational importance depends on the consumer's perception of the choice situation. The perceptual filters include performance risk, specific self-confidence, and social risk.

[49]The greatest amount of explained variance was recorded for persons who were 100 percent brand loyal. Explained variance decreased directly with brand loyalty.

[50]J. N. Fry, "Personality Variables and Cigarette Brand Choice," *Journal of Marketing Research,* vol. 8 (August 1971), 298-304. Self-confidence was selected as a moderator variable because of its presumed influence on more specific personality dimensions. Fry readily admits the arbitrariness of this choice.

[51]R. P. Brody and S. M. Cunningham, "Personality Variables and the Consumer Decision Process, *Journal of Marketing Research,* vol. 5 (February 1968), 50-57; Fry, "Personality Variables."

are needed. Finally, research is still needed to determine situations in which personality variables are, or are not, relevant moderators. Solutions to these questions present formidable methodological problems.

The use of personality as a moderator variable shows promise as a means of explaining conflicting results. It is, however, an area that needs considerably more experimentation before a definitive assessment can be made.

Personality may be useful if the market is first segmented on some objective variable other than personality. Then each isolated subgroup is studied to determine any differences in psychological attributes. Any number of variables could be used for the initial market segmentation, including age, income, degree of product use, or others depending upon the nature of the problem. One approach that has proved useful is to differentiate buyers by the extent to which they use both the product and the brand. Then the inquiry focuses on why one person uses the brand while others do not.

One manufacturer followed this procedure, and it is useful to discuss briefly conclusions that resulted.[52] The Flavorfest Company (the company is real, but the name is fictitious) manufactures and distributes a well-known bottled condiment product. The firm has long dominated the market for this product line, which includes other spices and seasoning items.

Flavorfest could base a marketing program on the assumption that all potential customers are equally valuable prospects, but such an assumption must be verified by research to be successful. It is more likely that substantial consumer differences exist. Subsequent research disclosed three distinct market segments, each of which offered very different prospects for marketing success. These research findings were as follows:

Heavy Users (39 percent of the market)

1. Demographic attributes. Housewives aged 20-45; well educated; higher income categories; small families with most children under five; concentration in Northeast and Midwest regions and in suburban and farm areas.

2. Motivational attributes.

   a. Strong motivation not to be old-fashioned and a desire to express individuality through creative action and use of exciting new things.

   b. The traditional role as a housewife is viewed with displeasure, and experimentation with new foods is done to express her individuality, not to please her family.

   c. The image of Flavorfest suggests exciting and exotic taste, and the product is reacted to favorably in terms of taste, appearance, and food value. It is highly prized in experimental cooking. Hence, there

---

[52]This section is taken from James F. Engel, Hugh G. Wales, and Martin R. Warshaw, *Promotional Strategy* (Homewood, Ill.: Irwin, 1971), 160-162. Used by permission.

is substantial compatibility between values of the user and product image.

Light to Moderate Users (20 percent of the market)

1. Demographic attributes. Housewives aged 35-54; large families with children under 12; middle-income groups; location mostly in Southeast, Pacific states, and Southwest.

2. Motivational attributes.

    a. A strong desire to express individuality through creative cookery, but this desire is constrained somewhat by a conflicting desire to maintain tradition and subvert herself to her family's desires.

    b. The desire to experiment with new foods is also constrained by a lack of confidence in the results of her experimental cooking.

    c. The image of Flavorfest is favorable. The product is liked in all respects, but is confined largely to use with one type of food. It is viewed as unacceptable in other uses. Hence, her vision is limited regarding new uses for Flavorfest.

Nonusers (41 percent of the market)

1. Demographic attributes. Older housewives; large families; lower-income brackets; location mostly in the Eastern states and some parts of the South.

2. Motivational attributes.

    a. A strong motive to maintain tradition and emotional ties with the past; identification with her mother and her role in the home.

    b. A conservative nonventuresome personality.

    c. Her role as a mother and housewife discourages experimental cookery, and Flavorfest is thus looked upon unfavorably. The image of Flavorfest connotes exotic flavors and a degree of modernity that is unacceptable.

    d. No interest is expressed in new uses and experimentation with Flavorfest, for the product does not represent the values embraced by these housewives.[53]

From this research it is clear that there are important demographic differences between users and nonusers. Therefore, it is possible through skillful use of advertising media to avoid certain segments if this is deemed desirable. Specially designed questions also isolated some important personality differences.

The heavy-user segment is relatively large, and the product is well regarded by these housewives. Because of the product's use in experimental cookery and its role in expressing individuality, the potential exists for stimulating greater use.

The nonuser segment, on the other hand, presents a different mar-

[53]Engel et al., *Promotional Strategy*.

keting situation. While this segment now tends to be large, it is made up largely of people with relatively little purchasing power living in areas where population growth is stagnant. In addition, the potential for stimulating use of Flavorfest is not at all favorable. The existence of strong negative values increases the probability of selective perception of persuasive messages, and there would seem to be little market opportunity.

The light-to-moderate-user segment represents the greatest opportunity for increased sales. The desire for creative cookery is present but is constrained by a desire to maintain tradition and by a lack of confidence in results of experimental efforts. Yet the product is liked in nearly all respects. Lack of confidence, for example, might be minimized by stressing nonfail recipes. The interest in pleasing the family can be shown as compatible with creative cookery by stressing favorable family reaction to new tastes and recipes. Finally, Flavorfest can be featured as an ideal accompaniment to a variety of foods.[54]

As an intervening variable, personality may be helpful and is properly categorized as it should be—a variable that accounts for individual differences with broader categories of economic and social influence that are typically included in life-style studies. Some recent advances in personality research by Horton indicate that personality variables such as anxiety and self-confidence are in themselves related to consumer choice behavior but even in this encouraging research for the concept of personality, explanation is stronger in some specific stimulus settings than in others, primarily low-risk products.[55]

Advertisements are designed with personalities in mind, even if the research indicated less than very good prediction of behavior. And results are good. This appears to work best on products which need to be positioned in the minds of consumers through advertisements, probably products for which a personality can be developed to coincide with the self-concept or personality of the target audience. Examine Figures 7.7 and 7.8 and you will see two outstandingly successful examples of brands that have been able to communicate they are right for the personality of consumers in defined market targets.

MEASUREMENT AND ANALYSIS OF LIFE-STYLES

The final section of the chapter deals with some of the practical issues of measuring life-styles and serves to integrate the concepts *life-style* and *personality*. You will probably be pleased to know that life-style measurement is one of the simpler methodologies in consumer research. You should understand it readily by looking closely at the examples in the next few pages.

---

[54]This section is adapted from James F. Engel, David T. Kollat, and Roger D. Blackwell, "Personality Measures and Market Segmentation," *Business Horizons* (June 1969), 61-70. For additional materials related to this discussion on personality, also see John Walton, *Personality Research and Consumer Decisions*, unpublished M.A. thesis (Columbus, Ohio: Ohio State University, 1972).

[55]Raymond L. Horton, "Some Relationships Between Personality and Consumer Decision Making," *Journal of Marketing Research* (May 1979), 233-246.

**Figure 7.7
Advertisement
Appealing to Male
Personality**

Source: Courtesy of Marlboro.

Large Surveys

Psychographics—the measurement of life-styles—generally involves surveys of fairly large size. The surveys are most often administered by mail, often to families who have agreed to return questionnaires as part of nationwide panels operated by firms such as Market Facts in Chicago or National Family Opinion in Toledo. Typically, such surveys involve 1,000 or more respondents to provide ample cell sizes for analysis by specific classifications such as age, geographic region, and so forth.

Self-administered questionnaires are generally preferred because of

**Figure 7.8
Advertisement
Appealing to
Female Personality**

Source: Courtesy of Revlon.

the time required to fill out surveys which may have 200 to 300 or more AIO questions. It is possible to give smaller questionnaires in person or to hand them to consumers stopped in shopping centers (known as intercept studies). Sometimes respondents are asked to mail the completed questionnaire when they have time to finish it. AIO questions can be administered by phone, although the number of questions must be

**Table 7.5
Life-Style
Dimensions**

Activities	Interests	Opinions	Demographics
Work	Family	Themselves	Age
Hobbies	Home	Social issues	Education
Social events	Job	Politics	Income
Vacation	Community	Business	Occupation
Entertainment	Recreation	Economics	Family size
Club membership	Fashion	Education	Dwelling
Community	Food	Products	Geography
Shopping	Media	Future	City size
Sports	Achievements	Culture	Stage in life-cycle

Source: Joseph T. Plummer, "The Concept and Application of Life Style Segmentation," *Journal of Marketing,* vol. 38 (January 1974), 34. Reprinted from the *Journal of Marketing* published by the American Marketing Association.

reasonably small and care must be taken to write short, clear questionnaire items.

Likert Scales

The format used in most AIO studies is known as a Likert scale, named after the researcher who popularized the method of response in which individuals indicate whether they strongly agree, agree, are neutral, disagree, or strongly disagree. Numerous variations are possible, sometimes resulting in seven, nine or some other number of response categories to the AIO question.

Typical AIO studies measure subjects of the type shown in Table 7.5, compiled by Plummer. Some researchers include media as a separate category rather than include it under interests as Plummer does.

An example showing the specific format of AIO questions and categories of response is shown in Table 7.6. Questions can be *general* or *specific.* You can see that most of the questions displayed in Table 7.6 are activity-specific although some general questions are presented in the lower portion of the figure.

**Methods of
Analysis**

The simplest and often the most action-oriented form of analysis of AIO measures is simple cross-classification techniques. By that, it is meant that responses to a question are tabulated by a particular classification such as age, income or some other variable—including other AIO questions.

Notice that the responses in Table 7.6 were classified by sex. Some questions have very different responses by sex, such as "I like to go and watch sporting events." Other questions, such as "Our family travels together quite a bit," have almost identical responses for males as for females. This particular cross-tabulation illustrates a very important problem in relating AIOs (or any type of consumer research) to behavior. The *behavior* may be determined by the entire family or influenced heavily by one member but the responses of a specific spouse—who may or may not be the decision maker—are the measures of life-styles. Similarly, measures may be obtained about television or radio preferences, but

Table 7.6

An Example of AIO Questions, Classified by Sex

Activity statements	Females (N = 594)					Males (N = 490)				
	SA	A	N/O	D	CD	SA	A	N/O	D	CD
Vacation related										
Our family travels together quite a lot	38%	30%	7%	16%	9%	37%	33%	7%	15%	8%
A cabin by a quiet lake is a great place to spend the summer	44	28	10	11	7	45	30	9	11	5
On a vacation, I just want to rest and relax	31	30	7	23	9	34	30	4	21	11
I like to spend my vacations in or near a big city	6	13	12	30	39	4	10	11	28	47
On my vacations, I like to get away from mechanization and automation	23	33	16	19	9	28	37	14	16	5
Vacations should be planned for children	17	39	16	20	8	18	38	19	18	7
Entertainment related										
Television is our primary source of entertainment	26%	26%	6%	23%	19%	24%	31%	6%	19%	20%
I would rather spend a quiet evening at home than go out to a party	24	30	8	25	13	30	31	8	23	8
We do not often go out to dinner or the theater together	20	22	8	19	31	15	25	6	22	32
Sporting Related										
The best sports are very competitive	13%	21%	31%	21%	14%	28%	28%	20%	15%	9%
I prefer to participate in individual sports more than team sports	11	18	39	18	14	16	29	25	17	13
Whenever possible, I prefer to participate in sporting activities, rather than just watch them	15	27	15	19	24	25	29	12	18	16
I like to go and watch sporting events	18	40	13	15	14	34	37	10	12	7
Leisure time related										
I have enough leisure time	14%	23%	8%	28%	27%	13%	14%	8%	31%	34%
I tend to spend most of my leisure time indoors	16	35	6	29	14	7	22	7	32	32
Basically, I'm satisfied with my present leisure time activities	21	45	7	29	7	25	39	7	22	7
My leisure time tends to be boring	4	14	8	26	48	4	12	8	27	49
Specific Activity Related										
I do a lot of repair work on my car	1%	4%	23%	7%	65%	24%	24%	5%	16%	31%
I often work on a do-it-yourself project in my home	37	34	15	7	7	36	31	13	11	9
I am active in one or more service organizations	12	11	19	17	41	8	10	23	18	41
General Statements										
When it comes to my recreation, time is a more important factor to me than money	23%	29%	17%	21%	10%	25%	30%	15%	19%	11%
When it comes to my recreation, money is a more important factor to me than time	9	19	16	34	22	10	20	18	34	18
I watch television more than I should	21	28	7	23	21	20	29	9	24	18
My major hobby is my family	49	30	9	9	3	35	32	14	14	5

Note: SA = Strongly agree; N/O = Undecided or no opinion; D = Disagree somewhat; CD = Completely disagree.

Source: Douglas K. Hawes, W. Wayne Talarzyk, and Roger D. Blackwell, "Consumer Satisfactions from Leisure Time Pursuits," in M. J. Schlinger, (ed.), *Advances in Consumer Research* (Chicago: American Marketing Association, 1975), 833. Reprinted by permission.

these may be unrelated to actual viewing if other members of the family dominate the media decisions.

Multivariate Techniques

Most AIO studies also use some multivariate techniques of analysis in addition to cross-classification. Typically, factor analysis is used to reduce a great amount of data into its more basic structure. *Factor analysis* is a mathematical procedure for analyzing the high amount of correlation almost always existent in items into its most basic components or factors.[56]

Market Segmentation

The most frequent and perhaps useful application of life-style measurement currently is for market segmentation strategies. This application is based upon the premise that the more you know and understand about customers, the more effectively a communications and marketing program can be developed to reach that market target. Plummer analyzes the value of life-style segmentation and concludes that it provides a new view of the market, assists in product positioning, leads to more effective communication, helps develop total marketing and media strategies, suggests new product opportunities and, overall helps explain the why of a product or brand situation.[57]

Possibly the most advanced use of life-style research for market segmentation analysis is found in the VALS program of SRI in California. They have developed a consumer typology, shown in Table 7.7, based on three fundamental categories. *Need-Driven* consumers exhibit spending driven by need rather than preference and are subdivided into survivors and sustainers, the former among the most disadvantaged people in the economy. *Outer-Directed* consumers are the backbone of the marketplace and generally buy with awareness of what other people will attribute to their consumption of that product. Outer-Directed consumers have three subgroups with the characteristics shown in Table 7.7. *Inner-Directed* are a small, flamboyant and fiercely individualistic group of people who are mostly young. While their numbers are small, they may be important as trend setters or groups from whom successful ideas and products trickle up.

During the next ten years (the study was published in 1978), SRI expects the number of Inner-Directed consumers to more than double to almost 50 million adults, the number of Outer-Directed consumers to hold steady at around 110 million and the number of Need-Driven consumers to decline slowly to around 22 million.

How might a firm use life-style segmentation information? An exam-

[56]An easy-to-understand introduction to factor analysis is found in Joseph Hair et al., *Multivariate Data Analysis* (Tulsa: PPC Books, 1979), 215–249 and J. O. Kim and Charles Mueller, *Factor Analysis: Statistical Methods and Practical Issues* (Beverly Hills, Calif.: Sage Publications, 1978). Also see David Stewart, "The Application and Misapplication of Factor Analysis in Marketing Research," *Journal of Marketing Research* (February 1981), 51–62.

[57]Arnold Mitchell, *Consumer Values: A Typology* (Menlo Park, Calif.: SRI, 1978).

Table 7.7
VALS Life-Style Segmentation

Percentage of Population	Consumer Type	Values and Lifestyles	Demographics	Buying Patterns	Spending Power
	Need-Driven Consumers				

6	Survivors	Struggle for survival
		Distrustful
		Socially misfitted
		Ruled by appetites
			Poverty-level
			  income
			Little education
			Many minority
			  members
			Live in city slums
				Price dominant
				Focused on basics
				Buy for immediate
				  needs
					$13 billion

10	Sustainers	Concern with safety,
		  security
		Insecure,
		  compulsive
		Dependent,
		  following
		Want law and order
			Low income
			Low education
			Much
			  unemployment
			Live in country as
			  well as cities
				Price important
				Want warranty
				Cautious buyers
					$32 billion

	Outer-Directed Consumers				

32	Belongers	Conforming,
		  conventional
		Unexperimental
		Traditional, formal
		Nostalgic
			Low to middle
			  income
			Low to average
			  education
			Blue collar jobs
			Tend toward noncity
			  living
				Family
				Home
				Fads
				Middle and lower
				  mass markets
					$280 billion

10	Emulators	Ambitious, show-off
		Status conscious
		Upwardly mobile
		Macho, competitive
			Good to excellent
			  income
			Youngish
			Highly urban
			Traditionally male,
			  but changing
				Conspicuous
				  consumption
				"In" items
				Imitative
				Popular
				  fashion
					$120 billion

28	Achievers	Achievement,
		  success, fame
		Materialism
		Leadership,
		  efficiency
		Comfort
			Excellent incomes
			Leaders in
			  business, politics,
			  etc.
			Good education
			Suburban and city
			  living
				Give evidence of
				  success
				Top of the line
				Luxury and gift
				  markets
				"New and improved"
				  products
					$500 billion

	Inner-Directed Consumers				

3	I-Am-Me	Fiercely
		  individualistic
		Dramatic, impulsive
		Experimental
		Volatile
			Young
			Many single
			Student or starting
			  job
			Affluent
			  backgrounds
				Display one's taste
				Experimental fads
				Source of far-out
				  fads
				Clique buying
					$25 billion

5	Experiential	Drive to direct
		  experience
		Active, participative
		Person-centered
		Artistic
			Bimodal incomes
			Mostly under 40
			Many young families
			Good education
				Process over
				  product
				Vigorous, outdoor
				  sports
				"Making" home
				  pursuits
				Crafts and
				  introspection
					$56 billion

Table 7.7 (Continued)
VALS Life-Style Segmentation

Percentage of Population	Consumer Type	Values and Lifestyles	Demographics	Buying Patterns	Spending Power
4	Societally Conscious	Societal responsibility Simple living Smallness of scale Inner growth	Bimodal low and high incomes Excellent education Diverse ages and places of residence Largely white	Conservation emphasis Simplicity Frugality Environmental concerns	$50 billion
2	Integrated	Psychological maturity Sense of fittingness Tolerant, self-actualizing World perspective	Good to excellent incomes Bimodal in age Excellent education Diverse jobs and residential patterns	Varied self-expression Esthetically oriented Ecologically aware One-of-a-kind items	$28 billion

Source: Excerpted by permission from Arnold Mitchell, *Consumer Values: A Typology* (Menlo Park, Calif.: SRI, 1978).

ple is shown in Figure 7.9, a brochure describing Lifestyle Carpet Centers marketed by Lee's Carpets. After the firm completed its life-style segmentation research, it developed carpets that would be particularly appropriate for each segment identified in the study. A merchandising program was implemented insuring that atmospherics and trained salespersons would be available in retail outlets compatible with the life-style strategy. Finally an advertising and sales promotion program was implemented.

You can see in Figure 7.9 a portion of a booklet which is distributed to customers, describing life-style segments, the kinds of homes likely to fit those characteristics, and the type of carpet most appropriate. Only one segment, the "Contemplative Person" is described in Figure 7.9 because of lack of space. Perhaps you can think what types of carpets and life-style would best describe other segments of the market.

Life-style is related to many aspects of consumer decisions. Food shopping is related to life-styles[58] as are other kinds of retail choice behavior[59] although promotion decisions and especially media decisions have been among the most frequent applications.[60] Life-style analysis is also useful for social marketing issues.[61]

Overall, life-style research is most appropriate for products whose

[58] Mary Lou Roberts and L. H. Wortzel, "New Life-Style Determinants of Women's Food Shopping Behavior," *Journal of Marketing* (Summer 1979), 28–39.

[59] W. O. Bearden, J. E. Teel, Jr., and R. M. Durand, "Media Usage, Psychographic, and Demographic Dimensions of Retail Shoppers," *Journal of Retailing* (Spring 1978), 65–74.

[60] J. E. Teel, W. O. Bearden, and R. M. Durand, "Psychographics of Radio and Television Audiences," *Journal of Advertising Research* (April 1979), 53–56.

[61] Z. E. Schipchandler, "Inflation and Life Styles: The Marketing Impact," *Business Horizons* (February 1976), 90–96; S. A. Ahmed and D. M. Jackson, "Psychographics for Social Policy Decisions: Welfare Assistance," *Journal of Consumer Research* (March 1979), 229–239.

**Figure 7.9
Life-Style
Marketing by Lee's
Carpets**

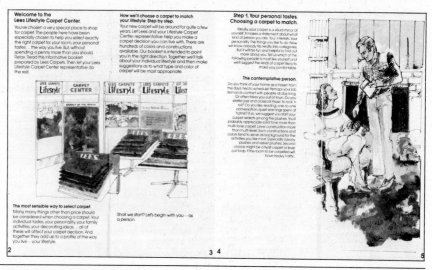

Source: Courtesy of Lee's Carpets.

function includes psychological gratification, or whose performance function cannot be evaluated objectively, products with high involvement, sometimes for products with high innovation, or those that are designed for a minority market segment, and are relatively expensive or symbolic. Life-style research is particularly helpful where advertising is a major tool in the product's marketing mix, where consumers are willing to switch brands when they are not completely satisfied, and where the category is not dominated by one or two brands. It is not so appropriate for commodities that are purchased on the basis of price primarily, or which have low involvement on the part of consumers.[62]

**A Concluding
Perspective**

This concludes Chapter 7 and it also concludes the first major part of this text. This chapter on life-styles, in a sense, serves the purpose of summarizing much of the material in Part 2 because all of the influences from the economic, cultural, family, and reference group are manifested in consumer life-styles—which, in turn, are measured through the technique of psychographics or AIO measures. All of these external or environmental variables become internalized through time to become a part of the decision-making influences within an individual. The sum of all of these and other influences is often described or thought of as personality. Traditionally, personality has been considered as an internal variable while influences such as family have been considered external variables. Yet, it can easily be concluded that all of the external variables cumulate

[62]Rudolph W. Struse, "Life Style Research Inappropriate for Some Categories of Products," *Marketing News* (June 17, 1977), 9.

and become a part of the life ways or patterns of an individual. In a sense, the term personality reflects an individual's characteristic ways of behaving or responding to these varied external and internal influences.

The discussion of personality in this chapter also provides a bridge to the rest of the book, for now we are ready to leave our analysis of environmental influences in Part 2, which, even though they are internalized within an individual, are basically external in measurement and analysis procedures. Now, we will turn our attention directly on the individual and will not return to these types of external topics until Parts 6 and 7 of the book. This part of the text in Part 2, however, is of critical importance in understanding the consumer because it focuses on the fact that *consumers purchase within the context of a life setting learned through socialization and interaction with others.*

Summary

Life-styles are the patterns in which people live and spend time and money. Life-styles are the result of the total array of economic, cultural, and social life forces that contribute to a person's human qualities. Most directly, life-style is a derivative of the social values a person internalizes and an individual's personality.

The concept of life-style is built upon the social-psychological theory that people develop constructs with which to interpret, predict, and control their environment. These constructs or patterns result in behavior patterns and attitude structure maintained to minimize incompatibilities and inconsistencies in a person's life—thus, it is possible to measure patterns among groups of people called life-styles. Psychographics or AIO measures are the operational form of life-styles, which marketing researchers measure. AIO stands for activities, interests, and opinions, and may be either general or product-specific.

The fundamental forces creating life-styles include the *cultural transfusive triad* and *early lifetime experiences.* The former refers to the influence of institutional influences such as the family, religion, and schools while the latter refers to basic intergenerational influences such as depressions, wars, and other major events.

Personality is linked to the concept of consistent responses to environmental stimuli and explains the differences in life-style that may be observed in individuals. Three theories of personality affecting consumer research include psychoanalytic, social-psychological, and trait-factor theories. Of these, trait-factor is most frequently used in marketing research, and it appears most useful as an intervening variable rather than a direct predictor of product or brand choice.

In this chapter, life-styles are analyzed from the perspective of: the society as a whole, groups of people within the society (segments), and individuals. Understanding the market through the analysis of life-styles has many applications to the development of product and communication strategies and the development of an integrated marketing strategy and program.

**Review and
Discussion
Questions**

1. Clearly distinguish among the following terms: life-styles, values, psychographics, AIO measures, benefits, personality.

2. Why do people have life-styles? Why are consistent patterns observable in a society, within groups of people, and between individuals?

3. Explain the difference between a general life-style measure and a specific life-style measure. Give two examples of each for a research project involving a soft drink.

4. Select from the topics of family, religious institutions, or schools and prepare a report documenting the changes that are occurring in these institutions.

5. Describe ways in which advertising directed to consumers raised during the Depression era might differ compared to that directed at consumers of the post-World War II era.

6. In what way is the rise of urbanism related to the changing values described in this chapter?

7. Assume that you are a marketing official for a large furniture manufacturer. Prepare a marketing program that would be successful in reaching consumers who might be young trendsetters. How should the manufacturer integrate retailers into this marketing program?

8. Describe the trait-factor theory of personality and assess its importance in past and future marketing research.

9. Assume that the marketing research director of a large consumer package goods firm is investigating the potential of personality variables as a basis for segmentation strategies. The director is familiar with several standardized psychological tests of personality but has been advised that tailor-made inventories might also be helpful. Citing the research in this chapter and other studies you may find in the literature, which approach would seem to have the highest probability of being useful?

10. Assume that you have recently been employed by a large department store and have been asked to prepare an analysis of the market for furniture in your city. The president of the store is interested in doing a psychographic study and has asked you to prepare a questionnaire that could be used in this city. Prepare a preliminary form of this questionnaire. Be sure to indicate the specific content of the questionnaire, some sample questions, the method of data collection, and methods of analysis.

PART THREE

PSYCHOLOGICAL FOUNDATIONS
OF CONSUMER BEHAVIOR

Two aspects of human behavior provide the foundation of all decision processes—information processing and learning. These basic topics are the subjects of Chapters 8 and 9.

Chapter 8 is addressed to learning processes. Clearly no single chapter can do justice to this broad subject, but the reader is introduced to various theories and concepts which are elaborated later. Moreover, learning is so important in the study of general psychology that an awareness of its variables and research generalizations is valuable in understanding human activity in any area of life.

The information processing arena has attracted droves of consumer researchers in recent years. This is understandable because the mechanics of memory hold the key to the whole process of persuasion. The literature has become vast, and therefore Chapter 9 is lengthy. The reader will find genuine rewards from perseverance, however, because the concepts developed there are used extensively in later chapters.

CHAPTER 8
LEARNING AND BEHAVIOR MODIFICATION

Wisdom is not always new, as this nineteenth century analysis of consumer behavior discloses:

The first time a man looks at an advertisement, he does not see it.
The second time he does not notice it.
The third time he is conscious of its existence.
The fourth time he faintly remembers having seen it before.
The fifth time he reads it.
The sixth time he turns up his nose at it.
The seventh time he reads it through and says, "Oh, brother!"
The eighth time he says, "Here's that confounded thing again!"
The ninth time he wonders if it amounts to anything.
The tenth time he thinks he will ask his neighbor if he has tried it.
The eleventh time he wonders how the advertiser makes it pay.
The twelfth time he thinks perhaps it may be worth something.
The thirteenth time he thinks it must be a good thing.
The fourteenth time he remembers that he has wanted such a thing for a long time.
The fifteenth time he is tantalized because he cannot afford to buy it.
The sixteenth time he thinks he will buy it some day.
The seventeenth time he makes a memorandum of it.
The eighteenth time he swears at his poverty.
The nineteenth time he counts his money carefully.
The twentieth time he sees it, he buys the article, or instructs his wife to do so.[1]

While the above quotation does not precisely describe how people learn to buy a product, it expresses the general theme of this chapter quite well. We need to understand as clearly as possible—how do people learn to buy one product instead of another?

---

[1] Thomas Smith, *Hints to Intending Advertisers* (London, 1885); quoted in Herbert E. Krugman, "An Application of Learning Theory to TV Copy Testing," *Public Opinion Quarterly*, (1962), 626-634.

BACK TO THE BASICS

Great football coaches like Bear Bryant or Woody Hayes often take their teams back to the basics. Sophisticated plays and superbly conditioned players are returned to the fundamentals of the game in order to get the team functioning well again. So it is sometimes with the study of consumer behavior; we need to return to the fundamentals of how people develop one behavior pattern instead of another or how people learn. In marketing, there has been a recent resurgence of interest in the fundamentals of human behavior and the modification of that behavior to achieve the marketer's own purposes. That is the topic of this chapter.

What Is Learning?

Most of what consumers do is learned behavior. People have some instincts or innate response tendencies, but when compared to the actions of other animals, a high proportion of human behavior is learned rather than instinctive. The great mental capacity of the human species, unlike that of other animals, permits great interpersonal variation in what is learned.

Everyday tasks—like walking and talking—are learned behavior, as every parent can testify. We also learn what other people expect from us. We learn attitudes, evaluative criteria, and expectations about the outcomes of our behavior. The grandfather of consumer behavior, George Katona, expressed it this way:

Learning in the broadest sense of the term is a basic feature of any organism. The human organism acquires forms of behavior, it acquires forms of action, of knowledge, of emotions. What has been done does not necessarily belong only to the past and is not necessarily lost. It may or may not exert influence on present behavior. Under what conditions and in what ways past experience affects later behavior is one of the most important problems of psychology.[2]

Definition of Learning

Learning may be defined in many ways, but in this book *learning* is defined as relatively permanent *changes in response tendencies due to the effects of experience.*[3] Often learning is defined as *changes in behavior* and many psychologists measure only overt behavior or performance. Behavior is the emphasis we focus on, but in consumer behavior we are also concerned with how people learn attitudes, emotions, evaluative criteria, and many other constructs which may not immediately be expressed in overt form.

Exclusions

There are changes in behavior that should not be considered learning. These include species-response tendencies (usually called instincts or reflexes), changes due to maturation (neuromuscular-glandular growth),

---

[2]George Katona, *Psychological Analysis of Economic Behavior* (New York: McGraw-Hill, 1951), 30. Reprinted by permission of the publisher.

[3]For a description of other definitions of learning, see John F. Hall, *The Psychology of Learning* (Philadelphia: Lippincott, 1966), 3-6. This book also serves as an excellent introduction to learning research.

and changes due to temporary states of the organism such as fatigue, drugs, or hunger. These latter states may affect learning and may be difficult to isolate from learning in certain cases of interest, but are fundamentally different from learning.

Types of Learning

There are two fundamental ways of classifying learning: associative and cognitive.[4] *Associative learning*, the most basic type of learning, involves *making a new association or connection between two events in the environment.* Sometimes you will see this described as connectionist approaches to learning. *Cognitive learning* is more complex and *involves interpreting present perceptions in the light of past information to reason our way through unfamiliar problems.* Some textbooks now describe cognitive learning as *information processing.* In this chapter, we will think mostly about associative learning since cognitive processes or information processing is presented in Chapter 9. Most of the material in this book is about cognitive learning, but in this chapter it will be helpful to look at some of the basics about associative learning.

Associative learning is further divided into two basic types, classical conditioning and operant conditioning. We will look at these in some depth. You should also know about a concept called *vicarious learning* or learning that *occurs by observing others*, changing our response tendencies after seeing the consequences of their behavior. Much of the behavior learned by young people arises from their observations of others. This is called *modeling*. There is much controversy about how vicarious learning occurs,[5] but it explains a lot about how people learn to behave—their sex roles, whether to smoke and drink, what kind of language is acceptable and so forth. The process by which society teaches these things is called *socialization*, which we will examine as one application of learning theory.

Behavior modification is another term used often today. It is not a different type of learning. Rather, it is an *application of learning theory involving intervention techniques to control behavior.* There are some interesting applications of behavioral modification which we will examine in the latter part of this chapter. Some theorists do not regard behavior modification as part of learning theory, but this chapter is a good place to discuss it.

The Study of Learning

No other field in psychology has generated the volume or quality of empirical research as has the study of learning. At one time, the experimental methods in psychology and learning theory were almost synonymous. Even today, learning experiments provide the classic methodological contributions.

[4]Actually, there are many ways of classifying learning. We are following the terminology found in Ernest Hilgard, Rita Atkins, and Richard Atkins, *Introduction to Psychology*, 7th ed. (New York: Harcourt Brace Jovanovich, Inc., 1979), Ch. 7.

[5]A good description of vicarious learning and the controversies about it are found in Paul Chance, *Learning and Behavior* (Belmont, Calif.: Wadsworth Publishing, 1979), Ch. 4.

With thousands of sophisticated research projects from which to draw and with a considerable amount of conceptual development, one might expect that learning would be one topic in which solid, indisputable generalizations would be possible. On the contrary, few topics are more disputed and tentative. Experimental results provide many contradictory findings and even more contradictory interpretations. Thus, it is impossible to speak meaningfully of the theory of learning; it is possible only to speak of learning theories. Good research supports leading proponents of these theories. This led Hilgard and Bower to comment on the dilemma one can fall into:

> The student of learning, conscientiously trying to understand learning phenomena and the laws regulating them, is likely to despair of finding a secure position if opposing points of view are presented as equally plausible, so that the choice between them is made arbitrary. He may fall into a vapid eclecticism, with the general formula, "There's much to be said on all sides."[6]

CLASSICAL CONDITIONING (S–R THEORY)

In classical conditioning, an unconditional stimulus (US) such as food, that is known to elicit an unconditional response (UR) such as salivation, is paired with a neutral stimulus, such as a bell or buzzer, which becomes a conditional stimulus (CS). As the unconditioned response (UR) is presented with the conditioned stimulus (CS), an increase will occur for the new (CS) stimulus (light) to elicit a similar, conditioned response (CR). The Pavlovian dog experiment is the model of classical conditioning.[7]

Advertising programs are sometimes built upon the principles of classical conditioning or what is often known as S–R Theory. Figure 8.1 shows how this might work. Seeing a US of a pleasant boy-girl situation produces for many people a UR of a pleasant emotion. When a consumer looks at such an ad (a US) at the same time a CS, such as a brand name, is presented, conditioning or learning will occur and a CR of pleasant emotion will be conditioned or associated with the brand.

Figure 8.2 represents an application of the principles illustrated in Figure 8.1. The advertiser apparently hopes the situation portrayed in the ad will elicit a response and that the brand will become conditioned to the same response. Read the copy carefully and you may conclude the advertiser is seeking a physiological as well as a visual response. There are significant ethical questions that should be raised about such ads, as we shall see later.

The explanation for classical conditioning is that some sort of connection occurs in the brain or nervous system, linking the stimulus (S)

---

[6]Ernest R. Hilgard and George H. Bower, *Theories of Learning*, 3rd ed. (New York: Appleton, 1966).
[7]Ivan P. Pavlov, *Conditioned Reflexes*, transl. by G. V. Anrep (London: Oxford University Press, 1927).

**Figure 8.1
Classical
Conditioning of
Brand Preference**

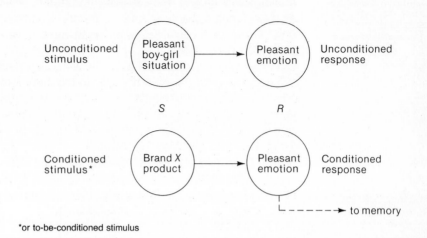

Unconditioned stimulus — Pleasant boy-girl situation → Pleasant emotion — Unconditioned response

S   R

Conditioned stimulus* — Brand X product → Pleasant emotion — Conditioned response

⌐ – – – – → to memory

*or to-be-conditioned stimulus

**Figure 8.2
Brand Learning through Sex Rewards**

Source: Courtesy of Paco Rabanne.

and a response (R). Hence, this approach is often called *connectionist* as well stimulus-response or S–R theory. People who study and theorize only about observable behavior, such as is done in S–R experiments, are called behavioralists.

John Watson was a behavioralist who, like Pavlov, influenced advertising significantly. Watson believed in the *contiguity theory,* which stated that the only thing necessary for learning was the mere fact that a response occurs in the presence of a stimulus. Thus, advertising would be effective merely through repetition and would not depend on a consumer liking the stimulus. You can probably think of some advertising campaigns that appear to be built on the contiguity theory!

Watson also described the frequency principle and the recency principle. According to the *frequency principle,* the more often a consumer experiences a conditional response in the presence of a stimulus, the more likely the response is to occur when presented with the stimulus in the future. If a consumer sees a slogan that says, "I'd walk a mile for a ———" or "Please don't squeeze the ———," the more likely the consumer is to recognize those brands in the store. According to the *recency principle,* a person is likely to respond to a stimulus the same way the person responded to it the last time he or she was presented with the stimulus. Therefore, if everything else were equal between two brands, a person might prefer—perhaps buy—the brand last advertised or last purchased. Both frequency and recency principles have had much effect upon the scheduling of advertising campaigns; although it is presumed they work best, if at all, for low-involvement products such as frequently purchased, low-unit price, consumer packaged goods.

Some psychologists do not accept a pure connectionist approach. Organisms (animal or human) seem to sometimes behave as if they expected an event to occur—a dog salivates when it expects the conditioned bell to ring. This approach to explaining behavior is called *expectancy theory.* It tends to emphasize the *relationship* between response and the stimulus and this leads us to another type of learning, *operant conditioning* or instrumental learning.

OPERANT CONDITIONING

Operant conditioning, also called *instrumental learning* or *respondent-reinforcement* (R-R), refers to *increasing the frequency or probability of a response by following the occurrence of a response with reinforcement.* The Skinner box illustrates operant conditioning.[8] An animal (rat, pigeon, etc.) is placed in a box with a bar that can be depressed to receive a reward (piece of grain) or avoid punishment (electrical shock from the floor). By manipulating the rewards, the experimenter can change the rate of pressing the bar. This is operant conditioning. The

[8]B. F. Skinner, *Behavior of Organisms: An Experimental Analysis* (New York: Appleton, 1966).

**Table 8.1
Suggested
Distinctions
between Two
Kinds of Learning**

Classical conditioning	Instrumental learning
(1) Outcome independent of what the learner does	Outcome depends on what the learner does
(2) A strong and reliable stimulus—response relationship already present	Variable responding prior to learning
(3) Change is mainly in the effectiveness of a stimulus	Change is mainly in the frequency of a response
(4) Typically involves behavior controlled by the autonomic nervous system	Typically involves behavior controlled by the somatic nervous system
(5) Involves involuntary responses	Involves voluntary responses
(6) Involves feelings or expectancies	Involves overt acts or directed thoughts
(7) Produces changes in opinions, tastes, and goals	Produces changes in goal-directed actions

Source: Winfred F. Hill, *Psychology: Principles and Problems* (Philadelphia: Lippincott, 1970), 62. Reprinted by permission of the publisher.

**Figure 8.3
Operant
Conditioning**

"I've got the people trained so that everytime I play those silly little horns they clap their hands together, and one of them throws me a fish!"

Source: *The Wall Street Journal*, 1980. Reprinted by permission.

rat's pressing the bar operates on the environment, producing or gaining access to the food. The differences between classical conditioning and operant or instrumental conditioning are summarized in Table 8.1.

Some people have observed that the experimenter is conditioned as well. Maybe the pigeon or the porpoise has the trainer conditioned to provide a reward when the trainee performs as expected, as Figure 8.3 indicates.

In many ways classical conditioning is analogous to low-involvement learning and the best strategy for developing brand preference may be coupling or associating a brand of toothpaste or some similar product with an S–R link-up like sex appeal. Imagery, repetition of basic themes on television and similar programs, would be most effective. High-involvement products, however, are more analogous to instrument (operant) learning. Consumers are seeking goal-oriented rewards and can be expected to "press the bar" of information search by reading print ads, talking to sales persons, and so forth. It is incorrect categorically to describe low- and high-level learning as classical conditioning and operant conditioning respectively, but the general comparison yields some insights into consumer learning.

ACQUISITION–HOW PEOPLE LEARN

The pairing of a stimulus and a response is called a *trial* and the period in which people are learning the association between the two is called *acquisition*. If we examine how new associations are learned, we may get some clues about creating brand preference for one product rather than another. To understand the learning process, it is necessary to describe the basic elements of drive, cue stimuli, responses, and reinforcement.[9]

Drive

Learning is most likely to occur in the presence of *drive*—any strong stimulus that impels action. Drive arouses an individual and keeps a person ready to respond; thus, analysis of drives in learning is similar to analysis of motivation. A motive differs from drive mainly in that motive is purposeful or directed toward a specific goal, whereas drive refers to an increased probability of activity without specifying the nature of the activity. A hungry person walking through a supermarket or looking at a magazine will have a probability of responding to food displays in the store or food advertisements. A motivated consumer, however, may not be hungry (low drive) but may be looking for the ingredients for tomorrow's meals and enter a store to buy the needed ingredients with a low probability of responding to other products the consumer may pass by.

The importance of drive is also illustrated by the belief of sales managers that, "a good salesperson should be hungry." The meaning of the statement is that a stimulus-deprived individual will exhibit a higher level of sales effort than a satisfied person.

Two types of drives are believed to exist. *Primary drives* are based upon innate physiological needs such as thirst, hunger, pain avoidance, and sex. *Secondary drives* are *learned* rather than innate and are derived from the primary drives. Examples of secondary drives include the desire for money, fear, pride, and rivalry, and the higher-order motives hypothesized by Maslow.[10]

Advertisers need to consider the drive state of consumers in planning communications programs. A hot summer day is the best time to run ads for *Country Time Lemonade*. Advertising for the product might be mostly wasted if the ads are run on cold days in the winter. Standard Oil prepares ads for fuel containing deicer with a media schedule that calls for the ads to be run only when the temperature is 20° F or less.

Umbrellas sell on rainy days, rarely on sunny days. Buyers of snow tires exhibit high levels of search activity the day it snows. Dry cleaners can run ads for 20 percent discounts in the summer and few people

[9]From Neal E. Miller and John Dollard, *Social Learning and Imitation* (London: Kegan, Trench and Co., 1945); also John Dollard and Neal E. Miller, *Personality and Psychotherapy* (New York: McGraw-Hill, 1950).

[10]A.H. Maslow, *Motivation and Personality,* (New York: Harper & Row, 1954).

respond or even attend to the ad; but on the first crisp, cool days of autumn a 10 percent discount ad is heavily attended by consumers and brings many responses.

Cue Stimuli

Cue stimuli are any objects existing in the environment perceived by an individual. The goal of the marketer is to discover or create cue stimuli of sufficient importance that they become *drive stimuli* or elicit other responses appropriate to his objects. It is common to speak of cue stimuli simply as stimuli.[11] Other experiments have verified generalization with other types of stimuli such as different hues of color, different light intensities, sizes of stimuli, temporal variation, and language or verbal stimuli.

Discrimination

Discrimination is the process whereby an organism learns to emit a response to one stimulus but avoids making the same response to a similar but somewhat different stimulus. Examples include a rat learning to respond to the color white but not to black, a pigeon learning to peck a green bar in order to obtain a reward but not a red bar, a child learning to call one tall male "Daddy" but not all tall males, or a consumer learning to prefer Wendy's as a place to eat over other fast food chains, or to take the "Pepsi Challenge" and tell a difference between colas.

Marketing Applications

Generalization and discrimination are important to understanding consumer behavior and marketing programming. Consumers form images about stores and products and generalize about unknown attributes, prices and quality levels on the basis of known or observable cues. The decor of a store leads a consumer to generalize about its pricing policies. We may generalize that American Airlines and Continental Airlines have similar service levels but discriminate that US Air is different.

Consumers make judgments about the believability of claims for new products based on what they have learned from experience with similar products. A marketer with a new product that complements and extends the marketing of currently accepted products may use a family or blanket brand in an attempt to stimulate generalization. A new product designed to replace an existing unsuccessful one or a competitor must insure that the colors, the verbal description and other features stimulate discrimination by consumers.

The meaning of a cue for one individual may be quite different than for another individual. The challenge for marketers is to understand these differences. Look at Figure 8.4 for example. The National Poison Center Network asked that the traditional symbol of poison be changed after research disclosed that children generalized the skull and crossbones with the mark of pirates and treasures and exciting backyard adventures. Adults might recognize the skull and crossbones as a symbol for poison

---

[11]Carl I. Hovland, "The Generalization of Conditioned Responses: I. The Sensory Generalization of Conditioned Responses with Varying Frequencies of Tone," *Journal of General Psychology* (1937), 125-148.

**Figure 8.4
Symbols
Generalized as
Attractive and
Unattractive by
Children**

Source: Paul Chance, *Learning and Behavior* (Belmont, Calif.: Wadsworth Publishing Company, 1979), 125. "Mr. Yuk" is reprinted by permission of the National Poison Center Network.

but for children the symbol was an invitation to gobble up the "pirate food" inside. The result was a number of accidental poisonings. The Poison Center proposed a change to the Mr. Yuk symbol, and a better warning for children.

When individuals have difficulty discriminating between stimulus situations, behavior becomes random. This was shown by Pavlov in his early experiments and has been repeated in many other experiments.[12] Pavlov used meat powder to condition a dog to salivate whenever it was presented with a luminous circle on a screen in front of it. After the dog had learned to salivate when presented with the circle, he began presenting a luminous ellipse *not* accompanied by meat powder. The dog gradually learned to salivate when presented with the circle and *not* to salivate when presented with the ellipse; it had learned to discriminate. Pavlov then began to make the ellipse more and more like the circle and alternated its presentation with the circle. The dog continued to make correct responses until the ellipse became very close to the shape of the circle (although still slightly different).

After several weeks of having difficulty discriminating, the dog had a nervous breakdown, which Pavlov termed "experimental neurosis." This and related experiments all point to the conclusion that when stimulus situations are quite similar and yet the individual must emit dichotomous responses, behavior becomes random. If this finding can be generalized to consumer behavior, one would expect that brand loyalty, for example, would be most unstable among products that are difficult to differentiate from one another. Buying decisions would either be subject to random switching or be decided on something other than learned preferences such as price cuts, deals, or special promotions. This would seem to be the best application for stochastic models of consumer behavior.

[12]Ivan P. Pavlov, *Conditioned Reflexes*.

Stimulus Sampling

Cue stimuli have been the primary units of analysis for some of the formal models of brand loyalty in consumer behavior. Estes describes the probability of a response not as a function of one stimulus but of a stimulus situation made up of many small stimulus elements.[13] Whenever a response occurs, all the stimulus elements sampled on that trial become conditioned to that response. If the same sample of stimuli were to occur again, the result would be the same response that was conditioned to the original, identical set of stimuli. Since it is unlikely that an identical set of stimuli will be sampled again, the probability of any act occurring as a response to a stimulus situation is a function of the number of stimulus elements in the common set.

With additional trials, it can be predicted that additional stimulus elements will become conditioned to the response act. Since something less than 100 percent of stimulus elements will be sampled, the probability of a response will be a probability less than one, not certainty. Thus, behavior is a stochastic process. Two other psychologists have developed a parallel approach to predicting behavior[14] as a function of learning, and it is the combined work of these men from which Kuehn's learning model[15] of brand loyalty evolved.

Responses

Responses can be as simple as jerking one's leg when struck with a rubber mallet or as complex as trying to rub one's stomach in a circular motion with the left hand while patting one's head with the right hand. Responses also include attitudes, familiarity, perception, and other complex phenomena. Usually, however, learning psychologists attempt measurement of learning in behavioral terms. That is, responses must be operationally defined and preferably physically observable.

In marketing, the responses of interest are usually purchases of a product although they may be immediate steps such as recall or recognition of an advertisement, returning a mail reply or looking at a display in a store. We shall need to look at such intermediate responses when we discuss behavior modification.

Reinforcement

Reinforcement (or reward—a synonymous term) is defined variously. Miller originally defined *reinforcement* as reduction in drive and Hull similarly defined it as reduction in stimulus. However, the application of some objects has been shown to be reinforcing without involving drive reduction or stimulus reduction. Thus, some learning psychologists define reinforcement merely as environmental events exhibiting the property of increasing the probability of occurrence of responses they accompany.

---

[13]William K. Estes, ''Toward a Statistical Theory of Learning,'' *Psychological Review* (1950) 94-107.

[14]R. R. Bush and F. Mosteller, *Stochastic Models for Learning* (New York: John Wiley & Sons, 1951).

[15]Alfred A. Kuehn, ''Consumer Brand Choice—A Learning Process?'' in Ronald E. Frank, Alfred A. Kuehn, and William F. Massy (eds.), *Quantitative Techniques in Marketing Analysis*, (Homewood, Ill.: Irwin, 1962), 390-403.

When animals are used in learning experiments, the rewards usually reduce some primary drive. Thus rats, cats, and dogs learn tasks and receive as a reward food, water, a receptive mate, or the removal of adverse stimuli.

Secondary rewards (objects or situations that have taken on reward properties because they have been conditioned to other rewards) are of more relevance to consumer analysts. These include praise or esteem for example.

Schedules of Reinforcement

Different *schedules of reinforcement* result in different and characteristic patterns of behavior. Learning will occur most rapidly when each correct response is rewarded (100 percent reinforcement). However, learning is more lasting when reinforcement is *partial*. There are many other variations in reinforcement schedules. In addition to the issue of partial or 100-percent reinforcement, there are many studies investigating the issue of whether a fixed ratio or variable ratio of reinforcement to responses is most effective and what the ratio should be.

A study by Deslauriers and Everett investigated the effects of small rewards given to encourage bus riding.[16] Although this study raised some methodological questions because it was done in unusual hours (at night), they concluded that the coupons given as rewards for riding the bus were just as effective when given on a partial (variable ratio of reinforcement) schedule as when given on a continuous schedule. Since it was much cheaper to give the discounts only part of the time rather than on every ride, considerable savings resulted from understanding the effectiveness of varying reinforcement schedules.

People use their memory of what happened in previous learning situations and this interaction of memory and reinforcement of trials produces learning or performance.[17] The individual uses past experience to store in memory an expectancy about the stimulus, the response, and the outcome. When learning occurs in memory, although not observed in performance at the time it is learned, it is considered to be *latent learning*, a goal frequently in the use of advertising programs.

Is Reward Necessary for Learning?

Many researchers have been concerned with the issue of whether or not reward is necessary for learning. Contiguity theory, you will remember, states that the only requirement for learning is that a response occur in the presence of a stimulus—which would mean that seeing an advertisement and attending it would be the only requirement for learning, at least latent learning—to occur.

Brogden carefully executed a study in which 11 kittens formed an

[16]B. C. Deslauriers and P. B. Everett, "The Effects of Intermittent and Continuous Token Reinforcement on Bus Ridership," *Journal of Applied Psychology* (August 1977), 369-375.

[17]Thomas Nelson, "Reinforcement and Human Memory," in W. K. Estes, *Handbook of Learning and Cognitive Processes: Approaches to Human Learning and Motivation,* vol. 3 (Hillsdale, N. J.: Halstead Press, 1976), 207-246.

experimental group and 12 other kittens formed a control group. Each group was placed in a cage that the kittens could rotate. The kittens were observed carefully, and when any kitten in the experimental group engaged in cage-turning activity, a 1000-cycle tone of moderate intensity was presented, until each kitten in the experimental group had been presented with the pairing of tone and response 30 times. Each of the control-group kittens was also observed engaging in cage-turning activity 30 times.

When pairing of contiguous stimulus and response had been accomplished, Brogden then presented the tone to each kitten in both groups. The kittens in the experimental group emitted the conditioned response five times as frequently as those in the control group. This result is interpreted to indicate that learning can occur without the presence of reinforcement or drive. Mednick commented on the experiment as follows:

Apparently all that is necessary for an association to develop between a stimulus and a response is that they occur together frequently. Reward does not seem to be necessary. When reward is used, however, conditioning proceeds far more rapidly and with greater vigor.[18]

Random Reinforcement

Responses sometimes are randomly reinforced. Those responses become associated with the stimuli in such instances simply because they occurred with the stimuli, not because they were elicited by stimuli. This may explain quite a bit about the types of human behavior that can be seen in consumer and many other types of behavior.

The classic description of random reinforcement is provided by Skinner in his experiment of how pigeons develop seemingly irrational behavior:

Suppose we give a pigeon a small amount of food every fifteen seconds regardless of what it is doing. When the food is first given, the pigeon will be behaving in some way—if only standing still—and conditioning will take place. It is then more probable that the same behavior will be in progress when the food is given again. If this proves to be the case, the "operant" will be further strengthened. If not, some other behavior will be strengthened. Eventually, a given bit of behavior reaches a frequency at which it is often reinforced. It then becomes a permanent part of the repertoire of the bird, even though the food has been given by a clock which is unrelated to the bird's behavior. Conspicuous responses which have been established in this way include turning sharply to one side, hopping from one foot to the other and back, bowing and scraping, turning around, strutting, and raising the head.[19]

---

[18]This experiment, conducted by W. J. Brogden, is described in Sarnoff A. Mednick, *Learning* (Englewood Cliffs, N.J.: Prentice-Hall, 1964), 25-26.

[19]B. F. Skinner, *Science and Human Behavior* (New York: Macmillan, 1953), 85.

Operant conditioning of this type accounts for superstitions and other forms of difficult-to-understand behavior. A student learns to use a lucky pen on exams or believes she does better wearing a certain type of clothing. Sure cures for colds or other illnesses are learned by primitive and not-so-primitive peoples. A consumer visits a supermarket much like other supermarkets but receives a random reinforcement on that trip—a special bargain, a good-tasting free sample or a friendly greeting from the manager—and thus the probability of returning to that store, and receiving more reinforcement, increases until the consumer develops loyalty for that store.

Superstitious or irrational habits are particularly difficult to extinguish. Consumers can endure many nonreinforced trials with only an occasional reinforcement because of the reinforcement schedule under which such responses are generally learned. Usually reinforcement in such situations has been infrequent and sporadic; this is the most difficult kind of learning to extinguish.

Amount and Timing of Reward

Learning increases as a function of the number of reinforced trials, although there is some controversy about the nature of the curve. Performance tends to increase as the *amount* of reinforcement increases up to some upper limit. Three components of the amount of reward have been identified. They include the volume or mass of the reward, the amount of consuming activity, and the quality of the reward, all of which influence performance. If a reward is *delayed* following the occurrence of a response, then performance drops off. If the reward is delayed too long, then learning will not occur at all.[20]

RETENTION AND EXTINCTION–HOW PEOPLE FORGET

Consumer analysts are more concerned with how much is retained than how much is learned. It is the content of memory that is likely to affect consumer behavior. But what is memory?

Memory is generally considered to involve three stages. *Encoding* is the process of coding physical phenomena from the sensory mechanisms into the code accepted by memory. *Storage* is the process of maintaining information until it can be used in the retrieval stage. The process looks like this:

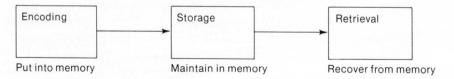

Encoding	Storage	Retrieval
Put into memory	Maintain in memory	Recover from memory

[20]A review of the reinforcement literature is found in John P. Houston, *Fundamentals of Learning and Memory* (New York: Academic Press, 1981) Ch. 7.

**Figure 8.5
Remembering and
Forgetting: Short-
Term Store and
Long-Term Store**

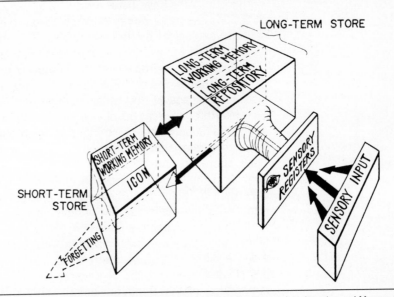

Source: Richard M. Shiffrin, "Capacity Limitations in Information Processing, Attention and Memory," in W. K. Estes, *Handbook of Learning and Cognitive Processes, Volume 4: Attention and Memory* (Hillsdale, N.J.: Lawrence Erlbaum Associates, 1976), 214. Reprinted by permission.

There appear to be two types of memory, short-term store (STS) and long-term store (LTS). Stimuli are thought to be imputed to memory through the sensory registers (auditory, visual, perhaps others) into what is called the sensory register or *sensory memory*. Sensory memory has a very brief duration period, something like one-half to one second and contains only very basic, unelaborated impressions of the external environment which decay rapidly unless processed on into one of the other stores (STS and LTS). The few stimuli (visual images or icons) to which consumers attend must be processed into STS before they fade away or they will never be remembered.[21]

Short-term store (STS) has a limited capacity and a limited duration. Many researchers think information will be lost from STS within one-half minute or so unless it is processed further. Items in STS may be maintained, however, through rehearsal. Or they can be displaced by new items entering STS. Items must be rehearsed if they are to be transferred to LTS and the longer items are held in STS by rehearsal, the higher the probability they are to be transferred to LTS and become part of permanent memory. This model of retention and extinction is built mainly upon the work of Atkinson and Shiffrin[22] and to some degree Waugh and Norman.[23] A picture of how the process works is shown in Figure 8.5.

[21]This section is based upon Houston, *Fundamentals*, 329-394.
[22]R. D. Atkinson and R. M. Shiffrin, "The Control of Short-Term Memory." *Scientific American* (August 1971), 82-90.
[23]N. C. Waugh and D. A. Norman, "Primary Memory," *Psychological Review* (March 1965), 890-904.

Two reasons have been advanced for why forgetting exists in LTS or STS. One theory is *decay* or *trace theory* based upon physiological or neuropsychological models of learning.[24] Trace theories postulate that each stimulus received by an individual leaves a neural trace which decays quickly unless repetition or rehearsal occur.

Interference theory postulates that the reasons people forget a learned message is that other learning of similar messages interferes. This interference may be of two types, and considerable debate exists about the importance or strength of each. Suppose that a consumer watched a television program and learned a message for Detergent *A*. Soon afterward and before she had an opportunity to remember Detergent *A* in the supermarket, she may have seen an advertisement for Detergent *B*. Since the *B* advertisement has an inhibitory effect on the retention of the earlier learned *A* advertisement, this type of forgetting (of *A*) is termed *retroactive inhibition* (RI). On the other hand, if the consumer learned the *A* advertisement and then viewed the *B* advertisement, a different type of interference would occur. If she tried to recall the *B* advertisement, the *A* advertisement would interfere with her remembering of the *B* advertisement. This latter type of interference is termed *proactive inhibition* (PI).[25]

Extinction

Extinction of a well-learned response is usually difficult to achieve. Under repeated conditions of nonreinforcement, however, there is a tendency for the conditioned response to decrease or disappear. One experiment illustrates the difficulty in achieving extinction. In this type of experiment dogs are conditioned to jump over a shoulder-high barrier in order to avoid a severe electrical shock. The dogs learn the response of jumping to the safe side of the box, then the dog must jump again to the other side of the box, over the barrier. If the dog does not jump every ten seconds, he receives another shock. Solomon[26] found, however, that after as few as 20 reinforcements, the electricity can be discontinued and the dogs will continue to jump, sometimes for hundreds of times.[27] Ex-

[24]D. O. Hebb, *The Organization of Behavior* (New York: John Wiley & Sons, 1949); also D. O. Hebb, "A Neuropsychological Theory," in S. Koch (ed.), *Psychology: A Study of a Science* (New York: McGraw-Hill, 1959), 622-643. Hebb explains the learning process by describing changes in the *neurons* of an organism's brain. When repetition of a neural pattern occurs, he believes that a microscopic growth or chemical change will decrease "synaptic resistance" and allow one neuron to activate another, thus producing response patterns. This *cell assembly* corresponds to a particular event sensed from the environment. Each item in the stream of thought going through an individual's brain is a *phase sequence* which, when assembled together, results in thinking or problem-solving ability.

[25]For a thorough analysis of interference and related topics see the collection of articles in W. K. Estes, *Handbook of Learning and Cognitive Processes, Volume 4: Attention and Memory* (Hillsdale, N. J.: Halstead Press, 1976). For a concise description of interference, see Winfred F. Hill, *Psychology: Principles and Problems* (Philadelphia: Lippincott, 1970), 312-321.

[26]Richard L. Solomon and Lyman C. Wynne, "Traumatic Avoidance Learning: Acquisitions in Normal Dogs," *Psychological Monographs,* (Washington, D.C.: American Psychological Association, 1953).

[27]Extinction is more difficult in this experiment than many examples, however, because secondary reinforcement appears to occur. If the dog does not jump within ten seconds, it experiences strong fear. Fear itself thus serves as a reinforcer.

tinction is virtually impossible to attain, unless the dogs are physically restrained by putting a ceiling on the box that prevents jumping.

Once something is learned, it appears that it is never truly *unlearned*. Thus, to say that a response tendency is extinguished merely means that the response in question has been *repressed* (through nonreinforcement) or it may be *replaced* by learning of an incompatible response. The return of response strength after extinction, without intervening reinforcement, is called *spontaneous recovery.* In experimental situations, animals that have had a particular response extinguished will often begin emitting the conditioned response after a period of rest. Spontaneous recovery is not unusual among people when they are confused, under stress, or in other unusual states. In such situations, they sometimes will recover response tendencies that have been extinguished for many years.

The original response strength of an extinguished habit can also be recovered instantly when a previously extinguished response is rewarded in an isolated instance. It is believed that undesirable habits are much more difficult to extinguish, therefore, by cutting down than by quitting entirely. These principles of extinction may serve to explain consumer preferences for a product, even in the face of numerous instances of using a competitive product.

Most research indicates that it is *easier to replace a conditioned response with an incompatible response than to extinguish the original response.* This would indicate that it should be easier to develop consumer preference for a new product than merely to develop consumer discontent with an existing product.

COGNITIVE LEARNING

The psychologists who studied learning until recently generally considered the topic to be limited to changes in behavior.[28] Today, there is much more emphasis upon cognitive learning or more complex forms of learning. The emergence of learning theory with measures of something other than behavior began around 1960 when neobehaviorist theories and stochastic-model theorists placed the emphasis on *probabilities of response.* The study of structure and process of memory also lead to inferences about what was occurring in the brain in addition to observable behavior. Even many of the behavioralists were involved in controversies about the nature of operant conditioning. Was the learning of how to run a maze by a rat merely a summary of S–R associations or was the rat applying thought or *insight* into solving the problem of obtaining the reward at the end of the maze? See Figure 8.6 for one of Charles Adam's ingenious cartoons concerning this question.

The future of learning theory is torn between two directions. Cogni-

---

[28]A good summary of the major philosophical issues in learning research is provided by James G. Greeno, "Psychology of Learning, 1960-1980," *American Psychologist* (August 1980), 713-728.

**Figure 8.6
Is Learning by S-R
or by Insight?**

Source: *The New Yorker* (March 16, 1981), 47. Drawing by Chas. Addams; © 1981 The New Yorker Magazine, Inc.

tive theory is the major direction and increasingly learning analysis centers upon the acquisition of knowledge in which modification and combination of cognitive structures are the basic processes. This has been stimulated by experiments on understanding language and problem-solving and is the major type of knowledge involved, not only in the next chapter, but most of this book. The other direction, however, is back toward an emphasis on behavior or only those things that can be measured without need to make inferences about cognitive structures or information processing. In marketing, an application of this behavioral direction—called behavior modification—is of substantial interest. We shall examine that topic next except for a brief look at the physiology of how the brain functions in learning.

**A Consumer's
Brain**

The human brain is composed of 10 to 12 billion cells called *neurons* which are the basic units of learning and mental functioning. Between these neurons are areas called *synapses* across which electrical impulses move from neuron to another neuron. The snyaptic junction between neurons is very important because it is there that nerve cells transfer signals. It is through this neurotransmission system that memory occurs.

Figure 8.7
How the Brain
Divides Its Work

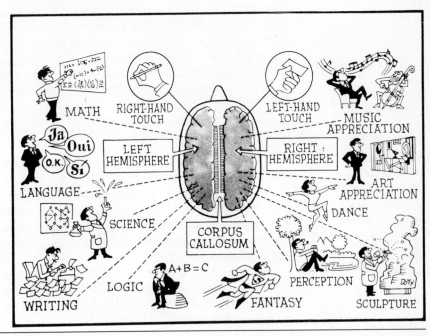

Source: "The Two Brains," *Newsweek*, August 6, 1973. Drawing by Roty Doty. Reprinted by permission.

A Divided Brain

The major areas of the brain (cerebral hemispheres) are divided. The left hemisphere controls the right side of the body and the right hemisphere controls the left side of the body. Usually the left side of the brain is slightly larger than the right. More importantly for consumer researchers, however, is the specialization of function in each side. The left cerebral hemisphere is specialized for the use of language while the right hemisphere is specialized for mental imagery and the understanding of spatial relationships.

Considerable research has been conducted showing the specialized activities of each side of the brain. Figure 8.7 shows how the work of the brain is divided. By looking at that figure, you can see how marketing researchers would be interested in the question of whether or not the right hemisphere would be most involved in watching television advertisements and forming overall images of a product and whether or not the left hemisphere would be more involved in print advertising and the processing of more detailed information about a product.[29]

[29]Sidney Weinstein, Valentine Appel, and Curt Weinstein, "Brain-Activity Responses to Magazine and Television Advertising," *Journal of Advertising Research* (June 1980), 57-63; Herbert E. Krugman, "Point of View: Sustained Viewing of Television," *Journal of Advertising Research* (June 1980), 65-68; John Rossiter, "Point of View: Brain Hemisphere Activity," *Journal of Advertising Research* (October 1980), 75-76.

BEHAVIORAL MODIFICATION AND MARKETING

Marketing analysts have often expressed peculiar interest in the principles of learning. While it is apparent that learning involves the most fundamental of human decision processes, consumer researchers have generally been more interested in psychological research dealing with perceptions, attitudes, and other more complex or inferential topics. The late Steuart Henderson Britt described how learning theory was relevant to marketing,[30] but little research was generated based on learning principles until recently.

Behavioral Modification Perspective

Behavioral modification is an application of learning theory. Behavioral modification, or behavior therapy as it is known in the psychology literature, refers to a group of *intervention techniques for controlling behavior.*[31] The Behavioral Modification Perspective (BMP) focuses upon the environmental, situational, and social determinants that influence behavior, *rather than the intrapsychic* (individual or internal) factors that determine behavior.

In marketing, a realistic approach to behavior modification was advanced by Nord and Peter who describe how the BMP could be used, but recommend that it be integrated with the internal psychological processes which also affect behavior.[32]

An outline of the behavior modification approach is provided by Kazdin. The distinctive characteristics of BMP include:

1. Focus on observable behavior.

2. Careful assessment of the behavior that is to be altered (behavioral objectives).

3. Evaluation of the effect of the program in altering behavior.

4. Concern for socially significant changes in behavior.[33]

The last concern is one that might be troubling in marketing if it were not for the implicit belief by marketers that influencing consumers to purchase the offering of the marketing is a socially significant change.

Reinforcement

The most important element in BMP is finding and applying reinforcement. Marketers usually are concerned with the application of positive reinforcement for the purpose of increasing the frequency of response of the desired behavior although in clinical practice, negative reinforcement—the removal of an adverse stimulus—is sometimes used to in-

---

[30]Steuart H. Britt, *Psychological Principles of Marketing and Consumer Behavior* (Lexington, Maine: D. C. Heath, 1978), especially chs. 19-24.

[31]Houston, *Fundamentals*, 531.

[32]Walter R. Nord and J. Paul Peter, "A Behavior Modification Perspective on Marketing," *Journal of Marketing* (Spring 1980), 36-47.

[33]Alan E. Kazdin, *Behavior Modification in Applied Settings*, (Homewood, Ill.: Dorsey Press, 1980).

crease the frequency of a desired response. Marketers must be aware in the development of BMP programs that an event may be positive for one person but not for others. Sometimes, an event may be a reinforcer in some circumstances but not at other times. That is why timing, cultural norms and other environmental elements are essential in developing a BMP program.

Reinforcers may be food or some other primary reward in institutional settings such as when autistic children are given bits of sugar coated cereal to encourage them to speak. For marketers, *social reinforcement such as praise is more likely to be used*. Children in a Head Start program were unwilling to eat unfamiliar foods, for example, until social reinforcers of praise and attention were given along with more primary reinforcers such as candy.[34] Sometimes rewards can simply be information. Winett, Neale and Grier found that the use of electricity could be reduced in a community simply by providing feedback concerning the amount of electricity consumed.[35] In another instance, energy use was reduced by rewarding families who achieved savings with a diamond-shaped decal which said, "We are saving oil," and which could be placed on the door of the house for others to see.[36]

Shaping

Shaping is a form of behavior modification that is particularly important to marketers. Shaping refers to the *reinforcement of successive approximations of a desired behavior pattern or response.* An animal that was expected to do a complex trick would never accomplish the trick if the trainer waited for the animal to do the complete trick and then rewarded the animal for doing so. Instead, the trainer rewards the animal for one step leading to the trick and then continues the reward as the dog adds additional steps.

A closely related technique called *prompting* can also be used. For example, a real estate agent might ask a prospective customer to meet the agent at a house. That is a cognitive approach—asking the customer internally to initiate behavior. Prompting, however, would involve the agent picking up the customer and taking the customer to the appointment; controlling the behavior is by intervention, in this case prompting.

Some forms of shaping that are sometimes used by marketers include the giving of a free product by a brush salesperson if the prospective customer "will simply allow me to show you my products, with no obligation to buy anything." Another example would be the use by insurance companies of a free road atlas or ballpoint pen given to customers who will simply write their name and birthday on a card and mail it to the

---

[34]C. H. Madsen, C. Madsen and F. Thompson, "Increasing Rural Head Start Children's Consumption of Middle-Class Meals," *Journal of Applied Behavior Analysis* (1974), 257-262.

[35]R. A. Winett, M. S. Neale, and H. C. Grier, "Effects of Self-Monitoring and Feedback on Residential Electricity Consumption," *Journal of Applied Behavior Analysis* (Summer 1979), 173-184.

[36]W. B. Seaver and A. H. Patterson, "Decreasing Fuel-Oil Consumption Through Feedback and Social Commendation," *Journal of Applied Behavior Analysis* (Summer 1976), 147-152.

company (allowing the salesperson to deliver personally, thereby manipulating the customer to get acquainted with the salesperson.) At state
fairs, some salespersons are very effective in picking someone from the
crowd and shaping his or her behavior to take initial steps in the purchase process just to help demonstrate this product. Not only does the
helper often buy the product but serves as a model for the vicarious
learning of other members of the audience.

Many sales-incentive systems are built upon the principle of shaping
by inducing with some reward—perhaps money or a gift item—calling
on a designated number of prospects or showing a product and getting
prospects "Merely to watch a demonstration so I can get practice before
I begin to work."

Marketing Applications

There are many applications of BMP in marketing. The commission form
of compensation for salespersons is one of the oldest and best-known
forms.

The *foot-in-the-door* approach is an application of behavior modification based upon the common folk knowledge, "If you give them an
inch, they'll take a mile." Freedman and Fraser investigated the hypothesis that asking people a small request first would get more results in
obtaining compliance with a large request than merely asking the large
request. Their study involved getting people to sign a petition by first
asking the people to put a "Drive Safely" sign in their front yard. The
results demonstrated that carrying out a small request increased the likelihood that people would agree to a similar larger request made later.
This was true, even when a different person made the larger request.[37]
Reingen found this technique could be used to induce people to donate
money to the Heart Fund[38] as well as increase the response rate to marketing surveys[39] and offered self-perception theory as an explanation for
such results.

An alternative approach—almost the opposite—is to use the *door-
in-the-face* technique in which the requester of some act by a consumer
makes an initial request so large that nearly everyone refused—the door
is slammed in the face. The requester then retreats to a smaller favor,
actually the one desired from the outset. Although the prior research suggested this should work as a compliance technique Reingen and Kernan
and Tybout did not find it to work.[40] Mowen and Cialdini commented on
several methodological problems in those works and found that if prop-

[37]Jonathon Freedman and Scott Fraser, "Compliance without Pressure: The Foot-in-the-Door Technique," *Journal of Personality and Social Psychology* (August 1966), 195-202.

[38]Peter Reingen, "On Inducing Compliance with Requests," *Journal of Consumer Research* (September
1978), 96-102.

[39]Peter Reingen and Jerome Kernan, "Compliance with An Interview Request: A Foot-in-the-Door, Self-
Perception Interpretation," *Journal of Marketing Research* (August 1977), 365-369.

[40]Reingen and Kernan, "Compliance"; Alice Tybout, "Relative Effectiveness of Three Behavioral Strategies as Supplements to Persuasion in a Marketing Context," *Journal of Marketing Research* (May
1978), 229-242.

erly implemented the door-in-the-face technique does allow the requester to get compliance with a relatively larger request than is possible with a simple direct solicitation.[41]

A considerable amount of research is developing on various aspects of compliance techniques generated from the behavior modification literature,[42] especially in the area of effects from discount or loss leaders, coupons, and so forth. There are some serious questions marketers must face about the ethics of such techniques, though.[43] How effective are they? Is it ethical to be more effective than in the past?

There are many unanswered questions about behavior modification, which promises to be an area of much interest and much application in the future. An outline of the possible applications and manner of developing those applications is shown in Table 8.2.

CONSUMER SOCIALIZATION

A final topic in thinking about learning is some consideration of the role of socialization—or social learning. How do people learn their roles in society, especially as they are growing up? Interest among consumer researchers is high in this topic, leading to such studies as Scott Ward's analysis of how children are affected by the media, especially television.[44]

There are several reasons for understanding socialization. First, this may allow consumer researchers to *predict some aspects of adult behavior* by knowing something about childhood experiences. Second, understanding processes by which children acquire consumption-related skills, knowledge, and attitudes is *important to public policy formulation, and the development of consumer education programs.* The study of consumer socialization is also important in understanding intergenerational changes in values and life-styles, which were discussed in Chapter 7. Consumer socialization is, of course, a special type of socialization and is concerned with the processes by which people acquire skills, knowledge, and attitudes relevant to their functioning as consumers in the marketplace.

Theories helpful in understanding the socialization process are re-

[41]John Mowen and Robert Cialdini, "On Implementing the Door-in-the-Face Compliance Techniques in a Business Context," *Journal of Marketing Research* (May 1980), 253-258.

[42]Anthony Doob, J. M. Carlsmith, J. L. Freedman, T. K. Landauer, and S. Tom, Jr., "Effect of Initial Selling Price on Subsequent Sales," *Journal of Personality and Social Psychology* (April 1969), 345-350; Carol Scott, "The Effects of Trial and Incentives on Repeat Purchase Behavior," *Journal of Marketing Research* (August 1976), 263-269; Alice M. Tybout, "Relative Effectiveness"; Peter Reingen and Jerome B. Kernan, "More Evidence on Interpersonal Yielding," *Journal of Marketing Research* (November 1979), 588-593; Carol Scott, "Modifying Socially-Conscious Behavior: The Foot-in-the-Door Technique," *Journal of Consumer Research* (December 1977), 156-164.

[43]O. Lee Reed, Jr., and John L. Coalson, Jr., "Eighteenth-Century Legal Doctrine Meets Twentieth-Century Marketing Techniques: F. T. C. Regulation of Emotionally Conditioning Advertising," *Georgia Law Review* (Summer 1977), 733-782.

[44]Scott Ward, "Consumer Socialization," *Journal of Consumer Research* (September 1974), 1-14.

Table 8.2
Illustrative Applications of the BMP in Marketing

I. Some applications of respondent conditioning principles

A. Conditioning responses to new stimuli

Unconditioned or previously conditioned stimulus	Conditioned stimulus	Examples
Exciting event	A product or theme song	Gillette theme song followed by sports event
Patriotic events or music	A product or person	Patriotic music as background in political commercial

B. Use of familiar stimuli to elicit responses

Conditioned stimulus	Conditioned response(s)	Examples
Familiar music	Relaxation, excitement, good will	Christmas music in retail store
Familiar voices	Excitement, attention	Famous sportscaster narrating a commercial
Sexy voices, bodies	Excitement, attention, relaxation	Noxema television ads and many others
Familiar social cues	Excitement, attention, anxiety	Sirens sounding or telephones ringing in commercials

II. Some applications of operant conditioning principles

A. Rewards for desired behavior (continuous schedules)

Desired behavior	Reward given following behavior
Product purchase	Trading stamps, cash bonus or rebate, prizes, coupons

B. Rewards for desired behavior (partial schedules)

Desired behavior	Reward given (sometimes)
Product purchase	Prize for every second, or third, etc., purchase
	Prize to some fraction of people who purchase

C. Shaping

Approximation of desired response	Consequence following approximation	Final response desired
Opening a charge account	Prizes, etc., for opening account	Expenditure of funds
Trip to point-of-purchase location	Loss leaders, entertainment, or event at the shopping center	Purchase of products
Entry into store	Door prize	Purchase of products
Product trial	Free product and/or some bonus for using	Purchase of product

D. Discriminative stimuli

Desired behavior	Reward signal	Examples
Entry into store	Store signs	50% off sale
	Store logos	K-Mart's big red "K"
Brand purchase	Distinctive brandmarks	Levi tag

Table 8.2 *(Continued)*

III. **Some applications of modeling principles**

Modeling employed	Desired response
Instructor, expert, salesperson using product (in ads or at point-of-purchase)	Use of product in technically competent way
Models in ads asking questions at point-of-purchase	Ask questions at point-of-purchase which highlight product advantages
Models in ads receiving positive reinforcement for product purchase or use	Increase product purchase and use
Models in ads receiving no reinforcement or receiving punishment for performing undesired behaviors	Extinction or decrease undesired behaviors
Individual or group (similar to target) using product in novel, enjoyable way	Use of product in new ways

IV. **Some applications of ecological modification principles**

Environmental design	Specific example	Intermediate behavior	Final desired behavior
Store layout	End of escalator, end-aisle, other displays	Bring customer into visual contact with product	Produce purchase
Purchase locations	Purchase possible from home, store location	Product or store contact	Product purchase
In-store mobility	In-store product directories, information booths	Bring consumer into visual contact with product	Product purchase
Noises, odors, lights	Flashing lights in store window	Bring consumer into visual or other sensory contact with store or product	Product purchase

Source: Reprinted by permission from Walter Nord and J. Paul Peter, "A Behavior Modification Perspective on Marketing," *Journal of Marketing* (Spring 1980), 41-42, published by the American Marketing Association.

lated to *learning theory.* In this conceptualization, the acquisition of social behavior is a process of trials or activities, some of which are reinforced and therefore increase in frequency. Learning can occur personally or vicariously. For example, a child may purchase a particular brand of candy bar and find it very tasty, thereby increasing the child's probability of purchasing the same brand in the future because of the child's personal learning experience. The child may also learn vicariously by accompanying a parent on a shopping trip and observing the behavior of this role model. Other role models may be observed and their reinforcing experiences may be vicariously learned. Experiences with one type of product or a particular brand may be *generalized* to new experiences with other brands. Products or brands of close similarity may be learned to be of different reinforcing values through the process of *discrimination* leading to different behavior on slightly different cues provided by brands that are basically equivalent.

A second group of studies and theories helpful in understanding are *cognitive* or *developmental* theories. In this stream of research the mind of the individual is seen as an independent force or organism that interacts with and is influenced by its environment but not entirely controlled by the learning environment. The mind of the individual selectively interprets environmental stimuli, reorganizes the new stimuli consistently with existing cognitive structures, and forms a new cognitive structure that controls behavior and continues to selectively interpret environmental stimuli.

In the family development literature, these cognitive structures are thought to progress through stages of development that are similar among most children. These theories are most often associated with the French researcher, Jean Piaget.[45] Research is increasingly focusing on these theories, investigating hypotheses that older children have more complex consumer learning skills than younger children, more negative attitudes toward advertising, and other related issues. This research is difficult to conduct, but generally supports the belief that youthful consumers make decisions progressing through different stages into their adult skills and motivations.[46]

LEARNING THEORY AND MARKETING

Learning theory is applied to the development of marketing strategy in many ways, as you have seen throughout the chapter. Fundamentally, marketing strategists are concerned with how people learn awareness, attitudes, and preferences that result in increased response tendencies to buy the product. Sometimes applications require us to go back to the basics, as we said at the beginning of the chapter. To conclude the chapter, let's look at a couple of examples.

The first example is Ziggy's, a supermarket chain that has applied the principle of repetition in almost the same way as the nineteenth century example given at the beginning of the chapter. This store, whose graphics are implemented by the internationally famed design firm of Don Watts in Toronto, repeats the name "Ziggy's" everywhere the customer looks. You can see in Figure 8.8 that "Ziggy's" is repeated on packages of everything from salami to coffee. This execution is not just a matter of carrying the store's identification; rather it is strong, grabbing use of the name to impact customer awareness and attention. In product areas where the brand cannot be placed directly on the product, such as produce, the name is still paired powerfully with the product to develop associative learning. In the advertising, the name is the predominant cue, even for a commodity product like veal. The famed cosmetic firm Revlon always places point-of-purchase materials on counters that are the same as customers have seen (learned) in advertising. Ziggy's implements this concept very effectively so that the learning that has occurred from advertising is reinforced (perhaps spontaneous recovery) in the store and

---

[45]Jean Piaget, *The Construction of Reality in the Child* (New York: Basic Books, 1954).

[46]Scott Ward and Daniel Wackman, "Family and Media Influences on Adolescent Consumer Learning," *American Behavioral Scientist* (January-February, 1971), 415-427; and Roy L. Moore and Lowndes F. Stephens, "Some Communication and Demographic Determinants of Adolescent Consumer Learning," *Journal of Consumer Research* (September 1975), 80-92.

**Figure 8.8
Repetition of
"Ziggy's" Brand
Name**

Source: Courtesy of "Ziggy's" and Don Watts Design, Toronto.

generalization of cues with a pleasant image is extended to a wide variety of products in the store.

Finally, another example of the application of learning theory to marketing programs can be seen in Figure 8.9. That ad is typical of many great advertising campaigns using the frequent repetition of a memorable theme with memorable execution. The ad combines a unique movie star—easily discriminated from other individuals—with a theme repeatedly paired with the name of a wine, "Paul Masson will sell no wine before its time." In a product category where the masses of customers are likely to be confused (fail to discriminate) by many brands and product types, Paul Masson has succeeded in getting consumers to learn one brand, Paul Masson, and presumably to associate that brand with correctness of product quality and compatibility with good food.

Figure 8.9
Repetition of "Paul
Masson's" Product
Theme

"Experts will tell you they drink Paul Masson
Pinot Chardonnay because of its full varietal
aroma, brilliant color and long pleasant finish.
What they mean is...it tastes good."

Paul Masson will sell
no wine before its time.

Source: Reprinted by permission of Paul Masson Vineyards, Saratoga, California.

Summary   The characteristic that produces a *dynamic* model of consumer behavior
is learning. Learning is the process by which consumer preferences are
constantly modified and updated. More specifically learning is defined as
changes in response tendencies due to the effects of experience. Nearly
everything humans do and feel is a result of learned responses.

The study of learning has a thorough and rigorous foundation. There
are many ways of categorizing learning, but two of the most fundamental

varieties are *classical conditioning* and *instrumental learning.* The principles underlying classical conditioning are useful in understanding how brands, products, and other symbols take on meaning for consumers; how stimuli that are neutral or unconditioned take on the meaning of other stimuli. The principles of instrumental learning help to explain problem-solving activities of consumers and deal with the ways specified response patterns are increased in their frequency or occurrence from among the variety of responses that might be chosen by a consumer.

This chapter describes in some detail five components of the learning process that receive considerable attention and research by psychologists. *Drive* is any impelling stimulus that energizes behavior. *Cues* and *stimuli* are any environmental objects sensed by an organism. *Behavior modification* is an *application* of learning theory concerned with intervention techniques to control behavior. *Reinforcement* tends to strengthen the association between stimuli and responses. *Retention* refers to the stability of learned material over time. Research indicates that materials learned well are difficult to extinguish and are more likely to be replaced with new material rather than unlearned.

Review and Discussion Questions

1. "Learning is the most fundamental of all human psychological processes." Defend or criticize this statement.

2. How should learning be defined? What problems exist in the definition you use?

3. Analyze the relative importance of learning theory to the understanding of human behavior compared to other forms of animal life.

4. Explain your views about the ethics of behavior modification in marketing.

5. Distinguish between classical conditioning and instrumental learning and assess the relative importance of each in an analysis of consumer behavior.

6. Are primary or secondary drives of more importance to marketing analysts? Defend your answer and give examples.

7. "The consumer can be taught to prefer any product a marketing firm chooses to offer." Analyze this statement fully. Do you agree?

8. Assess the importance of generalization and discrimination in consumer behavior.

9. How important is the concept of reinforcement in the learning of consumer preferences? Do rewards exist when a consumer watches a television commercial?

10. To what degree is the experimental neurosis finding with Pavlov's dog relevant to understanding brand choice with popular consumer goods?

11. What findings from learning psychology appear to have the most promise as stimulants to research in consumer behavior?

CHAPTER 9

INFORMATION PROCESSING

"Oh, you're the company with the blimp!" This was the common response of consumers in the early 1970s when they heard the name B. F. Goodrich. In reality, of course, this only symptomized the outright confusion in the minds of many people between Goodrich and Goodyear, both of which manufactured lines of automobile and industrial tires. Because Goodrich was being outspent three-to-one in consumer advertising by its major competitor, the "other guys" were receiving credit for innovations which were not even theirs. For example, consumers gave Goodyear more credit than Goodrich for introducing the first radial tire made in Amercia, even though Goodyear was not even marketing one at that time. The net result was that Goodrich was perceived by many consumers and even some of its dealers as being inferior to Goodyear.[1]

This is a classic example of the basic principle that each person actively processes and interprets information in a unique way. In fact, people tend to see and hear what they want to see and hear. B. F. Goodrich was an unfortunate victim of this basic human tendency, and its marketing efforts at that time certainly were not helping the problem.

Fortunately the staff at Grey Advertising understood what was happening and tackled the name confusion head-on with the now famous "non-blimp, we're the other guys" campaign. The strategy was to emphasize the B. F. Goodrich distinguished record of innovation through straightforward, low-key presentations making use of Goodrich president Patrick Ross as spokesperson. In so doing, a sharp contrast was established against competitive efforts which mostly featured low credibility torture tests. In two years Goodrich moved from last place to second place out of five major competitors in terms of consumer awareness for radial tires. Also it was ranked first as introducing the radial tire concept and making the best radial tires. Along with revamped efforts with its dealers, this campaign resulted in a substantial sales increase.

The authors often encounter this type of question: "Why study such things as memory when my need is for research to help me meet my

[1]*Advertising Age* (July 12, 1976), 40-42.

sales goals?" The Goodrich story is only one of many which illustrates the fact that it is essential to discover, if possible, why people respond (or fail to respond) as they do to various types of persuasion. Therefore, it is not a mere academic issue when we probe the whole subject of *cognitive processes* —the way in which information is "transformed, reduced, elaborated, stored, recovered, and used."[2] Probably *information processing* is a more palatable term, and it has come into common recent use in the literature of consumer research.[3] Memory, of course, is central to all that takes place, and the models of consumer behavior used in this book place it in a central position. Most agree with McGuire that analysis of the organization and functioning of memory ranks near the top in consumer research priorities.[4]

This chapter begins, then, with a discussion of how memory works. Then a distinction is made between information processing under high-involvement and low-involvement conditions. It will be demonstrated that the *consumer is sovereign* in every sense of the word—there is no magic power available for the marketer to use. This chapter provides the undergirding rationale for the basic proposition of this book: marketing success comes *only* through creative adaptation of all strategic efforts to consumer demand.

MEMORY ORGANIZATION AND FUNCTION

As might be expected, there are about as many theories on memory structure and functioning as there are writers on the subject. Here are several of the more popular conceptualizations; the perceptive reader will quickly detect the similarities among them.

One influential viewpoint is that memory consists of three different storage systems: (1) sensory memory; (2) short-term memory; and (3) long-term memory.[5] This is shown graphically in Figure 9.1. Briefly, memory is assumed to work in this way:

1. The stimulus enters and is processed first in sensory memory. Information is extracted about color, contour, and so on. No meaning is attributed at this stage.

2. The input then goes to short-term memory where it is held briefly. It is here that it is analyzed for meaning. It will fade from short-term storage

[2]Ulrich Neisser, *Cognitive Psychology* (New York: Appleton, 1966), 4.

[3]See especially James R. Bettman, *An Information Processing Theory of Consumer Choice* (Reading, Mass.: Addison-Wesley, 1979).

[4]William J. McGuire, "Some Internal Psychological Factors Influencing Consumer Choice," *Journal of Consumer Research,* vol. 2 (March 1976), 302-319.

[5]Lyle E. Bourne, Roger L. Dominowski, and Elizabeth F. Loftus, *Cognitive Processes* (Englewood Cliffs, N.J.: Prentice-Hall, Inc., 1979); Donald A. Norman, *Memory and Attention* (New York: John Wiley & Sons, 1969); Peter H. Lindsay and Donald A. Norman, *Human Information Processing* (New York: Academic Press, 1972); A. Newell and H. A. Simon, *Human Problem Solving* (Englewood Cliffs, N.J.: Prentice-Hall, 1972); J. W. Payne, "Heuristic Search Processes in Decision Making," in Beverlee B. Anderson, (ed.), *Advances in Consumer Research,* vol. 3 (Association for Consumer Research, 1976), 321-327; and James R. Bettman, "Issues in Designing Consumer Information Environments," *Journal of Consumer Research,* vol. 22 (December 1975), 169-177.

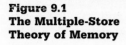

**Figure 9.1
The Multiple-Store
Theory of Memory**

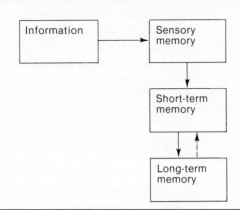

unless it is *rehearsed.* Rehearsal is a type of inner speech reflecting the fact that the input is being actively processed.

3. Information which is rehearsed then is transferred to long-term memory where it is stored permanently. It may be retrieved later if it is successfully integrated within the existing memory system. Forgetting occurs when means of retrieval are lost or when new information provides interference.

The multiple-store theory, however, has been thrown into question by recent research casting doubt on the assumption of the existence of separate memory systems.[6] Craik and Lockhart propose, for example, that there is one basic memory with various *levels* of information processing which encompass all of the components of Figure 9.1.[7] It is their hypothesis, accepted by some writers in the field of consumer behavior,[8] that long-term retention of incoming information is a function of the depth of information processing which takes place. If it only receives a sensory analysis, it will in essence become lost in terms of future use. An example would be the person who says, "I remember the picture of the mountain in the ad but nothing else." Deeper analysis occurs when the content is analyzed against current beliefs and interpreted in that context. If this does not occur, there will be no effective long-term memory.

Another widely accepted theory of memory is the *activation model.*[9]

[6]There are two excellent summaries to which the reader is referred. See Leo Postman, "Verbal Learning and Memory," in *Annual Review of Psychology,* vol. 26 (1975), 291-335; and Robert W. Chestnut and Jacob Jacoby, "Consumer Information Processing: Emerging Theory and Findings," in Arch G. Woodside, Jagdish N. Sheth, and Peter Bennett, (eds.), *Consumer and Industrial Buying Behavior* (New York: Elsevier North-Holland, 1977).

[7]F. I. M. Craik and R. S. Lockhart, "Levels of Processing: A Framework for Memory Research," *Journal of Verbal Learning and Verbal Behavior,* vol. 11 (1972), 671-684.

[8]See, for example, Joel Saegert, "A Demonstration of Levels-of-Processing Theory in Memory for Advertisements," in William L. Wilkie (ed.), *Advances in Consumer Research,* vol. 6 (Ann Arbor, Mich.: Association for Consumer Research, 1979), 82-84; and Jerry C. Olson, "Encoding Processes: Levels of Processing and Existing Knowledge Structures," in Jerry C. Olson (ed.), *Advances in Consumer Research,* vol. 7 (Ann Arbor, Mich.: Association for Consumer Research, 1980), 154-160.

[9]Allan M. Collins and Elizabeth F. Loftus, "A Spreading-Activation Theory of Semantic Processing," *Psychological Review,* vol. 82 (1975), 407-428.

Only one memory store is assumed. This model proposes that only limited portions can be activated at any point in time, and only the active portion is in use at any given moment. Further, that activation will be extinguished unless further effort is allocated.

None of these models is without its problems both conceptually and methodologically,[10] but these details are beyond the scope of this discussion. The authors agree with Bettman that it is quite appropriate to assume that there is one memory system with different internal functions.[11] We will refer, then, to sensory memory, short-term memory, and long-term memory as essential but different functions within one memory system.

Sensory Memory

In sensory memory,[12] incoming information receives an initial analysis for meaning based largely on such physical properties as loudness, pitch, and so on. Stimulus patterns thus become recognized as something meaningful. For example, a long thin object consisting of many pages receives preliminary classification as a book. Visual processing at this stage is referred to as *iconic* and auditory processing as *echoic*.[13] It takes place virtually instantaneously, with iconic processing requiring only one quarter of a second, for example.

Short-Term Memory

Once the stimulus passes through sensory processing, it enters short-term memory,[14] which is viewed by most theorists as the location of the primary processing activity which assigns meaning to that input. What it does, in effect, is to combine sensory input with the contents of long-term memory so that the new input is categorized and interpreted.

Short-term memory is limited in its capacity to process information at any given point in time. The term *chunk* is used in this context—a grouping of information familiar to the person which could be processed as a unit.[15] Depending upon which source one chooses to draw upon, processing capacity varies from four or five chunks [16] to as many as seven.[17]

Somehow the notion of chunk is pretty remote and abstract until we begin to look at it in a real world context. For example, a brand name is a chunk, and the more associations it can connote, the greater the infor-

[10]For a thorough and helpful review, see Bettman, ch. 6.

[11]Bettman, ch. 6. Also James R. Bettman, "Memory Factors in Consumer Choice: A Review," *Journal of Marketing,* vol. 43 (Spring 1979), 37-53.

[12]For more background, see Bourne, Dominowski, and Loftus, *Cognitive Processes;* Ulrich Neisser, *Cognitive Psychology* (New York: Appleton, 1966); Robert G. Crowsers, *Principles of Learning in Memory* (Hillsdale, N. J.: Lawrence Erlbaum, 1976); and Hershel W. Leibowitz and Lewis O. Harvey, Jr., "Perception," *Annual Review of Psychology,* vol. 24 (1973), 200-240.

[13]The standard source for research on echoic and iconic processing is D. F. Broadbent, *Perception and Communication* (New York: Pergamon, 1958). Also, see N. A. Moray, *Listening and Attention* (Baltimore, Md.: Penguin Books, 1969).

[14]Excellent reviews of pertinent literature are provided by Bettman, *An Information Processing Theory of Consumer Choice,* and Andrew A. Mitchell, "An Information Processing View of Consumer Behavior," In S. C. Jain (ed.), *Research Frontiers in Marketing: Dialogues and Directions* (Chicago: American Marketing Association, 1978), 188-197.

[15]Herbert A. Simon, "How Big Is a Chunk?" *Science,* vol. 183 (February, 1974), 482-488.

[16]Simon, "How Big Is a Chunk?"

[17]George A. Miller, "The Magical Number Seven, Plus or Minus Two: Some Limits on Our Capacity for Processing Information," *Psychological Review,* vol. 63 (1956), 81-97.

mation which can be conveyed by an ad. The Matex Corporation discovered this with its product *Thixo-Tex.*[18] Never heard of it? Neither had anyone else, as sales figures showed, even though some advertising had been done. Apparently *Thixo-Tex* was not much of a chunk. Then the name was changed to *Rusty Jones.* Sales increased from $2 million in 1976 to about $100 million in 1980 because of the remarkable connotation of "Rusty" as a way to prevent rust, extend the life of a car, and increase resale value.

Similarly, a product symbol or spokesperson may be viewed as a chunk. Just the sight of the Pillsbury Doughboy probably elicits thoughts such as bright, happy, modern, helpful, convenient, competitive, family, and so on.[19] The obvious conclusion is that it is well worthwhile to associate product attributes and evaluations with a name or symbol so that an entire grouping is triggered by sight or mention.

Another important property of short-term memory is transfer time—the amount of time necessitated to transfer an item or chunk into long-term memory. As will be stated later, rehearsal is required for this to take place. If information must later be recalled, evidence indicates that five to ten seconds are required to position one information chunk in long-term memory.[20] This becomes crucial in high-involvement decisions. As we will stress later in this chapter, recall is used most frequently in that situation, thus placing greater demands on information processing capacity. Recognition, on the other hand, requires between two and five seconds.[21] This type of response often triggers buying behavior under low involvement. This fact has some significant ramifications also, but more about that later.

Long-Term Memory

Long-term memory is generally viewed as an unlimited, permanent store. Its contents are often classified in this way:[22]

1. Episodic—ability to recall one's personal history.

2. Semantic—facts and concepts acquired which serve as a respository for meanings about the world.

3. Procedural—the repository for skills and knowledge of what can be done with stored facts, concepts, and episodes.

Others point out that this content combines in the form of memory schemata[23] or one's map of the world. Whatever term one prefers, these

---

[18]Hooper White, "Name Change to Rusty Jones Helps Polish Product's Identity," *Advertising Age* (February 18, 1980), 47-48.

[19]Harry W. McMahan, "TV Loses the 'Name Game' But Wins Big in Personality," *Advertising Age* (December 1, 1980), 54.

[20]Allan Newell and Herbert A. Simon, *Human Problem Solving* (Englewood Cliffs, N. J.: Prentice-Hall, 1972), 793-796.

[21]Herbert A. Simon, *The Sciences of the Artificial* (Cambridge, Mass.: MIT Press, 1969), 39.

[22]Bourne, Dominowski, and Loftus, *Cognitive Processes.*

[23]See, for example, Jean M. Mandler and Richard E. Parker, "Memory for Descriptive and Spatial Information in Complex Pictures," *Journal of Experimental Psychology: Human Learning and Memory,* vol. 2 (January 1976), 38-48.

memory structures allow the individual to organize new information in comparison with values and previous experience.

There are many theories about memory organization.[24] All center around the fairly obvious proposition that one element is logically related to another in some type of structure. Otherwise there would be chaos. There now is great interest in discovering whether product information is organized around brand names or product attributes. The growing consensus is that brand name is the organizing focus, although this is only a tentative generalization at this point.[25] We will return to this issue when discussing alternative evaluation in a later chapter.

Memory Control Processes

There have to be ways to control the flow of information in and out of memory. Atkinson and Shiffrin refer to these strategies as memory control processes,[26] and several of the more important ones are discussed in this section.

Rehearsal

Cognitive response theory is being used to shed some important new light on some aspects of memory control processes. Its basic postulate is that people are active participants in all that goes on in information processing—in other words, they are not just passive recipients.[27] They are always trying to relate new information to existing information stored in long-term memory. They do this by generating message-relevant thoughts through *rehearsal* (silent, inner speech).[28]

One function of rehearsal is to maintain information in short-term memory. An example would be rote repetition of a telephone number so it can be used without continual reference to a directory. It is not always sufficient to facilitate its transfer into long-term memory, however, since this is facilitated by *elaborative rehearsal.* At this stage new information is related to the existing cognitive structure and thereby transferred into long-term memory. What takes place during this stage is extremely important, and we will refer back to this concept a number of times later in the chapter.

Rehearsal, then, is best conceived as allocation of processing capacity to the stimulus in accordance with an individual's goals and the

---

[24]One good reference source is Bettman, *An Information Processing Theory,* ch. 6.

[25]See Eric J. Johnson and J. Edward Russo, "The Organization of Product Information in Memory Identified by Recall Times," in H. Keith Hunt (ed.), *Advances in Consumer Research,* vol. 5 (Ann Arbor, Mich.: Association for Consumer Research, 1978), 79-86.

[26]R. C. Atkinson and R. M. Shiffrin, "Human Memory: A Proposed System and its Control Processes," in K. W. Spence and J. T. Spence (eds.), *The Psychology of Learning and Motivation: Advances in Research and Theory,* vol. 2 (New York: Academic Press, 1968), 89-195.

[27]A good basic source on cognitive response theory is Richard M. Perloff and Timothy C. Brock, ". . . And Thinking Makes It So: Cognitive Responses to Persuasion," in Michael E. Roloff and Gerald R. Miller (eds.), *Persuasion: New Directions in Theory and Research* (Beverly Hills, Calif.: Sage Publications, 1979), 67-100.

[28]Donald A. Norman, *Memory and Attention: An Introduction to Human Information Processing,* 2nd ed. (New York: John Wiley & Sons, 1976), 86.

task at hand.[29] When rehearsal is elaborative, reflecting an active conscious interaction with incoming material, it leads to the constructive results suggested by Posner:

We must be able to reorganize information in order to solve problems, develop new structures, and interpret the world around us. To accomplish this we must operate upon the structures stored in our memories in a way analogous to the carpenter's shaping of wood.[30]

Coding

The individual must structure material in some appropriate way for rehearsal. Often such strategies as images, associations, and mnemonics will be used to code stimulus inputs so as to ensure the probability of later recall, recognition, or use. Bettman suggests, for instance, that brand names may be associated with a mental image that suggests or reflects that name.[31] Figure 9.2 contains an ad for *Sunlite* 100% Sunflower Oil, and it is easy to see how recall is facilitated by the association with the sun, the light it gives, the image of naturalness, and so on.

Transfer

Another type of memory control process is *transfer;* it shapes both the content and form of storage in long-term memory. The most clearly established proposition is that information which is appropriate for goal-oriented behavior is given highest priority. Actually, this is nothing more than just common sense. Those things which are of less personal relevance may never be transferred.[32]

Transfer also depends upon the ultimate expected use of the new information.[33] The person buying a new car, for instance, may do much brand comparison prior to a dealer visit. This necessitates reliance upon recall, with the result that attribute information probably will be stored in some detail.

Placement

This control function determines where a new bit of information is stored. The crucial determinant probably is the set of associations generated in the activity of processing. The association of the new input with existing memory categories (e.g. *Sunlite* Sunflower Oil associated with images of sunshine) will be a determining factor in *placement.*

[29]Bettman, "Memory Factors in Consumer Choice," 40.

[30]Michael I. Posner, *Cognition: An Introduction* (Glenview, Ill.: Scott Foresman, 1973), 92.

[31]Bettman, "Memory Factors in Consumer Choice," 40. For further discussion see Kathy A. Lutz and Richard J. Lutz, "Effects of Interactive Imagery on Learning: Application to Advertising," *Journal of Applied Psychology,* vol. 62 (1977), 493-498.

[32]Neisser has discussed this thoroughly under the heading "Analysis of Pertinence."

[33]A good basic source on transfer differences between recognition and recall is Barbara Tversky, "Encoding Processes in Recognition and Recall," *Cognitive Psychology,* vol. 5 (1973), 275-287.

**Figure 9.2
An Illustration of
Brand Imagery
Facilitating
Memory Coding**

Source: © 1980 Hunt-Wesson Foods, Inc. A Norton Simon Inc. Company. Reproduced with the permission of Hunt-Wesson Foods, Inc.

Retrieval

Retrieval is a complex and only partly understood process. About all that can be said without introducing unnecessary detail is that forgetting is now viewed by most theorists as a failure in retrieval as opposed to a loss or decay within long-term memory itself. The keeping of notes in a classroom is one way to facilitate retrieval, and this strategy is nothing more than common sense recognition that information may not otherwise be recalled in proper form when needed. Shopping lists serve the same purpose in a retail store, while other consumers scan the shelves to provide a memory jog for those things they previously intended to purchase on the shopping trip.

Response Generation

The last control operation is *response generation.* Rarely will the item retrieved from memory be an exact representation of the precise stimulus input. Rather, it is subject to some fairly major transformation as it is processed, rehearsed, coded, transferred, and stored. Because this is such a commonplace phenomenon, the marketer can learn much from pretesting advertising to see exactly what has happened in memory. The most common method is some type of realistic exposure followed by probing to determine what is recalled. The differences between input and output can be quite marked at times, and the only option is to try again until desired results are achieved.

INFORMATION PROCESSING UNDER HIGH INVOLVEMENT

As we mentioned in Chapter 2, consumer decision processes differ sharply depending upon the extent of involvement present. Involvement, in turn, reflects the extent of personal relevance of the decision to the individual in terms of his or her basic values, goals, and self-concept.[34] When involvement is present, there usually is a high degree of motivated information search and consequent information processing. Because this search is conscious and active, there is at least preliminary evidence that information is processed in the left hemisphere of the brain, the proposed seat of problem-solving activity.[35] Furthermore, it appears that print information is processed in the left hemisphere and the visual imagery of television in the right.[36] Finally, information is processed deeply in the left sector and apparently coded, transferred, and stored so that it can be *recalled,* rather than recognized.

The stages of information processing under high involvement are

[34]Refer to the various sources footnoted in Chapter 2. For an excellent single source reviewing the pertinent literature, see Michael Rothschild, "Advertising Strategies for High and Low Involvement Situations," in John C. Maloney and Bernard Silverman (eds.), *Attitude Research Plays for High Stakes* (Chicago: American Marketing Association, 1979), 74-93.

[35]For basic information on different functions in brain hemispheres, see Roger W. Sperry, "Lateral Specialization of Cerebral Function in the Surgically Separated Hemispheres," in F. J. McGuigan and R. I. Schoonover (eds.), *The Psychophysiology of Thinking* (New York: Academic Press, 1973). Also, Herbert E. Krugman, "Low Involvement Theory in the Light of New Brain Research," in Malone and Silverman, 16-22.

[36]There is growing evidence that verbal and visual processing uses different channels. See R. L. Clark, "Media, Mental Imagery, and Memory," *Educational Communication and Technology*, vol. 26 (1978), 355-363; Herbert C. Krugman, "Brain Wave Measures of Media Involvement," *Journal of Advertising Research*, vol. 11 (1971), 3-9. For a contradictory viewpoint, see Vallentine Appel, Sidney Weinstein, and Curt Weinstein, "Brain Activity and Recall of TV Advertising," *Journal of Advertising Research*, vol. 19 (1979), 7-18.

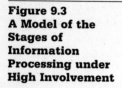

**Figure 9.3
A Model of the
Stages of
Information
Processing under
High Involvement**

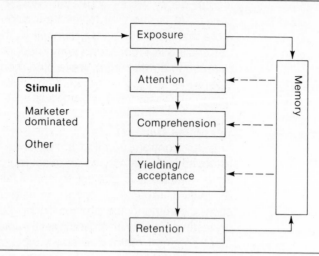

shown in Figure 9.3, and each is discussed in detail in this section. It is important to define these stages carefully:

1. *Exposure*—the achievement of proximity to a stimulus input such that opportunity exists for one or more of a person's five senses to be activated.

2. *Attention*—allocation of information processing capacity to the incoming stimulus.

3. *Comprehension*—the interpretation and meaning attributed to the stimulus.

4. *Yielding/acceptance*—the process whereby existing beliefs and cognitive structures are reinforced and/or modified by the stimulus input.

5. *Retention*—transfer of the stimulus input into long-term memory.

Many readers are wondering now what all this means when it comes to day-to-day reality. Perhaps it can best be illustrated this way. For any advertising or selling message to have an effect, it must survive all five stages of processing and enter into long-term memory. But many things can go wrong in the process with the result that attention is not attracted, it is miscomprehended, and so on. Let's assume that the odds of success are 50 percent at each stage, (i.e., only half are exposed, 50 percent of that group attend, and so on). This would mean that the probability of actually having some effect on beliefs and on ultimate behavior would be only .03125 (E .5 × A .5 ×C .5 × Y/A .5 × R .5).

    This represents a mighty meager return on marketing investment, and don't think for a minute that it cannot happen. A study of 1,800 TV commercials showed that only 32 percent of those exposed could even describe, and only 16 percent could remember, the brand that was advertised.[37]

[37]McMahan, "TV Loses the 'Name Game.'"

What this all says is that consumers are actively monitoring the environment for *relevant* information under high involvement, accepting that which is felt to be pertinent and rejecting that which is not. Furthermore, they will tend to resist influence attempts which are perceived as going against the grain. Anyone who ignores these facts will find his or her marketing effort to be fruitless, thus placing a strong premium on careful research. This is underscored by the fact that award winning (and presumably effective) ads are differentiated from their counterparts by the quality of the initial research which went into the message.[38]

Exposure

Information processing begins when patterns of energy in the form of stimulus inputs reach one or more of the five senses. For this to happen, of course, it is necessary for the communicator to select media, either interpersonal or mass, which reach that individual at the time and place where he or she happens to be. Exposure occurs from physical proximity to a stimulus input such that the individual has direct opportunity for one or more senses to be activated. This common sense principle of media selection is more difficult to implement than it might appear, however, because the first step is a very precise definition of audience target. It will not do, for example, to say that the target market for *Friskie's* dry cat food is all families who have a cat as a pet. Obviously any consumer has a variety of options in feeding a pet, and it will be necessary to determine beforehand exactly the type of person who prefers both a dry food and this particular brand. Next, research must disclose the types of media that actually will reach this particular audience. Now, all things being equal, the marketer at least stands a chance of delivering the message to the potential customer.[39]

The central nervous system possesses a vast capability to transmit information about numerous energy variations to the brain.[40] In vision, for example, the retina of the eye is stimulated by electromagnetic waves, and the result is the optic nerve activity.[41] The perception of different hues, on the other hand, results from changes in wave length.

Vibrations of the basilar membrane of the inner ear provide the basic sensations of hearing. Variations in experience of loudness, pitch, and timber, in turn, are a function of similar variations in the amplitude, frequency, and complexity of these vibrations.

Taste and smell seem to be activated by chemical interactions between stimuli and the membranes of the nose and taste buds. There is little else known about the physiology of these senses, other than the fact that different regions of the tongue detect one or more of four basic tastes—bitter at the base of the tongue, sour along the side, salty on the sides and top, and sweet along the top.

---

[38]James P. Murphy, "What Makes Ad Winner, Loser?" *Advertising Age* (October 20, 1980), S-32+.

[39]For a detailed review of the principles of media selection, see James F. Engel, Martin R. Warshaw, and Thomas C. Kinnear, *Promotional Strategy,* 4th ed. (Homewood, Ill.: Richard D. Irwin, 1979), ch. 13.

[40]For a useful but technical source on sensory processes, see S. S. Stevens (ed.), *Handbook of Experimental Psychology* (New York: John Wiley & Sons, 1951), chs. 3-11.

[41]Daniel J. Weintraub, "Perception," in *Annual Review of Psychology,* vol. 26 (1976), 263-289.

The skin senses provide information about pressure, pain, and temperature. Different receptors seem to exist for each type of sensation, and the types of energy submitted by each to the central nervous system are quite divergent.

Finally, there also are sensory receptors that provide information about internal states. Examples are the kinesthetic impulses, impulses from muscles or tendons, feelings of motion generating from the semicircular canals, an orientation to gravity resulting from the vestibular sacs, and various other types of pressure and pain.

The Concept of Threshold

There is a physiological constraint on whether or not exposure will take place, and this has come to be known as *threshold*—the intensity of stimulus energy required to activate various sensation levels.[42] There are three thresholds for each of the five senses:

1. Lower or absolute threshold—the absolute minimum amount of stimulus energy or intensity necessary for sensation or detection to commence.

2. Terminal threshold—the point at which additional increases in stimulus intensity have no effect on sensation.

3. Difference threshold—the smallest increment in stimulus intensity which will be noticed by an individual.

We will make some significant use of this concept later in the chapter when discussing the whole controversy surrounding subliminal perception.

The Measurement of Exposure

Apart from actually observing what a person does, exposure is difficult to measure directly. Therefore, it usually is inferred from data on radio or television listenership or readership of various periodicals.[43] The problem, of course, is that exposure to the medium does not necessarily reflect exposure to the advertising or selling message. There have been a few experimental efforts using such devices as photo-sensitive pages to isolate actual advertising exposure, and it appears that there is quite a gap between exposure measured in this way and actual recall of advertising content.

Selective Exposure

We have already established that people resist change in beliefs and behavior when involvement is high. One way to do this is to avoid exposure to unwanted information. It seems to be a commonplace thing for people to avoid contradictory information simply by not being in the au-

[42]See W. N. Dember, *The Psychology of Perception* (New York: Holt, Rinehart and Winston, 1961), ch. 2.

[43]For a review of media research methods, see Engel, Warshaw and Kinnear, chs. 12-13.

dience when they are forewarned that it is coming.[44] Katz argues that it happens in this way:

. . . (a) . . . an individual self-censors his intake of communications so as to shield his beliefs and practices from attack; (b) . . . an individual seeks out communications which support his beliefs and practices; and (c) . . . the latter is particularly true when the beliefs or practices in question have undergone attack or the individual has otherwise been made less confident of them.[45]

Not all authorities agree with Katz on this assessment,[46] but the balance of evidence certainly points this way. Also, every reader no doubt has done this at times in controlling the intake of mass media. Therefore, it should be accepted as a fact of life; selective exposure is one cornerstone of the proposition that the audience indeed *is* sovereign.

Attention

Attention is best viewed as the allocation of processing capacity once exposure has taken place.[47] One of the immediate outcomes is triggering the orientation reaction that prepares the individual to contend with a novel stimulus.[48] Activities previously underway are altered, along with these additional physical manifestations:

1. An increase in the sensitivity of the sensory organs. This occurs in the form of pupil dilation and photomechanical changes, which lead to lowered thresholds and reaction times for additional stimuli.

2. Changes in the skeletal muscles directing the sense organs. Turning the head is an example.

3. Changes in general skeletal musculature in the form of increased muscle tone and greater readiness for activity.

4. Generation of a state of arousal as indicated by electroencephalogram scores.

5. Elevation in galvanic skin response accompanied by increase in heart rate.

The Measurement of Attention Attraction

The most commonly used method is exposure of a group of people to one or more messages under conditions ranging from presentation of

[44]See, for example, M. T. O'Keefe, "The Anti-Smoking Commercials: A Study of Television's Impact on Behavior," *Public Opinion Quarterly*, vol. 35 (1971), 242-248; C. Atkin, et al., "Selective Exposure to Televised Violence," *Journal of Broadcasting*, vol. 23 (Winter 1979), 5-14; Elihu Katz, "The Uses of Becker, Blumler, Swanson," *Communications Research*, vol. 6 (January 1979), 74-83.

[45]Elihu Katz, "On Reopening the Question of Selectivity in Exposure to Mass Communication," in R. P. Abelson, et al. (eds.), *Theories of Cognitive Consistency: A Sourcebook* (Chicago: Rand McNally, 1968), 789.

[46]See, for example, D. O. Sears, "The Paradox of de Facto Selective Exposure Without Preferences for Supportive Information," in Abelson et al., 777-787; and J. T. Bertrand, "Selective Avoidance on Health Topics: A Field Test," *Communications Research*, vol. 6 (July, 1979), 271-294.

[47]Bettman, *Toward a Theory of Consumer Choice*, ch. 6.

[48]R. Lynn, *Attention Arousal and the Orientation Reaction* (Oxford: Pergamon, 1966).

three or four test advertisements in some type of booklet, to full-scale exposure to actual television or radio shows or print publications. Respondents then are questioned sometime after exposure and are asked to indicate what messages they recall or recognize. Obviously this measures *retention* rather than *attention.* It is to be expected that many more people attend to the message than will be revealed in this manner, because recall scores reflect the effects of selective information processing. For that reason considerable interest has been shown in recent years in laboratory measures that analyze attention without making use of verbal responses.[49] Among the methods attracting the most interest are (1) galvanic skin response (GSR) and pupil dilation response (PDR), (2) the eye movement camera, and (3) the tachistoscope.

GSR and PDR   Galvanic skin response (GSR) and pupil dilation response (PDR) seem to be measuring different aspects of information processing.[50] GSR measures two phenomena: (1) a decline in the electrical resistance of the skin to a passage of current and (2) a change in the potential difference between two areas of body surface.[51] When it elevates upon exposure to a stimulus, it is now felt to be an indicator of *arousal.*[52] PDR, on the other hand, measures minute differences in pupil size as it dilates and contracts.

Recent studies document that PDR is a sensitive measure of the amount of information or load processed within the central control unit from the incoming stimulus.[53] At one time it was felt that PDR measured affective or emotional response to a stimulus,[54] and several studies were published which purported to document that relationship in response to marketing stimuli.[55] The weight of later evidence, however, makes the load processing interpretation of PDR far more plausible. More recent research has underscored the potential of the GSR measure. First, the higher the arousal in response to an ad stimulus, the greater the extent of recall.[56] Furthermore, there is growing evidence that there also is a correlation with sales.[57]

If further replication verifies these apparent relationships, there are some significant practical implications. Different message variations can

---

[49]J. S. Hensel and D. T. Kollat, "Present and Projected Uses of Laboratory Equipment for Marketing and Advertising Research," paper presented at the American Marketing Association (September 1970).

[50]Paul J. Watson and Robert J. Gatchel, "Autonomic Measures of Advertising," *Journal of Advertising Research,* vol. 19 (June 1979), 15-26.

[51]R. D. Blackwell et al., *Laboratory Equipment for Marketing Research* (Dubuque, Iowa: Kendall Hunt, 1970), 42.

[52] Watson and Gatchel, "Autonomic Measures."

[53]For an extensive literature review see R. D. Blackwell, J. S. Hensel, and B. Sternthal, "Pupil Dilation: What Does it Measure?" *Journal of Advertising Research,* vol. 10 (1970), 15-18.

[54]E. H. Hess and J. M. Polt, "Pupil Size as Related to Interest Value of Visual Stimuli," *Science,* vol. 132 (1960), 349-350.

[55]See, for example, H. E. Krugman, "Some Applications of Pupil Measurement," *Journal of Marketing Research,* vol. 1 (1964), 15-18.

[56]Werner Kroeber-Riel, "Activation Research: Psycho-Biological Approaches in Consumer Research," *Journal of Consumer Research,* vol. 5 (March 1979), 240-250.

[57]"Psychogalvanometer Testing 'Most Predictive'," *Marketing News* (June 16, 1978), 11.

be analyzed prior to investment of funds in production to see which offers the greatest probability of attracting and holding attention. The advantage is that reliance need not be placed on verbal recall which can be inaccurate.

It is hard to predict whether or not such equipment will see widespread commercial use. In the first place, it can be quite expensive. The pupilometer alone can cost more than $20,000.[58] Moreover, findings have to be interpreted with a measure of both common sense and caution. One advertiser used the pupilometer to test an ad for frozen french fries. The designers were pleased with the amount of pupillary dilation recorded and assumed they had a winner until it was discovered that people were looking at the steak in the picture instead of the french fries.[59]

Eye Movement For many years it has been possible to track eye movement through advertising copy using a camera especially designed for this purpose. It was a highly artificial measure, however, in that the person's head was held in a fixed position in an uncomfortable manner. More recently this equipment has been dramatically improved (and vastly increased in price) through use of an infrared beam which tracks the eye as the consumer views or reads normally.[60] Some manufacturers report good results. It is possible to show which parts of a message capture and hold attention and whether or not various elements are perceived in the intended order. Avon Products has used this equipment to analyze pairs of ads, and those producing intended eye movement patterns have been found to produce highest sales.[61] Here are some other interesting results generated from use of this equipment at Cunningham & Walsh, a major advertising agency:[62]

1. People are found to be highly selective in what they view and see.

2. Greatest response is to representations of people.

3. The viewer scans rapidly and then zeroes in on one element at a time.

4. Product demonstrations vary widely in their ability to capture and hold attention.

5. The opening second of a commercial is most crucial in capturing attention.

[58]Berkeley Rice, "Rattlesnakes, French Fries, and Pupil-ometric Oversell," *Psychology Today* (February 1974), 55-59.

[59]Rice, "Rattlesnakes."

[60]James P. Forkan, "Oculometer Is Finding Out What Viewers See in Those TV Commercials," *Advertising Age* (April 11, 1977), 56.

[61]Joan Triesman and John P. Gregg, "Visual, Verbal, and Sales Response to Print Ads," *Journal of Advertising Research,* vol. 19 (August 1979), 41-47.

[62]Forkan, "Oculometer." Also see Neil Jesuele, "Combined Eye Tracking, Verbal Questioning Technique Now Helps Canadian Advertisers," *Marketing News* (April 18, 1980), 22. Edward W. Rhodes, Norman B. Leferman, Elizabeth Cook, and David Schwartz, "T-Scope Tests of Yellow Pages Advertising," *Journal of Advertising Research,* vol. 19 (April, 1979), 49-52. Also Clark Leavitt, "Intrigue in Advertising—The Motivational Effects of Visual Organization," in *Proceedings of the 7th Annual Conference* (New York: Advertising Research Foundation, 1961), 19-24.

The Tachistoscope   The tachistoscope is basically a slide projector with attachments permitting the presentation of stimuli under varying conditions of speed and illumination. It works much like a camera lens in this respect. Thus, it can be used to assess the rate at which a message conveys information. The amount of exposure needed to attract attention or stimulate any kind of awareness is recorded for various elements of the message (illustration, product, or brand name). It has been found that high readership scores and even sales correlate with the speed of recognition of the elements under analysis. In other words, the quicker it is recognized and processed, the better. The writer or designer thus has a useful basis to assess whether or not the message is being processed as intended.

Other Measures   Other measures have been tested experimentally, some of which are pretty debatable in terms of validity. One of the more interesting is binocular rivalry. This technique is used to measure which of two competing stimuli first attracts attention.[63] The stimuli are viewed through a stereoscopic device with an eye piece, and a different stimulus is projected to each eye. The underlying theory is that the input exerting the greatest potential for attention attraction will dominate, and this has been verified experimentally.[64]

More recently, some use has been made of brain patterns.[65] It is through this research that we have discovered the apparent differences between left and right brain functions, leading to the hypothesis that television is processed in the right sector whereas print is primarily processed in the left sector.[66] More verification is needed on this theory, but brain wave analysis may provide interesting insights into attention attracting potential of various messages and formats.

Probably it is just worth noting that others propose voice pitch[67] and facial analysis[68] as being useful physiological measures. The case is yet to be proved, however.

Selective Attention
An incredible number of stimuli vie for attention at any given moment. McKeachie and Doyle give the following estimates: (1) information comes into the central nervous system from over 260 million visual cells alone; (2) 48,000 cells are available for auditory perception; (3) the other

---

[63]J. M. Caffyn, "Psychological Laboratory Techniques in Copy Research," *Journal of Advertising Research,* vol. 4 (1964), 48.

[64]Ibid.

[65]See "Study of Brain Patterns Needed to Discover How Ads Affect Individual," *Marketing News* (June 16, 1980), 8+. Also, Appel, Weinstein, and Weinstein, "Brain Activity and Recall."

[66]Krugman, "Brain Wave Measures."

[67]Ronald G. Nelson and David Schwartz, "Voice-Pitch Analysis," *Journal of Advertising Research,* vol. 19 (October 1979), 55-62.

[68]"Facial Analysis Tests Response to TV Commercials," *Marketing News* (August 22, 1980), 7. Also John L. Graham, "A New System for Measuring Non-Verbal Responses to Marketing Appeals," in Richard P. Bagozzi et al., *Marketing in the 80s: Changes and Challenges* (Chicago: American Marketing Association, 1980), 340-343.

senses have at least 78,000 receptor cells; and (4) it would take a brain the size of a cubic light year to process just the information received by the eyes alone.[69] Obviously there are distinct limits on processing capacity in short-term memory, and it is to be expected that there will be selectivity in what is attended to and what is not.

Selective attention has been extensively documented in the psychological literature. It is too vast a subject to be discussed extensively here,[70] but some representative evidence will be reviewed under three headings:

1. the influence of need

2. perceptual vigilance and defense, and

3. maintenance of cognitive consistency.

The Influence of Need   Everyone is well aware from daily life that the onset of need affects those stimuli which receive attention and those which do not. Hungry people, for example, are far more receptive to food stimuli than they would be on other occasions. In fact, consumer economists have long contended that the worst time for food shopping is just prior to a meal because of the sharp increase in purchases which are made. Psychological need can have the same effect. Just to take one of hundreds of published examples, those with a strong motive for affiliation are more likely to isolate pictures of people from a larger grouping than will their counterparts who have a weaker need for affiliation.[71] The same people might also be expected to respond more readily to advertising appeals which stress social acceptance through avoidance of body odor.

Perceptual Vigilance and Defense   It has been found consistently that important values influence the speed of recognition for value-related words. For example, words that connote important values often are perceived more quickly, and this form of selective attention has come to be called *perceptual vigilance.*[72] It seems likely that consumers often avoid promotions for nonpreferred brands in this way. This hypothesis was confirmed in two studies that may shed light on why certain advertisements are noticed whereas others are ignored.[73] The key may lie in the extent to which the brand name is featured.

The opposite of perceptual vigilance is *perceptual defense,*

[69]Wilbert J. McKeachie and Charlotte L. Doyle, *Psychology* (Reading, Mass.: Addison-Wesley, 1966), 171.

[70]For a more extensive review see the first edition of this book published in 1968 by Holt, Rinehart and Winston, ch. 6.

[71]J. W. Atkinson and E. L. Walker, "The Affiliation Motive and Perceptual Sensitivity to Faces," *Journal of Abnormal and Social Psychology,* vol. 53 (1956), 38-41.

[72]L. Postman and B. Schneider, "Personal Values, Visual Recognition, and Recall," *Psychological Review,* vol. 58 (1951), 271-284. There has been some methodological controversy that may be of interest to some readers. See D. E. Broadbent, "Word-Frequency Effect and Response Bias," *Psychological Review,* vol. 74 (1967), 1-15.

[73]Homer E. Spence and James F. Engel, "The Impact of Brand Preference on the Perception of Brand Names: A Laboratory Analysis," in P. R. McDonald (ed.), *Marketing Involvement in Society and the Economy* (Chicago: American Marketing Association, 1970), 267-271.

whereby the recognition of low-valued stimuli being threatened is delayed or even avoided altogether.[74] Presumably the word itself has negative connotions to the individual, and it appears that barriers are thus erected to delay, inhibit, or abort information processing.[75] It is quite likely that consumers avoid promotion for nonpreferred brands in this way, although there is no direct evidence to cite. This would only be true, however, when high involvement is present.

Maintenance of Cognitive Consistency   Human beings have a persistent tendency to resist changes in strongly held attitudes and beliefs, especially those that are related in some way to their self-concept. This, of course, is the meaning of the term involvement as it has been used in this book. The cognitive structure functions, therefore, to enable the person to cope with his or her environment, and it is not surprising that change is resisted in order to maintain existing beliefs.[76] One way to do this is through selective attention. This happens in the world of marketing in that the typical advertising message is attended to by only a subset of those who are exposed. Bogart notes, "Advertising research data accurately reflect the fact that many messages register negative impressions or no impressions at all on many of the people who are exposed to the sight or sound of them."[77]

Selective attention to advertising will happen, of course, only when involvement is high, and the outcome from messages which go against the grain is questionable. For example, about ten percent of the flying public still have concern over the safety of the DC-10 aircraft after the disastrous crash in Chicago which took 273 lives May 25, 1979.[78] To combat these negative attitudes, an international advertising campaign was undertaken in 1980 utilizing print, radio, and television. Pete Conrad, former astronaut and current McDonnell Douglas official, was chosen as spokesperson. Presumably his credibility is expected to underscore testing and safety features and thus alleviate consumer anxiety. Whether or not this will happen is open to question. It could be completely screened out and never entered into long-term memory, in which case the messages have fallen on decidedly unfertile fields.

Comprehension   At the next stage in information processing (Figure 9.3), the individual now attempts to organize that subset of all possible stimuli and to come to some interpretation.

The principles of Gestalt psychology provide some insight into how stimuli are organized and interpreted. First, complexity is reduced as per-

[74]D. P. Spence, "Subliminal Perception and Perceptual Defense: Two Sides of a Single Problem," *Behavioral Science*, vol. 12 (1967), 183-193.

[75]This literature is thoroughly reviewed in D. P. Spence, "Subliminal Perception."

[76]For a good review, see E. E. Jones and H. D. Gerard, *Foundations of Social Psychology* (New York: John Wiley & Sons, 1967), ch. 7.

[77]Leo Bogart, "Where Does Advertising Research Go From Here?" *Journal of Advertising Research*, vol. 9 (March 1969), 6.

[78]Josh Levine, "DC-10 Worldwide Effort Selling Safety of Planes?" *Advertising Age* (July 14, 1980), 1+.

ceptions are organized into the simplest possible patterns. Second, we tend to produce a complete picture through a process referred to as *closure.* One famous advertising illustration is provided by the jingle, "You can take Salem out of the country but you can't take the country out of Salem." After this jingle was repeated with high frequency on television and radio, the company then played only the first part in subsequent advertising and left the remainder to be completed by the audience. Many more principles of this type could be mentioned, but space limitations do not permit further discussion.[79]

One interesting question is the minimum amount of stimulus input required to produce a perception of change. The point at which change is detected is called the *differential threshold,* and the following generalization, referred to as Weber's law, has emerged:

$$\frac{\Delta I}{I} = K$$

where

ΔI = the smallest increase in stimulus intensity that will be noticeably different from the established intensity

I = the intensity of the stimulus at the point where the increase occurs

K = a constant that varies across the various senses.

In other words, the stronger the initial intensity of one stimulus, the greater the intensity of the other if a difference is to be noticed.

Weber's law has some obvious applications in marketing. Assume, for example, that a price increase of $1 is to be put into effect. That increase would be highly apparent on a 50-cent item, whereas it probably would escape detection on an $80 item. Similarly, package designers would be required to engineer a larger increase in the size of a package for a change to be noticed if the item itself were large to begin with, and vice versa.

The Measurement of Comprehension

Comprehension is often tested through some type of recall procedure. The preferred method is to place test messages within, for example, a magazine or television program and then to allow for exposure under completely natural conditions. Recognition or recall is then assessed at some period after exposure, usually within 24 hours.

Grey Advertising, Inc., often will pretest the communicative ability of a piece of copy by placing it along with other material in a fictitious magazine entitled *Today.*[80] This magazine was created to duplicate the format of a new general interest magazine. Interviewers place it in homes,

[79]See the first edition of this book, ch. 5.

[80]See "W. T. Grant Company (B); Attitude Change Through Advertising," in Roger D. Blackwell, James F. Engel, and David T. Kollat, *Cases in Consumer Behavior* (New York: Holt, Rinehart and Winston, 1969), 88-94.

and people are asked to read it as they would any other magazine. Telephone interviews on the following day measure comprehension and recall as follows:

1. *Related recall.* The percentage of actual readers who can give: (1) aided or unaided identification of the brand; and (2) some playback on the message (either some specific detail or a general correct description).

2. *Comprehension and impact.* Ability to state the actual intended content of the copy correctly.

Selective Comprehension

Just because attention has been attracted does not imply that the stimulus will be correctly comprehended. Once again, there is a vast literature documenting this point, and only a few examples will be given here.

A landmark study undertaken in 1947 documented that children from the lowest economic classes overestimate the size of coins.[81] The assumption is that economic deprivation and resulting need affect the process of perception and comprehension. There is some contradictory evidence, but most authorities now accept that need and other personal characteristics can affect cognitive processes in this way.[82]

This type of physical stimulus distortion also occurs in consumer decision making. A soft-drink company introduced a new product that fell far short of its sales potential.[83] A taste test was conducted in which samples of this brand and competitors' were compared with and without labels. The findings disclosed that the brand under analysis received excellent ratings in comparison with others when it was unlabeled. The ratings were completely reversed, however, when labels were in place. It thus appears that the product image, name, or some other consideration affected taste ratings. As a result, the promotional program was totally revamped while product formulation was left unchanged.

Miscomprehension can enter in another way. Each person has certain expectations about the content of new information, and it is known that the reaction often reflects the expectation rather than the stimulus itself.[84] For example, a liquid cold remedy was introduced in a test market in the attempt to make inroads into the market share of Vick's *Nyquil,* and there was considerable evidence that consumers thought they were viewing *Nyquil* ads. The competitor's ads were quite similar to those used by *Nyquil* and the result was miscomprehension.

What this boils down to is that nearly every stimulus is subject to

[81]J. S. Bruner and Cecile C. Goodman,"Value and Need as Organizing Factors in Perception," *Journal of Abnormal and Social Psychology,* vol. 42 (1947), 33-44.

[82]Noel Jenkin, "Affective Processes in Perception," *Psychological Bulletin,* vol. 54 (1957), 100-127.

[83]Twink, "Perception of Taste," in Blackwell, Engel, and Kollat (eds.), *Cases in Consumer Behavior,* 38-43.

[84]For a classic study on this subject, see A. L. Edwards, "Political Frames of Reference as a Factor Influencing Recognition," *Journal of Abnormal and Social Psychology,* vol. 36 (1941) 34-50. Also it is discussed in Norman, *Memory and Attention.*

miscomprehension. Jacoby and his associates discovered that 96.5 percent of all people show at least some misunderstanding of what they view on television, whether it is news, a regular program, or advertising.[85] The range is from 11 percent to a high of 50 percent. Furthermore, as was mentioned earlier, only 32 percent of all television viewers in one test could remember seeing commercials to which they were exposed, and only 16 percent could describe the identity of a sponsor.[86] For every two persons who correctly named a brand, at least one named a competitor!

Very frequently the communicator is responsible for this problem, although the reasons for this are not always recognized. For example, one study showed that one of the favorite commericals aired during 1979 as measured by a vote of viewers was the series featuring James Garner and Mariette Hartley for the Polaroid *One Step* camera.[87] The commercials usually were built upon verbal sparring by a married couple, and there was no question that people liked them (see Figure 9.4). Unfortunately, many of those surveyed named Kodak as the brand being advertised. In the authors' opinion, this happened because the name was not mentioned often and also because the dialogue between the actors is so enjoyable that it obscures the main product message.

Other times, the choice of brand name can lead to some unfortunate connotations. Toro introduced a lightweight snowthrower named the *Snow Pup.* It proved to be unsuccessful because people comprehended the name to mean that it was a toy or was not powerful enough for its job. Changing the name (to *Snowmaster*) reversed this problem and made the product a success.[88]

Yielding/ Acceptance

Referring once again to Figure 9.3, the fact that a message is comprehended does not guarantee that it will have any effect on the existing cognitive structure and be accepted into long-term memory. Therefore, the next step in information processing is acceptance into the cognitive structure through reinforcement or change.

The key to understanding what happens at this stage lies in cognitive response theory which was mentioned earlier.[89] Let's refer once again to the concept of rehearsal—those silent, inner thoughts reflecting re-

[85] Jacob Jacoby, Wayne D. Hoyer, and David A. Sheluga, "Viewer Miscomprehension of Televised Communication: A Brief Report of Findings" in Kent B. Monroe (ed.), *Advances in Consumer Research,* vol. 8 (Ann Arbor, Mich.: Association for Consumer Research, 1981), 410-413.

[86] McMahan, "TV Loses the 'Name Game'."

[87] Dave Vedehra, "Coke, McDonald's Lead Outstanding TV Commercials," *Advertising Age* (May 26, 1980), 37-38.

[88] J. Neher, "Toro Cutting a Wide Swath in Outdoor Appliance Marketing," *Advertising Age* (February 25, 1979), 21.

[89] Good basic sources include A. G. Greenwald, "Cognitive Learning, Cognitive Response to Persuasion and Attitude Change," in A. G. Greenwald, T. C. Brock, and T. M. Ostrom (eds.), *Psychological Foundations of Attitudes* (New York: Academic Press, 1968); Peter L. Wright, "The Cognitive Processes Mediating Acceptance of Advertising," *Journal of Marketing Research,* vol. 10 (February 1973), 53-62; Perloff and Brock, ". . . And Thinking Makes it So"; and Richard M. Perloff and Timothy C. Brock, "The Role of Own Cognitive Responses in Persuasion: A Conceptual Overview," in Olson, *Advances in Consumer Research,* vol. 7, 741-744.

**Figure 9.4
Polaroid One Step
Camera**

Source: Courtesy of Polaroid Corporation.

sponses to the message which is being processed. The reader will recall
that nonrehearsed messages usually do not move beyond short-term
memory, let alone have much impact on cognitive structure under conditions of high involvement (we will argue differently for low involvement).
There are three major types of cognitive responses which are possible
during rehearsal:

1. Counter-arguments—refutations of and resistance to message claims,

2. Source derogations—negative evaluation of the source of the message,

3. Support arguments—agreement with message claims.

First, it is now known that generation of counter-arguments and source derogations are signs that the message is being actively resisted and hence will have little or no impact on cognitive structure.[90] The generation of support arguments, on the other hand, apparently is an accurate indicator of both acceptance and yielding.[91]

The Measurement of Yielding/Acceptance

There are two main ways yielding and acceptance can be measured. One is attitudinal—shifts in beliefs and attitudes from one period to the next following exposure to a persuasive message.[92] Another is actual measurement of cognitive responses through information monitoring methods.[93] People are either asked to verbalize what they are really thinking during exposure or to write their thoughts down afterwards. These protocols then are categorized as to what they represent—counter-arguments or whatever. It should be pointed out that this method is only in its infancy, but it offers greater promise than any other at this point.

Resistance to Persuasion

Whether or not a message is running against the grain can most clearly be detected at this stage. Let's take as an example the recruiting campaign undertaken on behalf of the U.S. Army by its advertising agency, N. W. Ayer ABH.[94] A consultant's report alleged that the Army was wasting its promotion dollars (approximately $60 million) by advertising a bad product. The campaign had emphasized the message, "Today's Army Needs You" to its target audience of about 800,000 youth. One can just imagine the counter-arguments expressed by some: "Oh yeah, tell me about it!" "You need me, huh; I don't need you!" These would be clear signs of message misfire. In reality, this whole effort seemed to contribute to rather than counteract an image that the Army is populated by the unskilled and the uneducated. This led to a new campaign built around the theme, "Be all you can be, 'cause we need you in the Army." The intent is to show that a stint in the army can provide valuable training for

---

[90]Wright, "Cognitive Responses Mediating Acceptance."

[91]Purloff and Brock, "The Role of Own Cognitive Responses." Also, Alice M. Tybout, Brian Sternthal, and Bobby J. Calder, "A Two-Stage Theory of Information Processing and Persuasion: An Integrative View of Cognitive Response and Self-Perception Theory," in Hunt, *Advances in Consumer Research,* vol. 5, 721-723.

[92]For an example of attitudinal measures, see Jerry C. Olson, Daniel Toy, and Philip A. Dover, "Mediating Effects of Cognitive Responses to Advertising on Cognitive Structure," in Hunt, *Advances in Consumer Research,* vol. 5, 72-78.

[93]A definitive source here is Peter Wright, "Message-Evoked Thoughts: Persuasion Research Using Thought Verbalizations," *Journal of Consumer Research,* vol. 7 (1980), 151-175. Also, John Swasy, "A Multi-Trait-Multi-Method Analysis of Cognitive Response Indicators Via Analysis of Covariance Structures," in Bagozzi, *Marketing in the 80s,* 362-365.

[94]Richard L. Gordon, "Army-Ayer Ad Program Takes Some Fire," *Advertising Age* (March 17, 1980), 78+ ; "Army Aims Higher," *Advertising Age* (December 29, 1980), 2.

civilian occupations. Perhaps it will work. Fortunately, it is possible to find out through monitoring cognitive responses.

Retention

The mechanics of memory were discussed thoroughly in the first section of the chapter. All that need be said here is that the last stage depicted in Figure 9.3 is the stimulus entrance into long-term memory. It now has survived quite a process, although what is stored there may bear little similarity to what has been entered because of the way it has been shaped and fitted along the way.

So, What Does It All Mean in Practice?

What does it all mean for marketing strategy? One very logical implication for mass marketers is that it often is wise to direct efforts, insofar as it is possible, to those who are already neutral or even sympathetic toward the content and to avoid those who are not. The probability of making inroads into this latter group may not be worth the effort. This is the underlying rationale for the concept of market segmentation. Another possibility is to search for those whose beliefs are wavering for one reason or another. Perhaps there is dissatisfaction with a competitor because of poor product quality. This could underscore profitable market opportunity.

Another way for marketing organizations to overcome the problem of selective attention is through the practice of what might be called controlled exposure. With this technique, consumers are placed in situations in which they have little or no choice but to give their attention to the message. In one such example, a real estate firm invites potential customers to a free meal and then makes a highly concentrated presentation during the meal concerning real estate development in Florida. The consumer is in a room with no windows and few distractions other than the sales presentation itself. This tactic may be highly debatable from an ethical point of view, given the frequency of fraudulent real estate deals. Yet many variants exist in the form of beauty seminars, cooking schools, sewing classes, and other situations in which consumers are brought into a situation in which attention can be controlled.

Marketers also are increasingly recognizing that a need exists for additional tools to overcome the problem of miscomprehension. One possibility is the use of materials to reinforce learning after the initial exposure. This includes the utilization of hang-tags on products to reinforce messages appearing in advertising or given through personal selling. Also, one trade association found that people were miscomprehending messages given in public meetings. As a result they prepared concise, informative brochures that restated the oral message. These brochures were attractive and were designed to fit into a coat pocket or purse. The intent was to induce the person to take the brochure home and discuss it with others in the hopes that miscomprehension of the oral presentation would be minimized.

In personal selling situations, firms also attempt to reduce miscomprehension through use of media involving both sight and sound. The oral presentation is either augmented or supplanted through use of a flip chart, a video cassette, a written outline, or some other similar tool.

Whatever strategy is undertaken, it is clear that the consumer *is* sovereign. He or she has full powers to screen out any message that contradicts a strongly held disposition. The only way this filtering ability can be overcome is if we can gain full control of their lives such as would be true in a prison camp setting.[95] Then we would have access to such tools of manipulation as hypnosis, psychotherapy, sensory deprivation (perhaps from solitary confinement), stimulation with drugs, the inducing of stress, or brain implantation with electrodes.[96] Needless to say, such means are not available to the business firm. Therefore, the only strategy is to design messages in such a way that they are (1) directed toward those whose dispositions and need states are consistent with the action being suggested, and (2) oriented toward reinforcing these tendencies, thereby leading to the desired action. As one authority observes,

. . . to the social scientist, A's influence of B is not a matter of art, but of the witting or unwitting application of known or unknown scientific principles, and must be looked upon as such. The scientific analysis of human behavior is perhaps the single most potent weapon in A's arsenal. If he fails to make use of this powerful tool, he does so at his own risk.[97]

INFORMATION PROCESSING UNDER LOW INVOLVEMENT

Thus far our discussion of information processing has assumed a high degree of involvement or personal relevance. That is, the purchase is sufficiently important to the consumer to activate motivated search and information usage. There is receptivity to relevant information and resistance to that which is not. Yet, a large percentage of buying decisions are not of this type. While there may be a need for the product or service, the actual alternative chosen is not especially crucial. There will be no search for information, and the primary effect on cognitive structure comes *after* purchase and product use rather than before.

Information processing is of quite a different nature now. Leo Bogart provides keen insight here:

Perhaps the main contribution that advertising research can make to this study of communications is in the domain of inattention to low-key stimuli, as exemplified by the ever increasing flow of unsolicited and unwanted messages to which people are subject in our over communicative civilization.[98]

---

[95]J. V. McConnell, *Persuasion and Behavioral Change* (Ann Arbor, Mich.: University of Michigan, 1959).

[96]See Robert N. Bostrom, "Altered Physiological States: The Central Nervous System and Persuasive Communications," in Roloff and Miller, *Persuasion: New Directions*, 171-196. Also, A. D. Biderman and H. Zimmer (eds.), *The Manipulation of Human Behavior* (New York: John Wiley & Sons, 1961).

[97]McConnell, *Persuasion*, 73.

[98]Bogart, "Where Does Advertising Research," 6.

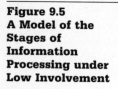

**Figure 9.5
A Model of the
Stages of
Information
Processing under
Low Involvement**

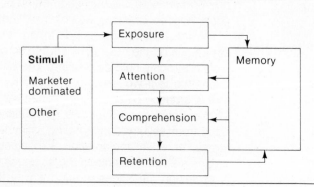

For the most part, attention is *involuntary* and occurs while the individual is exposed to a given medium for other reasons (entertainment and so on). There is an impact, nonetheless. There is growing evidence that a message indeed can be processed and stored in long-term memory *without having an effect at that point in time on cognitive structure.*[99] It seems that this is especially likely when television is used. Preliminary evidence indicates that it may be processed primarily in the right hemisphere of the brain in the form of visual images which enter long-term memory and *bypass the yielding/acceptance* stage.[100] This, in effect, represents passive, low-level learning. Bettman aptly classifies it as *incidental learning.*[101]

For the most part, information processing under low involvement is similar to that under high involvement as Figure 9.5 reveals. The only difference is the absence of the yielding/acceptance stage.

Now, how is this stored input later used in decision making? Most likely the consumer later receives a reminder through some type of point-of-sale stimulus where he or she saw a product advertised on television. There would be little or no recall; rather, memory would be activated in the form of *recognition.*[102] This is a crucial insight because it says that recognition, not recall, is the appropriate measure of incidental learning under low involvement. Krugman probably is right when he notes that we have understated the impact of television advertising because of widespread use of an inappropriate measure of impact—recall.[103] Recognition then could influence a "Why not try it?" response.

**The Problem of
Sensory Overload**

Because the level of interest is so low, the consumer will usually absorb very little from the advertising message—perhaps only one or two points. Furthermore, it should be stressed again that attention, by and large, is

---

[99]See especially Krugman, "Low Involvement Theory in the Light of New Brain Research;" and Krugman, "The Impact of Television Advertising," John C. Maloney and Bernard Silverman (eds.), *Attitude Research Plays for High Stakes* (Chicago: American Marketing Association, 1979).

[100]Krugman, "Low Involvement Theory."

[101]Bettman, *An Information Processing Theory,* ch. 4.

[102]Krugman, "Low Involvement Theory."

[103]For a more extensive discussion, see McGuire, "Some Internal Psychological Factors."

involuntary. This means that limitations on information processing capacity simply render the consumer unable to cope with all of the messages coming his or her way, thus giving rise to what is known technically as *sensory overload.* It is quite possible that a message will not capture and hold attention simply because it is lost in the noise.[104]

Let's look at one application of this. All too often it is naively assumed by some concerned with issues of consumer welfare that one answer to the problem of helping people to buy more wisely lies in providing more buying information. Under sensory overload, however, there is a very real sense that *more is not better!*[105] The potential error of such assumptions underscores the need for strategies for consumer welfare to be based on legitimate research in the same manner as marketing strategy decisions.

Besides overload, messages may also become lost in the noise because of excessive repetition. As commercial stimulation occurs repeatedly, the ability to attract attention fades. When this occurs a stimulus is said to have become *habituated.* Certain factors interact to bring this about:[106]

1. Stimulus intensity—the lower the intensity, the more rapidly habituation occurs.

2. Duration of stimulus—an extremely brief stimulus is less likely to habituate.

3. Difficulty of discrimination—the more difficult it is to grasp stimulus details, the less the likelihood of habituation.

4. Time—habituation occurs more rapidly as time between exposures decreases.

5. Conditioning—a stimulus that has become so conditioned that it is of personal significance to the recipient will not habituate, even when it is repeated.

Advertising is especially likely to fall victim to habituation. Most products are familiar, and it often is difficult to say much that is really new. This can place some real demands on design and format of message, the appeals used, and media placement.[107]

[104]Rothschild, "Advertising Strategies."

[105]These findings come from a large number of studies by the Purdue consumer psychology group. See, for example, Jacob Jacoby, "Consumer Reaction to Information Displays: Packaging and Advertising" (Advertising and Public Interest Workshop, American Marketing Association, May 1973); Jacob Jacoby, Donald Speller, and Carol Kohn, "Brand Choice Behavior as a Function of Information Load," *Journal of Marketing Research,* vol. 11 (February 1974), 63-69; Jacob Jacoby, Donald Speller, and Carol Kohn, "Brand Choice Behavior as a Function of Information Load: Replication and Extension," *The Journal of Consumer Research,* vol. 1 (June 1974), 33-42; and Jacob Jacoby et al., "Information Acquisition Behavior in Brand Choice Situations: A Cross-Cultural Extension" (Purdue Papers in *Consumer Psychology,* no. 162, 1976). For a dissenting point of view, see J. Edward Russo, "More Information Is Better: A Reevaluation of Jacoby, Speller, and Kohn," *The Journal of Consumer Research,* vol. 1 (December 1974), 68-72.

[106]David E. Berlyne, *Conflict, Arousal and Curiosity* (New York: McGraw-Hill, 1960).

[107]See Peter H. Webb, "Consumer Initial Processing in a Difficult Media Environment," *Journal of Consumer Research,* vol. 6 (December 1979), 225-236.

Resort is often made to various tactics which may seem to be little more than gimmicks, but remember that their sole purpose is to break through and capture attention under sensory overload conditions. Here are three possible means (all of which can also be used creatively when appealing to consumers under high involvement): (1) novelty and contrast; (2) manipulation of intensity through variations in size and position of the message; and (3) use of color.

Novelty and Contrast

Notice the Chiquita brand banana advertisement in Figure 9.6 because it makes effective use of novelty and contrast. The appearance of the banana in such a way that it stands on its end is quite unusual, with the result that attention is likely to be captured. This, of course, says nothing about the persuasive power of the message itself.

Numerous other illustrations could be given, only several of which are suggested here:

1. A black and white advertisement featuring an unusual amount of white space with no print or illustration can stand out clearly when competitive messages are in color.

2. An unusually shaped package captures attention when all others on a shelf are similar in design, shape, and color.

3. The announcer's voice advertising a product during a break in a classical music program is likely to be noticed because of the sharp stimulus contrast.

Size and Position of the Message

There have been a number of studies on the effects of increasing the size of an advertisement on the printed page; it has been found that doubling the size does not double the impact. Readership tends to increase in proportion to the square root of the increase in space.[108]

It also is possible to generalize on the relative value of different positions on the page in print media:

1. There is little variation in readership of advertisements appearing on the left- and right-hand pages in magazines or newspapers. The primary factor in readership is what the message says and how it says it.[109]

2. The greatest readership in magazines is usually attracted by advertisements on the covers or in the first 10 percent of the pages, but beyond this point location is a minor factor.[110]

3. Position within a newspaper does not appear to be crucial because of high page traffic throughout the paper.[111]

[108]R. Barton, *Advertising Media* (New York: McGraw-Hill, 1964), 109.

[109]"Position in Newspaper Advertising: 2," *Media/scope* (March 1963), 76-82.

[110]"Position in Newspaper Advertising: 2."

[111]"Position in Newspaper Advertising: 1," *Media/scope* (February 1963), 57.

**Figure 9.6
An Illustration of
Novelty and
Contrast**

Source: Chiquita Brands, Inc., is a registered trademark of the United Brands Co. Reprinted by permission.

4. Readership tends to be highest when the message is placed adjacent to compatible editorial features.

5. Position in the gutter (the inside fold) offers little advantage in print media. In fact, position on the page itself has no effect except when competing advertisements become especially numerous, in which case the upper right-hand position offers an advantage in newspapers.

Position in broadcast advertising has received less research, although it is known that commercials generally perform better when inserted as a part of the regular program rather than during the clutter of a station break. It also appears that commercials at the beginning and end of a program suffer a disadvantage because of the clutter of announcements and other distracting nonprogram material.

The Use of Color

It is widely recognized that color can add significantly to the effectiveness of an advertisement for a number of reasons:

1. The attention-attracting and holding power of the message may be sharply increased.

2. Contemporary social trends have encouraged experimentation with color in all phases of life, ranging from the factory to the home. Thus people have become responsive to innovative color stimuli.

3. Most products look better in color, especially food.

4. Color can be used to create moods, ranging from the somber appeal of dark colors to the freshness of greens and blues.

Some Additional Clues for Advertising Strategy

We have stressed at various points throughout this chapter that advertising often fails to register the brand name. This problem becomes especially acute under low-involvement information processing. If the brand name does not visually dominate, it is entirely probable that is will be lost.[112]

Furthermore, the primary impact seems to be visual—i.e., storage of a visual advertising impression. This probably explains the finding that print ads featuring photography rate nearly 50 percent above the norm in terms of impact.[113]

Another significant clue, according to Harry McMahan, is to develop a central character that signifies almost instantly everything that the message is trying to convey.[114] Examples are the Pillsbury Doughboy, Speedy Alka-Seltzer, Kellogg's Tony the Tiger, and the Esso Tiger. In turn, a point-of-sale tie-in featuring that same character will readily trigger recognition and stimulate either an initial or repeat purchase.

THE ISSUE OF DECEPTION

This chapter would not be complete without examination of the issue of deception from an information processing perspective. Gardner offers a definition of deception that states the issue with precision:

---

[112]Carl Hixon and John Fiedler, "Print: The Message, the Medium, the Environment," in John Eighmey (ed.), *Attitude Research under the Sun* (Chicago: American Marketing Association, 1979), 198-215.

[113]Hixon and Fiedler, "Print the Message."

[114]Harry W. McMahan, "Do Your Ads Have VI/P?" *Advertising Age* (July 14, 1980), 50-51.

If an advertisement (or advertising campaign) leaves the average consumer within some reasonable market segment with an impression(s) and/or belief(s) different from what would normally be expected if the average consumer within that market segment had reasonable knowledge and that impression(s) and/or belief(s) is factually untrue or potentially misleading, then deception is said to exist.[115]

Gardner's purpose here is to give a definition that will be accepted by legal authorities, but it makes a simple point—deception enters when people are left with an understanding that deviates from the truth. The emphasis is on how the message is comprehended and not only on the literal content of the message itself.

There is still another dimension of deception, however, and that refers to the use of devices which inhibit an individual's freedom of action.[116] Examples would be appeal to a strong but irrelevant emotion, use of such distractions as soft lighting or music, and so on. The person is deceived if he or she is somehow deterred from pursuing a course of action that would have been taken without the distorting effect of the message. When deception has entered, then the effects of audience sovereignty are blunted, and the communicator has opted for deliberate falsification and manipulation.

There also has been fear of manipulation through use of so-called *subliminal perception.* One of the raging controversies of the 1950s and the 1960s was over the question of whether or not people could be influenced without awareness on their part, thus giving rise to this term. This whole matter was triggered by an alleged advertising test in the late 1950s in which the words *Drink Coke* and *Eat popcorn* presumably were flashed on a movie screen at speeds well beyond the conscious awareness of audience members. To recall an earlier discussion, it would be said technically that the presentation was subliminal or below the threshold at which conscious discrimination is possible. Hence, the term subliminal perception. The sales of *Coca-Cola* were supposed to have increased 57.7 percent and popcorn sales 18.1 percent. In reality, these findings have unanimously been dismissed as being invalid, and all attempts at replication of that particular experiment have failed.

This issue lay dormant for years because of later evidence that there is no information processing leading to long-term storage without at least some degree of awareness.[117] It has come to life again, however, because an influential book by Dixon in which he presents new evidence and argues that subliminal perception does take place without awareness by the individual.[118] Furthermore, there is some additional evidence

[115]David M. Gardner, "Deception in Advertising: A Receiver Oriented Approach to Understanding," *Journal of Advertising,* vol. 5 (November 1976), 7.

[116]Emory Griffin, *The Mind Changers* (Wheaton, Ill.: Tyndale, 1976).

[117]See, for example, M. Wiener and P. H. Schiller, "Subliminal Perception or Perception of Partial Cues," *Journal of Abnormal and Social Psychology,* vol. 61 (1960), 124-137.

[118]Norman F. Dixon, *Subliminal Perception—The Nature of the Controversy* (Maidenhead-Berkshire, England: McGraw-Hill Publishing Co., Ltd., 1971).

that people can be motivated through a subliminally presented stimulus.[119] This immediately raises the spector of the hidden persuader and images of Big Brother. It is easy to jump to the conclusion that the advertiser now has unbridled power to manipulate the consumer. In fact, this simply is not true. These fears of unconscious manipulation are without basis in the ultimate sense because the evidence does *not* indicate that people can be induced to do something they otherwise would not do. All it says is that there is some information processing without awareness, but the individual still retains full powers to screen out unwanted messages. Unfortunately, the consumer never knows when subliminal persuasion is underway; therefore there is concern expressed by many that the potential exists for manipulation.

Dixon gives yet another reason why subliminal advertising has little to commend it as a strategy.[120] At best, only a fractional stimulus is presented. Because of sensory overload and all of the other problems we have discussed, this could easily be swamped by other messages presented under more normal conditions. As a result, the commercial persuader has nothing to gain by resorting to this means. Fears of a new-found tool of manipulation should be put to rest.

Summary

This has been a long chapter covering some essential material which provides the conceptual understanding of how people process incoming information. First, it was necessary to review the manner in which memory functions. Theorists now accept that memory is basically one coherent entity with three distinct components: (1) sensory memory; (2) short-term memory; and (3) long-term memory. It was shown how memory works as a stimulus enters and finally winds up in a long-term storage. Discussion then shifted to the differences in information processing under high involvement (i.e., situations where there is a strong degree of personal relevance or pertinence) and low involvement. The essential difference is that high involvement entails a motivated search for information. Therefore, the individual is receptive to relevant information but resistant to information which resists the grain.

It was shown that the following are steps in information processing: (1) exposure; (2) attention; (3) comprehension; (4) yielding/acceptance; and (5) retention. Low-involvement information processing differs in that information is accepted without having an effect on beliefs and attitudes. Therefore, the yielding/acceptance stage is bypassed, and information is stored in the form of visual images which then can be used later.

The essential point of all of this is that the consumer is sovereign and in full control of what enters long-term memory. Because of this, the burden is placed on the persuader to be an accurate researcher and to base all that is done on firm knowledge of human information processing.

[119]Joel Saegert, "Another Look at Subliminal Perception," *Journal of Advertising Research,* vol. 19 (February 1979), 55-58. Also, Dell Hawkins, "The Effects of Subliminal Stimulation on Drive Level and Brand Preference," *Journal of Marketing Research,* vol. 7 (August 1970), 322-326.
[120]Dixon, *Subliminal Perception.*

Review and Discussion Questions

1. Distinguish among sensory memory, short-term memory, and long-term memory. How does rehearsal enter as a stimulus is processed?

2. Listen to a series of radio commercials. As you listen, monitor your own thoughts. In what way do you detect source derogation, counter-argumentation, and support argumentation?

3. It was pointed out that information processed under conditions of high involvement is usually stored in memory so that it can be recalled. What is the significance of this fact in advertising strategy?

4. There is some controversy surrounding the subject of selective exposure. In your opinion, is there selective exposure to advertising? Why or why not?

5. Assume that a consumer cannot recall seeing advertisements for any brand of hair spray other than her preferred brand even though she had the opportunity in a given day to see 20 or more competing ads. What explanations can be given?

6. A leading critic of advertising contends that advertising has the power to influence people to buy unwisely—to act in a way which they would not otherwise do. In other words, advertising is a tool for manipulation of the consumer. What would your response be to this criticism?

7. Under what conditions is it possible for perceptual defense to affect the perception of brand names?

8. Assume that you have been given the assignment to investigate the possibility of subliminal presentation of advertisements on television for canned soup. What problems would occur? What would happen if a similar attempt were to be made with advertisements designed to appear in women's magazines?

9. A reader's attention is attracted by a two-page spread in *Time* advertising a new automobile. The advertisement is in four colors and features three pretty girls. What does it mean to say that attention is attracted? How does this happen?

10. The creative director of a leading New York advertising agency claims that creativity cannot be measured. He refuses to make any use of pretests of his copy and layouts and claims that his creative intuition is his best guide. If you were the director of research, what would your answer be?

11. Many critics contend that too much advertising today is gimmicky and cute. The argument is that creative people are carried away by flashy attention-attracting devices and are forgetting that good advertising must sell. How would you analyze this criticism?

12. In your opinion, will laboratory measures of attention see more or less use in the future? Why?

13. Search through a magazine and discover ads for products which you feel are likely to represent both high and low involvement. What differences would you expect in the way they are processed? Why?

14. What is the difference in motivated attention and involuntary attention in terms of advertising strategy?

15. What is meant by sensory overload? Have you experienced it? Can you explain it in terms of what you see happening in society today?

16. The next time you watch television, pay particular attention to detecting those ads you consider to be deceptive. What criteria are you using to make this determination? How can deception be measured?

PART FOUR

HIGH-INVOLVEMENT DECISION PROCESSES

Most of the published literature on consumer behavior has focused on high-involvement decisions—those which have a great deal of relevance and pertinence for the individual. Involvement leads to extended problem solving which begins with problem recognition and is followed up by search for information; considerable alternative evaluation which leads to changes in beliefs, attitudes, and intentions; choice; and post-choice outcomes. Therefore, there are more chapters in this part than anywhere else in the book. Yet, low-involvement behavior is more common than high-involvement. It is also far less complex and much simpler to describe and discuss as the chapters in Part 5 will indicate. In addition, many of the variables and processes discussed here apply to all types of behavior whether low or high involvement.

Chapter 10 is concerned with the first stage in the process. This is the point at which consumers recognize that some decision is necessary. The nature and determinants of problem recognition are discussed, followed by an analysis of procedures and techniques used for measurement and appraisal. The chapter also centers on the dilemma faced by marketers in triggering problem recognition.

After a problem is recognized, the consumer may or may not engage in an external search for information in order to learn about and evaluate the alternatives which are available. Chapter 11 focuses on the nature of this search process, with particular emphasis on those conditions and factors which trigger search. It also describes the nature and influence of various marketer-dominated information sources (advertising, personal selling, forms of promotion). Chapter 12 then analyzes the impact of interpersonal communication sources (i.e., nonmarketer-dominated sources), the characteristics of opinion leaders and methods of identifying them, and alternative models of interpersonal influence. Chapter 13 extends the discussion of search by focusing on the diffusion of innovations. Therefore, it serves as an integration of much that has been said in the preceding chapters. It reviews the manner in which new products and other types of innovation become accepted and adopted in a social setting. There is much research on this subject, and the marketing implications abound.

Once search has been finished, the next stage is alternative evaluation where information is processed and used to assess the pros and cons of the available options. Evaluative criteria, the specifications or expectations the consumer has formed to assess alternatives, come into play. Chapter 14 describes how they are formed and what their function is in this process.

The outcome of alternative evaluation is a belief that a given alternative expresses desired attributes. Beliefs, in turn, lead to an attitude reflecting a positive or negative evaluation of this belief, and attitudes are followed by an intention to act in an appropriate manner. Beliefs, attitudes, and intentions are the subject of Chapter 15, and the discussion is continued in Chapter 16 focusing more directly on the manner in which marketing efforts can lead to changes in these variables.

Choice and its outcomes are the last stage in the high-involvement decision process. Chapter 17 examines choice processes in both the retail and in-home environment. It also focuses on two outcomes of choice—satisfaction and dissonance (doubts). Satisfaction, in particular, assumes relevance in the context of the consumerism movement.

Finally, the consumer usually must visit a retail store sometime during the decision. Therefore, Chapter 18 is devoted to store choice and purchasing behavior. All too frequently retailing is ignored in the consumer behavior literature, but it will soon become apparent that consumer research is by no means the sole province of the manufacturer.

During the late 1960s and early 1970s, sales of panty hose boomed because of the popularity of the mini-skirt and the importance it gave to leg appearance. During that era, Hanes Hosiery emerged as a leader in the branded panty hose market with *L'eggs.* But then fashion trends changed and women began to wear slacks. As a result, they switched from panty hose to knee-high stockings or no hosiery at all. Now, how was Hanes to reverse this adverse sales trend? Was there any way to induce women to buy panty hose in spite of these adverse demand factors? The problem essentially was one of stimulating *problem recognition.* It is helpful to define this term formally before proceeding further with the Hanes dilemma: Problem recognition is *a perceived difference between the ideal state of affairs and the actual situation sufficient to arouse and activate the decision process.* In other words, it was necessary to help the consumer once again perceive a need for this product and to stimulate buying action.

The Hanes solution was market testing and introduction of *Underalls,* a new product designed to be worn with slacks as an accessory.[1] The reader will remember a brief discussion of this marketing strategy in Chapter 1. After extensive testing, a decision was made to introduce an entirely new product stressing the benefit of appearance—the elimination of panty lines appearing under slacks. To stay ahead of competition after an initial flurry of similar brands, management counteracted with *Slenderalls®,* designed to "get rid of bumps, bulges, and panty lines" all at once (see Figure 10.1). In so doing, the company was successful in stimulating people to buy something altogether new. This never would have happened without a keen awareness of an unmet consumer need.

Problem recognition, of course, is the first stage in any type of decision process behavior. When it occurs, the human system is energized and goal-orientation begins. Seemingly unrelated activities now become organized to satisfy this state of arousal. In short, the system is turned on and triggered to engage in purposeful activity.

---

[1]"Underalls' Success Due to 'Flanking Strategy,' Product Idea, Positioning," *Marketing News* (November 14, 1980), 11.

**Figure 10.1
Slenderalls**

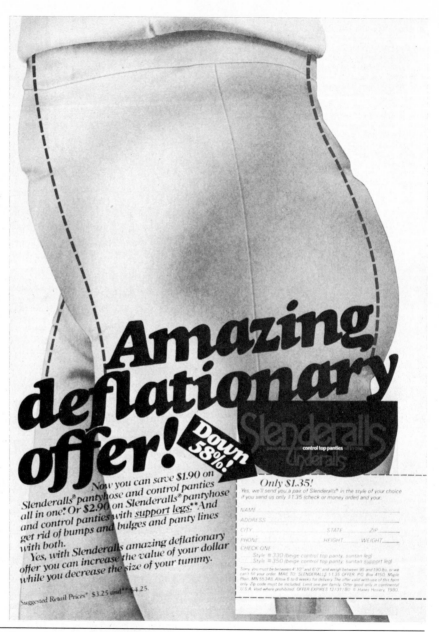

An abbreviated model of high-involvement consumer decision-process behavior appears in Figure 10.2. It represents two principal determinants of problem recognition; (1) motives and (2) incoming information and experience stored in memory. Motives are enduring predispositions to strive to attain specified goals and determine, to a large

**Figure 10.2
Determinants of
Problem
Recognition**

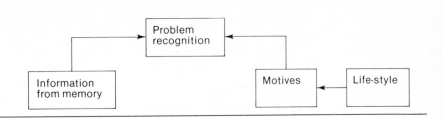

degree, the ideal state for an individual at any point in time. New information, on the other hand, often serves to reveal the extent to which present circumstances deviate from this ideal. The Hanes strategy is a case in point. Once this perceived deviation reaches a certain limit, the individual then is aroused to restore the disturbed balance.

This chapter begins with a discussion of the determinants of the ideal state. Motives are of central importance here, and insights are gained through reference to various theories of motivation and learning. Then the determinants of perceived inadequacy of the actual state are discussed. While there is emphasis on marketing implications throughout, the chapter concludes with an expanded consideration of the problems of marketing strategy.

THE IDEAL STATE

Perceptions of the ideal state can change for many reasons, but there are four determinants warranting special discussion: (1) motive activation; (2) reference group influence; (3) the influence of other decisions; and (4) marketing efforts.

**Motive
Activation**

A lifetime of learning and experience obviously serves to reinforce certain patterns of behavior that prove to be beneficial either in giving pleasure or in reducing discomfort and pain. These, in turn, become embedded in one's basic personality and life-style as motives—enduring predispositions that direct behavior toward certain goals. Motives function both to *arouse* and to *direct* behavior toward these ends.

Before proceeding further, it is well to stop and ask the important question of the relevance of *individual* motives to the marketer who must, of necessity, deal with *masses* in most situations. Fortunately, it usually is possible to uncover market segments with common strivings and goals. One authority puts it this way:

Motives are individually acquired but certain situations will produce pleasure or pain with such regularity either through biological or cultural arrangements that the probability of certain common motives developing in all people is very high.[2]

[2]David C. McClelland, *Personality* (New York: William Sloane Assoc., 1951), 474.

Motive arousal or activation occurs in three primary ways: (1) arousal of drive; (2) autistic thinking; or (3) environmental stimulation.

Arousal of Drive

A college student studying for a final examination suddenly says to his roommate, "I'm thirsty; I need to get a drink." He then rises and gets a drink of water. What has happened to activate this sequence of behavior? Clearly he felt discomfort that was recognized as thirst. It has become conventional in learning theory to explain that he felt a *need,* which then activated *drive* (a sense of discomfort or tension).

There is no general agreement on the causes of drive activation. Some postulate that it is generated by an internal disturbance of equilibrium stemming from physiological or even hereditary causes. Whatever the reason, drive leads to a change in the level of activity which then is channeled by motive patterns toward goals that have satisfied the aroused state in the past. It is in this sense that motive has both an arousing and a directing function.

Autistic Thinking

The human being possesses the unique capability of thinking about a person or object not present at the immediate time or of imagining the desirable consequences of engaging in some type of activity. This thought process, referred to as autistic thinking, can serve as a source of arousal in and of itself. Most people, for example, have been motivated to eat merely by thinking about a food object, even though no hunger drive was felt prior to that time.

Environmental Stimulation

A motive can be triggered by information coming from the environment. The smell of food can stimulate a desire to eat. In this instance the food aromas activate an expectancy that pleasure will be forthcoming, and the result is arousal of drive.

In other instances, the information provides cues about the probability of success if a desired course of action is pursued. This also can activate a motive. Assume that a consumer has a strong motive to succeed in situations in which it is known that behavior will be evaluated by others. In this case the person possesses a strong achievement motive.[3] Assume further that the person is exposed to the ad in Figure 10.3. Notice that success is virtually guaranteed each time a picture is taken using this advanced camera. Excellence in photography can be a real source of pride for some, with the result that the images of success stimulated by this appeal can activate the achievement motive.

Atkinson makes the important point that motives are *stable* because

---

[3]See David C. McClelland, *The Achieving Society* (Princeton, N.J.: D. Van Nostrand Company, Inc., 1961).

**Figure 10.3
An Appeal to the
Achievement
Motivation**

Source: Courtesy of Canon USA, Inc.

of the fact that they are established in childhood.[4] A motive will not be altered by outside influence, but persuasion from various sources *can* change the perception of success in motive satisfaction in a given situation. As a broad generalization, it is safe to conclude that one major role

[4]John W. Atkinson (ed.), *Motives in Fantasy, Action and Society* (Princeton, N.J.: D. Van Nostrand Company, Inc., 1958), 435.

for marketing communication is to show a product or service in the most favorable light in terms of the motive or motives it is designed to satisfy.

Classification of Motives

Psychologists and marketing people alike have tried their hand at classification and some lists attain great length. This often is little more than an exercise in ingenuity, however, because 100 people no doubt would produce 100 different lists. When an attempt is made to determine motive patterns on a more analytical basis, this is a different matter. A. H. Maslow brought important clarity to this difficult question.[5] While his thinking is based more on an intuitive than on an empirical foundation, it is worthy of note.

Maslow hypothesizes that motives are organized in such a way as to establish priorities and hierarchies of importance (prepotency). Through this means, internal conflict is avoided by one motive taking precedence over another. The following classification was suggested, proceeding from the lowest order to the highest:

1. Physiological—the fundamentals of survival, including hunger and thirst.

2. Safety—concern over physical survival, ordinary prudence, which might be overlooked in striving to satisfy hunger or thirst.

3. Belongingness and love—striving to be accepted by intimate members of one's family and to be an important person to them. This also can include nonfamily members.

4. Esteem and status—striving to achieve a high standing relative to others, including desires for mastery, reputation, and prestige.

5. Self-actualization—a desire to know, understand, systematize, organize, and construct a system of values.

Three essentially different categories are comprehended in this classification: (1) motives related to survival needs; (2) motives related to human interaction and involvement; and (3) motives related to competency and self. Each higher order of motive will not function until lower levels are satisfied, at least to some degree. The hungry person will care little about understanding nuclear physics. Undoubtedly it is reasonable to assume that some motives in each category are never fully satisfied, thus remaining as a continued source of problem recognition. A strong desire for status, for example, can be virtually insatiable.

The higher-order motives are of particular significance in understanding cross-cultural differences in consumer behavior. They generally will not be activated among the mass of people living in underdeveloped countries in which bodily survival is the primary concern. On the other hand, they will tend to predominate in the affluent societies of the Western world in particular. Witness the incidence of striving for individuality

[5]A. H. Maslow, *Motivation and Personality* (New York: Harper & Row, 1954).

through the inventory of consumer goods typical in suburban American homes—stereo sets, hobby activities of all types, a resurgence of interest in art and serious music, and so on. It is interesting also to point out that those who engage in such socially-conscious activities as the consumerism movement or civil rights are motivated to a large degree by self-actualization.[6]

Life obviously is more complex at these higher levels; greater individuality is exerted; and, accordingly, it becomes more difficult to isolate the motives underlying a particular buying action. Yet, this knowledge is all the more crucial for the business firm. This is because the exercise of individuality by buyers requires that all components of marketing strategy be precisely on target if sales potentials are to be attained.

It is unlikely that a classification such as Maslow's will prove very useful in explaining the specific motives in a given purchase. But the concept of prepotency (ordered relationships of motive strength) is of conceptual value. It has been verified that prepotency is reflected in consumer buying to the extent that previously ignored desires often exert themselves only after a purchase has satisfied a predominant (and perhaps lower order) motive.[7]

Unity and Stability of Motive Patterns

A major thesis of this book is that the consumer behaves in a consistent and purposeful manner. This implies that motives are integrated into a meaningful whole. There is widespread agreement in the behavioral sciences that one's entire psychological makeup is organized around the *self-concept*. It is not a governor against which behavior is referred. Rather, it is a means whereby social values and controls become internalized as behavioral standards. Rogers puts it this way:

The self-concept, or self-structure, may be thought of as an organized configuration of perceptions of the self which are admissible to awareness. It is composed of such elements as the perceptions of one's characteristics and abilities; the percepts and concepts of the self in relation to others and to the environment; the value qualities which are perceived as associated with experiences; and objectives, goals, and ideas which are perceived as having positive or negative valence.[8]

The self becomes a value to be enhanced, with the result that certain goal objects become internalized as permanent incentives. As Maslow indicated, self-actualization, self-esteem, and belongingness and love are all motives keyed to self-maintenance and enhancement.[9]

The self-concept integrates motives into a purposeful pattern that is

[6]George Brooker, "The Self-Actualizing Socially Conscious Consumer," *Journal of Consumer Research*, vol. 3 (September 1976), 107-112.

[7]George Katona, *The Powerful Consumer* (New York: McGraw-Hill, 1960), 132.

[8]Carl R. Rogers, *Client-Centered Therapy* (Boston: Houghton Mifflin Company, 1951), 492.

[9]Maslow, *Motivation and Personality*.

reflected in purchasing behavior. To take one example, cranberry sauce long has been a staple of the American diet, especially at Thanksgiving, Christmas, and other holidays. The heavy user of this product, however, uses it throughout the year as well. The heavy user was found through marketing research to have a very interesting self-concept and life-style. The core of her self-concept was found to lie in service to her family, and the same had been true of her mother and grandmother. Not surprisingly, her dominant values are highly traditional, and she adamantly rejects the modern liberation movement. The image of cranberry sauce, in turn, is remarkably consistent with her outlook on life in that it connotes tradition and engenders happy associations of family life, well-being, and the horn of plenty. Use of the product, then, represents highly self-approved behavior.

Quite an opposite life-style was found when the nonuser of cranberry sauce was studied. Her values reflect the now familiar concept of the liberated woman, even though this study was undertaken prior to the onset of the feminist movement. Traditional values, by and large, are rejected, and cranberries are rejected as well because of their old-fashioned image. Here is an example of a contradiction between self-concept and product image that will not be overcome through marketing effort, no matter how skillful. It is interesting to note, however, that this same person proved to be a heavy user of cranberry juice, which reflects quite a different image. Its values in nutrition, dieting, and modern cookery make it compatible with the life-style of those in this market segment.

The ad in Figure 10.4 is an interesting appeal to the woman who no longer is tied to the home. The product offered by Stouffer's facilitates her self-expression.

There have been more than 20 published attempts in the literature on consumer behavior to measure self-concept and relate it to particular aspects of buying behavior.[10] The results have been disappointing to say the least, and this should not be surprising. In the first place, measurement and analysis of this type belongs to the domain of counseling and psychological therapy. Furthermore, the now standard techniques of psychographic research discussed in Chapter 7 pretty largely reveal those aspects of self-concept that are reflected in purchasing behavior.

In summary, it is a basic principle that nonself-approved behavior is atypical in the market place, even though one writer has argued somewhat unconvincingly to the contrary.[11] Sometimes behavior appears to be irrational simply because it violates the observer's own standards and

---

[10]For a thorough review, see J. Paul Peter, "Some Observations on Self-Concept in Consumer Behavior Research," in Jerry C. Olson (ed.), *Advances in Consumer Research,* vol. 7 (Ann Arbor, Mich.: Association for Consumer Research, 1980), 625-626. Also see E. Laird Landon, Jr., "Self Concept, Ideal Self Concept, and Consumer Purchase Intention," *Journal of Consumer Research,* vol. 1 (September 1974), 44-51; Ira J. Dolich, "Congruence Relationships between Self Images and Product Brands," *Journal of Marketing Research,* vol. 6 (1969), 80-84; E. L. Grubb and G. Hupp, "Perception of Self, Generalized Stereotypes, and Brand Selection," *Journal of Marketing Research,* vol. 5 (1968), 68-63; and E. L. Grubb and B. L. Stern, "Self-Concept and Significant Others," *Journal of Marketing Research,* vol. 8 (1971), 382-385.

[11]Edward C. Bursk, "Opportunities for Persuasion," *Harvard Business Review,* vol. 36 (September-October 1958), 114-115.

**Figure 10.4
An Appeal to the
Self-Concept of the
Modern
Homemaker**

THE JOY OF NOT COOKING.

4:42—Your serve is beautiful today. And you've got the advantage.

When your game is going good, don't rush home. Let Stouffer's do the cooking.

Try Green Pepper Steak with Rice, ready after just 15 minutes in boiling water. Tender steak strips, savory sauce, delicious flavor. Or Salisbury Steak, grilled beef and onions, tasty beef broth gravy.

Or Chicken Stuffed Shells, big pasta shells chockful of chicken, blanketed with cheese sauce.

They're just some of the more than 40 good foods we make. To give you the time to do the things you want. And still put a good meal on the table. That's the joy of Stouffer's.

STOUFFER'S, ANYTIME.

Source: Courtesy of Stouffer's Foods.

criteria. Two decades ago, Snygg and Combs stated a philosophy of inquiry that should be assumed by all who claim to be objective analysts of consumer behavior.[12] It points out that behavior always is purposeful if analyzed from the point of view of the person in question. The problem

[12]Donald Snygg and Arthur W. Combs, *Individual Behavior* (New York: Harper & Row, 1949), 12.

enters when the analyst looking from the outside cannot fully grasp all of the relevant determinants of the behavior.

The Measurement of Motives

A number of pervasive motives such as achievement and affiliation have been studied in the literature. It is now generally felt, along with McClelland, that the following methodological criteria must be met:

1. The measure should reflect the presence or absence of a motive, as well as variations in its strength. This generally requires an independent measure of the motive against which the measure in question can be compared and validated. Needless to say, this can be extraordinarily difficult to attain.

2. The measure should reflect variations only in the motive under analysis, without contamination from other psychological variables. The various tests used often are not pure indicators in this sense and, as a result, contain considerable bias.

3. The measure should give the same reading for an individual at many points in time under approximately the same conditions. If this criterion is met, the measuring instrument can be said to be *reliable.*[13]

One of the most common methods is a self-rating in which the individual verbally gives responses that indicate the presence or absence of a motive. Another method is observer rating. Some of the best results have been obtained with various types of behavioral measures. McClelland, for example, measures achievement motivation through responses in which an individual is asked to tell a story about a situation he sees, thus revealing important underlying motivations.

The marketing researcher usually does not make use of these standardized measures, which have been developed largely for purposes of clinical diagnosis of the individual. Rather, motives are assessed most frequently through psychographic research discussed in Chapter 7. Interest in a product or particular type of behavior is isolated at the outset. Then a battery of AIO (activity, interest, and opinion) questions is administered to explore a variety of dimensions of life-style. These psychographic measures then are correlated with the behavior under analysis to reveal the underlying motivations.

A leading publishing house, for example, had to discover the motives satisfied through purchase of a Bible if a modern language version of the Bible were to be marketed successfully to the nonchurch-going public.[14] It was discovered that interest in the Bible in general and *The Living Bible* in particular was highest among housewives in the middle income and average education bracket with children still living at home. The psy-

[13]David C. McClelland, "Methods of Measuring Human Motivation," in John W. Atkinson, (ed.), *Motives in Fantasy, Action and Society* (Princeton, N.J.: D. Van Nostrand Company, 1958), 7-42.

[14]See Roger D. Blackwell, James F. Engel, and W. Wayne Talarzyk, *Contemporary Cases in Consumer Behavior* (Hinsdale, Ill.: Dryden Press, 1977), 350-359.

chographic profile revealed a basic conservative outlook toward life characterized by a traditional value profile and high premium placed on the family and child raising. *The Living Bible* thus was presented as an ideal guide for the concerned parent in raising children as they should be in today's world. *The Living Bible* quickly outdistanced its competition and found its way into nearly 40 percent of American homes.

The reader may well inquire at this point about so-called *motivation research*—an approach to consumer analysis much ballyhooed in the 1950s through the popularized writings of Vance Packard and others. Claims were made that researchers had discovered a set of miracle tools that could be used to plumb the depths of the consumer's psyche in some mysterious way so that he or she could be manipulated by the marketer. Actually the term was a real misnomer. The tools used at that time were not especially applicable to the measurement of motives any more than to attitudes, life-style, or a host of other influences on consumer behavior.

There were some, however, who designated motivation research as the use of certain techniques pioneered in the psychological clinic, including depth interviewing and projective tests. Depth interviewing is nothing more than nonstandardized questions and probes into reasons underlying behavior. Much can be learned, but the unconscious certainly cannot be penetrated in a one hour consumer interview. This might be possible following months of psychoanalysis, but even this is a debatable point.

The other tool of motivation research, the projective technique, is based on the accurate assumption that people can easily avoid such direct questions as, "Why do you shop at Kroger's?" and give an evasive or even deceptive answer. The projective question utilizes some type of indirect format, which elicits a response in such a way that the respondent is not completely aware that the answer given reflects his or her own feelings. There is no proof, however, that this method is superior to the more traditional directed question. Fortunately, the term motivation research has generally passed out of common use.

Reference Group Influence

It was stressed clearly in Chapter 6 that important reference groups, especially those performing a normative function, can be a powerful determinant of the ideal state. In fact, their expectations can set a rigid standard that makes deviation difficult unless a degree of social rejection can be tolerated. Many college freshmen quickly come into problem recognition, for instance, once they discover the vast difference between the types of clothing suitable on the high school campus and those acceptable at college.

The Influence of Other Decisions

Problem recognition also can be the outgrowth of other purchase decisions. Either acquiring a new residence or remodeling will likely affect perceptions of the desirability of carpeting and various pieces of furniture,

**Figure 10.5
Stimulation of
Problem
Recognition
Through Appeal to
Family and
Belongingness**

Funny stage they're at: George is older, but somehow he doesn't quite measure up to kid sister Shirley. "It's a stage," Dad consoles his son. "You'll outgrow it." The kids are growing up. Almost too fast. So, be sure to share those little moments, as well as the big, with faraway friends and family. Just reach out with a phone call, and they're sharing your day.

Bell System

Reach out and touch someone.

Source: Courtesy of American Telephone and Telegraph Company, Long Lines Department.

even though present options are not worn out.[15] Also consumers tend, at times, to arrange purchases in terms of acquisition priorities.[16] This means that acquisition of one item will be followed then by purchase of

[15]Donald H. Granbois, "A Study of the Family Decision Making Process in the Purchase of Major Durable Household Goods," unpublished doctoral dissertation, Indiana University Graduate School of Business, 1962, 84.

[16]See J. Paroush, "The Order of Acquisition of Consumer Durables," *Econometrica,* vol. 33 (January 1965), 225-235 and Hugh M. Sargent, *Consumer Product Rating Publications and Buying Behavior* (Urbana, Ill.; Bureau of Business and Economic Research, University of Illinois, 1959).

the next highest priority. Therefore, it often is possible to predict future buying actions from various consumer segments if one has information on present purchases plus established purchase intentions.[17]

Marketing Efforts

From the outset it must be recognized frankly that motive activation and other factors are far more likely to stimulate problem recognition through a changed perception of the desired state than any type of marketing effort. By and large, the very absence of existing problem recognition inhibits information processing. Nevertheless, it is possible at times to break through perceptual defenses with highly skilled appeals. The key lies in appeal to a dominant motive. In this sense, marketing inputs are another form of environmental stimulation discussed above.

Let's look at two examples. First, Figure 10.5 contains just one of the remarkable series of ads undertaken by the Bell System to encourage long distance calling. By its appeal to family love and desire to belong, it no doubt has encouraged many to make a call they previously were not contemplating. The Personal Products Company has carefully positioned *Deodorant Carefree Panty Shields* in terms of extra freshness and safety (Figure 10.6) and, in so doing, provided a new answer to an existing need.

DISSATISFACTION WITH ACTUAL STATE

Problem recognition also occurs when the individual sees that the actual situation or state of affairs falls short of the ideal. This can happen in two ways: (1) changed circumstances and (2) marketing efforts.

Changed Circumstances

A problem often is perceived when a present alternative is evaluated as being unsatisfactory. Perhaps it is broken, run down, worn out, or even seen to be overpriced. Until the present circumstances of high mortgage rates, for example, price savings were often a dominant motivating factor in the purchase of a home or town house in comparison with continuation of renting.[18] This no doubt will reoccur if economic circumstances change.

Changes within the nuclear family also can trigger problem recognition. The birth of a child results in modified requirements for food, clothing, furniture, and type of dwelling. Furthermore, new needs and redefinition of current circumstances occur as the family's size and age composition change.[19] Even a change in the place of employment can affect the perceived desirability of the present home.

---

[17]John McFall, "Priority Patterns and Consumer Behavior," *Journal of Marketing,* vol. 33 (October 1969), 50-55.

[18]Ruby T. Norris, "Processes and Objectives of House Purchasing in the New London Area," in Lincoln Clark (ed.), *The Dynamics of Consumer Reaction* (New York: New York University Press, 1955), 25-29; Peter Rossi, *Why Families Move* (New York: Free Press, 1955); William T. Kelley, "How Buyers Shop for a New Home," *Appraisal,* vol. 25 (1957), 209-214.

[19]See, for example, William D. Wells and George Gubar, "The Life Cycle Concept of Marketing Research," *Journal of Marketing Research,* vol. 3 (November 1966), 355-363.

**Figure 10.6
Stimulation of
Problem
Recognition
Through Providing
a New Solution to
an Existing
Problem**

Source: *Carefree Panty Shields* is the trademark of Personal Products Company, Milltown, N.J. 08850
© PPC 1980.

Changes in financial status or anticipated changes can have the same effect. Salary increases, tax refunds, temporary or unusual employment, cash gifts, and the retirement of debts all serve to activate new desires.[20] The opposite also is quite likely, especially in an era where inflation slowly eats away at earning power. In addition, financial expectations are quite important in the period immediately preceding the purchase of durable goods. A favorable outlook is an incentive for purchase and vice versa.[21]

As an example of the effect of anticipated change in financial status many students in the senior year of college purchase a car, clothing, or other items before they actually have a job. This may trigger other purchases as well either during the recruiting process or after the job has been accepted. One leading life insurance company maintains a highly developed sales force on campuses primarily to sell insurance to those who are graduating, on the anticipation of future earnings.

Marketing Efforts

It is possible through advertising or personal selling to present new products in such a way that the present alternatives are clearly perceived as being inadequate. If this is to be successful, however, the underlying motive, product characteristics, and product benefits in use must be stressed. Notice, first of all, how the *Formfit* ad by Rogers appeals to the athletic woman (Figure 10.7). It correctly captures one major motivation for running and demonstrates the need for a different type of bra. The ad in Figure 10.8 also features product attributes and refers to the consumer's basic motivations. The ad demonstrates that it really *is* a genuine improvement over other products.

FORMULATING A GENERAL MARKETING STRATEGY

Some people tend to respond to innovations sooner than others, thus underscoring individual differences in propensity to recognize a problem and undertake appropriate buying action. If they can be identified, these innovators are excellent targets for marketing efforts. The subject of diffusion of innovations is discussed in a later chapter in this section, but it is sufficient to note at this point that the early adopter tends to possess the following characteristics:[22]

1. More education

2. Higher income

3. Higher standard of living

4. More relevant product knowledge

[20]Granbois, "Study of the Family," 84.

[21]Eva Mueller, "The Desire for Innovations in Household Goods," in Lincoln Clark (ed.), *Consumer Behavior: Research on Consumer Reactions* (New York: Harper & Row, 1958), 37.

[22]Everett M. Rogers and J. David Stanfield, "Adoption and Diffusion of New Products: Emerging Generalizations and Hypotheses," in Frank M. Bass et al. (eds.), *Applications of the Sciences in Marketing Management* (New York: John Wiley & Sons, 1968).

**Figure 10.7
Stimulation of
Problem
Recognition
Through Appeal to
Dominant
Motivation and
Product Benefit**

Source: Courtesy of Formfit Rogers.

Figure 10.8
An Example Where
Emphasis on
Product by Itself
Does not Stimulate
Problem
Recognition

Are you ready for better looking skin?

There are no miracles when it comes to skin care. But Aapri®Apricot Facial Scrub comes close. Why? Because after just one use, you'll have fresher, better looking skin, no matter what type of skin you have.

What's more, it's simple. You just add water, rub into a lather and wash your face the way you normally

Just add water and rub into a lather. | You'll actually feel it working. | You'll have better looking skin in minutes!

would. You'll see that the secret ingredient in Aapri makes it so much more effective than soaps or ordinary cleansers.

Finely crushed apricot seeds are the secret.

The natural fiber of the apricot seed works in a unique way to help clean your skin like it's never been cleaned. Aapri is made with finely crushed seeds immersed in a creamy base that will actually get rid of that dead skin layer that can clog your pores and cause skin problems. Unless these skin cells are cleaned away, the skin takes on a dull appearance. So you may be hiding your best looking skin without knowing it.

Fresh healthy skin doesn't just happen.

It's just a matter of washing your face regularly with Aapri®Apricot Facial Scrub. And using good common sense. No matter what your age or skin type, there's really nothing like knowing your skin is as fresh and healthy looking as it can be. And there's nothing like Aapri.

Source: *Redbook,* December 1981. Courtesy of Aapri Cosmetics, Inc.

5. A positive outlook toward change in general

6. A strong achievement motivation

7. High aspirations for children and their success

8. Cosmopolitan interests

9. Higher than average exposure to the mass media

10. A tendency to deviate from group norms, accompanied by greater than average participation in groups

11. Higher than average exposure to interpersonal communication

12. Frequent service as an opinion leader to others

13. Possession of needs, attitudes, and behavioral patterns that are compatible with the innovation chosen.

Also, it was stressed in Chapter 6 that various family members interact and assume different roles in the purchase process. The role of husband and wife will vary considerably from product to product, especially in terms of initial problem recognition. Once again, the member recognizing the problem first will be the most responsive market target. From the data accumulated thus far, the following generalizations appear to be warranted:

1. The higher the price of the item, the greater the tendency for the husband to dominate in problem recognition.

2. The extent of husband-wife involvement in problem recognition tends to vary according to cultural norms of specialization. Husbands will dominate, for instance, when the product is technically or mechanically complex.

3. Younger and higher-income husbands play a greater role in problem recognition than their older and middle- to lower-income counterparts.

4. Working wives are more involved in problem recognition than those whose primary role is within the home.

Finally it has been pointed out that marketing efforts can play a role in triggering problem recognition either by highlighting the ideal state or by showing the inadequacies of the present state. Nevertheless, the stimulation of problem recognition through any type of marketing activity is far more difficult than it might seem from the discussion thus far. Keep in mind that each person has an ability to be completely oblivious to persuasion, to see and hear what he or she wants to see and hear. In fact, filters tend to be closed when problem recognition is not active. The very existence of an aroused motive, *per se,* makes one decidedly more responsive to relevant information. The reverse is also true, as Chapter 13 will stress at length.

In the final analysis, *problem recognition most frequently is triggered by factors beyond the control of the marketer.* Advertisements and other forms of promotion assume their greatest effectiveness *follow-*

ing problem recognition. The best strategy, then, is to uncover those who, for one reason or another, are dissatisfied with their present solution and are open to something different. Then appropriate changes can be introduced in product, package, price, promotion, and distribution to capitalize upon a responsive segment of prospective customers. The payout from this approach usually is greater than that achieved from attempts designed to stimulate problem recognition in a frequently indifferent consumer audience that is inundated with persuasion from all sides.

Summary

Behavior begins with the triggering of problem recognition. A problem is recognized when there is an intolerable gap perceived to exist between the ideal state of affairs and the present state of affairs.

Problem recognition can arise when something happens to highlight the ideal state and thus make the discrepancy between ideal and actual more apparent. One cause is the influence of other decisions in which one purchase often makes another necessary. Reference group members can stress only the allowable behavior and therefore make that the ideal through normative social influence. Sometimes problem recognition even occurs through novelty as the consumer seeks to bring about a change simply for the sake of change. Marketing efforts can trigger problem recognition as well when dominant motives are aroused by the appeals used. The most important factor, however, is motive activation.

Motives serve as the primary determinant of the ideal state. These learned predispositions embody goals that have been shown to be rewarding by past experience. As such, they are deeply imbedded in basic personality and are beyond change through marketing efforts. The best strategy is to uncover the motives associated with a particular purchase, highlight them, and demonstrate how the particular product or service is an adequate alternative to reduce the aroused drive.

Problem recognition also occurs when the present state is seen to be inadequate. Changes in circumstances (income, family life-cycle, financial expectations, and so on) are one important cause. Marketers also can show the present solution to be inadequate by stressing the benefits of improved products.

Review and Discussion Questions

1. A consumer goes into an automobile showroom planning to buy a four-door sedan and emerges with an air-conditioned hardtop costing $1,000 more than he intended to pay. When he was asked why he made this purchase, he was at a loss other than to say that he liked the car. He did mention, however, that he could not afford the extra cost. A professor from a nearby university observed this scene and concluded in disgust that this was just another example of irrational behavior. The implication was that this consumer acted in a nonpurposeful manner. Do you agree?

2. Can motives be changed through advertising? Why or why not?

3. Using Great Britain and India as examples, indicate how the concept of motive prepotency might explain certain cross-cultural differences in consumer behavior.

4. Discuss the problem-recognition process that occurred before you purchased your last bottle of soft drink. How did this differ from the one that preceded the purchase of a suit or slacks? What role, if any, did marketing activity play in problem recognition?

5. How did problem recognition underlie your decision to attend college or graduate school? Describe the process.

6. Use examples from your own experiences to illustrate how problem recognition resulted from: (a) depletion of previous solution, (b) dissatisfaction with present solution, (c) change in family characteristics or status, (d) change in reference groups, and (e) recognition of other problems.

7. What is the self-concept? How is it formed? Would measurement of self-concept be of any use to a brand manager who has full responsibility for the marketing of a new brand of household detergent? Would it be of greater use to the executive responsible for marketing stereo sets? Explain fully.

8. A manufacturer has developed a line of new power tools and has discovered that the husband is far more likely to feel the need for such a product and hence more apt to recognize the problem initially than is the wife. Of what use, if any, is such information in marketing strategy?

9. Assume that you are a consultant to a national manufacturer of air conditioners. Your firm has 60 percent of the market. The remainder is divided among seven competitors. Your firm wants to stimulate problem recognition among those who own second homes for vacation and weekend purposes. What are your recommendations concerning, first of all, the desirability of such a strategy and, secondly, the techniques that should be used for this purpose?

"Woofers," "tweeters," "flutter," "wow," "frequency response," "eight tracks," "four tracks," "dolby," and on we go. The buying of a stereo set has become no easy matter because of the "bells and whistles" now being added by manufacturers, and this trend is not dissipating.[1] In some ways the nonsophisticated consumer is at the mercy of the retail salesperson who has become expert in a high-price mix and match selling strategy. Most buyers, in short, simply do not possess the expertise to make an enlightened decision, and it is to be expected that they will actively search for relevant information.

The associate publisher of *Stereo Review* states, "The masses are intimidated by the hi-fi salon. Hi-fi audio has its own terminology and buying audio components is a complex purchase."[2] Until recently this mystique was not too serious as sales were growing from 20-25 percent yearly until the end of the 1970s. Then it became necessary to develop and market products in such a way that people other than hi-fi buffs would be attracted. One leader in the industry, the Fisher Corporation, recently introduced a $2,000 packaged system consisting of completely integrated components and marketed without making use of esoteric terminology. Furthermore, Technics, a Panasonic subsidiary, has broadened its advertising to include such publicatons as *Playboy, Time, Business Week,* and *Psychology Today.* Ads stress such features as styling and ease of operation. In turn, distribution patterns are changing to move beyond the audio specialist and thereby attract the general market.

Both Fisher and Technics have recognized the consumer's need for information in usable form stressing important features. In other words, they understand what is meant by search, the second stage in high-involvement decision making. *Search* is defined as *motivated exposure to information with regard to a given alternative.* It results when existing information, beliefs, and attitudes are found to be inadequate.

Figure 11.1 briefly depicts the search process. Notice, first of all, the

---

[1]Theodore J. Gage, "Gimmicks Grab the Crowd," *Advertising Age* (January 12, 1981), S-2.
[2]B. G. Yovovich, "Selling the New Technology," *Advertising Age* (January 12, 1981), S-12.

**Figure 11.1
A Model of the
Search Process**

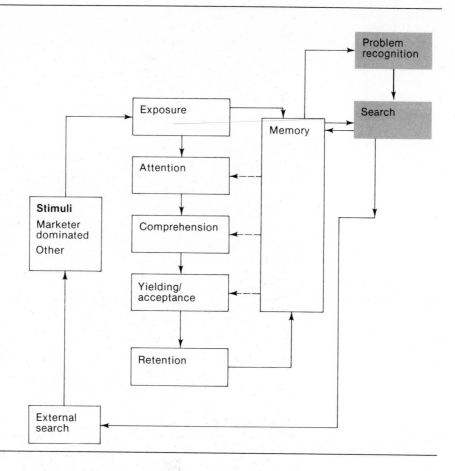

arrow from search into memory. What this means is that the individual searches memory first before turning to outside sources. If this is not sufficient, then external search begins, and the individual consults either marketer-dominated sources (ads, salesmen, and so on), or any other relevant input. This then is processed through memory as discussed in Chapter 9 and ultimately will have some type of effect on beliefs, attitudes, intentions, or behavior.

This chapter begins with a discussion of internal search followed by a review of the nature and extent of external search. Special attention then will be directed to problems of measurement. The next major consideration is the external sources which are consulted. These are discussed initially in overview form with in-depth consideration being given only to the marketer-dominated sources. Chapter 12 continues the discussion with a focus on personal sources (sometimes referred to as "opinion leadership"), and the subject is concluded in Chapter 13 under the broader heading, "diffusion of innovations."

INTERNAL SEARCH

Internal search is nothing more than a memory scan.[3] At times a past solution to the recognized problem is remembered and implemented.[4] This, of course, is the essence of habitual or routine response behavior, and it truncates other stages and leads directly to choice. In other instances, stored information will be much more fragmentary. Sometimes this information will not be suitable, an example being recall of a brand without any specifics regarding its performance capabilities. The consumer then is motivated to engage in active external search and will be receptive to information which is perceived as filling these memory gaps.

Internal search can only be detected through use of *protocol analysis.* The individual is asked to think aloud as he or she actually engages in some type of decision,[5] and it is hoped that actual use of stored memory content will be detected. Obviously this may not happen in any verbally discernible way, but no one has discussed a better measurement as of this writing.

THE NATURE AND EXTENT OF EXTERNAL SEARCH

External search, of course, represents a *motivated and completely voluntary decision* to seek new information. In general, the decision to search as well as the actual extent of search depends upon the person's perception of the *value* to be gained in comparison with the *costs* of obtaining and using that information.[6] New insights into product characteristics, financing arrangements, and the opinions of others are just a few of the possible benefits.[7] Costs may include time, travel, parking; and psychological frustrations, time away from more pleasurable pursuits, and so on.[8]

There also are some individual differences in propensity to search. Furthermore, people differ in the sequence of search—i. e., whether or not information is sought on product attribute, brand, or both. These subjects also are considered in this section.

---

[3]Internal search is rarely discussed in the consumer behavior literature. One of the few exceptions is James R. Bettman, *An Information Processing Theory of Consumer Choice* (Reading, Mass.: Addison-Wesley, 1979), 107-111.

[4]George Katona, *Psychological Analysis of Economic Behavior* (New York: McGraw-Hill, 1951), 47.

[5]For an example of protocol analysis see James F. Bettman and C. Whan Park, "Effects of Prior Knowledge and Experience and Phase of the Choice Process on Consumer Decision Processes: A Protocol Analysis," *Journal of Consumer Research,* vol. 7 (1980), 234-248.

[6]See, for example, Louis P. Bucklin, "Retail Strategy and the Classification of Consumer Goods," *Journal of Marketing,* vol. 27 (January 1963), 50-54; Richard H. Holton, "The Distinction between Convenience Goods, Shopping Goods, and Speciality Goods," *Journal of Marketing,* vol. 69 (June 1961), 213-225; Louis P. Bucklin, "Testing Propensities to Shop," *Journal of Marketing,* vol. 30 (January 1966), 22-27; Donald F. Cox, "The Audience as Communicators," in Stephen Greyser (ed.), *Toward Scientific Marketing* (Chicago: American Marketing Association, 1963), 58-72; Donald H. Granbois, "The Role of Communication in the Family Decision Making Process," in Greyser, 44-57; John U. Farley, " 'Brand Loyalty' and the Economics of Information," *Journal of Business,* vol. 37 (October 1964), 370-381.

[7]See, for example, W. Phillips Davidson, "On the Effects of Communication," *Public Opinion Quarterly,* vol. 3 (1959), 343-360.

[8]Wesley C. Bender, "Consumer Purchase Costs—Do Retailers Recognize Them?" *Journal of Retailing* (Spring 1964), 1-8.

The Perceived Value of Search

The following scenario pretty well describes the personal situation of the senior author as of this writing. It is obvious from the condition of a well-used 1973 car that a change must be made soon, yet no one in the family has paid much attention to the ads which have inundated them lately. The youngest member of the family, Karen, tries her best to convince the folks that *any* brand of imported car is superior to that "junk turned out of Detroit." The father quickly dismisses that argument by reminding everyone that the 1973 "problem car" is an imported lemon. Karen's mother chimes in with an obvious reminder about the precarious financial situation of the family at this time. The father will be the primary decision maker, and his dilemma is intensified by the inescapable fact that he knows nothing about engines, transmissions, and things like that. All three realize that they must do a good bit of investigation before a decision can be made.

This illustrates to one degree or another the major factors that can serve to motivate external search: (1) the quantity and quality of existing information; (2) ability to recall that information; (3) perceived risk; and (4) confidence in decision-making ability.

Quantity and Quality of Existing Information

First of all, the more a person knows, the lower the propensity to search, all things being equal. Research findings support the obvious conclusion that search is much less probable when a product has been bought repeatedly over time or when the consumer has had other means of gathering considerable previous information.[9] Similarly, the greater the number of brands of the generic product that have been purchased and used, the lower the likelihood of search.[10] Thus, as a general rule, both the presence and the extent of search vary inversely with the length and breadth of experience.[11] There is just one interesting exception documented by Bettman and Park, who found that those with no previous experience whatsoever are not prone to search, presumably because of a sense of being overwhelmed by the whole thing.[12] This could easily be the case, for example, with the hi-fi shopper, mentioned at the outset of the chapter, who simply does not know where to begin or

[9]Geoffrey C. Kiel, "An Empirical Analysis of New Car Buyers' External Information Search Behaviour" (doctoral dissertation, School of Marketing, University of New South Wales, 1977). Also see George Katona, *The Mass Consumption Society* (New York: McGraw-Hill, 1964), 289-290; and Joseph W. Newman and Richard Staelin, "Prepurchase Information Seeking for New Cars and Major Household Appliances," *Journal of Marketing Research,* vol. 9 (August 1972), 249-257. See also Peter D. Bennett and Robert M. Mandell, "Prepurchase Information Seeking Behavior of New Car Purchasers—The Learning Hypothesis," *Journal of Marketing Research,* vol. 6 (November 1969), 430-433 and Robert D. Woodruff, "Measurement of Consumers' Prior Brand Information," *Journal of Marketing Research,* vol. 9 (August 1972), 258-263.

[10]Katona, *Mass Consumption;* and Newman and Staelin, "Prepurchase."

[11]Paul E. Green, Michael Halbert, and J. Sayer Minas, "An Experiment in Information Buying," *Journal of Advertising Research,* vol. 4 (September 1964), 17-23; also G. David Hughes, Seha M. Tinie, and Phillippe A Naert, "Analyzing Consumer Information Processing," in Philip R. McDonald (ed.), *Marketing Involvement in Society and the Economy* (Chicago: American Marketing Association, 1969), 235-240.

[12]Bettman and Park, "Effects of Prior Knowledge and Experience."

even what questions to ask when faced with such an intimidating array of gadgetry.

The quality of stored information also is a factor, and there are several variables that affect its perceived relevance:

1. *Satisfaction*—the greater the satisfaction with the results of past purchases, the lower the probability that search will occur in the future when similar circumstances lead to problem recognition.[13]

2. *Interpurchase time*—the amount of time that elapses between purchases affects the appropriateness of stored information through the obvious effects of nonuse and forgetting. Thus, the greater the interpurchase time, the higher the probability of external search.[14]

3. *Changes in the mix of alternatives*—the appropriateness of stored information also is affected by the rate of price and style changes as well as by the frequency of new product introductions. The greater the rate of change, the higher the probability that search will occur.[15]

Ability to Recall Information

The ability to recall stored information through internal search depends in part on the degree to which the present problem is perceived to be similar to those which have arisen in the past.[16] Often this will not be the case, with the result that stored information is difficult, if not impossible, to retrieve.

Perceived Risk

During the 1960s in particular, the effects of perceived risk on decision making were extensively investigated.[17] Perceived risk can come from many sources, all of which share the common factor of a perceived uneasiness or fear that a wrong decision will be made. If perceived risk is present, it is reasonable to hypothesize that search will be activated[18] and here are some examples:

---

[13]Kiel, "An Empirical Analysis of New Car Buyers;" and Peter D. Bennett and Robert Mandell, "Prepurchase Information Seeking Behavior of New Car Purchasers."

[14]Katona, *Mass Consumption,* 289-290.

[15]Katona, *Psychological Analysis of Economic Behavior,* 67-68.

[16]Frederick E. May, "Adaptive Behavior in Automobile Brand Choices," *Journal of Marketing Research,* vol. 6 (February 1969), 62-65; John E. Swan, "Experimental Analysis of Predecision Information Seeking,"*Journal of Marketing Research,* vol. 6 (May 1969), 192-197. For more detailed relationships including some findings that contradict the above generalization, see Donald J. Hempel, "Search Behavior and Information Utilization in the Home Buying Process," in McDonald, *Marketing Involvement,* 241-249.

[17]Raymond A. Bauer, "Consumer Behavior as Risk Taking, in Robert S. Hancock, (ed.), *Dynamic Marketing for a Changing World* (Chicago: American Marketing Association, 1960), 389-398.

[18]Paul E. Green, "Consumer Use of Information," in Joseph Newman (ed.), *On Knowing the Consumer* (New York: John Wiley & Sons, 1966), 67-80; Scott M. Cunningham, "Perceived Risk as a Factor in Product Oriented Word of Mouth Behavior: A First Step," in L. George Smith (ed.), *Reflections on Progress in Marketing* (Chicago: American Marketing Association, 1964), 229-238; Scott M. Cunningham, "Perceived Risks as a Factor in the Diffusion of New Product Information," in Raymond M. Haas (ed.), *Science Technology and Marketing* (Chicago: American Marketing Association, 1966), 698-721.

1. *Price*—the higher the price, the greater the financial consequences of making an incorrect decision.[19]

2. *Length of commitment*—the greater the period of time the consumer is committed to use the product, the higher the risk and the greater the intensity of search.[20]

3. *Social influences*—recalling the discussion of reference groups in Chapter 6, the more visible a product is to others, the greater the risk of rejection by them and the need for additional information[21]

4. *Physiological considerations*—the consumption of some products may produce harmful or undesirable physiological effects, with the result that information is sought to reduce this type of risk.[22]

5. *The presence of competing decisions*—some purchases require multiple decisions on brand, color, size, style, and so on. To the degree that this is true, perceived risk and propensity to search both increase.[23]

Confidence in Decision-Making Ability

Often consumers have real doubts about their abilities to make a correct choice. In a sense, this could be considered as a dimension of perceived risk, but it is treated as a separate variable in some models of consumer behavior. The Howard-Sheth model is an example;[24] therefore, it is given similar treatment here.

Confidence as a determinant of choice and search behavior has been studied in two dimensions; (1) the degree of certainty perceived toward a brand[25] or (2) confidence in ability to judge or evaluate brand or product attributes.[26] Search is more likely when confidence is low, all

[19]William P. Dommermuth, "The Shopping Matrix and Marketing Strategy," *Journal of Marketing Research,* vol. 2 (May 1965), 128-132; George Katona and Eva Mueller, "A Study of Purchasing Decisions," in Lincoln H. Clark (ed.), *Consumer Behavior: The Dynamics of Consumer Reaction* (New York: New York University Press, 1955), 30-87, at 46; Henry Towery, "A Study of the Buying Behavior of Mobile Home Purchasers," *Southern Journal of Business,* vol. 5 (July 1970), 66-74. For an exception see Ruby T. Norris, "Processes and Objectives in Home Purchasing in the New London Area," in Clark, 25-29.

[20]Katona and Mueller, "Study of Purchasing Decisions," 30-80; Donald H. Granbois, "A Study of the Family Decision Making Process in the Purchase of Major Household Durable Goods," unpublished doctoral dissertation (Bloomington, Ind.: Indiana University Graduate School of Business, 1962).

[21]Katona, *Mass Consumption,* 289-290.

[22]See, for example, James F. Engel, David A. Knapp, and Deanne E. Knapp, "Sources of Influence in the Acceptance of New Products for Self-Medication: Preliminary Findings," in Haas, *Science Technology,* 776-782. This relation can also be inferred from Sidney P. Feldman and Martin C. Spencer, "The Effect of Personal Influence in the Selection of Consumer Services," in Peter D. Bennett (ed.), *Marketing and Economic Development* (Chicago: American Marketing Association, 1965), 44-52.

[23]Donald F. Cox and Stewart Rich, "Perceived Risk and Consumer Decision-Making—A Case of Telephone Shopping," *Journal of Marketing Research,* vol. 1 (November 1964), 32-39; Dommermuth, "Shopping Matrix," 130.

[24]See Donald R. Lehmann et al., "Some Empirical Contributions to Buyer Behavior Theory," *Journal of Consumer Research,* vol. 1 (December 1974).

[25]John A. Howard and Jagdish N. Sheth, *The Theory of Buyer Behavior* (New York: John Wiley & Sons, 1969).

[26]Peter D. Bennett and Gilbert Harrell, "The Role of Confidence in Understanding and Predicting Buyers' Attitudes and Purchase Intentions," *The Journal of Consumer Research,* vol. 2 (September 1975), 110-117; and Kiel, "An Empirical Analysis." For a more general source, see William B. Locander and Peter W. Hermann, The Effect of Self-Confidence and Anxiety on Information-Seeking in Consumer Risk Reduction," *Journal of Marketing Research,* vol. 17 (May 1979), 268-274.

things being equal. Yet, it is interesting to note that concern or anxiety of this nature was evidenced by fewer than one-third of those in the process of buying a major appliance and by only 10.6 percent of those who had just made a major purchase.[27]

The Costs of Search

One could certainly argue, theoretically at least, that greater information leads to increased consumer efficiency in terms of consumers forming preferences and making purchases which correspond with objective ratings of product quality.[28] If this is true, then the more the information the better! Unfortunately this overlooks the very real costs which must be incurred both to collect and process information.

Decision Delay

Bauer suggested that some buyers may shorten their deliberations in order to reduce the unpleasantness of the decision process itself.[29] He refers to an unpublished study now more than two decades old that also has been examined by the authors, demonstrating that some automobile buyers seem to go into a kind of panic as the point of decision is approached. A rush into purchase thus is a form of escape from the problem. There is no doubt that the predecision period can be one of frustration for some,[30] and the delay required for search often only compounds the dilemma. All things considered, then, the greater the perceived negative consequences of delaying the decision, the less the likelihood of extensive search.[31]

Expenditure of Time and Money

Some forms of search, particularly visits to retail outlets, require the consumer to spend considerable amounts of time. Moreover, a retail visit also tends to include a number of other purchases as well. Assuming that time is limited, search is reduced under such circumstances.[32]

The financial outlay required for search also can be considerable, especially if travel is required in the current era of energy shortages and high fuel costs.[33] Travel and parking costs can easily offset any gains

---

[27]"Consumer Satisfaction in the Purchase Decision Process' (Unpublished study reviewed by the authors).

[28]George B. Sproles, Loren V. Geistfeld, and Susanne B. Badenhop, "On Merging Consumer Efficiency Research into the Stream of Consumer Information Processing Research," in Jerry C. Olson (ed.), *Advances in Consumer Research,* vol. 7 (Ann Arbor, Mich.: Association for Consumer Research, 1980), 198-202.

[29]Bauer, "Consumer Behavior."

[30]Leon Festinger, *Conflict, Decision, and Dissonance* (Palo Alto, Calif.: Stanford University Press, 1964), esp. 152-156.

[31]John T. Lanzetta and Vera Kanareff, "Information Cost, Amount of Payoff and Level of Aspiration as Determinants of Information Seeking in Decision Making," *Behavioral Science,* vol. 7 (1962), 459-473; Green, "Consumer Use," 75; Green et al., "Experiment in Information," 23.

[32]Robert W. Chestnut and Jacob Jacoby, "The Impact of 'Time' Costs on Acquisition of Package Information" (Purdue Papers in *Consumer Psychology,* no. 155, 1976). Also Roger M. Swagler, "Information as Human Capital: Toward a Time-Usage Approach, in Olson, *Advances,* 195-197.

[33]Brian T. Ratchford, "The Value of Information for Selected Appliances," *Journal of Marketing Research,* vol. 7 (February 1980), 14-25.

from the information which is acquired. In fact, telephone shopping and the use of catalogs is rapidly growing for largely these reasons.

Information Overload

Acquiring additional information may have the desirable effect of increasing consumer confidence in decisions but actually inhibit buying behavior because of information overload.[34] As Jacoby et al. put it:

> It would appear that increasing package information load tends to produce: (1) dysfunctional consequences in terms of the consumer's ability to select that brand which was best for him, and (2) beneficial effects upon the consumer's degree of satisfactions, certainty, and confusion regarding his selection. In other words, our subjects felt better with more information but actually made poor purchase decisions.[35]

The public policy implications of this type of finding are substantial. All too often it is naively assumed that consumer welfare will be increased once the consumer has more information. This completely ignores the costs of information acquisition and use and assumes unlimited information capacity on the part of the individual. The error of such assumptions simply underscores the fact that strategies for consumer welfare must be based on legitimate research to the same extent as marketing decisions.

Psychological Costs

Search requiring a dealer visit also may carry certain psychological costs. The consumer may experience frustration, tension, and annoyance for several reasons, including fighting traffic, finding a place to park, standing in line to be waited upon, and dealing with incompetent sales personnel.[36] Any of these can serve as a real deterrent, to say nothing of the psychological burden required to process the information once it is collected.[37]

---

[34]These findings come from a large number of studies by the Purdue consumer psychology group. See, for example, Jacob Jacoby, "Consumer Reaction to Information Displays: Packaging and Advertising" (Advertising and Public Interest Workshop, American Marketing Association, May 1973); Jacob Jacoby, Donald Speller, and Carol Kohn, "Brand Choice Behavior as a Function of Information Load," *Journal of Marketing Research,* vol. 11 (February 1974), 63-69; Jacob Jacoby, Donald Speller, and Carol Kohn Berning, "Brand Choice Behavior as a Function of Information Load: Replication and Extension," *The Journal of Consumer Research,* vol. 1 (June 1974), 33-42; and Jacob Jacoby et al., "Information Acquisition Behavior in Brand Choice Situations: A Cross-Cultural Extension" (Purdue Papers in *Consumer Psychology,* no. 162, 1976). For a dissenting point of view, see J. Edward Russo, "More Information is Better: A Reevaluation of Jacoby, Speller and Kohn," *The Journal of Consumer Research,* vol. 1 (December 1974), 68-72.

[35]Jacoby, Speller, and Kohn, "Brand Choice Behavior."

[36]For a discussion of these and other costs, see Anthony Downs, "A Theory of Consumer Efficiency," *Journal of Retailing,* (Spring 1961), 6-12.

[37]J. Edward Russo, "The Decision to Use Product Information at the Point of Purchase," (paper delivered at the Retail Theory Conference, Institute of Retail Management, New York University, April 24-25, 1980). Also Steven M. Shugan, "The Cost of Thinking," *Journal of Consumer Research,* vol. 7 (September 1980), 99-111.

Individual Differences in Propensity to Search

It is known that some types of people are more likely to engage in search than others. Here are some of the more important correlates of search propensity:

1. *Personality characteristics:*

    a. Those who are information sensitive tend to have a higher confidence in the degree of control they have over their environment, whereas their counterparts tend to be more fatalistic.[38]

    b. Consumers demonstrating an open mind are more information sensitive than those with a closed mind.[39]

    c. The greater the tendency toward dependence on others, the lower the sensitivity to information.[40]

2. *Family role structure:*

    a. Liberal women (those interested in politics and uninterested in household chores) and traditionalist women (those basing their cooking and meal choices on their parents' patterns) have low proclivities to engage in search. The mother type (concerned with welfare of husband and children) is just the opposite.[41]

    b. Women are more likely to engage in search in the decision processes for major durable goods than are men.[42]

3. *Demographic characteristics:*

    a. Transient households living in a temporary status tend to withdraw from search. Aging, bleak future households (older and perceiving current social and economic position to be deteriorating) are most prone to search.[43]

    b. Those in the highest social status have a lower tendency than average to engage in search.[44]

    c. Consumers with education less than high school search the least, but there are no differences among those with varying degrees of education beyond high school.[45]

    d. Intensity of search is likely to be greater when the consumer is under 35 years of age and in the middle-income category as opposed to a higher or lower category.[46]

---

[38]Green, "Consumer Use," 76.

[39]Green, "Consumer Use," 76; also Gerald D. Bell, "Developments in Behavioral Study in Consumer Action," in Smith, *Reflections on Progress,* 272-282.

[40]Orville Brim et al., *Personality and Decision Processes* (Stanford, Calif.: Stanford University Press, 1962), 122.

[41]Louis P. Bucklin, "Consumer Search, Role Enactment, and Market Efficiency," *Journal of Business,* vol. 42 (October 1969), 416-438.

[42]Newman and Staelin, "Prepurchase Information Seeking."

[43]Bucklin, "Consumer Search," 416-438.

[44]Kiel, "An Empirical Analysis." But this relationship does not always hold. See, for example, Joseph N. Fry and Frederick H. Siller, "A Comparison of Housewife Decision Making in Two Social Classes," *Journal of Marketing Research,* vol. 7 (August 1970), 333-337.

[45]Newman and Staelin, "Prepurchase Information Seeking."

[46]Katona and Mueller, "Study of Purchasing Decisions," 30-87; Hempel, "Search Behavior," 241-249.

**Figure 11.2
An Ad Favoring
Choice by
Processing
Attributes**

Source: Courtesy Toyota Motor Sales USA, Inc.

Content and Sequence of Search

While the precise content to be gained through search is highly variable, a few generalizations are possible at this point. First, those with little or no prior experience with the product category may have to learn the appropriate evaluative criteria to use in the choice process. This is entirely likely in such complex purchases as an entire set of hi-fi components. Advertisements and other marketer-dominated sources are less used for this purpose than expert advice or product-rating agencies.

It is more likely that evaluative criteria are formed, with the result that information is required on product attributes. There are two possible ways in which information is processed and used. Borrowing Bettman's terminology, these may be referred to as Choice by Processing Brands (CPB) or Choice by Processing Attributes (CPA).[47] Sometimes people will search one brand at a time (CPB), centering on its attributes and features and then on to other alternatives in similar fashion.[48] Others will acquire information for several brands on a single attribute brand-by-brand and then do the same for other important attributes.[49]

The bulk of the evidence appearing thus far seems to favor the CPB strategy, but there is every reason to hypothesize that this depends largely on the stage in decision process. More recently Bettman and Park have reported that those in earlier stages process by attribute (CPA), as one might expect, and then switch to brand processing later.[50] A good illustration would be purchase of a front-wheel drive car. If most process by attribute early in the decision process (in this case front wheel drive) the ad for the Toyota Corolla Tercel in Figure 11.2 is especially appropriate because of its dominant emphasis on this feature. The Honda ad in Figure 11.3, on the other hand, stresses all features, including front-wheel drive and would be appropriate for those using CPB. Which would be more effective? The answer lies entirely in knowing the direction and sequence of the search process followed by most potential buyers.

It is also possible that the sequencing of search is explained by previous experience and knowledge. It appears that CPB is most likely when the consumer either has a fairly high level of product knowledge or previous purchasing experience.[51]

---

[47]Bettman, *An Information Processing Theory*, 132-133.

[48]James R. Bettman and Pradeep Kakkar, "Effects of Information Presentation Format on Consumer Information Acquisition Strategies," *Journal of Consumer Research*, vol. 3 (March 1977), 233-240.

[49]Noel Capon and Marian Burke, "Information Seeking Behavior and Consumer Durable Products," in Barnett A. Greenberg and Danny N. Bellenger (eds.), *Contemporary Marketing Thought* (Chicago: American Marketing Association, 1977), 110-115; Edward J. Russo and Barbara A. Dosher, "Dimensional Evaluation: A Heuristic for Binary Choice" (unpublished paper, Department of Psychology, University of California, San Diego, 1975); and Edward J. Russo and Larry D. Rosen, "An Eye Fixation Analysis of Multialternative Choice," *Memory and Cognition*, vol. 3 (May 1975), 267-276; and David A. Sheluga, James Jaccard, and Jacob Jacoby, "Preference, Search, and Choice: An Integrative Approach," *Journal of Consumer Research*, vol. 6 (September 1979), 166-176.

[50]Bettman and Park, "Effects of Prior Knowledge and Experience."

[51]Jacob Jacoby, Robert W. Chestnut, Karl C. Weigl, and William Fisher, "Pre-Purchase Information Acquisition: Description of a Process Methodology, Research Paradigm, and Pilot Investigation," in Beverlee B. Anderson (ed.), *Advances in Consumer Research*, vol. 3 (Chicago: Association for Consumer Research, 1976), 306-314. Also Bettman and Kakkar, "Effects of Information Presentation Format," and Bettman and Park, "Effects of Prior Knowledge and Experience."

**Figure 11.3
An Ad Favoring
Choice by
Processing Brands**

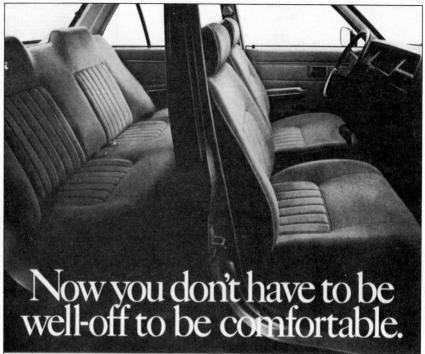

Now you don't have to be well-off to be comfortable.

The Honda Civic 4-Door Sedan.
With seats so comfortable they would be more at home in your living room, our newest Civic is a true sedan in every sense.

You'll feel equally comfortable at the steering wheel. Car and Driver magazine said the Honda wheel is better made than your average Mercedes wheel.

A tachometer, quartz digital clock, and even a remote trunk release will give you some idea of the kind of attention to detail that has gone into the building of this car.

SOME SIMPLE ENGINEERING FACTS

Naturally, being a Honda, the new Civic Sedan has front-wheel drive and a transverse-mounted 1500 CVCC* engine. So your passengers have more foot and legroom.

Available with the 5-speed gearbox or the optional 3-speed automatic transmission, this car is also a lot of fun to drive.

Due in part to the rack and pinion steering and 4-wheel independent suspension.

©1980 American Honda Motor Co., Inc.

INCREDIBLE GAS MILEAGE.
STILL A CIVIC RESPONSIBILITY.

With 5-speed, a gallon of gas takes you an EPA estimated 34 miles and 44 highway miles.

Use 34 mpg for comparison. Your mileage may differ depending on weather, speed and trip length. Actual highway mileage will probably be less. And figures for California will be lower.

Nevertheless, the Civic Sedan gives you gas mileage that's among the best in its class.

And that's bound to make you feel more comfortable. Not to mention well-off.

HONDA
We make it simple.

Source: Courtesy American Honda Motor Company, Inc.

Implications

It is now obvious that search for information is not the simple process it might appear to be on the surface. While there are definite benefits to be gained, there also are very real costs the consumer must weigh before taking this step.

The marketer cannot make any assumptions one way or another about the search process in a given decision situation. Strategy must be based on consumer research. In those instances in which it is verified that the benefits outweigh the costs from the consumer's perspective, then appropriate information can be provided at the time and place desired by the target audience. Usually the marketer can predict the necessity of this communication strategy by a largely common sense analysis. For example, search is most probable when the product is new or when, for other reasons, existing consumer beliefs and attitudes will prove to be inadequate. Furthermore, certain types of people are more likely to search than others (those under 35, etc.). Thus, it is possible to identify both the types of products and segments of consumers for which additional information is most necessary.

Again it must be stressed that the addition of more information does not necessarily lead to greater consumer confidence or satisfaction, regardless of the assumption of some who are concerned about consumer welfare. The necessity for more information can be determined *only* from the point of view of the user. As a case in point, unit pricing was advocated for many years before it was adopted by various retailers. In this method price is stated per ounce, per serving, and so on. It was widely alleged at the outset that the consumer would be an immediate beneficiary, but this does not appear to have taken place. Fewer than one-third of consumers actually have been found to use prices when stated in this manner, and those who do are mostly in the higher income and wealth segments.[52] Furthermore, actual buying behavior appears to be largely unaffected. Hopefully the future will witness increased use by those who need it most, but appear to be least aware of it—the poor.

SOURCES OF INFORMATION

Once it has been determined that search indeed will take place among most members of a market segment, the next question of importance for marketing strategy concerns the sources used and the importance of each. Four different categories are depicted in Table 11.1 based on whether or not the source is marketer dominated or general in nature, utilizing face-to-face or mass communication.

This section discusses, first of all, the major issues involved in isolating the importance of one medium in comparison with another. It is neces-

---

[52]See J. Edward Russo, "The Value of Unit Priced Information," *Journal of Marketing Research,* vol. 14 (1977), 193-201; and Joseph S. Coyle, "Dual Pricing," *Progressive Grocer* (February 1971), 46-50. The same holds true in use of nutrition information. See Jacob Jacoby, Robert W. Chestnut, and William Silberman, "Consumer Use and Comprehension of Nutrition Information," *Journal of Consumer Research,* vol. 4 (September 1977), 119-128.

**Table 11.1
Categories of
Consumer
Information
Sources**

	Face-to-Face	Mass Media
General	Word-of-mouth influence	General media
Marketer-dominated	Personal selling	Advertising and point-of-sale influence

sary to focus on criteria of importance as well as research methodology. Then it is possible to review, in overview fashion, the relative importance of each of the sources listed in Table 11.1. Then three of the four categories are explored in more detail: (1) general media; (2) advertising and point-of-sale influence; and (3) personal selling. Personal influence and word-of-mouth influences are discussed in the next two chapters.

Measuring the Importance of Information Sources

One way of expressing the importance of a given source is in terms of exposure and attraction of attention. This is probably the most commonly used criterion.[53] However, one must be cautious in judging one medium to be more important than another, simply because a greater percentage of people report attending to it. It does not necessarily indicate that the source had any particular impact on the decision process itself. As a consequence, there can be a major difference between *exposure* and *effectiveness* (i.e., actual use of the information provided).

The following typology can be helpful when comparing one source with another:[54]

1. *Decisive effectiveness*—the source was evaluated by the consumer as having a major impact on the decision—perhaps the dominant impact.

2. *Contributory effectiveness*—the source has played some specific role such as stimulating awareness or reducing uncertainty[55] but was not among the most important sources.

3. *Ineffective*—the source did not play any particular role in the decision, even though the consumer was exposed to it.

Regardless of the typology used, importance should always be stated in *relative* rather than absolute terms (i.e., importance relative to the degree of attention given each source). This is necessary because sources may vary in terms of exposure value, with the result that an absolute measure may reflect this fact and little else. Therefore it is best to use a measure that holds coverage or exposure constant. This can be done by comput-

---

[53]Frederick C. May, "An Appraisal of Buying Behavior Research," in Bennett, *Marketing and Economic Development*, 397.

[54]This is a slight modification of the typology used by Elihu Katz and Paul Lazarsfeld, *Personal Influence* (New York: Free Press, 1955), ch. 4.

[55]Woodruff, "Measurement of Consumers' Prior Brand Information."

ing an index such as the ratio of decisive effectiveness of a particular source to total exposure to that source.[56] When this index is less than 1.00, it means exposure exceeded effectiveness. The higher the ratio, the better.

There are five ways of measuring the importance of one source versus another: (1) retrospective questioning; (2) protocol records; (3) information display boards; (4) eye movement; and (5) observation.

Retrospective Questioning

The most common method is to survey people after a decision has been made.[57] Often this requires nothing more than an interview during or following the purchase. Another common approach is to use warranty card registration forms. Although this is relatively inexpensive, it has some limitations. First, and probably most important, is that in-depth questioning cannot be utilized because of the very nature of the form itself. Furthermore, those who return warranties may differ in important ways from those who do not. Finally, not all products offer warranties. Therefore, the warranty card should be viewed only as a supplementary method.

Careful attention should be given to the type, content, and sequencing of questions. One recommended approach is to utilize a series of *specific influence* questions, followed by *assessment* questions, followed by *exposure* questions.[58]

Influence questions should emphasize the process of decision, and the wording should not favor one channel of information over another. Considerable experimentation is needed to develop appropriate questions for the specific product, and it is often advisable to ask several questions. Examples of influence questions that have been used include: (1) "How did you happen to find out about the new brand?" (2) "How did you happen to choose this particular brand?" and (3) "How did you happen to start using the new brand of food?"

Assessment questions should be asked after specific influence questions have been administered. This increases the probability that the consumer will give some thought to the matter before answering. Relatively simple assessment questions seem appropriate, the following being examples: (1) "Summing up now, what was most important in causing you to purchase X?" or (2) "Summing up now, what do you think was the most important thing in causing you to change to this new brand?" While more sophisticated approaches to assessment are often necessary in other settings, this one appears sufficient for determining the effectiveness of information sources.

Exposure questions should be asked after the two preceding types of questions have been administered. It is appropriate to give consumers a check list itemizing sources of information and ask them to indicate

[56]Katz and Lazarsfeld, *Personal Influence.*
[57]This is the method used by Newman and Staelin.
[58]Katz and Lazarsfeld, *Personal Influence,* ch. 4.

whether they were exposed to various information sources. Representative questions are: (1) "Did you hear someone talk about it?" (2) "Did you read about it in a magazine?" and (3) "Did you see it on TV?"

There is, of course, no question about the validity of this approach.[59] It may not be possible to retrieve much of what was searched and learned from long-term memory, with the result that there always will be gaps. Nonetheless, it still should be possible to isolate major influences.

Protocol Records

In this method, the individual actually performs shopping-choice behavior, usually in some type of laboratory setting in which information use is possible. He or she then is asked to think out loud during the process, and a verbal record called a protocol is developed. This reveals the way in which information is used. Bettman has used this approach to construct what he calls *decision nets* depicting a flow chart of how consumers combine attribute and situational information.[60]

Information Display Boards

In the information display board method a person is presented with a board organized in the form of a matrix. The rows and columns of the board are intended to represent brands and attributes for the product class under consideration. Each cell of this matrix is a pocket containing information cards with actual values for brand-attribute combinations. The person is then free to use as much or as little of this information as desired when making a choice. This method is finding growing use.[61] Its obvious disadvantage lies in the artificial nature of the choice situation itself and the way in which information is both displayed and selected. Nonetheless, there is some tentative evidence that it may have validity.[62] Certainly there is no better way to assess choices of information items and sources and sequences of usage.

Eye Movement Studies

This method is similar in one respect to the information display board in that people are presented with a visual display of information alternatives in the form of a brand-attributes array.[63] Actual eye movements are then recorded as the individual chooses information items.

[59]Peter Rip, "The Informational Basis of Self-Reports: A Preliminary Report," in Olson, *Advances,* 140-145.

[60]James R. Bettman, "Toward a Statistics for Consumer Decision Net Models," *Journal of Consumer Research,* vol. 1 (June 1974), 71-80.

[61]See, for example, William L. Moore and Donald R. Lehman, "Individual Differences and Search Behavior for a Nondurable," *Journal of Consumer Research,* vol. 7 (December 1980), 296-307; and Jacob Jacoby, Robert W. Chestnut, and William A. Fisher, "A Behavioral Process Approach to Information Acquisition in Nondurable Purchasing," *Journal of Marketing Research,* vol. 15 (November 1978), 532-544.

[62]Donald R. Lehmann and William L. Moore, "Validity of Information Display Boards: An Assessment Using Longitudinal Data," *Journal of Marketing Research,* vol. 17 (November 1980), 450-459.

[63]Russo and Dosher, "Dimensional Evaluation," and Russo and Rosen, "An Eye Fixation Analysis."

Observation

To a limited degree field observation has been employed to reveal information selection and use in a retail setting.[64] Evidence thus far indicates that the incidences of information seeking are higher when observed than they prove to be when sole reliance is placed on retrospective questioning.[65]

The Relative Importance of Major Sources

There is a growing body of evidence that compares the relative role and impact of the various information sources, and the number of citations is too voluminous to be documented fully here.[66] The following are some of the major generalizations that emerge:

1. Consumers rarely rely exclusively on one source. Rather, search tends to be a cumulative process in that those who seek information from one source also turn to others. This suggests that the various media are *complementary* rather than *competitive.*[67]

2. The mass media (television, newspapers, etc.), whether dominated by the marketer or not, usually perform an *informing function* in high-involvement decision making. This is a *contributory* role, then, of providing such information as availability and brand features.

3. In high-involvement decisions, print media may play a more important role than electronic media.[68] The reason for this tentative proposition is that reading and speaking are left brain functions, and it also appears that extended problem solving thinking centers more in the left hemisphere than in the right.[69] Therefore, the more lengthy information-oriented print message may have a greater impact on consumer learning.[70]

[64]Joseph W. Newman and Bradley D. Lockeman, "Measuring Prepurchase Information Seeking," *Journal of Advertising Research,* vol. 11 (December 1975), 216-222.

[65]Newman and Lockeman, "Measuring Prepurchase."

[66]A large body of this evidence is summarized on 248-249 of the third edition of this text. Some of the more important recent sources include Michael A. Houston, "Consumer Evaluations and Product Information Sources," in James H. Leigh and Claude R. Martin, Jr. (eds.), *Current Issues & Research in Advertising 1979* (Ann Arbor, Mich.: Graduate School of Business, University of Michigan, 1979), 135-144; George P. Moschis and Roger L. Moore, "Purchasing Behavior of Adolescent Consumers," in Richard P. Bagozzi et al. (eds.), *Marketing in the 80s: Changes and Challenges* (Chicago: American Marketing Association, 1980), 89-92; Mary Jane Schlinger, "The Role of Mass Communications in Promoting Public Health," in Anderson, *Advances in Consumer Research,* vol. 3, 302-305; and Duane L. Davis, Joseph G. Guiltinan, and Wesley H. Jones, "Service Characteristics, Consumer Search, and the Classification of Retail Services," *Journal of Retailing,* vol. 55 (Fall 1979), 3-23.

[67]See, for example, George Katona and Eva Mueller, "A Study of Purchase Decisions," in Lincoln H. Clark (ed.), *The Dynamics of Consumer Reactions* (New York: New York University Press, 1955), 30-87, at 46; Bernard Berelson and Gary Steiner, *Human Behavior* (New York: Harcourt, 1964), 532; Cox, "The Audience as Communicators"; and Schlinger, "The Role of Mass Communications."

[68]Herbert E. Krugman, "Low Involvement Theory in the Light of New Brain Research," in John C. Maloney and Bernard Silverman (eds.), *Attitude Research Plays for High Stakes* (Chicago: American Marketing Association, 1979), 16-22; and Michael L. Rothschild, "Advertising Strategies for High and Low Involvement Situations," in Maloney and Silverman, *Attitude Research Plays,* 74-93.

[69]Roger W. Sperry, "Lateral Specialization of Cerebral Function in the Surgically Separated Hemispheres," in F. J. McGuigan and R. I. Schoonover (eds.), *The Psychophysiology of Thinking* (New York: Academic Press, 1973).

[70]Mary Jane Schlinger, "Attitudinal Reactions to Advertisements," in John Eighmey (ed.), *Attitude Research Under the Sun* (Chicago: American Marketing Association, 1979), 171-197.

4. In terms of *effectiveness,* the nonmarketer-dominated sources, especially word-of-mouth, assume a decisive role. Contact with friends and relatives typically assumes a legitimizing or evaluating function because of greater credibility and clarity.[71]

There is a growing body of evidence documenting why some information sources are more important than others, and the following factors enter: (1) the type of information desired; (2) perceived risk; (3) characteristics of the decision-making unit; and (4) the stage of market development.

As far as the type of information needed, it appears that marketer-dominated sources are most useful as sources of information on attributes that allow the consumer to judge the nature of the product visually.[72] Where this visual examination is not feasible or not reliable, the greater perceived objectivity of personal sources becomes a dominant consideration.

It has already been demonstrated that the occasional incidence of perceived risk of one type or another is a stimulus for search activity. It also affects the sources chosen, however. There is, for example, evidence that financial risk is a consideration, in that the role of personal sources increases as the cost of the item increases.[73] Second, the greater the visibility and social significance of a product (and hence the greater the perceived risk), the more likely that word-of-mouth influence will be dominant.[74] Finally, physiological risk can have an effect. As the severity of a disease increases, the need for authoritative information also increases, and the importance of marketer-dominated sources declines.[75]

In terms of the characteristics of the decision-making unit, the focus here is on the social status of the family, and word-of-mouth tends to dominate under the following circumstances:

1. The consumer is socially isolated rather than integrated into primary and/or secondary groups.[76]

2. Husband and wife's friends constitute separate social networks.[77]

---

[71]Houston, "Consumer Evaluations;" Davis, Guiltinan, and Jones, "Service Characteristics;" and Legrand and Udell, "Consumer Behavior."

[72]Houston, "Consumer Evaluations;" and Davis, Guiltinan, and Jones, "Service Characteristics."

[73]Granbois, "Study of Purchasing Decisions," 106.

[74]See, for example, Michael Perry and B. Curtis Hamm, "Canonical Analysis of Relations between Socioeconomic Risk and Personal Influence in Purchase Decisions," *Journal of Marketing Research,* vol. 6 (August 1969), 351-354; Robert B. Settle, "Consumer Attributional Information Dependence," unpublished paper (Gainesville, Fla.: University of Florida, September 1971).

[75]James F. Engel, David A. Knapp, and Deanne E. Knapp, "Sources of Information," 776-782, at 781. For additional studies dealing with the relationship between risk and the relative importance of information sources, see Scott M. Cunningham, "Perceived Risk as a Factor in Product-Oriented Word-of-Mouth Behavior: A First Step," in L. George Smith (ed.), *Reflections on Progress in Marketing* (Chicago: American Marketing Association, 1964), 229-238; Ted Roselius, "Consumer Rankings of Risk Reduction Methods," *Journal of Marketing,* vol. 35 (January 1971), 56-61.

[76]E. H. Schein, "Interpersonal Communication, Group Solidarity, and Social Influence," *Sociometry,* vol. 24 (June 1960), 148-161; Harold L. Wilensky, "Orderly Careers and Social Participation," *American Sociological Review,* vol. 26 (August 1961), 521-539; Harold L. Wilensky, "Social Structure, Popular Culture and Mass Behavior: Some Implications for Research," *Public Opinion Quarterly,* vol. 24 (Fall 1960), 497-499.

[77]Granbois, "Study of Purchasing Decisions," 105.

3. The decision-making process is performed independently by both parties in a family or by one spouse alone.[78]

The relative importance of sources also varies in part depending upon the length of time the product has been on the market. In the case of some farm products and practices, for instance, marketer-dominated sources tend to decline and personal sources increase in impact as the product matures.[79] This is covered in more depth in Chapter 13 under the subject of the diffusion of innovations.

General Media Sources: Product Ratings

Often the general media, especially those featuring product ratings, assume a significant role in decision processes. An unfavorable product rating can have an especially major impact.[80] This was demonstrated by the results of 1981 running shoe studies published in *Runner's World*.[81] Many manufacturers alleged that the ratings were invalid, but it is clear that many serious runners, including the senior author, made use of them in the absence of any other objective criteria. It is interesting to note, however, that *Consumers' Reports*, a widely-used testing source, was not evaluated as positively by its devotees in 1976 as compared with 1970, presumably because of their growing personal sophistication in product evaluation.[82]

The Marketer-Dominated Sources

The remainder of this section centers on the impact of media advertising, shopping behavior, point-of-sale information, and personal selling.

Media Advertising

Once consumers recognize a problem, they generally become more receptive to advertising they previously might have ignored entirely. Advertisements now are consulted for informational purposes. Although the informative role of advertising varies somewhat between products[83] and types of consumers,[84] the following are illustrative findings:

1. Consumers make considerable use of TV ads for information on style and design.[85]

[78]Granbois, 104, 106.

[79]Everett M. Rogers and George M. Beal, "The Importance of Personal Influence in the Adoption of Technological Changes," *Social Forces,* vol. 36 (1958), 329-335; Bruce Ryan and Neal Gross, "The Diffusion of Hybrid Seed Corn in Two Iowa Communities," *Rural Sociology,* vol. 8 (March 1943), 15-24.

[80]Mark G. Weinberger and William R. Dillon, "The Effects of Unfavorable Product Rating Information," in Olson, *Advances,* 528-532.

[81]Sam Harper, "Athletic Shoe Surveys Run into Industry Dispute," *Advertising Age* (September 22, 1980), 48.

[82]J. L. Engledow, R. D. Anderson, and H. Becker, "The Changing Information Seeker: A Study of Attitudes Toward Product Test Reports—1970 and 1976," *Journal of Consumer Affairs,* vol. 13 (Summer 1979), 75-85.

[83]See, for example, Elihu Katz and Paul F. Lazarsfeld, *Personal Influence* (New York: Free Press, 1955), ch. 5; Hugh W. Sargent, *Consumer Product Rating Publications and Buying Behavior* (Urbana, Ill.: Bureau of Economic and Business Research, University of Illinois, 1959), 41; K. L. Atkin, "Advertising and Store Patronage," *Journal of Advertising Research,* vol. 2 (December 1962), 18-23; and George H. Haines, Jr., "A Study of Why People Purchase New Products," in Raymond M. Haas (ed.), *Science, Technology and Marketing* (Chicago: American Marketing Association, 1966), 665-685.

[84]Donald H. Granbois, "The Role of Communication."

[85]Houston, "Consumer Evaluations."

2. Of those who bought a small electrical appliance, 25 percent consulted newspaper ads, 15 percent read magazine ads, 14 percent saw the product advertised on television, and 7 percent acquired information from radio commercials.[86] It was just such evidence as this that led Russell Colley in 1961 to state forthrightly that advertising performs primarily an informative function.[87] In his words:

Advertising's job purely and simply is to communicate to a defined audience information and a frame-of-mind that stimulates action. Advertising succeeds or fails depending on how well it communicates the desired information and attitudes to the right people at the right time and at the right cost.[88]

This philosophy has since become known as DAGMAR (Defining Advertising Goals, Measuring Advertising Results).

This seemingly common sense point of view has not been universally accepted, and it still generates controversy today. One of the primary criticisms is that advertising may accomplish communication goals yet have no influence whatsoever on buyer behavior. Assume, for instance, that 60 percent of potential customers are found to be unaware of a new brand of hi-fi equipment. Assume further that advertising has then communicated product benefits to 50 percent of this group. Does this automatically mean that the advertising has been successful? The answer may be negative because it is possible to convey facts without having any influence at all in terms of persuasion.[89] In fact, people can even be made *less* likely to buy after awareness has been stimulated. In such instances, the information actually conveyed and that needed by the consumer have little or no relationship. Great care must be exercised to verify that the information truly is relevant in terms of consumer decision processes.

Contrast the difference in this case example. A pilot study disclosed in sharp clarity that housewives over the age of 35, with children at home, and with average income and education were interested in modern language versions of the Bible.[90] The greatest felt need was to find help in establishing the moral and spiritual values of their children. At that point awareness of the *Living Bible*, one of several modern language versions, was only 18 percent. An advertising campaign then stressed the readability of this version and its role in the upbringing of children. Soon, awareness values quadrupled, and one out of two Bibles purchased in a recent year was a *Living Bible*.

[86]Jon G. Udell, "Prepurchase Behavior of Buyers of Small Electrical Appliances," *Journal of Marketing*, vol. 30 (October 1966), 50-52.

[87]Russell H. Colley (ed.), *Defining Advertising Goals* (New York: Association of National Advertisers, Inc., 1961).

[88]Colley, *Defining Advertising*, 21.

[89]Jack B. Haskins, "Factual Recall as a Measure of Advertising Effectiveness," *Journal of Advertising Research*, vol. 4 (1964), 2-8.

[90]See "The Living Bible" case in Roger D. Blackwell, James F. Engel, and W. Wayne Talarzyk, *Contemporary Cases in Consumer Behavior* (Hinsdale, Ill.: Dryden Press, 1977), 350-359.

Advertising, then, can change beliefs and attitudes, assuming that the information provided is relevant in terms of the consumers' evaluative criteria. Effectiveness cannot be measured, however, unless advertising objectives state the hoped for change in quantitative terms. Here is an example of a well-stated objective: increase the number mentioning Brand A when asked, "What brand of all-purpose flour claims it gives you a feeling of confidence when you use it?" from 35 percent to 45 percent.[91] All things being equal, this change in awareness should lead to a sales increase.

There are instances, of course, in which advertising will play a decisive role in the decision. In one recent study, about 50 percent of those interviewed actually purchased a product after seeing a magazine ad or a commercial for it.[92] Presumably the ad was a decisive influence, especially if it gave information on price reduction. Price advertising is a major sales trigger.

Shopping Behavior

The frequency and intensity of information search at the retail level is rather surprising. In one recent study Westbook and Fornell isolated four different shopping segments:[93]

1. *Objective shoppers*—this group is more highly educated, showing high incidence of joint husband-wife decision making. They consider a large set of alternatives, make many retail visits, and do not tend to consult personal sources.

2. *Moderate shoppers*—this group usually does not visit more than one store. They tend to be older, less educated, and relatively satisfied with previous purchases.

3. *Store intensive shoppers*—younger and well educated, these shoppers visit four or more stores and also make use of personal sources to help them differentiate between many alternatives being considered for purchase.

4. *Personal advice seekers*—these people usually visit only one store and make primary use of personal sources.

Here are some other illustrative findings:

1. Of those consumers purchasing major durable goods, 47 percent visited only the store in which the item was purchased; 15 percent visited two or three stores; and 26 percent visited more than three.[94] In an up-

---

[91]National Industrial Conference Board, *Setting Advertising Objectives* (New York, 1966).

[92]Opinion Research Corp., *A Study of Media Involvement* (New York: Magazine Publishers' Association, 1979).

[93]Robert A. Westbrook and Claes Fornell, "Patterns of Information Source Usage Among Durable Goods Buyers," *Journal of Marketing Research,* vol. 16 (August 1979), 303-312.

[94]Katona and Mueller, "Study of Purchasing," 45-46.

dating of this study 70 percent were found to have shopped at two or more outlets.[95]

2. Of those purchasing small electrical appliances, 60 percent shopped only in the store where the purchase was made, 16 percent shopped in two, and 22 percent visited three or more.[96]

3. Another study of electrical appliances found that the percentage of purchasers shopping in only one outlet was: for refrigerators, 42.4 percent; for television sets, 58.3 percent; for washing machines, 62.4 percent; for vacuum cleaners, 79.4 percent; for electric irons, 82.4 percent.[97]

Although the majority confine their efforts to the store where the product is purchased, some will visit that outlet more than once. Nearly one-fourth of the buyers of small electrical appliances, for example, made more than one shopping trip to the same store.[98]

Multiple shopping trips are most likely, first of all, when the price of the product is high.[99] And, as might be expected, the amount of information already in possession will affect shopping behavior, but the form of this relationship may be surprising. It seems that those who have the most or, conversely, the least information shop least extensively, whereas those in the middle do the most.[100] This may be explained by the fact that those with the least information also have the lowest incomes. Consumers with higher incomes, in turn, often minimize search behavior on the basis that the costs outweigh the benefits.

It is interesting to speculate about consumer behavior of this type in the future. On the one hand, it is possible to make a case for increased shopping because of the remarkable growth of specialty stores of all types. This, in turn, is accompanied by pressures to economize brought on by increased inflation and diminished growth of disposable income. On the other hand, the competing demands on leisure time are great, and these can reverse the balance between the benefits and costs of search, in which case shopping will diminish. Whatever the situation, changes are imminent, and there is a growing need for consumer research of this type. Far too much of the present evidence is becoming increasingly out-dated.

Point-of-Sale Information

In one study, nearly one-third of the prospective buyers of major appliances interviewed at the retail level expressed a need for more information.[101] While this will vary from product to product, much can be learned

---

[95]Joseph W. Newman and Richard Staelin, ''Prepurchase Information Seeking.''

[96]Udell, ''Prepurchasing Behavior,'' 52.

[97]William P. Dommermuth, ''The Shopping Matrix and Marketing Strategy,'' *Journal of Marketing Research,* vol. 2 (May 1965), 128-132.

[98]Udell, ''Prepurchasing Behavior,'' 52.

[99]Louis P. Bucklin, ''Retail Strategy and the Classification of Consumer Goods,'' *Journal of Marketing,* vol. 27 (January 1963), 50-54; also Dommermuth and Udell have found this relationship.

[100]Bucklin, ''Retail Strategy.''

[101]''Consumer Satisfaction in the Purchase Decision Process'' (unpublished study reviewed by the authors).

from package labels and other forms of point-of-purchase information. Indeed Bettman is correct when he notes that such sources as these readily serve as a type of *external memory* for the consumer.[102]

There is no question that consumers make some use of package labels during their decision process,[103] and, at times, the effects on behavior can be decisive.[104] The type of information and labeling used can shift consumer preference. For example, nutritional labeling tends to improve consumer perception of such quality attributes as "wholesomeness" and "tender."[105] It was also found that strictly promotional terms such as "sweet" and "succulent" leave people with an assurance of quality comparable to that of the more detailed nutritional information. This underscores the opportunity provided for outright deception, and one cannot help but wonder about the extent to which consumers have been misled in this way.

On the other hand, there is growing evidence that labels are not used as thoroughly as was previously thought. At times, they are misperceived, used only in part, or disregarded altogether.[106] This is a particularly disturbing finding when the content consists of safety warnings or precautions. A clue may lie in the fact that consumers with lower socioeconomic status make less use of this information and vice versa; just the opposite of what policy makers usually intend.[107] Also, Jacoby and his associates have demonstrated that information overload applies to labels also.[108] Use of this type of information ceases when the number of separate bits of information provided exceeds 12. All that can be said is that no assumptions can be made regarding label usage. Rather, actual use must be tested in the marketplace and both type and quantity of content adjusted until the desired effects are achieved.

Personal Selling

In high-involvement decision situations, personal selling still plays an important role. For example, the new energy-use labeling program for major appliances was found to be of little importance compared with the

---

[102]James F. Bettman, "Memory Factors in Consumer Choice: A Review," *Journal of Marketing,* vol. 43 (Spring 1979), 43.

[103]Dennis L. McNeill and William L. Wilkie, "Public Policy and Consumer Information: Impact of the New Energy Labels," *Journal of Consumer Research,* vol. 6 (June 1979), 1-11; and Kenneth C. Schneider, "Prevention of Accidental Poisoning Through Package and Label Design," *Journal of Consumer Research,* vol. 4 (September 1977), 67-73.

[104]McNeill and Wilkie, "Public Policy and Consumer Information."

[105]Edward H. Asam and Louis P. Bucklin, "Nutritional Labeling for Canned Goods: A Study of Consumer Response," *Journal of Marketing,* vol. 37 (April 1973), 32-37.

[106]Gary T. Ford and Philip G. Kuehl, "Label Warning Messages in OTC Drug Advertising: An Experimental Examination of FTC Policy-Making," in Leigh and Martin, *Current Issues & Research in Advertising 1979,* 115-128; Lorna Opatow, "How Consumers 'Use' Labels of OTC Drugs," *American Druggist,* vol. 177 (March 1978), 10+; and Jo-Ann Zybtniewski, "Keeping Pace with the Nutrition Race," *Progressive Grocer,* vol. 59 (July 1980), 29.

[107]James McCullough and Roger Best, "Consumer Preference for Food Label Information: A Basis for Segmentation," *Journal of Consumer Affairs,* vol. 14 (Summer 1980), 180-192.

[108]Jacob Jacoby, "Consumer Reaction to Information Displays: Packaging and Advertising" (paper delivered at the Advertising and Public Interest Workshop, American Marketing Association, May 1973). Also see Jacob Jacoby, George J. Szybillo, and Jacqueline Busato-Schach, "Information Acquisition Behavior in Brand Choice Situations," *Journal of Consumer Research,* vol. 3 (March 1977), 209-216.

input from salespersons.[109] Moreover, people still seek advice from druggists on many aspects of health and drug usage.[110]

Whether or not personal selling will have much impact comes from the nature of the customer-salesperson interaction (often referred to technically as "dyadic interaction").[111] Sometimes attempts to explain this interaction theoretically get pretty esoteric,[112] whereas the clues to successful salesmanship often are little more than common sense.

In one important study undertaken more than a decade ago, these transaction characteristics predicted whether or not a person would become a buyer: frequent reference to concession limits (bargaining ranges), reference to delivery, reference to styling, and reference to warranty.[113] Negative effects resulted, on the other hand, when the salesperson knocked a competitive product, attempted to change concession limits, made frequent reference to quality, or continually mentioned price. This conclusion can provide some invaluable clues to sales training which, by the way, has received renewed emphasis in business, with some stores reporting sales gains of 10 percent or more.[114]

In a related study, Engel analyzed the interaction between the salesperson and buyer in furniture outlets.[115] One of the most interesting findings was the distinction between dollar sales volume by the individual salesperson and his or her ability to convert a shopper into a buyer. Some salespeople achieve large volumes by highspotting—centering only on those who have pretty well decided what to purchase when approached. This type of retailing, however, often entails advice giving and negotiation. Many who excelled in this dimension had lower total sales volumes but, in the long run, were more useful in building a permanent clientele for the store. The problem was aggravated in this situation by compensation solely on the basis of commission. This serves only to encourage highspotting, whereas a combination of salary and commission will facilitate a greater focus on helpful information giving.

By the way, it is interesting to note that a highly dependent consumer tends to be suggestible and hence prefers assistance by a salesperson in decision making, whereas an independent person prefers a minimum of suggestion and assistance.[116] The independent person, in turn, seems

[109]John D. Claxton and C. Dennis Anderson, "Energy Information at the Point of Sale: A Field Experiment," in Olson, *Advances,* 277-282.

[110]"Public Goes on Strong 'Self-Medication Kick'," *Marketing News* (June 27, 1980), 6.

[111]This conceptualization is based on Ronald P. Willett and Allan L. Pennington, "Customer and Salesman: The Anatomy of Choice and Influence in a Retail Setting," in Haas, *Science,* 598-616. For an alternative conceptualization, see James H. Bearden, "Decision Processes in Personal Selling," *Southern Journal of Business,* vol. 4 (April 1969), 189-199.

[112]See, for example Robert E. Smith and Shelby D. Hunt, "The Effectiveness of Personal Selling Over Advertising: An Attributional Analysis," in S. C. Jain (ed.), *Research Frontiers in Marketing: Dialogues and Directions* (Chicago: American Marketing Associations, 1978), 158-163.

[113]Willett and Pennington, "Customer and Salesman."

[114]"Retailers Discover an Old Tool: Sales Training," *Business Week* (December 22, 1980), 51.

[115]See "The Columbia Furniture" case in Blackwell et al., *Contemporary Cases,* 247-256.

[116]M. Zuckerman and H. J. Grosz, "Suggestibility and Dependency," *Journal of Consulting Psychology,* vol. 26 (October 1958), 32-38.

to respond more positively to aggressive selling.[117] Women, on the other hand, are more likely to be negative to aggressive salespersons than their male counterparts.[118]

An important key to the interaction patterns reported above seems to lie in the extent to which the two parties are similar to one another.[119] In an experiment conducted by Brock, an expert salesman who was perceived as knowledgeable about the product being sold (paint) was less effective than one who identified his own paint consumption as being similar to that of his customers.[120] This seems to verify the communication principle that success usually lies in proportion to empathy or ability to put oneself in another's shoes.

There is no question that a consumer *can* benefit from an empathetic salesperson, but all too frequently the information transmitted (or not transmitted) has a negative effect. Engel found, for instance, that some furniture salespersons knowingly permitted customers to make a purchase that, for one reason or another, was very wrong for their own circumstances.[121] Couples had been specially trained for this project to pose as shoppers who offered a variety of situations to each salesperson who, by the way, had been formally trained in how to contend with each situation. More often than not the content of sales training never found its way to the sales floor. Outright indifference was not uncommon.

This problem becomes especially acute when one's physical well-being is threatened. In one unpublished study, shoppers visited many retail pharmacists in a major city and presented this question to one of the registered pharmacists: "I am on insulin, but I am having trouble with allergies and sinus. Would it be ok if I take Dristan?" The usual answer was, "Fine, go ahead," even though directions on the label clearly indicated that Dristan was *not* to be taken by those on insulin. A pharmacist of any repute should have known this, and failure to alert the consumer of the dangers is outright irresponsibility.

In a more recent study, pharmacists in various cities were evaluated to determine whether or not information on side effects of prescription drugs was ever communicated to the customer.[122] Most indicated that this was not their responsibility at all and that the doctor should do so. Not surprisingly it was verified that the physician also largely ignored this critical information. So where does this leave the consumer who must trust the professional in the field of health?

Unfortunately, personal selling is more difficult to regulate than me-

[117]James E. Stafford and Thomas V. Greer, "Consumer Preference for Types of Salesmen: A Study of Independence-Dependence Characteristics," *Journal of Retailing* (Summer 1965), 27-33.

[118]Stafford and Greer, "Customer Preference," 32; and Gilbert Burck, "What Makes Women Buy?" *Fortune* (August 1956), 93-94, 174-194.

[119]Timothy C. Brock, "Communicator-Recipient Similarity and Decision Change," *Journal of Personality and Social Psychology,* vol. 1 (June 1965), 650-654.

[120]Brock, "Communicator-Recipient Similarity."

[121]"The Columbia Furniture" case in Blackwell et al., *Contemporary Cases.*

[122]James C. McCullagh, "Is Your Medicine Chest a Relic from the Dark Ages?" *Prevention,* vol. 28 (December 1976), 95-113.

		Consumers Preferring Brand Before Information Seeking (Percent)	Consumers Preferring Brand After Information Seeking (Percent)
Table 11.2 Before-After Analysis of the Impact of Information- Seeking on Brand Preference	**Brand**		
	A	30	15
	B	40	40
	C	30	45
		100	100

dia advertising. Nevertheless, the consumerism movement has taken important steps both in legal action and in consumer education. Still, the best strategy is "let the buyer beware."

MARKETING RESEARCH AND DIAGNOSIS OF THE IMPACT OF SEARCH BEHAVIOR

The marketer always must ask what impact, if any, consumer search has had on the relative impact of a firm's brands. Some methods of data analysis can be of real help in answering this question.

Before-After Analysis

This procedure requires the measurement of brand preference before and after information seeking. Assuming that all other factors are held relatively constant, the difference between the two measurements roughly indicates the effect of information search on brand preference.

Examine the data in Table 11.2. In this situation, information search is hindering Brand A, helping Brand C, and having no particular effect on preference for Brand B. The essential question now is *why* this pattern exists, but further analysis is required before the answer can be given.

Information Utilization Analysis

The methodological requirements for information utilization analysis are less exacting than those discussed above. Table 11.3 illustrates the first phase in which Brand A is compared with the average for all other brands (AOB) in terms of exposure to sources of information. Exposure is classified into three categories: decisive, contributory, and ineffective. Brand A appears to be enjoying reasonable success in terms of *total exposure.* Compared with AOB, Brand A has received better total exposure in radio and television, and it is about average in terms of personal contacts and salesmen's influence. Purchasers are considerably less exposed than the average purchaser to magazines and newspapers.

Table 11.4 carries this analysis into a second phase. Brand A is now compared with AOB in terms of effectiveness indexes (decisive exposure versus total exposure) for the sources used by purchasers. This indicates that the brand is reasonably competitive with AOB for radio, television, magazines, and newspapers. Personal contacts and salesmen seem to be the major reasons why the brand is being hurt during the search process.

**Table 11.3
Exposure to
Sources of
Information**

Type of Exposure by Type of Information Source	Brand Purchased	
	Brand A (Percent)	Average For All Other Brands (Percent)
Personal Contacts		
Decisive exposure	28	34
Contributory exposure	18	25
Ineffective exposure	16	6
Total	62	65
Radio		
Decisive exposure	1	1
Contributory exposure	2	2
Ineffective exposure	6	4
Total	9	7
Television		
Decisive exposure	3	2
Contributory exposure	7	7
Ineffective exposure	8	2
Total	18	11
Magazines		
Decisive exposure	15	21
Contributory exposure	22	29
Ineffective exposure	8	12
Total	45	62
Newspapers		
Decisive exposure	3	4
Contributory exposure	15	22
Ineffective exposure	11	10
Total	29	36
Salesmen		
Decisive exposure	23	33
Contributory exposure	35	54
Ineffective exposure	37	10
Total	95	97

**Table 11.4
Effectiveness
Indexes for
Information
Sources**

Information Source	Purchasers of Brand A	Average for Purchasers of All Other Brands
Personal contacts	45.2	52.3
Radio	11.1	14.3
Television	16.7	18.2
Magazines	33.3	33.9
Newspapers	10.3	11.1
Salesmen	42.2	34.0

*These indexes are computed by calculating the ratio of decisive exposure to total exposure for each information source.

**Figure 11.4
Relationship
between Brand
Recommended
through Personal
Contacts and
Purchasing
Behavior**

Brand Recommended		Purchasing Behavior
Brand A	→ 35%	Purchased the brand recommended
	→ 65%	Purchased a different brand
Average for all other brands	→ 60%	Purchased the brand recommended
	→ 40%	Purchased a different brand

**Table 11.5
Net Gains and
Losses Resulting
from Switching
from the Brand
Recommended
through Personal
Contacts**

Brand	Number of Customers Switching to the Brand for Each 100 Switchings From the Brand	Net Gain or Loss (Percent)
A	45	−55
Average for all other brands	99	−01

Figure 11.4 extends the analysis by disclosing the relationship between the brand recommended through word-of-mouth influence and purchasing behavior. Compared with AOB, Brand *A* suffers from a low recommendation-fulfillment rate. This means that consumers have a lower than average tendency to purchase Brand *A* once it is recommended by another person. Furthermore, consumers have a below average tendency to switch to Brand *A* when other brands are recommended. As Table 11.5 indicates, Brand *A* loses 1.55 customers for each one who switches to it, and the other brands are doing much better.

In summary, information seeking adversely affects Brand *A,* and there is evidence that it is receiving poor word-of-mouth advertising. It has a low recommendation-fulfillment rate, and it is doing poorly at the point of sale even though it has achieved average exposure. Several steps are now required to complete the analysis:

1. The data should be analyzed by such characteristics as age, income, and life-style to determine which types of consumers are showing the most adverse reactions. There quite likely will be differences between segments.

2. Further analysis should determine why word-of-mouth is benefiting the other brands and hurting Brand *A.*

3. The reasons for the relative ineffectiveness of salespersons must be uncovered. There could be any number of reasons such as low commission, and so on.

Summary

Search refers to the process whereby the consumer seeks information to learn about the advantages and disadvantages of the various alternatives to satisfy a problem that has become recognized. Whether search will occur or not and the extent to which it occurs depends on the consumer's perceptions of the benefits and costs involved. The perceived benefit will be affected by the amount and appropriateness of existing information, the ability to recall that information, the type and degree of risk seen to be accompanying the purchase, and confidence. Costs include time, money, psychological discomforts, the satisfaction foregone by delaying purchase, and the dangers of information overload.

The information sources chosen vary from individual to individual and from one situation to the next. In general, it can be said that marketer-dominated sources (advertising, personal selling, and point-of-sale influence) are important in providing information in earlier stages of decision processes, but personal sources (word-of-mouth advertising) are most important in terms of effectiveness. The research techniques required to isolate the impact of one source versus another were presented.

The chapter continued the discussion of search processes by focusing on the role and functioning of the marketer-dominated stimuli. The first to be discussed was media advertising. It was stressed that the primary role of advertising is informative. The impact in terms of changing beliefs and attitudes can be great, and this predisposes the consumer to make a purchase at a later time. Only in certain instances will advertising actually trigger a purchase, and in those instances the purchase was imminent anyway.

The remainder of the marketer-dominated stimuli were evaluated within the context of the retail store. It was demonstrated that people do shop extensively and that point-of-sale is a significant source of information.

Finally, a case history was presented to illustrate what can be learned from diagnosis of the impact of search behavior on the purchase. Without such information the marketer will be at a loss to evaluate the dynamics underlying consumer decision.

Review and Discussion Questions

1. Define or otherwise describe the relevance of the following concepts: (a) external search, (b) interpurchase time, (c) physiological risk, (d) psychological costs, (e) changes in the mix of alternatives.

2. A product has a long interpurchase time, a low amount of social risk, a high degree of financial risk. Will external search occur? Discuss.

3. What are the consequences of external search?

4. "The majority of purchases a consumer makes are not preceded by external search." Why?

5. "Since consumers typically visit only one store before purchasing a product, store visits are not an important information source." Evaluate.

6. What problems, if any, are involved in determining the relative importance of information sources? How should these problems be overcome?

7. How does the type of information desired affect the utilization of information sources?

8. Assume you are a consultant to the research director of a large manufacturer of middle-priced ($1,000-$4,000) boats. The research director wants to know the relative importance of information sources and asks you to prepare a statement indicating how you would go about it.

9. Assume that your research recommendation was accepted and the research done. With the use of an index of relative effectiveness it was found that personal sources were five times more effective than advertising. Seeing this finding, the marketing vice-president has asked the advertising manager to justify the amount of money being spent on advertising. You are the advertising manager. What do you say?

10. The research director for Brand *C* presents you with the following data based on a rigorously controlled study:

Brand	Preferring Brand Before Information-Seeking (Percent)	Preferring Brand After Information-Seeking (Percent)
A	30	35
B	30	35
C	40	30
	100	100

The research director is uncertain as to what the problem is and does not know how to proceed. As a consultant to Company C, prepare an outline indicating what procedure will allow the company to determine what the problems are.

11. Your company manufactures a full line of mobile homes in all price ranges. Several studies have indicated that personal sources of information are considerably more effective than other sources. Prepare a statement indicating (a) the alternative strategies that can be used to utilize effectively consumers' use of personal information sources, (b) the alternative that you prefer and why.

12. Under what circumstances would a sales objective be appropriate for advertising? Under what circumstances would it be more appropriate to attempt to stimulate changes in awareness, attitude, or other so-called communication responses?

13. A leading manufacturer of recreational vehicles based its advertising campaign on this statement of objectives: "Our goal is to tell as many people as possible that travel and camping is fun for the family and that it is easier when you are traveling in your own 'motel.'" Evaluate.

14. Does the customer-salesperson similarity hypothesis describe your own preferences and responses when you have contact with salespeople? If not, is there an alternative hypothesis?

15. Of what use is the customer-salesperson similarity hypothesis in marketing planning?

After studying the last chapter, you may now feel better equipped to plan the advertising and sales program of an organization because you understand quite a bit about the effects of communications controlled by the marketing organization. Now suppose you were a marketing executive at Proctor & Gamble, and were faced with the situation described in this newspaper article.

It's easy to start a rumor, but it's hard to stamp it out.

Procter & Gamble Co. knows that. It's been trying for more than a year to kill a rumor that a reader called about Tuesday.

The caller said her mother, who lives in Natchez, Miss., wrote her that some people in her area were boycotting P&G products because the firm was controlled by the "Moonies." A reference to the followers of the Rev. Sun Myung Moon and his Unification Church.

The caller said she wanted to make sure her mother was right before organizing a boycott of her own.

Asked about the claim, a P&G spokesman in Cincinnati said, "That rumor has been spreading around the country for more than a year."

"There is absolutely no truth to the rumor," she said. "Neither Rev. Moon nor his Unification Church have any connection with Procter & Gamble Co."

She pointed out that "no one person holds more than one-half of one percent of P&G stock." She also noted that the Securities and Exchange Commission requires that a statement be filed when anyone owns more than 5 percent of any publicly held company.

Meanwhile, a quick check of Standard & Poor's *Stock Guide* revealed that if Moon and his followers sold flowers day and night, they would have a mighty tough time buying P&G.

There are 82,720,761 common shares of stock outstanding. Monday's price of $84 per share, that would come to about $6,948,543,924.

The Columbus caller said proof of the story was on P&G products: "They all have a moon and some stars on them," she said, which she said shows the Moonies' ownership.

But the P&G spokesman noted that the moon and stars insignia "is our copyrighted trademark and has been used since 1850."

She said the rumor became so prevalent in some areas that, "We sent letters to every television and radio station as well as all the newspapers," to make it clear the story had no basis in fact.

Source: Columbus *Citizen-Journal* (March 1981).

You might also have been a marketing executive at McDonald's, Wendy's or one of the regional hamburger chains recently and been confronted with "the additive problem." A rumor spread that the hamburger chain—and which one varied from city to city—was stretching the hamburger by adding ground worms. This rumor was serious business to the hamburger people. In some cities, it caused a 35-percent reduction in business. The companies took action in the communications under their control with advertisements delivered on TV by highly credible sources that stated the hamburger was "100% pure beef." The most effective counterattack, however, was probably a nonmarketing-dominated-communication—public information that informed consumers that hamburger cost about $1.50 per pound but that worms cost $4.00 per pound.

These examples are extremes of how nonmarketing-dominated communications can influence consumer behavior. Normally, as a consumer analyst, you won't have to deal with such serious rumor problems. Every day, however, products and marketing programs are affected by other forms of interpersonal communications. Consumer analysts, therefore, must understand to what extent consumers rely on opinions and experiences of other individuals in making purchasing decisions. What kinds of people do consumers look to for advice? Are there generalized opinion leaders or tastemakers? How does this flow of communication occur? These are the major issues discussed in this chapter.

INTERPERSONAL COMMUNICATIONS

Consumers obtain information about products and services from other people; particularly family members, friends and neighbors, and other acquaintances. This exchange of information between consumers is called *interpersonal communications,* while the effect of this behavior is termed *personal influence.* Individuals who influence the general and purchasing behavior of other people are called *opinion leaders.* Opinion leadership may be *positive* in its effect on promoting the purchase of a product or it may be *negative*, discouraging others from buying a product. This section discusses the impact and dynamics of interpersonal communication.

Interpersonal communications are frequently influential in purchasing decisions. Consider the following illustrative examples:

1. Almost 50 percent of male and female students at Florida State University discussed clothing brands, styles, retail outlets, and prices with their friends.[1]

2. A study of the diffusion of a new food product in a married students' apartment complex revealed that exposure to favorable word of mouth was found to increase the probability of purchase, while exposure to unfavorable comments decreased the probability.[2]

3. A large-scale study of Indianapolis housewives revealed that nearly two-thirds of those interviewed told someone else about new products they had purchased or tried.[3]

4. Another study found that the source of information most frequently consulted by durable goods buyers was friends and relatives. ". . . more than 50 percent of our buyers turned for advice to acquaintances and in most instances also looked at durable goods owned by them." Even more striking is the finding that one-third of durable goods buyers bought a brand or model that they had seen at someone else's house, often the house of relatives.[4]

5. A study of consumer attitudes toward health care found that the largest segment of consumers state the most important reason for choosing their doctor was a recommendation by a friend or relative.[5]

Other studies have also found interpersonal communications to be very important in the purchase of food items, soaps, and cleansing agents, in motion picture selections, hairdo styles, makeup techniques,[6] general fashions,[7] dental products and services,[8] farming practices,[9] physicians,[10] man-made fabrics,[11] and new products, to mention just a few.

[1]John R. Kerr and Bruce Weale, "Collegiate Clothing Purchasing Patterns and Fashion Adoption Behavior," *Southern Journal of Business* (July 1970), 126-133, at 129.

[2]Johan Arndt, "Role of Product-Related Conversations in the Diffusion of a New Product," *Journal of Marketing Research* (August 1967), 291-295.

[3]Charles W. King and John O. Summers, "Technology, Innovation and Consumer Decision Making," in Reed Moyer (ed.), *Consumer, Corporate and Governmment Interfaces* (Chicago: American Marketing Association, 1967), 63-68, at 66.

[4]George Katona and Eva Mueller, "A Study of Purchasing Decisions," in Lincoln H. Clark (ed.), *Consumer Behavior: The Dynamics of Consumer Reaction* (New York: New York University Press, 1955), 30-87, at 45.

[5]Roger D. Blackwell and W. Wayne Talarzyk, *Consumer Attitudes toward Health Care and Malpractice* (Columbus: Grid Publishing, Inc., 1977).

[6]Elihu Katz and Paul F. Lazarsfeld, *Personal Influence* (New York: Free Press, 1955).

[7]Charles W. King, "Fashion Adoption: A Rebuttal to the Trickle Down Theory," in Stephen A. Greyser (ed.), *Toward Scientific Marketing* (Chicago: American Marketing Association, 1963), 108-125.

[8]Alvin J. Silk, "Overlap among Self Designated Opinion Leaders: A Study of Selected Dental Products and Service," *Journal of Marketing Research* (August 1966), 255-259.

[9]Elihu Katz, "The Social Itinerary of Technical Changes: Two Studies in the Diffusion of Innovation," *Human Organization* (1961), 70-82; E. M. Rogers and G. M. Beal, "The Importance of Personal Influence in the Adoption of Technological Changes," *Social Forces* (May 1958), 329-335.

[10]James Coleman, Elihu Katz, and Herbert Menzel, "The Diffusion of an Innovation among Physicians," *Sociometry* (December 1957), 253-270; Herbert Menzel and Elihu Katz, "Social Relations and Innovation in the Medical Profession: The Epidemiology of a New Drug," *Public Opinion Quarterly* (Winter 1955-1956), 337-352.

[11]George M. Beal and Everett M. Rogers, "Informational Sources in the Adoption Process of New Fabrics," *Journal of Home Economics* (October 1957), 630-634.

Interpersonal Communication Dyads

Although considerable research has been conducted on the importance of interpersonal communication, research on the transmitter-receiver dyad is scarce. After reviewing the literature, King and Summers concluded that although the dimensions of analyses and the methodologies used have varied between studies, the research findings are remarkably consistent.[12]

1. The interaction dyad appears to be relatively homogeneous across many interaction contexts. In other words, studies comparing the social status and age of participants in an interaction dyad indicate that people tend to exchange information with other age and social status peers.

2. Perceived credibility and/or expertise of the person giving information on a topic is an important dimension in information-seeking behavior. Seekers search for referents more qualified than themselves on a topic. In contexts where expertise is not perceived as available within the seekers' peer level, sources higher or lower in age and social status may be consulted.

3. The family plays an important role in interpersonal communication in the socialization of children and in interaction within the extended family. The specific functions of family versus nonfamily interactions may be different, but this area has not been explored.

4. Proximity is important in facilitating interaction. Proximity as a variable is two-dimensional, including physical proximity and social proximity. Obviously, physical proximity—for example, living in the same neighborhood—makes possible physical contact and the settings for interpersonal exchange. Physical proximity also suggests a minimum social proximity in terms of some overlap of social status, interests, lifestyle, etc.

Decision Process Variations

The influence of interpersonal communications varies by stages of consumer decision making. While much of the research on interpersonal communications starts with models that recognize that consumer decisions are *processes*, in practice much of the research has failed to incorporate the process approach into the research design. Berning and Jacoby have noted this problem and set about to deal with it by analyzing one stage in decision making—the use of sources of information—both for new products and for established products. They concluded that the decision-making process preceding the purchase of new products is different than that in the purchasing of established products, and that the difference lies primarily in the search for information from friends.[13]

[12]Charles W. King and John O. Summers, "Dynamics of Interpersonal Communication: The Interaction Dyad," in Donald F. Cox (ed.), *Risk Taking and Information Handling in Consumer Behavior* (Boston: Division of Research, Graduate School of Business Administration, Harvard University, 1967), 240-264, at 261.

[13]Carol A. Kohn Berning and Jacob Jacoby, "Patterns of Information Acquisition in New Product Purchases," *Journal of Consumer Research* (September 1974), 18-22.

PERSONAL INFLUENCE

Other people—as referents or reference groups—play an important role in influencing the judgments and behavior of consumers. This personal influence has been recognized for nearly half a century dating back to the pioneering work of Sherif who demonstrated the impact others have upon an individual's judgment of an ambiguous stimulus situation. In a task involving the use of the autokinetic effect illusion (where a stationary spot of light on a screen in a dark room appears to move), isolated subjects were first asked to make a number of judgments regarding the light's movement. A subject was then seated together with a confederate who had been instructed to use judgmental standards that differed from the standards inferred from the subjects' prior judgments. Both the subject and confederate made their judgments aloud. As expected, subjects shifted their judgments toward the confederate, and this change persisted even when subjects later made their judgments alone.

In consumer research, such influence was often called normative compliance and interpreted as conforming to the expectations of others. As discussed in Chapter 6 in speaking of reference groups, this often created confusion. It lead to the belief in what was popularly called, "Keeping up with the Joneses," as if people were buying products in order to comply or identify with referent individuals. The research of Burnkrant and Cousineau[14] built upon a foundation laid by Kelman and Deutsch and Gerard,[15] lead astute consumer analysts to recognize that alternative motivations may underlie conformity. This interpretation is called *informational conformity*, which refers to *information accepted from others as evidence about reality*.

Informational influence leads to behavior that is in conformity to others who have personal influence but it is not based upon doing something to please the opinion leader. Rather, conformity is based simply on the belief that the consumer believes the person's position is right or correct. We may follow the advice of our tax lawyer simply because we believe she knows more than we do. We may buy a camera recommended by a knowledgeable photographer acquaintance—even if we personally disassociate ourselves from that individual—because we think he knows a lot about cameras.

When are consumers most likely to accept such influence? After reviewing the research in this area, Miniard concluded that social influence of an informational nature is most likely to occur when the individual:

1. lacks sufficient information,

2. is confronted with an ambiguous situation, or

3. is provided with information from others perceived to possess greater knowledge or expertise.

[14]Robert Burnkrant and Alain Cousineau, "Information and Normative Social Influence in Buyer Behavior," *Journal of Consumer Research* (December 1975), 206-214.

[15]H. C. Kelman, "Processes of Opinion Change," *Public Opinion Quarterly* (Spring 1961), 57-78; M. Deutsch and H. B. Gerard, "A Study of Normative and Informational Social Influences Upon Individual Judgment," *Journal of Abnormal and Social Psychology* (1951), 629-636.

**Attribution
Theory**

A recent development in understanding interpersonal influence is attribution theory. *Attribution* is a theoretical construct referring to *cognitive processes through which an individual infers the cause of the behavior of others or oneself.* Individuals come to know their own attitudes, emotions, and other internal states partially from inferring them from observations of their own behavior as "actors" in the circumstances in which the behavior occurs. To some degree, attribution theory (or self-perception theory, as it is sometimes also called) postulates that the individual is functionally in the same position as an outside observer who must rely on external cues to infer one's own inner state.

Shaver, in his textbook on attribution theory, explains the construct as it affects everyday life:

> In our everyday lives we are not dispassionate observers of human behavior, watching without evaluation. On the contrary, we try to understand behavior, to explain it, to determine what it means for us, and to make value judgments about it. Is another person complimenting me because I have behaved admirably, or is he flattering me because I have something he wants? Does the aspiring politician really believe his own campaign slogans, or is he simply taking positions he thinks will be popular with the voters? Is a particular criminal defendant to be held personally responsible for a crime, or were there extenuating circumstances that might serve as justification for the action? In each of these cases our main interest is not the action, but rather in the presumed reasons behind the action. In short, to what should each of these behaviors be attributed?[16]

The attribution process has been described by Calder and Burnkrant[17] and is shown in Figure 12.1. In the purchase and consumption of products, the consumer is a social actor whose behavior is usually observable by others. The consumer's behavior is informational input for the attribution processes of observers. These attributions or judgments about the consumer's behavior shape the observer's actions with respect to the consumer, which in turn may directly affect the original consumer's behavior. Attributions provide a psychological reason for the actions of the influencers as well as the influenced. For that reason, attribution theory is a step beyond the reference group studies described in Chapter 6.

Attribution theory has received considerable attention in the consumer literature although there is controversy about whether the theory has been correctly applied in experiments concerned with the subject.[18]

---

[16]Kelly Shaver, *An Introduction to Attribution Processes* (Cambridge, Mass.: Winthrop Publishers, Inc., 1975), ch. 5. This book serves as an easy-to-understand introduction to the subject.

[17]Bobby J. Calder and Robert E. Burnkrant, "Interpersonal Influence on Consumer Behavior: An Attribution Theory Approach," *Journal of Consumer Research* (June 1977), 29-38.

[18]Robert Hansen and Carol Scott, "Comments on Attribution Theory and Advertiser Credibility," *Journal of Marketing Research* (1976), 193-197. For reviews of self-perception and attribution research, see C. A. Scott, "Self-Perception Processes in Consumer Behavior: Interpreting One's Own Experiences," in Keith Hunt (ed.), *Advances in Consumer Research* (Chicago: Association for Consumer Research, 1978) and C. A. Scott, "Attribution Theory in Consumer Research," in Subhash Jain (ed.), *Research Frontiers in Marketing:* (Chicago: American Marketing Association), 169-173.

**Figure 12.1
An Attribution
Paradigm for the
Study of
Interpersonal
Influence**

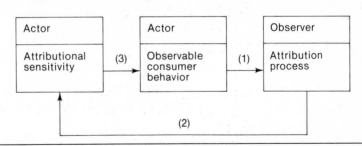

Source: Bobby J. Calder and Robert E. Burnkrant, "Interpersonal Influence on Consumer Behavior: An Attribution Theory Approach," *Journal of Consumer Research* (June 1977), 28. Reprinted by permission.

Attribution theory has been most often applied in the information processing area and gives guidance about the kinds of actors and their behaviors that should be shown in advertisements. A thorough review of the attribution theory literature by Mizerski, Golden and Kernan shows, however, that it offers an alternative explanation to cognitive dissonance and an explicit formulation for assessing self-fulfilling prophecy and social-stereotype phenomena, as well as insights into group-influenced decision making.[19] The way people learn to make attributions to validate their perceptions is also an integral concept in learning theory.

WHO ARE THE INFLUENCERS?

Marketers need to know what types of people are influencers. Who are the opinion leaders? How do we find them? As a consumer analyst, you may be asked to conduct research to determine the opinion leaders for the organization that employs you. How would you do it? The following paragraphs describe briefly important research considerations in finding opinion leaders.

Opinion leadership, you will remember, refers to the degree to which an individual influences others in a given choice situation. Those who do a disproportionately large amount of influencing others are called *opinion leaders* in those situations in which they exert influence. A number of methods have been used to find such persons.

**Identifying
Opinion Leaders**

Three basic types of techniques are used to measure opinion leadership:

1. The *sociometric* method involves asking respondents from whom they get advice and to whom they go to seek advice or information in making a specified type of decision.

2. The *key informant* method involves the use of informed individuals in a social system to identify opinion leaders in a given situation.

[19]Richard W. Mizerski, Linda Golden, and Jerome Kernan, "The Attribution Process in Consumer Decision Making," *Journal of Consumer Research* (September 1979), 123-140.

3. The *self-designating* method relies on the respondent to evaluate his or her own influence in a given topic area.

The advantages and disadvantages of these methods were evaluated by King and Summers.[20] The sociometric method has face validity but it is not effective when the social system to be investigated is not self-contained in terms of the flow of influence on the topic area of interest; or when the social system is too large to permit the interviewing of all of its members. For example, a retail store might wish to determine opinion leaders for fashion and appearance in a high school. The sociometric methods might be ideal from a theoretical perspective but not practical because of the cost and difficulty of the research.

The key informant method is useful when the objective is to study only opinion leaders, when financial and other constraints prohibit interviewing a large number of people, and/or when the social system is small and key informants can provide accurate information on the interaction process.

Since the conditions favoring these two methods do not usually exist in marketing settings, most consumer studies use the self-designating method.[21] This technique is a compromise between the other two methods, being simple to administer in survey research and not limited to small, self-contained social systems where a census is required.

An example of self-designation scales typically used in marketing studies is provided in Table 12.1. In practice, marketing researchers may only use one or two questions similar to those in Table 12.1 along with many other questions or may use several questions about opinion leadership. Generally, longer scales have greater validity and reliability[22] than methods involving fewer questions.[23]

The continuous scores from self-designating opinion leadership scales are divided into dichotomous categories of opinion leaders and non-opinion leaders.

Sometimes, opinion leadership is defined as including more than two categories such as low, medium, and high opinion leadership.

Clues to Opinion Leaders

Are there any clues to finding opinion leaders? Considerable research has been directed toward answering that question. This has focused on

[20]Charles W. King and John O. Summers, "Generalized Opinion Leadership in Consumer Products: Some Preliminary Findings," paper no. 224 (Lafayette, Ind.: Institute for Research in the Behavioral, Economic, and Management Sciences, Krannert Graduate School of Industrial Administration, January 1969).

[21]For examples, see Francesco M. Nicosia, "Opinion Leaders and the Flow of Communication: Some Problems and Prospects," in L. G. Smith (ed.), *Reflections on Progress in Marketing* (Chicago: American Marketing Association, 1965), 340-359; James S. Fenton and Thomas R. Leggett, "A New Way to Find Opinion Leaders," *Journal of Advertising Research* (April 1971), 22-25; Fred D. Reynolds and William R. Darden, "Mutually Adaptive Effects of Interpersonal Communication," *Journal of Marketing Research* (November 1971), 449-454; Stephen A. Blumgarten, "The Innovative Communicator in the Diffusion Process," *Journal of Marketing Research* (February 1975), 12-18.

[22]Everett M. Rogers and David G. Cartano, "Methods of Measuring Opinion Leadership," *Public Opinion Quarterly,* (Fall 1962), 43-45.

[23]The relative strengths and problems of alternative methods are reviewed in George Brooker and Michael J. Houston, "An Evaluation of Measures of Opinion Leadership," in Kenneth L. Bernhardt (ed.), *Marketing 1776-1976 and Beyond* (Chicago: American Marketing Association, 1976), 561-564.

**Table 12.1
Example of Self-
Designation Scales
of Opinion
Leadership**

(1) In general, do you like to talk about _____ with your friends?
Yes _____ —1   No _____ —2

(2) Would you say *you give very little information, an average amount of information, or a great deal of information* about _____ to your friends?
You give very little information _____ —1
You give an average amount of information _____ —2
You give a great deal of information _____ —3

(3) During the *past six months,* have *you told anyone* about some _____?
Yes _____ —1   No _____ —2

(4) Compared with your circle of friends, are you *less likely, about as likely,* or *more likely* to be asked for advice about _____?
Less likely to be asked _____ —1
About as likely to be asked _____ —1
More likely to be asked _____ —3

(5) If you and your friends were to discuss _____, what part would *you* be most likely to play? Would you *mainly listen* to your friends' ideas or would *you try to convince them* of your ideas?
You mainly listen to your friends' ideas _____ —1
You try to convince them of your ideas _____ —2

(6) Which of these happens more often? Do *you tell your friends* about some _____,
or do *they tell you* about some _____?
You tell them about _____ —1
They tell you about _____ —2

(7) Do you have the feeling that you are generally regarded by your friends and neighbors as a good source of advice about _____?
Yes _____ —1   No _____ —2

Source: Charles W. King and John O. Summers, "Generalized Opinion Leadership in Consumer Products: Some Preliminary Findings," paper no. 224 (Lafayette, Ind.: Institute for Research in the Behavioral, Economic and Management Sciences, Krannert Graduate School of Industrial Administration, January 1969), 16. Reprinted by permission.

demographic characteristics, social activity, general attitudes, personality characteristics, life-styles, and product related characteristics as well as the question of whether or not opinion leadership is generalized or specific.

Demographic Characteristics

There has been much effort devoted to determining if persons with certain demographic characteristics—such as high income, education, and so forth—would be opinion leaders. The answer seems to be that opinion leadership depends very much on the product category. In a product category where relatively high income is needed to purchase the product, people in higher income categories are likely to consider the product more feasible to buy, have higher ownership and experience, and therefore be opinion leaders for others. In other product categories, consumers with large families may dominate opinion leadership for household cleaning or maintenance items because they have greater experience with the product category. On the other hand, young women dominate for fashion products and movie-going. Some research has found that young persons are slightly more influential across many different products and have found some other demographic relationships. For the most part, however, demographic relationships are usually too weak to be very helpful.[24]

[24]James H. Myers and Thomas S. Robertson, "Dimensions of Opinion Leadership," *Journal of Marketing Research* (February 1972), 41-46.

One of the reasons why opinion leaders are not from specific demographic groups is that interpersonal communications tend to be homogeneous in terms of social class, age, and income. This is known as *homophily*, or the principle that the sources of communications and the receivers of communications tend to have similar attributes. *Homophilious* or highly similar communication dyads tend to interact with greater frequency than *heterophilious*, or highly dissimilar, dyads. Thus, influence (mass media or personal) tends to occur when source and receiver have similar or shared attitudes, meanings of language, belief structure, and so forth.[25]

Social Activity

Opinion leaders usually participate in more social activities and are more gregarious than non-opinion leaders.[26] In all of the factors used to identify opinion leaders, gregariousness is often one of the most important.

General Attitudes

In the case of new products, opinion leaders tend to have more favorable attitudes toward both new products as a concept and new products within their specific areas of influence. Where the norms of the population as a whole reflect positive attitudes toward new products, opinion leaders reflect even greater commitment to new products than do their counterparts. Thus leaders are usually more innovative than other individuals.[27]

Personality Characteristics

Robertson and Myers studied the relationship between personality characteristics and opinion leadership. Using the California Psychological Inventory to measure personality characteristics in eighteen major areas, they concluded that none of the basic personality variables related substantially to opinion leadership for any of the product areas studied (appliances, clothing, food).[28]

Other studies have found that opinion leaders do have some distinguishing personality characteristics. For example, Summers found that women's clothing fashion opinion leaders are more emotionally stable, assertive, likeable, less depressive or self-deprecating, and tend to be

[25]E. M. Rogers and D. K. Bhomik, "Homophily-Heterophily: Relational Concepts for Communication Research," *Public Opinion Quarterly* (Winter 1970), 523-538; George P. Moschis, "Social Comparison and Informal Group Influence," *Journal of Marketing Research* (August 1976), 237-244.

[26]Reynolds and Darden, "Mutually Adaptive," 449-454; John O. Summers, "The Identity of Women's Clothing Fashion Opinion Leaders," *Journal of Marketing Research* (May 1970), 178-185; Gary Armstrong and Laurence Feldman, "Exposure and Sources of Opinion Leaders," *Journal of Advertising Research* (August 1976), 21-27.

[27]John O. Summers and Charles W. King, "Interpersonal Communication and New Product Attitudes," in Phillip R. McDonald (ed.), *Marketing Involvement in Society and the Economy* (Chicago: American Marketing Association, 1969), 292-299.

[28]Thomas S. Robertson and James H. Myers, "Personality Correlates of Opinion Leadership and Innovative Buying Behavior," *Journal of Marketing Research* (May 1969), 164-168.

leaders and more self-confident.[29] Thus it appears that the relationship between personality characteristics and opinion leadership depends on the type of personality characteristic studied and the product under investigation. Tailor-made personality variables are probably more effective discriminators than are general personality characteristics.[30]

Life-style Characteristics

Tigert and Arnold constructed life-style profiles of general, self-designated opinion leaders, both in the United States and Canada. Using activity, interest, and opinion variables, they were able to construct a rich portrait of opinion leaders. Factor analysis revealed that eight factors— leadership, information exchanges, innovation, community and club involvement, independence, price consciousness, occupation, and fashion consciousness—were able to explain 27 percent in the variance of opinion leadership in Canada.[31]

The Tigert and Arnold study was concerned with a composite opinion leader for a broad variety of product categories. Had they constructed profiles of opinion leaders for specific products, or products in the same interest category, they probably would have been more successful. Nevertheless, their study points up the potential value of life-style profiles.

Product-Related Characteristics

Opinion leaders tend to have certain additional distinguishing characteristics related to the type of decision being made. First, they perceive themselves as more interested in the topic area. For example, in women's fashions, opinion leaders are more interested in fashions than are non-opinion leaders.[32]

Second, opinion leaders are more active in receiving interpersonal communications about products within their area of influence. In other words, other consumers talk to opinion leaders more than they do to non-opinion leaders about things that are related to the leaders' alleged area of expertise.[33] This varies by product category and between cultural groups and subgroups. In the United States, people tend to discuss grocery products more than in France. While word-of-mouth communications about grocery products were relatively low in France, they were relatively high with respect to retail services.[34]

Finally, opinion leaders are usually more exposed to certain additional sources of information. They may be more exposed to the mass

[29]Summers, "Identity," 180-181.

[30]See, for example, Reynolds and Darden, "Mutually Adaptive," 450.

[31]Douglas J. Tigert and Stephen J. Arnold, *Profiling Self-Designated Opinion Leaders and Self-Designated Innovators through Life Style Research* (Toronto: School of Business, University of Toronto, June 1971).

[32]Summers, "Identity," 178-185.

[33]Summers and King, "Interpersonal Communication," 292-299.

[34]Robert T. Green and Eric Langeard, "A Cross-National Comparison of Consumer Habits and Innovator Characteristics," *Journal of Marketing* (July 1975), 35-41.

media in general although not in every instance.[35] However, they are almost always more exposed to specific types of mass media that are relevant to their area of interest. Thus, for example, opinion leaders in women's fashions may not be more exposed to television in general, but they are usually more exposed to women's fashion magazines.[36]

Opinion Leadership Overlap

There is a great deal of interest in the question of whether opinion leadership is *monomorphic*—product specific—or *polymorphic*—overlapping many product areas. Much of the early literature supported the concept of monomorphic opinion leadership,[37] but more recently this has been clarified to support the conclusion that the same persons will be opinion leaders for related products but not for all products. For example, influence for women's clothing was found to be highly related to that for cosmetics. Also, personal care and influence for household furnishings correlated highly with that for household appliances in the research of Myers and Robertson.[38] Although the same persons may be opinion leaders for fashions and cosmetics, little overlap appears to exist between cosmetics and appliances.[39]

Montgomery and Silk found overlap in opinion leadership across most but not all of the categories studied. They also found that the patterns of overlap appeared to parallel the manner in which consumers' interests in these categories clustered together.[40] Further work by Montgomery and Silk found that patterns of association in opinion leadership for sixteen topics corresponded to the structure of interrelationships among measures of interest in the same topics.[41]

Thus research to date indicates that there are quasi-generalized opinion leaders. The nature of interest patterns seems to be one of the important factors that determine what constitutes their sphere of influence.

In summary, opinion leadership is an important phenomenon and marketing organizations need to understand what types of people are

---

[35]See, for example, Robert Mason, "The Use of Information Sources by Influentials in the Adoption Process," *Public Opinion Quarterly* (Fall 1963), 455-466.

[36]See, for example, Katz and Lazarsfeld, *Personal Influence*, 309-320; Summers, "Identity," 178-185; Reynolds and Darden, "Mutually Adaptive," 449-454.

[37]See, for example, Silk, "Overlap," 257; Katz and Lazarsfeld, *Personal Influence*, 334; Everett M. Rogers, *Diffusion of Innovation* (New York: Free Press, 1962), 30-36; Elihu Katz, "The Two Step Flow of Communication: An Up-to-Date Report on a Hypothesis," *Public Opinion Quarterly* (Spring 1957), 61-78.

[38]Myers and Robertson, "Dimensions," 45.

[39]Charles W. King and John O. Summers, "Overlap of Opinion Leadership across Consumer Product Categories," *Journal of Marketing Research* (February 1970), 43-50. For additional evidence see Edwin J. Gross, "Support for a Generalized Marketing Leadership Theory," *Journal of Advertising Research* (November 1969), 49-52.

[40]David B. Montgomery and Alvin J. Silk, "Patterns of Overlap in Opinion Leadership and Interest for Selected Categories of Purchasing Activity," in McDonald, *Marketing Involvement,* 377-386. For supporting evidence in other areas, see Herbert F. Lionberger, *Adoption of New Ideas and Practices* (Ames, Iowa: Iowa State University Press, 1960), 65-66.

[41]David B. Montgomery and Alvin J. Silk, "Clusters of Consumer Interests and Opinion Leaders' Spheres of Influence," *Journal of Marketing Research* (August 1971), 317-321.

leaders in a specific product category. Leaders are usually—although not always—similar to those they influence, and they typically differ from one sphere of interest to another. They tend to be more gregarious and innovative, are more interested in the area in question, and both receive and transmit more information about the topic.

MODELS OF PERSONAL INFLUENCE

A number of theories or models have been developed in an attempt to help marketers and others understand how the process of personal influence occurs. This section describes some of these models and the research that has developed from the models.

The Two-Step Flow Hypothesis

The two-step flow of communications is the traditional model of the link between mass media and interpersonal communication. Despite some revisions and modifications, the essential elements of the hypothesis remain unchanged from its original formulation in 1948. Briefly, this model states that influences and ideas flow from the mass media to opinion leaders and from them to the less active sections of the population.[42] The link between the passive masses and the mass media is the opinion leader.

Although the two-step flow was a historic breakthrough in understanding communications, it is no longer an accurate and complete model of the process. For one thing it views the audience as passive receivers of information. Yet several studies have found that up to 50 percent of word-of-mouth communications are initiated by consumers seeking information from opinion leaders.[43] Moreover, at least in some instances, word-of-mouth communication is affected by selective exposure and selective response.[44]

Multi-Stage Interaction Models

A more contemporary view of personal influence is built upon a multi-stage interaction approach. Much of this research is derived from the diffusion of innovations literature showing differences in personal communication and influence, depending upon whether consumers are earlier triers or later adopters of a product. A longitudinal study of *Maxim* coffee concluded that early adopters followed a pattern close to the two-step flow hypothesis but that later adopters engaged in a more conver-

---

[42]Paul F. Lazarsfeld, Bernard R. Berelson, and Hazel Gaudlet, *The People's Choice* (New York: Columbia University Press, 1948), 151. Many of the concepts and techniques utilized in this study were originated by Merton. See Robert K. Merton, "Patterns of Influence: A Study of Interpersonal Influence and of Communications Behavior in a Local Community," in P. F. Lazarsfeld and F. Stanton (eds.), *Communications Research* (New York: Harper & Brothers, 1949). An earlier exploratory study was conducted by Frank Stewart, "A Sociometric Study of Influence in Southtown," *Sociometry* (1947), 11-31, 273-286.

[43]Johan Arndt, "Selective Processes in Word-of-Mouth," *Journal of Advertising Research* (June 1968), 19-22.

[44]Russell W. Belk and Ivan Ross, "An Investigation of the Nature of Word of Mouth Communication across Adoption Categories for a Food Innovation," paper presented at the Association for Consumer Research Conference, University of Maryland, September 1971.

sational form of word-of-mouth that appeared to be devoid of opinion leadership.

Other studies have questioned the accuracy of a two-step flow. For example, King and Summers found in the case of women's apparel:[45]

1. About 39 percent of those who reported involvement in interpersonal communication mentioned participation as both a transmitter and a receiver.

2. Nearly 53 percent of those who reported participation as a receiver also reported participation as a transmitter.

3. Approximately 60 percent of those who reported participation as a transmitter also reported participation as a receiver.

Katz has also suggested that in some instances there may be chains of personal influence rather than simple dyads.[46] Sheth's study of the diffusion of stainless steel blades indicated that there may exist a three-or-more-step flow of communication.[47]

These findings suggest the need for more complex multistep, multisituation models that focus on consumers' needs for information, opinion leaders' motives for transmitting information, and situational determinants of the processes.

Why Do People Become Opinion Leaders?

In general, opinion leaders will not talk about products or services unless a conversation produces some type of satisfaction. Motivations to talk about products or services appear to fall into one or more of the following categories: (1) product involvement, (2) self-involvement, (3) concern for others, (4) message involvement,[48] or (5) dissonance reduction.

First, the *more interested an individual is in a given topic or product or service,* the more likely he or she is to initiate conversations about it. For example, Katz and Lazarsfeld found that public affairs and fashion leaders were more interested in their areas than were nonleaders. Similarly, marketing leadership was concentrated in wives of large families who were more interested and more experienced than were the girls or the small-family wives.[49] Apparently, in these and other situations, conversations serve as an outlet for the pleasure and/or excitement caused by or resulting from the purchase and/or use of the product or service.

Second, *self-involvement* may also play a major role in motivating opinion leaders to comment about a product or service. Dichter con-

---

[45]Charles W. King and John O. Summers, "Dynamics of Interpersonal Communication," in Cox, *Risk Taking,* 253-254.

[46]Katz, "Two Step Flow," 61-78.

[47]Jagdish N. Sheth, "Word-of-Mouth in Low-Risk Innovations," *Journal of Advertising Research* (June 1971), 15-18.

[48]This typology was developed by Ernest Dichter, "How Word-of-Mouth Advertising Works," *Harvard Business Review* (November-December 1966), 147-166.

[49]Katz and Lazarsfeld, *Personal Influence,* 249-252, 274-275, 239-242.

cluded that talking about a product or service often performs such functions as gaining attention, showing connoisseurship, suggesting status, giving the impression that the opinion leader has inside information, and asserting superiority.[50] Whyte found in a classic study of the diffusion of air conditioners, that some respondents subscribed to *Consumer Reports* to acquire conversational material.[51]

Concern for others may also precipitate talk by opinion leaders. Some conversations are motivated by a desire to help the listener make better purchasing decisions. In other instances, talking about a product or service allows the opinion leader to share the satisfactions resulting from the use of the product or service.

Advertising or *message involvement* is another type of opinion-leader motivation. Some people find it entertaining to talk about certain advertisements such as those for *Volkswagen* and *Rolaids.* Other people like to make jokes about advertising symbols such as the Jolly Green Giant, Mr. Whipple, or "It's not nice to fool Mother Nature."

Finally, some research suggests that under certain conditions word-of-mouth is used to *reduce cognitive dissonance* following a major purchase decision. Presumably the buyer attempts to reduce dissonance by persuading other people to buy the same product.[52] This motivation does not exist in all instances, however. Engel, Kegerreis, and Blackwell failed to find significant amounts of this behavior following the usage of an automotive diagnostic service.[53]

Why Do People Accept Opinion Leadership?

The conditions that are likely to cause consumers to seek information from opinion leaders are explained to some degree by attribution theory. They are also similar to general search determinants and include: (1) small amount of stored information, (2) stored information not appropriate, (3) high degree of perceived risk, and (4) low cost involved in using this source of information. Of those mentioned, perceived risk has received the most *empirical* attention. Situational determinants and product visibility are also relevant determinants.

Perceived Risk

Studies investigating the relation between perceived risk and information seeking from personal sources indicate that those consumers high in perceived risk are more likely to initiate conversations. And when they do, they are more likely to request information than those who are felt to

[50]Dichter, "How Word-of-Mouth, "147-166.

[51]William H. Whyte, Jr., "The Web of Word-of-Mouth," in Lincoln H. Clark (ed.), *The Life Cycle and Consumer Behavior* (New York: New York University Press, 1955), 113-122.

[52]Much of this section was based on a comprehensive literature review in Johan Arndt, "Word-of-Mouth Advertising," in Cox, *Risk Taking,* 188-239.

[53]James F. Engel, Robert J. Kegerreis, and Roger D. Blackwell, "Word-of-Mouth Communication by the Innovator," *Journal of Marketing* (July 1969), 15-19. See also James F. Engel, Roger D. Blackwell, and Robert J. Kegerreis, "How Information is Used to Adopt an Innovation," *Journal of Advertising Research* (December 1969), 3-8.

be low in perceived risk.[54] In other words, there appears to be a flow of information from those low in perceived risk to those high in perceived risk.[55]

A model for use by marketing organizations to analyze the relationship between perceived risk and word-of-mouth advertising has been proposed by Woodside and Delozier and is presented in Figure 12.2. It portrays the structure and mechanism they believe occurs in acquiring, transmitting and processing information from word-of-mouth advertising. The model, in Box 14, indicates that if informal groups consider a product to be a risk, this may cause consumers to search other sources of information such as professional organizations, noncommercial literature, personal salespersons and so forth; and to need different types of advertisements. They suggest that sellers of a product such as a Zenith color television—a relatively risky purchase for consumers—might want to inform consumers, "Tom has one, I have one, everyone has one."[56] It might also be possible for the company to arrange group discussions among influentials for the purpose of decreasing perceived risk.

Situational Determinants

Various situational and conversational determinants of word-of-mouth communication are important. Belk found that for both senders and receivers, food-related cues (drinking coffee, general conversations concerning food, shopping for food) were present in at least three-fourths of the reported incidents of word-of-mouth activity. Spontaneous word-of-mouth was rare. Based on the *Maxim* study and his previous research, Belk concluded:[57]

1. Much informal conversation regarding a new product does not involve opinion leader/follower pairs, and often such communications are exchanges of views and information.

2. The probabilistic occurrence of specific word-of-mouth conversations is more dependent upon the conversational and environmental context (cues) than upon the particular assemblage of persons present.

The first conclusion rejects the conventional concept of opinion leadership in favor of a more conversational form in which leader-follower role playing does not seem to occur. The second conclusion maintains that while spontaneous word-of-mouth may occur, a relevant context facilitates most word-of-mouth. An appropriate context may be created conversationally (that is, a relevant setting for discussing a certain type of product).

[54]Raymond A. Bauer, "The Initiative of the Audience," *Journal of Advertising Research* (1963), 2-7.

[55]Scott M. Cunningham, "Perceived Risk as a Factor in the Diffusion of New Product Information," in Haas, *Science,* 698-721; Johan Arndt, "Perceived Risk, Sociometric Integration and Word-of-Mouth in the Adoption of a New Food Product," in Haas, *Science,* 644-649.

[56]Arch G. Woodside and M. Wayne DeLozier, "Effects of Word of Mouth Advertising on Consumer Risk Taking," *Journal of Advertising* (Fall 1976), 12-19.

[57]Russell W. Belk, "Occurrence of Word-of-Mouth Buyer Behavior as a Function of Situation and Advertising Stimuli," paper presented at the American Marketing Association Fall Conference, August 1971.

Figure 12.2
Model of Word-of-Mouth Advertising and Consumer
Risk Taking

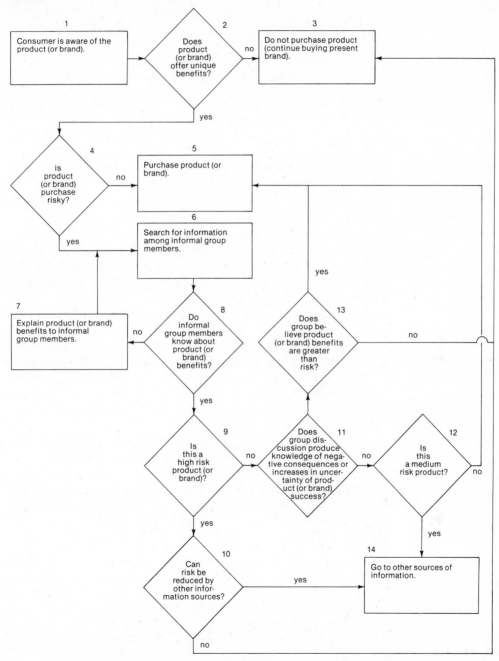

**Table 12.2
Reference-Group
Influence on
Product Decisions**

		Weak −	Strong +		
Strong +		Clothing Furniture Magazines Refrigerator (type) Toilet soap	Cars Cigarettes Beer (prem. vs. reg.) Drugs	+	Brand or Type
Weak −		Soap Canned peaches Laundry soap Refrigerator (brand) Radios	Air conditioners Instant coffee TV (black and white)	−	
		− **Product** +			

Source: Foundation for Research on Human Behavior, *Group Influence in Marketing and Public Relations* (Ann Arbor, Mich.: The Foundation, 1956), 8. Reprinted by permission.

Product Social Visibility

Interpersonal influence also varies by the social visibility of product categories. A conference report by Bourne is widely quoted to show that some products are more conspicuous and therefore more subject to reference group influences than are others.

Table 12.2 presents the Bourne report, showing that some products have significant interpersonal dimensions. These are called the product-plus, brand-plus categories.[58] People talk about and have norms concerning the purchase of automobiles, cigarettes, beer, and drugs and about specific brands of these proucts. To say that one drinks *Coors* may cause different attributions than if a person states a preference for *Blatz,* as an example of a product that has strong brand and product preference group dimensions.

The early conceptualization by Bourne has been challenged by Hendon[59] and others as not empirically based, (the assignment of products to cells was done mainly by guessing). Furthermore, the specific classifications for each product have probably changed since the 1950s. The conceptualization is still useful, however, as it communicates that product conspicuousness is an important determinant of whether or not products will be strongly influenced by reference groups. The authors conclude:

The conspicuousness of a product is perhaps the most general attribute bearing on its susceptibility to reference-group influence. There are two aspects to conspicuousness in this particular context that help to determine reference-group influence. First, the article

[58]Foundation for Research on Human Behavior, *Group Influence in Marketing and Public Relations* (Ann Arbor, Mich.: The Foundation, 1956).

[59]Donald W. Hendon, "A New and Empirical Look at the Influence of Reference Groups on Generic Product Category and Brand Choice: Evidence from Two Nations," *Proceedings of the Academy of International Business: Asia-Pacific Dimensions of International Business* (Honolulu: College of Business Administration, University of Hawaii, December 18-20, 1979), 752-761.

must be conspicuous in the most obvious sense that it can be seen and identified by others. Secondly, it must be conspicuous in the sense of standing out and being noticed. In other words, no matter how visible a product is, if virtually everyone owns it, it is not conspicuous in this second sense of the word.[60]

Other studies have also shown the effects of interpersonal communications even though they made little attempt to determine the reasons for opinion leadership. A famous study by Whyte, in Philadelphia, of early usage of room air conditioners indicated that interpersonal communication and imitation occurred next door and across the back yard but not across the street.[61] Other studies of beer, deodorant, after-shave lotion, and cigarettes show the variation that exists in group influence among product categories.[62] Even for a product such as bread, Stafford claimed that an opinion leader may exist whose choice of bread may influence others.[63]

STRATEGY IMPLICATIONS OF PERSONAL INFLUENCE PROCESSES

The above pages show the importance of the personal influence process for marketing organizations and indicate some of the variables and techniques that are available to analyze the process of influence as it applies to the products or services of an individual firm or other organization. The remaining task in this chapter is to analyze what marketing organizations can do to capitalize on this information about personal influence.

When discussing marketing implications, it is necessary to take an integrated view of the mass media and of personal influences. In the previous chapter on marketer dominated sources of information, the information was discussed so that the person might design advertising, sales personnel, point-of-sale materials, and so forth more effectively. In this chapter, however, the title implies that the material discussed is not controlled or dominated by marketing organizations. So, how can marketing organizations do anything about nonmarketer-dominated influences?

The answer is often a blend of efforts, combining mass media dominated by marketing (i.e., *advertising*) and mass media not dominated by marketing but which can be influenced through *public relations*. If a marketing organization understands how mass media and personal influences interact, it may be possible to develop an *integrated marketing*

---

[60]Foundation for Research on Human behavior, *Group Influence,* 7-8. Reprinted by permission.

[61]W. H. Whyte, Jr., "The Web of Word of Mouth," *Fortune,* (November 1954), 146 ff.

[62]Robert E. Witt and Grady D. Bruce, "Purchase Decisions and Group Influence," *Journal of Marketing Research* (November 1970), 533-555; Robert E. Witt, "Group Influence on Consumer Brand Choice," in McDonald, *Marketing Involvement,* 306-309.

[63]James E. Stafford, "Effects of Group Influence on Consumer Brand Preferences," *Journal of Marketing Research* (February 1966), 68-75. However, see Jeff Ford and Elwood Ellis, "A Reexamination of Group Influence on Member Brand Preferences," *Journal of Marketing Research* (February 1980), 125-132.

program including these influences even though they are not controlled by marketing organizations. Several possibilities are discussed in the following pages.

Reaching Opinion Leaders

The most formidable problem lies in identifying opinion leaders. Opinion leaders, it will be recalled, exist in all strata of society; they differ from other consumers in terms of competence, social location, the personification of certain values, and exposure to mass media; and they are only quasipolymorphic. Thus a marketer must conduct research to identify opinion leaders.

Even when opinion leaders are identified, it may not be profitable to direct advertising to them. For example, Tigert and Arnold found that opinion leaders in the US could not be reached through print media any more effectively than the average consumer in the population. However, in Canada they found that it was possible to reach general opinion leaders through several television and print vehicles.[64]

In situations where opinion leaders can be identified and reached effectively, several strategies are possible. First, as mentioned above, advertisements in the mass media or direct mail—if not too expensive—can be directed to them. It is possible to buy very specific mailing lists of groups such as high school coaches, physicians by specialties, church members of various denominations, and so forth. A number of organizations sponsor research that has a high probability of being read in journals or through press releases in order to reach key opinion leaders. Effective use of press conferences and releases can thus generate information directed toward opinion leaders, if a company's marketing research has provided a good profile of the opinion leaders for a product.

Second, many companies maintain advisory committees or boards of reference to help evaluate new products and programs. Knowing some of the reasons why people like to be opinion leaders, which were discussed earlier in this chapter, it could be predicted that if members of these advisory boards were carefully selected, they could be very important as opinion leaders when the product is introduced or when a consumer asks about a store or other aspect of the marketing program. Many sales organizations and many charitable organizations maintain advisory boards that are important adjuncts to the marketing-dominated efforts of the organization.

A third way of using opinion leaders is to give them, or loan them, a product for usage in a natural setting (where they are likely to be opinion leaders). Chevrolet and other auto manufacturers have sponsored projects in which students are loaned a new car. Ostensibly the car is for research, but it is also driven by students and professors in the business school who may be active as information transmitters to others on campus. In some instances, retailers have given products that were not sell-

---

[64]Tigert and Arnold, *Profiling Self-Designated*, 28-29.

ing well to opinion leaders in a community and have observed large quantities of the product sold later.

Finally, opinion leaders can be hired by a firm, as sales clerks or in other positions. Department stores and clothing retailers sometimes hire the most popular young people as clerks and give large discounts on the clothing they purchase, knowing of their influence as opinion leaders. Sometimes persons who are obvious opinion leaders are hired as "vice-president of community affairs" or "director of special projects" to capitalize on their influence in interpersonal relationships.

In situations where it is not possible or practical to identify real opinion leaders, an alternative strategy is to simulate them. One technique is to use advertising to replace or reduce the need for personal influence. Advertisements can communicate the idea that the consumer's reference group buys the product and that buying it is therefore appropriate for him. A related technique is to use testimonial advertising by a famous person who is perceived as competent to give advice about the product or service.

Reaching Proxy Opinion Leaders.

Since opinion leadership and innovativeness are often highly correlated, it is sometimes possible to use innovators as quasileaders, or a proxy variable for leaders. This strategy is appealing when innovators can be effectively reached through the mass media but opinion leaders cannot.

Using people who have a high degree of public exposure is another potential method of reaching proxy opinion leadership. In the introduction of the *Mustang,* for example, the Ford Motor Company used several promotional approaches where college newspaper editors, disc jockeys, and airline attendants were loaned *Mustangs.*[65] Some restaurants and bars offer cab drivers and bellhops meals and drinks at cost if they refer traveling executives and other out-of-towners to their establishments.

Creating New Opinion Leaders

An alternative or complementary strategy is to create opinion leaders. This may be an attractive approach when it is impossible to identify and/or reach real opinion leaders.

This approach has been used to transform unknown songs and unknown singing stars into hits. The initial step was to seek out social leaders among the relevant buyers, high school students.[66] Class presidents, secretaries, sports captains, and cheerleaders were selected from geographically diverse high schools. Later research revealed that most of these students were not opinion leaders for phonograph records.

The social leaders were contacted by mail and invited to join a select

[65]Frederick D. Sturdivant et al., *Managerial Analysis in Marketing* (Glenview, Ill.: Scott, Foresman, 1970), 233.
[66]Jerry Shulman, "Measuring Consumer Tastes in Popular Music," in Jerry Olson (ed.), *Advances in Consumer Research,* vol. 7 (Ann Arbor: Association for Consumer Research, 1980), 25-27.

panel to help evaluate rock-and-roll records. The introductory letter stressed several major points:

1. The recipient had been carefully selected, and the organizers felt that he or she, as a leader, should be better able than fellow students to identify potential rock-and-roll hits.

2. In return for help, the person would receive a token of appreciation for cooperation—free records.

3. The person was encouraged to discuss choices with friends and to weigh opinions before submitting a final vote.

4. The person would be told something about each specific record and the singing star. In addition, *Billboard Magazine* and record stores were suggested as sources of information to verify attitudes and eventual choices.

5. The person was a member of a panel of leaders, and after the panel members had voted s/he would be informed of the outcome.

6. S/he was under no obligation to join the panel and could withdraw from it at any time.

7. The experiment was essentially unstructured, but s/he would be informed of any expected or unexpected results.

8. An informal two-way atmosphere was encouraged and any new ideas or suggestions would be welcomed and, if appropriate, adopted.

9. The reader would be asked also to answer a few simple questions each month, and the results of the previous month's questionnaire would be made available to respondents the following month.

The total cost of the experiment was less than $5,000. The results were impressive: several records reached the top ten charts in the trial cities but did not make the top ten selections in any other cities. Thus, without contacting any radio stations or any record stores, rock-and-roll records were pulled through the channels of distribution and made into hits.[67]

Stimulating Information Seeking

Another family of strategies consists of various techniques designed to stimulate information seeking. These techniques may be used instead of, or in addition to, those mentioned above.

One approach is to generate curiosity and interest in products through planned secrecy. This technique was apparently successful for the new *Mustang* which was "the most talked about—and least seen—auto of this year."[68]

Another technique is to use advertisements that capture the imagination of the public through various techniques, particularly slogans or

---

[67]Joseph R. Mancuso, "Why Not Create Opinion Leaders for New Product Introductions?" *Journal of Marketing* (July 1969), 20-25.
[68]*Time* (March 13, 1964), 91.

phrases that become part of the everyday language. For example, early Volkswagen ads were thought to stimulate conversations. Alka-Seltzer's "Try it, you'll like it" advertisements also appeared to generate considerable word of mouth, as did "Hot and Juicy" and "We will sell no wine before its time," and the *Blue Nun.*

Another approach is to use advertisements that ask consumers to seek information. "Tell your friends," "Ask your friends," and "Ask the person who owns one" are examples of this technique.

Demonstrations, displays, and trial usage are methods that can be used to encourage consumer experience with more expensive products. For example, color television manufacturers sell their sets to hotels and motels at low prices partly because they feel it increases the chances that consumers will purchase their brands. Similarly, new types of telephones are placed in public locations because the practice is thought to accelerate adoption. Automobile manufacturers make deals with the rental companies on cars like the Lincoln *Continental,* (at Budget-Rent-a-Car) or the AMC *Eagle* in snow country rental locations.

Summary and Evaluation

In spite of the impressive amount of research that has been done on how consumers use personal sources of information, little information has been given to the problems involved in practically implementing these processes. Specific questions about how to combine mass media and word-of-mouth advertising are rarely raised, let alone studied. Yet the potential benefits to marketers can be impressive. Consider:

1. Advertising of a certain type for a household product was able, over a period of several months, to increase steadily word-of-mouth activity, particularly among people who might be regarded as prospective users of the product.

2. A study of a novel consumer service found that 73 percent of consumers who had tried the service as the result of direct-mail advertising, and who had responded to a mail questionnaire, indicated that they had recommended the service to friends and relatives. Furthermore, 8 percent of these respondents claimed that they had told at least ten people about the new service.

3. One company in a highly competitive consumer product category regularly spent only one-third as much on advertising as its two major competitors, yet retained a market share roughly equal to that of the two leading competitors. The apparent reason for their ability to succeed with relatively little advertising was the fact that their brand received vastly more word-of-mouth activity than did the other two brands, which had about the same market shares. The other brands were moved by muscle. The word-of-mouth brand had developed an advertising program that apparently aroused curiosity, which, in turn, stimulated some of the information seeking. In addition, the company had a good product that was well regarded by certain opinion leaders, and this resulted in favorable word-of-mouth activity.[69]

Research designed to discover the success requirements for the above types of strategies is necessary if the gap between research findings and operational strategies is to be bridged.

At the present stage of development it seems appropriate to conclude that whatever use is made of personal sources of information, it is necessary that advertising and distribution strategies be coordinated and consistent with personal communication. The firm needs to monitor informal channels to determine how actively they are being used, as well as the content of the communications.

Summary

This chapter discussed the personal-sources component of the search and alternative evaluation stage in the decision-making process. The first part of the chapter documented the fact that interpersonal communications are very influential in many purchasing decisions. These conversations usually occur between consumers who have similar characteristics, providing the referent is perceived to be competent and there is sufficient proximity to facilitate the interaction. Attribution theory offers an explanation for some forms of interpersonal influence.

The second part of the chapter discussed communications interactions in greater detail, noting both the consistencies and inconsistencies with the generalizations advanced earlier. Techniques for isolating opinion leaders were identified and evaluated and the characteristics of opinion leaders were described.

Alternative models of interpersonal communications and personal influence were presented in the last section of the chapter. It was concluded that the two-step flow hypothesis is no longer an accurate depiction of the processes involved. Consequently, an effort was made to synthesize the relevant literature into a provisional multistep interaction model and to identify some ideas and guidelines for future research projects.

Finally, this chapter concludes that there are a number of programs that marketing organizations can implement to capitalize on nonmarketer-dominated influences on consumer search processes. These include various ways of reaching opinion leaders, ways of reaching proxy opinion leaders, and methods for stimulating information seeking.

Review and Discussion Questions

1. Can personal influence be negative as well as positive? Explain your answer.

2. Assume that you are a consultant for a manufacturer of men's clothing. Discuss how you would go about identifying campus opinion leaders.

---

[69]Cox, *Risk Taking*, 185-186.

3. Describe the two-step flow hypothesis. Is this hypothesis a complete model of communication flows? Why or why not?

4. Recall the last time you volunteered information to someone about a product or service. What caused you to talk about the product or service? How does this compare with the general reasons that opinion leaders pass on information?

5. How do opinion leaders differ from those they influence?

6. Why do consumers seek information from opinion leaders?

7. Your company manufactures a full line of mobile homes in all price ranges. Several studies have indicated that personal sources of information are considerably more effective than other sources. Prepare a statement indicating (a) the alternative strategies that can be employed to utilize effectively consumers' use of personal information sources, and (b) the alternative that you prefer and why.

8. Assume that you are a public relations consultant for a state medical association that is concerned about the attitudes of the general public about malpractice claims. Specifically, the concern is that a general view may be developing that filing a malpractice claim against a doctor is an easy way to pay one's medical bills or to get something for nothing. Using the knowledge from this chapter, what advice would you give the state medical association?

Have you ever watched a stone fall into a pool of water? From the initial splash, concentric circles move out through the rest of the pool. At first the small waves reach only the area immediately surrounding the splash, but with time the widening waves reach across the expanse of water into nearly every area of the pool.

The acceptance of a new product by large numbers of people is in some ways analogous to the waves caused by a stone dropped into the pool. A few people purchase a product. Those around the initial purchasers then try the product, and eventually the acceptance of the product may diffuse throughout the entire population.

From this simple illustration, however, there are a number of questions that can be asked about the diffusion of new products:

1. How is the initial splash accomplished? Are certain types of people more likely than others to accept new products? Can we predict ahead of time who these people will be?

2. How rapidly do the waves of acceptance of new products move from those who are the first to adopt to other members of the population?

3. What is the pattern of the waves of acceptance that move through the population?

4. How can the diffusion process be influenced by interpersonal communications and marketing activity?

These questions illustrate the importance of understanding the diffusion process defined as the *process by which adoption of new products or ideas spreads through the population.*

Importance of New Product Decisions

Diffusion has spawned much research in the past few decades. This research has been prompted by a variety of micro- and macrosocietal problems. Three specific problems have caused the interest in learning how consumers react to new ideas and products.

The first problem is the economic waste caused by investing resources in the introduction of new products that are rejected by consumers. A study of leading companies by Booz-Allen & Hamilton reported that only one new product is successful out of each 58 ideas.[1] In the food-processing areas, Buzzell and Nourse found that only about two out of each 58 ideas are successful new products.[2] These failures are expensive and can cost millions of dollars.[3] Furthermore, firms often make serious errors in their prediction of sales levels of products that do succeed. Tull found in a study of 63 new products an average error of sales forecasts of 65 percent and an average error for profit forecasts for 53 new products of 128 percent.[4]

The second reason for concern with diffusion research is the desire to persuade people to accept socially desirable ideas and products. Rural sociologists have been particularly interested and helpful in obtaining acceptance of new ideas that contribute to increased efficiency in farming practices or the health of a community. The motivation for such studies stems from the notion that people should change to what is good for society. This has led to research (with the goal of changing behavior) on improved sanitation techniques, birth control methods, and increased use of political information. This is sometimes referred to as *social marketing,* a topic we will return to in the last chapter of this book.

A third reason for studying diffusion lies in the criticality of new product acceptance in the survival and growth of contemporary business firms. Growth industries in advanced economies have relied heavily on new products to attain that growth. The product life-cycle, which you probably studied in a basic marketing course, is shown in Figure 13.1 and you may want to review it. Just as all products grow and mature, so do they decline and fail. Thus, new product introduction and life-cycle renewal are major responsibilities of marketing managers.

In the product life-cycle, profit margins peak during the latter state of the growth phase and then continuously decline during subsequent stages. Profits of a firm are therefore enormously affected by the success of new products. A company must systematically introduce new products and/or modified products not only to maintain sales volume but in order to command adequate margins and profits. Planning of aspects of the firm's marketing program is very much affected by the product life-cycle as Figure 13.1 shows.[5] The problem is exacerbated by what Olshavsky and others show to be a rate of adoption of innovations that is increasing over time, causing a rapidly shortening product life-cycle.[6]

[1]*Management of New Products* (New York: Booz-Allen & Hamilton, 1965).

[2]Robert D. Buzzell and Robert E. M. Nourse, *Product Innovation in Food Processing 1954-1964* (Boston: Division of Research, Harvard Business School, 1967).

[3]Theodore L. Angelus, "Why Do Most New Products Fail?" *Advertising Age* (March 24, 1969), 85-86.

[4]Donald S. Tull, "The Relationship of Actual and Predicted Sales and Profits in New-Product Introductions," *Journal of Business* (July 1967), 233-250.

[5]For amplification of this topic see Roger Blackwell, David Kollat and James Robeson, *Marketing Management: A Strategic Approach* (Hinsdale, Ill.: Dryden Press, 1982), ch. 12.

[6]Richard Olshavsky, "Time and the Rate of Adoption of Innovations," *Journal of Consumer Research* (March 1980), 425-428.

Figure 13.1
Impact of the Product Life-Cycle on Marketing

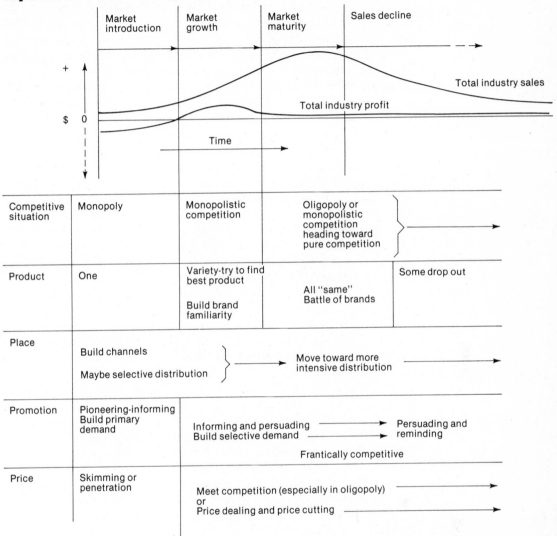

Source: Adapted by permission from Jerome McCarthy and Andrew Brogowicz, *Basic Marketing: A Managerial Approach* (Homewood, Illinois: Richard D. Irwin, Inc., 1981), 308 and 313.

WHY ALL THE FUSS ABOUT DIFFUSION?

You might be asking, Why should there be an entire chapter on the diffusion of new products? There are three primary answers to the question.

The first reason for a special chapter about diffusion is the emphasis placed upon the *social structure of communication rather than on the individual.* This relational approach to consumer decisions places the emphasis upon the flow of information between consumers rather than on the processing of the information by an individual consumer. A *relational* approach to how new products are adopted examines how social-structural variables affect diffusion flows in a system, analyzes the networks of communication flows on a sociometric basis and is concerned about the attitudes and behavior of other persons (non-adopters) in the social structure. A *monadic* approach, in contrast, focuses upon the personal and social characteristics of individual consumers.[7] Although the theory used in diffusion research is relational, much of the research, reported later in this chapter, is monadic in approach.

A second reason for a chapter on the topic of diffusion of innovation is the importance of the adoption process. *Adoption* is defined as the *process by which an individual becomes committed to continued use of an innovation.* Adoption includes not just the act of buying a new product but also includes the mental and behavioral sequence through which consumer's progress, potentially leading to acceptance and continued use of a product or brand.[8] Without the adoption process, there is no adaptation in the society and no opportunity for marketing organizations.

A third reason for studying diffusion of innovations in a special chapter is the quantity of research that has accumulated about this subject and the diversity of disciplines that have contributed to that research. At least 12 identifiable disciplines have studied the diffusion of innovations. These include anthropology, sociology, rural sociology, education, medical sociology, communication, marketing, agricultural economics, psychology, general economics, geography, and industrial engineering.

The most influential research in the diffusion literature is that done by Everett Rogers, whose book *Diffusion of Innovations,* provided the basic structure for diffusion research in marketing and other disciplines.[9] Over 400 empirical studies on the adoption of new products existed before Rogers wrote his book, so he did not originate the field. Nevertheless, his book brought together research from many disciplines and served to publicize the topic as a respectable academic discipline. Later publications and revisions[10] have continued to summarize the more than 2,000 studies of diffusion and have provided guidelines for research for marketing and other disciplines to branch out from this basic framework.[11]

Diffusion studies completed outside the marketing discipline are

[7]Everett M. Rogers, "New Product Adoption and Diffusion," *Journal of Consumer Research* (March 1976), 290-301, especially see Table 2 on 298.

[8]Thomas S. Robertson, "A Critical Examination of 'Adoption Process' Models of Consumer Behavior," in Jagdish Sheth (ed.), *Models of Buyer Behavior* (New York: Harper & Row, 1974), 271-295.

[9]Everett Rogers, *Diffusion of Innovations* (Glencoe, Ill.: The Free Press, 1965 and 1971).

[10]Everett Rogers and F. Floyd Shoemaker, *Communications Innovations* (New York: The Free Press, 1971); Everett Rogers, *Communication Strategies for Family Planning* (New York: The Free Press, 1973); Everett Rogers and Rehka Agarwala-Rogers, *Communication in Organizations* (New York: The Free Press, 1976).

[11]Everett M. Rogers, "A Personal History of Research on the Diffusion of Innovations," in Alan R. Andreasen and Seymour Sudman (eds.), *Public Policy and Marketing Thought* (Chicago: American Marketing Association, 1976), 43-63.

often of interest to consumer analysts because the studies involve consumer products. Some of the products studied in well-known diffusion studies include health-care practices, child-rearing practices, health insurance, leisure and recreational activities, new synthetic fabrics, floridation, self-medication, new food products, durable goods, auto insurance, women's apparel, the selection of a physician, new drug products, new retail stores, automobiles and automobile services, vacations, furniture, movies (such as "In Cold Blood"), and new types of telephones.[12]

Marketing strategists must use care in applying detailed findings of the diffusion traditions to marketing problems because of such differences in studies as type of innovation, type of respondents and so forth. But, in general, the consistency between disciplines is one of the basic reasons for the impact diffusion research has achieved.

ELEMENTS OF THE DIFFUSION PROCESS

The diffusion process has four basic elements, or analytical units. These elements or structural variables have been identified as: (1) the innovation, (2) the communication of the innovation among individuals, (3) the social system, and (4) time.[13]

The Innovation

An innovation can be defined in a variety of ways. The most commonly accepted definition, however, is that an *innovation* is *any idea or product perceived by the potential innovator to be new.* This may be called a *subjective* definition of innovation, since it is derived from the thought structure of a particular individual.[14]

Innovations can also be defined *objectively* on the basis of criteria external to the potential adopter. The anthropologist Barnett described innovations in such a way, defining them as "any thought, behavior, or thing that is new because it is qualitatively different from existing forms."[15] In consumer behavior, classifying an innovation using this definition focuses upon product characteristics to determine if differences occur between new products and previously existing ones. The question that arises is how different a new product must be to be considered qualitatively different. Look at Figure 13.2 for an example of a "questionably new" product.

The *operational* definition of innovation that is frequently used by consumer researchers is, "any form of a product that has recently become available in a market." Using this definition, an innovation is a brand of coffee that was not previously available in a given geographical

[12]For a review of diffusion research by marketing researchers as well as studies in other disciplines of interest to marketing analysts, see Charles W. King, "Adoption and Diffusion Research in Marketing: An Overview," in Raymond M. Haas (ed.), *Science, Technology and Marketing* (Chicago: American Marketing Association, 1966), 665-684; and Johan Arndt, "New Product Diffusion: The Interplay of Innovativeness, Opinion Leadership, Learning, Perceived Risk and Product Attributes," in Sheth, *Models*, 327-335.

[13]Everett Rogers, *Diffusion of Innovations*, 12-20. This conceptualization is retained in the later edition by Rogers and Shoemaker.

[14]This definition is used by Rogers, *Communication*, 13; King, "Adoption and Diffusion," 666.

[15]H. G. Barnett, *Innovation: The Basis of Cultural Change* (New York: McGraw-Hill, 1953), 7.

**Figure 13.2
Possibly an
Unneeded Product**

"Until this moment, I never realized we needed a food chopper
with a built-in transistor radio."

Source: *Wall Street Journal* (April 22, 1977), 18. Courtesy of Sidney Harris/Wall Street Journal

area. Other examples include modifications of existing products, such as
new features in the annual model change on automobiles or a new package for a food. An innovation can also be, of course, a totally new product such as television, video games, hospital computers or automobile
diagnostic centers. It can also be the opening of a new retail store.

In many *marketing studies* an innovation is defined as any product
that has achieved less than x percentage of market penetration. Typically, innovations are operationally defined as new products which have
not attained 10 percent (of their ultimate) market share.

The variety of definitions of innovation dictates an important caveat:
diffusion findings developed in varied research traditions do not necessarily apply to all types of new-product purchase decisions. Most of the
research in the diffusion tradition was conducted on major technological
innovations which are often high-involvement products. The process may
differ considerably when the innovation is a product of less consequence,
although this area needs further investigation.

There is a need for a classification system to handle widely differing
types of product innovations. One such classification system is based on
the impact of the innovation on the social structure accepting the innovation. In this taxonomic system, innovations may be classified as: (1)
continuous, (2) dynamically continuous, and (3) discontinuous.

1. A *continuous innovation* has the least disrupting influence on established patterns. Modification of an existing product is characteristic of this
type rather than the establishment of a totally new product. Examples
include adding fluoride to toothpaste, new-model automobile change-
overs, adding menthol to cigarettes.

2. A *dynamically continuous innovation* has more disrupting effects than
a continuous innovation, although it still does not generally alter established patterns of customer buying and product use. It may involve the
creation of a new product or the alteration of an existing product. Exam-

ples include electric toothbrushes, the *Mustang* automobile, *touch-tone* telephones.

3. A *discontinuous innovation* involves the introduction of an entirely new product that causes buyers to alter significantly their behavior patterns. Examples: television, computers.[16]

Many of the conflicting findings that exist in the diffusion literature stem from the fact that diffusion models developed for dynamically continuous or discontinuous innovations are being applied to research on continuous innovations. This may be appropriate in developing a broad conceptual framework for analyzing innovations, but when applied to such details as the amount of decision making involved in a purchase or the sources of information, the assumption that the same generalizations are applicable to each type of innovation is tenuous. Unfortunately, research on the marketing of new products often has not clarified these issues.

Communication

Communications are central to the study of diffusion and may be of two types, informal and formal. *Informal* communications are nonmarketer-dominated, such as reference-group and family influences. There is a temptation to assume that the people who first adopt a product are the ones who influence others to purchase and that their communications are therefore instrumental in the diffusion process. Interpersonal influence appears to be much more complex, however.[17]

Formal communications are those dominated by marketers. They include advertising, various forms of reseller support, and personal salespersons. When control of communications is possible, questions arise such as these: What types of media are most likely to transmit messages to those persons who are most likely to be the first adopters of an innovation? What media are most likely to be considered authoritative? What messages are most likely to influence new product acceptance?

Understanding the role of communications in the diffusion process is sufficiently important to justify a special section later in the chapter describing what is known about this topic.

The Social System

The diffusion of innovations is a social phenomenon. The word diffusion has little meaning except as it relates to a group of people. Adoption or rejection of a product refers to an individual person, but diffusion refers to a group or society of individuals. Consequently, diffusion research should focus not only on characteristics of a decision-making unit (individual or family) but also on the environment provided by the social system.

The diffusion of new product adoption is a temporal phenomenon and needs to be analyzed as such. The decision to adopt a new product, like all other consumption decisions described by the model in this book,

[16]Thomas S. Robertson, "The Process of Innovation and the Diffusion of Innovation," *Journal of Marketing* (January 1967), 14-19, at 15.

[17]Thomas S. Robertson, "Group Characteristics and Aggregate Innovative Behavior: Preliminary Report," in Sheth, *Models*, 310-326.

is a *process rather than an event.* People recognize problems, search for alternatives, evaluate new products as potential alternatives, decide to purchase the new product, and perhaps eventually purchase it. The adoption process is not considered complete, however, until postpurchase evaluation and repeat usage or purchases are generated. This is because adoption implies the decision to continue full use of an innovation.[18] To study the rate of diffusion in a social structure, it is necessary to evaluate the exact position of individual consumers in the process that leads to adoption.

There is a striking incongruity between the theoretical concept of adoption as a process and the way it is often measured. The theoretical concept of adopter should be measured by determining the intention of the consumer to incorporate the new product into his or her habitual pattern of consumption. In actual practice, the measurement of adoption is usually a "has or has not purchased" measure. If a consumer is observed to have purchased a new product or patronized a new store, the person is considered to be an adopter. Those who have not done so at the time of the study are considered to be nonadopters. This may cause misleading results when the product has been purchased as well as when it has not been purchased. This can happen because of some variable unrelated to the consumer's long-run intention to adopt the product (such as an out-of-stock situation for the consumer's true preference); or when the consumer has begun the process that leads to adoption (such as deciding in the mind to try the product at the next purchase occasion) but has not yet purchased the new product.

The Adoption Process

The adoption process is multistage in nature, as shown in Figure 13.3, with several kinds of variables that influence each stage.[19] The stages described below are knowledge, persuasion, decision (which may lead to adoption or rejection), and confirmation. However, Zaltman and Wallendorf have described the adoption process as having nine identifiable stages.[20]

Knowledge Awareness

The *knowledge* stage begins when a consumer receives physical or social stimuli that gives exposure and attention to the innovation's existence and some understanding of how it functions. The consumer becomes aware of the product but has made no judgment concerning the relevance of the product to an existing problem or need.

Knowledge is a result of selective perception, but beyond this many questions remain unanswered. Do some consumers have more knowledge of new products in general than do other consumers? Of all the information about new products constantly bombarding the consumer,

---

[18]Rogers, *Communication,* 17.
[19]This section is a condensation of Rogers and Shoemaker, 10-33.
[20]Gerold Zaltman and Melanie Wallendorf, *Consumer Behavior* (New York: John Wiley & Sons, 1979).

Figure 13.3
Paradigm of the Innovation-Decision Process
(for simplicity, only consequences of process
are shown, not of innovation)

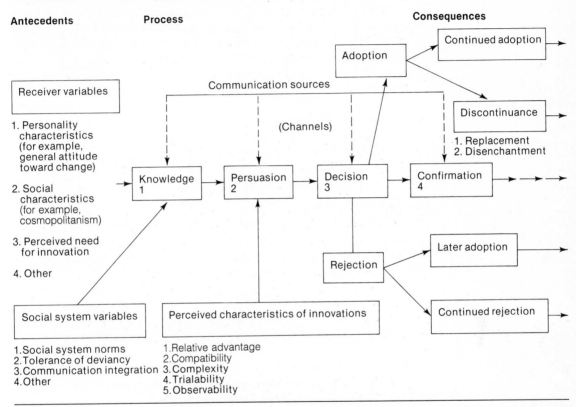

Antecedents   Process   Consequences

Source: Reprinted with permission of Macmillan Publishing Co., Inc., from *Communication Innovations* by Everett M. Rogers and F. Floyd Shoemaker. Copyright © 1971 by The Free Press, a division of the Macmillan Company.

what makes some information have an impact and be remembered while other information has no impact and is lost to consciousness?

Persuasion

Persuasion, in the Rogers-Shoemaker paradigm, refers to the formation of favorable or unfavorable attitudes toward the innovation. During evaluation, the individual may mentally imagine how satisfactory the new idea might be in some anticipated future use situation before deciding whether to try it (called "vicarious trial").

Persuasiveness is related to perceived risk in the new product. When an individual considers a new product, s/he must weigh the potential gains from adopting the product against the potential losses from switching from the product now used. If the new product is adopted, it may be inferior to a present product, or the cost (price of the product plus possible disadvantages) may be greater than the increased value. Thus, adopting the new product has a risk that can be avoided by postponing acceptance until the value has been clearly established. If, however, the product is designed to solve a problem that is of significant concern to the consumer, there is also the risk that value may be lost by delaying adoption of a product that is truly superior to the present product.

The consumer can reduce the risk of adopting the new product—and therefore uncertainty about the buying situation—by acquiring additional information. A person may seek out news stories, pay particular attention to advertising for the product, subscribe to product-rating services, talk with individuals who have already tried the product, talk with experts on the subject, or in some instances, even try the product on a limited basis. Each of these information search and evaluation strategies, however, has an economic and/or psychological cost. Moreover, they are unlikely to yield information that will completely reduce uncertainty.

Decision

The *decision* stage involves activities that lead to a choice between adopting or rejecting the innovation. The immediate consideration is whether or not to try the innovation, which is often influenced by the ability to try the innovation on a small scale (including vicarious trial by observing the use of the innovation by others). Innovations that can be divided are generally adopted more readily. Trial can sometimes be stimulated by the use of free samples. Perceived risk can also be reduced by allowing the consumer to buy a trial quantity smaller than what is normally bought.[21]

Figure 13.3 shows that the output of decision can be either rejection or adoption. Rejection can be continuous or may be reversed by later adoption. Conversely, adoption may be continuous or may lead to later discontinuance.

Confirmation

Confirmation refers to the process through which consumers seek reinforcement for the innovation decision. Consumers sometimes reverse previous decisions, especially when exposed to conflicting messages about the innovation. This state involves the issue of cognitive dissonance, discussed in a later chapter.

Discontinuance is, of course, as serious a concern to marketers as the original process of adoption. The rate of discontinuance may be just as important as the rate of adoption, with the corresponding need for marketing strategies to devote attention to preventing discontinuance of innovations. Rogers and Shoemaker report that later adopters are more likely to discontinue innovations than earlier adopters and are generally

---

[21]Robert Shoemaker and F. R. Shoaf, "Behavioral Changes in the Trial of New Products," *Journal of Consumer Research* (September 1975), 104-109.

likely to have the opposite characteristics (in education, social status, change agency contact, and the like) to those of the innovators. Offutt found discontinuance is most likely to occur when the innovation is not integrated into the practices and way of life of purchasers, or when the innovation conflicts with other aspects of consumer life-styles.[22]

Marketing and the Rogers Paradigm

The early Rogers paradigm and the revised Rogers-Shoemaker paradigm serve as theoretical models for diffusion research by consumer analysts. In spite of its emphasis on the process approach, however, the Rogers approach has generated limited amounts of process research in the consumer behavior field. Instead, diffusion research typically has treated adoption as dichotomous (that is, adopt or reject).

A more serious problem is that the Rogers paradigm deals mostly with discontinous innovations, whereas most marketing decisions involve continuous or dynamically continuous innovations. Conceptually, it is probably helpful to use a general model of consumer behavior that permits analysis of all types of products. The determination of when a product is sufficiently different to be an innovation fitting the conditions of the Rogers paradigm and when it is merely a modification of an existing product appears to be an arbitrary decision.

CORRELATES OF NEW PRODUCT SUCCESS

Will a new product be a success or will it fail? If you can make accurate predictions about that topic, you will have a highly desired ability. It is natural therefore that marketing analysts should study with great interest the findings about diffusion of innovation seeking clues to predict and enhance new product acceptance.

When a major bank—one with a reputation for successful introduction of innovative products and services—introduced Electronic Funds Transfer (EFT) to its city, the bank first carefully studied findings from the diffusion research tradition. Marketing officers of the bank made predictions from the literature about the economic, social, personal and communication characteristics most likely to be associated with trial and adoption of EFT. The introductory site was chosen to match the characteristics of innovators, as described in the literature. A communications program was developed on the basis of mass media to create awareness and interest and personal influence to induce trial, with a series of special meetings at clubs and organizations where opinion leaders could be shown the new bank machines.

What does the research about diffusion and adoption reveal? Over 2,700 publications have reported studies on this topic. Of these, 1,800 report empirical research and 900 report nonempirical analyses or dis-

[22]Nancy Offutt, *"Perception of Product Attributes and the Innovation Decision Process,"* PhD dissertation (Columbus: The Ohio State University, 1981).

**Table 13.1
Consumer
Characteristics
Related to
Innovativeness**

	Number of Empirical Findings Indicating Relation to Innovativeness (percent)					Total Number of Published Findings
	Positive	**None**	**Negative**	**Conditional**	**Total**	
Sociodemographic						
(1) Education	74.6	16.1	5.2	4.1	100	193
(2) Literacy	70.4	22.2	3.7	3.7	100	27
(3) Income	80.3	10.7	6.3	2.7	100	112
(4) Level of living	82.5	10.0	2.5	5.0	100	40
(5) Age	32.3	40.5	17.7	9.5	100	158
Attitudinal						
(6) Knowledgeability	78.8	16.7	1.5	3.0	100	66
(7) Attitude toward change	73.6	14.5	8.2	3.8	100	159
(8) Achievement motivation	64.7	23.5	0.0	11.8	100	17
(9) Aspirations for children	82.6	8.7	4.3	4.3	100	23
(10) Business orientation	60.0	20.0	20.0	0.0	100	5
(11) Satisfaction with life	28.6	28.6	42.8	0.0	100	7
(12) Empathy	75.0	0.0	25.0	0.0	100	4
(13) Mental rigidity	20.8	25.0	50.0	4.2	100	24

Source: Modified with special permission from Everett M. Rogers and J. David Stanfield, "Adoption and Diffusion of New Products: Emerging Generalizations and Hypotheses," paper presented at the Conference on the Application of Sciences to Marketing Management, Purdue University (July 12-15, 1966), Tables 4 and 5.

cussions.[23] The following paragraphs summarize the findings of Rogers' synthesis of this literature under the general categories of *consumer characteristics* associated with innovativeness, *product characteristics* associated with acceptance of new products, and *communication variables* associated with diffusion.

Consumer Characteristics Associated with Innovativeness

Some variables are correlated with innovativeness or adoption of new products. These results are shown in Table 13.1. *Sociodemographic variables* most correlated with early adoption are education, literacy, income, and level of living. *Attitudinal variables* most often correlated with early adoption include aspirations for children, knowledgeability (awareness that an individual has of the external world and events in general), and attitude toward change. Mental rigidity or satisfaction with life leads to rejection of innovations.[24]

[23]Everett Rogers and P. C. Thomas, *Bibliography on the Diffusion of Innovations* (Ann Arbor, Mich.: Department of Population Planning, University of Michigan, 1975).

[24]Everett M. Rogers and J. David Stanfield, "Adoption and Diffusion of New Products: Emerging Generalizations and Hypotheses," paper presented at the Conference on the Application of Sciences to Marketing Management, Purdue University (July 12-15, 1966).

Marketing Applications

Much effort has been directed toward profiling of innovators in a manner helpful to marketing strategists.[25] Income is almost always important in profiling the innovator. Sometimes it is more useful to use the concept of *privilegedness* than income. This refers to the amount of income an individual has relative to the other individuals with whom s/he normally associates.[26] When the product is a frequently purchased low-priced product, however, income (and education and occupation) may have little relation to early adoption.[27] In one study a curvilinear relationship was found between income and innovativeness, with the middle-income group containing fewer innovators because of unwillingness to take risks.[28]

Marketing strategists probably should assume that income will be important in profiling the innovator but it should be weighed in direct proportion to the price of innovation. Also, the ability to try or to sample the new product with little risk may mitigate the importance of income in innovation.

Social status appears also to be positively related to consumer innovation. Using the Reiss index of occupational status, one study revealed that among the earliest adopters of a new automobile service, one in three had an occupational index higher than 75. This is compared to a ratio of only one in seven for the population at large (or noninnovators). The 75-point level of the socioeconomic index consists of only the highest status professions such as architects, scientists, lawyers, doctors, engineers, auditors, and top management positions.[29]

Highly mobile people are more likely to be early adopters of new products. Shaw found that people who traveled extensively, had advanced in their jobs and income, and moved around were more likely to accept new products than stay-at-homes, even with income held constant.[30] *Heavy users* of a product were found by King[31] to be more likely to accept a new style of millinery, although this was not found to be true for heavy coffee users when faced with a new brand of coffee.[32]

Of various personality or attitudinal variables that explain early adoption by consumers, the most explanatory is *venturesomeness.* Robertson

[25]An excellent summary and synthesis of this literature is available in Thomas S. Robertson, *Innovative Behavior and Communication* (New York: Holt, Rinehart and Winston, 1971). The authors express their gratitude for Professor Robertson's kind permission to rely heavily on his book in the revision of this chapter.

[26]Richard P. Coleman, "The Significance of Social Stratification in Selling," in Martin L. Bell (ed.), *Marketing: A Maturing Discipline* (Chicago: American Marketing Association, 1960), 171-184.

[27]Frank et al., "The Determinants of Innovative Behavior," 318.

[28]Frank Cancian, "Stratification and Risk-Taking: A Theory Tested on Agricultural Innovation," *American Sociological Review* (December 1967), 912-927.

[29]Robert J. Kegerreis, James F. Engel, and Roger D. Blackwell, "Innovativeness and Diffusiveness: A Marketing View of the Characteristics of Earliest Adopters," in Kollat et al., *Research in Consumer Behavior,* 671-689, at 678.

[30]Stephen J. Shaw, "Behavioral Science Offers Fresh Insights on New Product Acceptance," *Journal of Marketing* (January 1965), 9-14, at 10.

[31]Charles W. King, "The Innovator in the Fashion Adoption Process," in Smith, *Reflections,* 324-339, at 335.

[32]Frank et al., "The Determinants of Innovative Behavior," 318-320.

and Kennedy found that the trait of venturesomeness was able to explain about 35 percent of the difference between innovators and noninnovators for a new telephone product.[33] Jacoby found in a study of 15 product categories that *openmindedness* was significantly related to innovative responses.[34] Scores on *dogmatism* have also been investigated as a variable in innovativeness. Jacoby found that persons *low in dogmatism* were most likely to be innovators and the findings of Jacoby have been substantially supported in a replication by Coney.[35]

In a study of Ford *Maverick* buyers, when that car was first introduced, the early adopters were found to be more *inner directed* than *other directed*. This study used Kassarjian's *I. O. Social Preference Scale* and is also significant as it found that the early adopters of a new product may be significantly different in social character than later adopters of the same new product.[36]

Innovativeness: Who are the prime prospects? If there are some people who are more likely to adopt new products—who are innovation prone—marketing executives would like to know who they are. Such persons are said to possess the characteristic of innovativeness.

Innovativeness is usually defined as the *degree to which an individual is relatively earlier in adopting an innovation than other members in the system.* The construct is measured in one of two ways in the marketing literature. The first measure is based upon time of adoption, such as those *individuals who purchase in the first X weeks, months, etc.* The second measure is a count of *how many of a prespecified list of new products a particular individual has purchased at the time of the survey.*[37]

Everyone has some degree of innovativeness. Hirschman explains the importance of understanding this principle:

Few concepts in the behavioral sciences have as much immediate relevance to consumer behavior as innovativeness. The propensities of consumers to adopt novel products, whether they are ideas, goods, or services, can play an important role in theories of brand loyalty, decision making, preference, and communication. If there were no such characteristics as innovativeness, consumer behavior would consist of a series of routine buying responses to a static set of products. It is the inherent willingness of a consuming population

---

[33]Thomas S. Robertson and James N. Kennedy, "Prediction of Consumer Innovators: Application of Multiple Discriminant Analysis," *Journal of Marketing Research* (February 1968), 64-69.

[34]Jacob Jacoby, "A Multiple-Indicant Approach for Studying Innovators," *Purdue Papers in Consumer Psychology*, no. 108 (Lafayette, Ind.: Purdue University, 1970).

[35]Jacob Jacoby, "Personality and Innovation Proneness," *Journal of Marketing Research* (May 1971), 244-247; Kenneth A. Coney, "Dogmatism and Innovation: A Replication," *Journal of Marketing Research* (November 1972), 453-455. Inconclusive results were obtained, however, in Brian Blake, Robert Perloff, and Richard Heslin, "Dogmatism and Acceptance of New Products," *Journal of Marketing Research* (November 1970), 483-486.

[36]James H. Donnelly, Jr. and John M. Ivancevich, "A Methodology for Identifying Innovator Characteristics of New Brand Purchasers," *Journal of Marketing Research* (August 1974), 331-334.

[37]David F. Midgley and Grahame R. Dowling, "Innovativeness: The Concept and Its Measurement," *Journal of Consumer Research* (March 1978), 229-241.

to innovate that gives the marketplace its dynamic nature. On an individual basis, every consumer is, to some extent, an innovator; all of us over the course of our lives adopt some objects or ideas that are new in our perception.[38]

The question of innovation proneness has been investigated in studies to see if the person who is an innovator for one product is also the innovator of other products. Robertson and Myers found that appliance, clothing, and food innovators were statistically related but with such a low level of correlation as to dispute the notion of a general trait of innovativeness.[39] Arndt concluded that a general receptiveness to innovation exists, but his investigation was in closely related product lines related to food consumption.[40]

The earliest adopters of a new automobile service, compared to the population as a whole, were found to be:

1. Much more willing to experiment with new ideas,

2. More likely to buy new products (in general) earlier,

3. Less likely to switch brands because of a small change,

4. Less interested in low price *per se,*

5. Less likely to try new convenience items if the innovation represented only minor changes.[41]

The success of this study opened up consideration that AIO questions might be used to identify innovative prone persons. Questions were included on the socioeconomic and attitudinal characteristics associated with innovativeness in a psychographic study. Persons who strongly agreed with those questions (such as "Generally, I approve of the feminist movement," representing attitude toward change and "I often go to a symphony concert" representing cosmopolitanism) were counted on five traits the literature suggested were associated with innovativeness. Using this process, innovators were identified and were 2.5 percent of the sample. The behavior of those determined by the scale to be innovators was measured concerning two innovations at that time—disco dancing and a new type of city magazine. The persons identified as innovators were much higher in their acceptance of these two innovations than the population.[42] While this is exploratory research, the process could be valuable to a firm because of the need to identify potential adopters before a new product is introduced. If they can be identified,

[38]Elizabeth C. Hirschman, "Innovativeness, Novelty Seeking, and Consumer Creativity," *Journal of Consumer Research* (December 1980), 283-295, at 283.

[39]Thomas S. Robertson and James H. Myers, "Personality Correlates of Opinion Leadership and Innovative Buying Behavior," *Journal of Marketing Research* (May 1969), 164-168.

[40]Johan Arndt, "Profiling Consumer Innovators," in Johan Arndt (ed.), *Insights into Consumer Behavior* (Boston: Allyn and Bacon, 1968), 71-83.

[41]Kegerreis et al., "Innovativeness," 687.

[42]Roger D. Blackwell, H. Lee Mathews, and Thomas M. Murnane, "A Psychological Testing Scale for Innovativeness Utilizing Five Major Traits," Working Paper (Columbus: The Ohio State University, March 1981), ch. 3.

**Figure 13.4
Adoptive and
Vicarious
Innovativeness**

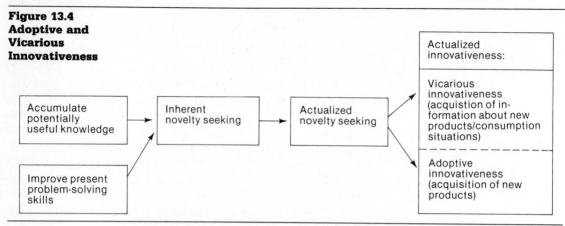

Source: Elizabeth C. Hirschman, "Innovativeness, Novelty Seeking, and Consumer Creativity," *Journal of Consumer Research* (December 1980), 283–295. Reprinted by permission.

media and other marketing activity can be targeted more efficiently in the introduction of new products.

While innovativeness may not exist across all products, there is hope for marketers. After a rigorous assessment of the literature in this area, Robertson concluded, "The consistency of innovativeness cannot be expected across product categories, but can be expected within product categories, and, sometimes, between related product categories."[43]

An individual may possess a trait of innovativeness but not actually be an adopter of the product. Situational variables may prevent the person from adopting (trying and liking) the product. The person could, however, "try" the product in the person's mind. Figure 13.4 shows how an inherent novelty seeker might be either an adopter or merely exhibit *vicarious* innovativeness.

**Product
Characteristics**

The acceptance of a new product by innovators is determined to a large degree by characteristics of the product itself or what consumers perceive the product to be. Product characteristics associated with the early adoption of the product are presented in Table 13.2 and are described briefly below.

Relative advantage of the new product is an important determinant of a product's success. The product must be perceived by consumers to be superior to the product it supersedes or to offer a benefit recognized as more attractive than present products. Similarly, the stronger the fulfillment of felt needs as perceived by the consumer, the more readily s/he seeks information about a new product, maintains interest, and undertakes trial and adoption. The more immediate the benefit, the more likely the consumer is to try the product. This same principle applies in

[43]Robertson, *Innovative Behavior*, ch. 3.

**Table 13.2
Product
Characteristics
Related to
Innovativeness**

	Number of Empirical Findings Indicating Relation to Innovativeness (Percent)					Total Number of Published Findings
	Positive	None	Negative	Conditional	Total	
(1) Relative advantage	78.8	15.2	3.0	3.0	100	66
(2) Compatibility	86.0	14.0	0.0	0.0	100	50
(3) Fulfillment of felt needs	92.6	3.7	3.7	0.0	100	27
(4) Complexity	18.8	37.5	43.7	0.0	100	16
(5) Trialability	42.9	42.9	14.3	0.0	100	14
(6) Observability	75.0	25.0	0.0	0.0	100	8
(7) Availability	55.6	22.2	16.7	5.6	100	18
(8) Immediacy of benefit	57.1	28.6	14.3	0.0	100	7

Source: Modified with special permission from Everett M. Rogers and J. David Stanfield, "Adoption and Diffusion of New Products: Emerging Generalizations and Hypotheses," paper presented at the Conference on the Application of Sciences to Marketing Management, Purdue University (July 12-15, 1966), Table 7.

the adoption of innovations by organizations; the more profitable is an innovation, the greater the rate of adoption.[44]

The *compatibility* of a new product is the degree to which the product is consistent with existing values and past experiences of the adopter and is an important determinant of a new product's acceptance. The norms of the relevant reference group will retard acceptance of products that are not compatible with the social system. If the consumer perceives the product to be too similar to previously tried and rejected products, however, acceptance of the new product will also be retarded. The color and design of the package, product, and promotional material accompanying the product act as a symbol to the consumer, communicating the compatibility of the new product with existing values and cognitive structure.

The *observability* (or communicability) of an innovation influences its rate of acceptance. Products that are visible in social situations or that have significant impact upon the social system appear to be those that are most communicable.

Products must have *perceived newness* to be attractive to early triers, Lambert found.[45] Promotional messages often stress newness, of course, but it is important for marketers to assess empirically consumers' perceptions of newness before committing substantial resources to the introduction of a product which management perceives to be new.

Some product characteristics have been identified that appear to *inhibit the rate of adoption.* One such characteristic is *complexity,* or the degree to which a new product is difficult to understand and use. Prod-

[44]Joseph P. Martino, "Adopting New Ideas," *Futurist* (April 1974), 88-89; Vijay Mahajan and R. A. Peterson, "First Purchase Diffusion Models of New Product Acceptance," *Technological Forecasting and Social Change* (November 1979), 127-146.

[45]Zarrel V. Lambert, "Perceptual Patterns, Information Handling, and Innovativeness," *Journal of Marketing Research* (November 1972), 427-431.

**Table 13.3 Social and Communications Variables
Related to Innovativeness**

	Number of Empirical Findings Indicating Relation to Innovativeness (percent)					
	Positive	**None**	**Negative**	**Condi-tional**	**Total**	**Total Number of Published Findings**
(1) Cosmopolitanism	80.8	11.0	2.7	5.5	100	73
(2) Mass media exposure	85.7	12.2	0.0	2.0	100	49
(3) Contact with change agencies	91.9	6.6	0.0	1.5	100	136
(4) Deviance from norms	53.6	14.3	28.6	3.6	100	28
(5) Group participation	78.8	10.3	6.4	4.5	100	156
(6) Interpersonal communication exposure	70.0	15.0	15.0	0.0	100	40
(7) Opinion leadership	64.3	21.4	7.1	7.1	100	14

Source: Modified with special permission from Everett M. Rogers and J. David Stanfield, "Adoption and Diffusion of New Products: Emerging Generalizations and Hypotheses," paper presented at the Conference on the Application to Sciences of Marketing Management, Purdue University (July 12-15, 1966), Table 6.

ucts that require detailed personal explanation, for example, are unlikely to diffuse rapidly. Although the research is far from conclusive, it appears that the trialability of a product affects the rate of acceptance. This is due to the desire of the consumer to try the product in a small quantity before deciding to adopt it. When the consumer is forced to buy a large unit at one time, s/he is likely to perceive more risk in the purchase than if able to purchase a little at a time.

Social and Communication Variables Associated with Innovativeness

The relations between a consumer and other members and objects of the social system influence the rate of adoption of new products. The relations that affect new product acceptance are of two basic types: market dominated and nonmarket dominated. The effectiveness of one is often influenced by the other.

Marketer-Dominated Influences

Contact with the mass media and commercial change agents tends to produce people who accept innovations more readily than others. This is indicated in items 2 and 3 of Table 13.3.

The mass media affect the adoption process most strongly at the awareness stage, their most important function being to inform the public of new products or ideas. At later stages in the adoption process—evaluation and decision—personal influences become more important. Effective use of the media by marketers is complex because of the interactions of variables. In a study by Eskin, it was found that both advertising and price were important determinants of the sales levels for a new food product, but that the effectiveness of the advertising in stimulating adoption depended upon the level of price charged.[46] The more experience with a product category a potential adopter has, the more the person is likely to use advertising as an information source.[47]

The type of product or service affects the role of media also. Green, Langeard and Favell found that the print media were more important as a source of innovation for innovators of a new *service* than for innovators of a new *product.* These investigators found that heavy television viewing was a characteristic of innovators in both categories, however.[48]

Other activities under the control of the marketing organizations have a significant impact on adoption. Sampling has been shown to be one of the most effective techniques for informing consumers of a new product. Also, personal salespeople play an important role in providing information to the consumer.

Word-of-Mouth Communications

Word-of-mouth or interpersonal communications play a critical role in the adoption of new products, as indicated in item 6 of Table 13.3. As an individual moves through early stages toward adoption, s/he increasingly turns to other individuals for confirming information. The individual seeking information turns either to someone who has already purchased the new product or to an *expert*—someone who by reason of training or experience has superior ability to judge the product. For example, a consumer interested in buying a new model of a camera may ask a professional photographer or a serious camera hobbyist to help evaluate the new model. Consumers turn to personal sources of influence as the amount of perceived risk in the new product increases and when the choice between products is ambiguous.

How can a marketing organization gain control over opinion leaders—the experts that influence adoption by others? A creative effort to do this is shown in Figure 13.5 for Hoodins Restaurant. The restaurant introduced a new concept to its operation, substantially changing its operation as a general restaurant to become a high-quality beefburger specialist. How could it identify the experts on hamburgers? Hoodins found the experts by advertising for them and then bringing them together for a tasting party. The comments of the experts became part of an integrated communications program, publicizing the comments of local experts who became transmitters of information to all those who saw local people in the ads and asked them about the new product.

Word-of-mouth influence about new products is a two-way information flow. Myers and Robertson concluded that the opinion leader is moderately more innovative than nonopinion leaders and is only relatively more influential than the average person. The homemaker who is an

[46]Gerald J. Eskin, "A Case for Test Market Experiments," *Journal of Advertising Research* (April 1975), 27-33.

[47]Kjell Gronhaug, "How New Car Buyers Use Advertising," *Journal of Advertising Research* (February 1975), 49-53.

[48]Robert T. Green, Eric Langeard, and Alice C. Favell, "Innovation in the Service Sector: Some Empirical Findings," *Journal of Marketing Research* (August 1974), 323-326.

**Figure 13.5
Hoodins
Hamburger
Experts**

IT'S OFFICIAL!

Hoodins Has The World's Greatest Hamburger!

Recently, an open advertisement was placed in the Columbus Dispatch requesting that all people who considered themselves hamburger "gourmets" fill out a statement of their credentials. Of the hundreds of responses we received, eight people were selected to form an unbiased jury of "experts" to taste-test the new Hoodins hamburger. On July 25, 1977 the results were announced. Their conclusion? There are a lot of great hamburgers in the world, but only one "greatest", and Hoodins has it.

The Panel

• **Ron Sherwood,** a gourmet cook, fish and chips specialist, restaurant reviewer, five-way chili sampler and hamburger eater "extraordinaire."
• **Jennifer Cross,** a homegrown product of Columbus, her expertise in hamburger tasting is formidable. According to Jennifer, "Hamburger is king in Columbus; one merely has to visit the restaurants trafficking in such fare to become an expert."
• **Diane Euerle/Richard Euerle,** are our only husband/wife taste-testing team. This well-traveled couple has sampled hamburgers from coast-to-coast, border-

to-border. Their opinion? "A great hamburger is every bit as good as a fine continental repast."
• **Sandoll Andromeda,** is a man who considers the integrity of preparation of any meal a paramount factor to its outcome. He even goes so far as to grind the meat for his hamburger, personally.
• **Ken Brenner,** an Akron native and busy man-about-town, has found, through experience, that hamburgers are virtually the staff of life among the working class. He insists on a presentation with integrity, when his meal is served.
• **Caroline Markson,** brought to the group an international element. She has eaten hamburgers from Hawaii to Holland, from Canada to Cayman. Turtle burgers, shark burgers, perhaps tulip burgers and milk-fed veal burgers are included in her repertoire. She claims, unabashedly, to be the Carol Lawrence of Hamburgers.
• **Suzy Kramer,** considered herself a natural candidate for the panel of experts because she is a student, which automatically makes her a hamburger connoisseur; and because she is a Public Relations major at Otterbein University, who can distinguish between advertising "hyp" and a healthy hamburger.

The Comments

• "The bun was delicious, the meat was fantastic."   *—Sandoll Andromeda*
• "It's delicious...haven't tasted any better."   *—Richard Euerle*
• "One's about all you can eat...it was terrific."   *—Ken Brenner*
• "This has got to be the best hamburger I've ever had."   *—Jennifer Cross*
• "I say it *is* the world's greatest hamburger."   *—Suzy Kramer*
• "My family used to brag about my home-cooked hamburger, but I couldn't make anything as good as this."   *—Caroline Markson*
• "I can't even get my mouth around it...it's a dynamite hamburger."   *—Diane Euerle*
• "One of the largest hamburgers I've ever had ...a lot of meat...I was shocked."   *—Ron Sherwood*

Hoodins

Rt. 161 at I-71 Open Monday-Thursday, 6:30 A.M. to Midnight • Friday and Saturday, 6:30 A.M. to 2:00 A.M. • Sunday, 7:30 A.M. to 11:00 P.M.

Suzy Kramer   *Diane Euerle*   *Richard Euerle*   *Ken Brenner*

Ron Sherwood   *Jennifer Cross*   *Caroline Markson*   *Sandoll Andromeda*

These people can't all be wrong...try the World's Greatest Hamburger...Only at Hoodins.

Source: Courtesy Hoodins Restaurants and Shelly Berman Communications.

opinion leader and innovator is also a "recipient of influence, not a dominant leader influencing a passive set of followers."[49]

Marketing strategists also need concern about unfavorable as well as favorable word-of-mouth communications. Arndt found that consum-

[49]James H. Myers and Thomas S. Robertson, "Dimension of Opinion Leadership," *Journal of Marketing Research* (February 1972), 41-46.

Figure 13.5 (continued)

Be the 1st to try THE WORLD'S GREATEST HAMBURGER

If You're A Hamburger "Expert", Tell Us About It! You May Be One Of The 8 Lucky People Who Will Taste Test "The World's Greatest Hamburger."

The "World's Greatest Hamburger" is being developed right here in Columbus, and we're looking for 8 hamburger gourmets to taste test this incredible burger. To qualify for this select panel, simply complete the statement below, in 25 words or less, and mail it to: SBC, Incorporated
P.O. Box 652
Columbus, Ohio 43215

I'm a hamburger expert and should be one of the taste-testers of "The World's Greatest Hamburger" because.

All entries must be received by midnight, July 20. Taste-testers will be notified on or before August 1. All entries become the property of SBC, Inc. Judging will be the sole responsibility of SBC, Inc. and their decision will be final. Associates of SBC, Inc., their families or clients of SBC, Inc. are ineligible.

Mail entry to: SBC Incorporated, P.O. Box 652, Columbus, Oh. 43215

Source: Courtesy Hoodins Restaurants and Shelly Berman Communications.

ers who received unfavorable word-of-mouth comments were 24 percentage points less likely to purchase a new product than other consumers; while persons who received favorable word-of-mouth comments were only 12 percentage points more likely to buy.[50]

[50]Johan Arndt, "Role of Product Related Conversations in the Diffusion of a New Product," *Journal of Marketing Research* (August 1967), 291-295, at 292.

**Figure 13.6
Market Segments
Identified by Time
of Adoption of
New Product (as
proportion of total
who eventually
adopt product)
(X = mean time
for adoption)**

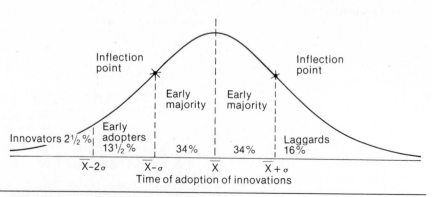

Source: Reprinted with permission of Macmillan Publishing Co., Inc. from *Diffusion of Innovations* by Everett M. Rogers. Copyright © 1962 by The Free Press.

Social Integration

Consumers who are well integrated into the social system and who are respected by a group appear to adopt new products more rapidly than those who are less integrated.

Arndt studied a new food product that was introduced into a social system. Consumers who were named most often as "a relatively good friend" were also among the earliest adopters of the product.[51] Coleman and co-workers, in studies of physicians, demonstrated that the reliance upon highly respected members of the group increases markedly with the amount of risk perceived to be associated with adopting a new product.[52]

Gregariousness is a trait usually associated with innovativeness, both on the part of the opinion leader and the individual being influenced.[53] King found that the fashion innovator is characterized by an active life-style in which innovators were likely to visit or entertain friends frequently, attend church or synagogue frequently, attend spectator sports, eat at restaurants frequently, and attend teas, concerts, plays, and club meetings.[54]

Marketing as a Change Agent

The marketing organization plays a role that in diffusion studies is described as a *change agent*—stimulating the adoption of a new idea or product in a social system. The process of bringing about acceptance of a new product does not occur instantly, however. It is a process that occurs *over time*.

The process of adoption over time is illustrated in Figure 13.6 as a classical normal distribution. Although not all products follow this distri-

[51]Johan Arndt, "Role of Product," 291-295 at 293.

[52]James Coleman, Elihu Katz, and Herbert Menzel, "The Diffusion of an Innovation among Physicians," *Sociometry* (December 1957), 253-269.

[53]The classic documentation of this finding is Elihu Katz and Paul F. Lazarsfeld, *Personal Influence* (New York: Free Press, 1955), chs. 10 and 11; also W. Erbe, "Gregariousness, Group Membership and the Flow of Information," *American Journal of Sociology* (March 1962), 502-516.

[54]Charles W. King, "The Innovator in the Fashion Adoption Process," in L. George Smith (ed.) *Reflections on Progress in Marketing* (Chicago: American Marketing Association, 1964), 324-339 at 335.

bution, some persons are innovators, others are early adopters, others fall in the early or late majority, and some persons who eventually adopt a product may be called laggards.

Acceptance of a new idea does not come all at once in a social system. The idea is transmitted to a few innovators who must pass through various stages to acceptance or rejection. After some innovators have adopted the product, others may follow, depending on the value of the innovation and other characteristics of the product. The process continues throughout the social system and its speed as well as eventual penetration of the system will be determined by many factors.

Marketing organizations can use the knowledge gained about the adoption process to be more effective change agents. To gain acceptance of a new discount store, *Gold Circle,* Shelly Berman Communications applied many concepts from the diffusion literature. This new type of department store was to open in Pittsburgh. The store was essentially a discount store but positioned as a new type of store, upscale in merchandise offering and target market. Evaluation of the diffusion literature suggested that mass media could create awareness and even interest. Personal communications would be necessary, however, to persuade people in the market target to try the store.

A procedure was devised to locate people in Pittsburgh who had a high amount of personal integration; generally people who are in many organizations and recognized as opinion leaders. A number of these people were flown to Columbus, where the company already operates stores of the new type. The Pittsburgh opinion leaders were given a moderate amount of money to spend in the store in a special after-hours occasion and were treated to a wine and cheese party. At the conclusion, television commercials were filmed in which these opinion leaders were shown giving testimonials. When the TV testimonials of these visible opinion leaders were shown in Pittsburgh, an enormous amount of interpersonal communication was stimulated, leading to trial of the store and a successful introduction of the new concept.

It should be concluded that the acceptance of new products does not occur for one reason or because of a single influence. A variety of forces is necessary to stimulate adoption. Some of these influences are marketer dominated such as advertising, sampling, and the sales force. Effective utilization of these marketing forces depends upon knowledge of the diffusion characteristics of the product category. At the same time, other variables which are beyond the control of the marketing strategist influence the adoption process. In the latter instance, the consumer analyst provides information helpful in adapting to consumer realities rather than trying to change them.

PREDICTING DIFFUSION AND ADOPTION SUCCESS

Marketing strategists are interested in predicting the behavior of aggregates of consumers rather than individual behavior. There are a number of models that, with varying degrees of success, have been used to predict market acceptance of new products. The output of these models usually involves predictions of the number of consumers who will accept a new product and the timing of acceptance.

New product models can be placed into two categories.[55] The first category can be called diffusion models, which are based upon fitting a mathematical curve to new product sales, using a parsimonious set of parameters. The parameters may or may not have definite behavioral content. The mathematical curves are determined from historical situations or theoretical propositions and applied to current problems. The variables in diffusion models are such things as the time the product has been introduced and number of persons in the market (with assumptions about interaction between consumers). Numerous types of diffusion or *stochastic* models are possible.

The second category of models is adoption models. These focus upon variables that describe consumer decision making concerning the new product and are called *deterministic* models. Some of them also include variables that describe marketer activity. Both kinds of models are included in the following discussion.

Penetration Models

The most basic stochastic models of new product acceptance permit predictions of the level of penetration by a new product in a given time period based upon early sales results. These models require data with which the analyst can separate the initial purchasers in early time periods from repeat purchasers. Thus these models separate the triers from the adopters.

Penetration models assume some ceiling penetration—a percentage of households that represents the maximum proportion that can be expected to purchase a product of this type. The ratio of repeat purchasers in a period to triers can be represented by r, and the ceiling proportion can be represented by x. The penetration in the first period would be rx. The penetration in the second period would be equal to rx less those first-period triers who did not repeat their purchase. The penetration in period two, therefore, would be

$$rx \ (1 - r).$$

In period three, penetration would be

$$rx \ (1 - r)^2,$$

and similarly for other periods until the ceiling is reached. Frequently, the effects of some external force (such as advertising) are added to the model as K. If this model were realistic, the marketer could project the total number of adopters at any point of time. Figure 13.7 shows how the penetration curve is calculated. Kelly found that the model was

---

[55]This categorization is from Philip Kotler, *Marketing Decision Making: A Model Building Approach* (New York: Holt, Rinehart and Winston, 1971). See ch. 17 of this source for an excellent overview of new product models.

**Figure 13.7
Explicit Character
of the Penetration
Model**

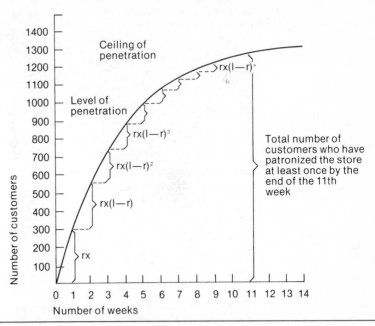

Source: Robert F. Kelly. "Estimating Ultimate Performance Levels of New Retail Outlets." *Journal of Marketing Research*, vol. 4 (February 1967), 18. Reprinted by permission from the *Journal of Marketing Research* published by the American Marketing Association.

useful in predicting the penetration of the market area for a new dairy store.[56]

The penetration model was introduced by Fourt and Woodlock.[57] It depends upon adequate data (usually from a consumer panel) to ascertain early penetration ratios and stability of these ratios over time. In spite of the impracticality of many of its assumptions for most innovations, it is one of the general group of brand share models that has influenced diffusion thought and research.[58]

**Epidemiological
Models**

A number of models have been developed that view new product diffusion as a process of social interaction about the product in which innovators and early adopters "infect" the rest of the population. Thus, these models, which are based upon social-interaction assumptions, have been compared to disease epidemics that move through the population. Predictions are usually based upon acceptance-rejection criteria in a time

[56]Robert F. Kelly, "Estimating Ultimate Performance Levels of New Retail Outlets," *Journal of Marketing Research* (February 1967), 3-19.

[57]L. A. Fourt and J. W. Woodlock, "Early Prediction of Market Success for New Grocery Products," *Journal of Marketing* (October 1962), 31-38; also William D. Barclay, "Probability Model for Early Prediction of New Product Market Success," *Journal of Marketing* (January 1963), 63-68.

[58]For a description of the fundamentals underlying these early brand-switching models, see Vijay Mahajan and Eitan Muller, "Innovation Diffusion and New Product Growth Models in Marketing," *Journal of Marketing* (Fall 1979), 55-68.

setting. The assumptions of these models and the number of variables are usually simple, although the mathematics involved may be sophisticated.

One model that has yielded good predictions of actual data was developed by Bass.[59] The assumptions underlying this model are that initial purchases of a new product will be made both by innovators and imitators, the distinction between the two being buying influence. Innovators are influenced in their initial purchase by marketing-controlled communications, but imitators are influenced by the number of previous buyers; imitators learn from the experiences of those who have already bought. Bass defines p as the coefficient of innovation and r as the coefficient of imitation. The importance of innovators is greater at first and diminishes monotonically with time.

The Bass model is described in the following manner:[60]

$$S(T) = mf(T) = [P(T)] \, m - Y(T)] = [p + q\int_0^T S(t)dt/m] \, [m - \int S(t)dt]$$

where

$$
\begin{aligned}
q/m &= \text{initial purchase rate (a constant)} \\
p &= \text{probability of initial purchase (a constant)} \\
f(T) &= \text{likelihood of purchase at } T \\
Y(T) &= \text{total number purchasing in the } (O,T) \text{ interval} \\
S(T) &= \text{sales at } T
\end{aligned}
$$

Using standard maximization techniques, it is possible to predict the peak and timing of peak sales for the product. Bass has applied this model to sales of eleven durable goods and it has generally yielded excellent predictions. Using regression analysis with data for three years, Bass was able to predict sales of room air conditioners that coincided with actual sales with a coefficient of determination of $R^2 = 0.92$. For color television, the predictors of sales through 1970 using the Bass model apparently were more accurate than the forecasts made by the manufacturers. An example of the closeness of fit between actual and predicted sales for power lawnmowers is shown in Figure 13.8.

An advance in epidemiological models was developed by Midgley in Australia, who dealt explicitly with the problem of interpersonal contacts. "Contagion" can be either positive or negative or neutral, with regard to new product information.[61] Figure 13.9 displays the Midgley model, which relates four categories of the population. The number of *potential adopters* is represented as X and from that group, which is the total population before the new product is introduced, X becomes a smaller number as some *potential* adopters become adopters. Some will become *active*

[59]Frank M. Bass, "A New Product Growth Model for Consumer Durables," *Management Science* (January 1969), 215-227.

[60]Bass, "New Product," 217.

[61]David F. Midgley, "A Simple Mathematical Theory of Innovative Behavior," *Journal of Consumer Research* (June 1976), 31-41.

**Figure 13.8
Actual Sales and
Sales Predicted by
Bass Model of New
Product Diffusion
(power lawn
mowers)**

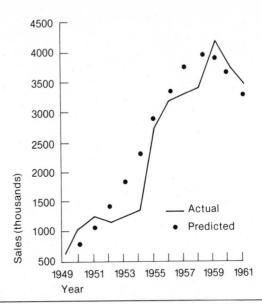

Source: Frank M. Bass, "A New Product Growth Model for Consumer Durables," *Management Science*
vol. 15, no. 5 (January 1969), 223, Figure 7. Reprinted by permission.

adopters *(Y),* some *active rejectors (Z),* and some *passives (P).* The
cumulative number of adopters *(C)* is then:

$$C = Y + Z + P$$

In a fixed population size of *N,* it will be true that

$$N \text{ (population size)} = X + Y + Z + P$$

At the time a new product is launched, *Y, Z* and *P* must equal zero and
the number of potential adopters therefore equals the population size
(X = N). This means that the process must be initiated by the marketing
mechanisms *(B* in Figure 13.9) since the influences *(A, C, D)* must be
zero before the product is introduced. It is possible to derive the equations for such influences. Midgley tested the theory with some data from
a consumer panel for toothpaste, candy, detergent, and biscuits and
found support for the theory from the data.

The Midgley model indicates the potential that is developing for forecasting new product adoption. The fact that the methodology is at least
partially successful indicates the possibilities for future consumer researchers to derive better and better estimates of the parameters needed
for use of such models by marketers in a wide range of product categories and marketing programs.[62]

[62]For other stochastic approaches to new product acceptance, see William F. Massey, "Forecasting the
Demand for New Convenience Products," *Journal of Marketing Research* (November 1969), 405-412;
and David H. Ahl, "New Product Forecasting Using Consumer Panels," *Journal of Marketing Research*
(May 1970), 160-167.

**Figure 13.9
Mathematical
Model of
Innovative
Behavior**

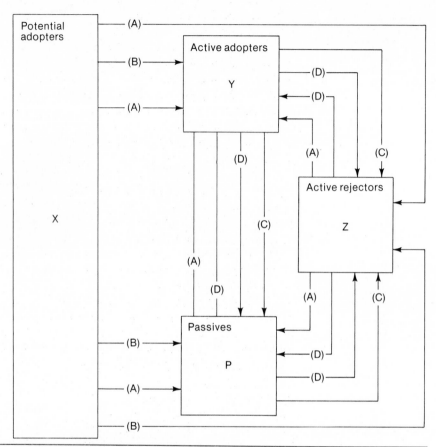

Key
(A) Due to the influence of active adopters
(B) Due to the influence of marketing activities
(C) Due to the influence of active rejectors
(D) Other state change mechanisms

Source: David F. Midgley, "A Simple Mathematical Theory of Innovative Behavior," *Journal of Consumer Research*, vol. 3 (June 1976), 33–34. Reprinted by permission.

**Deterministic
(Adoption)
Models**

Various mathematical models have been developed that relate adoption of a new product to specific consumer variables, which, if they can be measured, determine outcome variables of intermediate stages leading to trial of a new product.

The DEMON model is an example of the multistage model in which an assumption is made that consumers pass through stages of decision making leading to purchase of a new product. As each stage is reached, it is assumed that a higher probability of purchase results than in the preceding stage.[63]

[63]David B. Leamer, "Profit Maximization through New-Product Marketing Planning and Control," in Frank Bass (ed.), *Application of the Sciences in Marketing Management* (New York: John Wiley & Sons, 1968), 151-167.

DEMON was developed at the advertising agency of Batten, Barton, Durstine, and Osborne to predict acceptance of new products and to improve management decisions concerning marketing strategy for new products. DEMON is represented in Figure 13.10. The figure shows the stages involved in acceptance of a product new to a customer. In the model, awareness is an important variable. Awareness is predicted by measuring the ratio of advertising dollars spent to the number of delivered gross impressions and the ratio of impressions to the level of attained reach and frequency.[64]

In the DEMON model, each variable is first dependent, then independent. Thus, trial depends on awareness; but once activated, trial becomes the independent variable for prediction of *usage.* Each of these variables is influenced in turn by variables (such as advertising) which are marketer dominated. Although Figure 13.10 does not show the relationships between variables, the computer program for DEMON does contain such explicit equations. Components of this model have been further refined by Light and Pringle, using a set of recursive regression equations called NEWS (new product, early warning system).[65]

A number of other deterministic models have been developed by marketing organizations such as the N. W. Ayer Advertising Agency. Ayer uses a model that includes recall of advertising claims as an important determinant of initial purchases of new products.[66] The most ambitious of these models is probably one developed by Amstutz, which was used to obtain a good simulation of physical adoption of new drugs.[67] Another model that has received considerable managerial attention is SPRINTER, developed by Urban. This model simulates new product adoption based upon an assumption of buying activity leading to trial in the following stages: (1) awareness, (2) intent, (3) search, (4) selection, and (5) postpurchase behavior.[68]

Market Structure Models

Diffusion models in consumer behavior have mostly focused upon the consumer, either as an individual or in the stochastic models of aggregate consumers. In the future, diffusion models will increasingly focus on

---

[64]Reach and frequency are commonly used terms in advertising. *Reach* is the percentage of the population contacted at least once by an advertisement. *Frequency* is the average number of times each person is reached, or gross impressions divided by reach.

[65]Lawrence Light and Lewis Pringle, "New Product Forecasting Using Recursive Regression," in Kollat et al., *Research in Consumer Behavior,* (New York: Holt, Rinehart and Winston, 1970), 702-709; and Abraham Charnes et al., "NEWS Report: A Discussion of the Theory and Application of the Planning Portion of DEMON," in Sheth, *Models,* 296-309.

[66]Henry J. Claycamp and Lucien E. Liddy, "Prediction of New Product Performance: An Analytical Approach," *Journal of Marketing Research* (November 1969), 414-420.

[67]Arnold Amstutz, *Computer Simulation of Competitive Market Response* (Cambridge, Mass.: MIT Press, 1967); and Henry J. Claycamp and Arnold E. Amstutz, "Simulation Techniques in the Analysis of Marketing Strategy," in Frank M. Bass, Charles W. King, and Edgar Pessemier (eds.), *Applications of the Sciences in Marketing Management* (New York: John Wiley & Sons, 1968), 113-150.

[68]Glen L. Urban, "A New Product Analysis and Decision Model," *Management Science* (April 1968), 490-517; also David B. Montgomery and Glen L. Urban, *Management Science in Marketing* (Englewood Cliffs, N. J.: Prentice-Hall, 1969).

**Figure 13.10
DEMON Model of
New Product
Acceptance**

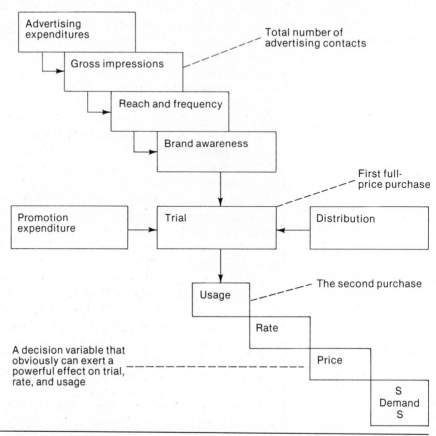

Source: James K. DeVoe. "Plans, Profits, and the Marketing Program," in Frederick E. Webster, Jr. (ed.), *New Directions in Marketing* (Chicago: American Marketing Association, 1965). Reprinted by permission.

more values, especially ones that incorporate the market structure and market strategy. The rate of diffusion is affected by diffusion change agencies in areas such as pricing, infrastructure and organizational development, promotional communications, market selection, segmentation, and so forth. Recent studies have attempted to take such factors into account and have studied the case of marketing organizations such as McDonald's, Friendly Ice Cream, bank cards, cable television and other innovative products and services.[69] In the marketing literature, many of the advances in developing models that relate diffusion to characteristics of organizations and the market structure have been contributions of Mahajan.[70]

[69]Lawrence Brown, Marilyn Brown and Samuel Craig, "Innovation Diffusion and Entrepreneurial Activity in a Spatial Context," in Jagdish Sheth (ed.), *Research in Marketing, Volume 4* (Greenwich, Conn.: JAI Press, 1981), 69-115.

[70]Vijay Mahajan and R. A. Peterson, "Innovation Diffusion in a Dynamic Potential Adopter Population," *Management Science* (November 1978), 127-146.

Evaluation of Models of Diffusion and Adoption

There has been a rapid expansion of knowledge in recent years concerning the development of models for new product acceptance. In many cases, extensive data have been presented to show the efficacy of respective models. To date there has been little application of a model developed by one individual or group to data or problems faced by other individuals or groups. That is the ultimate test of a model's generality. This type of testing is occurring (with NEWS and the Ayer model, for example), but the situations involved are often proprietary business applications, which do not lend themselves to widespread publication of the results. Perhaps, also, if the results were more conclusive, publication would be more widespread.

Summary

The diffusion of innovations is a topic of study and research that grew rapidly in the past few decades, dealing with how a new product is adopted in a society. It is a topic of immense importance to marketing organizations because of the necessity to bring out new products continuously in order to survive.

The purchase of a new product is analyzed as a special category of consumer decision making for three reasons. First, much of the research in the diffusion tradition has focused upon the decision to *continue or discontinue* future use of a product rather than upon the individual decision for a product or brand that is more typically analyzed with general consumer behavior models. A second reason for the special nature of diffusion studies is their emphasis upon the *social structure of communication* rather than individual processing of information. Thus, diffusion theory is generally *relational* rather than *monadic*. A third reason for an emphasis upon diffusion research is the simple volume of research to be assimilated. Over 2,700 publications exist in this field, reporting over 1,800 empirical investigations.

The elements of the diffusion process to be studied are (1) the *innovation,* (2) the *communication* of the innovation among *individuals,* (3) the *social system,* and (4) *time.* The most commonly accepted definition of an innovation is *any idea or product perceived by the potential innovator to be new.* Most marketing studies simply consider an innovation to be any form of a product that has recently become available in a market. Innovations may be classified as continuous, dynamically continuous and discontinuous.

Everett Rogers is the most influential analyst of the diffusion process. His model has become well-known in many disciplines, including consumer research. This model describes the adoption process as one of *knowledge* or awareness by the consumer, *persuasion* that the new product is valuable and worth the risk of trying it, a *decision* to adopt or reject the product, and *confirmation* of the trial and decision.

Marketing studies have focused on several correlates of new product adoption and the results of these studies are described in this chapter. The variables analyzed may be grouped together as *consumer charac-*

teristics related to innovativeness, product characteristics, and social and communication variables.

The final section of this chapter described some of the mathematical models that are currently being developed in an attempt to predict levels and timing of new product acceptance. Some of these are *stochastic* in that they represent aggregate behavior with relatively simple mathematical equations. Examples include models by Bass and by Midgley as well as early penetration models by others. Deterministic models attempt to explain product acceptance (outcome) as determined by intermediate stages (inputs). One of the most developed of these models is DEMON. Although the deterministic models are probably more realistic and helpful in advancing knowledge about how consumers make decisions, the stochastic models are currently more feasible and economical than the complex models.

Review and Discussion Questions

1. The interest of a marketing manager in the topic of diffusion of innovations is rather obvious. Why might an economist concerned with macroeconomic problems be interested in this topic?

2. Several definitions of innovation are presented in this chapter. Which would you use to conduct research in marketing or in another discipline? Defend your choice.

3. Explain as precisely as possible the differences between continuous, dynamically continuous, and discontinuous innovations.

4. What is meant by *relational* and *monadic* approaches to diffusion studies? Explain how research would be affected by one approach compared to the other.

5. A new bakery product is being introduced by a large firm. The company believes that it should obtain about 20 percent penetration in a market of 20 million people. In a test market, it was found that 3 percent of the people tried the product within the first week of introduction and that of those who tried it about half purchased the product again. However, of those who repurchased, usage was only one unit every two weeks. The bakery has asked you to help estimate the amount of production that will be needed each week until the product reaches a stable market position. Prepare a method to use.

6. The manufacturer of a new product is attempting to determine who the innovators for the product might be. The product is a game that requires players to answer each other with phrases from various foreign languages. Who would you identify as the most likely innovators? What appeals would you suggest be used in promoting the product?

7. A large manufacturer of drug and personal grooming products wants to introduce a new toothpaste brand in addition to the three he already markets. Evaluate for the firm what information might be used from innovation studies to guide in introducing the product.

8. A large pharmaceutical firm has successfully marketed an infant formula for several years. This product has good acceptance among pediatricians, who recommend the product for babies up to six months. In an attempt to expand their market, the firm has developed a new liquid food for babies between the ages of six and eighteen months. The new food is flavored with vegetables, fruits, or cereal, yet is fed through a bottle. It will compete directly with regular strained baby food, and the firm knows that competition will be keen. However, the firm is prepared to release an authoritative report by a well-known medical school to show that morbidity rates among liquid-fed babies are significantly lower than among strained-food-fed babies. This report indicates that it takes 100 spoonfuls of strained food each day to give a baby a nutritionally sound diet. Since babies tend to throw the food on the floor, they often receive a deficient diet and the liquid food will remedy this. The firm is convinced it must receive the endorsement of the liquid food by pediatricians to be successful. Your job is to outline a program to gain adoption of liquid food as the food recommended by pediatricians.

At one time, Scripto was virtually a household name in the writing instrument field which now totals annual sales in excess of $1 billion. Its market dominance in the 1950s, however, had been steadily eroded by aggressive competitive action, but 1978 marked a significant turning point.[1] It became apparent that the product line needed revamping, especially in view of the successful introduction of the *Eraser Mate* by the Gillette Company. This was the first erasable ball point pen, selling for $1.69.

Scripto management quickly turned to consumer research to evaluate the market success of *Eraser Mate*, because it also was about to introduce an erasable ball point. A trade audit disclosed that *Eraser Mate* captured a 40 percent share when compared with *Flair* markers and *Paper Mate* $.98 ballpoint pens, despite its higher price (ranging as high as $9.50). A survey of 2,000 households further revealed that an *Eraser Mate* was found in 11 percent of them, and 86 percent of users questioned said they would buy the product again. Even more surprising was the fact that two-thirds of users were under the age of 18, and 42 percent fell into the 11 to 14 age bracket.

What could Scripto do, given the success of *Eraser Mate*? Further analysis showed that teenagers prefer an inexpensive, disposable pen. Therefore, Scripto designed and introduced the *Scripto Erasable Pen* selling for $.98, backed with a $1.5 million network television and consumer magazine advertising budget (see Figure 14.1). The key copy point emerged from focus group research: "erases the ink, not the paper." When commercials were first tested, 98 percent surveyed remembered this benefit and 91 percent indicated strong interest in buying the product. This later was confirmed by sales figures when the product hit the market.

This is a good example of a company taking the process of alternative evaluation seriously. Management was aware that consumers make use of evaluative criteria which are used to compare alternatives, and these desired product attributes influence choice. If existing products and

[1]"Success of Scripto Erasable Pen Due to Marketing Research: CEO," *Marketing News* (January 23, 1981), 8.

**Figure 14.1
The Scripto
Erasable Pen**

Source: Courtesy Scripto, Inc.

brands fall short in any way (in this case the *Eraser Mate* was not disposable), a marketing opportunity exists.

Various aspects of alternative evaluation are discussed in the next two chapters. The purpose here is to provide an overview of the process itself and to center specifically on the nature and function of evaluative criteria. These criteria play a central role, and here is a more formal definition: *desired outcomes from choice or use of an alternative expressed in the form of the attributes or specifications used to compare various alternatives.*

ALTERNATIVE EVALUATION

Let's return once again to the beleagured American automobile industry discussed in Chapter 1. Obviously there are various segments of potential buyers, some of whom still are interested in the traditional Detroit options. The alternative evaluation process could take place in the following way for the buyer of the Ford *Granada*.[2]

Obviously problem recognition has occurred and usually there will be fairly extensive search because of the high-involvement nature of this purchase. Prospects typically look at ads, talk with friends, consult such rating services as *Consumer's Reports*, and shop various dealers. These people are part of the intermediate or standard car market whose evalu-

[2]Norman Krandall, "Fewer Arrows: More Moving Targets," *Proceedings of the 20th Annual Conference* (New York: Advertising Research Foundation, 1974), 9-10.

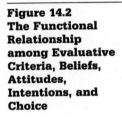

**Figure 14.2
The Functional
Relationship
among Evaluative
Criteria, Beliefs,
Attitudes,
Intentions, and
Choice**

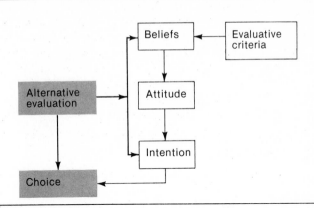

ative criteria are not especially oriented toward styling, prestige, and sporty appeal. Rather, their criteria focus much more on low price, relatively high gas mileage, comfort, space, and size. These, then, are the desired product features, and search will focus on appropriate information along these dimensions.

As information is acquired through search and processed, the outcome is formation of beliefs about the various makes, including the *Granada*. For example, will the *Granada* really deliver relatively economical performance plus the desired comfort not present in the smaller cars? The decision arrived at then becomes stored in long-term memory as a *belief* which specifies the consequences of purchasing a particular make in terms of each evaluative criterion which is used. The sum total of all these beliefs and evaluations represents an *attitude*, either favorable or unfavorable, toward the act of purchasing and using the *Granada* and other makes being considered.

All things considered, the prospect will purchase that make toward which attitude is most positive. Usually a positive attitude toward the act of purchase will be accompanied by an *intention to act*. Intentions are a statement of the subjective probability that a specified action (in this case the purchase of a *Granada*) will be undertaken. Again, all things being equal, this intention will culminate in an actual purchase.

This example has illustrated some central concepts in the model of high-involvement consumer behavior, a portion of which is reproduced in Figure 14.2. While omitting some detail to be discussed in the next chapter, it shows the functional relationship among evaluative criteria, beliefs, attitudes, intentions, and choice.

The starting point is the consumer's own evaluative criteria. As will be elaborated below, these generally must be accepted as a given by the marketing planner. The response of the business firm is to adapt product, price, promotion, and distribution to these important buying determinants. It can be a fatal mistake to proceed otherwise, as some later examples will illustrate.

**Figure 14.3
The Determinants
of Evaluative
Criteria**

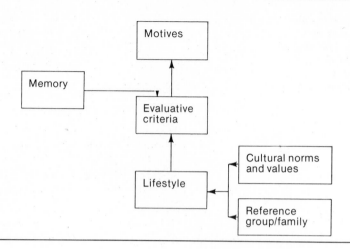

**The Nature of
Evaluative
Criteria**

Evaluative criteria find their specific representation in the form of those physical product attributes as well as strictly subjective factors the consumer considers to be important in the purchase decision. They can be *objective* (e.g., specific physical features such as front-wheel drive or "location within two blocks of public transportation") or *subjective* (i.e., symbolic values or benefits such as the perceived sportiness of the product).[3] It is not uncommon for virtually identical products to receive widely varying evaluations because of perceived subjective differences. One airline may be preferred over another, for example, because it is seen as being more exciting and energetic than a more conservative counterpart.

Psychological Foundations

The diagram in Figure 14.3 indicates that evaluative criteria are shaped by two basic factors: (1) motives and (2) memory. In this context, motives function in a highly specific manner to shape preferences for product attributes and benefits that will contribute most to motive satisfaction. Memory content, on the other hand, primarily refers to incoming information gathered through search as well as various forms of first-hand experience.

 Motives, of course, are personal goals that find their roots in life-style. Life-style, in turn, is shaped to a meaningful degree by cultural norms and values as well as various forms of social influence (reference groups and family). All of this is depicted in Figure 14.3. The reader will note that the model of high-involvement decision process behavior is gradually becoming more complex the further we delve into its various phases.

 While many examples could be given of the ways in which motives

[3]Irving S. White, "New Product Differentiation: 'Physical and Symbolic Dimensions,' " in B. A. Morin (ed.), *Marketing in a Changing World* (Chicago: American Marketing Association, 1960), 100.

shape the evaluative criteria which are used, consider the studies on achievement motivation by McClelland and his colleagues. Some of the major findings resulting from more than two decades of research follow:

1. American males with a high achievement need most often come from the middle class, have a good memory for incomplete tasks, and are active in college and community affairs.[4]

2. Those high in achievement are more likely to take risks in situations where achievement is possible through individual efforts.[5] Furthermore, they stay at a task longer than the average person if they perceive a chance for success.[6]

3. A need for achievement is reflected in development of internal standards; there is little desire to conform to social pressure in situations where internal and external standards conflict.[7]

The marketer would never measure achievement motivation directly, but its effects might clearly be observed in the criteria utilized to evaluate types and brands of cameras. These are just a few of the possible ways in which it might be reflected: "allows me to take the best pictures," "allows me to make my own settings and adjustments without automatic gadgets," "gives pictures I can be proud of." The nonachievement-oriented consumer, on the other hand, might place far greater importance on automatic features that would guarantee an acceptable picture with fewer risks. Here are two distinct market segments with widely variant product specifications, and such data cannot be ignored in marketing planning. It is unlikely that either could be induced to switch the evaluative criteria used without changes first taking place in the underlying motive pattern.

Evaluative criteria are not static, however. They will undergo modification and change based on new information and experience. Products enter the market, for example, with previously unheard-of features. Friends mention various attributes which they have found to be helpful in decision making, and so on. It should not be assumed at this point that these desired product attributes may be easily changed by advertising and promotion. For reasons elaborated later, quite the opposite is likely to be the case, and this has some potent implications for marketing strategy.

Characteristics

The two most important characteristics of evaluative criteria include the number used in reaching a decision and the relative importance (salience) of each.

[4]D. C. McClelland, *The Achieving Society* (Princeton, N.J.: Van Nostrand, 1961), 43-46.

[5]McClelland, *Achieving Society,* 43-46.

[6]N. T. Feather, "The Relationship of Persistence at a Task to Expectation of Success and Achievement-Related Motives," *Journal of Abnormal and Social Psychology,* vol. 63 (1961), 552-561.

[7]R. M. deCharms et al., "Behavioral Correlates of Directly and Indirectly Measured Achievement Motivation," in D. C. McClelland (ed.), *Studies in Motivation* (New York: Appleton, 1955), 414-423.

Number Used Most studies show that six or fewer criteria generally are used by most consumers, although Fishbein suggests that the number may go as high as nine.[8] The extent of involvement present is a determining consideration. Present evidence indicates this relationship: the higher the degree of involvement, the greater the number of evaluative criteria which enter into the decision.[9] A correlate is that each criterion will be characterized by a narrow latitude of acceptance.[10] In other words, the consumer will not positively evaluate an alternative that deviates very far from his or her specifications.

Salience Some criteria obviously will be viewed as more important than others. There has been some terminological difficulty in the literature on this point. It is probably best to use the term *salience* as a synonym for importance and *determinance* to identify those product attributes that are felt to be *most important.*[11] In that sense, front-wheel drive as a criterion could be both salient and determinant if it were the dominant factor in alternative evaluation.

Types of Evaluative Criteria

Evaluative criteria, of course, are expressed in terms of desired product attributes. Several types deserve special comment because of the attention afforded them in published research.

Reputation of Brand

Brand reputation frequently emerges as a determinant criterion as it did in a study of purchases of dress shirts and suits.[12] It also proved to be significant in use of over-the-counter drugs.[13] The brand name appears to serve as a surrogate indicator of product quality, and its importance as a criterion seems to vary with the ease by which quality can be judged objectively. If ease of evaluation is low, the consumer sometimes will perceive a high level of risk in the purchase.[14] Reliance on a well-known brand name with a reputation of long-standing quality thus can be an effective way to reduce risk.

[8]This is a cardinal principle of the Fishbein extended behavior model to be discussed in the next chapter. For a general review, see Martin Fishbein, "Attitude, Attitude Change, and Behavior: A Theoretical Overview," in Philip Levine (ed.), *Attitude Research Bridges the Atlantic* (Chicago: American Marketing Association, 1975), 3-16.

[9]Michael L. Rothschild and Michael J. Houston, "The Consumer Involvement Matrix: Some Preliminary Findings," in Barnett A. Greenberg and Danny N. Bellenger (eds.), *Contemporary Marketing Thought* (Chicago: American Marketing Association, 1977), 95-98; and Michael L. Rothschild, "Advertising Strategies for High and Low Involvement Situations," in John C. Maloney and Bernard Silverman (eds.), *Attitude Research Plays for High Stakes* (Chicago: American Marketing Association, 1979), 74-93.

[10]Rothschild, "Advertising Strategies."

[11]See Mark I. Alpert, "Unresolved Issues in Identification of Determinant Attributes," in Jerry C. Olson (ed.), *Advances in Consumer Research,* vol. 7 (Ann Arbor, Mich.: Association for Consumer Research, 1980), 83-88.

[12]D. M. Gardner, "Is There a Generalized Price-Quality Relationship?" *Journal of Marketing Research,* vol. 8 (1971), 241-243.

[13]J. F. Engel, D. A. Knapp and D. E. Knapp, "Sources of Influence in the Acceptance of New Products for Self-Medication: Preliminary Findings," in R. M. Haas (ed.), *Science, Technology and Marketing* (Chicago: American Marketing Association, 1966), 776-782.

[14]R. A. Bauer, "Consumer Behavior as Risk Taking," Robert S. Hancock (ed.), *Dynamic Marketing in a Changing World* (Chicago: American Marketing Association, 1960), 389-398.

In the case of headache and cold remedies, there is no way in which the average consumer can judge purity and quality. Brand thus becomes especially crucial as a surrogate indicator of quality. It is such a dominant factor with many consumers, for example, that they will pay many times more for a branded item even though they are aware that government regulations require all aspirin products to contain the same basic therapeutic formulation.[15]

Price

There has been considerable interest over the years in both the role and salience of price as an evaluative criterion, probably because of the relation of marketing to its parent field of economics.[16] A number of recent studies have focused on the price-quality relationship, and there is additional evidence on the ways in which price is used in alternative evaluation.

The Price-Quality Relationship   One premise of economic theory is that price can be used as a surrogate indicator of quality, in which case the demand curve will show a backward slope. In his review of 76 studies, Monroe reports that the findings tend to be mixed; the most he could conclude was that there are indications that this positive relationship does exist, at least over some ranges of prices in some product categories.[17] Additional recent supportive evidence has been reported by Shapiro[18] and by Cimball and Webdale.[19]

It now seems quite clear that there is a definite range of prices people are willing to pay as well as a reference price that influences price judgments.[20] Consumers appear to group unacceptably low and unacceptably high prices into categories and completely disregard price differences when they fall outside of what they consider to be the acceptable range.[21] This zone of acceptable prices may be the result of the consumer's perception of prices asked or paid in the past, his or her attitude about what the fair price should be, and the price that will allow the seller to cover costs and earn a reasonable profit.[22]

Most of the above studies have looked at price in isolation as the

---

[15]Engel, Knapp, and Knapp, "Sources of Influence."

[16]For an interesting perspective, see Jacob Jacoby and Jerry C. Olson, "Consumer Response to Price: An Attitudinal, Information-Processing Perspective," *Purdue Papers in Consumer Psychology,* no. 157 (Lafayette, Ind.: Purdue University, 1976).

[17]Kent B. Monroe, "Buyer's Subjective Perceptions of Price," *Journal of Marketing Research,* vol. 10 (February 1973), 70-80.

[18]Benson P. Shapiro, "Price Reliance: Existence and Sources," *Journal of Marketing Research,* vol. 10 (August 1973), 286-294.

[19]Richard S. Cimball and Adrienne M. Webdale, "Effects of Price Information on Consumer-Rated Quality" (paper presented at American Psychological Association, 1973).

[20]Kent B. Monroe, "The Influence of Price Differences and Brand Familiarity on Brand Preferences," *Journal of Consumer Research,* vol. 3 (June 1976), 42-49.

[21]P. S. Raju, "Product Familiarity, Brand Name and Price Influences on Product Evaluation" (State College, Pa.: Working Paper no. 38, College of Business Administration, Pennsylvania State University, 1976).

[22]A. O. Oxenfeldt, *Establishing a New Product Program: Guides for Effective Planning and Organization* (New York: American Management Association, 1958), 17-18.

sole criterion of quality judgments. This has tended to overstate the effects on quality perceptions.[23] Stafford and Enis report, for example, that quality judgments are affected by an interaction of price and store image.[24] In other situations, price has relatively little influence on perceived quality, especially when other information cues are available such as the merchandise itself, product ratings, and brand familiarity.[25]

It appears that a positive price-quality relationship is most probable under these conditions:

1. When the consumer has confidence in price as a predictor of quality.[26]

2. When there are real and perceived quality variations between brands.[27]

3. When quality is difficult to judge in other ways, especially when there are no quality-connoting criteria such as brand name or store location.[28]

Other Factors Affecting Price Apart from the price-quality question, the use of price as an evaluative criterion varies from product to product.[29] One study, for example, found that concern with price was high for detergents but low for cereal.[30] In some cases, price is of greater significance when the product is felt to be socially visible.[31]

Second, the role of price is often overrated. Consumers are not always looking for the lowest possible price or even the best price-quality ratio; other factors often assume greater importance.[32] In addition, consumers frequently are completely unaware of the price when decisions are made. In one study, for example, 25 percent of those interviewed did not know the relative price of the brand of toothpaste they had just purchased.[33]

Finally, there is some indication that the importance of price is affected by the number of alternatives under consideration. The greater

[23]R. A. Peterson, "The Price-Perceived Quality Relationship: Experimental Evidence," *Journal of Marketing Research,* vol. 7 (1970), 525-528.

[24]James E. Stafford and Ben M. Enis, "The Price-Quality Relationship: An Extension," *Journal of Marketing Research,* vol. 6 (1969), 456-458.

[25]David M. Gardner, "Is There a Generalized Price-Quality Relationship?" 241-243; J. Jacoby, J. C. Olson, and R. A. Haddock, "Price, Brand Name, and Product Composition Characteristics as Determinants of Perceived Quality," *Journal of Applied Psychology,* vol. 55 (1971), 570-580; and V. R. Rao, "Salience of Price in the Perception of Product Quality: A Multidimensional Measurement Approach" (paper presented at the American Marketing Association, 1971).

[26]Z. V. Lambert, "Product Perception: An Important Variable in Price Strategy," *Journal of Marketing,* vol. 34 (1970), 68-76.

[27]Lambert, "Product Perception."

[28]Monroe, "Influence of Price Differences."

[29]A. Gabor and C. W. J. Granger, "Price Sensitivity of the Consumer," *Journal of Advertising Research,* vol. 4 (1964), 40-44; A. Gabor and C. W. J. Granger, "Price as an Indicator of Quality: Report on an Enquiry," *Economica,* vol. 33 (1966), 43-70.

[30]W. E. Wells and L. A. LoSciuto, "Direct Observation of Purchasing Behavior," *Journal of Marketing Research,* vol. 3 (1966), 227-233.

[31]Lambert, "Product Perception."

[32]Monroe, "Buyer's Subject Perceptions."

[33]George Haines, "A Study of Why People Purchase New Products," in Haas, *Science,* 665-685, at 683.

the number of available options, the less important price tends to become.[34]

Other Criteria

The literature on other criteria used is quite meager, with the exception of isolated studies documenting the influences in a specific decision. For example, it was found that the selection of a bank is based primarily on five criteria: (1) friends' recommendations; (2) reputation; (3) availability of credit; (4) friendliness; and (5) service charges on checking accounts.[35] Obviously there are substantial variations between products and between consumers.[36] It is worth emphasizing once again that consumers do not always use physical or objective criteria to evaluate alternatives; indeed subjective factors easily can be the dominant consideration.[37]

Information Processing and Alternative Evaluation

There has been much recent research on the way in which comparisons are made between alternatives, making use of various evaluative criteria. The methods used for this purpose were discussed in Chapter 11 on the subject of search: (1) retrospective questioning; (2) protocol records; (3) information display boards; (4) eye movement; and (5) observation. In many instances the consumer makes use of a rule of thumb of some type stored in memory, and these strategies have come to be known as *choice heuristics*.[38] At other times these rules of thumb are more or less developed as the person proceeds through the alternative evaluative process, in which case it is said that a *constructive method* is used.[39]

Choice Heuristics: Compensatory Models

If a consumer uses a compensatory strategy in alternative evaluation, a perceived weakness on one attribute may be compensated for by strengths on others. Here are the approaches that have been discussed the most in the literature.[40]

(1) The Expectancy-Value Model This model assumes from the outset that there will be more than one evaluative criterion or attribute along which the alternative will be evaluated. Judgments are based on beliefs that assess whether or not the object actually possesses the attribute in question plus an evaluation of the goodness or badness of that

[34]L. K. Anderson, J. R. Taylor, and R. J. Holloway, "The Consumer and His Alternatives: An Experimental Approach," *Journal of Marketing Research,* vol. 3 (1966), 64.

[35]W. Thomas Anderson, Jr., Eli P. Cox III, and David G. Fulchur, "Bank Selection Decisions and Market Segmentation," *Journal of Marketing,* vol. 40 (January 1976), 40-45.

[36]S. A. Smith, "How Do Consumers Choose between Brands of Durable Goods?" *Journal of Retailing,* (Summer 1970), 18-26.

[37]White, "New Product Differentiation."

[38]James R. Bettman, *An Information Processing Theory of Consumer Choice* (Reading, Mass.: Addison-Wesley, 1979), 179-185.

[39]Bettman, *An Information Processing Theory,* 179.

[40]See Bettman, *An Information Processing Theory.* Also, Flemming Hansen, "Psychological Theories of Consumer Choice," *Journal of Consumer Research,* vol. 3 (December 1976), 132-137.

belief. This, in effect, is the Fishbein multi-attribute attitude model described in much more depth later. It is hypothesized that brands are evaluated one at a time along all attributes and that the total evaluation or judgment is the sum of the ratings along each attribute. The brand with the highest sum wins, and a relatively poor rating on one attribute may be offset by higher ratings on the others.

(2) The Attribute Adequacy Model   The expectancy-value model makes no particular assumptions about the degree to which the rating of a brand or product along an attribute approaches or even exceeds the ideal the consumer has in mind for that attribute. In the attribute adequacy model, the evaluation is arrived at in a similar manner to that discussed above, with the exception that an explicit assessment is made of the difference between ideal and actual on each attribute.[41] While there has not been much research to report, this may be a closer approximation of actual consumer behavior in extended problem-solving situations.

Choice Heuristics: Noncompensatory Models
The noncompensatory model (weakness in one attribute is not compensated for by the strengths of another) has received less attention in the literature, but four major variations have been isolated: (1) conjunctive; (2) disjunctive; (3) lexicographic; and (4) sequential elimination.

(1) The Conjunctive Model   When this model is used, the consumer establishes a minimum acceptable level for each product attribute. A brand will be evaluated as acceptable only if *each* attribute equals or exceeds that minimum level. A lower than acceptable rating on one attribute will lead to a negative evaluation and rejection. For example, a stereo component system may be evaluated as completely satisfactory in terms of sound reproduction and mechanical characteristics, yet be rejected because it is not compact in size.

(2) The Disjunctive Model   When following this approach, acceptable standards are established for each criterion. A brand will then be evaluated as acceptable if it exceeds the minimum specified level on any of these attributes. The choice rule used is to select the first satisfactory alternative.

(3) The Lexicographic Model   Now the consumer has ranked product attributes from most important to least important. The brand that dominates on the most important criterion receives the highest evaluation.[42] If two or more brands tie, then the second attribute is examined and so on until the tie is broken.

(4) Sequential Elimination   Here the consumer has established minimum cut-off points for each attribute. One criterion is selected for use,

[41]For one illustration see James L. Ginter and Frank M. Bass, "An Experimental Study of Attitude Change, Advertising, and Usage in New Product Introduction," *Journal of Advertising,* vol. 1 (1972), 33-39.

[42]A. Tversky, "Intransitivity of Preferences," *Psychological Review,* vol. 76 (January 1969), 31-48.

and all alternatives whose attributes do not pass that cut-off point are eliminated. Then the processing proceeds to the next attribute. There is some indication that this strategy is used when people must make relatively hasty judgments and imagine that a final product decision is imminent.[43]

Choice Heuristics: Constructive Processes

There will be other times in which the consumer does not make complete use of either a compensatory or noncompensatory strategy rule stored in memory. Rather, fragments or elements of stored rules are used, often during actual purchase, in a *constructive* fashion. This approach is probably most used when consumers have little product experience[44] plus the availability of relevant information at point of sale.[45]

Evaluation and Implications   Of all the choice heuristics discussed above, it is important to note that there is a growing consensus that compensatory strategies are utilized under high involvement.[46] Most likely there is a relatively large set of evaluative criteria, and product attributes are then combined in compensatory fashion. The compensatory approach also is more likely to be utilized by those with more formal education.[47] Finally, this strategy is favored when the number of alternatives is small.[48] Where there are many, a noncompensatory conjunctive strategy often is used to eliminate unacceptable alternatives, followed by a shift to compensatory assessment of the remaining acceptable alternatives.

All of the heuristics except the lexicographic and sequential elimination assume that consumers process information by brand (CPB) rather than by attribute (CPA). Some of the issues surrounding CPB and CPA were previously discussed in Chapter 11, but there is more to be said here. One could legitimately argue that CPB is the most logical method for the consumer to use, simply because this is the way information is presented in advertising, personal selling, and retail display.[49] Attribute

---

[43]Cartin Weitz and Peter Wright, "Retrospective Self-Insight on Factors Considered in Product Evaluation," *Journal of Consumer Research,* vol. 6 (December 1979), 256-269.

[44]James R. Bettman and Pradeep Kakkar, "Methods for Implementing Consumer Choices in Product Class Experience," S. C. Jain (ed.), *Research Frontiers in Marketing: Dialogues and Directions* (Chicago: American Marketing Association, 1978), 198-201; and James R. Bettman and Michel A. Zins, "Constructive Processes in Consumer Choice," *Journal of Consumer Research,* vol. 4 (September 1977), 75-85.

[45]James R. Bettman and C. Whan Park, "Implications of a Constructive View of Choice for the Analysis of Protocol Data: A Coding Scheme for Elements of Choice Processes," in Olson, *Advances in Consumer Research,* vol. 7, 148-153.

[46]Rothschild, "Advertising Strategies."

[47]Stephen A. Goodwin and Guy Gessner, "Educating the Consumer About Safety: Effect on Preferences for Power Lawn Mowers," in Richard P. Bagozzi et al., (eds.), *Marketing in the 80s. Changes and Challenges* (Chicago: American Marketing Association, 1980), 420-423.

[48]Denis A. Lussier and Richard W. Olshavsky, "Task Complexity and Contingent Processing in Brand Choice," *Journal of Consumer Research,* vol. 6 (September 1979), 154-165.

[49]David C. Arch, James R. Bettman, and Pradeep Kakkar, "Subjects' Information Processing in Information Display Board Studies," in H. Keith Hunt (ed.), *Advances in Consumer Research,* vol. 5 (Ann Arbor, Mich.: Association for Consumer Research, 1978), 555-560. Also James R. Bettman and Michel A. Zins, "Information Format and Choice Task Effects in Decision-Making," *Journal of Consumer Research,* vol. 6 (September 1979), 141-153.

processing, on the other hand, may be simpler from the consumer's point of view.[50] For this reason, it might be utilized in routinized buying decisions or in those situations in which evaluative criteria are fixed and the consumer already possesses some understanding of the various alternatives. It should be stressed, however, that the information display board, perhaps the most widely used method in this type of research, favors attribute processing by its very format and design.[51] Therefore, the incidence of actual use of this approach may be overstated.

What does all of this say for marketing strategy? Frankly, it can be pretty esoteric stuff at this point in time, rather far removed from the world of reality. Nevertheless, this does represent important basic research. At the very least, it does indicate the necessity of discovering in practical settings whether or not consumers actually prefer CPB or CPA. If the former is true, then information on salient attributes should be given in one package, so to speak, in the context of a given brand. If the latter is preferred, then the attribute itself should be predominantly featured. This has much to say for retail display since it would be necessary to group products and brands by salient attribute—something of a departure from what is done now. Because of the great need for further research, however, it would be a bit early to encourage any revolutionary changes based on what we know so far.

MEASURING EVALUATIVE CRITERIA

Because of the necessity to understand the evaluative criteria that consumers use, considerable attention must be paid to the problems of measurement. There are four categories of research methods: (1) direct approaches; (2) indirect approaches; (3) perceptual mapping; and (4) conjoint analysis. It also is necessary to utilize some type of measure of attribute saliency.[52]

Direct Approaches

It is possible to come right out and ask what considerations are used when comparing various alternatives in a purchase situation.[53] The assumption is made that the individual is aware of salient criteria and will state them when asked. Those that receive the most frequent mention or highest ranking then are considered to be the dominant or determinant factors. But what if the consumer really has given the matter little thought? It is quite possible that only some very obvious and socially acceptable product features will be mentioned. The validity of the data gathered in this way thus can be suspect.

[50]Bettman, "Data Collection and Analysis."

[51]Arch, Bettman and Kakkar, "Subjects' Information Processing" and Bettman and Zins, "Information Format."

[52]For a general discussion of various methods, see James H. Meyers and Richard F. Chay, "A Comparison of Two Methods Determining Optimum Levels of Product Characteristics," in William L. Wilkie (ed.), *Advances in Consumer Research,* vol. 6 (Ann Arbor, Mich.: Association for Consumer Research, 1979), 259-262.

[53]John W. Payner and E. K. Easton Ragsdale, "Verbal Protocols and Direct Observation of Supermarket Shopping Behavior: Some Findings and a Discussion of Methods," in Hunt, *Advances in Consumer Research,* vol. 5, 571-577.

Assume, for example, that a consumer says that price is the most important consideration in the purchase of an electric iron. S/he might mean one or more of several things: (1) "I will not pay $8-$10 more for the built-in sprinkling mechanism," (2) "I will not purchase an iron costing more than $25," (3) "I will seriously consider a brand only if it is within the $8-$14 range," or (4) "I know there are price differences between stores, so I will shop around." Obviously the questioning procedure should go into depth and probe the meaning of attribute labels. This can be done through a free-form guided (depth) interview in which respondents, either individually or collectively, expand on their answers.

Another difficulty with the direct questioning approach is that a criterion such as style may not be mentioned for the reason that all available alternatives are essentially similar.[54] Under different circumstances it might well be quite significant. This can be detected by dual questioning that calls for a two-phase query: (1) indication of the attribute and its importance in the decision and (2) the extent of perceived differences between alternatives along the dimension in question.[55] These two ratings then are combined into one overall score.

Indirect Approaches

Sometimes a marketer may believe that the consumer will not verbalize the true reasons for a choice when asked directly.[56] One proposed remedy is to elicit a response in third person through some type of *projective question.* An example would be, "What product features do most of the people around here consider to be important in buying a dishwasher?" Response biases presumably are overcome through a feeling by the respondent that he or she is not revealing personal opinions. The underlying premise of the projective method has not been verified experimentally,[57] so it is seldom used.

Perceptual Mapping

It is an undeniable fact that many persons find great difficulty in spelling out the rationale of alternative evaluation and choice behavior. Therefore, a research approach that can avoid this type of questioning has intuitive appeal. There has been some use in recent years of a family of research techniques grouped under the label of *perceptual mapping.* The most widely used method is *nonmetric multidimensional scaling* (MDS).[58]

In this method, respondents are asked only to rate similarities between alternatives, two at a time, usually on a 10 to 12 point scale rang-

[54]T. T. Semon, "On the Perception of Appliance Attributes," *Journal of Marketing Research,* vol. 6 (1969), 101.

[55]M. I. Alpert, "Identification of Determinant Attributes: A Comparison of Methods," *Journal of Marketing Research,* vol. 8 (1971), 184-191.

[56]See, for example, E. Dichter, *The Strategy of Desire* (New York: Doubleday, 1960).

[57]J. F. Engel and H. G. Wales, "Spoken versus Pictured Questions on Taboo Topics," *Journal of Advertising Research,* vol. 2 (1962), 11-17.

[58]For a definitive introduction, see P. E. Green and J. J. Carmone, *Multidimensional Scaling and Related Techniques in Marketing Analysis* (Boston: Allyn and Bacon, 1970). For practical examples, see Larry Percey, "An Application of Multidimensional Scaling and Related Techniques to the Evaluation of a New Product Concept," in Beverlee B. Anderson (ed.), *Advances in Consumer Research,* vol. 3 (Atlanta: Association for Consumer Research, 1976), 114-118; and Russell I. Haley, "Strategy Research, 1976," *Proceedings of the 22nd Annual Conference* (New York: Advertising Research Foundation, Inc., 1977), 23-33.

ing from similar to dissimilar. The computer then takes over and generates a visual output indicating the extent to which the various alternatives are seen to be similar. Usually they will be depicted graphically in two dimensions as the example in Figure 14.4 indicates. The two dimensions or axes of this so-called perceptual space are assumed to be the evaluative criteria along which the ratings of similarity were made. Now the analyst must infer the nature of these criteria and label these axes. That can be a demanding task indeed.

Looking at Figure 14.4, the problem here was to evaluate the success of a company that opened ten fast-food outlets in two midwest cities. An attempt was made to gain competitive advantage through a higher-price, higher-quality menu. After one year of operation it was felt that a survey was needed to evaluate the success to date. Part of the study focused on the ratings of the ten leading competitors, as well as Company X, the company under consideration here.

Consumers were asked to rate the similarity between each of these 11 competitors, two at a time, on a ten-point scale ranging from "very similar" to "very dissimilar." The appropriate computer program was used,[59] and the result was the output in Figure 14.4. Originally there were no labels whatsoever on these axes. Rather, these must be provided by the analyst who infers their content either by his or her own subjective intuition or by the presence of other data. In this case it appeared from prior research that the dimensions were *service* and *quality/price*. There was no way to be sure, however, and this is one of the real disadvantages of this technique. If the inferences were correct, the computer computation revealed that the price/quality criterion was most important in the perceived similarity ratings (it explained 63 percent of the variance).

MDS was most helpful in this instance in verifying that management had indeed been successful in differentiating its restaurants from others in the fast-food field. Notice that it stands alone in terms of higher quality and better service as was intended. MDS is no panacea, however, in revealing the evaluative criteria that were used. The labeling of axes can be quite subjective and even erroneous.[60] Another disadvantage is that the evaluative criteria cannot be determined until after the alternatives are rated, thus necessitating a cumbersome research process just to arrive at this type of output. Finally, there is evidence that other methods may produce equally good, and even superior, results.[61]

Conjoint Analysis

Most methods require a respondent to rate an evaluative criterion, one at a time, and the possibility of interaction effects is overlooked. An automobile that provides front-wheel drive, EPA overall fuel economy of 38 MPG, and a full set of gauges (not "idiot lights") may be rated more

[59]See F. W. Young and W. S. Torgerson, "TORSCA, A Fortran IV Program for Shepard-Kruskal Multi-dimensional Scaling Analysis," *Behavioral Science,* vol. 12 (1967), 498-499.

[60]Volney Stefflre, "Multi-dimensional Scaling as a Model of Individual and Aggregate Perception and Cognition," in Jain, *Research Frontiers,* 17-21.

[61]John R. Hauser and Frank S. Koppelman, "Alternative Perceptual Mapping Techniques: Relative Accuracy and Usefulness," *Journal of Marketing Research,* vol. 16 (November 1979), 495-506.

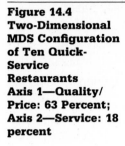

Figure 14.4
Two-Dimensional
MDS Configuration
of Ten Quick-
Service
Restaurants
Axis 1—Quality/
Price: 63 Percent;
Axis 2—Service: 18
percent

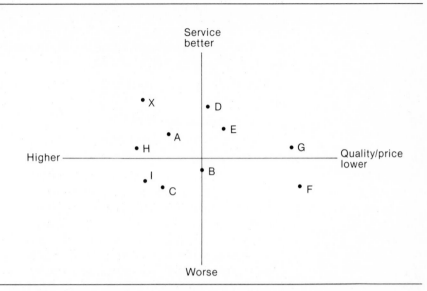

positively when all three factors are considered than it would be if any factor were considered by itself. A relatively new development in mathematical psychology called *conjoint measurement* permits assessment of bundles of benefits as well as part-worth contributions of each benefit to an overall rating of preference.[62]

Usually there is some type of preliminary questioning which determines the salient attributes. In what is called the "full profile approach,"[63] product stimuli are presented verbally or pictorially utilizing from five to six different attributes in combination. Then various scaling devices and computer models can be used to predict preferences.[64]

In one published example, conjoint analysis was employed to find out what people wanted in terms of financial service alternatives.[65] These attributes were checked: type of bank, accessibility to banking service, quality of service, hours of service, and cost of checking account. Some real differences were found among three consumer segments:

1. For two segments, a service charge of 15 cents per check is preferred to a $200 minimum balance.

[62]P. E. Green and V. R. Rao, "Conjoint Measurement for Quantifying Judgmental Data," *Journal of Marketing Research,* vol. 8 (1971), 355-363. Also see Richard M. Johnson, "Trade-off Analysis of Consumer Values," *Journal of Marketing Research,* vol. 11 (May 1974), 121-127; and John O'Neill, "The Use of Conjoint Measurement for Product Planning," in William Locander (ed.), *Marketing Looks Outward* (Chicago: American Marketing Association, 1977), 96-100.

[63]Paul E. Green and V. Srinivasan, "Conjoint Analysis in Consumer Research: Issues and Outlook," *Journal of Consumer Research,* vol. 5 (September 1978), 103-123.

[64]See Franklin Acito and Arun K. Jain, "Evaluation of Conjoint Analysis Results: A Comparison of Methods," *Journal of Marketing Research,* vol. 17 (February 1980), 106-112; Arun K. Jain, Naresh K. Malhotra, and Vijay Mahajan, "Aggregating Conjoint Data: Some Methodological Considerations and Approaches," in Neil Beckwith et al., (eds.), *1979 Educators' Conference Proceedings* (Chicago: American Marketing Association, 1979); and James B. Wiley and James Low, "A Generalized Logit Model to Aggregate Conjoint Data," in Beckwith, *1979 Educators',* 78-81.

[65]Arun K. Jain and Naresh K. Malhotra, "Designing New Products to Fit Markets in the Banking Service Sector: A Conjoint Measurement Approach," in Beckwith, *1979 Educators',* 524-529.

2. All three segments indicated a preference for locally based financial institutions.

3. All three segments showed clear preference for location within a short distance as well as better service.

4. Segments one and two indicated a preference for longer opening hours.

5. In terms of relative importance, cost is most important for segments one and two, whereas service is most important for segment three when they make a decision on bank choice.

Based on these findings, various modifications were made in the service mix, and bank usage was accurately predicted.

Conjoint analysis has found widespread use. In fact, Green and Srinivasan have been able to identify at least several hundred studies undertaken by corporate market research groups and consulting firms.[66] The method is not without its problems, however. One of the difficulties is that data collection can become unwieldy, especially if the number of attributes being studied is large.[67] Also data collection costs can be high, although it is possible to reduce these outlays by confining the analysis only to evaluative criteria already demonstrated to have a measure of salience in the choice process.[68]

Measuring Attribute Salience

Conjoint analysis can isolate salience through what can be referred to as *part-worth analysis.*[69] Also it is possible to use direct rating scales. The most common procedure is simply to ask people to assess the salience of each criterion using some type of scaling approach. In the fast food restaurant example given earlier it was known from a previous study that consumers by and large make use of nine criteria when evaluating alternatives. They were asked to rate the importance of each of these attributes in the following manner:

	Important					Unimportant			
Good products	1	2	3	4	5	6	7	8	9
Good service	1	2	3	4	5	6	7	8	9
Low prices	1	2	3	4	5	6	7	8	9
Clean facilities	1	2	3	4	5	6	7	8	9
Open 24 hours	1	2	3	4	5	6	7	8	9
Well-known company	1	2	3	4	5	6	7	8	9
Wide range of choices	1	2	3	4	5	6	7	8	9
Convenient location	1	2	3	4	5	6	7	8	9
Many outlets	1	2	3	4	5	6	7	8	9

[66]Green and Srinivasan, "Conjoint Analysis."

[67]Herb Hupfer, "Conjoint Measurement—A Valuable Research Tool When Used Selectively," *Marketing Today,* vol. 14 (1976), 1 ff.

[68]See Hupfer, "Conjoint Measurement," for more practical suggestions on use of this method.

[69]P. E. Green and V. R. Rao, "Conjoint Measurement for Quantifying Judgmental Data," *Journal of Marketing Research,* vol. 8 (1971), 355-363. Also see Richard M. Johnson, "Trade-off Analysis of Consumer Values," *Journal of Marketing Research,* vol. 11 (May 1974), 121-127; and John O'Neill, "The Use of Conjoint Measurement for Product Planning," in William Locander (ed.), *Marketing Looks Outward,* 96-100.

An alternative is to employ paired adjectives such as "nutritious" and "not nutritious" using a similar numerical rating scale.[70] Also, some prefer to ask respondents to allocate 100 points across the categories to reflect their ranking of importance.

There always is the question of proper phrasing for the scale intervals. Only one study has specifically focused on methods for assigning weights to evaluative criteria, and the following results are reported:[71]

1. Rank orders of attribute importance appear to be quite stable across versions; simple "yes-no" or "1-6" judgments work as well as a more difficult task such as assigning points to attributes ranging from 0 to 100.

2. The use of a "1-6" gradient scale seems to generate finer distinctions when used alone than an arbitrary dichotomy such as "yes-no."

3. There are some differences between these versions, which raises the question of the wisdom of using a single measuring device.

Two other studies have focused on differing ways of measuring salience. Heeler and his colleagues contrasted three methods—conjoint analysis, self-questionnaire report, and information-display board and found the results to be sharply different.[72] The greatest convergent validity (i.e., parallel patterns of results) was found between self reports and conjoint analysis. Saegert and Cassis, on the other hand, asked people to make two ratings: (1) importance and (2) the extent to which available brands are differentiated on each of these attributes.[73] Importance ratings multiplied by similarity ratings gave good predictions of choice.

Obviously more needs to be done. One methodological refinement is to ascertain just what importance means. Is an attribute important because people desire it or because they do not desire it? Not only must it be determined how relative rankings of attribute importance change from one measurement to the next, but further inquiries also must employ some type of external criterion of importance against which varying approaches can be assessed. In the absence of this type of evidence, it is recommended that a nondichotomous rating scale be used, with the number of scale positions being a matter of the researcher's personal preference.

IMPLICATIONS FOR STRATEGY

Can evaluative criteria be changed through marketing strategy or consumer education? Or is the best strategy to accept these criteria as givens and proceed accordingly? These are not trivial questions.

[70]For useful insights into the wording of these adjectives, see J. H. Myers and W. C. Warner, "Semantic Properties of Selected Evaluation Adjectives," *Journal of Marketing Research*, vol. 5 (1968), 409-412.

[71]D. E. Schendel, W. L. Wilkie, and J. M. McCann, "An Experimental Investigation of 'Attribute Importance'," in D. M. Gardner (ed.), *Proceedings of the 2nd Annual Conference of the Association for Consumer Research* (College Park, Md.: College of Business and Public Administration, University of Maryland, 1971), 404-416.

[72]Roger M. Heeler, Chike Okechuku, and Stan Reid, "Attribute Importance: Contrasting Measurements," *Journal of Marketing Research,* vol. 16 (February 1979), 60-63.

[73]Joel Saegert and Jimmy Cassis, "More on Determinant Attribute Analysis on Bank Selection Criteria," in Beckwith, *1979 Educators',* 520-523.

Changing Evaluative Criteria

It was pointed out earlier that evaluative criteria have their roots in basic life-style. As a result, they can be highly resistant to change under conditions of high involvement. Here is an example of the dilemma marketers often face.

A market research study was undertaken and results indicated that the following criteria are used by a large segment of people to evaluate headache remedies (on a scale of 1 to 6, where 1 represents very important and 6 represents very unimportant):

Speed of relief	1.5
Reputation of brand	1.7
Quality of ingredients	2.3
Price	4.3
No side effects	4.8
Used by friends	5.6

Brand *A* was found to rate relatively well on most criteria, especially on price, but it rated poorly on reputation of brand. The brand has a six percent share of market and sells at a price roughly 40 percent below that of the three leading competitors.

Management now is faced with a dilemma. Its price advantage is of comparative unimportance to most buyers, and reputation of the brand is weak. This latter factor is especially critical because, as was discussed earlier, reputation of brand often is a surrogate indicator of product quality.

One alternative for remedial action is to convince buyers that all brands are identical; hence, the rational consumer should buy on the basis of price. From a strictly objective point of view, this could be in the best interest of consumers since government ratings (USP) do guarantee that all products sold contain the same chemical formulation. An advertising message with this theme, however, probably would prove ineffective with most of the members of this market segment. Reputation of brand is a strongly held evaluative criterion, and, similarly, there are strong negative views regarding the importance of price. The message probably will be screened out in the information-processing stage through selective attention. Even if the consumer is aware of the advertisement, he or she will probably distort the content and retain views unchallenged. The reasons for this selective screening were discussed earlier, and it can be a major inhibitor to promotional success.

Others have tried this first option with minimal success. Aluminum manufacturers tried for many years to convince consumers that a lightweight cooking utensil could be as high in quality as the more traditional heavier product. It was found that this belief was exceedingly difficult to change. Similarly, a manufacturer of ceiling tile found that it was impossible to sell a tile without holes. The reason was a deep-seated conviction that sound absorption capability was in proportion to the numbers of holes per square foot.

Let's also refer back once again to the automobile industry. The so-called "Big Three" futilely tried to unload unwanted intermediate- and large-size cars during 1979 and 1980 by heavy advertising and price discounting. The more popular front-wheel drive cars, on the other hand, were in short supply. There seemed to be a pervasive feeling among administrators that enough high pressure salesmanship could override consumer preferences. Detroit discovered once again what now should be an unquestioned principle: it is not possible to go against the grain of consumer preference, particularly under high-involvement circumstances. Some six decades of serious study of marketing should have made this clear. Isn't it about time that we stop ignoring the obvious?

Marketers, for the most part, must accept evaluative criteria as given and adapt strategy to these demand determinants. But this does not by any means indicate that unwise and even harmful buying practices should be accepted or tolerated. An example where some type of action is warranted comes from a study of the purchase of generic brands where real price savings are possible.[74] People who are most disadvantaged economically are most reluctant to use these brands, mostly because they fear lower quality. The headache remedy cited earlier also is a good case in point. A lower purchase expenditure will provide comparable therapeutic effects. Unfortunately, many consumers tend to be ignorant of such facts, especially those with minimal educational backgrounds. This is the situation in other product categories as well.[75] Therefore, there is a real need for consumer education, especially to provide help in the use of objective criteria, where possible, instead of subjective criteria.

Former Federal Trade Commissioner Mary Gardiner Jones points to yet another factor that underscores the need for consumer education.[76] It is her contention (and the authors' as well) that advertisers will provide consumer information only with respect to those evaluative criteria over which they have some competitive advantage. The consumers will be left in ignorance on other factors that quite often are of greater significance in their welfare.

Consumers' Union has been in the vanguard of the consumer education movement for many years, and the circulation of *Consumers' Reports* now approaches two million. This magazine publishes product tests that compare alternatives on many dimensions which are impossible for the consumer without extensive testing equipment. He or she thus is able to make a decision on a more objective basis. The purchaser of a high-fidelity speaker, for instance, can make a selection on the basis of performance curves, compatibility with various types of inputs, and other objective considerations in addition to the way in which it sounds.

[74]Roger A. Strang, Brian F. Harris, and Allan L. Hernandez, "Consumer Trial of Generic Products in Supermarkets: An Exploratory Study," in Beckwith, *1979 Educators',* 386-388.

[75]Arch G. Woodside and James L. Taylor, "Predictive Values of Product Information: An Application of the Brunswick Lens Model to Consumer Behavior" (unpublished working paper, Columbia, S. C.: University of South Carolina, 1976).

[76]Mary Gardiner Jones, "A Critical Analysis of the Howard Report" (Advertising and Public Interest Workshop, American Marketing Association, 1973).

Figure 14.5
The Maytag Lonely
Repairman: An
Illustration of
Appeal to
Consumer Benefits

Source: Courtesy the Maytag Company.

There is increasing emphasis on the consumer in the schools. It seems especially appropriate to offer this subject so that the young consumer can learn how to be a wise buyer before actually entering the market in a major way.

Corporations also can offer real service in consumer education. The "Shell Answer Book" series that ran in a number of consumer magazines provided much useful information on automobile performance, maintenance, and energy saving. While the company obviously gained some promotional benefit, the book also helped many people buy more wisely.

Appeal to
Benefits, Not
Attributes

In a recent study of new product introductions in the United Kingdom, 70 percent of those which were actually test-marketed never were introduced nationally and thus could be classified as failures.[77] The most common reason was that the product was nothing more than an indistinctive "me too," which offered no significant price or performance advantage to the consumer. Chin points out that one of the most common marketing errors is to advertise product attributes that may not be a real

[77]J. Hugh Davidson, "Why Most New Consumer Brands Fail," *Harvard Business Review,* vol. 54 (March-April 1976), 117-122.

benefit to the consumer.[78] In his words, "After all is said and done, consumers are only interested in one thing, 'What's in it for me?' "[79]

The obvious strategy, then, is to make the consumer's evaluative criteria the starting point of marketing strategy. Advertising should feature only *true* benefits. If there are no such distinctives, then it is time for a marketing overhaul of some type to remedy the deficiencies.[80]

One could scarcely imagine a more effective use of this strategy than that exemplified by the Maytag Company.[81] Even though it is a relatively small manufacturer, the company has won the status of being the largest independent marketer of washing machines, dryers, and dishwashers. For several decades it has stressed one major benefit delivered by its products—dependability. The lonely Maytag repairman shown in Figure 14.5 has been at the center of its successful television and magazine advertising since 1967.

Benefit Segmentation

Often good market opportunities are discovered by analysis of consumer attribute preferences. It is not unusual to uncover one or more segments not being served adequately by existing product alternatives—a process known as benefit segmentation.[82] This was the strategy used by Scripto as described earlier in this chapter.

Benefit segmentation lies at the heart of many of the new product successes in recent years, and it is helpful to look at several examples.[83] The pet food market must rank as one of the most competitive in terms of the number of product offerings. Not surprisingly, sales are made by appealing to the pet owner; the pet's preferences are decidedly secondary in spite of the claims of some advertisers. Ralston Purina, for example, successfully focused on convenience and introduced its *Whisker Lickins* soft moist cat food in single serving pouches.[84] Presumably the cats also will eat the stuff, but the greatest benefit is to the owner who avoids both touching and smelling it.

Growing numbers of people now are taking music with them wherever they go, even onto the jogging track or while roller skating. Head-

[78]Theodore G. N. Chin, "New Product Success and Failures—How to Detect Them in Advance," *Advertising Age* (September 24, 1973), 61-64.

[79]Chin, "New Product Success," 61.

[80]Eric J. Johnson and J. Edward Russo, "Product Familiarity and Learning New Information," in Kent B. Monroe (ed.), *Advances in Consumer Research,* vol. 8 (Ann Arbor, Mich.: Association for Consumer Research, 1981), 151-155.

[81]"Maytag Repairman Still Lonely," *Advertising Age* (April 30, 1980), 112.

[82]R. I. Haley, "Benefit Segmentation: A Decision-Oriented Research Tool," *Journal of Marketing,* vol. 32 (1968), 30-35; R. I. Haley, "Beyond Benefit Segmentation," *Journal of Advertising Research,* vol. 11 (1971), 3-8.

[83]For a more general discussion of the issues of benefit segmentation see the following: Roger J. Calantone and Alan Sawyer, "The Stability of Benefit Segments," *Journal of Marketing Research,* vol. 15 (August 1979), 395-404; Shirley Young, Leland Ott, and Barbara Feigin, "Some Practical Considerations in Market Segmentation," *Journal of Marketing Research,* vol. 15 (August 1978), 405-412; and Yoram Wind, "Issues and Advances in Segmentation Research," *Journal of Marketing Research,* vol. 15 (August 1978), 317-337.

[84]*The Gallagher Report,* vol. 24 (November 15, 1976).

Figure 14.6
The Bone Fone: An
Example of Benefit
Segmentation

Bone Fone Clone

If you thought the Bone Fone was great, wait until you hear what's new. Here's the latest on the Bone Fone spin-offs.

It started with the Bone Fone. And this very unusual stereo system has created a whole new series of products.

The Bone Fone is an AM/FM stereo radio that drapes around your neck like a scarf. Two speakers, placed near your ears, not only provide excellent stereo separation, but vibrate slightly through your bones to give you the same sensation as standing in front of your home stereo system.

UNEXPECTED APPLICATIONS

Shortly after it was introduced, the Bone Fone became a very popular product for a variety of reasons. A lady in Helena, Montana who bought the unit for her son told us, "It's made a significant contribution to my sanity. No more rock n' roll blasting through the house, the sound goes where my son goes."

A jogger in Rowlett, Texas wrote us "Amazing separation, fantastic stereo response, helps my jogging tremendously. I wasn't really expecting this type of quality through a magazine ad at this price."

But one of the most unexpected letters came from a man in Belle Center, Ohio. "You don't have to be young and jog to enjoy Bone Fone. You see, I'm 73 years old. I just sit and listen."

LETTERS EVERYWHERE

Letters have come from mailmen, roller skaters, skiers, cyclists, motrocycle enthusiasts, hikers and even people who listen to the Bone Fone stereo while walking their dog. The Bone Fone appeals to practically every American.

The Bone Fone was designed by an engineer who wanted to listen to good stereo music without carrying heavy box radios or bulky headphones. Headphones block out all other sounds—even warnings which could be dangerous outdoors, and box radios are heavy and disturb those around you. So he invented the Bone Fone—"the stereo sound you wear around."

Weighing only 17 ounces and powered by 4AA cell batteries the Bone Fone stereo provides a sound that would be impossible to describe in an advertisement. The cliche, "you've got to hear it to believe it," certainly applies here. And for **$69.95** it's the lowest priced stereo entertainment product available.

But what about the sport enthusiast who can care less about stereo music? Or the person who wants just the news? Or simply the person that just listens to AM radio and doesn't want to spend $69.95?

The Bone Fone drapes around your neck like a scarf and has a sound that you find incredible when you first hear it.

Enter NUTS! NUTS is the AM version of the Bone Fone for sports nuts, news nuts, jogging nuts or anybody who wants a low cost Bone Fone without FM or stereo. NUTS sells for **$39.95** complete with two speakers and a strap that firmly attaches the unit to you for any physical activity.

Sitting at a football game, walking your dog, jogging—NUTS gives you a convenient way to listen to music, news and sports without paying a premium for stereo.

But the Bone Fone spinoffs don't end there. There's the Neck Fone—a device you place over your shoulders and plugs into your home stereo system. This lets you enjoy your home stereo without disturbing those around you and without the bulk of headphones. The Neck Fone sells for **$34.95**.

So there you have it. Three exciting products—Bone Fone, NUTS, and the Neck Fone—three unusual solutions designed to solve any gift-giving problem.

LOWEST-PRICED STEREO

Compare the Bone Fone price with any box radio, stereo system or even the new $200 Sony Walkman. The Bone Fone is the lowest-priced quality personal stereo system you can buy. It is also safer than headphones as it leaves you free to hear the sounds around you and keeps you in touch with the environment.

To order any of the above products, simply send your check or money order for the amount listed above plus $2.50 for postage and handling (Ill. residents add 6% sales tax) to the address below, or credit card buyers may call our toll-free number below. Each unit is backed by a 90-day limited warranty and a service-by-mail facility as close as your mailbox. Service should rarely be required as the units use solid-state components and are designed to take rugged treatment. JS&A is America's largest single source of space-age products—further assurance that your modest investment is well protected.

The Bone Fone started a small revolution. Be part of that revolution with the space-age way to listen to music, news and sports. Order a Bone Fone product at no obligation, today.

JS&A

Dept.RW   One JS&A Plaza
Northbrook, Ill. 60062   (312) 564-7000
Call TOLL-FREE **800 323-6400**
In Illinois Call .... **(312) 564-7000**
©JS&A Group, Inc.,1980

Source: Courtesy of JS&A Group, Inc.

phone sets with self-contained radios have been on the market for several years, but consumers have not found them to be satisfactory. Therefore, a new product has been marketed called the *Bone Fone* which allows sounds to resonate through the wearer's bones to the inner ear and avoids the cumbersomeness of headsets.[85] Initial sales have far exceeded expectations. (See Figure 14.6.)

The marketing problem becomes especially acute when efforts are made to attack an entrenched leader. The Hertz Corporation reports car rental revenues of $1.1 billion for 1979, whereas Avis Rent A Car reported $811 million.[86] Avis long has taken aim at its larger competitor and has steadily gained. Using a recent survey which discovered that travelers tend to be "anxious, ulcerous and uptight" (they must have been observing the authors with our peripatetic travel life), Avis developed its new "Leave your worries behind" theme.[87] While its $12 million advertising budget still will retain the "We try harder" tag line, the new strategy says that "Avis is the one thing you don't have to worry about." In so doing, it is following a benefit segmentation strategy.

Skillful Personal Selling   The discussion thus far has assumed that use will be made mostly of the mass media that offer the greatest opportunities for selective avoidance by the consumer. Another approach, however, is to utilize personal selling. At times consumers will be receptive to help from a salesperson, especially when they have had little relevant past experience, when something has happened to change previous beliefs, or when there is high perceived risk surrounding the purchase. Training of salespeople to suggest more appropriate evaluative criteria has proved highly successful for the EMBA Mink Company, the Royal Worcester Porcelain Company, and many others.[88] Unfortunately personal selling all too often has become a lost art.

Summary

This chapter is the first of two which analyze how people evaluate alternatives and form new beliefs, attitudes, and intentions. An overview of this process was provided at the outset. Most of the discussion focused on the nature and role of evaluative criteria—desired outcomes from choice or use of an alternative expressed in the form of attributes or specifications used to compare various alternatives. It was demonstrated that these desired attributes are formed largely by the individual's lifestyle and reflect important motives.

Much has been learned recently on how people actually evaluate alternatives against these criteria using what are now referred to as *choice heuristics.* Those most seen in high-involvement situations favor

---

[85]Bernard F. Whalen, "Inventor of Bone Fone Radio Resonates His Way to Success," *Marketing News* (March 21, 1980), 4.

[86]"Hertz Claims World Lead," *Advertising Age* (October 13, 1980), 6.

[87]Josh Levine, "Avis Attempts to Allay Travelers' Worries," *Advertising Age* (October 13, 1980), 6.

[88]James F. Engel, W. Wayne Talarzyk, and Carl M. Larson, *Cases in Promotional Strategy* (Homewood, Ill.: Irwin, 1971), 361-366, 373-380.

processing by brand and are *compensatory* (a weakness on one attribute may be compensated for by strengths on others).

Because of roots in such basic dispositions, evaluative criteria are difficult to change through marketing influences and usually must be accepted as given and adapted to accordingly. Examples were given of price, and product reputation. Considerable emphasis was placed on measurement and several different methodologies were discussed. Finally, several marketing strategies were suggested, and the need for consumer education was underscored.

Review and Discussion Questions

1. What are evaluative criteria? What criteria did you use when you purchased your last pair of shoes? How did these differ, if at all, from those used by others in your family?

2. It is frequently alleged that the consumer is irrational and fails to buy wisely if he or she does not make maximum use of objective criteria in purchasing decisions. Evaluate.

3. One of the major criteria mentioned by many college girls in the purchase of an underarm deodorant is that "it makes me feel more confident in the presence of others." From your understanding of psychological and social influences on behavior, assess the probable underlying determinants of this evaluative criterion.

4. How important is reputation of brand as an alternative criterion in each of these product classes: Hand soap, toilet paper, panty hose, men's shirts, china and glassware, and gasoline? What are the reasons for your answers?

5. Summarize the evidence on the price-quality relationship. Would you expect this relationship in each of the types of products mentioned in question 4? Why or why not?

6. Think of the last time you made a purchase that required some thought and contemplation. Did you use a compensatory or a noncompensatory strategy in arriving at your final judgment?

7. Ask a friend to think out loud regarding a recent purchase that also required some thought and contemplation. In effect you will be using a retroactive protocol method of research. Was the judgment strategy compensatory or noncompensatory? Can you be more specific and use such labels as expectancy-value, disjunctive, conjunctive, or lexicographic?

8. Before World War II, the Customer Research Department of the General Motors Corporation regularly asked people to appraise the relative importance of certain product attributes using direct questions. It usually was found that highest marks were given to dependability and safety; styling was rated lower, and price was somewhere in between. What uses, if any, can be made of these data in marketing planning?

9. What are surrogate indicators? Why are they used?

10. Using a product of your own choice, prepare a research proposal indicating how you would determine the evaluative criteria which are being used in the purchase process.

11. Today considerable importance is being placed on consumer education. What are the causes of the so-called consumer movement? What is the role of the business firm in educating consumers on how to buy wisely?

CHAPTER 15

ALTERNATIVE EVALUATION:
BELIEFS, ATTITUDES AND INTENTIONS

"We've only just begun." This was the theme of an advertising campaign for the Crocker Bank of San Francisco starting in the late 1960s. Featuring significant events in young people's lives (marriage, first job, etc.), the outcome was a significant attitude shift toward Crocker Bank among young adults. But it became obvious by 1974 that some major marketing changes were needed.[1]

Consumer research focused on the problems people most frequently had with banks and whether or not any competitor was providing answers. The four major problems that emerged became the basis for a multi-media campaign theme line featuring, "Crocker's Changing Banking." Here were the problems and resulting changes in the service mix that led to sharp earnings increases for the bank:

1. *Short banking hours.* Crocker instituted "people's hours" as opposed to "banker's hours" and generated many new accounts.

2. *Checking account charges.* Crocker announced free checking accounts for people 62 and older.

3. *Lower interest on savings accounts than those offered by savings and loan associations.* Crocker quickly narrowed the gap to the legal limit, and other banks followed suit. Yet research showed that more people were aware of Crocker's action than that of any other bank, and Crocker's share of the bank savings market rose five percent in one year.

4. *Complicated bank forms.* Crocker was the first bank in the West to introduce simplifed loan agreements and other forms.

The net result of this marketing strategy was a 60 percent revenue gain in one year.

Crocker, of course, was following a strategy of benefit segmentation. First, research isolated important evaluative criteria which served, in effect, as unmet consumer needs. Crocker then instituted changes and communicated these changes to its public. The outcome was clearly a

---

[1]Virginia Miles, "Research Is Key in Changing Your Brand Strategy," *Advertising Age* (July 12, 1976), 32-34.

shift in *belief* that Crocker was "delivering the goods" in these areas, followed by a favorable shift in *attitude* toward the action of patronizing the Crocker Bank. Intent to use its services and an upsurge in customer traffic followed in short order.

This is an illustration of what has come to be known as the *hierarchy of effects,* in which a shift in awareness on important dimensions of a product or service leads to a corresponding change in beliefs, attitudes, intentions to act, and buying behavior. As we have stated before, this is part of the extended problem-solving behavior seen under conditions of high involvement, and this point need not be elaborated further.[2]

The purpose of this chapter is to continue the discussion of alternative evaluation, focusing more explicitly on beliefs, attitudes, and intentions. Even though attitude has been the most discussed and researched variable of these three, many researchers and practitioners still are bothered by this basic question: Will a change in attitude lead to a change in behavior? In order to provide a thorough answer, it is necessary to begin with a historical note documenting developments in attitude theory and research. Then we will focus explicitly on the so-called *multi-attribute model.* It has dominated research in consumer behavior until recently, and it has provided important clarifications of the nature and function of these three variables.

DOES A CHANGE IN ATTITUDE LEAD TO A CHANGE IN BEHAVIOR?

Until the 1970s, attitude research and theorizing dominated the literature of social psychology. In fact, many people agreed that an understanding of the nature and functioning of attitudes was the greatest contribution of social psychology to its parent field.

Notice that we are referring only to attitude as a single variable here. This is because beliefs and intentions were not singled out for separate consideration until recently. More about that later, because this single variable concept has led to some real problems. The classic definition is that an *attitude* is a mental and neural state of readiness to respond, which is organized through experience and exerts a directive and/or dynamic influence on behavior.[3] It soon became popular to theorize that there are three underlying attitude dimensions: (1) *cognitive*—the manner in which the attitude object is perceived; (2) *affective*—feelings of like or dislike; and (3) *behavioral*—action tendencies toward the objective. Unfortunately, these three components became confounded in measurement, leading to many of the problems discussed below.

From the outset, the assumption has been that a change in attitude will be followed by a change in behavior. The entire theory of persuasion to be discussed in the next chapter rests on this premise. Yet, it re-

---

[2]For the important references on involvement, see the footnotes in ch. 2.

[3]G. Allport, "Attitudes," in C. Murchison (ed.), *Handbook of Social Psychology* (Worcester, Mass.: Clark University Press, 1935), 798-884.

mained unverified for many years, and two camps soon formed. One alleged, largely without evidence, that behavior change indeed does follow attitude change. The other, acting on an equally shaky foundation, held strongly to the contrary. Some even dismissed attitude as a "phantom variable."

On the negative side, it was shown as early as 1934 that behavior was not predicted from written statements which presumably reflected attitudes toward minority groups.[4] Festinger was unable to find any consistent published evidence that attitudes and behavior are related in any direct way, although it must be pointed out that his review neglected vast numbers of relevant finds.[5] A similar review led Deutscher to state, "Disparities between thought and action are the central methodological problem of the social sciences."[6] Fishbein concluded:

After more than 70 to 75 years of attitude research, there is still little, if any, consistent evidence supporting the hypothesis that knowledge of an individual's attitude toward some object will allow one to predict the way he will behave with respect to that object. Indeed, what little evidence there is to support any relationship between attitude and behavior comes from studies that a person tends to bring his attitude into line with his behavior rather than from studies demonstrating that behavior is a function of attitude.[7]

Those on the positive side of this argument tended, almost without exception, to come from the applied fields of public opinion or consumer research. There are a number of studies clearly documenting that a change in attitude, usually through some type of persuasive campaign, is followed by behavioral change among large numbers of people.[8] In fact, many marketing researchers feel that attitude change should be a primary goal of promotional strategy. DuBois, for example, reported that the better the level of attitude, the more users you hold and the more nonusers you attract.[9] Studies at Grey Advertising, Inc. over a number of years led to this conclusion:

More and more psychologists are coming to the conclusion that to result in a sale an advertisement must bring about a positive change in the *attitude* of the reader or viewer. . . . That there is a

[4]R. T. LaPiere, "Attitudes vs. Actions," *Social Forces,* vol. 13 (1934), 230-237.

[5]Leon Festinger, "Behavioral Support for Opinion Change," *Public Opinion Quarterly,* vol. 28 (Fall 1964), 404-417.

[6]L. Deutscher, "Words and Deeds: Social Science and Social Policy," *Social Problems,* vol. 3 (1966), 235.

[7]M. Fishbein, "Attitude and the Prediction of Behavior," in M. Fishbein (ed.), *Attitude Theory and Measurement* (New York: John Wiley & Sons, 1967), 477.

[8]For just a few references, see Alvin A. Achenbaum, "Advertising Doesn't Manipulate Consumers," *Journal of Advertising Research,* vol. 12 (April 1972), 3-14; and "Ads Can Change Attitudes, Hike Sales; Effects Are Measurable," *Marketing News* (February 13, 1976), 5; and Steven J. Gross and C. Michael Niman, "Attitude-Behavior Consistency: A Review," *Public Opinion Quarterly,* vol. 39 (Fall 1975), 358-368.

[9]C. DuBois, "Twelve Brands on a Seesaw," *Proceedings of the 13th Annual Conference* (New York: Advertising Research Foundation, 1968).

**Figure 15.1
The Relationships
among Evaluative
Criteria, Beliefs,
Attitudes, and
Intention under
High Involvement**

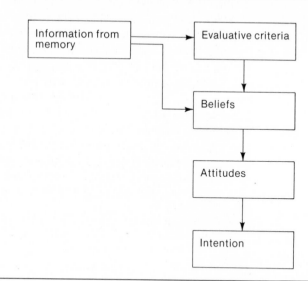

definite relationship between change of *attitude* toward a brand
and buying action is not only a logical conclusion but is supported
by a preponderance of *evidence.*[10]

**Why Should the
Marketer Care?**

There clearly are arguments on both sides of the attitude/behavior question, but so what? Does it make any difference in marketing practice?

Perhaps the best way to answer these questions is to refer once
again to the distinction between high and low involvement. High involvement leads to extended problem solving which seems to lead to the relationships in Figure 15.1. In other words, new information *does* affect
the consumer's cognitive structure and leads to a change in evaluative
criteria under some circumstances (although rarely, as discussed in the
previous chapter) in beliefs, attitudes, and intentions. This, in turn, is followed by a change in behavior. Therefore, advertising, selling, or any
other type of promotional activity can legitimately be undertaken to help
move a person from one stage to the next in his or her decision process.
A change in belief and/or attitude, then, *is* a valid marketing goal.

Quite the reverse is true under many low-involvement situations. Often a behavioral act is undertaken *followed* by a change in beliefs and
attitudes. In these cases, attitude change is *not* a valid marketing goal.
Everything should be aimed at stimulating purchase or trial in the hopes
that satisfaction will lead to reuse.

The distinction between high and low involvement, then, is usually
obscured in the discussions held on this subject to date. No wonder there
is such controversy. One can argue either way, depending upon whether
or not involvement is present.

[10]*Grey Matter*, vol. 39 (New York: Grey Advertising, Inc., November 1968), 1.

Assuming high involvement, there is yet another advantage to inclusion of attitude in one's strategy. Heller argues convincingly that behavioral measures such as market share tell only what happened in the past and not what will happen in the future.[11] Futhermore, there are no reasons revealed for behavior. He contends, instead, that the work of marketing research must be futuristic and that it is possible to alter market performance by understanding the attitude lying behind purchase decisions. In other words, a product may be evaluated poorly on one or two evaluative criteria, in which case changes could be made which later would increase market share. Attitude share, then, is just as important as market share from a *diagnostic perspective.*[12] The reader will discover later in this chapter and the next just how important this diagnostic advantage can be for marketing strategy.

The Terminological/ Methodological Confusion

Part of the controversy over the relation between attitude and behavior has its roots in how the variable has been defined and measured over the years. Here are some of the more important considerations:

1. *Varying conceptions and definitions.* Fishbein and Ajzen reviewed 750 articles published between 1968 and 1970 and found almost 500 different ways of conceptualizing the variable of attitude.[13] The upshot is that published studies often centered on very different phenomena.

2. *Varying measurement methods.* The number of ways to measure attitude is virtually endless as a review of any book on survey research will show. Only in recent years has there been any serious attempt to compare various approaches to ascertain which, if any, have validity, and these have been few and far between.[14] Bonfield underscored the problem by a review of those studies published in the major consumer research sources which made use of attitude as a variable.[15] He found only three that included a serious attempt at validation.

3. *Time interval.* Attitudes predict behavior with some accuracy only when the time interval between measurement and actual behavior is short.[16]

4. *Assignment of too much weight to a single variable.*[17] Common sense

---

[11]" 'Attitude Share of Market' Predicts Better Than Behavioral Measures," *Marketing News* (May 16, 1980), 7.

[12]" 'Attitude Share of Market'."

[13]Martin Fishbein and Icek Ajzen, "Attitudes and Opinions," *Annual Review of Psychology,* vol. 23 (1972), 188-244.

[14]See, for example, Russell I. Haley and Peter B. Case, "Thirteen Attitude Scales for Agreement and Brand Discrimination," *Journal of Marketing,* vol. 43 (Fall 1979), 20-32; and Joel N. Axelrod, "Attitude Measurements That Predict Purchases," *Journal of Advertising Research,* vol. 8 (March 1968), 3.

[15]E. H. Bonfield, "A Comment on the State of Attitude Measurement and Consumer Research: A Polemic," William L. Wilkie (ed.), *Advances in Consumer Research,* vol. 6 (Ann Arbor, Mich.: Association for Consumer Research, 1979), 238-244.

[16]"Broad Attitude Trends Don't Always Predict Specific Consumer Behavior," *Marketing News* (May 16, 1980), 8+.

[17]Icek Ajzen and Martin Fishbein, "Attitude-Behavior Relations: A Theoretical Analysis and Review of Empirical Research," *Psychological Bulletin,* vol. 84 (1977), 888-918.

ought to indicate that attitude alone cannot fully explain a complex behavioral act; yet this has often been the expectation. Consideration also must be given to the moderating effect of social pressure,[18] economic circumstances and expectations,[19] attitude toward the situation in which the behavior takes place,[20] and a variety of other factors. Examples could be exposure to new information, opportunity to make brand choice, the influence of competing brands, the effect of store environment, price and financial constraints, and family decision processes.[21]

5. *Lack of specificity in the attitude measure.* When the object of the attitude is very broad (e.g., attitude toward nutrition) there is no reason to expect that it will necessarily predict a specific type of behavior (e.g., consumption of low sugar products).[22]

Some Lifting of the Fog

When the first edition of this text was published in 1968, the authors could do little more than cite the conflicting evidence reviewed here and leave unanswered the all-important question of whether or not attitude change is a valid communication goal. During that period, however, the writings of Milton Rosenberg[23] and Martin Fishbein[24] came into vogue. Fishbein, in particular, drove home the crucial point that the cognitive, affective, and behavioral components of attitude need to be treated as separate variables and not be confounded in one measurement as has traditionally been the case.[25] This proved to be a major step forward and shed much needed light on the attitude-behavior linkage. In fact, the Fishbein model, in particular, dominated published consumer research in the 1970s.

The distinction between high- and low-involvement behavior also is a significant forward step for the reasons already stressed. As more research is done from these two perspectives, we can expect to see some real payout.

MULTI-ATTRIBUTE MODELS

Following the lead of Rosenberg and Fishbein, consumer researchers have come to view attitude differently in recent years. First, single-attitude scores (e.g., like or dislike of a given brand) are giving way to multidimensional models. In particular, growing use is being made of the so-

[18]Icek Ajzen and Martin Fishbein, "Attitudes and Normative Beliefs as Factors Influencing Behavioral Intentions," *Journal of Personality and Social Psychology,* vol. 21 (1972), 1-9.

[19]George Katona, *The Powerful Consumer* (New York: McGraw-Hill, 1960).

[20]Milton Rokeach, "Attitude Change and Behavioral Change," *Public Opinion Quarterly,* vol. 30 (Winter 1966-67), 529-550.

[21]George Day, *Buyer Attitudes and Brand Choice Behavior* (New York: Free Press, 1970).

[22]"Broad Attitude Trends."

[23]Milton J. Rosenberg, "Cognitive Structure and Attitudinal Effect," *Journal of Abnormal and Social Psychology,* vol. 53 (1956), 367-372.

[24]Martin Fishbein, "The Relationships Between Beliefs, Attitudes and Behavior," in Shel Feldman (ed.), *Cognitive Consistency* (New York: Academic Press, 1966), 199-223.

[25]Martin Fishbein and Icek Ajzen, *Belief, Attitude, Intention and Behavior: An Introduction to Theory and Research* (Reading, Mass.: Addison-Wesley, 1975), 12.

called *multi-attribute* model which begins with evaluative criteria as specified in Figure 15.1 and views attitude as the outcome of the consumer's beliefs about each competing brand or alternative in terms of these attributes. Because the remainder of this chapter makes such extensive use of the variables in Figure 15.1, it is helpful to define them with precision at the outset:

1. *Evaluative criteria:* desired outcomes from choice or use of an alternative expressed in the form of the attributes or specifications used to compare various alternatives.

2. *Beliefs:* information that links a given alternative to a specified evaluative criterion, specifying the extent to which the alternative possesses the desired attribute.

3. *Attitude:* a learned predisposition to respond consistently in a favorable manner with respect to a given alternative (referred to earlier as the affective dimension).

4. *Intention:* the subjective probability that beliefs and attitudes will be acted upon.

Pioneering Consumer Research Applications

This heading almost makes it sound as if we are reaching into the deep, dark past to dredge up old moth-eaten research. Notice that we do not go back much beyond a single decade. Many of these earlier applications are still important, because the research and conceptual formation has provided the basis for the more sophisticated Fishbein behavioral intentions model discussed below.

The Rosenberg Model

Rosenberg's model as originally published contained two variables: (1) *values* (equivalent to evaluative criteria) and their importance in arriving at an attitude; and (2) *perceived instrumentality* (a complex term that simply estimates the degree to which the taking of a point of view or following an action will either enhance or block the attainment of a value).[26] Assume that low price is an important value (evaluative criterion) and that the consumer has come to believe that Brand A offers low price. The perceived instrumentality of Brand A thus would be high.

His attitude model took this form:

$$A_0 = \sum_{i=1}^{N} (VI_i)(PI_i)$$

where:

A_0 = the overall evaluation of the attractiveness of alternative 0
VI_i = the importance of the ith value
PI_i = the perceived instrumentality of alternative 0 with respect to value i
N = the number of pertinent or salient values

[26]Rosenberg, "Cognitive Structure."

In its pure form, the Rosenberg model calls for the measurement of value importance on a scale containing 21 categories ranging from "gives me maximum satisfaction" ($+10$) to "gives me maximum dissatisfaction" (-10). Using our earlier example, low price might receive a rating of $+10$. Perceived instrumentality is assessed using 11 categories ranging from "the condition is completely attained through a given action" ($+5$) to "the condition is completely blocked through undertaking the given action" (-5).[27] Perhaps Brand *A* in the above example would be given a score of $+5$.

Probably the best test of this approach in its pure form was published by Hansen in 1969.[28] He successfully predicted choices among modes of travel, menu items, hairdryers, and restaurants. He also found that the two basic terms (value importance and perceived instrumentality) are independent and will not predict response when used separately. Similar results were reported by Bither and Miller.[29]

The Fishbein Model

Fishbein's original model is similar to Rosenberg's, but there are subtle differences.[30] His first component is *belief,* defined as the probability that an object does or does not have a particular attribute. The second component is an *affective term* normally stated in terms of good or bad. It specifies whether or not the possession or failure of possession of the attribute in question is positive or negative. The model takes this form:

$$A_0 = \sum_{i=1}^{N} B_i a_i$$

where:

A_0 = attitude toward the object
B_i = the ith belief about the object
a_i = the evaluation of the belief
N = the total number of beliefs

In his initial research, Fishbein measured attitudes toward Negroes.[31] It was his hypothesis that attitudes are a function of beliefs about the characteristics of members of this race (B_i) and the evaluative aspects of those beliefs (a_i). For example, the characteristic "uneducated" was rephrased into the belief statement, "Negroes are uneducated." The belief

[27]Rosenberg, "Cognitive Structure."

[28]Flemming Hansen, "Consumer Choice Behavior: An Experimental Approach," *Journal of Marketing Research,* vol. 4 (November 1969), 436-443.

[29]Stewart W. Bither and Stephen Miller, "A Cognitive Theory of Brand Preference," in Philip R. McDonald (ed.), *Marketing Involvement in Society and the Economy* (Chicago: American Marketing Association, 1969), 210-216.

[30]Martin Fishbein, "An Investigation of the Relationships between Beliefs about an Object and the Attitude toward that Object," *Human Relations,* vol. 16 (1963), 233-240.

[31]Fishbein, "An Investigation of the Relationships."

statements were measured with a five-point scale with the poles labeled with such terms as "probable/improbable" and "likely/unlikely." A five-point scale also was used to measure evaluative aspects of each belief with such terms as "good/bad."

The formula calls for belief (B_i) and evaluation (a_i) scores to be multiplied for each belief. Then these scores are summed to arrive at a single attitude ranking. While this model has seldom been applied to marketing in its pure form, as the next section points out, Bettman and his associates verified that people do multiply beliefs in their evaluation as Fishbein has hypothesized.[32] Whether or not these are then summed was less clear. It also was found that both the B_i and the a_i terms make substantial contributions to the evaluation and hence must be retained in this type of research. They feel, however, that both should be scored with a scale ranging from -3 to $+3$.[33]

Hybrid Models

Most of the marketing applications did not follow Rosenberg or Fishbein without some often substantial modifications. Here is one example which embodies a formulation close to the Rosenberg model but with different measurements:[34]

$$A_b = \sum_{i=1}^{n} W_i B_{ib}$$

where:

A_b = attitude toward a particular alternative b
W_i = weight or importance of evaluative criterion i
B_{ib} = evaluative aspect or belief with respect to utility of alternative b to satisfy evaluative criterion i
n = number of evaluative criteria important in selection of an alternative in category under consideration

In this formula W_i is the weight or importance of the evaluative criterion, and B_{ib} is the evaluation of the alternative along that criterion. This rating is performed for each evaluative criterion, and the summed score is attitude toward the alternative.

Much of the resulting research attempted to validate these varying approaches through correlating the attitude scores produced through the Rosenberg, Fishbein, or hybrid model of some type with other independently derived measures of attitude. This did serve to measure what is technically known as *convergent validity*, and there are some excellent

[32]James R. Bettman, Noel Capon, and Richard J. Lutz, "Multi-Attribute Measurement Models and Multi-Attribute Attitude Theory: A Test of Construct Validity," *Journal of Consumer Research,* vol. 1 (March 1975), 1-15.

[33]Bettman, Capon, and Lutz, "Multi-Attribute Measurement Models."

[34]W. W. Talarzyk and R. Meinpour, "Comparison of an Attitude Model and Coombsian Unfolding Analysis for the Prediction of Individual Brand Preference" (paper presented at the Workshop on Attitude Research and Consumer Behavior, Bloomington, Ill.: University of Illinois, December 1970).

summaries for the reader to refer to.[35] Unfortunately, *predictive validity* (the hypothesized relationship between beliefs, attitudes, intentions, and behavior) remained elusive.

Some Insights Which Were Gained

There were several attempts to assess which of these models or their variants performed best as was mentioned above, and overall predictive validity proved to be disappointing. In other words, the hypothesized relationship between changes in beliefs and attitudes leading to corresponding changes in intention and behavior was rarely demonstrated conclusively.

There are several reasons why ability to predict behavioral response is low. First, attitude toward an object takes no account whatsoever of the situation in which the behavior is undertaken. Situational influence has now been documented thoroughly, and it must be given proper emphasis in behavioral prediction.[36] Consider Burdus's words on this subject:

> When my colleagues talk about my ideal cigarette, I am tempted to ask them whether they mean ideal for work or ideal for play, ideal for the beginning of the month when I'm rich or ideal for the end when I am poor. When they talk about shampoos, another so called homogeneous market, I want to know whether the ideal they are asking me about is my ideal when I am on holiday sea-bathing, my ideal when the shopping has to be done as quickly as possible. The markets may be homogeneous—it seems I am not.[37]

A second major omission is failure to consider the existence of conformity pressures from various reference groups and family. These often can dominate beliefs and attitudes as a determinant of both intention and behavior.[38]

Finally, there is a host of both anticipated and unanticipated circumstances that will affect intentions and choice. Examples are financial circumstances, assumed availability of goods, and so on.

The net result is that beliefs and attitudes, defined in terms of attitudes toward an object, have been expected to carry an impossible

[35]See especially M. B. Holbrook and J. M. Hulbert, "Multi-Attribute Attitude Models: A Comparative Analysis," in Mary Jane Schlinger (ed.), *Advances in Consumer Research,* vol. 2 (Chicago: Association for Consumer Research, 1975), 375-388; and W. L. Wilkie and E. A. Pessemier, "Issues in Marketing's Use of Multi-Attribute Attitude Models," *Journal of Marketing Research,* vol. 10 (November 1973), 428-441.

[36]For some of the recent literature, see Russell W. Belk, "The Objective Situation as a Determinant of Consumer Behavior," in Schlinger, *Advances in Consumer Research,* 427-437; Richard J. Lutz and Pradeep Kakkar, "The Psychological Situation as a Determinant of Consumer Behavior," in Schlinger, *Advances in Consumer Research,* 439-453; Russell W. Belk, "Situational Variables in Consumer Behavior," *Journal of Consumer Research,* vol. 2 (December 1975), 157-164; and Richard J. Lutz and Pradeep Kakkar, "Situational Influence in Interpersonal Persuasion," in Anderson, *Advances in Consumer Research,* 370-378.

[37]J. S. Burdus, "Attitude Models—The Dream and the Reality," in Phillip Levine (ed.), *Attitude Research Bridges the Atlantic* (Chicago: American Marketing Association, 1975), 161.

[38]Herbert C. Kelman, "Attitudes Are Alive and Well and Gainfully Employed in the Sphere of Action," *American Psychologist,* vol. 29 (May 1974), 310-324.

weight of prediction. This fact has led to the development of the extended Fishbein model discussed in the next section.

The Fishbein Behavioral Intentions Model

As his research program matured, Fishbein, along with his colleague Ajzen, came to realize that attitude toward the object (A_O) was a limited concept. Consider their words:

. . . it really doesn't make a lot of difference how much a person likes a given product, or how good that product's "brand image" is—if the consumer doesn't believe that buying that product will lead to more "good consequences" (and fewer "bad consequences") than buying some other product, they (*sic*) will tend to buy the other product. Thus, one of the factors that contributes to a person's intention to engage in some behavior is the attitude toward engaging in the behavior . . . not the attitude toward the object of the behavior. Fortunately, however, everything we know about attitudes toward objects also applies to attitudes toward actions.[39]

Therefore, the first modification was to substitute *attitude toward performing a particular behavior under a given set of circumstances* (A_B) for attitude toward the object (A_O).

The second modification was to take explicit account of the norms governing behavior and a person's motivation to comply with those norms. This component is referred to as *subjective norm* (*SN*).[40]

Fishbein and Ajzen contend that A_B and *SN* taken together will provide an accurate prediction of a person's intention to perform a given behavior *(BI)*. Intention, in turn, will give an approximate prediction of behavior, all things being equal. The resulting general model appears as follows:

$$B \approx BI = w_1(A_B) + w_2(SN)$$

where:

B = *overt behavior*
BI = behavioral intention
A_B = attitude toward performing the behavior
SN = the subjective norm
w_1
w_2 = empirically determined weights

A_B and *SN* must be measured, whereas the weights reflecting the importance of these factors are estimated statistically through use of regression analysis.

Notice that Fishbein and Ajzen make no claim to be able to predict behavior perfectly. The most they will say is that behavioral intention will approximate behavior.

[39]Martin Fishbein, "Attitude, Attitude Change, and Behavior: A Theoretical Overview," in Levine, *Attitude Research,* 12.

[40]Fishbein and Ajzen, *Belief, Attitude, Intention and Behavior,* esp. 301 and following.

There are some computational formulae used for A_B and *SN*. It is necessary to review these next, after which we will show the Fishbein behavioral intentions model in flow chart form and provide a practical illustration of how it can be used in practice.

Attitude toward the Behavior (A_B)

Remember that A_B is attitude toward performing a particular behavior under a given set of circumstances. It is estimated using this formula:

$$A_B = \sum_{i=1}^{n} b_i e_i$$

where:

    A_B = attitude toward performing the behavior
    b_i = belief that performing behavior *B* leads to consequence *i*
    e_i = the person's evaluation of consequence *i*
    n = number of beliefs

This looks pretty abstract, so let's put it in more understandable terms, focusing on a specific purchase and use situation. A_B will be interpreted as attitude toward purchasing and using a given brand in a product class. Belief may be viewed as the person's estimate of whether or not the product under consideration will possess a desired attribute. The *e* component really is a measure of attribute salience, in that it provides an evaluation of the goodness or badness of that particular product attribute.

For purposes of illustration, assume that a serious runner needs a new pair of running shoes and is engaged in alternative evaluation. Assume further, that these evaluative criteria have been isolated through preliminary research:

The shoe must provide shock absorbence to permit running on hard surfaces.

The price must be under $40.

The sole should be designed to provide maximum wear on hard surfaces.

The shoe must provide built-in arch support.

It must be available in a variety of colors.

It must feel comfortable when worn.

It should receive a five-star rating by *Runner's World* (an annual rating of runners' shoes appearing in *Runner's World*)

This, by the way, would represent a high-involvement purchase situation, because proper foot gear is one significant key to prevention of injury.[41] Furthermore, there is high perceived risk that the wrong shoe might be purchased.

[41]Gabe Mirkin and Marshall Hoffman, *The Sports Medicine Book* (Boston: Little, Brown and Company, 1978), chs. 10-11.

The e score or evaluation of salience of each of these desired attributes is assessed usually through use of a six-point scale in this form:[42]

The shoe must be priced under $40

	+3	+2	+1	−1	−2	−3	
Very good	___	___	___	___	___	___	Very bad

This would be done, of course, for each of the seven attributes and the average value computed across a sample of people would be a measure of salience. The higher the value in the positive direction, the more determinant the attribute is viewed to be.

The belief that a given brand (say Brand A) actually possesses an attribute would be measured this way for each of the salient attributes:

The shoe is priced under $40.

	+3	+2	+1	−1	−2	−3	
Very likely	___	___	___	___	___	___	Very unlikely

Again, the higher the score in a positive direction, the stronger the belief that the brand meets the specification.

A_B now is derived by multiplying the b and e components for each belief and then summing across the total number of beliefs (n). The e component is measured only once for the product class as noted above, whereas a b score must be computed for each brand. The illustration begun here appears in completed form in Figure 15.3, discussed later.

Subjective Norm (SN)

The second component of this expanded model, SN, represents an individual's perception of what other people think he or she should do. It is a function of the person's beliefs about the expectations of these people and his or her motivation to comply with what they say. It is depicted in this formula:

$$SN = \sum_{j=1}^{n} NB_j MC_j$$

where:

SN = subjective norm
NB_j = normative belief (the person's belief that reference group or individual j thinks he or she should or should not perform the behavior)
MC_j = motivation to comply with the influence of referent j
n = number of relevant reference groups or individuals

---

[42]These questions are phrased following the guidelines given in Fishbein and Ajzen, *Belief, Attitude, Intention, and Behavior.*

Social norms were discussed extensively in an earlier chapter, and they were defined, in general, as internalized, socially sanctioned forms of behavior. Pressures to act in certain ways can be severe under some circumstances. The existence of such an influence, however, is of no consequence unless the individual is motivated to comply. This is why these two variables appear in the above equation.

According to Fishbein and Ajzen, normative beliefs are measured on a scale such as this:

The people I run with think I:

	+3	+2	+1	−1	−2	−3	
should	___	___	___	___	___	___	should not

purchase Brand A running shoe.

Motivation to comply then would be assessed in this way:

In general:

	+3	+2	+1	−1	−2	−3	
I want to do	___	___	___	___	___	___	I want to do the opposite of

what the people I run with think I should do.

These scores would also be multiplied and summed for the number of relevant social influences there might be in a given situation. Again, we will complete this illustration in the next section.

Practical Implications

Perhaps it would be helpful now to diagram the Fishbein extended model. This appears in Figure 15.2 and hence becomes part of the model of high-involvement behavior used in this book. Notice that it shows intention to be a function of attitude (A_B) and social influence as hypothesized by Fishbein. The arrow from reference group/family to normative compliance is meant to depict the (NB)-(MC) relationship. Attitude, in turn, is shown as a function of beliefs.

Now, let's return to the running shoe example. Table 15.1 contains the complete set of data obtained from a sample of people on A_B making use of seven product attributes, and Table 15.2 shows SN (assuming that other runners are the only possible reference group).

The only remaining step now is to obtain the weights for A_B and SN. These are obtained statistically by regressing the two sets of scores on

**Figure 15.2
Incorporation of
the Fishbein
Behavioral
Intentions Model
into the Model of
High-Involvement
Decision Process
Behavior**

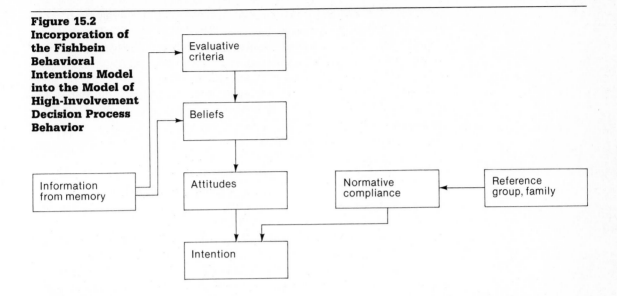

**Table 15.1
Attitudes (A_B)
toward Three
Brands of Running
Shoe**

Attribute	Evaluation (e_i)	Beliefs (b_i)		
		Brand A	Brand B	Brand C
Shock absorbence	+1	+3	+1	+2
Price under $40	+3	−2	+3	+2
Wearability of sole	+2	−1	+2	+1
Arch support	+1	+2	−1	+2
Colors	+1	+1	+3	+2
Comfort	+2	+3	+1	+2
Five-Star rating	+3	+3	−1	+1
Total score (A_B)		+13	+15	+21

**Table 15.2
Social Influence
(SN) toward the
Purchase of Three
Brands of Running
Shoe**

Source	Motivation to Comply (MC)	Normative Beliefs About Brands (NB)		
		Brand A	Brand B	Brand C
People I run with	−1	+1.5	+2	+3
Total score (SN)		−1.5	−2	−3

an independently derived measure of intention (*BI*). A question of this type is usually worded in this way: "What is the probability that you will purchase Brand A between now and two weeks from now?"[43] The time period, of course, would vary from product to product depending upon the frequency of purchase.

The scores in Table 15.1 were computed by multiplying each belief

[43]Paul R. Warshaw, "Predicting Purchase and Other Behaviors from General and Contextually Specific Intentions," *Journal of Marketing Research*, vol. 17 (February 1980), 26-33.

score for each product, one attribute at a time, by the evaluation score (e_i) and summing to arrive at the total. This was done for Brand A, for example, by starting with "shock absorbence" and multiplying a rating of $+3$ (b_i by $+1$ (e_i), moving onto "price" $(+3)(-2)$ and so on to reach a total of $+13$. Clearly, Brand C is the winner with a total score of $+21$. The social influence (SN) score was arrived at similarly by multiplying MC times the NB rating for each brand. While Brand C was preferred, once again, this time by other runners, there is a negative motivation to comply. Hence it comes out lowest.

All we need now are the weights (w) for the A_B and SN components. In this example, it would be completely reasonable to assume that SN would be of little or no relevance because of the known fact that runners tend to be loners.[44] Hence their decision would be made on their own judgment. The BI (behavioral intention) measure, then, consists mainly of the attitude component, and Brand C comes out on top. Presumably intention to purchase will come close to predicting actual purchase.

There are a number of ways to measure these component scores,[45] and not all follow Fishbein to the letter in methodology. The most important use of these data does *not* lie in ability to predict intentions or even behavior. Rather, the greatest benefit is in the diagnostic information which is provided. Notice, for example, that salient criteria are clearly identified: "price" and the "five-star rating by *Runner's World*." If a brand rates low on either of these, this is a definite danger sign although not necessarily a fatal one. The Fishbein model assumes that consumers make use of a compensatory strategy in alternative evaluation. Remember our discussion of choice heuristics in Chapter 14? This means that a perceived weakness on one attribute may be compensated for by strengths on others. Nevertheless, the low rating received by Brand A on price might be a signal either that price should be lowered if it exceeds $40 or a better promotion job be done to inform consumers if that is not the case. More will be said on this type of diagnostic analysis in the next chapter.

Validity of the Behavioral Intentions Model

It should be stated once again that the model discussed here is designed to predict intentions and not behavior itself, which it can only approximate. Therefore, its validity must be assessed by comparison against an independently derived measure of intentions. Preliminary research of this type has been undertaken, but something should be said first about the way in which intentions should be measured.

As we mentioned earlier, the usual approach to measurement of BI following Fishbein's lead is wording such as this: "What is the probability that you will purchase the 'given brand' between now and next Monday

[44]See James F. Fixx, *The Complete Book of Running* (New York: Random House, 1977).

[45]See, for example, David T. Wilson, H. Lee Matthews, and James W. Harvey, "An Empirical Test of the Fishbein Behavioral Intention Model," *Journal of Consumer Research*, vol. 1 (March 1975), 39-48; and Michael A. Ryan and E. H. Bonfield, "The Fishbein Extended Model and Consumer Behavior," *Journal of Consumer Research*, vol. 2 (August 1975), 118-136.

morning?"[46] Pavasars and Wells would modify this wording slightly because of their finding that intentions predict behavior best when defined as the "probability of buying a particular brand relative to the probabilities of buying competitive brands on the next purchase."[47] Wells recommends that these probabilities be assessed by the constant-sum method in which a fixed number of points, say 100, is allocated by the consumer to a set of brands in proportion to the estimated likelihood of buying that brand on the next purchase. The number of points allocated to each, divided by the total number of points, then represents the probability of purchase.[48]

Warshaw recommends going a step further, making use of what he calls "conditional intentions."[49] Very high predictions of behavior were obtained with wording such as this: "Assuming that you do make one or more purchases of soft drink from a given location L between now and next Monday, what is the probability that you will buy _____?"[50]

In the validity tests conducted to date, positive results have been reported by Wilson, Mathews, and Harvey;[51] Harrell;[52] Wilson, Mathews, and Monoky;[53] Ryan and Bonfield;[54] Oliver and Berger;[55] and Siebold and Roper.[56] These studies have encompassed a wide range of behavior, although it is not certain that all can be classified as high involvement. Earlier Ryan and Bonfield were not as optimistic, stating that the predictive power obtained in a series of marketing studies both in the United States and Great Britain is lower than that reported by Fishbein and others working in a less real world situation.[57]

Perhaps the most that can be said with certainty thus far is that the expanded Fishbein model predicts both intentions and behavior far better than the various A_O models discussed earlier.

[46]Warshaw, "Predicting Purchase."

[47]John Pavasars and William D. Wells, "Measures of Brand Attitudes Can Be Used to Predict Buying Behavior," *Marketing News* (April 11, 1975), 6.

[48]Pavasars and Wells, "Measures of Brand Attitudes."

[49]Warshaw, "Predicting Purchase."

[50]Warshaw, "Predicting Purchase."

[51]David T. Wilson, H. Lee Mathews, and James W. Harvey, "An Empirical Test of the Fishbein Behavioral Intention Model," *Journal of Consumer Research*, vol.1 (March 1975), 39-48.

[52]Gilbert D. Harrell, "Physician Prescribing: Behavioral Intention, Attitudes, Normative Beliefs, Risk and Information" (unpublished doctoral dissertation, State College, Pa.: Pennsylvania State University, 1977).

[53]David T. Wilson, H. Lee Mathews, and John F. Monoky, "Attitude as a Predictor of Behavior in a Buyer-Seller Bargaining Situation: An Experimental Approach," Working Series in Marketing Research, (State College, Pa.: Pennsylvania State University, February 1972).

[54]Michael J. Ryan and E. H. Bonfield, "Fishbein's Intentions Model: A Test of External and Pragmatic Validity," *Journal of Marketing*, vol. 44 (Spring 1980), 82-95.

[55]Richard L. Oliver and Philip K. Berger, "A Path Analysis of Preventive Health Care Decision Models," *Journal of Consumer Research*, vol. 6 (September 1979), 113-122.

[56]D. R. Siebold and R. E. Roper, "Psychological Determinants of Health Care Intentions: Test of the Triandis and Fishbein Models," in D. Nimmo (ed.), *Communication Yearbook*, vol. 3 (New Brunswick, N.J.: Transaction Books, 1979), 625-643.

[57]Michael A. Ryan and E. H. Bonfield, "The Fishbein Extended Model and Consumer Behavior," *Journal of Consumer Research*, vol. 2 (August 1975), 118-136; and Michael J. Ryan and E. H. Bonfield, "The Extended Fishbein Model: Additional Insights . . . Problems," in Schlinger (ed.), *Advances in Consumer Research*, 265-283.

Still, there are some conceptual and methodological difficulties with this model which should be noted briefly. Those interested in more detail are referred to two comprehensive literature reviews by Miniard[58] since only several of the more major issues are discussed here.

(1) Validity of the Component Weights   This model will be accurate in prediction of intention only if the relative weights for the two components (A_B and SN) correctly reflect the true influence of each variable. Direct evidence on this point is lacking, but inspection of the regression data from some of the experiments undertaken to date gives rise to suspicions that the weights may not accurately reflect relative importance.[59] More research is clearly needed.

(2) Accurate Reflection of Situational Influence   It is assumed that anticipated circumstances such as financial status, availability of goods, access to retail stores, and general economic attitudes are all captured within the A_B measure, but there is some evidence that this may not be the case.[60] If this proves to be true upon further analysis, then one can agree with Warshaw that a case can be made for separating out these influences as opposed to aggregating them within one measure.[61]

(3) The Additive Assumption   Troutman and Shanteau raised this relevant question: "Do consumers evaluate products by adding or averaging attribute information?"[62] The Fishbein model, of course, assumes the former in that a combined score is arrived at from a series of separate judgments for each product. An alternative perspective is provided by the *information integration theory* of Norman Anderson and his associates who assume that people are more likely to arrive at an average judgment across beliefs.[63] If this is true, then some very different outcomes would be observed.[64] Cohen and his associates theorize that the

---

[58]See Paul W. Miniard, "Examining the Diagnostic Utility of the Fishbein Behavioral Intentions Model," (working paper 80-71, Columbus, Ohio: College of Administrative Science, Ohio State University, August, 1980); and Paul W. Miniard and Joel B. Cohen, "An Examination of the Fishbein Behavioral Intention Model's Concepts and Measures," *Journal of Experimental Social Psychology* (in press).

[59]See, for example, Paul W. Miniard and Joel B. Cohen, "Isolating Attitudinal and Normative Influences in Behavioral Intentions Models," *Journal of Marketing Research,* vol. 16 (1979), 102-110; Michael J. Ryan, "An Examination of an Alternative Form of the Behavioral Intention Model's Normative Component," in H. Keith Hunt (ed.), *Advances in Consumer Research,* vol. 5 (Ann Arbor, Mich.: Association for Consumer Research, 1978), 283-289; and Paul R. Warshaw, "A New Model for Predicting Behavioral Intentions: An Alternative to Fishbein," *Journal of Marketing Research,* vol. 17 (May 1980), 153-172.

[60]Kenneth E. Miller and James L. Ginter, "An Investigation of Situational Variation in Brand Choice Behavior and Attitude," *Journal of Marketing Research,* vol. 16 (1979), 111-123.

[61]Warshaw, "A New Model."

[62]C. Michael Troutman and James Shanteau, "Do Consumers Evaluate Products by Adding or Averaging Attribute Information?" *Journal of Consumer Research,* vol. 3 (1976), 101-107.

[63]See Norman H. Anderson, "Averaging Versus Adding as a Stimulus-Combination Rule in Impression Formation," *Journal of Experimental Psychology,* vol. 70 (1965), 394-400; and Norman H. Anderson, "How Functional Measurement Can Yield Validated Interval Scales of Mental Quantities," *Journal of Applied Psychology,* vol. 61 (1976), 677-692.

[64]O. B. Ahtola, "Toward a Vector Model of Intentions," in Beverlee B. Anderson (ed.), *Advances in Consumer Research,* vol. 3 (Ann Arbor, Mich.: Association for Consumer Research, 1976), 481-484.

situation itself may determine whether one enters into averaging or adding,[65] but any kind of definitive conclusion awaits further research.

(4) Measurement of the Normative Component   The reader will recall that motivation to comply (*MC*) with normative social influence is measured on the following type of scale if one follows Fishbein and Ajzen:

In general:

| I want to do | _____ _____ _____ _____ _____ _____ | I want to do the opposite of |

what referent *x* thinks I should do.

There now is growing doubt as to whether or not such general wording should be used, and some feel a case can be made for much more specific probing into this factor.[66]

Some Concluding Comments

There is no question that the literature on consumer research has been occupied with the various multi-attribute models for more than a decade. Until recently, however, the models' popularity has been pretty much confined to academic ranks, although there are definite signs that this is changing.[67]

Why has this gap existed? One reason, quite frankly, is because multi-attribute models became a kind of fad for a period of time. Much of the earlier published research split hairs to such a degree that those with a more applied interest tended, perhaps too quickly, to dismiss the output as being irrelevant. In part, this always will be a problem when the focus of one group lies on basic research more than does the other, but this is not the total picture.

Industry researchers have been increasingly concerned over issues of methodological validity, and there have been some breakthroughs in ability to predict behavior from modified attitude scales or through such methods as multidimensional scaling and conjoint analysis. Industry researchers have quietly moved ahead on these fronts, and that may be why there has been less explicit interest in the Fishbein type of model.

It also should be noted that the gap may be more apparent than real. The authors have kept a foot in both camps, so to speak, for many years. Much consumer research undertaken in the so-called real world is designed to measure evaluative criteria, assess the strengths and weak-

---

[65]Joel B. Cohen, Paul W. Miniard, and Peter R. Dickson, "Information Integration: An Information Processing Perspective," in Jerry C. Olson (ed.), *Advances in Consumer Research,* vol. 7 (Ann Arbor, Mich.: Association for Consumer Research, 1980), 161-170.

[66]See, for example, Martin Fishbein, "Extending the Extended Model: Some Comments," in Anderson, *Advances in Consumer Research,* vol. 3, 491-497; M. Glassman and N. Fitzhenry, "Fishbein's Subjective Norm: Theoretical Considerations and Empirical Evidence," in Anderson (ed.), *Advances in Consumer Research,* vol. 3, 477-480; Miniard and Cohen, "Isolating Attitudinal and Normative Influences"; and Miniard and Cohen, "On the Adequacy."

[67]" 'Attitude Share of Market' Predicts."

nesses of competitive alternatives in these terms, and to predict intentions. While there may be some differences in approaches, the basic outcome often is surprisingly similar.

Resolution only will come through application of multi-attribute models in actual consumer buying and decision-making situations apart from the laboratory. Academic and business researchers both have much to gain from cooperative endeavors in this respect.

IMPLICATIONS FOR MARKETING STRATEGY

This chapter has dealt with attitude from the specific perspective of multi-attribute models. In that context, it has been explicitly assumed that high involvement is present. If that were not the case, then changes in belief and attitude would follow purchase, not precede it, and there would be little to gain from measuring these variables and pursuing strategies for change as discussed in the next chapter.

It should be noted that attitude as a variable used to explain human behavior usually is conceived much more broadly than A_B. It is conceived as a component of world view, much in the same sense as was presented under the subject of psychographics in an earlier chapter.[68] Accordingly, there is a substantial variety of approaches to attitude measurement which can be reviewed in any basic text on marketing research or communication research.[69] Psychographic measurement, of course, has real value in marketing, but its findings are used in a very different manner than A_B, because one can rarely expect a general attitude statement to predict specific intention or behavior. For yet another case in point, Wells reports a slight increase from 1968 to 1978 in agreement with the statement, "I like to feel attractive to members of the opposite sex," but there was a much sharper increase in the use of shampoo than would have been expected.[70] The reason for this was a change in hairstyles which encouraged more frequent shampooing at home, and the issue of attractiveness to the opposite sex had little to do with it. Proper use of a multi-attribute model might have detected more of these factors and discouraged a naive and misleading conclusion.

Keep in mind that multi-attribute models are uniquely applicable to an analysis of the alternative evaluation process and can provide strategically helpful information. The diagnostic benefit of data such as that il-

[68]For other perspectives on attitude, see Richard J. Lutz, "A Functional Approach to Consumer Attitude Research," in Hunt (ed.), *Advances in Consumer Research,* vol. 5, 360-369; Richard P. Bagozzi and Robert E. Burnkrant, "Single Component Versus Multi-Component Models of Attitude: Some Cautions and Contingencies for Their Use," in Olson (ed.), *Advances in Consumer Research,* vol. 7, 339-343; and David Brinberg, "A Comparison of Two Behavioral Intention Models," in Kent B. Monroe (ed.), *Advances in Consumer Research,* vol. 8 (Ann Arbor, Mich.: Association for Consumer Research, 1981), 48-52.

[69]For a review of other approaches used in marketing see Haley and Case, "Testing Thirteen Attitude Scales."

[70]See "Broad Attitude Trends Don't Always Predict," which quotes the research of William D. Wells at Needham, Harper & Steers.

lustrated in Tables 15.1 and 15.2 has already been demonstrated, and more will be said in the following chapter. In this sense, use is made of the disaggregated data from the A_B measure (i. e., the ratings from which the A_B score is computed).

The aggregated single measure of A_B for a company's brand as well as the competitor's also can provide useful input for marketing strategy. It is one measure of the effectiveness of marketing efforts when it is correlated with market share and computed over a period of time. Once the attitude-share relationship is known, changes in the index can serve as a forecasting tool. If it declines, this is a signal that a diagnosis of marketing strategy is needed for remedial purposes. If it increases, on the other hand, it may foreshadow a gain in market share. When the same measurements are taken for competitors, advance warnings may be provided of potential inroads or decline in market share.

Finally, there is no necessity to make precise use of the Fishbein formulation when using a multi-attribute model. No doubt it can be varied and improved without diminishing the many benefits which are offered. Therefore, we should anticipate and utilize modifications and alterations when it is clear that better diagnosis and prediction are possible.

Summary

This chapter examined an important phase of alternative evaluation: the formation and function of beliefs, attitudes, and intentions. It began with a historical perspective of the progress that has occurred in the years since the first edition of this book was published. Previously the nature of the relationship between attitudes and choice, if any, was an open question. But recent years have seen a concentration of research on the expectancy-value models pioneered by Rosenberg and Fishbein. Now it can be said with some certainty that attitudes predict intentions, which in turn will predict buying action, all things being equal. Attitudes are the outcome of beliefs, which state the probability that an alternative under consideration actually possesses the desired attributes specified by the evaluative criteria discussed in the preceding chapter.

Until recently, most attention was directed toward attitude toward an object (A_O). The models used for this purpose and some of the methodological and conceptual questions were analyzed. Deficiencies in the predictive power of the A_O model has led to widespread acceptance of the extended Fishbein model, which predicts buying intentions through a combination of attitude toward the act of purchasing a brand (A_B) plus the existence of normative social pressures and a motivation by the individual to comply. This model has resulted in much sharper predictive power, but it also was shown that predictions can be increased if specific account also is taken of anticipated circumstances. These factors then were combined in a model that is part of the consumer behavior model used in this book. The chapter concluded with a review of implications for marketing strategy.

Review and Discussion Questions

1. Consult five basic textbooks in introductory social psychology and list the definitions of attitude. What differences can you detect? Why do different authorities offer varying definitions of such a familiar concept?

2. What explanations can you give for the contradictory evidence in the literature until recently regarding the relationship of a change in attitude to a change in behavior? Is attitude change a valid marketing goal?

3. What are the relationships among evaluative criteria, beliefs, attitudes, and intentions?

4. Contrast the Rosenberg and Fishbein models of attitude toward an object, A_o. Are they really measuring the same thing as some authorities have contended? Or are there some basic differences?

5. What are some of the reasons why measures of A_o often are not very good predictors of both intention and purchase?

6. In what specific ways does Fishbein's extended model differ from his earlier model of A_o? In your estimation, is this an improvement or not?

7. Reviewing the running shoe purchasing example discussed in the text, why is it easier to change a b component than the e component? You may need to refer to the preceding chapter to answer this question with precision.

8. One leading New York advertising agency refuses to use attitude change as a criterion of advertising success or failure. Another agency uses only attitude change for this purpose. What reasons could be given for such a major difference?

9. A marketing research study undertaken for a major appliance manufacturer disclosed that 30 percent of those polled plan on purchasing a trash compactor in the next three months and 15 percent plan on purchasing a new iron. How much confidence should be placed in the predictive accuracy of these intention measurements? Are there differences in predictive accuracy between products? Why or why not?

L'Oreal is the largest marketer of haircolor and hair care products in Europe, but it never established much penetration in the United States market until the middle 1970s.[1] Prior to that time the market was dominated by Clairol, and there was very little brand switching due to the high-involvement nature of this product. One could scarcely conceive of a product class which has more implications for the user's ego.

To counteract the Clairol domination, it was decided to concentrate all marketing efforts behind *Preference* haircolor, the highest-priced item within the L'Oreal line. The agency, McCann-Erickson, positioned this product as "the most expensive hair color in the world," and this selling point was internalized by many to infer superior quality. By accompanying this theme with the phrase, "because I'm worth it," L'Oreal positioned *Preference* haircolor and other items in its product line in terms of product quality, a sense of self-esteem, sophistication, and classical beauty. The outcome? A doubling of market share, moving L'Oreal into the second spot just behind Clairol.

The strategy in this case was well-conceived for a high-involvement product where it is necessary to understand the evaluative criteria used in purchase, important buyer motivations, and to create the correct perception of brand attributes in these terms.[2] The goal, of course, is to change beliefs and attitudes in the expectation that buying behavior also will change, a necessity when high involvement is present.

In this chapter we will review some of the major principles that have evolved from the broad field of persuasion. The chapter begins with a discussion of the general strategies required to change beliefs and attitudes in the context of multi-attribute models. This will provide needed conceptual understanding in the *message content*. Design and structure of appeals are considered later. The most important factor in this latter context is discrepancy between the beliefs of members of the target audience and the position advocated by the communicator. Then additional

[1]Virginia Miles, "Research is Key in Changing Your Brand Strategy," *Advertising Age* (July 12, 1976), 39.

[2]Michael L. Rothschild, "Advertising Strategies for High and Low Involvement Situations," in John C. Maloney and Bernard Silverman (eds.), *Attitude Research Plays for High Stakes* (Chicago: American Marketing Association, 1979), 74-93.

variations in message content and structure are reviewed, including such topics as the fear appeal, and one-sided versus two-sided messages. Also it is necessary to touch briefly on whether there ever will be a definitive science of persuasion complete with rules and theorems.

GENERAL STRATEGIES TO CHANGE BELIEFS AND ATTITUDES

Referring once again to Fishbein's behavioral intentions model, the reader will recall that the formula for attitude toward the action of performing a particular behavior under a given set of circumstances (A_B) takes this form:

$$A_B = \sum_{i=1}^{n} b_i e_i$$

where:

A_B = attitude toward performing the behavior

b_i = belief that performing behavior B leads to consequence i

e_i = the person's evaluation of consequence i

n = the number of beliefs

Changes can be brought about in two basic ways: (1) changing an existing b element,[3] and (2) changing an existing e element.[4]

Changing an Existing b Element

Let's refer once again to the running shoe example used in the previous chapter. Most of the pertinent data are reproduced in Table 16.1. "Price under $40" and "five-star rating by *Runner's World*" are the two most valued attributes, followed closely by "wearability of sole" and "comfort."

The first step is to examine how competitive brands are evaluated along these attributes. If the company's offerings received a low rating, two questions must be asked. First, is the product, in fact, inferior on this dimension? If so, the logical strategy is product redesign. On the other hand, the product may indeed be competitive but not be perceived in this manner by consumers. Then the strategy requires revamped promotion.

Table 16.1 Attitudes (A_B) toward Three Brands of Running Shoe

Attribute	Evaluation (e_i)	Beliefs (b_i) Brand A	Brand B	Brand C
Shock absorbence	+1	+3	+1	+2
Price under $40	+3	-2	+3	+2
Wearability of sole	+2	-1	+2	+1
Arch support	+1	+2	-1	+2
Colors	+1	+1	+3	+2
Comfort	+2	+3	+1	+2
Five-star rating	+3	+3	-1	+1
Total score (A_B)		+13	+16	+21

[3]James L. Ginter, "An Experimental Investigation of Attitude Change in Choice of a New Brand," *Journal of Marketing Research,* vol. 11 (February 1974), 30-40.

[4]These options were suggested by Lutz. See Richard J. Lutz, "Changing Brand Attitudes through Modification of Cognitive Structure," *Journal of Consumer Research,* vol. 1 (March 1975), 49-59.

Let's take the example of Brand B. which is rated as unlikely to have a five-star rating from *Runner's World*. It could be that it has not always received this prized accolade in the past but recently has been a consistent winner. The strategy then is to tell this story clearly and dramatically. An ad something like that used by Pony Sports & Leisure, Inc. would be most appropriate (Figure 16.1). *Pony,* by the way, is only used as an illustration here and has usually been a highly rated shoe.

**Figure 16.1
A Strategy
Featuring a
Determinant
Product Attribute**

Source: Courtesy Pony Sports & Leisure, Inc.

**Figure 16.2
An Advertising
Strategy Featuring
a Salient Attribute**

Source: Courtesy of Brooks Shoe Co.

Brand A, on the other hand, is known to have the five-star rating but is not evaluated favorably on price and wearability of sole. Here the strategy might be to feature ruggedness and sole design, making the case that these features required a higher price. This approach is followed in promoting the Brooks *Hugger GT* shown in Figure 16.2. Once again, this is not to imply that Brooks is, in fact, Brand A in this example, and this ad is only used for illustrative purposes.

Here the intent is to undertake a strategy designed to move a large number of people in a more positive direction on salient attributes. Usually it is possible to state such objectives in quantifiable terms. An example might be to convince 60 percent of *Runner's World* readers that Brand A is very likely to have a long-wearing sole. Changes then would be detected by actually measuring the number of prospects giving this response after the marketing plan has been executed.

This type of objective is quite common in advertising management.[5] It is based on the premise, first of all, that the attributes in question are salient to the individual. If not, it matters little whether movement in the desired direction occurs or not, because attitudes and behavior will remain unchanged. One of the authors once served as a consultant to a manufacturer of refrigerators. In that year, the only distinctive feature of this brand was unexposed cooling coils. Unfortunately consumers did not care one way or another about this product feature. An advertising campaign might have been undertaken that successfully communicated this attribute, but it would represent utter waste.

Fishbein also points out that systems of beliefs are interrelated.[6] If you change one, you often will change another in an unexpected fashion. For instance, an advertiser might succeed in convincing a large part of the market that Brand X is low in price. However, this may lead to the conclusion that it also is low in quality. This can be avoided by awareness of the interrelationship between these attributes and stressing that low price does not mean low quality.

Changing an Existing *e* Element

The manufacturer of Brand B in our example could decide to try a frontal attack on consumer beliefs that a five-star rating is important. Ads and retail selling tools could denigrate the credibility of *Runner's World* and stress that true world class runners make their own judgments. Some name endorsements might help in this respect.

Such a strategy, however, is downright dangerous. It completely overlooks the fact that determinant attributes reflect underlying evaluative criteria which can have some pretty deep roots. In this case, the average prospect may be saying, in effect, that he or she does not feel competent to evaluate the features of running shoes without this presumably objective information. The manufacturer's appeal thus will fall on deaf ears. The principle is that determinant evaluative criteria usually are strongly held and should be taken as a given.

Maintenance of Belief Levels

Frequently there is merit to a strategy that focuses on maintaining favorable ratings on determinant and salient attributes. Any erosion could, of course, undermine market share. This is precisely the strategy followed

---

[5]For further discussion, see James F. Engel, Martin R. Warshaw, and Thomas C. Kinnear, *Promotional Strategy*, 4th ed. (Homewood, Ill.: Richard D. Irwin, 1979), ch. 10.

[6]This is particularly stressed in Martin Fishbein, "Attitude, Attitude Change, and Behavior: A Theoretical Overview," Philip Levine (ed.), *Attitude Research Bridges the Atlantic* (Chicago: American Marketing Association, 1975), 9.

**Figure 16.3
A Strategy of
Maintenance of
Positive Beliefs on
a Determinant
Attribute**

Source: Courtesy of Brooks Shoe Co.

by the Brooks Shoe Manufacturing Company in Figure 16.3 featuring its longstanding record of winning five-star ratings.

GENERAL PRINCIPLES OF MESSAGE CONTENT

Continuing with our same example, the manufacturer of Brand A must attempt to convince consumers that it does offer a sole that gives long wear and, if this indeed is the case, that the price is under $40. At the moment, the majority do not believe either of these to be very likely. Two factors now must be weighed seriously in marketing decision making: (1) the latitude of acceptance around existing beliefs, and (2) the credibility of the company in the eyes of consumers.

The Latitude of Acceptance

A general principle of persuasion theory is that attitudes are resistant to change to the extent that the individual's beliefs are anchored in his or her conception of self-worth. This, of course, is what we mean by high involvement. Sherif and his colleagues discovered some years ago that involvement is revealed by the degree to which the individual will tolerate or accept a position that is different from his own along a scale of belief.[7] The range of positions felt to be acceptable is referred to as the *latitude of acceptance.* Conversely, the range of unacceptable belief statements is the *latitude of rejection.* Involvement is reflected when the latitude of acceptance is low and the latitude of rejection is large. In fact, involvement may be so high that the individual says, in effect, "Nothing you say can change me." In this case, the latitude of acceptance includes only the present belief and all other possibilities fall into the latitude of rejection.

In the context of consumer buying, there is growing consensus that a highly involved consumer will have a narrow latitude of acceptance and wide latitude of rejection around beliefs on salient attributes.[8] When this is the case, the best strategy is to design a message in such a way that it falls at the outer edge of the latitude of acceptance.[9] If this latitude is exceeded, it is probable that the message will not be accepted into long-term memory in information processing. It will take some skillful marketing research to discover just how great this level of discrepancy can be.

Usually latitudes are measured by a set of belief statements ranging from acceptable to nonacceptable, and an example appears in Table 16.2. Here the present position of most nonusers of Brand B is that it is "not as comfortable to wear as most other shoes." They will accept the fact, however, that "Brand B has been improved this year so that many runners think it is more comfortable" (this is still within the latitude of

[7]C. W. Sherif, M. Sherif and R. E. Nebergall, *Attitude and Attitude Change* (New Haven, Conn.: Yale University Press, 1961). For an alternate approach, see N. T. Hupfer and D. M. Gardner, "Differential Involvement with Products and Issues: An Exploratory Study" (paper presented at the Association for Consumer Research September 1971).

[8]See John L. Lastovicka and David M. Gardner, "Components of Involvement," in Maloney and Silverman, *Attitude Research Plays*, 53-73; Michael L. Rothschild and Michael J. Houston, "The Consumer Involvement Matrix: Some Preliminary Findings," in Barnett A. Greenberg and Danny N. Bellenger (eds.), *Contemporary Marketing Thought* (Chicago: American Marketing Association, 1977), 95-98; and Richard E. Petty and John T. Capicoppo, "Issue Involvement as a Moderator of the Effects on Attitude of Advertising Content and Context," in Kent B. Monroe (ed.), *Advances in Consumer Research,* vol. 8 (Ann Arbor, Mich.: Association for Consumer Research, 1981), 20-24.

[9]This is the fundamental tenet of belief change stressed in Martin Fishbein and Icek Ajzen, *Belief, Attitude, Intention, and Behavior: An Introduction to Theory and Research* (Reading, Mass.: Addison-Wesley, 1975), ch. 11. Also see C. Insko, F. Murashima, and M. Saiyadain, "Communicator Discrepancy, Stimulus Ambiguity and Influence," *Journal of Personality,* vol. 34 (1966), 52-66; H. Johnson, "Some Effects of Discrepancy Level on Responses to Negative Information about One's Self," *Sociometry,* vol. 29 (1966), 52-66; J. Whittaker, "Opinion Change as a Function of Communication-Attitude Discrepancy," *Psychological Reports,* vol. 13 (1963), 763-772.

**Table 16.2
Latitudes of
Acceptance and
Rejection of Beliefs
on Comfort of
Brand B**

Latitude of Acceptance	Present→ Position	1. Brand B is a brand of running shoe. 2. Brand B is used by many runners. 3. Many runners prefer Brand B. 4. Brand B is not as comfortable to wear as most other shoes. 5. Brand B has been improved this year so that many runners think it is more comfortable. 6. Brand B has been improved so that it is about as comfortable as most other shoes. 7. Brand B has been improved so that it is more comfortable than most other shoes. 8. Brand B has been improved so that it is the most comfortable of all running shoes.

acceptance). If the goal is to make inroads into the share of market held by Brands A and C, then this defines what can be stated in advertising and selling copy.

What will tend to happen is that the various latitudes change over time. In other words, the consumer may be moved a position or two on the belief scale now. A new belief position is thus established, accompanied by a new set of latitudes. Then reexposure takes place, hopefully accompanied by another shift up to the limits of the latitude of acceptance and so on until the desired goal is achieved.

It is necessary to pause here and point out that there is a school of thought with roots in the theory of cognitive dissonance which holds that attitude change is a linear function of the extent of discrepancy between the individual's position and message content.[10] In other words, the more the message deviates, the greater the probability of change in the desired direction. It is now generally recognized, however, that this principle *only* holds true under conditions of low involvement.[11]

All things being equal, people with a negative attitude accompanied by a narrow latitude of acceptance (indicating high involvement) are poor prospects. Whenever possible, efforts should concentrate on those who show the highest probability of change. The likelihood of profitable return on substantial marketing investment directed toward the former group is too low. In effect, this type of thinking is the root principle of market segmentation—"Fish where the fishing is good."

It should be pointed out, by the way, that the discussion thus far has assumed that primary use will be made of the mass media. A negatively disposed prospect can be changed much more readily through personal selling. In fact, one of the attributes of a good salesperson is ability to detect the limits of the latitude of acceptance and work skillfully up to that point by countering objections and stressing product strong points.

[10]See, for example, S. Goldberg, "Three Situational Determinants of Conformity to Social Norms," *Journal of Abnormal and Social Psychology*, vol. 49 (1964), 325-329; H. Helson, R. Blake, and J. Mouton, "An Experimental Investigation of the 'Big Lie' in Shifting Attitudes," *Journal of Social Psychology*, vol. 48 (1958), 51-60; R. Tuddenham, "The Influence of a Distorted Group Norm upon Influential Judgment," *Journal of Psychology*, vol. 46 (1956), 227-241; P. Zimbardo, "Involvement and Communication Discrepancy as Determinants of Opinion Conformity," *Journal of Abnormal and Social Psychology*, vol. 60 (1960), 86-94.

[11]For a pertinent illustration, see Frederick W. F. Winter, "A Laboratory Experiment of Individual Attitude Response to Advertising Exposure," *Journal of Marketing Research*, vol. 10 (May 1973), 130-140.

Beliefs frequently will change in a tangible manner right on the spot as the sales person keeps moving toward the objective. The key, of course, is the opportunity for feedback and interaction provided by the face-to-face communication situation.

Source Credibility

It has long been felt that a highly credible source will produce more belief change than a noncredible source,[12] and this principle has been used by advertisers since the very beginning. A recent example is Robert Morley, the spokesperson for British Airways, who was selected by *Advertising Age* as the Star Presenter for 1980.[13] (See Figure 16.4.) Largely because of his, "We'll take good care of you," assurance, the airline has captured first place in the highly competitive US–UK run.

More recently, it has become clear that the effects of source credibility depend upon the degree of involvement that is present. When involvement is high, people will carefully evaluate the message and counter argue when the content is inconsistent with beliefs and attitudes. From the perspective of cognitive response theory, Perloff and Brock contend that a high credibility source will reduce counter arguing under this circumstance and hence stimulate greater message acceptance.[14] When the person agrees with the position being advocated, however, a low-credibility source will do just as well.

It also has been found that there can be a greater discrepancy between a prospect's present belief position and message if the source is perceived as being credible.[15] In other words, people seem to place greater confidence in a trustworthy source and hence are more receptive to what is said, even when there is a substantial deviation from their own position. Similarly, there is a marked reduction in willingness to accept a discrepant message when the source is of moderate or low credibility.

The moderating effect of source credibility has distinct managerial significance. It is quite difficult to make an advertisement credible when it is obvious that the whole intent of the message is to persuade. The recipient generally recognizes that the source is anything but impartial and unbiased. Therefore, a message that deviates substantially from the recipient's own position is likely to be screened out as he or she processes the stimulus. Given this relationship it becomes necessary to pre-

[12]See, for example, C. Samuel Craig and John M. McCann, "Assessing Communication Effects on Energy Conservation," *Journal of Consumer Research,* vol. 5 (September 1978), 82-88; and Gary Cronkhite and J. R. Liska, "The Judgement of Communicant Acceptability," in Michael E. Roloff and Gerald R. Miller (eds.), *Persuasion: New Directions in Theory and Research* (Beverly Hills, Calif.: Sage, 1980), 101-140.

[13]Josh Levine, "Morley's Airline Image: 'It's Basically Who I am,' " *Advertising Age* (June 2, 1980), 3+.

[14]Richard M. Perloff and Timothy C. Brock, ". . . 'And Thinking Makes it So:' Cognitive Responses to Persuasion," in Roloff and Miller, *Persuasion,* 67-100. Also see R. R. Dholakia and Brian Sternthal, "Highly Credible Sources: Persuasive Facilitors or Persuasive Liabilities?" *Journal of Consumer Research,* vol. 3 (1977), 223-232; Brian Sternthal, R. R. Dholakia, and Clark Leavitt, "The Persuasive Effect of Source Credibility: Test of Cognitive Response," *Journal of Consumer Research,* vol. 4 (1978), 252-260; and Richard W. Mizerski, James M. Hunt, and Charles H. Patti, "The Effects of Advertising Credibility on Consumer Reactions on an Advertisement," in S. C. Jain (ed.), *Research Frontiers in Marketing: Dialogues and Directions* (Chicago: American Marketing Association, 1978), 164-168.

[15]This literature is thoroughly reviewed in Brian Sternthal, "Persuasion and the Mass Communication Process" (unpublished doctoral dissertation Columbus, Ohio: Ohio State University, 1972), ch. 4.

Figure 16.4
Use of a Credible
Source in
Consumer
Advertising

Source: Courtesy of British Airways Corporation.

dict the boundary of acceptable discrepancy, but attempts to predict this point have repeatedly failed to date.

Implications   It now seems apparent that the effects of message discrepancy on attitude change are moderated by source credibility and ego involvement.

Two recent studies that manipulated both of these moderating variables confirmed this conclusion.[16] In each instance highly involved subjects changed their attitudes significantly less upon exposure to a discrepant message than did those who were less involved, and there was a greater tendency for this group to disparage the communication source.

Given that marketing communications usually are not perceived as highly credible, the message should deviate from the attitude position of members of the target audience only to a small extent. Attitude change is best achieved by successive exposures, each of which encompasses only small discrepancy. This generalization is especially critical when recipients' attitudes are based on ego involvement.

VARIATIONS IN MESSAGE CONTENT AND STRUCTURE

The remainder of this chapter focuses selectively on the literature of persuasion. This literature is vast, with over 7000 references on advertising alone.[17] One redeeming factor is that there has been a distinct decline in the number of irrelevant persuasion studies published during the 1970s.[18] The person reviewing this literature immediately must face the fact, however, that there has been no clear distinction between high- and low-involvement issues until recently. Therefore, it is difficult to isolate approaches that might be effective in one circumstance but not in another.

The first part of this section focuses on several broad categories of research on variations in message content and appeal: (1) comparative advertising; (2) fear appeals; (3) humor; (4) drawing a conclusion; (5) distraction; and (6) nonovert appeals. Then discussion shifts to another major consideration—manipulation of such structural factors as one-sided versus two-sided messages, order of presentation, degree of internal structure, repetition, and time-compressed speech.

Variations in Message Content

Comparative Advertising

The Joseph Schlitz Brewing Company recently finished a series of tests in which Schlitz beer was taste-tested against major competitors during telecasts of the pro-football playoffs and the Super Bowl. Many distributors reported sharp sales increases through what is referred to as comparative advertising.[19] Thousands of such ads have been run in the past decade, leading to a genuine controversy in the trade.

In theory, comparative advertising can be to the consumer's benefit as pertinent sales points are driven home in head-to-head product comparisons in ads. But, does this in fact happen? Some argue that the

---

[16]See, for example, Homer Johnson and Ivan Steiner, "The Effects of Source on Responses to Negative Information About One's Self," *Journal of Social Psychology,* vol. 74 (1968), 215-224.

[17]Robert W. Chestnut, "Persuasive Effects in Marketing: Consumer Information Process Research," Roloff and Miller, *Persuasion,* 267-283.

[18]Michael E. Roloff and Gerald R. Miller, "Forward"; Roloff and Miller, *Persuasion,* 7-10.

[19]Elizabeth Brenner, "Schlitz Test Just Beginning," *Chicago Tribune* (February 1, 1981), 4-5.

consumer does show some gain in the information acquired, thus supporting the consumerists' contentions in this respect.[20] The preponderance of evidence, however, shows little or no effect on beliefs or attitudes, to say nothing of eventual buyer behavior,[21] although there are some case histories of successful sales results.[22] Others even show that there can be decided boomerang effects in terms of consumer dislike of the ads,[23] increased counterargumentation,[24] or favoring the attacked competitor.[25]

One main point stands out: comparative ads work *only* when clear differences between brands can be objectively verified by consumers.[26] Even then, best results are attained when the print medium used allows for more deliberation and careful consideration.[27] Here are some additional guidelines given by Stanley I. Tannenbaum, Chairman of Kenyon & Eckhardt, Inc.:[28]

1. Employ the comparison technique only in situations where there is a clear superiority on a salient product attribute and where the major competitor is perceived more positively.

2. When the comparison is strongly inconsistent with consumer beliefs, credibility suffers.

3. Identify but never disparage the brand leader.

4. The goal is to gain increased attention from users of the competitive brand or from those who regard it as a quality standard.

5. Other brands can be named when your brand has a distinct advantage and when it takes time for competitors to counteract.

6. Great care must be taken to avoid being misinterpreted as promoting the brand against which comparison is being made.

7. Comparisons are not helpful when a competitor could counterattack in an area where its brand has clear superiority on a salient attribute.

[20]R. Dale Wilson and Aydin Muderrisoglu, "Strength of Claims in Comparative Advertising: A Study of Competitive Vigor," Neil Beckwith et al. (eds.), *Proceedings: 1979 Educators' Conference* (Chicago: American Marketing Association, 1979), 361-366.

[21]Linda O. Golden, "Consumer Reactions to Explicit Brand Comparisons in Advertisements," *Journal of Marketing Research,* vol. 16 (1979), 517-532; W. M. Pride, C. W. Lamb, and B. A. Plechter, "The Informativeness of Comparative Advertisements: An Empirical Investigation," *Journal of Advertising* vol. 8 (Spring 1979), 29-35; most commercial research tests also document this point as reported by Andrew Kershaw, "Mischief of Comparative Advertising" (paper given at the 1976 annual meeting of the American Association of Advertising Agencies).

[22]See Nancy Giges, "Comparative Ads: Better Than . . . ?" *Advertising Age* (September 22, 1980), 59-62.

[23]Giges, "Comparative Ads."

[24]R. Dale Wilson and Aydin Muderrisoglu, "An Analysis of Cognitive Responses to Comparative Advertising," in Jerry C. Olson (ed.), *Advances in Consumer Research,* vol. 7 (Ann Arbor, Mich.: Association for Consumer Research, 1980), 566-571.

[25]Giges, "Comparative Ads."

[26]Giges, "Comparative Ads."

[27]Kershaw, "Mischief of Comparative Advertising."

[28]Stanley I. Tannenbaum, "Comparative Advertising: The Advertising Industry's Own Brand of Consumerism" (paper given at the 1976 annual meeting of the American Association of Advertising Agencies).

8. Every effort must be made to leave the impression that the named competitor has not been deceiving the consumer.

9. The consumer must be able to verify the comparison and prove it to his or her satisfaction.

When such guidelines as these are carefully followed, comparative advertising perhaps can offer some benefit, especially when introducing a new product.[29]

The Fear Appeal

A study undertaken in 1953 by Janis and Feshbach indicated that a communication stressing the unfavorable physical consequences (fear) of not taking the suggested course of action can have an adverse effect on attitude if this fear appeal is too intense.[30] This negative relationship between fear arousal and persuasion was confirmed in several subsequent investigations undertaken between 1953 and 1963,[31] with the result that fear appeals were used only in such isolated instances as promotion of medical products and sale of life insurance.[32] More than 100 studies have been undertaken since 1953, however, and the great majority contradict the early findings and show a positive relationship between fear and persuasion.[33] In fact, of 16 relevant experiments undertaken between 1965 and 1971, all reported positive findings.[34] Not surprisingly, Ray and Wilkie concluded that marketers have neglected a promising area of inquiry.[35]

(1) The Effect of Source Credibility It now appears that an increased threat of physical consequences enhances a persuasion only when credibility of the source is high.[36] When this is not the case, coun-

---

[29]Douglas J. Lincoln and A. Coskun Samli, "Empirical Evidence of Comparative Advertising's Effects: A Review and Synthesis," Beckwith, *Proceedings,* 367-372.

[30]I. L. Janis and S. Feshback, "Effects of Fear-Arousing Communication," *Journal of Abnormal and Social Psychology,* vol. 48 (1953), 78-92.

[31]See, for example, I. L. Janis and R. Terwilliger, "An Experimental Study of Psychological Resistance to Fear Arousing Communications," *Journal of Abnormal and Social Psychology,* vol. 65 (1962), 403-410.

[32]J. Stuteville, "Psychic Defenses against High Fear Appeals: A Key Marketing Variable," *Journal of Marketing,* vol. 34 (1970), 39-45.

[33]There have been a number of literature reviews. See K. Higbee, "Fifteen Years of Fear Arousal: Research on Threat Appeals: 1953–1968," *Psychological Bulletin,* vol. 72 (1969), 426-444; I. Janis, *The Contours of Fear* (New York: John Wiley & Sons, 1968); H. Leventhal, "Findings and Theory in the Study of Fear Communications," in L. Berkowitz (ed.), *Advances in Experimental Social Psychology,* vol. 5 (New York: Academic Press, 1970), 119-186; W. McGuire, "Nature of Attitudes"; and Brian Sternthal and C. Samuel Craig, "Fear Appeals: Revisited and Revised," *Journal of Consumer Research,* vol. 1 (December 1974), 22-34.

[34]Sternthal, "Persuasion," ch. 5. For a more recent published example, see John J. Burnett and Richard L. Oliver, "Fear Appeal Effects in the Field: Segmentation Approach," *Journal of Marketing Research,* vol. 16 (May 1979), 181-190.

[35]M. Ray and W. Wilkie, "Fear: The Potential of an Appeal Neglected by Marketing," *Journal of Marketing,* vol. 34 (1970), 59-62.

[36]These studies are reviewed in Sternthal, "Persuasion," ch. 5.

terargumentation seems to be generated, with the outcome that the source is rejected as being biased.

It has been stressed earlier that the credibility of advertising, in general, is not high. This fact, in itself, should be a warning light to those who would use this type of appeal indiscriminately. Furthermore, there are wide variations in credibility between manufacturers. The credibility of both medium and communicator must be established, therefore, before serious consideration is given to this type of strategy.

(2) Type of Fear Almost without exception, the published studies have centered on threats of physical consequences. Thus marketing applications are pretty much limited to those purchase situations in which physical fear is a potential motivator. Yet, social disapproval can be an even more powerful motivation, but only one study has examined the consequences of fear of disapproval.[37] The findings were that threat of disapproval is even more persuasive than a promise of social approval. This clearly warrants further investigation.

(3) The Need for Further Research[38] While there is merit in considering use of this type of message in appropriate situations, caution must be exercised in generalizing too extensively from published evidence to date. First, the range of topics investigated has been quite narrow, encompassing mainly such issues as health and politics. Furthermore, most investigations have employed only two levels of fear (referred to variously as "minimal-high," "weak-strong," and so on), and there is no confirmation that the full range of fear has been explored. Finally, the effects of temporal delay on response should be investigated more fully. It is quite possible that different results will be achieved through the passage of time.

Humor

At one time, especially during the 1950s and 1960s, there was a tendency to avoid the use of humor on the pretext that it can quickly overwhelm the product message and thus lead to failure to achieve creative objectives.[39] While this is always a possibility, humor has been used much more frequently in recent years. In fact, a content analysis of 2000 television commercials showed that 15 percent made use of humorous appeals, many of which were for low-involvement products.[40] Yet McMahan and others have long contended that humor can sell, regardless of the product type.[41]

Sternthal and Craig reviewed the literature on the role of humor in persuasion and concluded that humorous messages particularly excel in

---

[37]Ray and Wilkie, "Fear."

[38]See Sternthal and Craig, "Fear Appeals."

[39]David Ogilvy, "Raise Your Sights! Tips for Copywriters, Art Directors and TV Producers—Mostly Derived from Research" (Internal publication, Ogilvy & Mather, Inc.).

[40]J. Patrick Kelly and Paul J. Solomon, "Humor in Advertising," *Journal of Advertising*, vol. 4 (Summer 1975), 31-35.

[41]Harry Wayne McMahan, "No Joking; Humor Sells!" *Advertising Age* (December 29, 1980), 19.

**Figure 16.5
Life Cereal's
"Mikey": An
Example of Humor
Integrated with
the Main Selling
Point**

Source: Reprinted with permission of the Quaker Oats Company.

terms of attention attraction.[42] Furthermore, humor can serve to enhance source credibility, something the advertiser certainly can use to his benefit.

More can be learned from the study of the effectiveness of 40 different factors in television commercial content and execution.[43] Humorous appeals can produce above average change in brand preference if these precautions are observed.[44]

1. The brand must be identified in the opening ten seconds, or there is the real danger that humor can inhibit recall of important selling points.[45]

2. The type of humor makes a difference. Subtlety is more effective than the bizarre.

3. The humor must be relevant to the brand or key idea. Recall and persuasion both are diminished when there is not this linkage. An example of especially effective strategy in this sense is Life cereal's "Mikey" in Figure 16.5. Most readers will recall the two kids who said, "Cereal which

[42]Brian Sternthal and C. Samuel Craig, "Humor in Advertising," *Journal of Marketing,* vol. 37 (October 1973), 12-18.

[43]Harold L. Ross, Jr., "How to Create Effective Humorous Commercials Yielding above Average Brand Preference Changes," *Marketing News* (March 26, 1976), 4.

[44]Ross, "How to Create."

[45]This danger also was found by Sternthal and Craig, "Humor in Advertising."

is good for you can't taste good. Let's try it on Mikey. Hey, Mikey! He *likes it!*"

4. Humorous commercials that entertain by belittling the potential user usually do not perform well. A better strategy is to make light of the brand, the situation, or the subject matter.

Drawing a Conclusion

In recent years, growing use has been made of what some now refer to as *cool commercials.*[46] A cool message is unstructured; the viewer is told a fragment of the story or impressions are invoked so that he or she must fill in from his or her own imagination (see Figure 16.6). The hot message, on the other hand, is more structured and tells a complete story logically and sequentially, with a definite conclusion stated (see Figure 16.7).

From the results of a number of communication studies, the unstructured approach of the cool commercial would appear to be ineffective. This is because experimental research has determined repeatedly that explicit conclusion-drawing is more persuasive than allowing the audience to draw its own conclusions.[47] Presumably the audience is not sufficiently motivated or intelligent enough to draw conclusions on its own. There is strong contradictory evidence, however, from a series of ads on various mental health issues. The best ads turned out to be those that asked questions and let the reader or viewer come to his or her own conclusion.[48] The implication derived from this test is that ads ". . . should make our brains itch, not anesthetize them."[49]

There also is evidence that the message which states a conclusion only implicitly approaches the structured message in terms of impact *over time.*[50] When the audience is highly intelligent or motivated, this approach may be particularly effective. As Brehm has pointed out, many people seem to react negatively when a conclusion is stated and feel that an attempt is being made to influence and thereby limit their freedom of choice. When this is the reaction a boomerang effect can occur in the form of solidification of initial opinion.[51]

[46]The authors are indebted here to Bill Taylor of Ogilvy & Mather, Inc.

[47]E. Cooper and H. Dinerman, "Analysis of the Film 'Don't Be a Sucker': A Study of Communication," *Public Opinion Quarterly,* vol. 15 (1951), 243-264; B. Fine, "Conclusion-Drawing, Communicator Credibility and Anxiety as Factors in Opinion Change," *Journal of Abnormal and Social Psychology,* vol. 54 (1957), 369-374; H. Hadley, "The Non-Directive Approach in Advertising Appeals," *Journal of Applied Psychology,* vol. 37 (1963) 496-498; C. Hovland and W. Mandell, "An Experimental Comparison of Conclusion-Drawing by the Communicator and by the Audience," *Journal of Abnormal and Social Psychology,* vol. 47 (1952), 581-588; N. Maier and R. Maier, "An Experimental Test of the Effects of 'Developmental' versus 'Free' Discussion on the Quality of Group Decisions," *Journal of Applied Psychology,* vol. 4 (1957), 320-323.

[48]"Ads Without Answers Make the Brain Itch," *Psychology Today,* vol. 9 (November 1975), 78.

[49]"Ads Without Answers," 78.

[50]A. Cohen, *Attitude Change and Social Influence* (New York: Basic Books, 1964), 10; W. McGuire, "A Syllogistic Analysis of Cognitive Relationships," in C. Hovland and M. Rosenberg (eds.), *Attitude Organization and Change* (New Haven, Conn.: Yale University Press, 1960); E. Stotland, D. Katz and M. Patchen, "The Reduction of Prejudice through the Arousal of Self-Insight," *Journal of Personality,* vol. 27 (1959), 507-553.

[51]Jack W. Brehm, *A Theory of Psychological Reactance* (New York: Academic Press, 1966), ch. 6.

**Figure 16.6
A Cool Commercial**

Source: Courtesy of the Dr Pepper Company and Young & Rubicam of New York, New York.

Given that the net persuasive effect of explicit versus implicit conclusion drawing does not appear to differ, the choice between the two approaches must be resolved on the basis of other considerations. The cool commercial, for example, appears to be used more appropriately to build a long-range image. Also it is effective when a product has no apparent advantage; when competitors are running hot commercials; and when the basic product appeal is primarily emotional rather than logical (as is the case with cosmetics, for example).

**Figure 16.7
A Hot Commercial**

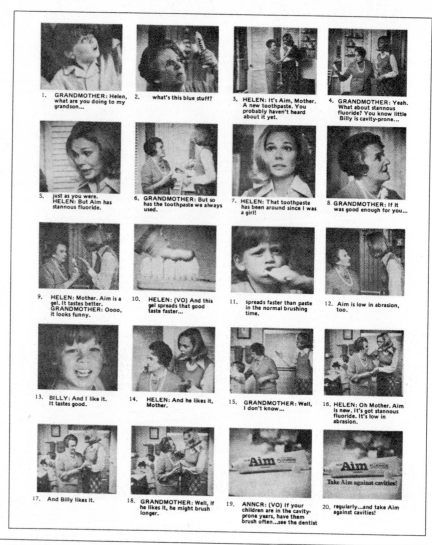

1. GRANDMOTHER: Helen, what are you doing to my grandson...

2. what's this blue stuff?

3. HELEN: It's Aim, Mother. A new toothpaste. You probably haven't heard about it yet.

4. GRANDMOTHER: Yeah. What about stannous fluoride? You know little Billy is cavity-prone...

5. just as you were. HELEN: But Aim has stannous fluoride.

6. GRANDMOTHER: But so has the toothpaste we always used.

7. HELEN: That toothpaste has been around since I was a girl.

8. GRANDMOTHER: If it was good enough for you...

9. HELEN: Mother. Aim is a gel. It tastes better. GRANDMOTHER: Oooo, it looks funny.

10. HELEN: (VO) And this gel spreads that good taste faster...

11. spreads faster than paste in the normal brushing time.

12. Aim is low in abrasion, too.

13. BILLY: And I like it. It tastes good.

14. HELEN: And he likes it, Mother.

15. GRANDMOTHER: Well, I don't know...

16. HELEN: Oh Mother. Aim is new. It's got stannous fluoride. It's low in abrasion.

17. And Billy likes it.

18. GRANDMOTHER: Well, if he likes it, he might brush longer.

19. ANNCR: (VO) If your children are in the cavity-prone years, have them brush often...see the dentist

20. regularly...and take Aim against cavities!

Source: Courtesy of Lever Brothers Company.

Distraction

People counterargue with a message that contradicts their present beliefs and attitudes, thus impeding any change. Therefore, any strategy that serves to interfere with or reduce counterargumentation is worthy of consideration. One possible means is to distract the reader or viewer during exposure.[52] This is especially applicable under high-involvement

[52]One of the first pieces of evidence on this subject is by Leon Festinger and Nathan Maccoby, "On Resistance to Persuasive Communications," *Journal of Abnormal and Social Psychology*, vol. 68 (1964), 359-366. For excellent reviews of research see R. A. Osterhouse and T. C. Brock, "Distraction Increases Yielding to Propaganda by Inhibiting Counterarguing," *Journal of Personality and Social Psychology*, vol. 15 (1970), 344-358; Baete Barton, "Distract and Conquer. Distraction as an Advertising Strategy" (working paper, International Series, (Institut Fur Konsum-Und Verhaltensforschung, Im Spadtwald, West Germany: The University of Saarland, 1980).

conditions when the individual is opposed to the position being taken in the message. Guarantees must be built in to avoid interference with comprehension.[53] Distraction might be introduced, for example, through use of humor[54] or competing stimuli such as background music or noise.[55]

Only one study thus far has successfully used distraction in an advertising context,[56] while others report failure.[57] Frankly it seems to be stretching matters a bit to try this strategy in a real world setting. First of all, it is pretty hard to do in practice, especially in a television or print ad. It may be more feasible in a personal selling situation where staged interruptions, background music, and such can be manipulated. More crucial, however, is the fine line between reduction of counterargumentation and interference with comprehension. From what we have studied on information processing, people tend to screen out much of what we say anyway, so why make it easier for them? Perhaps this type of strategy is best left to the academic laboratory.

Nonovert Appeals

This one will be mentioned quickly and more or less in passing because it is intriguing. Walster and Festinger reported success in bringing about changes when people felt they were overhearing a message.[58] Presumably it was felt that those who were speaking were making no conscious attempt to persuade. This may suggest that the slice of life commercial,[59] ostensibly showing real-life situations with ordinary people who normally would not be commercial spokesmen, stands a better chance of success than a more overt attempt to persuade. This hypothesis, however, can only be tentative, because the Walster and Festinger study did not possess the degree of experimental control normally required for verified findings.

Use of Structural Variables

One-Sided versus Two-Sided Messages

In a variety of studies undertaken in a noncommercial context, it has been found that a *two-sided message* (that is, information and persuasive arguments favorable and unfavorable to the advocated position are

---

[53]Osterhouse and Brock, "Distraction Increases"; Perloff and Brock, ". . . 'And Thinking Makes it So' "; and R. E. Petty, G. O. Wells, and T. C. Brock, "Distraction Can Enhance or Reduce Yielding to Propaganda: Thought Disruption Versus Effort Justification," *Journal of Personality and Social Psychology*, vol. 34 (1976), 874-884.

[54]Sternthal and Craig, "Humor in Advertising."

[55]Barton, "Distract and Conquer."

[56]S. W. Bither, "Effects of Distraction and Commitment on the Persuasiveness of Television Advertising," *Journal of Marketing Research*, vol. 9 (February, 1972), 1-5.

[57]David Gardner, "The Distraction Hypothesis in Marketing," *Journal of Advertising Research*, vol. 10 (December 1970), 25-31; and M. Venkatesan and G. A. Haaland, "Divided Attention and Television Commercials: An Experimental Study," *Journal of Marketing Research*, vol. 5 (1968), 203-205.

[58]E. Walster and L. Festinger, "The Effectiveness of 'Overheard' Persuasive Communications," *Journal of Abnormal and Social Psychology*, vol. 65 (1962), 395-402.

[59]Kenneth Roman and Jane Maas, *How to Advertise* (New York: St. Martin's Press, 1976), 23-24.

contained in the message) induces more attitude change than a one-sided appeal. In a widely quoted study, Hovland and others reported the following findings:[60]

1. Giving both sides produced greatest attitude change in those instances where individuals were initially opposed to the point of view advocated.

2. For those convinced of the main argument, presentation of the other side was ineffective.

3. Those with higher education were most affected when both sides were presented.

More recent evidence documents that the two-sided appeal may have a positive effect on perceived source credibility. Walster and others, for example, showed that presentation of both pro and con arguments appeared to increase audience perception of source credibility sufficiently to allow for successful utilization of a widely discrepant communication message.[61] Similar results were reported by Chu, who also found that the one-sided message induced significantly more counterargumentation than a two-sided version.[62]

While it may appear that advertisers never could capitalize upon these findings, Faison suggests that such a conclusion is premature.[63] He presented both favorable and unfavorable product attributes in advertisements for automobiles, ranges, and floor waxes. The influence of the two-sided appeal was significantly greater, and this suggests a previously overlooked way to increase promotional effectiveness. It might be quite a task, however, to convince a manufacturer that his advertising campaign also should mention product flaws. More recently, Golden and Alpert were unable to detect any advantage in using a two-sided appeal.[64] So, what is the best strategy here? Who knows? Probably most marketers also would say, Who cares?

Before dismissing this subject, we note that the policy of corrective advertising instituted by the Federal Trade Commission in 1971 may have some unintended effects. The goal is to require manufacturers to admit blame in their advertisements once they have been found guilty of false and misleading appeals. This admission in a certain percentage of its future messages presumably will serve to offset past misleading ef-

[60]C. I. Hovland, A. A. Lumsdaine, and F. D. Sheffield, *Experiments on Mass Communication*, vol. 3 (Princeton, N.J.: Princeton University Press, 1948), ch. 8.

[61]E. Walster, E. Aronson, and D. Abrahams, "On Increasing the Persuasiveness of a Low Prestige Communicator," *Journal of Experimental Social Psychology*, vol. 2 (1966), 325-342.

[62]G. Chu, "Prior Familiarity, Perceived Bias, and One-Sided versus Two-Sided Communications," *Journal of Experimental Social Psychology*, vol. 3 (1967), 243-254.

[63]E. W. Faison, "Effectiveness of One-Sided and Two-Sided Mass Communications in Advertising," *Public Opinion Quarterly*, vol. 25 (1961), 468-469.

[64]Linda L. Golden and Mark I. Alpert, "The Relative Effectiveness of One-Sided and Two-Sided Communication for Mass Transit Advertising," in H. Keith Hunt (ed.), *Advances in Consumer Research*, vol. 5 (Ann Arbor, Mich.: Association for Consumer Research, 1978), 12-18.

forts, and there is evidence that counteradvertising works in this way.[65] The opposite also can happen, however, in that the admission of blame will enhance the present credibility of the advertiser in the consumer's eyes and hence increase promotional effectiveness. This, of course, would be contrary to the result intended by the Federal Trade Commission.

Order of Presentation

There now is a considerable body of evidence on the subject of the order in which dominant appeals should be presented. This assumes, of course, that there are two or more main arguments either related to each other or pro and con. Some say that the argument presented first will prove to be most effective (*primacy*), whereas others say that the most recently presented argument will dominate (*recency*). Research investigations have focused both on the order of two-sided appeals as well as the order of major arguments in a one-sided message.

(1) Two-Sided Appeals   The available evidence of order of presentation of two-sided appeals presents an equivocal picture. Roughly equal numbers of studies report primacy, recency, or no significant order effect.[66] Attempts to explain these wide differences to date have been unfruitful, with the result that no firm generalizations can be advanced.

(2) One-Sided Appeals   Should the strongest argument in a commercial message be presented first or last? Again the empirical evidence is contradictory. Although one experimenter reports that presentation of the strong argument first is most effective,[67] the majority of published studies report no differences whatsoever.[68]

While there is no empirical resolution of the question at this point in time, there are some logical guidelines for strategy. First, initial presentation of the strongest argument may have a stronger effect on attention attraction and receptiveness to subsequent arguments. Moreover, material presented first usually is best learned.[69] On the other hand, presentation of successively weaker arguments may tend to diminish the overall persuasive effect of the message. Therefore, saving the strongest arguments for last may boost reception when it is most needed.

[65]H. T. Hunt, "Measuring the Impact and Effectiveness of Counter Messages" (Conference on Advertising and the Public Interest, American Marketing Association, May 1973); and Michael B. Mazis and Janice E. Adkinson, "An Experimental Evaluation of a Proposed Corrective Advertising Remedy," *Journal of Marketing Research,* vol. 13 (May 1976), 178-183.

[66]This evidence is reviewed in Sternthal, "Persuasion," ch. 8.

[67]H. Sponberg, "A Study of the Relative Effectiveness of Climax and Anti-Climax Order in an Argumentative Speech," *Speech Monographs,* vol. 13 (1946), 35-44.

[68]H. Gilkinson, S. Paulson, and D. Sikkink, "Effects of Order and Authority in an Argumentative Speech," *Quarterly Journal of Speech,* vol. 40 (1954), 183-192; H. Gulley and D. Berlo, "Effect of Intercellular and Intracellular Speech Structure on Attitude Change and Learning," *Speech Monographs,* vol. 23 (1956), 288-297.

[69]Sternthal, "Persuasion," ch. 8.

Time Compression

Recently there has been considerable interest in a technique where it is possible to compress an ad by electronic means so that about 30 seconds of content can be delivered in only 24 seconds without distortion in speech or sound characteristics.[70] Preliminary research by MacLachlan and his colleagues seems to indicate that time-compressed ads are even more effective than their longer counterparts in terms of recall.

Certainly this offers some benefits for advertisers who can say more in less time. Whether it is a benefit for the consumer who often is a victim of information overload is something else again. Obviously, time compression will help both parties only if the message itself is appropriate in terms of salient attributes, and so on.

Repetition

The benefit of repetition is a fundamental tenet of learning theory. Most authorities agree that repetition of a persuasive message generally is beneficial. It is argued that preceding advertisements may have made too weak an impression to stimulate much buying interest. Later ads, then, can be effective in strengthening weak impressions, with the result that a prospect's disposition to think and act favorably is enhanced.

In addition, markets are not static; people continually enter and leave. Therefore, a repeated message will reach new prospects. If this fact is overlooked a firm can quickly experience erosion of its market share as loyal buyers diminish.

Once one goes beyond a general agreement on the benefits, the issues become less clear. What effect does multiple exposure have on each stage of the communication process? Can repetition be overdone to the point that a reverse or boomerang effect occurs? In short, decision makers perceive an acute need for knowledge of the effects of repeated messages, but available evidence is inconclusive. Consider the comments of Cacioppo and Petty:

Given the social implications of advertising and the large sums of money spent each year to promote favorable attitudes toward the product or concept, it is surprising that one can think of few influences on persuasion that currently are more confusing than the effects of message repetition. . . Accurate predictions of the effects of repetition have been elusive.[71]

(1) The Way Repetition Functions It must be restated at the outset that exposure to information under high involvement and extended prob-

---

[70]P. LaBarbera and J. MacLachlan, "Time-Compressed Speech in Radio Advertising," *Journal of Marketing,* vol. 43 (1979), 30-36; and J. MacLachlan and M. H. Siegel, "Reducing the Cost of TV Commercials by Use of Time Compressions," *Journal of Marketing Research,* vol. 17 (1980), 52-57.

[71]John T. Cacioppo and Richard E. Petty, "Persuasiveness of Communications Is Affected by Exposure Frequency and Message Quality: A Theoretical and Empirical Analysis of Persisting Attitude Change," in James R. Leigh and Claude R. Martin, Jr. (eds.), *Current Issues and Research in Advertising 1980* (Ann Arbor, Mich.: Graduate School of Business, University of Michigan, 1980), 97.

lem solving conditions is entirely voluntary. When that is not the case under low involvement, repetition assumes a different function.

There is no question that repetition can be an aid to information processing.[72] Through moderate repetition, each additional exposure provides more opportunity to process the message, comprehend it, and respond to it (either through elaboration or counterargumentation). Thus it can be argued that belief and attitude change is enhanced through moderate repetition by helping people to overcome limitations on both the desire and capacity to engage in information processing.[73]

Mitchell and Olson expand further on the value of repetition from an information processing perspective:[74]

1. Due to situational distractions or because of message complexity, it may be necessary to repeat a message a number of times before information is completely processed.

2. Information is moved from short-term memory into long-term memory through repetition, which enhances cognitive rehearsal.

3. Repetition creates a new belief linking attribute and brand, which in turn functions to change attitude.

4. The continued pairing of an attribute and a brand through repetition increases strength of belief.

5. Repetition reduces or stops forgetting by continually activating the process of information retrieval from long-term memory.

Notice that the emphasis here has been upon *moderate* levels of repetition. Studies thus far under conditions of high involvement postulate that there is a definite limit past which further repetition is not worthwhile. Many writers will indicate that this is reached with only several exposures.[75] The point at which further repetition is not worthwhile is termed *wearout*.

Two types of wearout have been identified in laboratory situations.[76] The first is simply increased inattention, regardless of what one tries to do to stimulate continued viewing, listening, or reading. The second occurs when there is a shift in cognitive responses given upon exposure from message-related thoughts (a positive outcome) to an increase in one's own thoughts. The latter, of course, can take the form of counterargumentation, which is to be avoided at all costs. Since this point can be reached quickly, only moderate repetition is recommended under high involvement.

[72]Cacioppo and Petty, ''Persuasiveness of Communications.''

[73]Cacioppo and Petty, ''Persuasiveness of Communications.''

[74]Andrew A. Mitchell and Jerry C. Olson, ''Cognitive Effects of Advertising Repetition'' (working paper no. 49, State College, Pa.: College of Business Administration, Pennsylvania State University, 1976).

[75]Rothschild, ''Advertising Strategies.''

[76]Bobby J. Calder and Brian Sternthal, ''Television Commercial Wearout: An Information Processing View,'' *Journal of Marketing Research*, vol. 17 (May 1980), 173-186.

(2) Effects of Repetition on Changes in Beliefs and Attitudes   In his definitive literature review, Sawyer reports that repetition can result in increased liking for a repeated stimulus.[77] To a lesser extent, repetition may result in a more positive attitude, but it also is possible that there will be no effect whatsoever or even a negative effect over time.

On the favorable side, Zajonc marshalled data from a variety of published research studies, most of which are only indirectly related to the subject under consideration; his conclusion was that "mere exposure" (that is, repeated exposure) is a sufficient condition for attitude modification and change.[78] Since most of the data he cited traditionally have not been considered as pertinent to an understanding of repetition, this conclusion must be accepted only as tentative. More recently, it was demonstrated that overexposure can lead to a boomerang effect in which the initial effects on attitudes are largely offset by diminution.[79]

More definitive positive evidence is provided by several published studies. It is reported, for example, that positive evaluations toward a brand increased from 29.2 percent prior to advertising exposure to 38.2 percent after two exposures.[80] Similarly, the findings from the Schwerin Research Corporation indicate that repetition helps a strong campaign.[81] Gardner reports that successive repetition causes the audience to move in the direction intended by the message.[82] The Grey Advertising Agency found that frequent exposure to television shows carrying a brand's advertising is reflected in a higher attitude level and in a greater likelihood of positive attitude change.[83] And McCullough demonstrated that exposure of individuals to print messages five times produced greater attitude change than did a single exposure.[84] Finally, it may be a general phenomenon that consumers attribute higher quality to a heavily advertised brand than to its less frequently advertised counterpart.

Repetition also can have negative effects, however. Capitman reported that a decline in preference often occurs after the fourth exposure to the same commercial.[85] This is especially likely if the claim is perceived by consumers as debatable and open to challenge. Similarly, continued acceptance of a commercial probably is associated with the level

[77]For a definitive review of over 200 published studies, see Alan G. Sawyer, "The Effects of Repetition: Conclusions and Suggestions about Experimental Laboratory Research (paper presented at the Workshop on Consumer Information Processing, University of Chicago, November 1972).

[78]R. Zajonc, "The Attitudinal Effects of Mere Exposure," *Journal of Personality and Social Psychology*, monograph supplement, vol. 9 (1968), 1-27.

[79]Richard L. Miller, "Mere Exposure, Psychological Reactance and Attitude Change," *Public Opinion Quarterly*, vol. 40 (Summer 1976), 229-233.

[80]"Frequency in Print Advertising: 1," *Media/scope* (February 1962).

[81]"Frequency in Broadcast Advertising: 2," *Media/scope* (March 1962).

[82]As cited in H. Cromwell and R. Kunkel, "An Experimental Study of the Effect on Attitude of Listeners of Repeating the Same Oral Propaganda," *Journal of Social Psychology*, vol. 35 (May 1952), 175-184.

[83]"How Advertising Works: A Study of the Relationship between Advertising, Consumer Attitudes, and Purchase Behavior" (unpublished study, New York: Grey Advertising, 1968).

[84]J. L. McCullough, "The Use of a Measure of Net Counterargumentation in Differentiating the Impact of Persuasive Communications" (unpublished doctoral dissertation, Columbus, Ohio: Ohio State University, 1971).

[85]"Frequency in Broadcast Advertising: 2," *Media/scope* (March 1962).

of good taste; a weak commercial seems to be especially vulnerable to a negative result.[86] Ray and Sawyer also found that attitudinal responses toward certain products were not influenced by repetition of the message.[87] A possible explanation for these results is that Ray and Sawyer reexposed subjects immediately after first exposure, and the effects of reexposure have been found to be most effective after sufficient time has elapsed to allow some decay in the impact of the original message.[88]

The factor of density (the proportion of the firm's messages to all messages received by the consumer) also is important. In his study, Light discovered a negative relation between frequency and attitude when density is high, thus showing the effects of saturation from many messages.[89]

The key also lies in the message itself, with favorable results occurring when a strong message is repeated, and vice versa. What, however, is the essential ingredient of a good message? While it is difficult to generalize, it appears that too frequent repetition without reward leads to loss of attention, boredom, and disregard of the communication.[90] The consumer, in other words, must perceive the appeal favorably and glean from its content some continuing positive reinforcement of his own predispositions. A commercial that stresses product improvement and continued excellence, for example, is likely to be rewarding to a prospective purchaser of color television.

It is unlikely that any message, no matter how strong, can be repeated ad infinitum without variation. Capitman's warning of wearout following approximately the fourth exposure is worthy of note. The best strategy is to *repeat the basic theme with variation* so that the reward level can remain high.[91] Product excellence can be demonstrated in many ways, and a campaign can clearly register the theme by varying the message and thus avoiding boredom and loss of attention from overexposure. The proper strategy, of course, is unique to each situation.

Other findings, mostly focusing on low-involvement products, are more positive and build a stronger case for repetition. This evidence will be reviewed in a later chapter.

(3) Implications The review here shows that moderate levels of repetition can be of value when high involvement is present, but there is that all-pervasive problem of wearout. Perhaps it would be helpful to pull things together by citing the main conclusions of an extensive review of

[86]"Frequency in Broadcast Advertising: 2," *Media/scope* (March 1962).

[87]Sawyer, "Effects of Repetition."

[88]T. Cook and C. Insko, "Persistence of Attitude Change as a Function of Conclusion Reexposure: A Laboratory-Field Experiment," *Journal of Personality and Social Psychology*, vol. 9 (August 1968), 243-264.

[89]M. Lawrence Light (unpublished paper, Columbus, Ohio: Ohio State University).

[90]C. I. Hovland, I. L. Janis, and H. H. Kelley, *Communication and Persuasion* (New Haven, Conn.: Yale University Press, 1953), 249.

[91]C. Samuel Craig, Brian Sternthal, and Clark Leavitt, "Advertising Wearout: An Experimental Analysis," *Journal of Marketing Research*, vol. 13 (November 1976), 365-372.

published and unpublished research by the Association of National Advertisers.[92]

1. One exposure of an ad message has little or no effect in all but a minority of circumstances.

2. Since one exposure is usually ineffective, the main goal of a media strategy is to place emphasis on enhancing frequency through repetition rather than extensive audience reach.

3. Evidence suggests that an exposure frequency of two within a purchase cycle is an effective level, but there is no hard and fast rule in this respect.

4. The optimal exposure frequency appears to be at least three within a purchase cycle (a four-week period).

5. Beyond three exposures within a brand purchase cycle or over a period of about four weeks, increasing frequency builds response at a decreasing rate.

6. Wearout is not always a function of too much frequency *per se*, because it also is affected by copy and campaign content.

7. In general, the smaller and less well known brand will benefit most by repetition.

8. There is no evidence to suggest that frequency response principles or generalizations vary by medium.

THE QUEST FOR DECISION RULES

A large volume of evidence has been reviewed in this chapter, and the reader may be bothered by the fact that the state of present knowledge makes it a virtual impossibility to advance firm generalizations. Fishbein's analysis of the state of the art is a discouraging one indeed:

> . . . at this time despite an incredible amount of research on this problem, we are still in the position of almost total ignorance. There is not a single generalization that can be made about the influence of source, message, channel, or audience effects on persuasion . . . the traditional approach to communication has also been more harmful than helpful.[93]

Fishbein probably has some truth in his assessment, but such a negative outlook is not warranted. Even though definitive decision rules are not available, the present evidence gives rich insights into *certain approaches that might work under certain situations*. This heuristic value, in itself, should not be dismissed with such a quick wave of the academic hand.

More critically, one should question whether it will be possible or even desirable to arrive at definitive rules of persuasion. The words of

---

[92]Michael J. Naples, *Effective Frequency: The Relationship Between Frequency and Advertising Effectiveness* (New York: Association of National Advertisers, Inc., 1979), ch. 7.

[93]Fishbein, "Attitude, Attitude Change, and Behavior," in Levine, *Attitude Research*, 10.

the distinguished advertising practitioner Harry W. McMahan are of more value in this context:

Examples can help. Guidelines can help. But rules often only lead the advertising novice astray. In our 20,000 commercials we can disprove almost any "rule." Why? Because, for one thing, different product fields require different handling in communication and persuasion. Cosmetics are more on the emotional side . . . Gasoline and cigarets are more emotional than rational. Coca Cola and Pepsi, instead, vie in "personality" battles. . . . Share-of-the-market definitely influences the advertising. No one in the product field continues on top, many times, even with a mediocre campaign. Why? *Momentum.* . . . It is this difference in market position and the difference in product fields that make most "rules" inapplicable to all advertising.[94]

There is no question that the trend is away from the tried-and-true in persuasion techniques.[95]

Decisions always must be made on three bases: (1) experience; (2) creativity and intuition; and (3) research. No one is sufficient by itself. A slavish reliance on rules, if indeed any did exist, would short-circuit the expression of creativity and would lead to ignoring some obvious research facts. The type of evidence reviewed in this chapter only should be viewed as guidelines of what *might* be tried under certain circumstances. To go any further would be to violate the very nature of enlightened decision making.

There always is a controversy as to whether research can be used in the so-called creative process. Some contend that it interferes with originality and even that it leads to dullness and sameness in advertising.[96] Admittedly this can happen if a committee is responsible for designing and reviewing advertising and selling copy, because the tendency is to stay within the boundaries of the safe and narrow. Research findings often become quoted in that context as a straightjacket. This, however, is not proper use of research which is intended, first of all, to reveal those influences on demand which can be affected through advertising and selling. *How* this should be done in an ad is rarely revealed by research but must be the product of creative minds. Research can also help through the whole set of copy-testing methods that have been used for decades.[97] Any enlightened designer or writer can learn a great deal from this kind of analysis.

[94]Harry W. McMahan, "Advertising: Some Things You Can't Teach—and Some You Can," *Advertising Age* (November 8, 1976), 56. Reprinted by permission from the November 8, 1976, issue of *Advertising Age.* Copyright 1976 by Crain Communications Inc.

[95]Arthur Bellaire, "Bellaire Survey IV Finds Trend Away from Tried-and-True in TV Commercial Techniques," *Advertising Age* (January 2, 1978), 17-18.

[96]Merle Kingman, "Who's to Blame for Sameness in Ads? Not Us: Researchers," *Advertising Age* (February 2, 1981), 41-42.

[97]For a good review, see Lyman E. Ostlund, "Advertising Copy Testing: A Review of Current Practices, Problems, and Prospects," in James Leigh and Claude R. Martin, Jr. (eds.), *Current Issues & Research in Advertising 1978* (Ann Arbor, Mich.: Graduate School of Business, University of Michigan, 1978), 87-105.

Hopefully future research on persuasion will be more definitive. As a start, the focus should be much more directly on change in beliefs.[98] As we stressed in the previous chapter, belief change is the heart of the process that leads to eventual changes in behavior. Much of the present literature is quite ambiguous in this sense. In fact, it is this awareness that led Fishbein to the highly negative conclusion cited before.

Next, much greater attention needs to be paid to methodological details and to variations in nature of product and competitive context. Sawyer has provided some very useful insights that should be considered by anyone interested in future research in this very important field.[99]

Summary

It was the purpose of this chapter to review a wide variety of research findings that document appropriate strategies for attitude change. Three specific questions were asked: (1) How great should the distance be between attitude position of members of the target audience and the position advocated by the message? (2) How can message content be varied to achieve a maximum effect? (3) What changes can be made in message structure (that is, the order of arguments and repetition)?

It appears that the optimum discrepancy between attitude position of recipients and that of the message should be small. This is because increasing the discrepancy appears to induce attitude change only when the message source is perceived as credible. Marketing stimuli such as advertising are viewed as having an obvious intent to persuade and usually suffer in credibility for this reason.

An extensive body of literature then was reviewed on the effects of variations in the creative message. Much is now known about the possible influence of fear appeals, distraction, nonovert appeals, and stated conclusions. Such evidence, however, is primarily of heuristic value only in its suggestion of possible clues for strategy. The type of research upon which most of it is based is, by nature, artificial, and one must be cautious in generalizing to more natural circumstances.

The chapter concluded with a discussion of manipulation of structural variables. Of special importance are the effects of repetition. A substantial body of research evidence was reviewed that indicates that repetition can increase awareness, retention of content, and attitude change. The most important question then becomes, at which point does the value of repetition stabilize or decline? It has been shown, for example, that repetition can have a negative effect on attitude change. One determinant appears to be message density—that is, the proportion of the firm's messages to the total received by the individual over a period of time. The higher this proportion, the greater the probability of a declining or even negative effect from repetition. It seems obvious that continual field study is needed to monitor message effects and detect points of wearout.

---

[98]Fishbein and Ajzen, *Belief, Attitude, Intention, and Behavior*, ch. 11.
[99]See Sawyer, "Effects of Repetition," 35-62.

Removing a campaign either prior to or after the point of diminishing returns is not a profitable business practice.

After discussion of a vast amount of evidence, it was asked whether or not it will be possible to arrive at decision rules for those engaged in persuasion. The answer was that there are too many variables underlying any situation to permit such generalization. Furthermore, decisions are made on the basis of experience, creativity, and research. Undue reliance on rules could short-circuit the natural workings of the creative mind.

Review and Discussion Questions

1. Compare the various theories on placement of communication messages relative to the recipient's own position on the topic. Of what use would these approaches be to a manufacturer of toothpaste? a manufacturer of pianos and organs?

2. A large, nationally known drug firm is interested in expanding market acceptance of its birth control pill. Would you recommend that a fear appeal be used? Why or why not?

3. The EXY Corporation sells aluminum cookware through door-to-door solicitation only. Although some advertising is used, the company relies primarily on its familiar company name and reputation for quality as the prime reasons for justifying a high price. How might the findings on source credibility be used by the sales manager?

4. In a laboratory story study it is discovered that a foreign make of automobile is regarded more favorably when advertising messages feature positive selling points as well as the fact that problems have existed in the past with respect to brake fade, door leaks and rattles, faulty ignition, and spark-plug fouling. Would you, as the director of advertising research, recommend that this company use a two-sided campaign? What arguments might be advanced?

5. A well-known brand of refrigerator has two distinct features: (1) a mechanically excellent meat keeper, and (2) a thin-wall construction, which gives greatest interior capacity per foot of exterior space. Using the findings on primacy versus recency, in which order should these appeals be presented, assuming that thin-wall construction seems to be of greater importance to consumers?

6. "*Zoomo* Reduces Headache Pain." What might happen if this slogan is repeated for one year on a saturation basis in newspapers, magazines, and on radio and television? What reasons can you give for your answers?

7. What might be done to reduce campaign wearout in the situation described in Question 6?

8. Does advertising influence buying action? With what degree of certainty would you want to predict such an effect in the advertising of *Zoomo* for headache pain (Question 6)? Would your answer differ if the product in question were an electric range?

9. What factors lead to campaign wearout? Give examples of each.

10. If your library still retains copies, secure an advertising book from the 1920s, the 1930s, the 1940s, the 1950s, the 1960s, and the 1970s. What conclusions can you come to with respect to rules for advertising design? Have there been changes in thinking?

CHAPTER 17

CHOICE AND ITS OUTCOMES

This chapter and the one following focus on the last two phases of the consumer decision process: choice and the outcomes of choice. The selection and purchase of an alternative often requires an accompanying decision process to select an appropriate retail outlet. This whole subject is considered in the next chapter. Our concern here is more with choice in a nonretail setting.

The decision process does not stop, however, once choice has been made. Under circumstances of high involvement there is considerable post-decision evaluation which has two dimensions: (1) satisfaction or dissatisfaction with the purchase, and (2) dissonance (doubt that a correct decision was made). The whole issue of satisfaction, in particular, is a major concern of the burgeoning consumerism movement, and there are many implications for both marketing and consumer education.

THE CHOICE PROCESS

Our model of high-involvement consumer decision making behavior in Figure 17.1 is now almost complete, and it shows that choice is the outcome of two determinants: (1) intentions and (2) unanticipated circumstances. Since the subject of intention and its correlates was thoroughly discussed in preceding chapters, the primary purpose here is to discuss those unanticipated factors leading to nonfulfillment of purchase intentions. Then the focus shifts to purchase behavior in a nonretail setting.

Unanticipated Circumstances

The list of possible unanticipated circumstances could, of course, be endless. One common one would be lack of funds at the moment. This could cause the purchase to be aborted or lead to brand substitution. Furthermore, the influence of a normative reference group does not necessarily cease once intentions have been formed, and it is possible that its pressures could be exerted in such a way as to change intentions. Finally, there can be a whole set of in-store influences leading to brand substitution.

Figure 17.1
The Choice Process under High Involvement

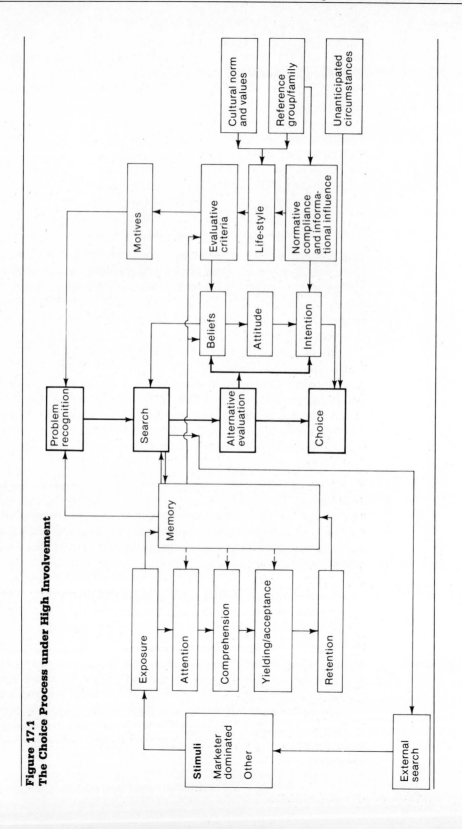

Display and Exposure

A major triggering influence on brand substitution is exposure to another alternative. This new information, in effect, causes the consumer to re-evaluate established beliefs and attitudes, with the result that intention to act changes.

Price Reductions

Some brand switching occurs as a result of a lowered price, but this does not necessarily signal any real change in beliefs and attitudes. At times the consumer has a set of alternatives that are about equal in prefer-ence, and a reduced price often leads to a temporary shift in choice. Restoration of relative price parity most frequently is accompanied by a return to the preferred brand, all other things being equal.

Out-of-Stock Conditions

Consumer reactions to out-of-stock conditions are another influence on choice. Unfortunately published research on this subject is limited, and most of it pertains to low-involvement products.[1] The determining factor is the degree of brand loyalty, and this varies widely by product class. For example, 62 percent of those studied in drugstores and supermar-kets refused to buy a substitute brand of toothpaste.[2] Consumers also react when a new product is not available on the shelves. One study showed that nearly 50 percent said they would go elsewhere to find a desired item.[3]

In-Home Buying

A growing percentage of consumer shopping and buying activity now takes place in the home rather than at the retail level. One authority estimated that this type of buying accounted for 12 percent of all con-sumer purchases in 1976.[4] That translated to a sales volume of about $60 billion in 1976, and estimates are that this figure will increase to $120 billion by the end of 1981.[5]

Strategies used to reach consumers in this way are now referred to as *direct marketing*. Here is a useful definition from the Direct Mail/Mar-keting Association (DMMA):

Direct (response) marketing is the total of activities by which prod-ucts and services are offered to market segments in one or more media for informational purposes, or to solicit a direct response from a present or prospective customer or contributor by mail, telephone or other access.[6]

---

[1]See, for example, "Out-of-Stocks Disappoint Shoppers, Force Store Switching," *Progressive Grocer* (November 1968), S-26 to S-32.

[2]"Out-of-Stocks Disappoint."

[3]James D. Peckham, "The Consumer Speaks," *Journal of Marketing,* vol. 27 (October 1963), 21-26.

[4]Estimates by Bob DeLay, president of the Direct Mail/Marketing Association (DMMA) cited in Bob Stone, *Successful Direct Marketing Methods,* 2nd ed. (Chicago: Crain Books, 1979), 3.

[5]Stone, *Successful Direct Marketing,* 4.

[6]Stone, *Successful Direct Marketing,* 3.

Stone notes that there are a number of factors which have contributed to the rapid growth of direct marketing and in-home buying:[7]

1. Changing consumer life-styles resulting from greater emphasis placed on leisure, the number of working wives, and demand for more services and conveniences in shopping.

2. Availability of credit, especially credit cards (150 million were in circulation in 1977).

3. Problems encountered when shopping at retail stores. Examples are congested parking lots, inadequate parking, uninformed sales personnel, long lines, and in-store congestion during peak hours.

4. Changes in consumer demand due to increased levels of discretionary income.

5. Innovations in computer technology which have permitted personalization of messages at high speed, mathematical models that predict the effects of varying levels of direct marketing expenditures, and reliable prospect lists.

In-home buyers generally rank above the average in terms of socio-economic status, but there are no other demographic differences.[8] There are some interesting psychographic differences, however, and this type of buyer is described as follows:

1. Venturesome and self-confident.[9]

2. Innovative and price conscious.[10]

3. Cosmopolitan in outlook and shopping behavior.[11]

The heaviest buyers also appear to be least patronage loyal and use a variety of buying modes and information sources.[12] Convenience, product assortment, price, and availability of unique products are the most common motivations.

Telephone Shopping

Unfortunately, there is little evidence on telephone shopping. The problem is complicated by the fact that many stores that sell by telephone do not categorize their sales according to whether the merchandise was purchased in the store or over the telephone. Moreover, most of the empirical studies that have been conducted group telephone shoppers with

---

[7]Stone, *Successful Direct Marketing*, 4.

[8]Peter L. Gillett, "In-Home Shoppers—An Overview," *Journal of Marketing*, vol. 40 (October 1976), 81-88.

[9]Fred D. Reynolds, "An Analysis of Catalog Buying Behavior," *Journal of Marketing*, vol. 38 (July 1974), 48.

[10]Christie Paksoy, "Lifestyle and Psychographic Analysis of Catalog Shoppers," presented at American Council of Consumer Interests, 1975.

[11]Isabella C. M. Cunningham and William H. Cunningham, "The Urban In-Home Shopper: Socioeconomic and Attitudinal Characteristics," *Journal of Retailing*, vol. 49 (Fall 1973), 42.

[12]Gillett, "In-Home Shoppers," 86.

catalog purchasers and/or consumers who purchase from door-to-door salesmen.[13] Studies investigating consumers purchasing from combinations of nonstore sources are reviewed in the last part of this section.

One study attempted to determine why some consumers are more likely to shop by phone than are others.[14] The study was part of a larger study of department store shopping behavior.[15] The first stage involved interviews with 2,092 New York homemakers and 853 Cleveland homemakers. The second stage involved telephone interviews with 723 New York homemakers and 461 in Cleveland who had recently ordered something by telephone.

Three general customer characteristics were most commonly associated with telephone shopping.[16]

1. *Need for convenience.* Telephone shoppers tended to have a greater need for convenience in shopping. They placed a high value on shopping quickly, were more likely to have young children, and were more likely to be residing in the suburbs.

2. *Means to shop by telephone.* Possession of the means to shop easily by phone was also an important determinant of telephone shopping. Volume of phone ordering increased with income and the possession of a charge account.

3. *Risk perceived in phone shopping.* When shopping in person, a customer has the opportunity to reduce uncertainty by personally evaluating the merchandise, by comparing brands, by comparing prices, colors, sizes, and so on. In contrast, the telephone shopper is limited to two methods of uncertainty reduction: reliance on past experience with the store, brand, or product; or reliance on a newspaper advertisement that may or may not picture the product.

Nonphone shoppers perceived intolerable amounts of risk in telephone shopping and were unwilling and/or unable to use newspaper advertising as a useful means of obtaining information and reducing uncertainty.

Purchasing by Mail

As used here, mail-order shopping is differentiated from catalog purchasing in that response here comes from some kind of direct mail or direct marketing piece other than a catalog. *Better Homes & Gardens* surveyed the readers of their publications to discover attitudes toward shopping by mail. The two major reasons given were "can't find items elsewhere" (33

[13]See, for example, Peter L. Gillett, "A Profile of Urban In-Home Shoppers," *Journal of Marketing,* vol. 34 (July 1970), 40-45; Laurence P. Feldman and Alvin D. Star, "Racial Factors in Shopping Behavior," in Keith Cox and Ben Enis (eds.), *A New Measure of Responsibility for Marketing* (Chicago: American Marketing Association, 1968), 216-226.

[14]Donald F. Cox and Stuart U. Rich, "Perceived Risk and Consumer Decision Making—The Case of Telephone Shopping," *Journal of Marketing Research,* vol. 1 (November 1964), 32-39.

[15]Stuart U. Rich, *Shopping Behavior of Department Store Customers* (Cambridge, Mass.: Division of Research, Harvard Business School, 1963).

[16]Cox and Rich, "Perceived Risk and Consumer Decision Making," 34.

percent) and "convenience" (27 percent).[17] Other reasons given were "fun," "price," and "better quality."

One study was undertaken to evaluate whether or not a consumer will perceive greater risk in the act of buying by mail as compared with purchase from a store or directly from a salesman.[18] The primary product investigated was a supplementary hospitalization insurance plan marketed solely through the mail. Using in-home interviews, a quasiexperimental study was conducted with three groups of 100 respondents respectively. Group A was a random sample of policy holders living in the Columbus, Ohio, area. Group B was selected randomly from the prospect list who had received a promotional mailing from that company one week before the study but had not yet purchased. Group C, the control group, consisted of respondents selected randomly from geographical areas matched to those of Group B, but they received no promotional mailings.

The study found in general that people perceived more risk in the act of buying by mail than in buying from a store or a salesman. However, mail-order buyers of hospitalization insurance did *not* perceive significantly less risk in the mail-order purchase of such insurance than nonbuyers. Thus, although there was a general tendency for people to perceive more risk in buying by mail than in buying from a store or a salesman, there was an apparent inconsistency between this finding and the finding that mail-order buyers could not be distinguished from nonbuyers in terms of risk perception.[19]

In another study, Feldman and Star[20] analyzed the purchasing behavior of 760 white and 240 nonwhite participants in the 1963 *Chicago Tribune* study, "Chicago Shops."[21] Grouping phone with mail-order shopping, they found on an overall basis that the proportion of whites shopping over the phone *or* by mail order (30 percent) was more than twice that of the 13 percent proportion of nonwhites. However, when further classified by income, there was a general similarity in the pattern of phone or mail-order usage by both racial groups. Specifically, as income increased, the proportion of *each* racial group shopping over the phone or by mail order increased.[22]

Catalog Buying

Catalog shopping also is experiencing rapid growth. The number of catalog companies in existence today (excluding department stores) is approximately 7000. Sears issues 19 catalogs in 24 different editions accounting for about 300 million copies annually, and major catalogs such

[17]Stone, *Successful Direct Marketing*, 4.

[18]Homer E. Spence, James F. Engel, and Roger D. Blackwell, "Perceived Risk in Mail-Order and Retail Store Buying," *Journal of Marketing Research*, vol. 7 (August 1970), 364-369.

[19]Spence, et al., "Perceived Risk," 367-368.

[20]Feldman and Star, "Racial Factors," 216-226.

[21]"Chicago Shops," *Chicago Tribune* (1963).

[22]Feldman and Star, "Racial Factors," 218.

as this one can have has many as 150,000 items listed.[23] Feldman and Star earlier found that approximately 40 percent of whites and 18 percent of nonwhites purchased merchandise from catalogs.[24] For both races, catalog buying tended to increase as income increased. The only difference between the two racial groups was found at the lowest income level. The apparent explanation was the lack of credit available to nonwhites at this income level combined with a lower level of literacy.[25]

Door-to-Door Purchasers

Door-to-door sales are important for some products, especially cosmetics and household cleaning items. Peters and Ford conducted a survey in which they defined "heavy" buying from a particular source as being 50 percent or more of total cosmetic purchases.[26] The heavy in-home buyer was different from her counterparts in the following ways:[27]

1. Had less access to a car for daytime shopping.

2. Tended to be less educated.

3. Was more likely to have children living at home.

4. Was more likely to have a family income under $15,000 annually.

5. Had a greater chance that the head of household would be a blue-collar worker, clerical employee, or a salesman rather than a professional.

Purchase Through Television

Soon it will be possible to reproduce on the television screen virtually any information the consumer desires. Referred to as videotex, anything that can be typed on a computer terminal keyboard can be transmitted to the home screen and even copied if the television set has facsimile capability.[28] This methodology was pioneered in Great Britain by the British government, and it has now spread to 22 countries and at least 12 states in the US. Within five years it is estimated that videotex systems will be in a significant number of middle-class US homes.[29]

One of the most interesting tests of this technology is being undertaken in Columbus, Ohio, and Houston, Texas, by Warner Communications. It is a form of interactive cable television marketed under the trade name *QUBE* which gives the consumer full capability of responding to a

[23]Stanley H. Slom, "While Retail Sales Have Ups and Downs Catalog Shopping Gains in Popularity," *Wall Street Journal* (June 6, 1975), 30.

[24]Feldman and Star, "Racial Factors."

[25]Feldman and Star, "Racial Factors."

[26]William H. Peters and Neil M. Ford, "A Profile of Urban In-Home Shoppers: The Other Half," *Journal of Marketing,* vol. 36 (January 1972), 62-64.

[27]Peters and Ford, "Profile of Urban In-Home Shoppers."

[28]Bernard F. Whalen, "Videotex: Moving From Blue Sky to Black Ink," *Marketing News* (October 3, 1980), 1T.

[29]Whalen, "Videotex."

central source by the push of a button in his or her home.[30] By this means, purchases are made instantly once an item is mentioned or displayed on the screen.

The authors confidently predict that we are just seeing the beginning of an electronic revolution here. While videotex is only in its infancy, we agree with many others who predict that it can virtually change the face of buying behavior in the future, to say nothing of the impact on television programming and viewing.[31]

Composite In-Home Shoppers

Gillett conducted a study of in-home shopping in which he defined this type of behavior as comprising placement of a mail or telephone order from the home, or ordering in person from a catalog or a catalog counter of a retail store.[32] In-home shopping was found to be widespread: 70 percent of the women surveyed had shopped at home at least once during the 11-month period of the study. About 43 percent had shopped by direct mail, 38 percent by phone, and 29 percent from catalogs. Only a small fraction of total family expenditures for general merchandise was purchased from these sources, however.

In-home shoppers were not found to be a captive market, consisting of those actively avoiding the retail store. Rather, this type of purchasing was most often discretionary. Avoiding an extra trip to pick up a needed item and buying in response to an advertisement were typical motivations. Most also considered themselves to be active store shoppers who do not find that form of purchase to be difficult or unpleasant. They were flexible in choice of shopping alternatives; they were not bound by shopping traditions; and they perceived lower-than-average risk in buying by mail or telephone.[33]

Marketing Implications

In view of the dollar volume importance of in-home buying, it is surprising to find so little consumer research in this area.[34] Several provisional statements can be made, however, on the basis of the evidence to date.

First, a longstanding misconception by retailers must be changed. They historically have been reluctant to promote nonstore sales on the assumption of greater expense and the theory that this would detract from total sales rather than to provide additional business. Now, however, it appears that much, if not most, in-home buying represents incremental volume.

Many factors must be considered, of course, in deciding whether to

---

[30]Whalen, "Videotex."

[31]For more information see "Television's Fragmented Future," *Business Week* (December 17, 1979), 61-66.

[32]Gillett, "In-Home Shoppers."

[33]Gillett, "In-Home Shoppers."

[34]Gillett's review provides an up-to-date source. See Gillett, "In-Home Shoppers."

develop volume over the telephone or by mail or catalog.[35] For example, it is always possible that there is greater perceived risk in nonstore buying. If so, the strategy should be designed in cognizance of this danger. Advertisements and catalogs should be informative and written to facilitate ordering by brand, size, or color. Liberal return privileges are also important.

The greatest need now is for further research.[36] It is obvious that the in-home buyer has developed a high level of sophistication. Marketers and consumer educators alike will require definitive data on the in-home shopping decision process. There is much futuristic talk of completely automated in-home buying systems,[37] but such developments seem premature until the necessary basic research is undertaken.

THE OUTCOMES OF CHOICE

Figure 17.2 completes the model of high-involvement decision process behavior by adding the outcomes of choice: (1) satisfaction and (2) dissonance. Both outcomes can have a strong effect on future behavior.

Satisfaction

In Chapters 1 and 2, we took a hard and sometimes critical look at the marketing practices of US automobile manufacturers in recent years, and the reader may recall that satisfaction with the purchase is a crucial factor. The numbers of complaints about low quality and poor performance reached epidemic proportions, leading the manufacturers, at long last, to place a premium on quality. Further loss of loyal customers to the imports as well as negative word-of-mouth communication were too high a price to pay.

In the past few years, satisfaction or dissatisfaction is a subject which has received a great deal of attention from academic researchers.[38] The reason, as Ralph Day notes, is the recognition that those concerned with governmental regulation and punitive action resulting from complaint behavior required an empirical basis for their actions.[39] From this pragmatic beginning, research has grown both in terms of quantity and conceptual and methodological sophistication.

---

[35]See, for example, Cyrus C. Wilson, "Telephone Order Promotion Strategy as an Aspect of Merchandising Strategy for Full Service Retail Stores in the Central Business District" (unpublished paper, Columbus, Ohio: Ohio State University, Department of Marketing, 1964).

[36]Gillett has provided some useful suggestions for future research. See "In-Home Shoppers."

[37]See William G. Nickels, "Central Distribution Facilities Challenge Traditional Retailers," *Journal of Retailing,* vol. 49 (Spring 1973), 45-50.

[38]For a thorough review of the literature, see Ralph L. Day, "How Satisfactory Is Research on Consumer Satisfaction?" in Jerry C. Olson (ed.), *Advances in Consumer Research,* vol. 7 (Ann Arbor, Mich.: Association for Consumer Research, 1980), 593-597; Stephen A. LaTour and Nancy C. Peat, "Conceptual and Methodological Issues in Consumer Satisfaction Research," William L. Wilkie (ed.), *Advances in Consumer Research.* vol. 6 (Ann Arbor, Mich.: Association for Consumer Research, 1979), 431-437; and Carol A. Scott, "Consumer Satisfaction: Perspectives From Self-Perception Theory" (working paper no. 89, Center for Marketing Studies, University of California at Los Angeles, 1980).

[39]Day, "How Satisfactory is Research?"

Figure 17.2
The Complete Model of High-Involvement Decision Process, Showing the Outcomes of Choice

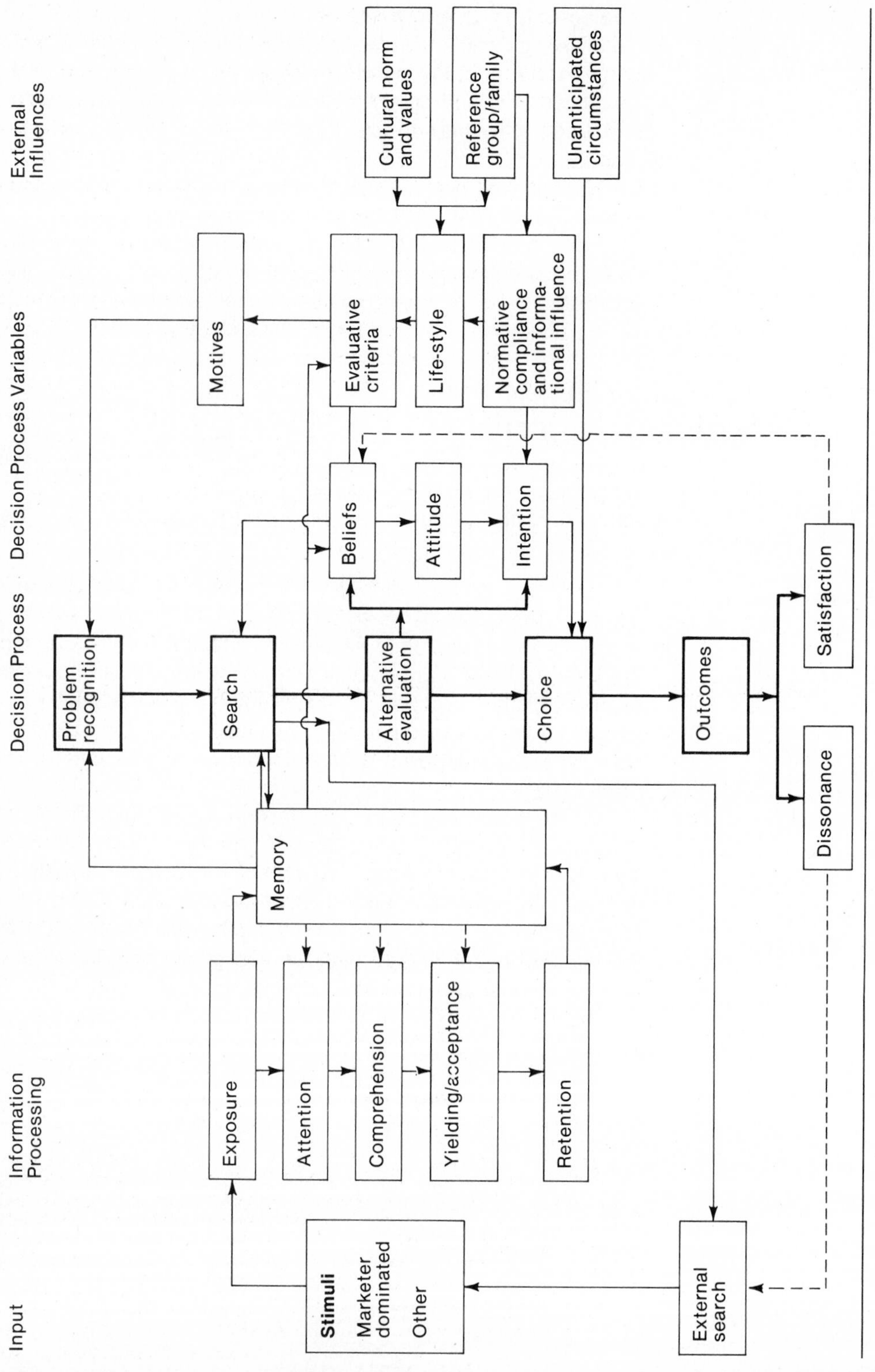

The Concept of Satisfaction

As the reader will recall, a fundamental tenet of learning theory is that a given response is reinforced either positively or negatively to the extent that it is followed by reward. Reward, in turn, leads to an evaluation that the purchase was satisfactory. In the present context, *satisfaction* is defined as *an evaluation that the chosen alternative is consistent with prior beliefs with respect to that alternative*. Dissatisfaction, of course, is the outcome when this does not prove to be the case.

Notice in Figure 17.2 that an evaluation of satisfaction (or dissatisfaction) becomes a part of long-term memory, and hence it can exert an effect on brand beliefs and attitudes. The probability of engaging in a similar buying act will be increased if there are positive consequences in the act of purchase and use and vice versa. It may be concluded that brand loyalty will develop and be strengthened as long as there is positive reinforcement of beliefs, *all other things being equal*. This conclusion must be qualified for the reason that the relationship between response tendencies and behavior is not necessarily one-to-one. Other factors intervene to affect buying action, and it must not be overlooked that the consumer will, on occasion, seek novelty and deliberately go against established beliefs and attitudes.

The implication of this definition is that satisfaction implies a conscious and deliberate evaluation of outcomes. As would be expected, this is much more prevalent with high-involvement as opposed to low-involvement products.[40] Previous experience is a factor in this evaluation, and it apparently can work in two ways. As one might expect, high levels of satisfaction with a previously owned product are commonly followed by low levels of dissatisfaction with a replacement purchase.[41] At other times, however, those with a poor prior experience evidently are pleasantly surprised and indicate higher levels of satisfaction than their counterparts who had a better prior experience.[42] Perceived personal competence also is a factor in that greater satisfaction is voiced by those with low or medium levels of competence in comparison with those with higher levels.[43] Finally, one's demographic status (age, education, occupation, and income) does not seem to affect this outcome.[44] The only other correlate found in the literature thus far is some relationship of purchase satisfaction with overall life satisfaction.[45]

[40]John E. Swan and I. Frederick Trawick, "Triggering Cues and the Evaluation of Products as Satisfactory or Unsatisfactory," in Neil Beckwith, et al. (eds.), *1979 Educators' Conference Proceedings* (Chicago: American Marketing Association, 1979), 231-234.

[41]Robert A. Westbrook and Joseph W. Newman, "An Analysis of Shopper Dissatisfaction for Major Household Appliances," *Journal of Marketing Research,* vol. 15 (August 1978), 456-466.

[42]Stephen A. LaTour and Nancy C. Peat, "The Role of Situationally-Produced Expectations, Others' Experiences, and Prior Experience in Determining Consumer Satisfaction," in Olson, *Advances in Consumer Research,* vol. 7, 588-592.

[43]Westbrook and Newman, "An Analysis."

[44]Westbrook and Newman, "An Analysis."

[45]Robert A. Westbrook, "Intrapersonal Affective Influences on Consumer Satisfaction with Products," *Journal of Consumer Research,* vol. 7 (June 1980), 49-54.

It is now generally agreed that confirmation of expectation is the key to satisfaction.[46] What is meant is simply this: the set of beliefs about a given brand or option function, in effect, as a kind of hypothesis regarding the consequences of an action of purchase and use. The input of information after purchase either serves to confirm or reject the hypothesis. If confirmed, beliefs, attitudes, and future purchase intentions will be strengthened, thus leading to greater brand loyalty.[47] If not confirmed, the most probable outcome is an unfavorable evaluation that will lead to a weakening of these dispositions. If beliefs are not based on salient attributes, of course, these effects will not occur.[48]

One interesting result of satisfaction noted by Bettman is the likelihood that the choice heuristic used in future decisions will be simplified.[49] The reader will recall our earlier discussion of compensatory and noncompensatory approaches to alternative evaluation, some of which are quite complex. It is entirely reasonable to expect brand loyalty to lead to simple rules such as this: "Make the same choice again unless there is information that other brands have been improved."

Dissatisfaction and Complaint Behavior

How extensive is dissatisfaction? The evidence here is somewhat mixed. Westbrook and his colleagues found very little negative response expressed in the period after purchase of a major appliance and concluded that assumptions of pervasive consumer discontent should be challenged.[50] Others have discovered a less optimistic picture, however, and here are some of the representative findings:

1. In a nationwide survey undertaken in 1976, about one-third of those interviewed reported consumer problems occurring during the previous year, an average of 1.9 per household.[51]

2. About one in five purchasers of clothing and textiles can report specific dissatisfaction usually involving a physical performance characteristic.[52]

[46]Richard L. Oliver's studies are especially worthy of note. See Richard L. Oliver, "Theoretical Bases of Consumer Satisfaction Research: Review, Critique, and Future Direction," in Charles W. Lamb, Jr. and Patrick M. Dunne (eds.), *Theoretical Developments in Marketing* (Chicago: American Marketing Association, 1980); 81-84; Richard I. Oliver and Gerald Linda, "Effect of Satisfaction and Its Antecedents on Consumer Preference and Intention," in Kent B. Monroe (ed.), *Advances in Consumer Research,* vol. 8 (Ann Arbor, Mich.: Association for Consumer Research, 1981), 88-93; and Richard L. Oliver, "A Cognitive Model of the Antecedents and Consequences of Satisfaction Decisions," *Journal of Marketing Research* (in press). Also James R. Bettman, *An Information Processing Theory of Consumer Choice* (Reading, Mass.: Addison-Wesley, 1979), ch. 9; and I. Frederick Trawick and John E. Swain, "Inferred and Perceived Disconfirmation in Consumer Satisfaction," in Richard P. Bagozzi, et al. (eds.), *Marketing in the 80s. Changes and Challenges* (Chicago: American Marketing Association, 1980), 97-100.

[47]Jacob Jacoby and Robert W. Chestnut, *Brand Loyalty, Measurement and Management* (New York: John Wiley & Sons, 1978).

[48]John E. Swan and Linda J. Combs, "Product Performance and Consumer Satisfaction: A New Concept," *Journal of Marketing,* vol. 40 (April 1976), 25-33.

[49]Bettman, *An Information Processing Theory,* ch. 9.

[50]Robert A. Westbrook, Joseph W. Newman, and James R. Taylor, "Satisfaction/Dissatisfaction Purchase Decision Process," *Journal of Marketing,* vol. 42 (October 1978), 54-60.

[51]Mark A. Grainer, Kathleen A. McEvoy, and Donald W. King, "Consumer Problems and Complaints: A National View," in Wilkie, *Advances in Consumer Research,* vol. 6, 494-500.

[52]George B. Sproles and Loren V. Geistfeld, "Issues in Analyzing Consumer Satisfaction/Dissatisfaction with Clothing and Textiles," in H. Keith Hunt (ed.), *Advances in Consumer Research,* vol. 5 (Ann Arbor, Mich.: Association for Consumer Research, 1978), 383-391.

3. Of those who bought a clothing item, 45 percent discovered it to be defective in some way, and 70.7 percent of those purchasing prepackaged foods found quality to be lower than expected.[53]

4. There are higher reported incidences of dissatisfaction with repairs and other forms of consumer services.[54]

Some consumers will complain and seek redress, especially if they are active in the consumerism movement in some way.[55] The percentages reported to complain, however, vary widely from one study to the next. The highest incidences are reported by Grainer and his colleagues, who found that 69 percent of those voicing dissatisfaction submitted a complaint.[56] Unfortunately only 40 percent who complained received adequate redress and many were completely rebuffed.[57] Day and Boder report that only about 20 percent of those they studied took no action whatsoever, and those who did often would boycott the source or give a warning to friends.[58] Sproles and Geistfeld, however, discovered that less than a fourth of those with unsatisfactory experience with clothing and textiles registered a complaint to the retailer or manufacturer.[59] This variation in reported behavior probably underscores the obvious point that there will be differences across products and situations.[60]

Dissatisfaction and the Consumerism Movement

Every reader could report his or her own story of dissatisfaction. For a period of time it seemed that the business community was nearly oblivious to the consumer voice, and it is not surprising that Ralph Nader and other consumer spokepersons soon attracted a vast following. The public hue and cry has finally penetrated corporate boardrooms, and some responsible businessmen are undertaking necessary remedial action. While consumerism is discussed in more depth in the concluding chapter, it is worthy to ponder the remarks of Thomas A. Murphy, Chairman of the General Motors Corporation:

. . . public sentiment is clearly against big business. . . . It has been building for many years, and for a number of reasons—but principally, in my judgment, because business has been falling short of customer expectations. And today's customer dissatisfaction is both the sorry evidence and the sad result. . . . We simply are not being believed. . . . We move in the right direction every time we

[53]John O. Summers and Donald H. Granbois, "Predictive and Normative Expectations in Consumer Dissatisfaction and Complaining Behavior," in William D. Perreault (ed.), *Advances in Consumer Research,* vol. 4 (Atlanta, Ga.: Association for Consumer Research, 1977). 155-158.

[54]Ralph L. Day and Muzaffer Boder, "Consumer Response to Dissatisfaction with Services and Intangibles," in Hunt, *Advances in Consumer Research,* vol. 5, 263-272.

[55]James G. Barnes and Karen R. Kelloway, "Consumerists: Complaining Behavior and Attitudes Towards Social and Consumer Issues," in Olson, *Advances in Consumer Research,* vol. 7, 329-334.

[56]Grainer, McEvoy, and King, "Consumer Problems."

[57]Grainer, McEvoy, and King, "Consumer Problems."

[58]Day and Boder, "Consumer Response."

[59]Sproles and Geistfeld, "Issues in Analyzing."

[60]This point is made by Ralph L. Day and Stephen B. Ash, "Consumer Response to Dissatisfaction with Durable Products," in Wilkie, *Advances in Consumer Research,* vol. 6, 438-444.

emphasize quality as well as quantity in our products, every time we focus on service as well as sales, every time we welcome criticism and act upon it rather than avoid it and condemn it . . . . we are going to have to fulfill the businessman's first, last, and always responsibility: the responsibility to satisfy these customers—today, right now, not tomorrow.[61]

A needed warning is sounded for marketing management. A case can be made for realistic research that documents consumer desires as well as product capabilities. Advertisement and selling messages, then, should be designed to create expectancies that will be fulfilled by the product insofar as is possible.[62] The extent to which this seemingly common sense precaution is violated through use of cute exaggerations and other forms of creative gimmickry in advertisements is, at times, appalling.

Similarly, product designers should be keenly aware of the way in which a product fits into the consumer's life-style. What does it mean to the consumer? How is it used? The product should be designed and promoted so that performance will be satisfactory under conditions actually experienced in the home. Many consumers, for example, use electric toasters for English muffins, rolls, and other forms of baked goods besides bread. If the toaster will not handle these items satisfactorily, unconfirmed expectancies and buyer dissatisfaction are the probable result.

Many consumers, in turn, become quite vocal when they are dissatisfied and do not hesitate to spread unfavorable word-of-mouth communication. One low-priced brand of automobile seems to have been particularly damaged in this fashion by product performance that violated its advertising claims. This, in turn, becomes compounded in that those who become aware of this fact will tend to screen out advertisements for this make. Little opportunity thus exists to turn these people into prospects.

Post-Decision Dissonance

Returning once again to the automobile buyer of the 1980s, let's create a scenario that might have some interesting outcomes. A consumer has just completed some fairly extensive search activity and narrowed the choice to four makes—two imports and the new Ford *Escort* and Plymouth *Reliant*. During family discussions and alternative evaluation there is some real disagreement on which make is best. Each has its desirable features, but none clearly stands out as being superior. While one is finally chosen, there never is a complete meeting of minds.

This situation contains all of the prerequisites for post-choice disso-

---

[61]Thomas A. Murphy, "Businessman, Heal Thyself," *Newsweek* (December 20, 1976), 11.

[62]The dangers of creation of unrealistic expectations are underscored by Bruce G. Vanden Bergh and Leonard N. Reid, "Effects of Product Puffery on Response to Print Advertisements," in James H. Leigh and Claude R. Martin, Jr. (eds.), *Current Issues and Research in Advertising 1980* (Ann Arbor, Mich.: Graduate School of Business, University of Michigan, 1980); and Gerald Linda and Richard L. Oliver, "Multiple Brand Analysis of Expectation and Disconfirmation Effects on Satisfaction (paper given at the meeting of Division 23, American Psychological Association, 1980).

nance—*post-choice doubt motivated by awareness that one alternative was chosen and the existence of beliefs that unchosen alternatives also have desirable attributes.* Dissonance occurs when two cognitions or beliefs do not fit together, and the result is a state of psychological discomfort. The person now is aware that he has purchased the car, but this is dissonant with his favorable evaluation of the other makes. He can reduce dissonance by (1) reevaluating the desirability of the unchosen alternatives in favor of the choice he has made or (2) by searching for information to confirm his choice (see the "search" arrow in Figure 17.2). Post-decision doubts of these types are most probable when:

1. A certain minimum level of dissonance tolerance is surpassed. Individuals can live with inconsistency in many areas of their lives until this point is reached.[63]

2. The action is irrevocable.[64]

3. Unchosen alternatives have desirable features.[65]

4. A number of desirable alternatives is available.[66]

5. The individual is committed to his decision because of its psychological significance to him.[67]

6. Available alternatives are qualitatively dissimilar—that is, each has some desirable unique features (referred to in the terminology of dissonance theory as low "cognitive overlap").[68]

7. Perception and thought about unchosen alternatives is undertaken as a result of free will (volition) with little or no outside applied pressure.[69] If pressure is applied, the individual will do what he is forced to do without letting his own point of view or preference really be challenged.

The automobile purchase decision described above fully meets these criteria: presumably a dissonance tolerance threshold has been passed, the decision is irrevocable, there are other unchosen desirable alternatives that apparently are dissimilar, there is commitment to the decision,

---

[63]M. T. O'Keeke, "The Anti-Smoking Commercials: A Study of Television's Impact on Behavior," *Public Opinion Quarterly,* vol. 35 (1971), 242-248.

[64]H. B. Gerard, "Basic Features of Commitment," in R. P. Abelson et al. (eds.), *Theories of Cognitive Consistency: A Sourcebook* (Chicago: Rand McNally, 1968), 456-463.

[65]See, for example, H. J. Greenwald, "Dissonance and Relative vs. Absolute Attractiveness of Decision Alternatives," *Journal of Personality and Social Psychology,* vol. 11 (1969), 328-333.

[66]J. W. Brehm and A. R. Cohen, "Re-evaluation of Choice Alternatives as a Function of Their Number and Qualitative Similarity," *Journal of Abnormal and Social Psychology,* vol. 58 (1959), 373-378.

[67]C. A. Kiesler, "Commitment," in Abelson et al., *Theories of Cognitive Consistency,* 448-455; Gerard, "Basic Features of Commitment"; J. W. Brehm and A. R. Cohen, *Explorations in Cognitive Dissonance* (New York: John Wiley & Sons, 1962), 300.

[68]Brehm and Cohn, *Explorations in Cognitive Dissonance.*

[69]A. R. Cohn, H. I. Terry, and C. B. Jones, "Attitudinal Effects of Choice in Exposure to Counter-Propaganda," *Journal of Abnormal and Social Psychology,* vol. 58 (1959), 388-391; L. Festinger and J. M. Carlsmith, "Cognitive Consequences of Forced Compliance," *Journal of Abnormal and Social Psychology,* vol. 58 (1959), 203-210; A. R. Cohen, J. W. Brehm, and W. H. Fleming, "Attitude Change and Justification for Compliance," *Journal of Abnormal and Social Psychology,* vol. 56 (1958), 276-278; T. C. Brock, "Cognitive Restructuring and Attitude Change," *Journal of Abnormal and Social Psychology,* vol. 64 (1962), 264-271.

and no pressure was applied to make the decision. Obviously post-decision dissonance is largely confined to extended problem-solving situations. Indeed, avoidance of such doubts can be an incentive for establishment of purchasing routines.

1. Reevaluation of Alternatives   When dissonance occurs it can be reduced by increasing the perceived attractiveness of the chosen alternative and/or downgrading the desirability of those not chosen.[70] In addition, it is possible to accomplish the same result by concluding that all alternatives are essentially identical, even though this was not felt to be true during prepurchase deliberations.[71] By so doing, of course, none would stand out over others, and doubts would be removed.

There have been a number of studies in the marketing literature that confirm that consumers do spread apart alternatives in order to reduce dissonance. LoSciuto and Perloff, for example, found that a chosen record album was reranked as more desirable than the unchosen alternative, which was then downgraded in desirability.[72] In addition, this tendency was found one week after the first post-decision rating. Similar findings are reported by Anderson et al.,[73] Cohen and Goldberg,[74] Holloway,[75] and Sheth.[76]

One interesting possibility is that this state of post-decision regret is only a temporary phenomenon.[77] It may well be that reestablishment of the original state of equilibrium through bolstering one's choice will make selection of that alternative more probable in the future. Mittelstaedt verified this hypothesis and showed that the probability of purchasing the same brand again is increased in proportion to the magnitude of post-decision dissonance surrounding the initial purchase.[78] This may shed useful light on the psychological mechanisms of brand loyalty.

The findings reported here are perhaps of greatest interest to those with a scholarly interest in understanding consumer behavior. Those with a more applied interest, however, are more likely to question their relevance. In reality there is little the marketer can do to affect or capitalize upon post-decision reevaluation of alternatives. The marketer, of course, desires to differentiate his firm's offerings as much as possible from com-

---

[70]L. Festinger, *A Theory of Cognitive Dissonance* (Evanston, Ill.: Row, Peterson, 1957).

[71]Festinger, *Theory of Cognitive Dissonance.*

[72]L. A. LoSciuto and R. Perloff, "Influence of Product Preference on Dissonance Reduction," *Journal of Marketing Research,* vol. 4 (1967), 286-290.

[73]L. K. Anderson, J. R. Taylor, and R. J. Holloway, "The Consumer and His Alternatives: An Experimental Approach," *Journal of Marketing Research,* vol. 3 (1966), 62-67.

[74]J. Cohen and M. E. Goldberg, "The Dissonance Model in Post-Decision Product Evaluation," *Journal of Marketing Research,* vol. 7 (1970), 315-321.

[75]R. J. Holloway, "An Experiment on Consumer Dissonance," *Journal of Marketing,* vol. 31 (1967), 39-43.

[76]J. N. Sheth, "Cognitive Dissonance, Brand Preference and Product Familiarity," in J. Arndt (ed.), *Insights into Consumer Behavior* (Boston: Allyn and Bacon, 1968), 41-54.

[77]E. Walster and E. Berscheid, "The Effects of Time on Cognitive Consistency," in Abelson et al., *Theories of Cognitive Consistency,* 599-608.

[78]R. Mittelstaedt, "A Dissonance Approach to Repeat Purchasing Behavior," *Journal of Marketing Research,* vol. 6 (1969), 444-447.

petitors and to induce the consumer to make a purchase. All things being equal, dissonance will be generated in the presence of qualitatively dissimilar alternatives, and it often is resolved to the company's benefit by reinforcing the decision. This process takes place as a result of what has happened *before* purchase, so there are no significant implications for marketing planning.

2. Post-Decision Information Search Doubts following purchase also can be reduced by searching for additional information that serves to confirm the wisdom of the choice. This is shown by the search arrow in Figure 17.2. In the purchase of an automobile, for example, dissonance cannot be reduced by changing the behavior and admitting a mistake because of great financial loss if the car is returned to the dealer. Also, most people are reluctant to admit that a wrong decision was made and to live with that knowledge. Although both of these acts would reduce dissonance and restore consonance, it is more likely that a person experiencing dissonance will buttress choice through procuring additional information. This information-seeking tendency has been widely documented,[79] although much of the evidence must be regarded as tentative for methodological reasons.

It is a reasonable extension of the discussion thus far to predict that a consumer who is not especially confident in his or her choice would be receptive to advertisements and other literature provided by the manufacturer. The selling arguments and points of alternative superiority stressed there could prove useful in bolstering a perception that the decision was wise and proper. There has been some evidence that confirms this hypothesis,[80] but none of it has conclusively verified that dissonance reduction is the motivation for post-decision search.[81] It is equally possible that a new owner will be set to notice advertisements simply because of the fact that an important new product has entered his or her life. This is a common phenomenon unrelated to dissonance.

Even though the published evidence is inconclusive, most purchasers have experienced dissonance in one form or another following an extended decision process. At one point in history it was reported that the Ford Motor Company designated certain advertisements to help new purchasers reduce dissonance.[82] This probably is unnecessary in that

[79]See, for example, J. S. Adams, "Reduction of Cognitive Dissonance by Seeking Consonant Information," *Journal of Abnormal and Social Psychology,* vol. 62 (1961) 74-78; J. Mills, E. Aronson, and H. Robinson, "Selectivity in Exposure to Information," *Journal of Abnormal and Social Psychology,* vol. 59 (1959), 250-253.

[80]See D. Ehrlich et al., "Post Decision Exposure to Relevant Information," *Journal of Abnormal and Social Psychology,* vol. 54 (1957), 98-102; James F. Engel, "The Psychological Consequences of a Major Purchase Decision," in W. S. Decker (ed.), *Marketing in Transition* (Chicago: American Marketing Association, 1963), 462-475; J. H. Donnelly, Jr. and J. M. Ivanevich, "Post-Purchase Reinforcement and Back-Out Behavior," *Journal of Marketing Research,* vol. 7 (1970), 399-400; and S. B. Hunt, "Post-Transaction Communications and Dissonance Reduction," *Journal of Marketing,* vol. 34 (1970), 46-51.

[81]William H. Cummings and M. Venkatesan, "Cognitive Dissonance and Consumer Behavior: A Review of the Evidence," *Journal of Marketing Research,* vol. 13 (August 1976), 303-308.

[82]George Brown, "The Automobile Buying Decision within the Family," Nelson N. Foote (ed.), *Household Decision-Making* (New York: New York University Press, 1961), 193-199.

the messages designed to attract the consumer in the first place probably will stress the very points that are needed to reduce any dissonance. Yet it is a wise strategy to stress product superiority in instruction manuals and other material enclosed in the package. In addition, some manufacturers and retailers follow the beneficial practice of contacting consumers shortly after purchase to assert once again the wisdom of their choice and to affirm their appreciation.[83]

3. A Research Dilemma   The theory of cognitive dissonance until recently has generated more research in social psychology than any other theoretical contribution. This explains, in part, why there were so many published applications in marketing at one point in time. Indeed, it almost became a fad. Nearly 20 years of experience with this theory, however, have given rise to methodological insights that often have been ignored in applications of the theory to marketing. Some serious methodological critiques have been published,[84] and there has been a recent assessment of the 23 marketing-related studies by Cummings and Venkatesan.[85] Cummings and Venkatesan documented that the conditions necessary for arousal of dissonance, which were stated at the outset of this section, usually have not been fully met. Therefore, the evidence must be interpreted with some caution. Their conclusion is worthy of note:

Certainly none of the findings in this literature have presented a major challenge to the validity of the theory, because of the methodological problems involved. However, no single study has provided evidence which conclusively supports the application of dissonance theory to consumer behavior. In brief, the evidence is far from definite. But it should be noted that the evidence in favor of the applicability of dissonance theory is more voluminous and somewhat more substantial than the evidence against.[86]

Summary

This chapter examined the choice process and the outcomes of choice. Choice is a function of two major variables: buying intentions and unanticipated circumstances. A variety of unanticipated circumstances can lead to brand substitution at the retail level; they include display and exposure, price reduction, and out-of-stock conditions.

   Not all shopping takes place in a retail store. In-home shopping is becoming increasingly common through telephone, mail order, catalog, and purchase from a door-to-door salesman. The marketing implications

---

[83]See J. Ronald Carey et al., "A Test of Positive Reinforcement of Customers," *Journal of Marketing*, vol. 40 (October 1976), 98-100.

[84]E. Aronson, "Dissonance Theory: Progress and Problems," in Abelson et al., *Theories of Cognitive Consistency*, 5-27; N. Chapanis and A. Chapanis, "Cognitive Dissonance: Five Years Later," *Psychological Bulletin*, vol. 61 (1964), 1-22; S. T. Margulis and E. Songer, "Cognitive Dissonance: A Bibliography of its First Decade," *Psychological Reports*, vol. 24 (1969), 923-935. Also see R. A. Wicklund and Jack W. Brehm, *Perspectives on Cognitive Dissonance* (Hillsdale, N. J.: Lawrence Fulbaum Associates, 1976).

[85]Cummings and Venkatesan, "Cognitive Dissonance and Consumer Behavior."

[86]Cummings and Venkatesan, "Cognitive Dissonance and Consumer Behavior." 305.

were examined, and it was demonstrated that retailers, in particular, must take cognizance of this type of shopping and capitalize upon the opportunities.

Finally, choice can have two outcomes: satisfaction or dissatisfaction and post-decision dissonance (doubt). The growth of dissatisfaction has been a major incentive for the rise of the consumerism movement, and there are many implications. Post-decision dissonance, on the other hand, is of much less importance. First, studies have suffered from severe methodological limitations, and, secondly, there is little the marketer must do if dissonance indeed is found to follow a major purchase decision.

Review and Discussion Questions

1. Prepare an outline indicating an appropriate method of determining whether or not customers who order by mail differ from those who do not.

2. Suppose that customers who order by mail differ from other customers in the following ways: (a) higher income (over $15,000), (b) greater tendency to have charge accounts, and (c) greater tendency to live in the suburbs. How can this information be used in designing specific marketing strategies? (Optional: design a marketing program based on this information.)

3. What types of behavior can be triggered by a purchase other than those mentioned in the chapter? What implications can you suggest for marketing management?

4. What is meant by the statement, "Manufacturers and resellers are well advised to undertake research that leads to a greater understanding of the *total purchase act*"?

5. The brand manager for a laundry detergent sees an article on cognitive dissonance and goes to his advertising agency with the question of whether or not consumers of this product should experience dissonance. What would your answer be? How would you arrive at this conclusion?

6. Would dissonance be likely if the product in Question 5 were a new stereophonic sound system featuring speakers no larger than a book? Why or why not?

7. Assuming that dissonance is experienced by a purchaser of the stereo set mentioned in Question 6, what would be the possible outcomes? Would the purchaser search for consonant or discrepant information? What would determine his course of action in information search?

8. Assume that a research report indicates a pronounced tendency for purchasers of power lawnmowers to notice advertisements for their brand. What explanations could you offer? What are the implications, if any, for advertising management?

9. What is an expectancy? How are expectancies formed regarding products and services?

10. Research documents the fact that consumers were surprised to discover the excellent sound output of the small speakers in the stereophonic system mentioned in Question 6. Is this finding necessarily favorable? Explain.

11. Some tentative findings indicate that satisfaction with a product increases to the extent that the consumer has expended considerable shopping effort. What would you recommend if you were research director for a large retail department store chain?

12. What is meant by commitment? Why is it so important if cognitive dissonance is to be demonstrated?

13. What are the requirements of research in cognitive dissonance? What difficulties are presented when this theory is applied to marketing?

Along with the decision with respect to product or brand choice, the consumer also must decide where the purchase is to be made—in home, as discussed in the last chapter, or in a retail outlet. Retailing itself is a fascinating area for consumer research because there is a dynamic rate of innovation and change.

Two trends are especially dramatic. The first is the growth of the limited-line specialty store. It features narrow product lines but deep assortments and hence can meet the service needs of a customer on a personalized basis. Often this is tailored to specific life-style segments. The second trend is the growth of the mass merchandiser providing strong price appeal because of the economics of scale associated with self-service and wide assortment. Caught in the middle is the conventional outlet, which is having increasing trouble competing and surviving.[1]

The appeal of the specialty store lies in the fact that everything it does can be carefully tailored to meet a life-style segment with a unique product mix.[2] Such stores often achieve inventory turnover rates which are twice those of conventional stores, and return on net worth follows suit. A good example appears in Figure 18.1—The Limited. The Limited operates about 200 outlets in carefully selected locations throughout the nation, maintains an ongoing program of consumer research to determine product and store criteria used by members of its market segment, and creates an exciting in-store atmosphere for presentation of high fashion merchandise.

At the other end of the spectrum are the mass merchandisers. These can take many forms such as discount department stores like Gold Circle (a division of Federated, which also owns conventional department outlets) and K-Mart, probably the most successful retailer in the United States during recent years. A number of newer forms are emerging such

---

[1]These trends have been described by Management Horizons based upon its computerized retail data base, which contains the SEC 10-K reports of all publicly held retail firms and their photographic data base, which contains over 260,000 slides of retail firms related to the statistical data base.

[2]A comparison of specialty shopping characteristics and conventional store characteristics is described in Daniel J. Sweeney and Richard C. Reizenstein, "Developing Retail Market Segmentation Strategy for a Women's Specialty Store Using Multiple Discriminant Analysis," Boris Becker and Helmut Becker (eds.), 1972 Combined Proceedings (Chicago: American Marketing Association, 1972), 466-472.

Figure 18.1
The Limited

Source: Courtesy of The Limited.

as warehouse furniture stores (Levitz and Wickes) and supermarkets for commodities other than foods (examples are Toys R Us, Standard Brands Paint, and Herman's Sporting Goods).

The most dramatic and innovative of the mass merchandising forms is the hypermarket. These are stores in the 60,000 to 200,000 square foot range carrying both convenience and shopping goods with a heavy emphasis on general merchandise as well as food. They have incorporated breakthrough technology in materials handling in a warehouse operating profile that provides both a warehouse feel for consumers as well as strong price appeal. Some other features of hypermarkets are the use of total store graphics programs which coordinate all of the customers' visual impressions of the store, strong use of vertical space in merchandise presentations wherever possible, and use of classification dominance in selected merchandise categories—giving the customer the visual (and perhaps actual) impression that the merchandise assortment contains virtually any item that could possibly be desired.

**Figure 18.2
The Hypermarket**

Source: Courtesy of Management Horizons, Inc.

The hypermarket has been most successful in Europe although Stein's in Montreal and Jewel in Chicago have adapted the concept to North America. Figure 18.2 shows some views of Carrefour in France, showing the massive amounts of merchandise, total store graphics, and classification dominance that create excitement and price appeal; as well as some of the operating economies involved in the technology of palletized product display and storage; and the cash registers which will each ring up over a million dollars per year in some stores.

All of these examples underscore the rapidity of change and the consequent need for retailers to have a keen understanding of the implications of these kinds of consumer research issues: How do consumers choose stores in which to shop? How important is location? How important is a store's image in determining store patronage? What factors determine image? What can be done to build store loyalty and to reduce shopper switching? These are the topics of concern in this chapter.

THE STORE-CHOICE DECISION

The retail store-choice decision can be one of high involvement or low involvement. At times it will be a highly important decision, especially if the products being purchased also are high involvement. At other times, especially with convenience items, the decision is much simpler—choose the nearest store. Most of the research on this subject does show that the consumer has well-formed evaluative criteria and hence exhibits an evaluative process prior to choice, and that is the perspective taken in this chapter.

Initial Factors in Store Choice

The most obvious factor in initial store choice is to culminate a brand choice decision, although at times the choice is completely nonproduct related. Sometimes consumers simply go shopping with no direct purchase in mind. This may reflect a desire to get out of the house, window shop or to get out with the family for a day of leisure. These types of influences may be especially important in large regional shopping centers offering such diverse attractions as good restaurants, movies, special exhibits, and concerts. Other such reasons are described in Table 18.1.

Table 18.1 Why Do People Shop?

Personal Motives

Role playing. Many activities are learned behaviors, traditionally expected or accepted as part of a certain position or role in society—mother, housewife, husband, or student.

Diversion. Shopping can offer an opportunity for diversion from the routine of daily life and thus represents a form of recreation.

Self-gratification. Different emotional states or moods may be relevant for explaining why (and when) someone goes shopping. Some people report that often they alleviate depression by simply spending money on themselves. In this case, the shopping trip is motivated not by the expected utility of consuming, but by the utility of the buying *process* itself.

Learning about new trends. Products are intimately entwined in one's daily activities and often serve as symbols reflecting attitudes and life-styles. An individual learns about trends and movements and the symbols that support them when the individual visits a store.

Physical activity. Shopping can provide people with a considerable amount of exercise at a leisurely pace, appealing to people living in an urban environment. Some shoppers apparently welcome the chance to walk in centers and malls.

Sensory stimulation. Retail institutions provide many potential sensory benefits for shoppers. Customers browse through a store looking at the merchandise and at each other; they enjoy handling the merchandise, the sounds of background music, the scents of perfume counters or prepared food outlets.

Social Motives

Social experiences outside the home. The marketplace has traditionally been a center of social activity and many parts of the United States and other countries still have market days, country fairs, and town squares that offer a time and place for social interaction. Shopping trips may result in direct encounters with friends (e.g., neighborhood women at a supermarket) and other social contact.

Communications with others having a similar interest. Stores that offer hobby-related goods or products and services such as boating, collecting stamps, car customizing, and home decorating provide an opportunity to talk with others about their interests and with sales personnel who provide special information concerning the activity.

Peer group attraction. The patronage of a store sometimes reflects a desire to be with one's peer group or a reference group to which one aspires to belong. For instance, record stores may provide a meeting place where members of a peer group may gather.

Status and authority. Many shopping experiences provide the opportunity for an individual to command attention and respect or to be waited on without having to pay for this service. A person can attain a feeling of status and power in this limited master-servant relationship.

Pleasure of bargaining. Many shoppers appear to enjoy the process of bargaining or haggling, believing that with bargaining, goods can be reduced to a more reasonable price. An individual prides himself in his ability to make wise purchases or to obtain bargains.

Source: Excerpted from Edward M. Tauber, "Why Do People Shop?" *Journal of Marketing*, vol. 36 (October 1972), 46-59. Reprinted from the *Journal of Marketing* published by the American Marketing Association.

Outcome of Purchase

Hopefully, the purchase occurs as the shopper finds an alternative that satisfies purchase intentions. On the other hand, it may halt or abort when this is not true. If the outcome is satisfactory and fulfills expectations, store loyalty is the hoped-for outcome, and the reverse, of course, is also true. This is an important subject which is discussed in more depth later.

The Store-Choice Decision Process

Monroe and Guiltinan have developed a useful flow chart of what takes place in store choice (Figure 18.3).[3] In most respects, it does not differ in concept from the high-involvement product decision model used in this book. It is assumed that certain buyer characteristics (life-style and so on) will lead to some general outlooks and activities on shopping and search behavior. The retailer can have an influence here with advertising and promotional strategies. These buyer characteristics also affect the importance of store attributes which lie at the heart of what has traditionally been called *store image* (referred to in Figure 18.3 as perceptions of attributes and attitude toward stores). Store image, in turn, affects store choice and the eventual product or brand purchase.

Obviously, consumers do not go through this process before each store visit. If past experiences have been satisfactory, the choice will be pretty much habitual unless there are other factors which have changed since the last visit.

SHOPPER PROFILES

Turning now to the first factor in the model in Figure 18.3 (buyer characteristics), it sometimes is possible to understand store choice and loyalty by examining the profiles of those who shop there. Demographics and psychographics are particularly useful in this respect.

Demographic Profiles

Usually, a store survives and prospers because it appeals to a specific market segment. If this market is properly understood in such terms as age, income, and place of residence, the outlet then can maximize its appeal through its product and service mix.[4]

The most important variable is probably geography. In a study of grocery shopping for coffee, Winn and Childers investigated a number of demographic variables but found that geographical census regions and central city size were the most important correlates explaining shopping concentrations. The second set of variables that were also of importance were social class related and included household income, education of household head, and occupation of household head.[5] There is a rich ar-

---

[3]Kent B. Monroe and Joseph P. Guiltinan, "A Path-Analytic Exploration of Retail Patronage Influences," *Journal of Consumer Research*, vol. 2 (June 1975), 19-28.

[4]A. Coskun Samli, "Use of Segmentation Index to Measure Store Loyalty," *Journal of Retailing*, vol. 51 (Spring 1975), 51-60.

[5]Paul R. Winn and Terry L. Childers, "Demographics and Store Patronage Concentrations: Some Promising Results," in Kenneth L. Bernhardt (ed.), *Marketing: 1776-1976 and Beyond* (Chicago: American Marketing Association, 1976), 82-86.

Figure 18.3
Sequence of Effects in Store Choice

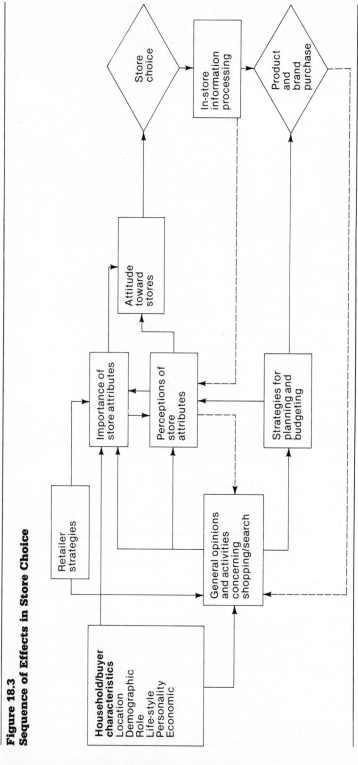

Source: Kent B. Monroe and Joseph P. Guiltinan, "A Path-Analytic Exploration of Retail Patronage Influences," *Journal of Consumer Research*, vol. 2 (June 1975), 21. Reprinted by permission.

ray of demographic data, categorized by census tracts and other geographic regions; and one of the useful techniques for retailers, once they have identified the demographic variables associated with patronage of their store, is to use computerized mapping of the trade area to prepare visual displays of the market according to the concentration of each demographic variable in a region.[6]

Many other demographic variables may be used to develop store profiles. Race is correlated with type of store shopped, days of the week shopped, and degree of shopping activity.[7] Even religion has been found to have some relevance in predicting purchase of certain types of furniture.[8] One of the more promising areas of demographic research is in the construction of profiles of the entire shopping process including awareness of stores, search processes, price perception and store loyalty. Woodside has demonstrated how this can be accomplished in a study of franchised food outlets.[9]

Psychographic Profiles

The greatest use of psychographic analysis for retailers appears to be the description of life-style of the user, especially the heavy user, thereby providing some clues on what should be in the product and service mix. In one interesting study, Tigert and his colleagues surveyed the heavy user of carry-out fried chicken and discovered that the heavy user is described in this way:[10]

1. A young working wife in a family with an above-average number of children.

2. Socioeconomic and educational status is about average.

3. She is optimistic about her personal and financial future, fashion and appearance conscious, pro-credit, active, and ready to take risks.

4. She seems to have liberal attitudes.

5. She seems to spend some of her time in a dream world.

Knowing this profile, management might well adjust hours of operation and peak staffing, pricing, and advertising strategy. It would not be wise, for example, for ads to depict an over-40, overweight, somewhat haggard person closely tied to her home.

At a more basic level, McCall analyzed changing life-styles and pointed out some of the changes that successful retailers probably will

[6]For examples of how to prepare these maps, see David W. Cravens, Thomas L. Bell, and Robert B. Woodruff, "Application of Geographic Mapping to Urban Market Analyses," in C. Curhan (ed.), *1974 Combined Proceedings* (Chicago: American Marketing Association, 1974), 183-189.

[7]Donald E. Sexton, Jr., "Differences in Food Shopping Habits by Area of Residence, Race, and Income," *Journal of Retailing,* vol. 50 (Spring 1974), 37-49.

[8]Howard A. Thompson and Jesse E. Raine, "Religious Denomination Preference as a Basis for Store Location," *Journal of Retailing,* vol. 52 (Summer 1976), 71-78.

[9]Arch G. Woodside, "Patronage Motives and Marketing Strategies," *Journal of Retailing,* vol. 49 (Spring 1973), 35-44. Also see Joseph Barry Mason and Morris L. Mayer, "Empirical Observations of Consumer Behavior," *Journal of Retailing,* vol. 48 (Fall 1972), 17-31.

[10]Douglas J. Tigert, Richard Lathrope, and Michael Bleeg, "The Fast Food Franchise: Psychographic and Demographic Segmentation Analysis," *Journal of Retailing,* vol. 47 (Spring 1971), 81-90.

have to make.[11] For example, the demand for stores with night openings to serve families with more than one working member will increase in geometric proportions as will the need for night repair services. Small stores will have to develop superior salespersons to compete with large store offerings preferred by some consumer segments, and the increase of numbers of working women may require use of media other than newspapers which women formerly relied upon most heavily for shopping information.

Shopper Typologies

Several studies in past years attempted to classify consumers into categories depending upon their attitudes toward shopping and shopping behavior.[12] Stone, for example, isolated these four types: (1) the economic shopper; (2) the personalizing shopper; (3) the ethical shopper; and (4) the apathetic shopper.[13] The assumption is that there is a kind of shopping life-style that cuts across purchases, but that seems a bit naive in view of what we know today. This study is highly product specific and dependent upon individual and situational differences. Any attempt to generalize in this way is unwarranted.

RETAIL IMAGE

Whether or not a consumer patronizes a given store depends both on the evaluative criteria of the consumer and the perception of store attributes. This overall perception is what has traditionally been referred to as *store image*. This concept has been defined in various ways,[14] but no one has ever improved significantly on Martineau's concept of store personality: "the way in which a store is defined in the shopper's mind, partly by its functional qualities and partly by an aura of psychological attributes."[15] In this section we will examine, first of all, some of the measurement methods, but most of the attention is focused on important store attributes.

Retail Image Measurement

Retail image is one type of attitude, measured across a number of dimensions hopefully reflecting salient attributes. Not surprisingly, almost the entire gamut of attitude research methods has been used for this

[11]Suzanne McCall, "Analytical Projections of Lifestyle Identification in Consumer Behavior," in Kenneth L. Bernhardt (ed.), *1976 Combined Proceedings* (Chicago: American Marketing Association, 1976), 354-359.

[12]See Gregory P. Stone, "City Shoppers and Urban Identification: Observations on the Social Psychology of City Life," *American Journal of Sociology,* vol. 60 (1954), 36-45; and R. Ronald Stephenson and Ronald P. Willett, "Analysis of Consumers' Retail Patronage Strategies," in Philip R. McDonald (ed.), *Marketing Involvement in Society and the Economy* (Chicago: American Marketing Association, 1969), 316-322.

[13]Stone, "City Shoppers." For a tentative verification of this theory, see William R. Darden and Fred D. Reynolds, "Shopping Orientations and Product Usage Rates," *Journal of Marketing Research,* vol. 8 (November 1971), 505-508.

[14]See Jay D. Lindquist, "The Meaning of Image," *Journal of Retailing,* vol. 50 (Winter 1974-1975), 29-38; Robert A. Hansen and Terry Deutscher, "An Empirical Investigation of Attribute Importance in Retail Store Selection," *Journal of Retailing,* vol. 53 (Winter 1977-1978), 59-72; and Leon Arons, "Does Television Viewing Influence Store Image and Shopping Frequency?" *Journal of Retailing,* vol. 37 (Fall 1961), 1-13.

[15]Pierre Martineau, "The Personality of the Retail Store," *Harvard Business Review,* vol. 36 (January-February 1958), 47.

Table 18.2
Belief and Importance Scores for Retail Stores

Attribute	Impor- tance scores	Store A	Store B	Store C	Store D	Store E	Store F	Store G	Store H
Price	6.13	3.71	3.91	4.48	5.14	3.93	4.11	3.92	4.06
Assortment	6.11	4.79	4.56	4.21	4.68	4.33	4.23	4.39	4.46
Personnel	5.15	4.70	4.56	4.31	4.40	4.39	4.34	4.34	4.43
Atmosphere	4.84	4.86	4.64	4.24	4.56	4.50	4.35	4.42	4.53
Service	5.63	4.89	4.67	4.23	4.47	4.62	4.47	4.49	4.50
Quality	6.37	5.15	5.02	3.97	4.35	4.80	4.65	4.71	4.69

Source: Don L. James, Richard M. Durand, and Robert A. Dreves, "The Use of Multi-Attribute Attitude Model in a Store Image Study," *Journal of Retailing,* vol. 52 (Summer 1976), 23-32. Reprinted by permission.

purpose; including the semantic differential,[16] customer prototypes,[17] the O-sort,[18] the Guttman scale,[19] multidimensional scaling,[20] and psycholinguistics.[21]

All things considered, the multi-attribute approach discussed in Chapter 15 offers the greatest promise and is finding increased use.[22] An illustration is presented in Table 18.2. This research focuses on men's clothing stores in a college town. Potential customers were asked to list attributes, characteristics, or terms coming to mind when one thinks of men's clothing stores. From that list, the six attributes perceived as having the most salience were assortment, personnel, atmosphere, service, quality, and price. Then stores were rated on a one-to-seven scale along each attribute, providing some very useful information for diagnostic purposes.[23] Store C, for example, rated poor on quality, the most salient attribute. This could be a major cause of low patronage.

Salient Attributes in Store Choice

The determinants of this type of choice decision obviously vary by product class,[24] a point that is sometimes overlooked. Nevertheless, salient attributes usually fall into the following categories: (1) location; (2) nature and quality of assortment; (3) price; (4) advertising and promotion; (5) sales personnel; (6) services offered; (7) physical store attributes; (8)

[16]G. H. G. McDougall and J. N. Fry, "Combining Two Methods of Image Measurement," *Journal of Retailing,* vol. 50 (Winter 1974-1975), 53-61.

[17]W. B. Weale, "Measuring the Customer's Image of a Department Store," *Journal of Retailing,* vol. 37 (Spring 1961), 40-48.

[18]See, for example, William Stephenson, "Public Images of Public Utilities," *Journal of Advertising Research,* vol. 3 (December 1963), 34-39.

[19]Elizabeth A. Richards, "A Commercial Application of Guttman Attitude Scaling Techniques," *Journal of Marketing,* vol. 22 (October 1957), 166-173.

[20]Peter Doyle and Ian Fenwick, "How Store Image Affects Shopping Habits in Grocery Chains," *Journal of Retailing,* vol. 5 (Winter 1974-1975), 39-52.

[21]Richard N. Cardozo, "How Images Vary by Product Class," *Journal of Retailing,* vol. 50 (Winter 1974-1975), 85-98.

[22]See, for example, Don L. James, Richard M. Durand, and Robert A. Dreves, "The Use of a Multi-Attribute Model in a Store Image Study, *Journal of Retailing,* vol. 52 (Summer 1976), 23-32; and Hansen and Deutscher, "An Empirical Investigation."

[23]For a useful discussion, see Eleanor G. May, "Practical Applications of Recent Retail Image Research," *Journal of Retailing,* vol. 50 (Winter 1974-1975), 15-20.

[24]Cardozo, "How Images Vary."

nature of store clientele; (9) store atmosphere; and (10) posttransaction satisfaction.[25]

Location

Of all the factors named in store choice, location has received the lion's share of research.[26] The general conclusion (subject to some notable exceptions) is that purchase probability increases as travel distance decreases. This probably reflects a great deal of common sense, especially in the present era of escalating energy costs.

During the past 50 years, numerous attempts have been made to sharpen knowledge of the effect of location and distance on patronage. These investigations have focused on cities, trading areas, shopping centers, and individual stores.

1. Cities and Trading Areas   There have been a number of investigations of the impact of the location of a town, city, or trading area as a determinant of store patronage. To take just one example, it was found that the large majority living in small towns in Georgia shopped beyond the town boundaries,[27] and similar results were found by others.[28]

Several attempts have been made to explain this type of patronage behavior. In the 1920s, William J. Reilly studied patronage in Texas and then postulated that two cities attract retail trade from an intermediate town in the vicinity of the breaking point (where 50 percent of the trade is attracted to each city) in direct proportion to their population and in inverse proportion to the square of the distances from the two cities to the intermediate town.[29]

Two decades later, Converse found the following modification of "Reilly's law" useful in explaining intercity shopping patterns.[30]

$$\left(\frac{B_a}{B_b}\right) = \left(\frac{P_a}{P_b}\right)\left(\frac{D_b}{D_a}\right)$$

where:

B_a = proportion of trade attracted from intermediate town by City A
B_b = proportion of trade attracted from intermediate town by City B
P_a = population of City A
P_b = population of City B

[25]For a helpful review of research and conceptual thinking on this subject see Lindquist, "The Meaning of Image."

[26]This literature is reviewed in Gunnar Olsson, *Distance and Human Interaction: A Review and Bibliography* (Philadelphia: Regional Science Research Institute, 1965).

[27]John R. Thompson, "Characteristics and Behavior of Out-Shopping Consumers," *Journal of Retailing,* vol. 47 (Spring 1971), 70-80.

[28]Robert O. Herrmann and Leland L. Beik, "Shoppers' Movements Outside Their Local Retail Area," *Journal of Marketing,* vol. 32 (October 1968), 45-51.

[29]William J. Reilly, *Methods for the Study of Retail Relationships* (Austin, Tex.: Bureau of Business Research, University of Texas Press, 1929), 16.

[30]Paul D. Converse, "New Laws of Retail Gravitation," *Journal of Marketing,* vol. 13 (October 1949), 379-388.

D_a = distance from intermediate town to City A
D_b = distance from intermediate town to City B

Converse found, in 1942, that this formula predicted the actual flow of trade to two Illinois towns from an intermediate town with an error of 3 percent.

Although these early models were useful, they were simplistic. Among other things, they ignore the relative incomes of the populations, merchandise assortments in the two cities, and consumer preferences. More recent research has gone beyond these early foundational studies and has included other variables, especially product category. For example, Herrmann and Beik found that the percentage of purchases made out of town varied from 43.8 percent for women's coats, to 8.8 percent for housewares.[31] Similarly, in Thompson's studies, over 50 percent of respondents purchased women's coats as well as curtains and drapes, rugs and carpets, men's suits and women's fancy dresses out of town; but purchased major appliances, automobiles, furniture and jewelry out of town much less frequently.[32]

What kind of a person is the *outshopper* (one who shops outside of a local trading area)? Socioeconomic status appears to be a big factor, especially in explaining the well-known tendency of ghetto residents to shop in their neighborhood.[33] Outshoppers show some important psychographic differences, however:[34]

1. They are significantly more exposed to non-local media and exhibit high knowledge of the outside world.

2. They are more innovative, fashion conscious, gregarious, and socially active.

3. They invest a great deal of time and effort in shopping and consult all relevant sources of information to a greater extent than their counterparts.

4. They are more mobile and more cosmopolitan in their outlook.

The outshopper would be attracted, then, by regional media, strong variety of both product lines and shopping options, unique specialty stores, and similar advantages.

2. Shopping Centers The effect of location on shopping center choice is uncertain. Gentry and Burns found that it was not an important consid-

---

[31]Herrmann and Beik, "Shoppers' Movements," 46.

[32]Thompson, "Characteristics and Behavior of Out-Shopping Consumers," 79. For more recent results on outshopping, see W. R. Darden and William D. Perreault, Jr., "Identifying Interurban Shoppers: Multiproduct Purchase Patterns and Segmentation Profiles," *Journal of Marketing Research*, vol. 13 (February 1976), 51-60.

[33]Karen F. Stein, "Explaining Ghetto Consumer Behavior: Hypotheses from Urban Sociology," *The Journal of Consumer Affairs*, vol. 14 (Summer 1980), 232-242.

[34]William R. Darden, John J. Lennon, and Donna K. Darden, "Communicating with Interurban Shoppers," *Journal of Retailing*, vol. 54 (Spring 1978), 51-64.

eration at all, compared with price and variety.[35] On the other hand, Brunner and Mason's analysis of the Toledo, Ohio, market led them to conclude that the propensity to shop at a center is inversely associated with the driving time to reach the center, and that a time limitation of 15 minutes would be applicable for approximately three-fourths of the center's patrons.[36] However, a study of the Cleveland market found wider variation, with the percentage of customers living within 15 minutes' driving time ranging from 55.5 percent to 83.7 percent for the seven centers studied.[37]

The Cleveland study, like others that could be cited, found that variables in addition to distance must be considered in order to predict shopping center patronage. For example, the authors of the Cleveland study found that 98 percent of the variation in the percentage of customers who drove more than 15 minutes to a shopping center was accounted for by the size of the shopping center in square feet and the limiting effect of Lake Erie on some shopping centers.

Huff has developed a model that estimates the probability that consumers in each relatively homogeneous statistical unit (neighborhood) will go to a particular shopping center for a particular type of purchase.[38]

$$P_{ij} = \frac{\dfrac{S_j}{T_{ij}\lambda}}{\displaystyle\sum_{j=1}^{n} \dfrac{(S_j}{T_{ij}\lambda)}}$$

where:

P_{ij} = probability that consumers from each of the *ith* statistical units will go to specific shopping center *j*

S_j = size of shopping center *j*

T_{ij} = travel time to shopping center *j*

λ = a parameter estimated empirically for each product category, for example, clothing, furniture

Huff has used this equation to plot isolines that are equiprobability contours that consumers will shop in center *j*. The probability of patronage declines as the distance to other centers becomes less and the distance to center *j* becomes greater.[39]

[35]James W. Gentry and Alvin C. Burns, "How 'Important' are Evaluative Criteria in Shopping Center Patronage?" *Journal of Retailing,* vol. 53 (Winter 1977-1978), 73+.

[36]James A. Brunner and John L. Mason, "The Influence of Driving Time upon Shopping Center Preference," *Journal of Marketing,* vol. 32 (April 1968), 57-61.

[37]William E. Cox, Jr. and Ernest F. Cooke, "Other Dimensions Involved in Shopping Center Preference," *Journal of Marketing,* vol. 34 (October 1970), 12-17.

[38]David L. Huff, "A Probabilistic Analysis of Consumer Spatial Behavior," in William S. Decker (ed.), *Emerging Concepts in Marketing* (Chicago: American Marketing Association, 1962), 443-461.

[39]For an excellent discussion of other techniques for estimating shopping center patronage, see Bernard J. LaLonde, *Differentials in Super Market Drawing Power* (East Lansing, Mich.: Bureau of Business and Economic Research, Michigan State University, 1962). For dissenting findings about these types of models, see Joseph B. Mason and Charles T. Moore, "An Empirical Reappraisal of Behavioristic Assumptions in Trading Area Studies," *Journal of Retailing* (Winter 1970-1971), 31-37.

Although Huff's model has proved helpful, other factors are involved in store choice, making the variable of location even more complex.[40] For example, there is every reason to think that overall store image might be another significant consideration. Nevin and Houston, however, included image as a component of the Huff model and found that it did *not* improve predictions of consumer choice.[41] Obviously, more research must be done to see how these various factors interact.

3. Cognitive Mapping The perception consumers have concerning location of stores or shopping areas is more important in explaining shopping behavior and preferences than is actual location.[42] Consequently, research increasingly is focusing upon environmental cognitions of consumers. These cognitive maps can refer both to cognized distances between stores or shopping centers and cognized traveling times.

Consumers generally overestimate both functional (actual) distance and functional time. Such variations between *cognitions of distance* and actual (functional) distance appear to be related to things such as ease of parking in the area, quality of merchandise offered by area stores (inversely), and the display and presentation of merchandise by stores (inversely). Variations between *cognized time* and actual time appear to be related to things such as ease of driving to the area (inverse), the price of merchandise (direct), the quality of merchandise (inverse), and the helpfulness of salespeople (direct).[43]

Nature and Quality of Assortment

The depth, breadth, and quality of assortment often emerge as a determinant store attribute. This is especially likely to be the case with department stores and shopping centers.[44] This factor seems to be near the top whether research is done in a laboratory or actually in the field.

Price

The importance of price as a determinant of store patronage logically varies by type of product. For example, recent studies of supermarket shoppers show it to be a dominant factor, as one might expect, given

[40]J. D. Forbes, "Consumer Patronage Behavior," in Robert L. King (ed.), *Marketing and the New Science of Planning* (Chicago: American Marketing Association, 1968), 381-385. Also see Thomas J. Stanley and Murphy A. Sewall, "Image Inputs to a Probabilistic Model: Predicting Retail Potential," *Journal of Marketing*, vol. 40 (July 1976), 48-53.

[41]John R. Nevin and Michael J. Houston, "Image as a Component of Attraction to Intraurban Shopping Areas," *Journal of Retailing*, vol. 56 (Spring 1980), 77-93.

[42]David B. Mackay and Richard W. Olshavsky, "Cognitive Maps of Retail Locations: An Investigation of Some Basic Issues," *Journal of Consumer Research,* vol. 2 (December 1975); and Edward M. Mazze, "Determining Shopper Movement Patterns by Cognitive Maps," *Journal of Retailing,* vol. 50 (Fall 1974), 43-48.

[43]R. Mittelstaedt et al., "Psychophysical and Evaluative Dimensions of Cognized Distance in an Urban Shopping Environment," in R. C. Curhan (ed.), *1974 Combined Proceedings,* 190-193.

[44]Hansen and Deutscher, "An Empirical Investigation"; Lindquist, "The Meaning of Image"; Gentry and Burns, "How 'Important' ", and John D. Claxton and J. R. Brent Ritchie, "Consumer Prepurchase Shopping Problems: A Focus on the Retailing Component," *Journal of Retailing,* vol. 55 (Fall 1979), 24-43.

high rates of inflation.[45] At one time it was not important in selection of a department store,[46] but that has changed more recently.[47] This depends to a large degree, however, on the nature of the buyer. Some preferring other factors such as convenience will, in effect, trade off that consideration against higher prices.[48] It is probably less of a factor also when there are strong brand preferences.[49]

It is important to note that the consumer's perception of price, or *subjective price,* may be more important than actual price.[50] This is not always an easy matter, as Figure 18.4 illustrates. There also is some evidence to indicate that advertised specials are often unavailable or mispriced on the shelf.[51] This kind of thing does little more than build skepticism and undermine store loyalty.

Advertising and Promotion

Advertising certainly has proved to be the clue for Farm Fresh stores. Through advertising they have tripled volume over the past five years without increasing the number of outlets.[52] Advertising stressed low prices, and managers conscientiously monitored competitive ads to guarantee that Farm Fresh prices always were on a par or lower. The impact on consumers was backed up by testimonials appearing in the ads.

Others question the efficacy of price advertising, despite the fact that it is so widespread.[53] All it may do is to shift market share from one competitor to the next. Nevertheless it must be done to maintain competitive parity. Apparently, a segment of the population—as large as a third or more of the total—is affected by price advertising. Still, their loyalty may be short-lived until the next set of advertised prices attracts that segment elsewhere.

The effects of price advertising are filtered by the recipient through the dimensions of their overall image. Keiser and Krum concluded

other information cues besides advertised low price would seem to influence consumer choice of retailers. These information cues are

---

[45]See Jo-Ann Zbytniewski, "Consumer Watch," *Progressive Grocer* (June 1980), 31; Jo-Ann Zbytniewski, "How do Shoppers Choose a Super Market?" *Progressive Grocer* (August 1979), 105-107; "7th National Consumer Survey," *Merchandising* (October 1979) 18+; and Jo-Ann Zbytniewski, "Shoppers Raise Their Consciousness About Prices," *Progressive Grocer* (June 1978), 29.

[46]Stuart U. Rich and Bernard D. Portis, "The Imageries of Department Stores," *Journal of Marketing,* vol. 28 (April 1964), 10-15.

[47]Gentry and Burns, "How 'Important'."

[48]Robert H. Williams, John J. Painter, and Gerbert R. Nicholas, "A Policy-Oriented Typology of Grocery Shoppers," *Journal of Retailing,* vol. 54 (Spring, 1978), 27-42.

[49]William R. Davidson, "The Shake-Out in Appliance Retailing," *Home Appliance Builder* (March 1965), 21-29.

[50]Kent B. Monroe, "Buyers' Subjective Perceptions of Price," *Journal of Marketing Research,* vol. 10 (February 1973), 73-80.

[51]J. B. Mason and J. B. Wilkinson, "Mispricing and Unavailability of Advertised Food Products in Retail Food Outlets," *Journal of Business,* vol. 49 (April 1976), 219-225.

[52]Ronald Tanner, "Building a Store Image with Careful Ad Planning," *Progressive Grocer* (March 1979), 35.

[53]Joseph N. Fry and Gordon H. McDougall, "Consumer Appraisal of Retail Price Advertisements," *Journal of Marketing,* vol. 38 (July 1974).

**Figure 18.4
The Problem of
Price Perceptions**

Source: Reprinted with permission from the December 15, 1980, issue of *Advertising Age,* p. 16. Copyright 1980 by Crain Communications Inc.

received from personal shopping experience, from friends, and from many other sources besides newspaper advertisements.[54]

There is no question that advertising, along with other forms of sales promotion, can affect store choice,[55] but its impact is difficult to assess. It may depend in part on the type of purchase and the nature of the store itself. For example, a study documenting the sources of awareness of a new dairy products outlet found that advertising accounted for only 16.9 percent of this awareness, compared with 50.5 percent for visual notice and 32.6 percent for word-of-mouth.[56] Word-of-mouth, in turn, proved to be the most decisive influence on choice.

[54]Stephen K. Keiser and James R. Krum, "Consumer Perceptions of Retail Advertising with Overstated Price Savings," *Journal of Retailing,* vol. 52 (Fall 1976), 27-36.

[55]Linquist, "The Meaning of Image."

[56]Robert F. Kelly, "The Role of Information in the Patronage Decision: A Diffusion Phenomenon," M. S. Moyer and R. E. Vosburgh (eds.), *Marketing for Tomorrow . . .Today* (Chicago: American Marketing Association, 1967), 119-129.

The role of sales promotion devices on store patronage also varies widely. Consider the case of trading stamps, which are not used as much today as they used to be. Some studies found that few consumers attached enough significance to them to make stamps a determining factor in the decision.[57] Others found substantial share deterioration when they were discontinued.[58]

Sales Personnel

Knowledgeable and helpful salespeople were rated as an important consideration in choice of a shopping center by more than three-fourths of those interviewed in five major metropolitan areas.[59] The necessity of skillful personal selling was previously stressed under the discussion of search, so this finding is not surprising. But does performance match expectations? Current evidence indicates that consumer confidence in retail sales people is clearly ebbing.[60] Less than half of those interviewed in a nationwide survey in 1979 said they believe what a salesperson tells them, down ten percent from the previous year. Furthermore, they are not prone to switch brands because of selling efforts. If this trend continues, a substantial weeding out will occur at the retail level, with those who place proper emphasis upon sales training and performance surviving while others fall more and more behind.

Services Offered

The presence of convenient self-service facilities, ease of merchandise return, delivery, credit, and overall good service all have been found to be considerations affecting store image.[61] This varies, of course, depending upon the type of outlet and consumer expectations. For instance, the 90 Giant supermarkets in the Washington, D.C. area began a year-long pilot nutrition education program in cooperation with the National Heart, Lung, and Blood Institute with good effects. The program is called "Foods for Health," and various tips are presented through shelf-talkers, posters, and other forms of display.[62] Similarly, a *Chain Store Age Executive* survey of managers revealed that the presence of in-store banking facilities such as automated teller machines raised traffic levels by 10 to 15 percent annually.[63] Others have found that provision of in-store restaurants increased total sales by five to six percent.[64] These are just

[57]See, for example, T. Ellsworth, D. Benjamin, and H. Radolf, "Customer Response to Trading Stamps," *Journal of Retailing,* vol. 33 (Winter 1957-1958), 165-169.

[58]Bernald J. LaLonde and Jerome Herniter, "The Effect of a Trading Stamps Discontinuance on Supermarket Performance: A Panel Approach," *Journal of Marketing Research,* vol. 7 (May 1970), 205-209.

[59]"Why They Shop Some Centers," *Chain Store Age Executive,* vol. 54 (May 1978), 31-35.

[60]"7th National Consumer Survey," *Advertising Age.*

[61]Lindquist, "The Meaning of Image."

[62]Jo-Ann Zbytniewski, "Just-the-Facts-Ma'am on Health and Nutrition Posted in Giant Stores," *Progressive Grocer* (February 1979), 29.

[63]"Retailers Asking: Is There Money in In-Store Banking?" *Chain Store Age Executive,* vol. 54 (October 1978), 35-39.

[64]Jo-Ann Zbytniewski, "Eating Out in Supers," *Progressive Grocer* (June 1980), 68-72.

several examples of the variety of services that warrant experimentation because of their high potential payout.

Physical Store Attributes

Reference is made here to such facilities as elevators, lighting, air conditioning, convenient and visible washrooms, layout, aisle placement and width, carpeting, and architecture. All have been found to be factors in and of themselves in store image,[65] but their presence or absence also affects perception of the other features discussed in this section. In this sense, they probably play more of an image-facilitating role rather than a determining role.

Store Clientele

Not surprisingly, the type of people who shop in a store affects choice because there is a pervasive tendency to attempt to match one's self-image with that of the store.[66] This is strongly affected by the clientele, as one writer stated succinctly a number of years ago:

Their personality concept is not primarily the result of physical features of the store—it is rather the result of the group of customers who have come to shop there. Customers associate themselves with a social group, shop where that group shops, and attribute to the store characteristics of the group.[67]

Store Atmosphere

At one time, nothing could have been more mundane and unexciting than the purchase of men's shoes, but Nunn-Bush has attempted to change this by opening a chain of stores called the Brass Boot.[68] A Brass Boot store recreates the atmosphere of a "Victorian English Club" with customers relaxing in leather-covered seats beneath ornate chandeliers. Goblets of red wine and piped-in music are all intended to "stimulate the buying hormones."[69] While this example gets a bit overdone in its hoped-for hormonal impact, it is an illustration of what is often referred to as *atmospherics*.[70] It is defined as the conscious designing of space to create certain effects in buyers, and it is most appropriate as a competitive tool under these circumstances:[71]

1. There is a large and growing number of competitors.

---

[65]Lindquist, "The Meaning of Image."

[66]Bruce L. Stern, Ronald F. Bush, and Joseph F. Hair, Jr., "The Self-Image/Store Image Matching Process: An Empirical Test," *The Journal of Business,* vol. 50 (January 1977), 63-69.

[67]John H. Wingate, "Developments in the Super Market Field," *New York Retailer* (October 1958), 6.

[68]"Sex, Wine, and Sitars: Shoe Fashion for the Groovy Male," *Journal of Footwear Management* (Spring 1970), 22.

[69]"Sex, Wine, and Sitars."

[70]Philip Kotler, "Atmospherics as a Marketing Tool," *Journal of Retailing,* vol. 49 (Winter 1973-1974), 48-63.

[71]Kotler, "Atmospherics."

2. Produce and/or price differences are small.

3. Product entries are aimed at distinct social classes or life-style groups.

The Limited stores shown in Figure 18.1 also are excellent examples of sophisticated use of atmospherics to create an image of high and even trendy fashion.

Posttransaction Service and Satisfaction

Those who purchase such high-involvement products as furniture, appliances, and automobiles and who frequent department stores are most likely to mention postsale service as a factor in continued patronage.[72] This refers to returns, replacements, adjustments, and so on. Those who seem to voice the greatest dissatisfaction with food stores are younger, more mobile, with well-educated spouses.[73] This segment of the population is growing, as earlier chapters disclosed, with the result that retailers cannot overlook these factors if they hope to retain continued patronage.

Determinants of Store Choice in Certain Industries

We have noted a number of times that preferred store attributes vary by product class and type of customer. Thus, it is not especially helpful to focus only on general determinants. In the following paragraphs some examples of research are described in specific retailing outlets including department stores, food stores, specialty stores, and discount stores.

Department Stores

The choice of a department store seems to be influenced most by quality of merchandise and ease of the shopping process,[74] store location,[75] and postsale service.[76] Frequent shoppers, in turn, show a distinct demographic and psychographic profile:[77]

1. Frequent patrons tend to be slightly younger, with better educations and slightly higher incomes than their counterparts. Demographics are not a strong predictor of patronage, however.

2. The frequent shopper is more active in life, travels more, patronizes restaurants and hotels more frequently, participates in sports, is involved in community activities, likes to entertain friends, and participates in various cultural activities. In short, there are real differences between frequent and nonfrequent patrons in what might be termed a cosmopolitan, active life-style.

3. The frequent shopper has a strong fashion emphasis accompanied by

[72]Claxton and Ritchie, "Consumer Prepurchase Shopping Problem"; and Hansen and Deutscher, "An Empirical Investigation."

[73]John Miller, "Store Satisfaction and Aspiration Theory," *Journal of Retailing*, vol. 52 (Fall 1976), 65-84.

[74]Hansen and Deutscher, "An Empirical Investigation."

[75]Leon G. Schiffman, Joseph F. Dash, and William R. Dillon, "The Contribution of Store-Image Characteristics to Store-Type Choice," *Journal of Retailing*, vol. 53 (Summer 1977), 3-14.

[76]Hansen and Deutscher, "An Empirical Investigation."

[77]Melvin R. Crask and Fred D. Reynolds, "An In-depth Profile of the Department Store Shopper," *Journal of Retailing*, vol. 54 (Summer 1978), 23-32.

readership of fashion magazines and purchase of individualized fashion items.

4. Almost 80 percent of frequent shoppers returned an unsatisfactory product during the past year, compared with only 50 percent of their counterparts.

The findings place some strong pressures on the department store retailer to take atmospherics into consideration to reflect travel, culture, and other dimensions of preferred life-styles. Merchandise lines also must be consistent, and care must be taken with layout and display to make the shopping process both easy and pleasant. Also, failure to provide liberal return privileges and other forms of postsale service will reduce the chances of retaining a loyal customer.

Food Stores and Supermarkets

Consumers do not appear to use any one store attribute as determinant when choosing a food store but rather seem to weigh several in a noncompensatory manner.[78] There is real convergence of research findings on the following attributes listed in order of salience:[79] (1) cleanliness; (2) low prices; (3) all prices clearly labeled; (4) good produce department; (5) freshness—with date marked on the package; (6) accurate and pleasant checkout clerks; and (7) well-stocked shelves. Of much less importance are good assortment of nonfood items, carrying of purchase to car, in-store bakery, eye-catching displays, knowing a person's name, trading stamps and other extras, and sale of hot foods to take out or to eat in the store.

Demographics do not seem to be a good predictor of food shopping preferences and styles,[80] but shoppers do seem to fall into some segments which vary as to the attributes which are preferred:[81]

1. *The apathetic shopper.* This accounts for 22 percent of the shoppers, and most of these do not express a preference for any particular attribute.

2. *The demanding shopper.* While this accounts for only 8.6 percent, they demand excellence and quality at competitive prices. Trading stamps are unimportant.

3. *The quality shopper.* Comprising 19 percent of the shoppers, this group wants fresh produce and quality meat cuts and little else.

4. *The fastidious shopper.* Those in this group (15 percent) want a supermarket with spick-and-span facilities and expect a wide assortment of brands.

[78]Jo-Ann Zbytniewski, "How do Shoppers Choose a Super Market?" *Progressive Grocer,* (August 1979), 105-107.

[79]Hansen and Deutscher, "An Empirical Investigation"; Zbytniewski, "How do Shoppers Choose"; Zbytniewski, "Consumer Watch"; and Zbytniewski, "Shoppers Raise Their Consciousness."

[80]Williams, Painter, and Nicholas, "A Policy-Oriented Typology."

[81]William R. Darden and Dub Ashton, "Psychographic Profiles of Patronage Preference Groups," *Journal of Retailing,* vol. 50 (Winter 1974-1975), 99-112.

5. *The stamp preferer.* Shoppers in this group, representing only 12 percent, want trading stamps but also expect quality products, competitive prices, variety, friendly personnel, and clean stores.

6. *The convenient-location shopper.* Just 15 percent fall into this category, with this being the only preferred attribute.

7. *The stamp haters.* Just eight percent are classified in this way, and they prefer stores not offering stamps.

While there are other ways of profiling supermarket shoppers,[82] this research does indicate the variety of segments which exist. Obviously no one type of outlet can satisfy all demands. Therefore, a conscious decision must be made as to which target group is the market objective and then appropriate attributes for that group must be offered. Sometimes more than one segment can be served within a single outlet by offering various shopping zones, creating a store within a store. This is becoming more and more common in the largest supermarkets. Cleanliness and low price, of course, are determinant attributes, and their presence may override other considerations and permit attraction of multiple segments.

Specialty Stores

As we mentioned at the outset, specialty stores offering such specific products as hi-fi equipment or health foods are growing by leaps and bounds. Because of the nature of the products offered, customers expect expert sales assistance, as well as a wide assortment of the product.[83] Product guarantees and after-sale service also are important.[84]

Specialty-store shoppers are unique in many ways. Looking specifically at consumers purchasing audio equipment, about half score high on a product knowledge test compared with only 10 percent shopping for the same items in a department store; 40 percent shopped at three or more stores; and there was a greater tendency to be exposed to specialized magazines and manufacturer's literature.[85]

If the specialty outlet is to thrive, then, it must recognize the sophistication of the shopper and offer the breadth and depth of product lines, information and sales help, and after-sale services which are expected. If this is done, such outlets offer real advantages that mass retailers cannot begin to match. Personalization is the key.

Discount Stores

The discount store was a post-World War II phenomenon which started from a bare-bones warehouse type of environment and has grown into such mass outlets as the highly successful K-Mart chain. Convenient lo-

[82]See, for example, Williams, Painter, and Nicholas, "A Policy-Oriented Typology."

[83]Schiffman, Dash, and Dillon, "The Contribution of Store-Image."

[84]Schiffman, Dash, and Dillon, "The Contribution of Store-Image."

[85]Joseph F. Dash, Leon G. Schiffman, and Conrad Berenson, "Information Search and Store Choice," *Journal of Advertising Research,* vol. 16 (June 1976), 35-40.

cation is the most important attribute in store choice, followed closely by low price and broad merchandise selection as would be expected.[86] Shoppers tend to be younger families with children, most of which have a full-time working wife.[87] Income and education levels tend to be somewhat below average, and the majority of the heads of household are blue collar workers,[88] although these factors will vary by nature of outlet.

These types of retail outlets obviously succeed best when located by a shopping center of some type close to the consumer's home. Self-service is virtually demanded to permit low price, and there must be a wide variety of lines carried especially in health and beauty aids, household items (excluding appliances), and hardware and paints.[89] Services can be minimal if these requirements are met.

Retail Store Loyalty

Whenever possible, all retailers want to build up a sizeable loyal clientele that can be counted upon for repeat purchase. This issue has not been researched as extensively as one might expect, at least in terms of published literature. Enis and Paul have suggested, however, that loyal segments are potentially very profitable for food retailers. More specifically they found that: (1) store-loyal behavior is independent of the total amount spent; (2) more loyal customers allocated larger proportions of total purchases to first choice stores; (3) stores with the largest percentage of loyal customers have the largest market share; and (4) those who are loyal are no more expensive to serve than others.[90] The financial gains, then, appear to be considerable. Yet many within the food industry predict that store loyalty will sharply decline in the middle and late 1980s because of energy costs.[91] Closeness of location could become the dominant consideration.

What kind of person tends to be store loyal? This no doubt varies by product class and customer type, but some generalizations are possible. First, those who are most store loyal tend to engage in less comparison among stores, have a low knowledge of existence of other stores, and rarely visit more than one or two stores.[92] In terms of socioeconomic status, two studies show that the store-loyal consumer, especially one who is loyal across store types, tends to be older, have a lower educational attainment, and a lower family income than his or her less loyal counterparts.[93] Also s/he tends not to be a fashion opinion leader, not

[86]"Definition of Discount Store," *The Direct Merchandiser,* vol. 18 (May 1978), 22+.

[87]John L. Pagliaro, "Who is the Typical Warehouse Store Shopper? Support to 'Blue Collar' Theory," *Supermarketing,* vol. 33 (June 1978), 26.

[88]Pagliaro, "Who is the Typical."

[89]"Definition of Discount Store."

[90]Ben M. Enis and Gordon W. Paul, " 'Store Loyalty' as a Basis for Market Segmentation," *Journal of Retailing,* vol. 46 (Fall 1970), 42-56.

[91]Jo-Ann Zbytniewski, "Lower Store and Brand Loyalty and More Splintering in Wants," *Progressive Grocer* (October 1979), 111-118.

[92]Arieh Goldman, "The Shopping Style Explanation for Store Loyalty," *Journal of Retailing,* vol. 53 (Winter 1977-1978), 33+.

[93]Goldman, "The Shopping Style Explanation"; and Fred D. Reyonds, William R. Darden, and Warren S. Martin, "Developing an Image of the Store-Loyal Customer," *Journal of Retailing,* vol. 50 (Winter 1974-1975), 73-84.

venturesome in trying new products, not urban-oriented, not gregarious, and not a credit user. On the positive side, s/he is time conscious and actively exposed to radio and television, although s/he is not a newspaper reader.

If these socioeconomic and psychographic profiles tend to be true on a wider basis, then merchants appealing to this segment should not overemphasize an urban-oriented or cosmopolitan image. Rather, they should stress local ties and community traditions. Furthermore, there is merit in stressing the convenience of local shopping given the relationship between time consciousness and store loyalty.

SOME CLUES FOR RETAILING STRATEGY

It is helpful to probe more deeply into some of the ways in which leading retailers as well as manufacturers are capitalizing on knowledge of consumer retail store-choice processes.[94]

Making Proper Use of Retailing Research

Do retailers really understand consumer preferences for store attributes and respond properly? Jolson and Spath focused particularly on supermarkets and answered this question negatively.[95] It seems almost inevitable that this naiveté can only lead this kind of manager to the oblivion many stores are certain to face during the period of economic crunch during the 1980s[96] Furthermore, this is totally unnecessary given the availability of existing research and readily-accessible research technology to be used by any responsible manager.

Vertical Marketing Systems

Consumer needs at the retailing level are increasingly being met through the emergence of vertical marketing systems. A vertical marketing system is defined as a tightly programmed network of horizontally coordinated and vertically aligned establishments managed as a total system. They are in contrast to traditional channels of distribution in which each channel member performs independently a historical set of marketing functions. Instead, a VMS relies upon the concept of functional shiftability to improve total system performance. That is, establishments of each level are reprogrammed so that marketing functions within the system are performed at the most advantageous level of position.[97] The salient characteristics of conventional channels and vertical marketing systems are summarized in Figure 18.5.

Three major types of vertically aligned networks are generally rec-

[94]This section relies heavily on materials from Management Horizons, Inc. The authors acknowledge the assistance of staff members, especially Dr. William R. Davidson, chairman.

[95]Marvin A. Jolson and Walter F. Spath, "Understanding and Fulfilling Shopper's Requirements," *Journal of Retailing,* vol. 49 (Summer 1973), 38-47.

[96]Zybtniewski, "Lower Store and Brand Loyalty."

[97]William R. Davidson, "Changes in Distributive Institutions," *Journal of Marketing,* vol. 34 (January 1970), 7-10.

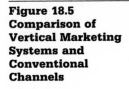

**Figure 18.5
Comparison of
Vertical Marketing
Systems and
Conventional
Channels**

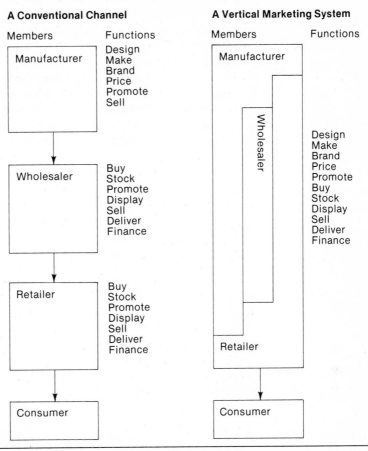

A Conventional Channel

Members | Functions

Manufacturer
Design
Make
Brand
Price
Promote
Sell

Wholesaler
Buy
Stock
Promote
Display
Sell
Deliver
Finance

Retailer
Buy
Stock
Promote
Display
Sell
Deliver
Finance

Consumer

A Vertical Marketing System

Members | Functions

Manufacturer

Wholesaler

Design
Make
Brand
Price
Promote
Buy
Stock
Display
Sell
Deliver
Finance

Retailer

Consumer

Source: David T. Kollat, Roger D. Blackwell, and James F. Robeson, *Strategic Marketing* (New York: Holt, Rinehart and Winston, 1972), 289. Reprinted by permission of Holt, Rinehart and Winston.

ognized[98] A *corporate* VMS is based on ownership of various parts of the system. A classic example is an operation such as Sears. Other examples include Sherwin-Williams, a paint manufacturer that operates over 2,000 retail outlets, or Hart Schaffner & Marx, which owns more than 200 retail stores. A *contractual* VMS is based upon a long-term contractual agreement in which independent parties agree to exchange some autonomy in order to position marketing functions (advertising, inventory control, buying, and so forth) at their most efficient level. Examples include IGA, a chain of grocery stores organized by wholesalers, and American Hardware stores, which supplies most of the items in a group of independent hardware stores. Other famous contractual systems are the major franchisers such as Holiday Inn, McDonald's, and Wendy's, although some of these are in the process of converting to

[98]For more details, see David T. Kollat, Roger D. Blackwell, and James Robeson, *Strategic Marketing* (Hinsdale, Ill.: Dryden Press, 1972), 287-292.

corporately owned systems. An *administered* VMS is based upon the ability of one party to take control or exert leadership over the distribution system because of the expertise of that party. Examples include Kraft, which dominates the dairy case in most grocery stores, or *L'eggs* hosiery products in drug and grocery stores.

How does a VMS allow a retailer to respond more closely to the evaluative criteria and purchasing processes of consumers? An answer to this question is provided by considering the example of *L'eggs,* an administered VMS. Traditionally, women's hosiery products have been distributed through department stores and independent specialty stores. Based upon a $400,000 consumer research program,[99] Hanes found that women would like to buy more hosiery in supermarkets and drugstores but were not particularly impressed by the offerings of those stores because of their price promotion and lack of uniform quality control for many private labels. From the research, a number of key elements were discovered concerning the product features, promotion, pricing and distribution necessary to satisfy consumer purchases in drugstores and supermarkets. Hanes developed a new brand, *L'eggs,* an effective advertising program to communicate the primary product quality ("Our *L'eggs fit* your legs"), and a price that permitted enough margin to satisfy retailers. To help overcome the out-of-stock and service problems that hurt other manufacturers in supermarkets and drugstores, *L'eggs* employed a computerized control system to provide data on manufacturing, warehouses, retailing inventory balance, sales and market analysis—including model stocks tailored to individual neighborhoods, and other variables.

Several lessons are possible from this example. First, it would probably have been impossible for any individual food or drug retail chain to develop a marketing mix that was so research-based and carefully programmed. Thus, this type of retailer made an explosive gain in effectiveness relative to department and specialty stores by relying on the manufacturer to perform some marketing functions. Second, other manufacturers who failed to understand the underlying shift in consumer shopping preferences were left at a serious disadvantage, and many were displaced. Third, consumers are probably more satisfied with the convenience and offering of the VMS than was true previously with the independent or unprogrammed conventional channel.

Acceleration of Institutional Life Cycles

Retailers, like other institutions, have life cycles; and movement through those cycles is accelerating.[100] The life cycle of retailing and other institutions has four main parts, beginning with the *introduction* and early growth of an innovative retailing form. Examples would be the depart-

[99]This research and other details of the *L'eggs* example are contained in W. Wayne Talarzyk, *Contemporary Cases in Marketing* (Hinsdale Ill.: Dryden Press, 1974), 285-296.

[100]William R. Davidson, Albert D. Bates, and Stephen J. Bass, "The Retail Life Cycle," *Harvard Business Review,* vol. 54 (November-December 1976), 89-96.

Table 18.3
Life-Cycle Characteristics of Five Retail Institutions

Institution	Approximate Date of Innovation	Approximate Date of Maximum Market Share	Approximate Number of Years Required To Reach Maturity	Estimated Maximum Market Share	Estimated 1975 Market Share
Downtown department store	1860	1940	80	8.5% of total retail sales	1.1%
Variety store	1910	1955	45	16.5% of general merchandise sales	9.5%
Supermarket	1930	1965	35	70.0% of grocery store sales	64.5%
Discount department store	1950	1970	20	6.5% of total retail sales	5.7%
Home improvement center	1965	(estimate) 1980	15	35.0% of hardware and building material sales	25.3%

Source: William R. Davidson, Albert D. Bates, and Stephen J. Bass, "The Retail Life Cycle," *Harvard Business Review,* vol. 54 (November-December 1976), 89-96. Copyright © 1976 by the President and Fellows of Harvard College; all rights reserved.

ment store in the 1800s, a supermarket in the 1930s, the discount store in the 1950s, or the catalogue showroom of the 1970s.

After the innovative form is introduced and catches on, it moves into an *accelerated development* stage. The growth is fast because the form is competing with the older, traditional retailer who is typically complacent and does not realize the nature of the new competition. In the accelerated development of discount stores, for example, department stores attempted programs of retaliation on the theme, "We will not knowingly be undersold." This failed because it focused on only one evaluative criterion of consumers rather than recognizing other criteria of importance to consumers such as the suburban location of most discounters, the convenience of night and Sunday openings, and the availability of and appeal of self-service merchandising.

The third stage is *maturity* when market share of the innovation levels off, a proliferation occurs of similar stores with no differential advantage, and frequently, overstoring or excess square footage becomes an industry problem. The result of such difficulties is a severe reduction in profitability. Finally, unless some new strategies are used, there is a *decline* in growth and profitability as one type of retailer gradually becomes replaced with new forms of retailing. This process has always occurred. The significance of the point is that such life cycles are accelerating dramatically, as Table 18.3 indicates.

The acceleration in life cycles has been caused in part by increased communications, better transportation, new technology and other variables. The implication for marketers, however, is an accelerated need for sophisticated consumer research that identifies potential new customers as well as potential *dis*consumption by existing customers and their impact on market structure and competitive developments. This requires managerial flexibility in merchandising and operations on the part of retailers but it also requires improved monitoring systems on the part of manufacturers and suppliers. In the past, manufacturers and wholesalers often refrained from selling to new types of retailers for fear of disrupting existing channel relationships. To do so today often leaves the door open for minor suppliers who proceed to take market share away from the larger companies by selling to more innovative outlets. All levels of suppliers must become increasingly concerned about not being locked into one type of retail outlet for a product, and therefore are becoming more responsive to new retail ventures than they probably were in the past.

Summary

Purchasing processes is a term that refers to the interaction between consumers and retail outlets. Decisions about stores are fundamentally the same as decisions about products or brands and involve problem recognition, search, alternative evaluation, choice, and outcomes and consequences. Problem recognition leading to shopping behavior may be initiated by product problem recognition or by nonproduct related motives such as the desire to get out of the house or engage in family related leisure activity.

Store choice is a complex process consisting of four variables: (1) evaluative criteria; (2) perceived characteristics of stores; (3) comparison process; and (4) acceptable and unacceptable stores. In general, the determinants of store choice are location, depth and breadth of assortments, price, advertising and word-of-mouth communications, sales promotions, store personnel, services, physical attributes, and store clientele.

Store image is the *perception of consumers* about the objective characteristics of stores. The most common method of measuring store image is with the semantic differential. Other recently developed techniques include multi-attribute measures and multidimensional scaling.

Shopper profiles are important in analyzing the comparison process by which consumers pick acceptable and unacceptable stores. Demographic variables, especially age, income and place of residence, are often used to define patronage of a store. Psychological variables such as psychographics and personality or perceived risk are sometimes used for store profiles, as well as retailing specific typologies such as one developed by Stone.

Generic retailing responses are those that cut across all lines of trade. They include the emergence of vertical marketing systems, the acceleration of institutional life cycles, the growing polarity of retail trade and the expanded use of positioning strategies.

Review and Discussion Questions

1. Why is it important to understand purchasing processes as part of the decision process approach to understanding consumer behavior?

2. Think of the last time you bought a product. How did you decide which store to patronize? How does your behavior compare with the conceptualization of the process as presented in this chapter?

3. Define the term store image and explain why it is important as a concept for retail management.

4. What is the image of the two largest stores in your area? How do your perceptions of these stores compare with your friends' images? Your parent's? Why do these differences exist?

5. Assume you are a consultant for a major department store. Describe how you would go about determining whether the types of shoppers found in the Stone study exist for your store. Of what value are shopper categories identical or similar to those used in the Stone study?

6. Assume that you are asked to measure the image of the dominant grocery chain in your area. How would you recommend this be done? Why?

7. Of what importance is location in analyzing the patronage of retail stores?

8. Several generic retailing responses were described in this chapter. Briefly outline the salient characteristics of each and list some examples other than those mentioned in the chapter.

9. Describe the importance of price in the patronage decision for supermarkets.

10. Is the acceleration of institutional life cycles a problem or an opportunity for retailers? Explain your answer.

PART FIVE

LOW-INVOLVEMENT DECISION PROCESSES

Consumer behavior is differentiated from choice behavior in other areas of life to a large extent by the fact that much of it is low involvement—many products which are purchased and used have only modest relevance and importance in life itself. What difference does it make, for example, which brand of toilet paper is purchased this time? When involvement is low, the choice process is radically different, as Chapter 19 will indicate. Problem recognition leads directly to choice, which is followed, not preceded, by alternative evaluation. The role of advertising and point-of-sale influences are different than they would be if there were a higher level of involvement.

Brand switching is commonplace when involvement is low. Therefore, brand loyalty and repeat purchase is of considerable importance to the marketer. Various models and concepts have been developed on the subject of brand loyalty, and these are reviewed in Chapter 20. Those who have only moderate quantitative capability may wish to skim or even to skip the last part of the chapter which unavoidably delves into quantitative modeling.

While low involvement characterizes the majority of consumer decisions, only two chapters are devoted to this purpose. In part, this reflects the research priorities in published literature to date. But it also reflects the fact that much of what we discussed in previous chapters provides essential foundations for this subject as well.

CHAPTER 19

THE LOW-INVOLVEMENT DECISION PROCESS

In 1975 Airwick Industries, Inc., was losing $2 million on US sales of $35 million. Fortunately it has reversed its fortunes by a series of successful product introductions.[1] Part of this upsurge occurred through the purchase of the *Glamorene* brand from Lever Brothers in 1978. Airwick then unveiled *Carpet Fresh,* a rug cleaner and room deodorizer. Sales targeted at $34 million the first year hit $50 million.

Carpet Fresh inspired others to enter the market. Lehn & Fink rushed out *Love My Carpet,* for example, but Airwick has maintained about a 60 percent share of an $85 million market through extensive advertising. Emboldened by that success, it then introduced *Plush,* a dry rug cleaner and conditioner for use in heavy-traffic areas of the home. Backed by $14 million in advertising, it has gained 50 percent of the $65 million market for that type of product.

These product successes are not accidents; rather they reflect the skillful use of marketing research. Early studies showed that the original formulation of *Carpet Fresh* as a granular product was negatively rated by consumers out of fear that granules would lodge under furniture. The formula then was changed to a more powdery one.

Carpet Fresh and *Plush* are just two of literally thousands of examples of products that are bought with little or no decision process, at least in the sense that we have been considering up to now. The consumer says, in effect, "I think I have heard of that; why not give it a try?" Search and extensive alternative evaluation simply are not present. We agree with Olshavsky and Granbois, who came to the following conclusion after review of an extensive body of research:

A significant proportion of purchases may not be preceded by a decision process. This conclusion does not simply restate the familiar observation that purchase behavior rapidly becomes habitual, with little or no pre-purchase processes occurring after the first few purchases. We conclude that for many purchases a decision process never occurs, not even on the first purchase.[2]

[1]"Airwick's Discovery of New Markets Pays Off," *Business Week* (June 16, 1980), 139-140.
[2]Richard W. Olshavsky and Donald H. Granbois, "Consumer Decision-Making—Fact or Fiction?" *Journal of Consumer Research,* vol. 6 (September 1979), 93-100.

The purpose of this chapter is to look at low-involvement decisions, showing as clearly as we can what makes them different from high-involvement decisions. As we will see, advertising plays a very different role and usually is less important than point-of-purchase display and promotion. What is done at the retail level, then, may well provide the key to successful marketing.

WHAT MAKES LOW-INVOLVEMENT BUYING DIFFERENT?

Why is a product such as *Carpet Fresh* low involvement for most people? The answer is simple—it just doesn't have personal relevance[3] in the sense that there is little perceived risk that a wrong decision will be made,[4] a weak sense of relationship between the product purchased and one's self-concept,[5] or little anxiety about the outcome.[6] So the product doesn't quite perform as expected, so what? Probably only one or two attributes are even considered, with a wide latitude of acceptance when the evaluation is made.[7] There will be no extensive problem solving involving search and alternative evaluation, making use of noncompensatory evaluation styles.[8]

The decision process under these circumstances is quite simple. The reader will recall the model we introduced in Chapter 2. It is reproduced once again in Figure 19.1. The information processing component will be discussed below, so the important thing to note here is the very abbreviated decision process in which problem recognition leads to choice, with alternative evaluation *following* choice rather than *preceding* it as is the case under high involvement.

Information Processing

This subject also was discussed in some depth earlier (Chapter 8), but some review is helpful. First of all, there is little or no active search (i.e., voluntary exposure). Rather, attention is *involuntary* for the most part and occurs as the individual is exposed to a medium for other reasons. There is growing evidence that the right sector of the brain dominates in low-involvement situations, with information stored in the form of holistic im-

---

[3]Richard E. Petty, John T. Capicoppo, "Issue Involvement as a Moderator of the Effects on Attitude of Advertising Content and Context," in Kent B. Monroe (ed.), *Advances in Consumer Research,* vol. 8 (Ann Arbor, Mich.: Association for Consumer Research, 1981), 20-24.

[4]Richard Vaughn, "The Consumer Mind: How to Tailor Ad Strategies," *Advertising Age* (June 9, 1980), 45-46.

[5]Vaughn, "The Consumer Mind"; and John L. Lastovicka and David M. Gardner, "Components of Involvement," John C. Maloney and Bernard Silverman (eds.), *Attitude Research Plays for High Stakes* (Chicago: American Marketing Association, 1979), 53-73.

[6]Vaughn, "The Consumer Mind."

[7]Michael L. Rothschild, "Advertising Strategies for High and Low Involvement Situations," in Maloney and Silverman, *"Attitude Research Plays,* 74-93; John L. Lastovicka and David M. Gardner, "Low Involvement Versus High Involvement Cognitive Structures," in H. Keith Hunt (ed.), *Advances in Consumer Research,* vol. 5 (Ann Arbor, Mich.: Association for Consumer Research, 1978), 87-92; and Michael L. Rothschild and Michael J. Houston, "The Consumer Involvement Matrix: Some Preliminary Findings," in Barnett A. Greenberg and Danny N. Bellenger (eds.), *Contemporary Marketing Thought* (Chicago: American Marketing Association, 1977), 95-98.

[8]Rothschild, "Advertising Strategies."

Figure 19.1
The Low-Involvement Decision Process

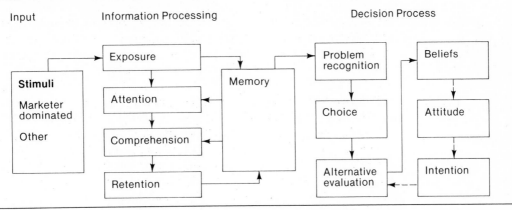

ages without having much effect on cognitive structures.[9] In fact, the consumer will have little awareness that this is taking place. Consequently, questioning which focuses on *recall* can seriously understate the impact of a message, especially if it is aired over television.[10] It now appears that recognition is a much more appropriate measure.[11] What happens, in effect, is that there is passive low-level learning which enters into long-term memory, bypassing the yielding/acceptance stage which is so crucial under high involvement.

The outcome, then, is a kind of belief about the existence of an object. It really is little more than stored information which is held until a later point, at which time it becomes activated and helps to trigger product trial.

Problem Recognition

Problem recognition really does not occur upon initial exposure to advertising or other promotional stimuli. The most that can be hoped for is a kind of low-level interest which says, in effect, "That might be worth looking into sometime." True problem recognition more likely is stimulated within the retail store when the product is actually seen or observed on display. Purchase and use is similar in many ways to hypothesis testing in which the consumer sees if it lives up to expectations.

Once the product has been used with positive outcomes, future problem recognition most likely takes the form of stock out. In other words, the product is used up and something must be done. A mental note is made which finds its way into a shopping list, and choice proceeds more

---

[9]See Herbert E. Krugman, "Low Involvement Theory in the Light of New Brain Research," in Maloney and Silverman, *Attitude Research Plays,* 16-22; Flemming Hansen, "Hemispheral Lateralization: A Implications for Understanding Consumer Behavior," *Journal of Consumer Research* (June 1981), 23-36; and Flemming Hansen and Niels Erik Lundsgaard, "Developing an Instrument to Identify Individual Differences in the Processing of Pictorial and Other Non-Verbal Information," in Monroe, *Advances in Consumer Research,* vol. 8, 367-373.

[10]Krugman, "Low Involvement Theory."

[11]Krugman, "Low Involvement Theory."

or less automatically unless some other brand comes in with a lower price or some other form of advantage.

Choice and Alternative Evaluation

In a way, most low-involvement products are presold by advertising, as we will elaborate later. Some awareness is there, but the most crucial role is played by point-of-sale stimuli designed to encourage product trial. During trial, alternative evaluation takes place. For instance, *Carpet Fresh* is supposed to clean and deodorize carpets with little muss and fuss. Does this happen or not? If it does, then a belief is formed that the product indeed does qualify in terms of salient attributes. This, in turn, will be followed by a positive attitude toward the act of buying and using the product and by an intention to repurchase once the supply is used up. In a sense, this can be said to be brand loyalty, but it certainly is not based on any degree of true commitment. Most probably several brands are seen to be essentially equal, and switching is quite probable if one offers some type of price break or other inducement. This subject is discussed in depth in the next chapter, because brand loyalty always is a crucial concern of the marketer.

The Importance of Low-Involvement Theory

It is somewhat surprising to note the fact that the vast majority of published research in consumer behavior has assumed high involvement. All of the multi-attribute models, compensatory-choice heuristics, recent studies on counter argumentation have made this assumption. Yet, as we have noted above, the majority of consumer buying has little or no involvement. Bogart's quote is worth repeating here:

> Perhaps the main contribution that advertising research can make to this study of communications is in the domain of inattention to low-key stimuli, as exemplified by the ever increasing flow of unsolicited and unwanted messages to which people are subject in our over communicative civilization.[12]

Kassarjian hits the nail on the head when he contends that research on this topic will alter most of our conceptions of consumer behavior models and theories. Hopefully, his research will lead to greater relevance in terms of focusing on behavior as it is in most buying situations.[13]

PRECHOICE INFLUENCES ON THE LOW-INVOLVEMENT DECISION PROCESS

Advertising, of course, is one way to reach the consumer, but the strategy used under low involvement may differ somewhat from that discussed earlier. The emphasis here must be on registering brand name

---

[12]Leo Bogart, "Where Does Advertising Research Go From Here?" *Journal of Advertising Research,* vol. 9 (March 1969), 6.

[13]Harold H. Kassarjian, "Low Involvement: A Second Look," in Monroe, *Advances in Consumer Research,* vol. 8, 31–34.

**Figure 19.2
The Relationship
between
Awareness and
Market Share**

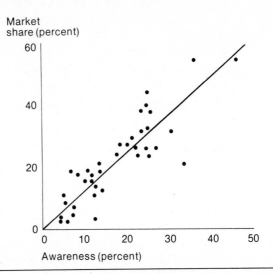

Source: Reprinted by permission from "Brand Awareness Increases Market Share, Profits: Study," *Marketing News* (November 28, 1980), 5, published by the American Marketing Association.

so that it will be recognized later. Another method the marketer can use is some form of product sampling. Each has its role.

Advertising

The role of advertising, simply put, is to build awareness of brand name first and to register some information on salient attributes. The Payout Council of the Advertising Research Foundation undertook a very interesting study in which product movement in a Kansas City food store (part of the Milgram's chain) was monitored in terms of the various kinds of marketing efforts which were undertaken.[14] It was possible to trace the effects of such variables as price dealing and consumer advertising on actual sales. It was discovered that the presence or absence of advertising immediately affected purchases of major brands. Specifically, manufacturers of five advertised brands spent $23.24 on media advertising that produced $55.37 in added sales.[15] Opposite effects were noted when this was not done. Unknown brands, in other words, simply do not move from the retail shelves.

In another important study undertaken by the Strategic Planning Institute (SPI), brand awareness was found to correlate directly with market share, as Figure 19.2 documents.[16] Market share, in turn, correlated directly with pretax return on investment. SPI executive Sidney Schoeffler made reference to the fear that brand awareness is merely a concept dreamed up by advertising agencies to justify their existence and voiced this conclusion:

[14] *Project Payout. A Review and Appraisal of the Pilot Study in Milgram's Store #40* (New York: The Payout Council, Advertising Research Foundation, 1980).

[15] *Project Payout,* 32.

[16] "Brand Awareness Increases Market Share, Profits: Study," *Marketing News* (November 28, 1980), 5.

Marketers and advertisers can now heave a collective sigh of relief. The programs that increase brand awareness and the programs that convert it into market share should be a major concern of senior management.[17]

What differentiates successful from unsuccessful advertising when the products have low involvement? Several factors are especially important: (1) name registration; (2) memorability; (3) source credibility; and (4) repetition.

Name Registration

Harry W. McMahan notes, "The name of the game is the name. . . Here is where all advertising starts and where so much of television advertising misses."[18] Research testing 1800 TV commercials aired on 29 nights in Atlanta, Georgia, showed that fewer than one-third of those interviewed could remember and describe a commercial and only 16 percent could remember the name of the sponsor.[19] To make matters worse, for every two persons who correctly named a brand, at least one named a competitor.[20] This may be a major reason why so many new products fail—the name never is registered.

The brand name itself has much to do with this process. The name *Carpet Fresh* pretty much describes what the product is and can do for the buyer. Other names are so abstract that no amount of advertising can establish the benefits offered. It must be remembered that watching or reading is done *involuntarily,* and very little in the way of content can be registered on one exposure. This is why the brand name itself must stand out and dominate if there is to be any chance of success whatsoever.[21]

Memorability

We have discussed the problem of information overload at some length in Chapter 9. This refers to the obvious fact that people in the western world live in an over-communicative age. There are distinct limits on information-processing capacity, with the result that many advertising messages simply get lost in the noise. They fail to capture attention. Therefore, it is necessary under conditions of involuntary exposure to resort to many devices to break through the noise, so to speak, and establish a degree of memorability for the commercial.

Probably there is no end to the creative approaches which can be used for this purpose, including jingles, whimsy, humor, and slice of life situations just to mention a few.[22] One of the strategies that seems to

[17]"Brand Awareness Increases," 5.

[18]Harry W. McMahan, "TV Loses the 'Name Game' but Wins Big in Personality," *Advertising Age* (December 1, 1980), 54.

[19]McMahan, "TV Loses the 'Name Game'."

[20]McMahan, "TV Loses the 'Name Game'."

[21]This is a widely accepted principle. For further detail, see Kenneth Roman and Jane Maas, *How to Advertise* (New York: St. Martin's Press, 1976).

[22]See Roman and Maas, *How to Advertise;* and Harry W. McMahan, "McMahan's '100 Best' Commercials of 1977," *Advertising Age* (January 30, 1978), 43+.

**Figure 19.3
Morris the Cat: An
Example of VI/P**

Source: "Morris"—the 9-Lives Spokescat. Reprinted by permission.

work the best according to McMahan is what he calls VI/P (Visual Image/Personality).[23] Symbols such as the Pillsbury Doughboy, Speedy Alka Seltzer, Tony the Tiger, and others all serve to provide continuity and identification to television advertising. This is especially important in view of the fact that television apparently is processed mostly in the right hemisphere of the brain and retained in the form of visual images. One of the all-time winners in this respect was the late Morris the Cat (Figure 19.3) who even had his own fan clubs. Incidentally *9-Lives* became a best seller through this use of VI/P.

It must not be assumed, however, that the role of advertising is to entertain. In 1979, 15,000 people were asked to list the most outstanding television commercial they had seen in the last four weeks. Almost two-thirds could list at least one, but a dangerously high proportion could not remember the product being advertised.[24] When creative execution dominates the essential message, then advertising can be evaluated as a failure, no matter how much it is liked.

[23]Harry W. McMahan, "Do Your Ads Have VI/P?" *Advertising Age,* (July 14, 1980), 50-51.
[24]Dave Vadehra, "Coke, McDonald's Lead Outstanding TV Commercials," *Advertising Age* (May 26, 1980), 37.

Source Credibility

It has been hypothesized that source credibility is an especially important consideration when low involvement is present.[25] This is entirely plausible given the marginal conditions of reading and viewing in which all messages have a high probability of being screened out. If there is no measure of familiarity with at least neutral credibility or if there has been bad previous experience with a company or any of its brands, the prospects of capturing and holding attention are reduced.

Repetition

Most of the writers cited here on low involvement agree that high repetition is a key to success.[26] Given the fractional exposure to any given message, it may take a great many exposures to register the brand name and any degree of familiarity with salient attributes.

As we have mentioned previously, the literature on this subject is vast. It leads to the conclusion that repetition indeed does enhance learning but also that there is a point of wearout when increased repetition actually leads to a diminished response.[27]

In one of the most definitive investigations appearing in the published literature, Steward underscored the value of repetition in building and sustaining brand awareness.[28] In more detail:

1. Advertising causes a rapid initial rise in awareness and then levels off in its effects. When repeat messages sustain awareness, it tends to fall once promotion is stopped.

2. At least 15 consecutive exposures are needed to produce the lowest costs in terms of attracting additional prospects per dollar of advertising. Only three or four insertions proved to be inefficient.

3. One of the two products studied was a failure primarily because of the content of the advertising and the product itself rather than the duration of repetition.

We must stress once again, however, that *high levels of repetition are appropriate only under conditions of low involvement.* High involvement is quite different, as we pointed out in Chapter 16. There, only limited repetition is permissible before counter argumentation sets in.

If awareness can be influenced positively by repetition, one would expect the same impact on beliefs and attitudes, as was confirmed by Sawyer in his definitive literature review.[29] It is interesting to refer once

[25]Rothschild, "Advertising Strategies."

[26]See especially Herbert E. Krugman, "Low Involvement Theory."

[27]This is demonstrated conclusively in Sawyer's review of over 200 published studies. See Alan G. Sawyer, "The Effects of Repetition: Conclusions and Suggestions about Experimental Laboratory Research" (paper presented at the Workshop on Consumer Information Processing, University of Chicago, November 1972).

[28]J. B. Stewart, *Repetitive Advertising in Newspapers: A Study of Two New Products* (Boston: Harvard Business School, 1964).

[29]Sawyer, "Effects of Repetition," 17.

again in this context to the "mere exposure" hypothesis put forth by Zajonc.[30] Drawing upon literature which is usually not cited in this context, he concluded that "mere exposure" (i.e., repeated exposure) is a sufficient condition for attitude change. This can only be accepted as a tentative hypothesis, however, given the evidence that overexposure can at some point lead to a boomerang effect in which the initial effects on attitudes are largely offset by diminution.[31] One explanation for a wearout effect when low-involvement stimuli are repeated is simply that people cease drawing the same meaning from a stimulus when it is seen or heard too often. This loss of meaning is referred to as *semantic satiation.*[32] Just how and why satiation occurs is not well understood, but it has been documented as a factor with which advertisers must contend.[33]

Probably one major factor in a satiation effect is the common conclusion that no message, no matter how strong, can be repeated *ad infinitum* without variation. The reward from the twelfth exposure to the same beer ad is likely to be minimal, for example, and it probably will be negative. The best strategy is to *repeat the basic theme with variation* so that the reward level can be sustained.[34] The brand name can be registered and product excellence demonstrated in many ways, and a campaign can thus avoid boredom and loss of response from overexposure. The proper strategy, of course, is unique to each situation.

It is interesting that much of the evidence gathered in a laboratory setting indicates that repetition seems to have less effect on buying action than it does on brand evaluation or purchasing intentions.[35] Sawyer's findings are reproduced in Figure 19.4, and it will be noticed that repetition strengthened recall far more than behavior as measured by coupon return after five or six exposures. The findings from field experiments are more positive, however. In one methodologically sophisticated investigation, for example, du Pont researchers verified the negative effect of discontinued advertising on sales.[36] Purchases of *Teflon* cookware were significantly higher in those cites where high levels of advertising were maintained. Steward also reported these findings from his study:[37]

[30]R. Zajonc, "The Attitudinal Effects of Mere Exposure," *Journal of Personality and Social Psychology,* monograph supplement, vol. 9 (1968), 1-27.

[31]Richard L. Miller, "Mere Exposure, Psychological Reactance and Attitude Change," *Public Opinion Quarterly,* vol. 40 (Summer 1976), 229-233.

[32]Harriett Amster, "Semantic Satiation and Generation: Learning? Adaptation?" *Psychological Bulletin,* vol. 62 (1964), 273-286; D. E. P. Smith and A. L. Raygor, "Verbal Satiation and Personality," *Journal of Abnormal and Social Psychology,* vol. 52 (1956), 323-326; M. F. Basette and C. J. Warne, "On the Lapse of Verbal Meaning with Repetition," *American Journal of Psychology,* vol. 30 (1919), 415-418; W. E. Lambert and L. A. Jakobovits, "Verbal Satiation and Changes in the Intensity of Meaning," *Journal of Experimental Psychology,* vol. 60 (1960), 376-383.

[33]R. C. Grass, "Satiation Effects of Advertising," in *Proceedings of the 14th Annual Conference of the Advertising Research Foundation* (New York: Advertising Research Foundation, 1968), 20-28.

[34]C. Samuel Craig, Brian Sternthal, and Clark Leavitt, "Advertising Wearout: An Experimental Analysis," *Journal of Marketing Research,* vol. 13 (November 1976), 365-372.

[35]Sawyer, "Effects of Repetition," 24.

[36]J. C. Beckness and R. W. McIsaac, "Test Marketing Cookware Coated with Teflon," *Journal of Advertising Research,* vol. 3 (1963), 2-8.

[37]Stewart, "Repetitive Advertising."

**Figure 19.4
Effects of
Repetition on
Recall, Brand
Evaluation,
Purchase
Intention, and
Coupon
Redemption**

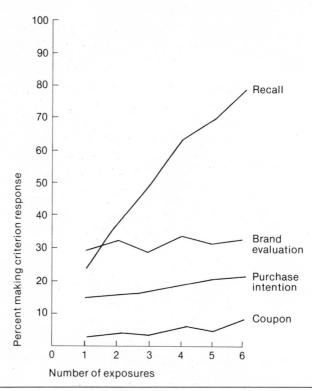

Source: Alan G. Sawyer, "The Effects of Repetition: Conclusions and Suggestions about Experimental Laboratory Research" C. D. Hughes and M. L. Ray (eds.), *Buyer/Consumer Information Processing* (Chapel Hill: University of North Carolina Press, 1974), 190-219. Reprinted by permission.

1. When no advertisements were used, few tried the two new products under investigation (*Lestare* and *Chicken Sara Lee*).

2. Four weekly insertions served to encourage some people to buy sooner than they otherwise would.

3. Eight ads doubled the number of customers, but 15 insertions produced the best results per dollar of advertising expenditure.

4. Twenty advertisements produced the most customers, but costs exceeded sales gains.

Generally, it is safe to say that repetition can help in terms of stimulating awareness, changing beliefs and attitudes, and triggering behavior. Yet there is that ever present problem of wearout—the point where maximum return begins to diminish. Perhaps it will be helpful to provide a summary of known ways in which repetition can be used sensibly without unnecessarily generating wearout:

1. Repetition aids consumer learning and hence can be effectively utilized at the start of a new campaign.

2. Repetition can help establish products or brands that are new to a particular medium.

3. A pool or group of commercials should not wear out as quickly as a single commercial, given the same frequency of exposure.

4. When it is not possible to produce a number of varied commercials, introduce several claims within the message to lengthen the learning process.

5. When several commercials are produced, introduce significant variations, or they are likely to be perceived as the same and hence wear out more quickly.

6. A commercial with humor or a single point wears out quickly.

7. Commercials for infrequently purchased products wear out more slowly for the reason that only a fraction of the audience are prospects at any given point of time.

8. The greater the time span between repetition, the longer a message can be run.

9. A message can be reintroduced after a period of absence from the air and hence be perceived as new.

10. Wearout is greatest among heavy television viewers.

11. If the budget is limited, a single commercial spread out over a period of time may produce greater learning than airing of a pool of commercials.

12. Commercials that involve the viewer wear out more slowly than those with a straightforward message.

13. Copy testing predicated on a single exposure can shed little light on wearout.

14. Performance must be tracked over time to assess wearout.

15. Only good commercials wear out—those that are ineffective to begin with will lose nothing.[38]

Product Sampling

The offering of a product sample either door-to-door or in-store is one of the oldest and most widely used marketing methods. The objective, of course, is to encourage trial and subsequent use. Does this, in fact, take place? Three recent controlled studies provide solid affirmative evidence:[39]

1. Product samples were offered of a dessert product in Stop & Shop stores in New England, and sales were compared with stores where this

---

[38]A. Greenberg and C. Suttoni, "Television Commercial Wearout," *Journal of Advertising Research,* vol. 13 (1973), 53.

[39]Dan Ailloni-Charas, "Sampling Short-Circuits Product Trial Process, Strengthens Brand's Permanent Home at Retail," *Marketing News* (March 6, 1981), 7.

was not done. On the aggregate, the sampled stores outsold the control stores more than four times.

2. In a similar test with a beverage product, actual product purchase and use was 47 percent in the group receiving a sample versus 8.7 percent in the nonsampled group.

3. In-home sampling increased product movement of a dry dog food by 60 percent during the sampling period and 233 percent by the twelfth week after sampling ceased.

There are some precautions to be followed, however, because sampling often does not return its costs in increased sales.[40] First, the product must be viable and competitive. Next, the whole program must be merchandised to the trade outlets to achieve their support. Finally, sampling alone is not a successful strategy. It works only when it is a part of a total program of advertising and trade support.

IN-STORE INFLUENCES ON THE LOW-INVOLVEMENT DECISION PROCESS

While there is no question that advertising and sampling can have a role in building some product familiarity and interest, the real impact on the purchase of low-involvement items takes place at point-of-sale. Reference is made here to the so-called impulse or unplanned purchase which is defined for our purposes as a *buying action undertaken without a problem previously having been consciously recognized or a buying intention formed prior to entering the store.* Studies show that the incidences of unplanned purchases range from 38.7 percent in a department store[41] to nearly two-thirds of all purchases in supermarkets.[42] Of course, this varies by product since both high- and low-involvement items are offered for sale in each type of outlet. Also, it varies by types of customer with those under 35 and over 65 being more prone to purchase by impulse in the department store.[43]

There are several reasons why unplanned purchasing takes place.[44] The first centers around the effects of in-store exposure. Sometimes the product is actually seen for the first time with no prior exposure, with the result that problem recognition and choice more or less occur on the

---

[40]Ailloni-Charas, "Sampling Short-Circuits."

[41]Danny N. Bellenger, Dan H. Robertson, and Elizabeth C. Hirschman, "Impulse Buying Varies by Product," *Journal of Advertising Research,* vol. 18 (December 1978), 15-18.

[42]"Consumer Buying Decisions Made In-Store," *Beverage Industry* (July 22, 1977), 22-23; and "Industry Retail Selling Strategies Designed to Induce Impulse Sales," *Beverage Industry* (June 3, 1977), 6+.

[43]Bellenger, Robertson, and Hirschman, "Impulse Buying Varies."

[44]For the most thorough discussions on this subject, see David T. Kollat, "A Decision-Process Approach to Impulse Purchase," in Raymond M. Haas (ed.), *Science, Technology and Marketing* (Chicago: American Marketing Association, 1966), 626-639; and David T. Kollat and Ronald P. Willett, "Is Impulse Purchasing Really a Useful Concept for Marketing Decisions?" *Journal of Marketing,* vol. 33 (January 1969), 81.

spot. At other times, seeing the item on display triggers recognition, reflecting the effects of previous advertising, and the choice is made. Furthermore, some consumers use displays as a reminder of shopping needs rather than relying on a shopping list.

This all boils down to the fact that in-store promotion is a major factor in the low-involvement purchase. In this section we will examine the role of quite a variety of point-of-purchase methods: (1) package design; (2) display; (3) pricing; (4) in-store advertising; (5) contests and promotions; (6) combination methods; and (7) store layout.

Package Design

No matter how much advertising is undertaken, the package design can make or break the outcome at the point-of-sale. As Walter Stern points out, "Consumers generally do not distinguish clearly between a product and its package; to them package and product are part of an entity, and the product is the package and vice versa."[45] One crucial issue, then, is whether or not the package accurately conveys the intended product image. The Ralston Purina Company underwent a major packaging change which moved it away from too many different symbols and lack of brand cohesion to a new design that communicates "stew-like goodness" and capitalizes on the western heritage of the brand name through a desert atmosphere. The outcome proved to be revitalized sales.[46]

Another equally important factor is shelf visibility. This, of course, is profoundly affected by color, and the research carried out on that subject goes far beyond our space limits here.[47] The goal, of course, is to make the package stand out so that recognition is achieved easily and quickly. There are any number of success stories which could be cited in this context. A representative case in point is the recent upsurge of consumer interest in *Columbo* yogurt, sold primarily in New England.[48] Because of the influx of competitive brands, *Columbo* was being lost in the noise. So the logo was redesigned and the container was made to stand out with a strong visual image on the shelf. The outcome has been maintenance of sales leadership in the New England and New York markets. This redesign was intended to produce these results: (1) visual excitement; (2) easy identification of corporate name from a distance; (3) establishment of a family identity between various package sizes and shapes; (4) a simplified look; (5) consolidated type faces; and (6) use of color to the best advantage.[49]

Package design also must take into account the use of the package to obtain additional information at point-of-sale. Jacoby and his associ-

[45]Walter Stern, "Design Research: Beauty or Beast," *Advertising Age* (March 9, 1981), 43.

[46]"Packaging Design Seen as Cost-Effective Marketing Strategy," *Marketing News* (February 20, 1981), 1+.

[47]See, for example, Walter P. Margulies, "Color it Motivational," *Advertising Age* (October 13, 1969), 69+.

[48]"Packaging Design Seen."

[49]"Packaging Design Seen."

ates have demonstrated that consumers do refer to package information, but there is a definite point at which benefits cease.[50] This occurs when the number of separate bits of information exceeds 12—further evidence of the problems of information overload mentioned earlier.

The type of information and labeling provided can shift preference and buying action. For example, nutritional labeling tends to improve perception of quality attributes such as "wholesomeness" and "tender."[51] Vague labels, on the other hand, have no such effect. It also was found that strictly promotional terms such as "sweet" and "succulent" leave the consumer with an assurance of quality comparable to that of more detailed nutritional information.

Point-of-Purchase Display

This term is usually meant to refer to such devices as counter cards, banners, window streamers, shelf extenders, racks, and the like. Studies of the effects vary in purpose and sophistication,[52] but one thing is clear—display can increase sales dramatically. Indeed, it can be the ultimate key to low-involvement purchases. Consider these comments from Joseph Plamara, sales promotion manager for Coty:

Successful displays must tell what the product is, what it will do, and what variations are available. It should arouse consumer interest and hold it until a sale is made.[53]

Once again the literature, especially trade publications, offers a plethora of examples, and a few representative studies are cited here:

1. In one major study of the impact of point-of-purchase stimuli undertaken nearly two decades ago, it was discovered that 82 percent of people studied recalled seeing at least two test displays, 44 percent said they used displays to help in the purchase, and 33 percent actually bought one or more of the displayed items.[54]

2. Display increased the sales of canned soup approximately 150 percent during a test of the impact of various promotion methods.[55]

3. Overall sales of dairy products increased from 15 to 35 percent from use of point-of-purchase display, depending upon the product itself and in-store conditions.[56]

4. Stores that doubled the number of shelf facings on new beverage

---

[50]Jacob Jacoby, "Consumer Reaction to Information Displays: Packaging and Advertising" (paper delivered at the Advertising and Public Interest Workshop, American Marketing Association, May 1973).

[51]Edward H. Asam and Louis P. Bucklin, "Nutritional Labeling for Canned Goods: A Study of Consumer Response," *Journal of Marketing*, vol. 37 (April 1973), 32-37.

[52]For a theoretical discussion, see Evan E. Anderson, "An Analysis of Retail Display Space: Theory and Methods," *Journal of Business*, vol. 52 (1979), 103-108.

[53]"Impulse Buying: Display Makers Have Good Case," *Product Marketing* (October 1978), 26-27.

[54]*Awareness, Decision Purchase* (New York: Point-of-Purchase Advertising Institute, 1961), 14.

[55]*Project Payout.*

[56]"Dairy. How to Turn P-O-P into Sales Dollars," *Progressive Grocer* (June 1977), 83+.

products during the first few weeks of introduction showed 85 to 160 percent increases over stores that did not make this adjustment.[57]

5. Displays of new health and beauty-aid items in supermarkets increased sales from 100 to 400 percent above normal levels.[58]

As one might expect, the type of display and its locations make a real difference under some circumstances. Here are some examples: (1) end of aisle displays often produce the greatest results;[59] it is especially important that the product be displayed at eye level whenever possible;[60] and there are benefits to be gained from making the display stand out through movement or special design so that it is not perceived as part of the usual display.[61] Getting such displays accepted by retailers, however, is no easy matter, and many are placing strong restrictions on what they accept. Therefore, manufacturers are finding it necessary to ensure that the display clearly communicates product benefits in a format which is compatible with store layout while keeping displays up-to-date with current advertising and other forms of promotion.[62]

On the basis of evidence to date, much of which could not be cited here, these conclusions are warranted:

1. Display typically increases sales.

2. Sales of some products increase to a greater extent than others, but the reasons for this are not always clear.[63]

3. Sales of substitute, nondisplayed items tend to decrease.

4. The effectiveness of displays is often overstated.

There are two basic reasons why the effectiveness of displays is exaggerated. First, most studies do not determine the extent to which consumers respond by accumulating inventory rather than increasing the rate of consumption. Second, many studies do not determine the extent to which customers purchase from the display instead of from the product's regular location. Despite these factors, the evidence is clear that displays of various types *do* increase sales in most situations.

One explanation is that exposure to display can trigger consumer problem recognition on the spot. Mere exposure to the product in ques-

[57]Carla Selinger, "Industry Retail Selling Strategies Design to Induce Impulse Sales," *Beverage Industry* (June 3, 1977), 6+.

[58]"How In-Store Merchandising Can Boost Sales," *Progressive Grocer* (October 1971), 94-97.

[59]George J. Kress, *The Effect of End Displays on Selected Food Product Sales* (New York: Point-of-Purchase Advertising Institute, undated).

[60]"Dairy. How to Turn P-O-P."

[61]"HBA Firms Spend Close to $3 Million," *Product Marketing* (June 1979), 58-61.

[62]Cameron S. Foote, "Space Limitations Put Squeeze on P. O. P. Promotional Material," *Advertising Age* (February 4, 1980), 58.

[63]Some studies have investigated some of the reasons why end-aisle displays increase the sales of some products more than others. See, for example, "Displays Add Sales, Profit, and Personality to Kroger of Bay Village," *Progressive Grocer* (January 1967), 63-70; Kress, *Effect*, 18-22; Robert Kelley, "An Evaluation of Selected Variables of End Display Effectiveness" (unpublished doctoral dissertation, Cambridge, Mass.: Harvard University, 1965).

tion can either serve as a reminder of a previously-recognized need or activate a latent need. Furthermore, it can stimulate conscious recall of previous advertising or other forms of influence and hence activate buying behavior. In these instances, the consumer usually will not have entered the store with specific intent to buy this product or brand.

Displays also have the effect of leading the consumer to believe that prices have been lowered. Discussion in the next section will demonstrate that most consumers do not know the prices of products, particularly those sold in supermarkets. Therefore, they can easily be misled when a particular item stands out from its competitors. The tendency for sales of display items to increase even when price is increased lends support to the hypothesis. The manufacturer and retailer, of course, are beneficiaries, but the effect on the consumer is little less than outright deception. Since this practice is completely legal at this point in time, the only remedy is consumer education stressing the value of price comparison shopping.

It will be interesting to watch the trends in point-of-sale merchandising, because some significant changes are imminent. First, more use of modular units is expected.[64] This refers to a relatively large shelf-type display which holds only the items from a single manufacturer. It has been proved to have good effects when there is substantial national advertising backup. A second trend is toward the use of audio-visuals—films, videotapes, and projectors.[65] The Wella Corporation boosted sales of five hair products as much as 500 percent by this method. Probably the most interesting development of all is the computerized display.[66] Helena Rubinstein, Inc. is generally credited with the first major computer application at point-of-sale with its *Skin Life Instant Beauty Analyzer* introduced in 1977.[67] While it costs about $5,000, sales have gone up as much as 400 percent from its use. The obvious benefit for the consumer is the opportunity to get on-the-spot answers to problems simply by dialing into the computer. All parties stand to gain as the trend intensifies.

Pricing

The reader will recall that low price ranks nearly at the top as the most preferred attribute in choice of a supermarket. There is no question that price will continue to be a major consideration in outlets offering mostly low-involvement products as long as inflation continues largely unabated.[68] The no-frills supermarket is commonplace now,[69] and some predict that low overhead, low price outlets will double their market share before 1990.[70]

---

[64]Norman Topping, "Modular Units: Low-Cost Way to Added Sales," *Product Marketing* (October 1979), 41.

[65]"HBA Firms Spend."

[66]Louis J. Haugh, "Computers are P. O. P. Trend of the Future," *Advertising Age* (October 2, 1978), 70+.

[67]Haugh, "Computers are P. O. P. Trend."

[68]Ed Meyer, "Life Styles Hold Key to the 1980s," *Advertising Age* (January 28, 1980), 47-48.

[69]"No-Frills Food. New Power for the Supermarkets," *Business Week* (March 23, 1981), 70-80.

[70]"Carbon Copy Stores Are Out as 'Positioning' Takes Over," *Progressive Grocer* (October 1979), 61+.

As important as price is becoming, it is surprising how inaccurate consumer price perceptions tend to be. On the average, food shoppers knew the correct price only 27 percent of the time in 1977, compared with 30 percent in 1974.[71] Furthermore, this type of misperception seems to be pretty much the same throughout all types of people.[72]

The Effects of Price Dealing

Reference is made here to any type of retail price incentive except couponing which is discussed separately. There is clear evidence that price deals (as contrasted with an overall policy of low pricing referred to above) can have a dramatic effect on sales. These effects usually are immediate and positive resulting in increases as high as 500 percent for margarine.[73] One of the most extensive recent investigations went beyond initial sales effects, however, and here are some of the major findings:[74]

1. Promotional deals result in substantial increases in levels of purchase of dairy products, especially while the deal is effective. Carry-over effects into later periods, however, are much lower.

2. The response to a deal is much greater than an equivalent reduction in price.

3. The response to a promotional deal is lower for familiar products.

There has been some interesting speculation on the long-run effects when purchase is stimulated primarily by a price deal. Drawing from attribution theory, Scott and Yaltch found that people who received some kind of reward (low price, for example) for testing a new product and who were encouraged to attribute their behavior to this factor were receptive to unfavorable product information and unreceptive to more favorable information.[75] In effect, then, this could lead to a kind of boomerang effect and reduced probability of future purchase.[76] This finding must be taken as highly tentative, however, until there is further evidence.

Couponing

Couponing, of course, is just a specific form of price deal, but it is worthy of separate mention because of its widespread use. In 1980 over 90

[71]Robert Dietrich, "Poor Price-Quiz Scores Give Shoppers No Cause for Pride," *Progressive Grocer* (January 1977), 33.

[72]F. E. Brown, "Who Perceives Supermarket Prices Most Validly?" *Journal of Marketing Research,* vol. 8 (February 1971), 110-113.

[73]*Project Payout,* 55.

[74]B. C. Cotton and Emerson M. Babb, "Consumer Response to Promotional Deals, *Journal of Marketing,* vol. 42 (July 1978), 109-113.

[75]Carol A. Scott and Richard F. Yaltch, "Consumer Response to Initial Product Trial: A Bayesian Analysis," *Journal of Consumer Research,* vol. 7 (June 1980), 32-41.

[76]See Carol A. Scott, "Attribution Theory and Consumer Research: Scope, Issues and Contributions," in S. C. Jain (ed.), *Research Frontiers in Marketing: Dialogues and Directions* (Chicago: American Marketing Association, 1978), 169-173.

billion coupons were distributed, compared with 16.4 billion in 1970![77] Yet, only five percent are redeemed by consumers, and, of those which are, only one in five (one percent of the total) ever is exchanged for an actual product.[78] In spite of low redemption, the definitive in-store test, referred to as Project Payout, found that a cost of $20.40 in coupon redemptions leads to a sales increase of $29.45.[79]

There is some basis now for the conclusion that many retailers and manufacturers are using coupons indiscriminately to move products which probably never should have been distributed in the first place or which are due to be scrapped. If redemption rates continue to decline, then this method of price dealing should decrease from its presently astronomical level.[80]

Unit Pricing

Knowing that price misperception exists and that people have a growing sensitivity to price information, many retailers have switched to unit pricing where price is stated per ounce, per serving, and so on. Early studies showed that the impact on consumer buying was not especially large,[81] even though those arguing from a perspective of consumer welfare strongly favor its use.[82] Later studies found a shift toward less expensive items when an improved display of unit price information was used.[83] The clue seems to lie in the way in which information is presented. When unit prices are in the form of an organized list, consumers have greater savings and retailers benefit too in the form of a shift to higher-profit store brands.[84]

In-Store Advertising

Reference is made here to various types of banners, signs, and other similar forms of sales boosters. While many retailers object and claim they will not use run-of-the-mill merchandising materials, this does not prove to be the case in practice.[85] One of the most effective strategies is a tie-in promotion or cross merchandising where related products are promoted jointly in one effort.[86] In just one example, a cross-merchandis-

[77]William Nigut, Sr., "Is the Boom in Cents-Off Couponing Going to Burst?" *Advertising Age* (December 15, 1980), 41-44.

[78]Nigut, "Is the Boom?"

[79]*Project Payout,* 30.

[80]Nigut, "Is the Boom?"

[81]"Dual Pricing, *Progressive Grocer* (February 1971), 46-50; William E. Kilbourne, "A Factorial Experiment on the Impact of Unit Pricing on Low-Income Consumers," *Journal of Marketing Research,* vol. 11 (November 1974), 453-455; T. David McCullough and Daniel I. Padberg, "Unit Pricing in Supermarkets," *Search: Agriculture,* vol. 1 (January 1971), 1-22.

[82]Esther Peterson, "Consumerism as a Retailer's Asset," *Harvard Business Review,* vol. 52 (May-June 1974), 91-101.

[83]McCullough and Padberg, "Unit Pricing"; and J. Edward Russo, Gene Krieser, and Sally Miyashita, "An Effective Display of Unit Price Information," *Journal of Marketing,* vol. 39 (April 1975), 9-11.

[84]J. Edward Russo, "The Value of Unit Price Information," *Journal of Marketing Research,* vol. 14 (May 1977), 193-201.

[85]Weil, "Use of Sales Boosters; In-store Tape Ads Hypo Co-op," *Chain Store Age Executive* (April 1977), 25.

[86]"PMA Hears: In-Store Signs, Ads Hike Impact of Cross-Display," *Supermarketing* (December 1978), 1+.

ing promotion produced sales gains of 87 percent for mushrooms and 62 percent for steak,[87] and this type of outcome is not unusual.

Contests and Promotions

Country Time lemonade has run a "Good Old-Fashioned" sweepstakes with "good old-fashioned" prizes—first prize is an $18,000 replica of a 1931 Ford. *Morningstar Farms* offers grocery prizes with the lead line, "Fill your grocery bag for two years. Free." This type of contest promotion can have a strong effect on sales, as numerous convenience goods manufacturers have discovered.[88] Supermarket traffic is being boosted as much as 15 percent by the use of various types of games (crossword puzzles, Bingo, etc.) offering prizes to winners, although there are wide geographic variations in outcomes.[89] While such devices may appear to be outright gimmicks to the reader, consumers *can be* attracted in positive ways, and product sales follow accordingly. When such devices do not generate favorable consumer reactions (and this is often the case), they inevitably fail.

Combination Promotions

Perhaps the best strategy of all is to undertake an integrated campaign making use of national and local advertising along with various forms of in-store promotion. We have frequently referred to Project Payout, the carefully designed experiment undertaken to isolate the effects of any type of promotion on actual product movement. In this study, it was found that a combination of price reduction, in-store display, and newspaper advertising increased the sales of *Star Kist* tuna 6.75 times, whereas another brand not undertaking such efforts, *Chicken of the Sea,* saw its sales index drop from 1.00 to 0.61.[90]

In-Store Layout and Design

Product exposure, of course, is the goal of all we have been discussing here, and one of the most helpful means to this end is careful study of traffic patterns. This method is used most often in supermarkets where interviewers actually observe and track consumers as they shop. The patterns then are summed and entered on a small replica of the store layout. These paths show the density of customer traffic in different parts of the store (Figure 19.5) and are then converted into the number of customers who pass and buy from major product groups (Table 19.1). Generally it is found that a direct relation exists between locations passed and purchase.

Often passing-buying ratios are used to make store-layout decisions. The premise is that products having a high passing-buying ratio should be scattered throughout the store to maximize customer exposure to

[87]"PMA Hears."

[88]"HBA Firms Spend."

[89]"The Supermarket Game Boom," *Chain Store Age Executive* (June 1977), 42.

[90]*Project Payout.*

Figure 19.5
Density of Customer Traffic in Different Parts of a Supermarket

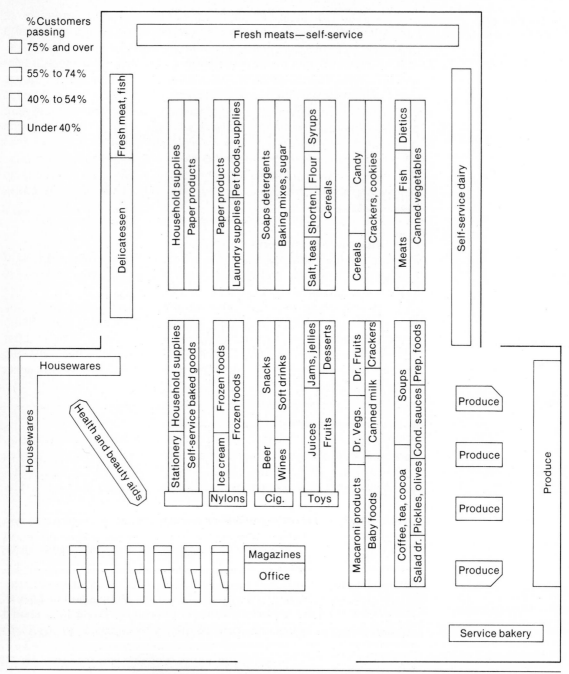

Source: "Colonial Study," *Progressive Grocer* (January 1964), C-90. Reprinted by permission of the publisher.

**Table 19.1
Number of
Customers Who
Pass and Buy from
Major Product
Groups in an
Average
Supermarket**

Out of 100 customers 94 pass and 80 buy fresh meats
Out of 100 customers 90 pass and 56 buy produce
Out of 100 customers 93 pass and 78 buy dairy products
Out of 100 customers 63 pass and 28 buy frozen foods
Out of 100 customers 61 pass and 14 buy ice cream
Out of 100 customers 70 pass and 41 buy self-service baked foods
Out of 100 customers 64 pass and 15 buy service baked foods
Out of 100 customers 57 pass and 18 buy service deli products
Out of 100 customers 45 pass and 12 buy baby foods
Out of 100 customers 53 pass and 24 buy baking mixes, needs, flour
Out of 100 customers 57 pass and 13 buy beer
Out of 100 customers 49 pass and 11 buy candy
Out of 100 customers 63 pass and 25 buy cereal
Out of 100 customers 65 pass and 13 buy cigarettes, tobacco
Out of 100 customers 61 pass and 21 buy coffee, tea, cocoa
Out of 100 customers 75 pass and 17 buy condiments, sauces
Out of 100 customers 68 pass and 35 buy crackers, cookies
Out of 100 customers 59 pass and 16 buy desserts
Out of 100 customers 55 pass and 7 buy dietetic foods
Out of 100 customers 63 pass and 13 buy fish, canned
Out of 100 customers 53 pass and 20 buy fruit canned
Out of 100 customers 55 pass and 9 buy fruit, dried
Out of 100 customers 61 pass and 14 buy household supplies
Out of 100 customers 72 pass and 19 buy jams, jellies, spreads
Out of 100 customers 55 pass and 13 buy juices, canned
Out of 100 customers 53 pass and 10 buy macaroni products
Out of 100 customers 64 pass and 19 buy meat, canned
Out of 100 customers 49 pass and 12 buy milk, canned
Out of 100 customers 64 pass and 37 buy paper products
Out of 100 customers 48 pass and 15 buy pet food supplies
Out of 100 customers 66 pass and 15 buy pickles, olives, relishes
Out of 100 customers 56 pass and 10 buy prepared foods
Out of 100 customers 59 pass and 19 buy salad dressing, mayonnaise
Out of 100 customers 57 pass and 13 buy salt, seasoning, spices
Out of 100 customers 49 pass and 12 buy snacks
Out of 100 customers 61 pass and 24 buy soaps, detergents, laundry supplies
Out of 100 customers 55 pass and 22 buy soft drinks
Out of 100 customers 62 pass and 24 buy soups
Out of 100 customers 60 pass and 29 buy vegetables, canned
Out of 100 customers 55 pass and 12 buy vegetables, dried
Out of 100 customers 46 pass and 18 buy health and beauty aids
Out of 100 customers 30 pass and 6 buy housewares
Out of 100 customers 38 pass and 13 buy magazines, books
Out of 100 customers 36 pass and 2 buy stationery
Out of 100 customers 35 pass and 4 buy toys
Out of 100 customers 39 pass and 1 buys records

Source: "Colonial Study," *Progressive Grocer* (January 1964), C-91. Reprinted by permission of the publisher.

other product assortments. But such decisions should be made with caution, because they measure association rather than causation. The conventional explanation for the observed relationship is that customers buy an item because exposure to in-store stimuli either triggers a buying decision or serves as a reminder of a latent need. An equally plausible explanation, however, is that shoppers obviously must pass an item if they intend to purchase it. In other words, intention leads to a shopping pattern rather than the reverse. Actually both explanations are plausible. We are saying traffic-pattern studies are incomplete without consumer surveys which document what the person actually was doing and why.

THE NEED FOR ANALYTICAL RESEARCH

The discerning reader who bothers to look at the footnotes (if you have done that, you deserve a special reward for unusual valor) will notice that the vast majority in this chapter have represented anecdotal trade reports. One major exception is Project Payout, which has been cited a number of times. For some reason, research on display, layout, and so on has not attracted the attention of many in academic ranks; yet it is high on the priority list of industry analysts. Is low-involvement behavior somehow beneath the conceptual and methodological dignity of the academe? It almost seems as if this is the case, given the paucity of the literature. High-involvement behavior research has carried the day too long, because what we have described here encompasses the lion's share of consumer behavior as it actually takes place out there. Of course the clear-cut distinction between high and low involvement has only recently become accepted. Hopefully this fact in-and-of itself will lead to a change in research priorities.

Summary

This is the first of two chapters on low-involvement decision process behavior. Low-involvement buying differs from that discussed in previous sections for these reasons: (1) lack of high personal relevance; (2) low perceived risk; (3) little relationship between consequences of the purchase and one's self-concept; and (4) low anxiety about outcomes. A model of this type of buying behavior was presented showing that problem recognition leads directly to choice with alternative evaluation (formation of beliefs, attitudes, and intentions) being an *outcome of* rather than an *influence on* behavior.

Advertising and product sampling can affect the choice by stimulating some product knowledge and interest. This is done most frequently, it now appears, through use of television in which visual images are stored and then activated at point-of-sale through recognition. This places in-store promotion, then, as the most important set of influences on choice. In particular, we examined the role of displays, pricing, package design, in-store advertising and contests, layout, and so on. It is here that the greatest marketing emphasis must be placed if there is to be any hope of success. The chapter concluded with a brief discussion of the need for further research in this important area.

Review and Discussion Questions

1. Assume you have been called in as a marketing consultant to suggest an advertising strategy for a new brand of dry cat food. Is this likely to be a high-involvement or a low-involvement product? Why? What factors would you look for?

2. Continuing with the example in Question 1, assume that your answer is low involvement. Also assume that management has asked for a general discussion of the type of advertising which might be undertaken. What would your answer be? Why?

3. Would in-store sampling likely be a good strategy for this new pet food? Why or why not?

4. Many customers object to the highly repetitive advertising often used for low-involvement products. Others list some of the approaches used as being high on their "least liked" list. Does this imply lack of advertising effectiveness, or might the reverse also be true?

5. What is impulse buying? What possible explanations can be given?

6. It has been stressed that in-store promotion is the key to stimulating purchase of low-involvement products. Why is this so? What role do these influences play?

7. From the perspective of involvement theory, what differentiates a good package design from a poor one? What role might aesthetics and artistic sensibility have, if any?

8. Referring back to the new pet food mentioned in Question 1, what strategy would you suggest in terms of display, pricing, in-store advertising, and so on? What is your rationale?

9. Some say that in-store contests and promotions are only gimmicks to attract customers and that they should be abolished. If that is so, why do they still continue to succeed?

CHAPTER 20

BRAND LOYALTY AND REPEAT-PURCHASE BEHAVIOR

Under conditions of low involvement, alternative evaluation follows purchase and hopefully results in a positive attitude toward the brand and an intention to repurchase. When this occurs, the manufacturer has gained a great asset known as *brand loyalty*.

When serious research on consumer behavior became popular around the late 1950s and early 1960s, the subject of brand loyalty carried the day. Quite an extensive literature has resulted, much of which is cited in this chapter. Since this subject also leads to quantitative modeling, much of what has been published demands some sophistication to comprehend and apply. Thus, the reader should be prepared for some tough going in the latter parts of this chapter, but there is no way that can be avoided.

Why is brand loyalty discussed in the context of low involvement and not earlier? The reason is that the study of loyalty requires repeat purchase patterns, and a large proportion of those items bought in this way are low-involvement products. Therefore, the reader will notice references to frozen orange juice, paper products, and similar items. Loyalty also develops under high involvement as we have noted previously, but most of the research has not been done in that context.

The discussion begins with a consideration of the meaning of brand loyalty and research results supporting the existence of the phenomenon. The second section analyzes the structural and behavioral correlates of brand loyalty. Various models relating some of these correlates to measures of brand loyalty are presented in the third section. The chapter concludes with some additional discussion of marketing strategy implications.

WHAT IS BRAND LOYALTY?

The definition of brand loyalty has generated considerable confusion as well as controversy. Whether or not brand loyalty exists and, of course, the extent to which it exists, depend partly on how it is defined. A distinction is sometimes made between *repeat purchase behavior* and *loyalty*.

The differences in these terms can be understood by examining the usage of the term brand loyalty by various investigators.

Brand loyalty is *conceptual* in nature. As a conceptual variable, it has been used both as an output variable—the result of consumer decisions; and as an input variable—the cause of consumer decisions. In either case the concept of brand loyalty to be used in consumer research must be *operationally defined.* How the concept is defined may have a very great effect on the research results that will be obtained. The operational definitions described below include: (1) brand-choice sequences; (2) preferences over time; (3) proportion of purchases; and (4) other measures, including an extended definition of brand loyalty based both on preferences and purchases.

Brand-Choice Sequences

One of the earliest studies defined brand loyalty according to the *sequence of purchasing a specific brand.* The purchase records of 100 households in a *Chicago Tribune* panel were analyzed for such frequently purchased items as coffee, orange juice, soap, and margarine. For each product category, each household making five or more purchases was placed in one of four brand-loyalty categories depending on the sequence of brands purchased. Thus, if A, B, C, D, E, F . . . are various brands (*Snow Crop, Minute Maid,* etc.) in a particular product category such as orange juice, then households could be classified as having the following types of loyalty:

1. *Undivided loyalty* is the sequence AAAAA.

2. *Divided loyalty* is the sequence ABABAB.

3. *Unstable loyalty* is the sequence AAABBB.

4. *No loyalty* is the sequence ABCDEF.

Using this definition of brand loyalty, Brown observed that the percentage of households demonstrating some degree of loyalty varied from 54 to 95 percent, depending on the product involved. In fact, the percentage of households that were undividedly loyal varied from 12 percent to 73 percent across products.[1]

This operational definition of loyalty was important in the development of the concept and in studies such as those of Tucker[2] and Stafford[3] who defined brand loyalty as three successive choices of the same brand in their empirical studies. While the concept developed in these early studies is still valid, the practical problems of this definition have

[1]George Brown, "Brand Loyalty—Fact or Fiction?" *Advertising Age* (June 19, 1952), 53-55; (June 30, 1952), 45-47; (July 14, 1952), 54-56; (July 28, 1952), 46-48; (August 11, 1952), 56-58; (September 1, 1952), 80-82; (October 6, 1952), 82-86; (December 1, 1952), 76-79; (January 25, 1953), 75-76.

[2]W. T. Tucker, "The Development of Brand Loyalty," *Journal of Marketing Research,* vol. 1 (August 1964), 32-35.

[3]James E. Stafford, "Effect of Group Influences on Consumer Brand Preferences," *Journal of Marketing Research,* vol. 3 (February 1966), 68-75.

caused it to be little used today for the reasons that Charlton and Ehrenberg describe below:

> This approach has led to few generalizable results, because there is no simple way of summarizing purchase sequences quantitatively. Different consumers buy at different rates. Their purchase sequences are invariably out of phase with one another, and it is difficult to aggregate the buying behavior of one consumer with that of another who buys, say, more frequently. There is also no common time scale for relating any one measure of aggregate behavior to other aspects of buying behavior or to other events in the market place. The purchase sequence approach, therefore, does not facilitate the kinds of comparisons between consumers, brands, or product fields that are likely to lead to generalizable results.[4]

Preference over Time

Sometimes loyalty has been defined as preference statements over time rather than actual purchase. One such study involved data collected by Guest in 1941 concerning the brand awareness and preferences of students. In follow-up studies of these same persons 12 and 20 years later, Guest found suggestive evidence of a high degree of loyalty toward brand names (although not to specific brands).[5] This loyalty was most manifest when factors such as unavailability, price considerations, and respondent not being the buyer did not play a major part in brand selection.

In a literature review of operational definitions of brand loyalty, Jacoby found 17 studies employing preference statements over time, similar to the usage by Guest.[6] More recent research of brand loyalty, however, has favored definitions that emphasize actual purchase, described below.

Proportion of Purchases

The most frequently used definition of brand loyalty, at least in empirical research, is *the proportion of total purchases within a given product category devoted to the most frequently purchased brand (or set of brands)*. This is used both as a conceptual definition of brand loyalty in these studies as well as an operational measure.

Proportion of purchases has the advantage of being *quantifiable* and thus useful in a wide variety of mathematical models. In addition, using this definition of brand loyalty, Cunningham introduced the concept of *multibrand* loyalty in various forms.[7] *Dual-brand loyalty,* for example, would be the percent of total purchases devoted to the two most favorite

---

[4]P. Charlton and A. S. C. Ehrenberg, "McConnell's Experimental Brand Choice Data," *Journal of Marketing Research,* vol. 10 (August 1973), 302-307.

[5]Lester Guest, "Brand Loyalty Revisited: A Twenty Year Report," *Journal of Applied Psychology,* vol. 48 (1964), 93-97.

[6]Jacob Jacoby, "Brand Loyalty: A Conceptual Definition," *Proceedings of the 79th Annual Convention,* American Psychological Association (1971), 655-656.

[7]Ross M. Cunningham, "Brand Loyalty—What, Where, How Much?" *Harvard Business Review,* vol. 34 (January-February 1956), 116-128; Ross Cunningham, "Customer Loyalty to Store and Brand," *Harvard Business Review,* vol. 39 (November-December 1961), 127-137.

brands; *triple*-brand loyalty refers to the three most favorite brands; and so on. In a later study, Cunningham also used a similar approach to demonstrate store loyalty.[8]

Other researchers have used this concept of brand loyalty, including use in most of the mathematical models described later in the chapter. Each researcher tends to use the basic concept with some variation. Farley used two summary measures of brand loyalty, one a cross-sectional measure based on "the average number of brands bought by families of a given product during the period of study," and another, a time-series measure based on "the percent of families in a given market whose favorite brand is different in the first half of the period studied from the second half."[9] Small values of each measure indicate brand loyalty, whereas large values indicate frequent brand switching.

In the definition of brand loyalty used by Massy, Montgomery, and Morrison, a consumer is considered brand loyal if his or her preferred brand during the first half of the period under study is the same as the one during the second half, preferred brand being defined as the one which is purchased most often in a given period.[10] Blattberg and Sen have extended the "proportion of purchases" approach to segments that are loyal to national or private brands as a category as well as specific brands within each of those categories.[11] One segment of the population they found to be "high national brand loyal" and found that the proportion of purchases devoted to the favorite brand ranged from about 90 to 100 percent *within this segment*. Blattberg and Sen also used the concept of "last purchase loyal" (as have some other researchers) to define a consumer who buys one brand on several successive occasions, switches to another brand, buys that several times, switches again, and so on.[12]

Other Measures of Loyalty

Several researchers have employed a combination of two or more of the above criteria in defining brand loyalty. Thus, the factor analytic approach employed by Sheth uses a definition of brand loyalty based on both the frequency of purchase of a brand and the pattern of these purchases.[13] Pessemier used an entirely different approach based on the price increase in the most preferred brand relative to the price of the other brands necessary to induce brand switching.[14] Cunningham, on the other

---

[8]Ross M. Cunningham, "Customer Loyalty to Store and Brand," *Harvard Business Review,* vol. 39 (November-December 1961), 127-137.

[9]John U. Farley, "Why Does Brand Loyalty Vary over Products?" *Journal of Marketing Research,* vol. 1 (November 1964), 9-14; John U. Farley, "Brand Loyalty and the Economics of Information," *Journal of Marketing Research,* vol. 13 (October 1964), 370-381.

[10]William F. Massy, David B. Montgomery, and Donald G. Morrison, *Stochastic Models of Buying Behavior* (Cambridge, Mass.: M.I.T. Press, 1970), 119.

[11]Robert C. Blattberg and Subrata K. Sen, "Market Segments and Stochastic Brand Choice Models," *Journal of Marketing Research,* vol. 13 (February 1976), 34-45.

[12]Blattberg and Sen, "Market Segments," 35.

[13]John A. Howard and Jagdish N. Sheth, *The Theory of Buyer Behavior* (New York: John Wiley & Sons, 1969), 249; also Jagdish N. Sheth, "A Factor Analytic Model of Brand Loyalty," *Journal of Marketing Research,* vol. 5 (November 1968), 395-404; Jagdish N. Sheth, "Measurement of Multidimensional Brand Loyalty of a Consumer," *Journal of Marketing Research,* vol. 7 (August 1970), 348-354.

[14]Edgar A. Pessemier, "A New Way to Determine Buying Decisions," *Journal of Marketing,* vol. 24 (October 1959), 41-46.

hand, attempted to evaluate probable behavior when confronted with the absence of one's favorite brand as an indicator of brand loyalty.[15]

Limitations of Traditional Definitions of Brand Loyalty

The definitions discussed above have one common characteristic: they provide an operational measure of brand loyalty. Unfortunately, however, the large number of approaches causes several problems.

First, it is difficult to compare and synthesize findings. Assume, for example, that two consumers exhibit the following pattern of purchases during a given period:

Consumer 1 = *ABCABC.*
Consumer 2 = *ABCCCC.*

The definition—"number of brands purchased during the time period"—would treat both consumers alike. However, the "purchase sequence" definition would treat them differently.

Why did the second consumer buy Brand C on each of the last four purchase occasions? Is it because he really prefers Brand C and has developed a sort of loyalty toward that brand, or is it because the store he patronizes has stopped carrying the other brands? Maybe Brand C is being promoted with a long series of promotional deals, or the store has rearranged the merchandise, providing a better shelf display for C. This illustrates the importance of distinguishing between "intentional loyalty" and "spurious loyalty." As Day points out:

. . . the spuriously loyal buyers lack any attachment to brand attributes, and they can be immediately captured by another brand that offers a better deal, a coupon, or enhanced point-of-purchase visibility through displays and other devices.[16]

Another basic problem is that most traditional definitions do not deal with multiple-brand loyalty. Although Brown, Cunningham, and a few other pioneers conceived the possibility of loyalty to more than one brand, it has been dealt with seriously only in recent years.[17]

Finally, it seems risky to define and measure loyalty to accommodate empirical data. Instead, once a conceptual framework has been developed, a comprehensive set of relevant variables could be identified and studied.

Preference-Purchase Definitions of Brand Loyalty

A resolution of the limitations of traditional definitions can be achieved by a definition of brand loyalty that includes both *preferences* of consumers and *purchases* of consumers. A preference-purchase definition recognizes a difference between intentional loyalty and spurious loyalty or that *loyalty is something more than repeat purchase behavior.*

Day contends that to be truly brand loyal, the consumer must hold a

[15]Scott M. Cunningham, "Perceived Risk and Brand Loyalty," in Donald F. Cox (ed.), *Risk Taking and Information Handling in Consumer Behavior* (Boston: Harvard University Press, 1967), 507-523.

[16]George S. Day, "A Two-Dimensional Concept of Brand Loyalty," *Journal of Advertising Research,* vol. 9 (September 1969), 29-35.

[17]See, for example, Massy et al., *Stochastic Models;* Sheth, "Measurement of Multidimensional Brand Loyalty"; A. S. C. Ehrenberg and G. J. Goodhardt, "A Model of Multi-Brand Buying," *Journal of Marketing Research,* vol. 7 (February 1970), 77-84.

favorable attitude toward the brand in addition to purchasing it repeatedly.[18]

Jacoby concurs, suggesting that brand loyalty has at least two primary dimensions—brand loyal behavior and brand loyal attitude:

Brand loyal behavior is defined as the overt act of selective repeat purchasing based on evaluative psychological decision processes, while brand-loyal attitudes are the underlying predispositions to behave in such a selective fashion . . . . To exhibit brand loyalty implies repeat purchasing behavior based on cognitive, affective, evaluative and predispositional factors . . . .[19]

Following this line of analysis, an extended definition of brand loyalty would be: *Brand loyalty is the preferential attitudinal and behavioral response toward one or more brands in a product category expressed over a period of time by a consumer (or buyer).*

This definition has many implications. Foremost is the fact that any measure of brand loyalty should incorporate behavioral as well as attitudinal components. An example is a measure proposed by Day.[20]

$$L_i = \frac{P(B_i)}{kA_i^n} = f(X_a, X_b, \ldots, X_j)$$

where:

L_i = *brand-loyalty score for ith* buyer of brand *m*

$P(B)_i$ = proportion of total purchases of products that buyers devoted to brand *m* over period of study

A_i = attitude toward brand *m* at beginning of study, scaled so that a low value represents a favorable attitude

$X_a, \ldots, X_j$ = descriptive variables to be fitted to L_i by least squares

k = constants whose values are varied by trial and error to maximize fit between L_i and $X_a, \ldots, X_j$.

Day provides empirical evidence to demonstrate the superiority of such a measure over the traditional approaches that use only purchase data. His measure isolates spurious loyalty and achieves a better statistical fit with a set of descriptive variables.[21]

The extended conceptualization has several other attractive features. First, it explicitly recognizes the existence of multibrand loyalty. Second, brand loyalty is viewed as a *product-specific* phenomenon rather than a general attribute. Thus a consumer may be highly brand loyal in product category *X*, but not in categories *Y* or *Z*.

Third, the definition recognizes that brand loyalty is a temporal phenomenon. Model builders can specify the time span over which the behavior is to be studied. Fourth, the definition focuses on the responses

---

[18]Day, "Two-Dimensional Concept."

[19]Jacob Jacoby, "A Model of Multi-Brand Loyalty," *Journal of Advertising Research,* vol. 11 (June 1971), 25-31.

[20]Day, "Two-Dimensional Concept."

[21]Day, "Two-Dimensional Concept."

of the decision maker. Since the final consumer need not always be the buyer, it would be difficult otherwise to study the correlates of brand loyalty using data on buyers who are not consumers.

Fifth, the definition proposes a continuum of brand loyalty as opposed to the artificial loyal-disloyal dichotomy. Finally, the approach points out the need to incorporate variables affecting brand-loyal attitudes as well as purchase behavior.

The easiest to understand and perhaps the most complete definition of this approach to brand loyalty was formulated by Jacoby. While many other definitions are used as operational measures of brand loyalty, this form of an extended preference-purchase definition captures the full range of meaning of the concept brand loyalty:

Brand loyalty is (1) the biased (i.e., nonrandom) (2) behavioral response (i.e., purchase) (3) expressed over time (4) by some decision-making unit (5) with respect to one or more alternative brands out of a set of such brands, and is (6) a function of psychological (i.e., decision-making,evaluative) processes.[22]

This definition is consistent with the study of consumer behavior as a decision process and yet delineates it as a special phenomenon for scientific analysis and prediction. Jacoby's definition is very useful in distinguishing *repeat purchase behavior* that focuses only on behavior from *loyalty,* which encompasses the antecedents of behavior.[23]

It also specifically brings to attention the fact that brand loyalty is a concept that applies to a "decision-making unit" such as a family. The failure to make this recognition and the consequent correlation of *individual* variables with *family* purchases probably accounts for many of the problems in brand loyalty research. For example, attitudinal measures may reflect very well the preferences of the person who completes a questionnaire but correlate poorly with purchase behavior of the family over time (brand loyalty) because other members of the family are more influential in the family's purchases some or all of the time.

BRAND LOYALTY CORRELATES

Numerous attempts have been made to determine why brand loyalty varies across consumers and products. This section summarizes the consumer, shopping pattern, and market structure characteristics that are, or are not, associated with differential degrees of brand loyalty. Because of the wide variety of definitions of brand loyalty, the following correlates and noncorrelates should be viewed as provisional rather than definitive.

[22]Jacob Jacoby and Robert W. Chestnut, *Brand Loyalty, Measurement and Management* (New York: John Wiley & Sons, 1978), 80-81.

[23]Considerable discussion has been generated by Jacoby's definition of brand loyalty. See Lawrence X. Tarpey, Sr., "A Brand Loyalty Concept—A Comment," *Journal of Marketing Research,* vol. 11 (May 1974), 214-217; Jacob Jacoby, "A Brand Loyalty Concept: Comments on a Comment," *Journal of Marketing Research,* vol. 12 (November 1975), 484-487; Lawrence X. Tarpey, Sr., "Brand Loyalty Revisited: A Commentary," *Journal of Marketing Research,* vol. 12 (November 1975), 488-491.

Consumer Characteristics

In one of the earlier studies attempting to identify characteristics of brand-loyal consumers, the Advertising Research Foundation reported results based on toilet-tissue purchasing behavior for 3,206 members of the J. Walter Thompson panel.[24] They found virtually no association between personality (as measured by the Edwards personal preference schedule), socioeconomic variables, and household brand loyalty.

Employing the same data source, but analyzing beer, coffee, and tea purchasing behavior, Frank, Massy, and Lodahl observed only a modest association between socioeconomic, demographic, and personality variables and brand loyalty. Using a brand-loyalty score based on a large number of measures of household purchasing behavior, such as number of brands purchased, percentage spent on most frequently purchased brands, and so on, they observed some relationships between brand loyalty and certain personality measures from the Edwards test. Thus husbands' and wives' endurance, deference, and succorance scores, wives' need for autonomy and change, and husbands' need for affiliation seem to have been somewhat related to brand loyalty. The overall conclusions of the study, however, were that high brand loyal households apparently have a profile of personality and socioeconomic characteristics that is virtually identical to that of households exhibiting a lower degree of loyalty.[25]

Frank and Boyd, in their investigation of household brand loyalty to private brands, also concluded that socioeconomic variables could not differentiate between private and manufacturer brand-loyal consumers.[26] Similarly, Coulson found that knowledge of the brand preferences of other family members did not significantly affect whether respondents had a regular brand that was purchased more than others. He also observed that homemakers who tended to have a regular brand that was purchased more than others, did not differ from other homemakers in terms of age or social class.[27] Guest, in his 20-year study of brand preferences through time, also found that sex, intelligence, and marital status were unrelated to brand loyalty.

In a study attempting to relate the influence of reference groups on brand-loyal behavior, Stafford found no significant relation between level of group cohesiveness and member brand loyalty. However, in the more cohesive groups, the extent and degree of brand loyalty of members was closely related to brand-choice behavior of the informal leader.[28]

Carman used an entropy measure of loyalty based on purchase data

---

[24]*Are There Consumer Types?* (New York: Advertising Research Foundation, 1964).

[25]Ronald E. Frank, William F. Massy, and Thomas M. Lodahl, "Purchasing Behavior and Personal Attributes," *Journal of Advertising Research,* vol. 9 (December 1969), 15-24; Ronald E. Frank, "Correlates of Buying Behavior for Grocery Products," *Journal of Marketing,* vol. 31 (October 1967), 48-53.

[26]Ronald Frank and Harper Boyd, Jr., "Are Private-Brand-Prone Grocery Customers Really Different?" *Journal of Advertising Research,* vol. 5 (December 1965), 27-35.

[27]John S. Coulson, "Buying Decisions within the Family," in Joseph Newman (ed.), *On Knowing the Consumer* (New York: John Wiley & Sons, 1966), 66.

[28]Stafford, "Effect of Group Influences."

alone[29] and the Morgan-Sonquist automatic interaction detector scheme (AID) to analyze the results.[30] On the other hand, he was unable to relate most personality characteristics and consumer mobility—geographic, intergenerational, and social—to brand loyalty. However, he did find some relationships and concluded:

1. Personal characteristics of consumers will explain differences in store loyalty, which in turn is the single most important predictor of brand loyalty.

2. Loyalty is positively correlated with the extent to which the homemaker socializes with his or her neighbors. Why this is the case is not clear.

3. The characteristics of consumers that are associated with brand loyalty differ among products. Thus, a loyal coffee buyer possesses the characteristics representative of high self-confidence. Furthermore, in the case of coffee, reference-group influence is most obvious, with consumers most interested in status being the most loyal. For canned fruits and frozen orange juice, reference-group influence is insignificant.

As a result of the richness of the data bank and the versatility of the AID technique in handling a large number of predictor variables, Carman was able to identify relations that would normally go undetected. For example, he describes the characteristics of the brand-loyal coffee buyer as follows:

She respects the food-shopping opinion of her neighbors but, in general, trusts technical sources of food information more than personal sources. . . . (She indicates) stronger home or career orientation. She lives in the better neighborhoods of the shopping area, and she does not cook the kind of meals served in her parents' home. However, she considers herself a permanent part of the neighborhood. Loyal coffee buyers have a higher income consistent with the neighborhood than the nonloyal group. . . . (They have) high self-confidence. These results appear to be in agreement with the hypothesis of Brody and Cunningham[31] that brand-loyal coffee consumers should have self-confidence.[32]

Using the extended attitudinal/behavior measure of brand loyalty described earlier in the chapter, Day also detected significant associations

---

[29]Their measure θ, based on purchase data alone, is defined as

$$\theta = \Sigma \frac{K}{i = 1} P_i \log P_i$$

where P_i is the true proportion of purchases going to brand i and K the number of brands available on the market.

[30]James M. Carman, "Correlates of Brand Loyalty: Some Positive Results," *Journal of Marketing Research*, vol. 7 (February 1970), 67-76. It should be noted that some Monte Carlo studies with AID raise several questions regarding its unfortunate propensity for capitalizing on specific sample variation.

[31]Robert P. Brody and Scott M. Cunningham, "Personality Variables and the Consumer Decisions Process," *Journal of Marketing Research*, vol. 5 (February 1968), 50-57.

[32]Carman, "Correlates of Brand Loyalty," 73-74.

between loyalty and certain consumer characteristics.[33] He found the brand-loyal consumer to be very conscious of the need to economize when buying, confident of his or her judgments, and older in a smaller than average household (thus needing to satisfy the preferences of fewer family members).

It has also become fairly evident that brand loyalty is a product specific phenomenon; that is, some product categories are likely to have more loyalty than others. Some researchers have concluded that more brand switching will occur when price differences are significant between brands and that this will have the most effect on consumers in the extreme levels of both income and education, rather than in a linear relationship to these variables.[34] Possibly, brand switching is a function of the value of time to a consumer. This hypothesis suggests that upper income people have more natural loyalty to brands but when their preferred brand is out of stock or not carried by a convenient store, upper income consumers will switch to another brand rather than spend the time necessary to find their preferred brand.[35]

In an examination of brand loyalty for appliances, Newman and Werbel found some relationship between loyalty and a personality variable, specifically optimism about the future. The persons *least* optimistic about future business conditions were most likely to be brand loyal. This study also concluded, as one would expect, that a strong relationship exists between brand loyalty and satisfaction with a present product of that brand.[36] In thinking about the discussion of loyalty definitions earlier in this chapter, it is also worthwhile to note that the Newman and Werbel study concluded that measures of loyalty built upon preference (brand deliberation) as well as purchase are more useful than those built upon repeat purchases alone.

Shopping-Pattern Characteristics

Studies have also investigated the relationships between brand loyalty and various shopping-pattern characteristics, including store loyalty, shopping proneness, amount purchased, brand last purchased, and interpurchase time. The results of these studies are summarized below.

As was pointed out above, Carman found that store loyalty was the most important correlate of brand loyalty.[37] Other researchers have also demonstrated the importance of store loyalty in determining brand loyalty.[38] This relationship is due, in part, to the fact that store loyalty tends to restrict the number of brand alternatives available to the consumer.

---

[33]Day, "Two-Dimensional Concept."

[34]William A. Chance and Normal D. French, "An Exploratory Investigation of Brand Switching," *Journal of Marketing Research,* vol. 9 (May 1972), 226-229.

[35]Shmuel Shairir (Shraier), "Brand Loyalty and the Household's Cost of Time," *Journal of Business,* vol. 47 (January 1974), 53-55.

[36]Joseph W. Newman and Richard A. Werbel, "Multivariate Analysis of Brand Loyalty for Major Household Appliances," *Journal of Marketing Research,* vol. 10 (November 1973), 404-409.

[37]Carman, "Correlates of Brand Loyalty," 69-71.

[38]Tanniru R. Rao, "Consumer's Purchase Decision Process: Stochastic Models," *Journal of Marketing Research,* vol. 6 (August 1969), 321-329.

However, Carman maintains that the brand-store loyalty relationship is more complex than the simple reduction in available choices.[39]

Shopping proneness is another characteristic that has been related to brand loyalty.[40] Consumers who are not shopping-prone shop in relatively few stores. Within these stores, they tend to remain loyal to a small number of brands rather than make careful choices between the values being offered by these stores.

When the store in which a shopper normally makes a purchase undergoes substantial change (such as ownership), this may also affect a buyer's loyalty to the manufacturer's brands formerly purchased there, a study of auto buyers discloses.[41]

Studies investigating the relationship between the amount purchased and brand loyalty yield contradictory findings. Based on the purchase habits of 66 households in seven product categories including soap, cleansers, coffee, peas, margarine, orange juice, and headache remedies, Cunningham found very little relationship between purchasing activity and brand loyalty.[42] Massy, Frank, and Lodahl report similar findings for coffee and beer, although they found some association between activity and brand loyalty for tea.[43] In contrast, Kuehn, using frozen orange juice purchases from a *Chicago Tribune* panel of 650 households, found that brand loyalty was higher for heavy purchasers than for light purchasers.[44] Day, in a more recent study using certain convenience foods, also found that true brand-loyal buyers were also heavy users of the products.[45]

Some of the apparent contradictions in loyalty may be due to differences in loyalty caused by the length of time the product has been on the market. Some excellent experiments have been conducted by Ehrenberg and his associates in a continuing panel of households, called the RBL Mini Test Market Operation. In these studies, it was found that brand switching is much more prevalent immediately after the introduction of a product and equilibrium or brand loyalty is reached after the passage of an amount of time.[46]

Several studies have investigated the relationship between interpurchase time and brand loyalty. Based on purchases of frozen orange juice, Kuehn observed that the probability of a consumer's buying the

[39]Carman, "Correlates of Brand Loyalty."

[40]Carman, "Correlates of Brand Loyalty."

[41]Richard D. Norstrom and John E. Swan, "Does a Change in Customer Loyalty Occur When a New Car Agency is Sold?" *Journal of Marketing Research,* vol. 13 (May 1976), 173-177.

[42]Cunningham, "Perceived Risk."

[43]Massy et al., *Stochastic Models.*

[44]Alfred A. Kuehn, "Consumer Brand Choice as a Learning Process," *Journal of Advertising Research,* vol. 2 (December 1962), 10-17.

[45]Day, "Two-Dimensional Concept."

[46]A. S. C. Ehrenberg and P. Carlton, "An Analysis of Simulated Brand Choice," *Journal of Advertising Research,* vol. 13 (February 1973). Also see P. Carlton, A. S. C. Ehrenberg, and B. Pymont, "Buyer Behaviour under Mini-test Conditions," *Journal of the Market Research Society,* vol. 14 (July 1972), 171-183; and P. Carlton and A. S. C. Ehrenberg, "An Experiment in Brand Choice," *Journal of Marketing Research,* vol. 13 (May 1976), 152-160.

same brand on two consecutive purchases (a measure of brand loyalty) decreased exponentially with an increase in time between these purchases.[47] In a study of Canadian banks, it was also found that the longer the elapsed time, the greater the decay in loyalty.[48] Morrison[49] and Carman,[50] on the other hand, observed no significant change in brand loyalty as the time between purchases varied. These contradictory findings may very well be due to the use of different product categories by these researchers.

Finally, attempts have been made to relate factors such as perceived risk and cognitive dissonance to brand loyalty. Thus, Sheth and Venkatesan suggest, based on a laboratory study, that "perceived risk is a necessary condition for the development of brand loyalty assuming high involvement." The sufficient condition is the existence of well-known market brands on which the consumer can rely.[51] Using a different laboratory experiment, Mittelstaedt suggests that brand loyalty may be a function of the dissonance experienced at the time of purchase, and that the experience coupled with its subsequent reduction may lead one to repeat a choice.[52] This also would assume high involvement.

Market-Structure Characteristics

Several studies have investigated the relationship between brand loyalty and certain market-structure characteristics, such as the availability of brands, price fluctuations, and dealing activity. The importance of these types of variables was demonstrated by Farley's study of the purchases of 199 families in 17 diverse product categories.[53] He found that:

1. Consumers tended to be less loyal toward products with many available brands, where number of purchases and dollar expenditures per buyer are high, where prices are relatively active, and where consumers might be expected to simultaneously use a number of brands of the product.

2. Consumers tend to be loyal in markets where brands tend to be widely distributed, and where market share is concentrated heavily in the leading brand.

Based on these findings Farley concluded:

Much of the apparent difference over products in some important aspects of brand choice can apparently be explained on the basis of

---

[47]Kuehn, "Consumer Brand Choice."

[48]Joseph N. Fry et al., "Customer Loyalty to Banks: A Longitudinal Study," *Journal of Business,* vol. 46 (October 1973), 517-525.

[49]Donald G. Morrison, "Interpurchase Time and Brand Loyalty," *Journal of Marketing Research,* vol. 3 (August 1966), 289-291.

[50]James M. Carman, "Brand Switching and Linear Learning Models," *Journal of Advertising Research,* vol. 6 (June 1966), 23-31.

[51]Jagdish N. Sheth and M. Venkatesan, "Risk Reduction Process in Repetitive Consumer Behavior," *Journal of Marketing Research,* vol. 5 (August 1968), 307-310; Cunningham, "Perceived Risk."

[52]Robert Mittelstaedt, "A Dissonance Approach to Repeat Purchasing Behavior," *Journal of Marketing Research,* vol. 6 (November 1969), 444-446.

[53]Farley, "Why Does Brand Loyalty Vary?"

structural variables describing the markets in which the products are sold, and does not depend on specific characteristics of the products or on attitudes of consumers towards products.

Other researchers have also found relationships between market characteristics and brand loyalty. For example, Day found that the true brand-loyal buyer was less influenced by day-to-day price fluctuations and special deals than were others.[54]

Weinberg also believes that a wide range of competing brands contributes to disloyalty because of the information gained through experience with those brands.[55]

Not all researchers, however, are convinced of the influence of market structure variables on brand loyalty. Thus, if brand loyalty were successful in building up the resistance of buyers to switch to other brands in the face of changes in market conditions, one would expect that the elasticities for loyal buyers with respect to some of the major market structure variables would be less than those for the nonloyal group. Massy and Frank, however, found no statistically significant difference between the price, dealing, and retail advertising elasticities for families who were brand loyal and those who were not.[56]

Moreover, another study casts doubts on Farley's conclusions concerning the relationship between brand loyalty and the number of brands available in the market. Specifically, a laboratory experiment conducted by Anderson, Taylor, and Holloway found that the greater the number of alternatives available, the greater the concentration on the most frequently chosen alternative.[57]

Brand-Loyalty Correlates: Summary and Critical Appraisal

The major conclusions that can be drawn concerning the correlates of brand loyalty are:

1. Socioeconomic, demographic, and psychological variables generally do not distinguish brand-loyal consumers from other consumers when traditional definitions of brand loyalty are used.

2. When extended definitions of brand loyalty are used, some socioeconomic, demographic, and psychological variables are related to loyalty. However, these relationships tend to be product specific rather than ubiquitous across product categories.

3. There is limited evidence that the loyalty behavior of an informal group leader affects the behavior of other group members.

4. Store loyalty is commonly associated with brand loyalty. Moreover, store loyalty appears to be an intervening variable between certain consumer characteristics and brand loyalty. In other words, certain con-

[54]Day, "Two-Dimensional Concept."

[55]Charles B. Weinberg, "The Decay of Brand Segments," *Journal of Advertising Research,* vol. 13 (February 1973), 44-47.

[56]William F. Massy and Ronald E. Frank, "Short Term Price and Dealing Effects in Selected Market Segments," *Journal of Marketing Research,* vol. 2 (May 1965), 171-185.

[57]Lee K. Anderson, James R. Taylor, and Robert J. Holloway, "The Consumer and His Alternatives: An Experimental Approach," *Journal of Marketing Research,* vol. 3 (February 1966), 62-67.

sumer characteristics are related to store loyalty, which in turn is related to brand loyalty.

5. There is some evidence that brand loyalty is inversely related to the number of stores shopped.

6. The relationship between amount purchased and brand loyalty is uncertain because of contradictory findings.

7. The relationship between interpurchase time and brand loyalty is also uncertain due to contradictory findings.

8. There is limited evidence that perceived risk is positively related to brand loyalty.

9. Market-structure variables, including the extensiveness of distribution and the market share of the leading brand, exert a positive influence on brand loyalty.

10. The effects of the number of alternative brands, special deals, and price activity are uncertain due to contradictory findings.

The fact that many of the findings concerning brand-loyalty correlates are inconclusive and/or contradictory is due, in part, to the infancy of this type of research and, hence, the absence of a widely accepted research tradition. Future research efforts might be more productive if certain guidelines were adopted.

In attempting to isolate correlates, the evidence suggests that brand loyalty should be treated as a *product-specific rather than a general attribute*. Many studies have demonstrated that correlates vary across products. Thus, attempts to determine characteristics of consumers who are brand loyal across all product categories are confounded by inherent product differences. As such, a study based on product X showing a relationship between brand loyalty and certain characteristics is not necessarily contradicting another study based on product Y that concludes that the same characteristics are unrelated to brand loyalty.

Studies based on correlations also generally do not permit the researcher to impute cause and effect relationships. The latter require carefully controlled laboratory and field experiments. Greater use of panels specifically designed for a longitudinal analysis of brand loyalty (as contrasted with existing commercial panels) would probably accelerate progress.

Finally, progress may be improved by the use of more powerful statistical techniques. Simplistic analysis based on proportions and rank correlations should at least be supplemented with factor analysis, regression analysis, AID analysis, discriminant analysis, and various clustering approaches.

BRAND LOYALTY MODELS

A wide variety of mathematical models have been designed in an attempt to understand brand-loyalty behavior over time. The primary emphasis has been on *stochastic* models, which treat the response of consumers in the marketplace as the outcome of some probabilistic process. A stochastic model, with its built-in probability component, is distinguished from or contrasted with *deterministic* models, in which an attempt is made to predict behavior in exact or nonprobabilistic terms.

The consumer behavior model used throughout the book is deterministic. You might therefore ask why we switch to stochastic models when analyzing a special type of decision, namely brand loyal purchases. The reason stochastic models are used is to allow for a multitude of variables that are not or cannot be measured. Stochastic models are really a simplification of reality, although it may not seem that way when you look at some of the models.

There are two basic philosophies of stochastic models. The first philosophy recognizes that many factors determine the outcome of behavior even though most of these factors are not measured nor explicitly included in the model of market response. Such factors may include a wide range of individual consumer variables (personality, attitudes, income, and so forth) as well as a wide range of exogenous variables such as advertising, price, competitive activity. Even though these variables are not explicitly considered in the model, their effect is accounted for in the stochastic nature of the response. Montgomery and Urban conclude:

This procedure is parsimonious in that consumer behavior may often be described by relatively simple stochastic models, whereas the adoption of a deterministic approach would require exceedingly complex models.[58]

A second philosophy of stochastic models is based upon the premise that not only is the model of market response stochastic but the actual consumer process is stochastic. Stated alternatively, consumer choices are random (probabilistic) because there is a *stochastic element in the brain* that influences choice. Thus, it is less possible even in principle to provide an explanation for the (stochastic) component than it is to provide an explanation for the outcome of the toss of a coin.[59] This is in sharp contrast with the more dominant stream of consumer research. Here the underlying premise is that behavior is caused and can therefore be explained, at least in principle, even if adequate data do not exist to account for behavior at any point in time. Most of the stochastic models described in the remaining part of the chapter have not explicitly considered which philosophy is true, and similar models have been used by researchers of both philosophies. Bass, a proponent of the philosophy of stochastic brain processes, concluded:

It will never be possible to prove conclusively that behavior is fundamentally stochastic or fundamentally deterministic since it will

[58]David B. Montgomery and Glen L. Urban, *Management Science in Marketing* (Englewood Cliffs, New Jersey: Prentice-Hall, Inc., 1969), 54.

[59]Frank M. Bass, ''The Theory of Stochastic Preference and Brand Switching,'' *Journal of Marketing Research,* vol. 11 (February 1974), 1-20.

never be possible to measure all of the variables which influence choice.[60]

Following a brief overview of the basic logic and terminology of models, this section examines the most widely used ones, describing the basic characteristics of each without a high degree of mathematical sophistication, pointing out their strengths and limitations.[61] This section closes with a discussion of potentially useful areas for future research and application.

Overview of Brand-Loyalty Models

The models that follow describe a functional relationship between the probability of choosing a brand during a purchase occasion and the factors that have an effect on this probability.[62] Some of these factors include feedback from past purchases, influence of exogenous market forces, and factors indigenous to various households.

Purchase-event feedback is normally expressed in terms of the number of previous purchases that are allowed to have an effect on the present purchase. The effect of market forces is normally incorporated in the form of a time trend term in the model. Finally, population heterogeneity is treated by allowing the parameters of a given model to have a distribution over the entire population, by *a priori* dividing the population into more homogeneous groups and developing model parameters separately for each group, or by explicitly including in the model some of the factors causing heterogeneity. The models presented below cover a wide range of complexity, from the very simple Bernoulli model that treats the population as being homogeneous, with no purchase event feedback and no effect of external factors; to the more complex probability diffusion models that permit inclusion of effects due to most of the factors.

The study of brand loyalty models often requires considerable mathematical sophistication. In preparing this section of the chapter, an effort has been made to avoid those mathematical concepts that would keep many readers from understanding the material. It is necessary to use mathematical symbols to describe the models but an attempt is also made to explain the meaning of each model in words that can be understood by any reader who will make an effort to understand the concepts and basic relationships important to the model. Readers with more affinity for mathematical topics may want to refer to the source materials of the models, referred to in the footnotes.

[60]Bass, "Theory of Stochastic Preference," 2.

[61]For an excellent summary of these models, see Massy et al., *Stochastic Models.*

[62]In *Stochastic Models of Buying Behavior,* Massy, Montgomery, and Morrison provide a clear distinction between "brand choice models" and "purchase incidence models." Whereas the former deal with the probability of choosing a brand on a given purchase occasion, the latter are concerned with purchase timing and amount of purchase. Although brand choice models may be modified to include purchase timing, specialized purchase incidence models are often more useful when describing specific sales prediction during a given period. Because of the greater relevance of brand choice models to our discussion, the presentation is limited to models in this category. For a throrough analysis of some of the purchase incidence models, including the negative binomial, Poisson, logistic, exponential and others, the student is referred to chapters 8 and through 11.

Bernoulli Models

The earliest investigations of brand loyalty assumed, at least implicitly, that the behavior could be described as a Bernoulli process in which the consumer is assumed to have a constant probability p of purchasing the brand under study.[63] The probability p is determined from aggregate brand choice data and is assumed to be independent of all external influences, prior purchases, or consumer characteristics.

This process can be represented simply for some brand, A, and by a composite of all other brands, B. The probability of purchasing brand A at a purchase occasion t, is represented as $p(A_t)$ and is determined from aggregate brand choices between A and B.

The behavioral premise of early Bernoulli models suggests there is no feedback from the purchase event. The response probability may be free to change over time, however, which permits the model to reflect changes in anticipated or unanticipated circumstances such as the limited number of brands available at a store, specials, or out-of-stock conditions. Therefore, if Brand A becomes available in more stores, for example, the probability of buying Brand A can be expected to rise for many consumers who purchase that brand, all other factors remaining constant.

Modifications to the Bernoulli Model

Several variations of the basic Bernoulli model have been developed by explicitly considering the heterogeneity in the population. These include the compound Bernoulli model and the dynamic Bernoulli model.

1. Compound Bernoulli Model   In the compound Bernoulli model, the probability p is constant for each particular individual but varies over the entire population according to some prespecified probability distribution. In other words, different individuals in the population are permitted to have different fixed values of p.[64]

2. Dynamic Bernoulli Model   In the dynamic Bernoulli model, the purchase probability p is not only allowed to vary between individuals, but is also allowed to change from one purchase situation to another for the same customer.[65]

The basic model as well as its variations all assume a zero-order process; that is, they assume that past history has no effect on the present or future purchase probability. Several other models also are developed making such an assumption. Two of these—the probability diffusion model and the New Trier model—are described below.

Probability Diffusion Model

The probability diffusion model was proposed by Montgomery as a *zero-order model*;[66] that is, it does not consider purchase-event feedback. The

---

[63]Brown, "Brand Loyalty"; Cunningham, "Perceived Risk."

[64]Massy et al., *Stochastic Models*, 59.

[65]Ronald A. Howard, "Dynamic Inference," *Journal of Operations Research Society of America*, vol. 13 (September 1965), 712-733.

[66]Massy et al., *Stochastic Models*, ch. 6.

underlying probabilities are subject to change according to yet another stochastic process. Hence, an individual's response probability is said to be *nonstationary.* The model is also *heterogeneous* since different respondents may have different response probabilities, even though the same response probability change process holds for all respondents.

The Montgomery probability-diffusion model can be described by outlining the major underlying assumptions:

1. Let the brand-choice behavior be described as a dichotomous selection (as in the case of learning models).

2. Assume that each respondent possesses a number N of hypothetical elements, some of which are at any given response occasion associated with response A, and the remainder with response B.[67]

3. If at a particular response occasion t, the respondent has i of his N elements associated with response A, his probability p_t of making response A on that occasion is i/N.

4. The response elements change allegiance between A and B according to a mechanism that can be described as follows:

$$\lambda_i = (\alpha + \sqrt{i})(N - i)$$
$$\mu_i = (\beta + (N - i)v)i$$

where:

$\alpha =$ the probability of an element associated with response B to change to A

$\beta =$ the propensity of change from A to B

$v =$ a proportionality factor whereby the propensity of each element to change allegiance is increased by an amount for each element associated with the opposite response.

The first expression above is a product of the single-element propensity to change from response B to A and the number of response elements in B. The second expression is interpreted similarly.

The above assumptions, together with the assumption of no purchase feedback and independence of responses of various consumers, lead Montgomery to describe the behavior of the average probability of purchase over time. Thus he shows that the expected value of p_t can be described by the following functional relationship:

$$m(t) = E[p(t)] = p_j(t_0)e^{-(\alpha + \beta)(t - t_0)} + \frac{\alpha}{\alpha + \beta}[1 - e^{-(\alpha + \beta)(t - t_0)}].$$

In the function, t_0 is the time at which the model was first applied and $p_j(t_0)$ is the initial probability of purchase for individual j. The equation is represented by the curve in Figure 20.1.

The model represents a change over time in the expected probability of purchase, independent of any purchase feedback effect. The change

---

[67]Although these elements may have behavioral significance, they are proposed strictly as hypothetical constructs for modeling purposes.

**Figure 20.1
Behavior of
Expected Value of
p_t for the
Probability
Diffusion Model of
Brand Loyalty**

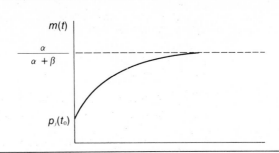

is therefore assumed to be the result of external environmental factors including promotion.

Modifications to the Probability Diffusion Model

The inability of the probability diffusion model to consider purchase event feedback led Jones to develop what he terms a dual-effects model.[68] In essence, Jones proposes a modification to the propensities of change of the response elements as follows:

$$\lambda_i = (\alpha_n + \sqrt{i})(N - i)$$
$$\mu_i = [\beta_n + \sqrt{(N - i)}]i$$

where subscript n denotes the nth purchase, and α_n and β_n are allowed to change from one purchase to another according to a certain mechanism.[69] Thus a simple mechanism would be

$$\alpha_n = \begin{cases} \alpha_{n-1} + \lambda & \text{if } A \text{ was purchased at } n \\ \alpha_{n-1} & \text{if } B \text{ was purchased at } n \end{cases}$$

$$\beta_n = \begin{cases} \beta_{n-1} & \text{if } A \text{ was purchased at } n \\ \beta_{n-1} + \phi & \text{if } B \text{ was purchased at } n \end{cases}$$

Using this model, the change in average purchase probability through time can be expressed by the curve in Figure 20.2.

New Trier Model

The New Trier model was developed specifically to model the brand choice behavior of a consumer who has purchased a brand that was previously unfamiliar. The brand does not have to be a new brand in the marketplace, only a brand not used before by that consumer or one used so long ago that the consumer has essentially forgotten it. This model was developed by Aaker and is a zero-order model as well as heterogeneous and nonstationary.[70]

[68]J. Morgan Jones, "A Dual-Effects Model of Brand Choice," *Journal of Marketing Research,* vol. 7 (November 1970), 458-464; also J. Morgan Jones, "A Comparison of Three Models of Brand Choice," *Journal of Marketing Research,* vol. 7 (November 1970), 466-473.

[69]Jones, "A Comparison of Three Models."

[70]David A. Aaker, "The New-Trier Stochastic Model of Brand Choice," *Management Science,* vol. 17 (April 1971), 435-450. Also see David A. Aaker, "A Measure of Brand Acceptance," *Journal of Marketing Research,* vol. 9 (May 1972), 160-167.

**Figure 20.2
Behavior of
Expected Value of
p_t for Dual-Effects
Model of Brand
Loyalty**

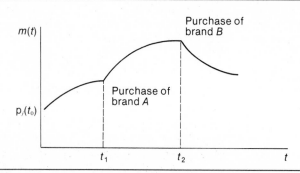

Source: J. Morgan Jones, "A Dual-Effects Model of Brand Choice," *Journal of Marketing Research,* vol. 7 (November 1970), 461. Reprinted with permission from the *Journal of Marketing Research* published by the American Marketing Association.

The model assumes that there is a trial period after the initial purchase, during which the probability of purchasing the brand for that family remains constant. After a number of trial-period purchases, which is assumed to vary from consumer to consumer, the consumer is assumed to reach a decision and therefore to have a new probability of purchasing the brand. The probabilities of purchasing the new brand during and after the trial period are assumed to be distributed across the population according to independent beta distributions, thus achieving interconsumer heterogeneity.

Aaker's New Trier model includes an opportunity for the consumer to reject the brand in the posttrial period. The probability of the consumer rejecting the brand is assumed to decrease with time. In the postdecision period, the consumer has a constant probability. The outputs and uses of the New Trier model are similar to those yielded by the probability diffusion model.

Zero-order models of the type described above have originated in fairly simplistic formulations of limited usefulness. They have developed, however, into the more sophisticated models incorporating heterogeneity and nonstationarity that have provided a good fit to empirical brand-data in specific product classes. The assumption of a zero-order process, however, limits the usefulness of the model, causing development of the Markov models described below.

Markov Models

Unlike Bernoulli models, Markov models consider the influence of past purchases on the probability of current purchases. The number of previous purchases that are assumed to affect the current purchases is designated by the *order* of the model. For example first order means the last purchase, second order means the last two purchases, and so on.

The First-Order Stationary Markov Model

To illustrate the characteristics of a first-order Markov model, consider a product category with three brands: *A, B,* and *C.* Based on past pur-

Table 20.1
Hypothetical
Markov
Transitional
Probabilities

	Next Purchase			
Last purchase	A	B	C	Total
A	0.7	0.1	0.2	1.0
B	0.3	0.6	0.1	1.0
C	0.4	0.1	0.5	1.0

chase data for a sample of consumers, the researcher estimates the conditional (or transitional) probabilities of moving from one state to another in *any two* consecutive time periods. These transitional probabilities are shown in Table 20.1.

Table 20.1 is interpreted as follows. If a consumer purchased Brand A during a certain period, then during the next period there is a 70 percent chance that he will buy *A* again, a 10 percent chance of buying *B*, and a 20 percent chance of buying *C*. Similarly, a buyer of Brand B during the last period would have a 30 percent probability of buying *A* during the next period, a 60 percent chance of buying *B*, and a ten percent chance of buying *C*.

Table 20.1 is called a transitional matrix. It is essentially a measure of brand-switching (or conversely, brand-loyal) behavior. Most Markov models assume that the matrix is stationary; that is, the transition probabilities remain unchanged through time.

To illustrate the mechanics of the Markov process, it is useful to compute the probabilities of a consumer's purchasing Brands A, B, or C during future purchase periods, given the actual purchase during the present period. Thus, if the consumers purchased Brand A during period 1, the probability of buying the different brands during periods 2, 3, 4, and 5 would be as follows:[71]

	Brand		
Period	A	B	C
2	0.70	0.10	0.20
3	0.60	0.15	0.25
4	0.57	0.17	0.26
5	0.55	0.19	0.26

[71]These probabilities can be computed by methods of matrix algebra or by simply tracing behavior by means of a tree diagram. Only sample computations are shown below.

For a consumer buying *A* during period 1, the probabilities during period 2 are obvious. The probability of his buying *A* during period 3 would be $0.7 \times 0.7 + 0.1 \times 0.3 + 0.2 \times 0.4 = .60$; for *B* it would be $0.7 \times 0.1 + 0.1 \times 0.6 + 0.2 \times 0.1 = 0.15$; and for *C* it would be $0.7 \times 0.2 + 0.1 \times 0.1 + 0.2 \times 0.5 = 0.25$. For the student familiar with matrix algebra, all nine probabilities for period 3 (three each for different purchases during period 1) can be obtained by multiplying the transition matrix by itself. The new matrix can be postmultiplied by the original transition matrix to obtain probabilities for period 4.

The probabilities that we have computed here should not be confused with the transition matrix probabilities. The latter simply refer to the effect of the *immediately preceding* purchase expressed in the form of the probability of purchase during the next period. The probabilities that we have computed (using the transition probabilities) correspond to many future periods *given* the actual purchase during the first period and *assuming a stationary transition matrix* between each pair of consecutive periods.

On the other hand, if Brand B were purchased during period 1, the corresponding probabilities for future periods would be as follows:

	Brand		
Period	A	B	C
2	0.30	0.60	0.10
3	0.43	0.40	0.17
4	0.49	0.30	0.21
5	0.52	0.25	0.23

Similar computations could be made for Brand C by following the procedures outlined in Footnote 71.

If this process were continued indefinitely, the probabilities of the consumer being in states *A, B,* and *C* during future periods will approach a set of equilibrium, or steady-state values. These steady-state probabilities are independent of past history; that is, regardless of the actual purchases during period 1, the probability of the consumer's buying *A, B,* or *C* after a theoretically infinite number of transitions would approach a predetermined set of values dependent only on the transition matrix. For the transition matrix in the example, these steady state probabilities would be 0.54, 0.20, and 0.26.[72]

For a more detailed discussion of Markov models and their characteristics, the reader is referred to the work of Herniter and Magee,[73] Maffei,[74] Lipstein,[75] Harary and Lipstein,[76] and others noted below.[77]

Criticisms of the First-Order Stationary Markov Model

The model described above is plagued with numerous problems. First, since there is evidence that brand choice is influenced by many past

[72]The steady-state probabilities p_1, p_2, and p_3 can be derived by solving the following set of simultaneous equations (stated in matrix notation):

$$(p_1 p_2 p_3) \begin{matrix} 0.7 & 0.1 & 0.2 \\ 0.3 & 0.6 & 0.1 \\ 0.14 & 0.1 & 0.5 \end{matrix} = (p_1 p_2 p_3)$$

and

$$p_1 + p_2 + p_3 = 1.$$

[73]Jerome D. Herniter and John F. Magee, "Customer Behavior as a Markov Process," *Operations Research,* vol. 9 (January-February 1961), 105-122.

[74]Richard B. Maffei, "Brand Preferences and Simple Markov Processes," *Operations Research,* vol. 8 (March-April 1960), 210-218.

[75]Benjamin Lipstein, "The Dynamics of Brand Loyalty and Brand Switching," *Proceedings of the 5th Annual Conference of the Advertising Research Foundation* (New York: The Foundation, 1959).

[76]F. Harary and B. Lipstein, "The Dynamics of Brand Loyalty: A Markovian Approach," *Operations Research,* vol. 10 (January-February 1962), 19-40.

[77] George P. H. Styan and H. Smith, Jr., "Markov Chains Applied to Marketing," *Journal of Marketing Research,* vol. 1 (February 1964), 50-55; J. E. Draper and L. H. Nolin, "A Markov Chain Analysis of Brand Preference," *Journal of Advertising Research,* vol. 4 (September 1964), 33-39; J. S. Stock, "Paired Market Choice Model—A Simplified Approach to Markov Chains," in Henry Gomez (ed.), *Innovation—Key to Marketing Progress* (Chicago: American Marketing Association, 1963), 99-105.

purchases, the first-order assumption has been challenged by many as being too restrictive.[78]

Second, the stationarity assumption underlying the transition matrix has been criticized. Thus although Maffei[79] and Styan and Smith[80] report the acceptability of the assumption in their research, they have been strongly challenged by Ehrenberg[81] and Massy,[82] the latter concluding that stationarity is the exception rather than the rule.

The homogeneity assumption is another problem. The model assumes that all buyers have the same transition probabilities. Several researchers have demonstrated that homogeneity is inconsistent with empirical evidence.[83]

The aggregation problem is a fourth criticism. This problem occurs because the probability of a particular consumer's buying a brand is actually inferred from the relative frequency of purchasing that brand in the aggregate sample. In other words, if 60 consumers in a group of 100 buy Brand A, each of the 100 customers is said to have a 60 percent probability of buying that brand. Howard[84] suggested a vector Markov model which, while resolving the aggregation problem, necessitates making other unacceptable assumptions.[85]

A fifth problem inherent in Markov models deals with interpurchase time. All consumers cannot be expected to purchase on a precise cycle with a prespecified interpurchase time. Approaches that attempt to overcome this objection include the introduction of a dummy no purchase brand to take the place of an actual purchase. However, a purchase versus no purchase decision is different from a brand-choice decision. As a result, Howard[86] has suggested a time-dependent semi-Markov model that explicitly treats time as a random variable. Kuehn and Rohloff[87] and Morrison[88] offer other approaches to incorporate different interpurchase times.

Other criticisms of the first-order Markov model revolve around the problem of inferring transition probabilities for the entire population based on sample estimates. Updating these probabilities, based on other rele-

---

[78]See, for example, Howard and Sheth, *Theory of Buyer Behavior,* 237-238.

[79]Maffei, "Brand Preferences."

[80]Styan and Smith, "Markov Chains."

[81]A. S. C. Ehrenberg, "An Appraisal of Markov Brand Switching Models," *Journal of Marketing Research,* vol. 2 (November 1965), 353.

[82]William F. Massy, "Order and Homogeneity of Family Specific Brand Switching Processes," *Journal of Marketing,* vol. 3 (February 1966), 53.

[83]See, for example, Ronald E. Frank, "Brand Choice as a Probability Process," *Journal of Business,* vol. 35 (January 1962), 43-56.

[84]Ronald A. Howard, "Stochastic Process Models of Consumer Behavior," *Journal of Advertising Research,* vol. 3 (September 1963), 35-40.

[85]Howard and Sheth, *Theory of Buyer Behavior,* 236-237.

[86]Howard, "Stochastic Process Models," 40.

[87]Alfred A. Kuehn and A. C. Rohloff, "New Dimensions in Analysis of Brand Switching," in Fred E. Webster (ed.), *New Directions in Marketing* (Chicago: American Marketing Association, 1965), 297-308.

[88]Donald G. Morrison, "Interpurchase Time and Brand Loyalty," *Journal of Marketing Research,* vol. 3 (August 1966), 289-292.

vant information, also presents problems. Under these conditions, Herniter and Howard recommend use of a Bayesian framework for revising *a priori* probabilities.[89]

A seventh problem lies in determining how issues such as multiple-brand purchases or multiple purchases of the same brand should be handled. Unfortunately, most of the recommended approaches necessitate forcing actual data into an artificial format suitable for Markov analysis.[90]

Finally, it is difficult to obtain valid purchase data unless expensive longitudinal designs are used.[91] This may limit the profitable use of the model.

Proposed Modifications to the First-Order Markov Model
A variety of attempts have been made to overcome the limitations of the first-order stationary Markov model. The most popular variations are discussed below.

1. Models Overcoming the Stationarity Assumption Lipstein attempted to deal with objections to the stationarity assumption by developing a Markov model of brand loyalty that has a nonstationary transition matrix.[92]

2. Models Overcoming the Homogeneity Assumption Morrison suggested a variety of ways of overcoming the unrealistic homogeneity assumption.[93] One approach is to divide consumers into two groups—hard-core loyal buyers and potential switchers. This dichotomous classification can be extended into a continuum of loyalty, yielding what are generally termed compound Markov models.[94] However, these models require a dichotomous treatment of the brands available; for example, the favorite brand versus all other brands. Examples of transition matrices under these conditions are discussed below.[95]

1. *The symmetric first-order Markov model.* In this model the transition matrix appears as follows and *p* varies over the entire population according to some prespecified probability distribution.[96]

[89]Jerome D. Herniter and Ronald Howard, "Stochastic Marketing Models," in D. B. Hertz and R. T. Eddison (eds.), *Progress in Operations Research,* vol. 2 (New York: John Wiley & Sons, 1964).

[90]See, for example, Draper and Nolin, "A Markov Chain Analysis," 33-39; Styan and Smith, "Markov Chains Applied to Marketing," 50-55.

[91]See, for example, Donald H. Granbois and James F. Engel, "The Longitudinal Approach to Studying Marketing Behavior," in Peter D. Bennett (ed.), *Marketing and Economic Development* (Chicago: American Marketing Association, 1965), 205-221.

[92]B. Lipstein, "A Mathematical Model of Consumer Behavior," *Journal of Marketing Research,* vol. 2 (August 1965), 265-269; B. Lipstein, "Test Marketing: A Perturbation in the Market Place," *Management Science,* vol. 14 (1968), 3437-3448.

[93]Massy et al., *Stochastic Models,* 92-93.

[94]Donald G. Morrison, "Testing Brand-Switching Models," *Journal of Marketing Research,* vol. 3 (November 1966), 401-409.

[95]Massy et al., *Stochastic Models,* 118-136.

[96]The β distribution has often been employed for this purpose. For details, see Massy et al., *Stochastic Models,* 60-61.

		Brand Purchased at time $t + 1$	
		A	**B**
Brand purchased at time t	A	p	$1 - p$
	B	$1 - p$	p

A = brand being studied
B = all other brands

2. *The brand-loyal model.* In this model p is distributed as before, but another parameter, k $(0 < k < 1)$, which is the same for all individuals, is also introduced. The reasoning, as seen in the matrix below, is that an individual with a high probability of remaining with his Brand A will also have a higher probability of leaving Brand B (other brands) to buy A, than another individual with a lower p.

		Time $t + 1$	
		A	**B**
Time t	A	p	$1 - p$
	B	kp	$1 - kp$

3. *The last purchase-loyal model.* This model uses somewhat different logic. It argues that a consumer with a high p is more loyal to the brand he purchased last—regardless of which brand it was—than a consumer with a lower p. (Both k and p are defined as before.)

		Time $t + 1$	
		A	**B**
Time t	A	p	$1 - p$
	B	$1 - kp$	kp

4. *The general first-order compound model.* In this model the parameters p and q are jointly distributed according to some prespecified distribution.

		Time $t + 1$	
		A	**B**
Time t	A	p	$1 - p$
	B	$1 - q$	q

Using the coffee purchases of 531 members of a *Chicago Tribune* panel, Massy, Montgomery, and Morrison obtained a very good fit between the data and "the brand loyal model" described above. They concluded that if strong loyalty exists, it is generated toward a particular brand and not toward the most recently purchased brand.[97] In addition, they concluded that loyal customers are more "Bernoulli" than nonloyals, meaning that recent purchase decisions have a smaller effect on the current purchase decisions of loyals than they do on nonloyals.[98]

3. Models Overcoming the First-Order Assumption   Another objection to the basic Markov model is that it is first-order; that is, it considers only the previous purchase when modeling the current purchase situation. One way of overcoming this objection is to use higher order Markov formulations. For example, a second-order Markov model considers the effect of two previous purchases. The transition matrix is as follows:

| | | Purchases During Times $t - 1$ and t | | | |
		AA	BA	AB	BB
Purchases	AA	p_1	—	$1 - p_1$	—
during times	BA	p_2	—	$1 - p_2$	—
$t - 2$ and $t - 1$	AB	—	$1 - q_2$	—	q_2
	BB	—	$1 - q_1$	—	q_1

Some of the entries in the matrix are blank because the corresponding combinations of states are not possible. For example, a consumer who purchased A in $t - 2$ and B in $t - 1$ could not purchase A in $t - 1$ and either A or B in time t.

Second-order models are unquestionably more realistic than first-order models. However, the data requirements of the higher order models are usually so large that they are unmanageable.

Linear Learning Models

Models in this category are an outgrowth of the work done by Kuehn[100] based on the learning theory constructs of Bush and Mosteller.[101] The primary concept underlying the development of these models is that past brand choices affect future behavior, and that there is a linear relationship between pre- and postpurchase probabilities. More specifically, let the purchasing process be represented in the form of dichotomous choice A representing the brand under study and B all other brands. Also let p_t be the probability of buying A during trial t. Using subscripts to represent trials, the model specifies two relationships termed the purchase operator and the rejection operator:

purchase operator: $p_{t + 1} = \alpha + \beta + \lambda p_t$, if Brand A is purchased at t

[97]Massy et al., *Stochastic Models*, 118-136.

[98]Note that when $k = 1$, the brand-loyal model is the same as the Bernoulli model. In other words, the higher the k ($0 < k < 1$), the more "Bernoulli" the group of consumers.

[99]The model does not allow the consumer to buy both brands during any one time period.

[100]Alfred A. Kuehn, "Consumer Brand Choice."

[101]Robert Bush and Frederick Mosteller, *Stochastic Models for Learning* (New York: John Wiley & Sons, 1955).

**Figure 20.3
Graphical
Representation of
Linear Learning
Model**

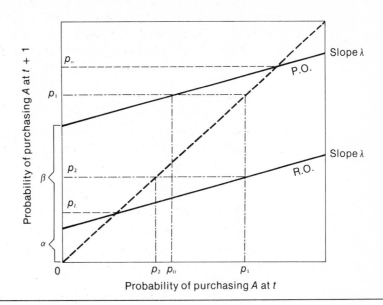

or

rejection operator: $p_{t+1} = \alpha + \lambda p_t$, if Brand B is purchased at t.

These two operators are graphically illustrated in Figure 20.3. The parameters α and β representing the intercepts ($\alpha + \beta$ for the purchase operator and α for the rejection operator) and λ, the common slope, are assumed to be the same for all consumers and are estimated from panel data.

Suppose at trial $t = 0$ there is a certain probability p_0 that a particular respondent would buy Brand A. If s/he actually buys Brand A during that trial, the probability of buying A on the next trial is determined by refering to the purchase operator. A perpendicular drawn from p_0 to intersect the purchase operator will yield the probability at t_1 on the Y axis. This can be transferred to the X axis with the help of the 45° line. Now at t_1, suppose the consumer buys a brand other than A (that is, B); the probability of buying A at trial t_2 can now be obtained by referring to the rejection operator. The purchase probabilities can thus be revised after each purchase by referring to the appropriate operator.

An interesting characteristic of the model is that the purchase probability approaches, but never exceeds, the maximum value p_u (obtained at the intersection of the purchase operator and the 45° line). Similarly it never falls below p_l (obtained at the intersection of the rejection operator and the 45° line). This is equivalent to saying that consumers generally will not develop such a strong brand loyalty as to ensure either complete acceptance or rejection of a given brand. Another characteristic of the model is that consecutive purchases of Brand A increase the probability of buying A on the next purchase, but only at a decreasing rate.

The model has been tested extensively using many branded nondurable consumer grocery and drug items and was found very useful in analyzing brand-switching data.[102] Practical applications of the model, in the form of analyzing effects of advertising and other merchandising influences, have also been suggested.[103] However, in general, learning models have been less popular than their Markov counterparts, especially among practitioners. This may be due to the fact that it is more difficult to estimate the parameters of the learning model, as well as the limitations imposed by the need to treat brand choice in a dichotomous fashion.

Modifications to the Learning Model

Modifications to the basic model include treatment of population heterogeneity, resulting in what is called a compound learning model. Another modification involves recasting the learning model into a special type of first-order Markov formulation.[104] The learning Markov model, so derived, treats the transition probabilities as a function of two effects—a retention effect and a merchandising activity effect. The former represents the fraction of purchases retained by a brand through habit, whereas the latter represents the effect of the brand's merchandising strategy. Finally, under special conditions the linear learning model would degenerate into a Bernoulli or Markov model. Thus if $\lambda = 0$ (the slope of the purchase or rejection operator), the relationships specifying the purchase and rejection operators are equivalent to the transmission matrix:

	Time $t + 1$	
	A	**B**
Time t A	$\alpha + \beta$	$1 - \alpha - \beta$
B	α	$1 - \alpha$

Similarly if $\alpha = \beta = 0$ and $\lambda = 1$, $p_{t+1} = p_t$, and we have the simple zero-order Bernoulli model.

Entropy Loyalty Model

One of the more interesting models to be developed is the entropy model discussed by Carman and Stromberg and more fully developed by Herniter.[105] The concept of entropy is borrowed from the study of thermody-

---

[102]Alfred A. Kuehn and Ralph L. Day, "A Probabilistic Approach to Consumer Behavior," in Revis Cox, Wroe Alderson, and Stanley Shapiro (eds.), *Theory in Marketing* (Homewood, Ill.: Irwin, 1964), 380-390.

[103]See, for example, Alfred A. Kuehn and Ralph L. Day, "Probabilistic Models of Consumer Buying Behavior," *Journal of Marketing*, vol. 29 (October 1964), 27-31: Alfred A. Kuehn, "How Advertising Performance Depends on Other Marketing Factors," *Journal of Advertising Research*, vol. 2 (March 1962), 2-10.

[104]Alfred E. Kuehn, "A Model for Budgeting Advertising," in Frank M. Bass et al. (eds.), *Mathematical Models and Methods in Marketing* (Homewood, Ill.: Irwin, 1961), 315-348; A. C. Rohloff, "New Ways to Analyze Brand-to-Brand Competition," in Stephen Greyser (ed.), *Toward Scientific Marketing* (Chicago: American Marketing Association, 1963), 224-232.

[105]Jerome Herniter, "An Entropy Model of Brand Purchase Behavior," *Journal of Marketing Research*, vol. 10 (November 1973), 361-375. Also see James M. Carman and John L. Stromberg, "A Comparison of Some Measure of Brand Loyalty" (working paper No. 26, Berkeley: Institute of Business and Economic Research, University of California, July 1967).

namics and is a measure of uncertainty in a probabilistic system. It is an objective function that can be used to maximize the unknown probabilities of a system. Herniter considered the problem that brand loyalty is not the same as purchase behavior but for operational purposes assumes a "customer's preference for a brand reflects his or her probability of purchasing the brand on any given occasion."[106]

The entropy model is based upon a multinominal distribution to account for changes in response probabilities. The basic data are market share of brands in a market, constrained by the number of brands. Thus, entropy is used as a measure of uncertainty. From this a measure of loyalty can be determined that is defined for all values of the parameters of the underlying multinominal model. It is derived as a natural extension of a likelihood ratio test of the null hypothesis for complete nonloyalty and therefore has a maximum value for the completely nonloyal state and a minimal value for a state that can reasonably be considered most loyal.

The entropy model is of considerable value to marketers because of its reliance on market share data that are more readily available than many other kinds of data based upon characteristics of individual consumers. The use of the model in empirical tests has resulted in good predictions although the model as originally proposed by Herniter was somewhat limited in applications because of the difficulty in applying it to a market with more than a few brands.[107]

Cognitive Brand Loyalty Model

The problem of omitting brand preferences in discussing brand loyalty and focusing only on repeat purchase behavior has been treated in research by Jarvis who developed a cognitive brand-loyalty model.[108] Jarvis recognized that brand-loyal behavior in most other models appears to have little or no relationship to the consumer's sensitivity to marketing variables such as pricing, advertising or the introduction of new brands. His study therefore examined the relationship between cognitive (or attitudinal) brand loyalty and several marketing-related variables. These variables included the price increase in one's usually purchased brand which is necessary to induce the consumer to switch to an alternative, the likelihood of purchasing a new brand within a product class, and the evaluation of a communication describing a new brand.

Cognitive brand loyalty was measured using a modified form of the social judgment ordered alternatives methodology. In this methodology, subjects were asked to place the brands with which they were aware in each product class into three "affective" regions according to their acceptability for the next purchase event. These regions were "acceptable, not acceptable, and uncertain."

[106]Jerome Herniter, "A Comparison of the Entropy Model and the Hendry Model," *Journal of Marketing Research,* vol. 11 (February 1974), 21-29.

[107]See Frank M. Bass, "Theory of Stochastic Preference," *Journal of Marketing Research,* vol. 11 (February 1974), 1-20, for methods of overcoming these problems.

[108]Lance P. Jarvis, "An Empirical Investigation of Cognitive Brand Loyalty and Product Class Importance as Mediators of Consumer Brand Choice Behavior" (doctoral dissertation from University Park, Pa: Pennsylvania State University, 1972).

These categories were classified as *AR* (acceptance), *RR* (rejection), and *NR* (noncommitment). Cognitive loyalty strength was measured by two indexes: (1) *RR/AR,* and (2) *RR/AR* [1.0 − *NR*], where each region was expressed as a proportion of the brands of which an individual was aware. For both criteria, cognitive loyalty was found to be stronger as the resulting index number increased. The value of a model such as this is its ability to analyze the intentions of consumers rather than utilizing only behavior that is difficult to observe and collect data on.

EVALUATION OF BRAND LOYALTY MODELS

A wide variety of models have been employed in an attempt to understand and predict brand-loyalty behavior. The complexity of brand choice behavior has been the reason so many different models have been developed, each trying to solve specific problems that vary between product categories and buying situations. Numerous assumptions, discussed in conjunction with each of the models, have been introduced by researchers in order to make the models manageable. At the same time, those assumptions frequently create artificialities. The zero-order assumption, suppression of population heterogeneity, and inability to incorporate the influence of external factors are some of the problems associated with many models.

Problems of Brand Loyalty Models

Some problems that are specific to stochastic models of brand loyalty include the following:

1. There may be a many-to-one mapping of models into a set of data; that is, several alternative models with quite different underlying structures may be consistent with the empirical data. Therefore, a need exists for developing methods that discriminate among competing models to determine the appropriate model for a specific product category, market structure and timing, or buying situation.

2. The effects of heterogeneity and nonstationarity of response probability may be confounded in stochastic models.

3. The stochastic process generating the response of probabilities may itself change. Although changes in the process will generally occur much more slowly than changes in choice probabilities, this still suggests the need for developing methods that assume only short-run stationarity, even for models that allow the choice probability to change.

4. A combining of classes may create a problem when an "n-alternative" real market is collapsed into a "2-alternative" model market. If combining all "other brands" into a composite brand (as is the case in some models) is to leave the structure of the system unchanged, then a stochastic operater on the state space of the system must be of a special form. (Both Markov and linear-learning models involve stochastic operators.)

5. Most of the loyalty models avoid the issue of multibrand loyalty. Yet, many researchers have empirically documented the commonsense notion that some consumers exhibit varying degrees of loyalty to several brands in a product category.[109] Some of the more recent work is making attempts at treating multibrand loyalty and provides a greater understanding of the true nature of brand loyalty.[110]

6. Most of the stochastic models do not consider the attitude component of brand loyalty or assume that preference and purchase probabilities are equivalent. This may be one of the factors introducing a degree of artificiality in the models.

Empirical Comparison of Models

Many brand loyalty models have been compared to each other in empirical research by fitting two or more of them to the same data base and then comparing their fit. The fit of the model to the data set is usually determined by a chi-square test with the model to be tested as the null hypothesis. A complementary method of evaluating the fit of models to the empirical data is to examine the estimated parameters of the model to see if any of them attain infeasible values.

Montgomery and Jones have fitted a number of models of the MRCA panel data for *Crest* toothpaste. Montgomery fitted four models: the brand-loyal and last-purchase loyal Markov models, the linear-learning model (modified to allow heterogeneity), and the probability-diffusion model to data for *Crest* toothpaste. The linear-learning and the probability-diffusion models seemed to provide a significantly better overall fit to this set of data than the Markov models. The probability-diffusion model seemed to be superior to the linear-learning model in the very unstable postendorsement period.

Jones, also using the *Crest* data, used considerably different criteria for including households in his sample, and classified people into average interpurchase interval segments on the basis of their postendorsement behavior, in contrast to Montgomery's use of their pre-endorsement behavior. This gave a slightly better overall fit for the linear learning model. In the same study, Jones also fitted the three versions of his dual-effects model to the *Crest* data. One version, where the transition intensities change by an additive mechanism, dominated the other two versions for this data base. Even this additive version of the dual-effects model was generally dominated by the linear learning and probability-diffusion models in most segments.

Aaker has also empirically compared his New Trier model and the heterogeneous linear learning model using two sets of panel data on a frequently purchased consumer goods product. In both cases, the linear learning model provided a better fit to the data, as indicated by the *p* levels associated with the chi-square goodness-of-fit test. As these *p* levels indicate, both models provide a good fit to the data. Aaker also

[109]Sheth, "Measurement of Multidimensional Brand Loyalty of a Consumer"; Jacoby, "Brand Loyalty Concept," 25-31.

[110]A. S. C. Ehrenberg and G. J. Goodhardt, "A Model of Multi-Brand Buying," *Journal of Marketing Research,* vol. 7 (February 1970), 77-84; also see Massy et al., *Stochastic Models.*

used the estimated models to predict the empirical proportions that purchase the brands on the *nth* purchase occasion ($n = 1,2, \ldots 10$) following the estimation period. In both cases, the New Trier model seemed to make better predictions of the empirical proportions, after the first four or five purchase occasions, than did the linear learning model.

Summary Evaluation

In summary, models, while providing a statistically significant fit to data in certain product categories, suffer from oversimplification. Explicit treatment of the influence of marketing variables as well as the differences between individual consumers needs to be emphasized. Also needed is a model (or set of models) that starts out with the determinants of brand loyalty and then attempts to relate these determinants to a valid measure of brand loyalty.

In the future it would seem useful to develop a typology of brand loyalty and focus some attention on explaining the why of loyalty as against simply providing correlates of the observed behavior. A plausible typology has been proposed by Engel, distinguishing brand loyalty resulting from inertia, psychological commitment, and marketer strategies.[111] Brand loyalty through inertia may represent an effort to reduce perceived risk and/or certain costs—time, energy, psychological frustration, and so on—incurred in a buying situation. In contrast, brand loyalty through psychological commitment may be the result of factors such as ego involvement, reference-group influence, or a dissonance-reducing strategy. Finally, brand loyalty from marketing strategy may be due to the availability of brands, advertising, or even certain contractual arrangements. More research needs to be done to substantiate or refute these suggested typologies and develop others that may be more relevant.

Finally, an area of research that may benefit from current developments in multidimensional scaling is the study of the relationship between brand loyalty and the perceptual and preference structures of consumers. Thus, questions such as the following may be raised and investigated: In a given product category, does the perceptual configuration of brand-loyal consumers differ from disloyal consumers? More specifically, do brand-loyal consumers perceive the various brands in a product category as being substantially dissimilar, whereas disloyal consumers perceive all the brands as being very similar? On the other hand, one may argue, in view of the concept of brand loyalty through inertia, that a brand-loyal consumer may indeed perceive all brands as being very similar and become loyal to one in order to reduce the effort necessary to choose among the many similar brands. A related question may be: Is the object of loyalty perceived as being very different from the other brands? Also, in the case of multiple-brand loyalty, is the consumer loyal to a group of brands that are perceived as being similar, or does he pick a few dissimilar brands and become loyal to them?

---

[111]James F. Engel, "The Influence of Needs and Attitudes on the Perception of Persuasion," in Greyser, *Toward Scientific Marketing*, 18-29.

MARKETING IMPLICATIONS

Some marketing implications have been discussed throughout the chapter. To avoid being redundant, the discussion that follows is confined to the general implications of brand loyalty to marketing strategists.

Brand loyalty is one way of segmenting a market. For example, some of the ways a manufacturer of Brand A could attempt to increase sales are:

1. Increase the number of consumers who are loyal to Brand A.

2. Decrease the number of consumers who are loyal to competing brands.

3. Increase the number of nonloyal consumers who purchase the product to purchase Brand A.

4. Increase the amount purchased among consumers who are loyal to Brand A.

5. Convince those who do not purchase the product to purchase Brand A.

Marketing programming to any of these segments is practical only if the consumers comprising these segments are identifiable. In some instances, brand loyalty is not a useful basis for segmenting markets. For example, in the case of grocery products, brand-loyal customers do not seem to differ from other customers in terms of attitudes, personality and socioeconomic characteristics, amount purchased, or sensitivity to pricing, dealing, retail advertising, or the introduction of new brands.[112] However, this finding may not be applicable to other product categories, and may not even hold for individual grocery products if the suggestions articulated in this chapter are implemented.

A previous section of the chapter identified typologies of consumer loyalty. Although the classification is only tentative, it is possible to indicate how marketing strategy would differ between types of loyalties. Thus, if loyalty is attributable to inertia, then significant product improvements, price reductions, effective advertisements pointing out unperceived product benefits, and several other strategies could all trigger a change in buying behavior. In other words, meaningful changes in marketing variables might not be screened out through selective perception, so that it might be possible to change brand loyalty through appropriate promotion, product, and pricing strategies.

These types of strategies, however, are less likely to be effective if loyalty is caused by psychological commitment to a brand. In these situations, the probability that selective attention, comprehension, and recall will weaken the effects of marketing strategies is probably much higher.

To illustrate a somewhat different approach, consider a market where a significant segment of consumers is loyal to a particular brand.

[112]Ronald E. Frank, "Is Brand Loyalty a Useful Basis for Market Segmentation?" *Journal of Advertising Research,* vol. 7 (June 1967), 33.

Assume that research indicated that these consumers consider certain other brands as falling in their region of acceptance, and the rest of the brands distributed over the regions of neutrality and rejection.

What is the most effective marketing strategy for brands in the various regions? The most preferred ("loyal") brand could emphasize the importance of the product attribute(s) that has led consumers to become loyal to that brand. Marketers of other brands in the region of acceptance could emphasize the comparability between themselves and the "loyal" brand on this attribute(s), and minimize any perceived or real differences. Marketers of brands in the regions of neutrality and rejection, on the other hand, would probably be better advised to focus their efforts on a different product attribute(s), and make that attribute(s) salient.[113]

Finally, consider the relevance of brand loyalty models—the Markov models as a specific example—to the marketing strategist. The transition matrix in the model represents brand switching behavior. In addition to the long-run steady-state probabilities, which approximate eventual market shares, a marketer may be particularly interested in the changes that take place in the transition matrix as the result of promotional efforts. Conceptually, the optimum level of promotional effort can be determined by relating changes in transition probabilities to the investment required to bring about the changes.

The transition probabilities also suggest certain general types of marketing strategies. For example, if all the diagonal entries of the matrix are of high magnitude (0.9), the implication is that the marketer should direct efforts toward inducing consumers to try the brand. If a reasonable degree of success is achieved, there is a high probability that these consumers will stay with the brand and become loyal consumers.[114]

Summary

This chapter was concerned with a temporal aspect of consumer behavior—brand loyalty. Researchers define loyalty in a wide variety of ways. Consequently, it is difficult to compare and synthesize findings. Therefore, the need for a new and extended definition of brand loyalty was articulated and a definition incorporating both behavioral and attitudinal components was presented.

Regardless of the precise definition, researchers have found conclusive evidence of the existence of brand loyalty. Attempts to determine the reasons for the variation in loyalty across products and consumers have, however, produced contradictory results. The chapter discussed at length numerous characteristics of consumers, their shopping patterns, and the market structure that have been investigated by researchers in attempts to identify correlates of brand loyalty. Studies concentrating primarily on the economic, demographic, and social-psychological characteristics of consumers have yielded the most discouraging results.

In recent years, many attempts have been made to develop and/or

---

[113]For more details, see Jacoby, "Model of Multi-Brand Loyalty," 30-31.

[114]For further discussion, see John U. Farley and Alfred E. Kuehn, "Stochastic Models of Brand Switching," in George Schwartz (ed.), *Science in Marketing* (New York: John Wiley & Sons, 1965), 446-464.

use stochastic models to relate probabilities of brand choice to factors such as purchase feedback, influence of external marketing activities, and characteristics of consumers. The most popular models were presented and evaluated. Unfortunately, the models usually begin with a mathematical formulation and manipulate empirical data to fit them. Future research in this area needs to concentrate on more valid measures of brand loyalty and an explicit treatment of marketing influences as well as consumer heterogeneity.

Finally, the marketing implications of brand loyalty were discussed. Brand loyalty is a useful way of segmenting markets provided that consumers exhibiting various kinds and degrees of loyalty can be identified and reached profitably. The approach used may vary depending on whether loyalty is due to inertia, psychological commitment, or marketer influence. Finally, it was shown how a Markov model transition matrix can be used to help formulate promotional strategy.

Review and Discussion Questions

1. Define or otherwise describe the following: (a) state; (b) brand loyalty; (c) transition probability; (d) stationary nature; (e) homogeneity; and (f) psychological commitment.

2. How does the learning model differ from a first-order Markov model?

3. What are the various definitions of brand loyalty? How should brand loyalty be defined?

4. Is brand loyalty a useful basis for market segmentation? Discuss.

5. What conclusions can be drawn concerning the correlates of brand loyalty?

6. What are the uses and limitations of first-order Markov models?

7. Give an example of a multidimensional definition of brand loyalty.

8. Discuss the limitations of the learning model.

9. How does brand loyalty through inertia differ from brand loyalty due to psychological commitment?

10. How would marketing strategy differ depending on whether brand loyalty is due to commitment or inertia?

11. Are Bernoulli models adequate representations of brand loyalty? Why or why not?

12. Formulate a hypothetical model postulating a relationship between brand loyalty and all the factors that have an influence on brand loyalty. Propose a quantifiable measure for each of the variables. What problems do you anticipate in operationalizing your model?

PART SIX
CONSUMER AFFAIRS AND PERSONAL VALUES

The study of consumer behavior is an applied discipline. The question that must be asked is applied to what? The answer that is most obvious throughout the book is that knowledge about consumers is applied to marketing strategies.

Marketing transcends many forms of organizations, and an understanding of consumer behavior is increasingly recognized as necessary in not-for-profit as well as for-profit organizations. Beyond these classifications for organizations is a broader type of organization or concern called society. Sometimes societal concerns are focused as organizational concerns, such as when governmental organizations become involved in regulatory activities. Sometimes an organization is affected by societal concerns through its own mechanism and norms of behavior regardless of regulatory pressure. In the final analysis, the design of marketing programs that are based upon knowledge of consumer behavior must involve the consumer researcher's own personal values. The final two chapters of this book concentrate on the topic of personal values.

CHAPTER 21
CONSUMERISM

President John F. Kennedy holds a special place in history for many people. For consumer analysts, however, one of his special contributions was the enunciation of four rights of the consumer that have become the foundation for business, government and other policies relating to consumers. Kennedy articulated the rights of the consumers as:

1. The right to safety.

2. The right to be informed.

3. The right to choose.

4. The right to be heard (redress).

But how should those rights be achieved? That is the question with which people are now struggling. The answers must necessarily involve economics, business, law, physical sciences, and other disciplines with a special role for consumer research and behavior.

Articulating the four rights of the consumer is a starting point, perhaps a platform. But more basic issues exist. What are the meanings to consumers of such terms as safety, information, choice, and redress? Before a business or government program can be developed stating the rights of the consumer, it is absolutely essential to develop an understanding of what those rights actually mean to consumers. Before a business firm can decide what information to disclose about a product or before a government agency can decide what information must be disclosed, more basic questions must be answered: What information is *relevant* to the consumer? Do all consumers consider the same information relevant or are there distinct needs among market segments? What trade-offs in price or other disadvantages justify the additional information? These are questions about which the study of consumer behavior can make productive and unique contributions. These are the issues discussed in this chapter.

Consumer behavior is a discipline similar to law in that it is useful—and even necessary—to parties with different and often conflicting interests. It is not unusual for a lawyer, as an example, to be employed by a government agency such as the Federal Trade Commission one year and to be employed by a business firm the next year. In the former role, the attorney may be prosecuting businesses concerning their consumer practices and in the next role, the attorney may be defending and designing the consumer practices. Basic law school training is not for one role or the other; it is simply basic training in the legal process, which may be applied to varied situations. Consumer behavior is very much the same. The study of consumer decision processes throughout this book and the specific study of consumerism in this chapter may be used by a person employed by a regulatory agency, business firm, consumer advocacy group, or for that matter, to further the consumer's own personal interests.

After defining consumerism and its causes, this chapter will focus on the issues of product safety, consumer information, competitive choice, redress, environmental protection, responsibility to minorities and the poor, and social marketing. This chapter contains basic materials about consumerism that are then applied in government, business, and personal decisions in Chapter 22.

DEFINITIONS OF CONSUMERISM

Consumerism has many meanings, which often mirror the various interests of business, government, consumer groups, and academic researchers. These definitions run the gamut from reflecting the basic search of people to get better values for their money to challenging society's goal which calls for an ever-increasing amount of material goods. Consumerists of the first type believe that prices are too high, quality and safety of goods are not adequate, and service facilities need to be improved. The latter range of meanings of consumerism leads to questions of whether the emphasis should be on increasing material wealth or whether it might be better to focus more resources on public welfare, health and education programs, and better leisure facilities and programs.[1]

Some analysts have defined consumerism as: . . . the organized efforts of consumers seeking redress, restitution, and remedy for dissatisfaction they have accumulated in the acquisition of their standard of living.[2]

This definition can be broadened usefully by dropping the requirement that consumerism be limited to organized efforts. Kotler achieves this in the view, "Consumerism is a social movement seeking to augment the

---

[1]Robert Ferber, "Rising Consumerism Primary Concern to Market Managers," paper presented to the American Marketing Association, Hawaii Chapter (May 7, 1970); reprinted in *Marketing News* (Mid-June 1970), 4 ff.

[2]Richard H. Buskirk and James T. Rothe, "Consumerism—An Interpretation," *Journal of Marketing* (October 1970), 61-65.

rights and power of buyers in relation to sellers."[3] Even this definition may be too limiting if it implies that pressure is focused only on *business*. Aaker and Day observe that consumerism

. . . encompasses the evolving set of activities of government, business, independent organizations that are designed to protect the rights of consumers . . . Consumerism is concerned with protecting consumers from all organizations with which there is an exchange relationship. There are consumer problems associated with hospitals, libraries, schools, police forces, and various government agencies, as well as business firms.[4]

This same notion was expressed by Senator Charles Percy, who describes the consumer movement as ". . . a broad public reaction against bureaucratic neglect and corporate disregard of the public."[5]

The broad concept of consumerism is used in this book because of the many industries and organizations with which consumer researchers are involved. Many consumer researchers are involved in understanding consumer research for business, but many others are concerned with the same issues in government agencies, charitable and charity-related institutions, and most any other organization that exists to serve the public.[6]

CAUSES OF CONSUMERISM

Consumerism is not entirely new. Even in the Middle Ages, St. Thomas Aquinas, Martin Luther, John Calvin, and other reformers represented a kind of consumerism by attacking deceptive selling practices of businessmen and advancing the concept of a just price rather than what the market would bear.[7] Three eras of consumerism leading to the contemporary situation were identified in a history of consumerism by Herrmann.[8] While these developments focus on history in the United States, similar phenomena have occurred on a world-wide basis, especially in more advanced nations.[9] A description of these eras in the rise of consumerism

[3]Philip Kotler, "What Consumerism Means for Marketers," *Harvard Business Review* (May-June 1972), 48-57.

[4]David A. Aaker and George S. Day, *Consumerism: Search for the Consumer Interest*, 2nd ed. (New York: Free Press, 1974), 17.

[5]Quoted in William T. Kelly, *New Consumerism: Selected Readings* (Columbus, Ohio: Grid Publishing, 1973), 2.

[6]The basic source on nonbusiness marketing is Philip Kotler, *Marketing for Nonprofit Organizations* (Hinsdale, Ill.: Dryden Press, 1975).

[7]Leon Garry, "Consumerism Began with Cyrus of Persia," *Business and Society Review* (Winter 1972-1973), 62-64.

[8]Robert O. Herrmann, "Consumerism: Its Goals, Organizations and Future," *Journal of Marketing* (October 1970), 55-60. This reference is the source of much of the material in this section, as is also William P. Anthony and Joel B. Haynes, "Consumerism: A Three Generation Paradigm," *University of Michigan Business Review* (November 1975), 21-26. The authors also wish to thank Roger Campbell for his assistance in preparing this section.

[9]Colson E. Warne, "The Worldwide Consumer Movement," in Ralph M. Gaedeke and Warren W. Etcheson (eds.), *Consumerism: Viewpoints from Business, Government, and the Public Interest* (San Francisco: Canfield Press, 1972), 17-19.

should put the current movement into a proper perspective for predicting its present and future course.[10]

The Early 1900s

Consumer activism in the early part of this century, resulted in substantial progress in consumer protection legislation before it gradually subsided. During the 1890s and again in 1902, attempts were made to enact pure food legislation, but each time the bill died in Congress.

In 1906, *The Jungle* by Upton Sinclair exposed the filth surrounding the meat packing industry in Chicago, creating such substantial public awareness and outcry that Congress was compelled to act. The Meat Inspection Act of 1906 was quickly enacted to provide federal inspection of meat packing and processing. Later that same year, the Food and Drug Act created the Food and Drug Administration, an agency charged with preventing the appearance of misbranded and adulterated food and drugs in interstate commerce. A few years later, in 1914, the Federal Trade Commission was established to curb monopoly and trade practices that might be unfair to competitive businesses. The business community remained largely indifferent to consumer protection, however, and the consumer movement gradually abated.

The 1930s

The consumerism movement of the 1930s had its inception in the immediately preceding years. During the 1920s, incomes rose rapidly and thus sales of new and unfamiliar consumer durables also rose rapidly. Consumers were deluged with advertising as radio and magazines grew rapidly as advertising media.

In 1927, the book *Your Money's Worth* by Stuart Chase and F. J. Schlink stirred the consumer movement once again. The book attacked the manipulation and deceit of advertising and called for scientific testing and product standards to provide consumers with information for making wise purchasing decisions. This attack resulted in the founding of a new consumer organization, Consumers Research, Inc., which was the forerunner of today's Consumers Union, publishers of the magazine *Consumer Reports*.

The stock market crash of 1929 forestalled a widespread consumer movement. Instead, efforts were focused upon consumer education. Budgeting and money management were emphasized to help the consumer identify the best buys at the lowest cost.

A book by F. J. Schlink and Arthur Kallett, *100,000,000 Guinea Pigs*, pointed to loopholes in the 1906 Food and Drug Act that allowed consumers to be forced into the role of guinea pigs for dangerous medicines, unsafe cosmetics, and adulterated foods. More consumer support was generated by the sulfanilamide scandal of 1937 which ended in 107 deaths and led to the passage of the Food, Drug and Cosmetic Act

---

[10]For more details concerning the history of consumerism, see Aaker and Day, *Consumerism: Search for the Consumer Interest;* Kelly, *New Consumerism: Selected Readings;* Gaedeke and Etcheson, *Consumerism: Viewpoints from Business;* and Joel R. Evans, *Consumerism in the United States: An Inter-Industry Analysis* (New York: Praeger, 1980).

of 1938. The bill, however, had been adulterated itself through five years of hearings and controversy so that it was too weak to suit many consumer activists.

In 1938, the Wheeler-Lea amendment to the Federal Trade Commission Act also was passed. Wheeler-Lea enlarged the powers of the Federal Trade Commission to prosecute unlawful, deceptive, or unfair trade practices—becoming a watchdog for the consumer rather than only regulating practices that were unfair to competition. During this period, an increasing concern about consumerism was observed by business leaders, partially stimulated by a national survey by Dr. George Gallup indicating that the consumerism movement was likely to increase. World War II, however, diverted attention of the nation away from consumer problems and toward national problems and the war effort.

The 1960s

The consumerism era of the 1960s, which forms the foundation for the current movement, also had antecedents in prior years. Just as the two previous eras had gained a part of their impetus from the publication of a book, so did this era. In 1957, Vance Packard's *The Hidden Persuaders* argued that the consumer was being manipulated by advertising without realizing the source of the manipulation. The reaction to this book showed that public interest in consumer problems continued but in a more sophisticated way than in past eras.

The problem of drug safety also was a prominent issue in the consumerism of the 1960s just as it had been in prior eras. Since 1959, Senator Estes Kefauver's Antitrust and Monopoly Subcommittee had been holding hearings on the prescription drug industry, with many revelations that created public awareness and concern. The thalidomide scare finally triggered public reaction that resulted in the passage of the Kefauver-Harris Amendment to the Food, Drug and Cosmetic Act.

The beginning of the new consumerism, however, is generally attributed to President John F. Kennedy's message to Congress on March 15, 1962, in which he outlined the consumer bill of rights listed at the beginning of this chapter. Kennedy's message clearly implied that government is the ultimate guarantor of consumer rights, and it set forth the basis for much of the role of the federal government in consumerism. Subsequent actions of administrators, legislators and consumer activists have broadened the movement so that today, the rights are still a dynamic and evolving force in the economy.

The 1980s

The new consumerism operative in the United States in the 1980s may be described as a blend of government and market regulation. The result is *deregulation* of some industries or perhaps more correctly, a *reregulation by the market.* This contemporary conservatism was observable in the election of both President Jimmy Carter (as a force in his election perhaps more than in implementation) and President Ronald Reagan. The basic force was an attitude by consumers that government efforts to help the consumer often resulted in more harm than help. The Gallup Poll disclosed that only 14 percent of Americans agreed with the statement, "The biggest threat to our nation is big government," in 1959 compared to 43 percent who agreed with that statement in 1979—many more than rated big labor, big business, or anything else as the major threat to the nation.

The new consumer and voter preference resulted in deregulation of the airline and other industries, a sharp reduction in the budget of the Federal Trade Commission and its influence, and statements to the effect that, "Parents rather than the government should control the television viewing of their children." In Scottsdale, Arizona, and other cities in the Southwest, even government agencies like the fire department were replaced by business firms providing fire services under contract for the city.

What are the effects of deregulation for consumers? The airline deregulation is perhaps the best example of how consumers are affected. After deregulation, many airlines cut prices on some routes and raised prices on other routes. Planes and services were added on some routes and deleted from others. Some cities were simply omitted from the schedules.

The trend toward market regulation produces some interesting effects on appropriate consumer strategies. For example, an airline passenger flying from Columbus, Ohio, to New York in 1981 would have paid $292 for a round-trip ticket before April 26, 1981. On that date, however, a new airline—People Express—entered the market as a competitor, charging only $110 round trip on weekdays or $70 round trip on Saturday and Sunday. TWA promptly matched that price making it seem that consumers greatly benefited from deregulation and the ensuing competition. However, the issue is a bit more complex. The fare on TWA applied only to nonstop flights to LaGuardia airport. If an uninformed consumer chose a route to Kennedy airport, or chose a schedule with a stop, say, Pittsburgh, the regular fare of $292 applied. Also, if a consumer chose first-class even to LaGuardia, the fare was $404—a premium on the weekend of $334. Regular fares applied to cities like Philadelphia and Albany, but a well-informed consumer might save about $200 by flying to New York and making a connection or taking a train or rental car to destinations between New York and Philadelphia. What type of consumer benefits most in this market-regulated form of consumerism? The one who is a better information-seeker, more experienced, or has more consumer education. You can see how consumerism might change its emphasis to consumer education or information distribution in the environment of the 1980s.

How should organizations respond to the new market-regulated consumerism of the 1980s? That issue promises to generate considerable research as proper responses are sought for business, government, and other organizations. A lot of research and perhaps a little prayer, as Figure 21.1 indicates.

**Figure 21.1
A Proper Response
to Deregulation**

*"... and please grant me and the rest of the board
the grace not to abuse deregulation."*

Source: *The New Yorker* (March 1981). Drawing by Reilly, © 1981 The New Yorker Magazine, Inc.

CATALYSTS TO CONSUMERISM

What causes consumers to stand up for their rights? To search for information about product capabilities? To seek redress when products are unsafe, deceptive, or unsatisfying? Those interested in both macromarketing and micromarketing policies need to know who the concerned consumers might be and what catalysts are likely to move them toward action. Several categories of variables have emerged from research on this topic to explain the activation of consumerism.

**Historical–
Societal
Variables**

An historical analysis reveals that consumerism increases most rapidly after an era of rapidly rising income followed by rising prices which cause a decrease in the rise of real purchasing power.[11] Usually the social environment must provide leadership for the consumerism movement, normally among highly educated and high-income individuals.

The rise of consumerism may be similar to the diffusion of innovations, described in Chapter 13. Hendon advances the proposition that consumerism is but a part of the theory of social adaptation to innovation, in which the innovation (consumerism) moves through phases of introduction (initial impact), growth, and reaction or widespread acceptance of regulatory and business actions which quiet things down until a new

[11]Herrmann, "Consumerism: Its Goals."

innovation occurs. Then the cycle begins again.[12] Hendon presents data
to support this hypothesis and suggests that organizations might profitably study such diffusion processes in order to predict the future direction
and magnitude of important social movements that affect organizations.

What stimulates consumerism in retailing? Hollander analyzed retailing practices to isolate those that attract consumer interest and stimulate
consumerism activities. These functions or practices include *poor sanitation* (especially in the handling of food), *inadequate shopping information* (in marking, labeling, and advertising practices), *price inflation*,
unfair credit practices, and *inadequate repair and warranty services*.[13]
Hollander concludes that the causes of consumerism are variables about
which retailers can implement helpful and positive remedies.

Sociopsychological Variables

Several studies investigate sociopsychological variables associated with
interest in consumerism activities.

Alienation, as that concept is used in sociology, is advanced as a
major cause for consumer discontent by Lambert and Kniffin, who believe that unless the basic causes that fuel consumer discontent are dealt
with successfully, relief is transitory and discontent later causes new
symptomatic issues and complaints.[14] In this analytical framework, alienation is manifested in five forms: *powerlessness, meaninglessness,
normlessness, isolation* and *self-estrangement*. Powerlessness, for example, results when consumers believe they cannot exert any influence
on business decisions concerning what products will or will not be placed
on the market, their quality level, warranty coverage, and so forth. Consequently, they harbor feelings like those of alienated voters who see
themselves as being able only to exercise a negative choice between
candidates offered to them by political bosses. The actions that business
firms can take to combat powerlessness and other forms of alienation
include cool lines, buyer protection plans, and a management system of
information and control to identify and correct practices that needlessly
produce dissatisfaction.

Socially conscious consumers, or those persons who not only are
concerned with their own personal satisfactions, but also buy with some
consideration of the social and environmental well-being of others, have
been investigated in a number of situations. Anderson and Cunningham
found that sociopsychological variables were more powerful in explaining
social consciousness than demographic variables. They also found that

[12]Donald Hendon, "Toward a Theory of Consumerism," *Business Horizons* (August 1975), 16-24.

[13]Stanley C. Hollander, "Consumerism and Retailing: A Historical Perspective," *Journal of Retailing*
(Winter 1972-1973), 6-21.

[14]Zarrel V. Lambert and Fred W. Kniffin, "Consumer Discontent: A Social Perspective," *California Management Review* (Fall 1975), 36-44; Zarrel V. Lambert, "Consumer Alienation, General Dissatisfaction,
and Consumerism Issues: Conceptual and Managerial Perspectives," *Journal of Retailing* (Summer
1980), 3-10.

the variables most negatively associated with such consumer interest were dogmatism, conservatism, and status consciousness while cosmopolitanism varied directly with social consciousness.[15]

The consumerist may have a different cognitive map than the nonactivist. This was the conclusion of Bourgeois and Barnes after a thorough review of the literature and their own empirical research in which they found consumerists to enjoy shopping less than average consumers, to be less exposed to the broadcast media but be heavier readers of the national and international sections of newspapers, be more negative toward advertising, be opinion leaders and be interested in other social issues such as women's rights, politics and environmental protection. Bourgeois and Barnes conclude that the consumerist is properly labeled by the more general trait of social activist.[16]

Sociodemographic variables have been analyzed by a number of researchers as an explanation for consumer activism, usually with regard to specific activities such as energy consumption, recycling activities, boycott participation, and so forth. Most of these studies have concluded that variables associated with consumer activism or dissatisfaction with marketing practices include the sociodemographic variables of being young, politically liberal or avant-garde, and well educated.[17]

CS/D or Who Complains?

Are consumers satisfied (CS) or dissatisfied (D) with the offerings of contemporary organizations? Most business firms with a good marketing research department know the answer to that question. Proctor and Gamble, for example, has a marketing research program that has carefully designed and executed surveys with thousands of consumers over many years. Consumers are asked to rate P & G products, as well as those of competitors, on many dimensions and describe any problems or complaints about the products and their intentions to buy each brand in the future. When there is any dissatisfaction, P & G knows about it quickly and reliably.

At Borden, on the other hand, a system is maintained that sends every complaint or inquiry received about any product any place in the

[15]W. Thomas Anderson, Jr., and William H. Cunningham, "The Socially Conscious Consumer, *"Journal of Marketing* (July 1972), 23-31. Less definitive results were found, however, in similar research reported in Frederick E. Webster, Jr., "Determining the Characteristics of the Socially Conscious Consumer," *Journal of Consumer Research,* (December 1975), 188-196.

[16]Jacques C. Bourgeois and James G. Barnes, "Viability and Profile of the Consumerist Segment," *Journal of Consumer Research* (March 1979), 217-228.

[17]Hiram C. Barksdale and William R. Darden, "Consumer Attitudes toward Marketing and Consumerism," *Journal of Marketing,* (October 1972), 28-35; Thomas P. Hustad and Edgar A. Pessemier, "Will the Real Consumer Activist Please Stand Up: An Examination of Consumers' Opinions about Marketing Practices," *Journal of Marketing Research* (August 1973), 319-324; Michael B. Mazis and John H. Faricy, "Consumer Response to the Meat Boycott," in Ronald C. Curhan (ed.), *1974 Combined Proceedings* (Chicago: American Marketing Association, 1974), 329-333. These results were not found, however, in W. Wayne Talarzyk and Glenn S. Omura, "Consumer Attitudes toward and Perceptions of the Energy Crisis," in Curhan, *1974 Combined Proceedings,* 316-322. Also, see Thomas C. Kennear, James R. Taylor, and Sadrudin A. Ahmed, "Ecologically Concerned Consumers, Who Are They?" *Journal of Marketing* (April 1974), 20-24; and Thomas J. Stanley and William Danko, "Correlates of Consumer Discontent Over Product Related Issues," in Richard Bagozzi (ed.), *Marketing in the 80s* (Chicago: American Marketing Association, 1980), 407-411.

world to a central information system. There each item is inspected by a consumer affairs representative. That person not only takes appropriate action (refund of money, instructions on how to use the product properly, and so on), but also puts the information into a computerized format to analyze trends and problem areas.

Two types of CS/D measures are illustrated by the P & G and Borden examples. One measure is volunteered complaint data; the other is survey data. The existence of the two methodologies did not escape the attention of public policy makers and consumer researchers either. They have attempted to develop a theoretical and methodological literature that considers both approaches to understanding consumerism. We aren't able to describe much of that literature here because it includes annual volumes of articles on the subject, and each volume is about the size of this textbook. The first conference to focus on CS/D was organized by Keith Hunt in 1976. The proceedings from these conferences provide a massive amount of research if you are interested in investigating the topic in depth.[18]

The most widely used source of complaint data is generated by the Council of Better Business Bureaus in Washington, D.C., reflecting the experiences of local bureaus throughout the United States.[19] In some instances, consumer agencies operate a hot line telephone number where consumers can call to report their problems.[20] Some scholars and policy makers believe volunteered complaint data do not adequately represent the total array of consumer complaints, however, because they over-represent professional, upscale persons and because the process does not generate the unvoiced complaints of consumers.[21]

The second type of methodology to measure dissatisfaction or complaints involves comprehensive surveys to representative samples of consumers. One of the most comprehensive of this type of survey is known as the Best and Andreasen study. These researchers found that about one in five purchases leads to perception of some problem (other than general concern about price) but that few of these problems are actually voiced in complaints to the seller. Further, respondents take action in only about 40 percent of the purchase instances for which they report problems.[22] This and other studies report that those who take ac-

[18]Keith Hunt (ed.), *Conceptualization and Measurement of Consumer Satisfaction and Dissatisfaction* (Cambridge: Marketing Science Institute, 1977); Ralph Day (ed.), *Consumer Satisfaction, Dissatisfaction and Complaining Behavior* (Bloomington: Indiana University, 1977); Ralph Day and Keith Hunt (eds.), *New Dimensions of Consumer Satisfaction and Complaining Behavior* (Bloomington: Indiana University, 1979); Keith Hunt and Ralph Day (eds.), *Proceedings of the Conference on CS/D, 1980,* in press.

[19]A statistical summary of complaints for the entire nation is issued each year by the Council of Better Business Bureaus, Inc., 1150 17th Street, N.W., Washington, D.C. 20036.

[20]Steven L. Diamond, Scott Ward, and Ronald Faber, "Consumer Problems and Consumerism: Analysis of Calls to a Consumer Hot Line," *Journal of Marketing* (January 1976), 56-62.

[21]J. P. Liefeld, F. H. C. Edgercombe, and Linda Wolfe, "Demographic Characteristics of Canadian Consumer Complaints," *Journal of Consumer Affairs* (Summer 1975), 73-80.

[22]Arthur Best and Alan R. Andreasen, *Talking Back to Business: Voiced and Unvoiced Consumer Complaints* (Washington, D.C.: Center for Study of Responsive Law, 1976).

tion are of a distinct socioeconomic group. Specifically, they are better educated, earn higher incomes, are in higher social classes, are more active in formal organizations, and are more politically committed and liberal than other groups.[23]

A study by Wall, Dickey and Talarzyk, however, indicates that product characteristics—in their instance, clothing—interact with such consumer variables as age and experience to predict CS/D.[24]

Most of the studies in the CS/D literature have been descriptive rather than theoretical studies. Some researchers have used fairly powerful analytical tools in the attempt to profile complainers.[25] Increasingly, there are attempts to develop a conceptual or theoretical basis for understanding CS/D.[26]

The problem in the CS/D research starts with the fact that there is little agreement on what consumer satisfaction means, as Day describes:

While everyone knows what satisfaction means, it clearly doesn't mean the same thing to everyone. It has been defined by researchers in a variety of ways including the following: a level of "happiness resulting from a consumption experience;" a cognitive state resulting from a process of evaluation of performance relative to previously established standards; a subjective evaluation of the various experiences and outcomes associated with acquiring and consuming a product relative to a set of subjectively determined expectations; a two factor process of evaluating a set of "satisfiers" and a set of "dissatisfiers" associated with the product; and, one step in a complex process involving prior attitude toward a product or service, a consumption experience resulting in positive or negative disconfirmation of expectancies, followed by feelings of satisfaction or dissatisfaction which mediate post-consumption attitude which subsequently influences future purchase behavior. The above definitions represent a range from the notion of a simplistic "black box" happiness function to a very complex set of concepts which overlap each other and are virtually impossible to operationalize. To say that there is no general agreement among satisfaction researchers on how to define satisfaction would indeed be an understatement.[27]

---

[23]Rex H. Warland, Robert O. Herrmann, and Jane Willits, "Dissatisfied Consumers: Who Gets Upset and Who Takes Action," *Journal of Consumer Affairs* (Winter 1975), 148-162.

[24]Marjorie Wall, Lois Dickey, and Wayne Talarzyk, "Correlates of Satisfaction and Dissatisfaction with Clothing Performance," *Journal of Consumer Affairs* (Summer 1979), 104-115.

[25]William Bearden, Jesse Teel, and Melissa Crockett, "A Path Model of Consumer Complaint Behavior," in Richard Bagozzi, *Marketing in the 80s* (Chicago: American Marketing Association, 1980), 101-104.

[26]See for example the expectancy approach in Frederick Trawick and John E. Swan, "Inferred and Perceived Disconfirmation in Consumer Satisfaction," in Bagozzi (ed.), *Marketing in the 80s,* 97-100; and the attribution approach in Marsha Richins, "Product Dissatisfaction: Causal Attribution Structure and Strategy," in Bagozzi (ed.), *Marketing in the 80s,* 105-108.

[27]Ralph Day, "How Satisfactory Is Research on Consumer Satisfaction?" in Jerry C. Olson (ed.), *Advances in Consumer Research,* vol. 7 (Ann Arbor, Mich.: Association for Consumer Research, 1980) 593-597.

One of the theories that has been advanced to explain consumer dissatisfaction is increased consumer expectations, especially on the part of the younger, affluent, and more sophisticated consumers, and exaggerated advertising claims concerning product performance.[28] These factors are more likely to affect dissatisfaction than deteriorating product and service offerings. While overexpectations may exist and produce dissatisfaction, there is empirical evidence to indicate that consumer expectations are not rising but are, in fact, decreasing.[29] Swan and Combs have shown the importance, however, of relating satisfactions to expectancies about products, and this appears to be an area likely to experience even more attention.[30]

Business Failures

Finally, in our discussion of the catalysts of consumerism, we must recognize the failures of business to provide good products and good service. This is analogous to the old joke about a firm that introduced a new dog food. In spite of putting the finest of ingredients in the dog food, spending enormous amounts on advertising, and gaining strong sales and distribution support, the dog food did not sell. The president of the company requested marketing research to determine if the product was positioned to the right segments, to evaluate the advertising appeals, and to measure the effectiveness of the sales force. All of these variables were excellent according to the research, and the president was distraught about the poor sales record. Finally, someone came forth and told the president why consumers did not buy the dog food, "The dogs don't like it!"

What types of firms generate the most complaints? The answer to that question is shown in Table 21.1 based upon complaint data from the Better Business Bureau. Table 21.1 shows that mail-order companies generated more complaints than any other type of business, followed by auto dealers and miscellaneous service establishments. Perhaps the reason for so many complaints at auto dealers can be understood by looking at Figure 21.2. Using survey measures of dissatisfaction, Best and Andreasen also found mail-order and car repair services to be among the highest levels of unsatisfactory performance, along with appliance repair purchases.[31]

Two reasons exist for studying the catalysts for consumerism. One concerns the development of business strategies to prevent and mitigate consumer complaints and dissatisfaction. The other concerns public policies to accomplish the same thing. In Chapter 22 , we take a close look at how both organizations attempt to accomplish these goals.

[28]Rolphe E. Anderson and Marvin A. Jolson, "Consumer Expectations and the Communications Gap," *Business Horizons* (April 1973), 11-16.

[29]Thomas R. Wotruba and Patricia L. Duncan, "Are Consumers Really Satisfied?" *Business Horizons* (February 1975), 85-90.

[30]John E. Swan and Linda Jones Combs, "Product Performance and Consumer Satisfaction: A New Concept," *Journal of Marketing* (April 1976), 35-38.

[31]Best and Andreasen, *Talking Back to Business,* 16.

Table 21.1
Types of Business Involved in Consumer Complaints, 1976

Type of Business	Rank	Number	Percent of total	Percent settled
Total		390,685	100.00	75.1
Mail-order companies	1	58,562	14.98	83.1
Auto dealers	2	27,239	6.97	78.5
Miscellaneous service establishments	*	19,073	4.88	67.9
Miscellaneous retail stores/shops	*	14,813	3.79	68.9
Home furnishings stores	3	13,618	3.48	76.2
Magazines, ordered by mail	4	13,522	3.46	85.1
Miscellaneous home maintenance	5	12,352	3.16	61.9
Department stores	6	11,671	2.98	88.3
Auto repair shops—exc. Transm.	7	10,214	2.61	64.9
Television servicing companies	8	9,394	2.40	
Home remodeling contractors	9	8,170	2.09	65.4
Insurance companies	10	8,078	2.06	84.3
Dry cleaning/laundry companies	11	8,077	2.06	70.1
Apparel and accessory shops	12	7,737	1.98	75.8
Appliance stores	13	7,652	1.95	76.2
Real estate sales/rental companies	14	7,567	1.93	69.7
Appliance service companies	15	7,106	1.81	72.9
Miscellaneous automotive	16	6,538	1.67	66.3
Direct selling—magazines	17	6,517	1.66	76.1
Manufacturers/producers	18	5,641	1.44	83.2
TV/radio/phono/shops	10	5,526	1.41	75.6
Photographic processing companies	20	5,465	1.39	77.1
Floor covering stores	21	5,284	1.35	69.6
Auto gasoline service stations	22	5,153	1.31	66.5
Auto tire, battery, accessory shops	23	4,768	1.22	76.4
Roofing contractors	24	4,481	1.14	60.7
Jewelry stores	25	4,373	1.11	77.1
Direct selling—miscellaneous	26	4,338	1.11	78.0
Heating and central air conditioning companies	27	4,117	1.05	75.2
Mobile/modular home dealers	28	4,092	1.04	72.3

Note: Percent is based on total number of complaints to BBB offices. The full report contains 86 business categories, but only those with more than 1 percent are reprinted here.

*Unranked because category includes a variety of businesses.

Source: *CBBB Statistical Summary of Better Business Bureau Activity, 1976* (Washington, D.C.: Council of Better Business Bureaus, 1976). Reprinted by permission of the Council of Better Business, Inc., 1150 17th Street, N. W., Washington, D.C.

Understanding Consumer Rights and Needs

Consumer research has an important role to play in the analysis of consumer rights and needs. The role of research in developing an empirically based understanding of the rights and needs of consumers is described below. Following that, illustrative research findings that are beginning to emerge are described concerning the following topics: product safety, consumer information, competitive choice, redress, environmental protection, responsibility to minorities and the poor, and social marketing.

**Figure 21.2
Consumer
Attitudes toward
Car Repair May
Not Be Unfounded**

"There won't by any extras. $895.50 includes
everything I can think of."

Source: *The Wall Street Journal,* 1980. Reprinted by permission of Cartoon Features Syndicate.

**The Critical
Nature of a
Research
Approach**

A rigorous research framework for investigating issues in consumerism is critical to the resolution of disparate views of diverse groups seeking to respond to consumerism. Both business and government need the objectivity of information that is the output of well-designed research on consumer behavior. By fulfilling this critical need, consumer researchers have the potential for being boundary-spanning agents in the arena of conflict and subjectivity that has often surrounded the discussion of consumer rights and needs. The design of consumer information programs by public policy makers has traditionally *not* put the information needs of consumers first in the program planning. As a result there have been frequent instances of information programs looking for consumers to use them.

A research approach to consumerism emphasizes the collection of data that help understand consumer preferences and behavior rather than specifying policies that should be implemented to achieve those rights. Stated alternatively, a research approach to consumerism is not so much concerned with what business or government ought to do as it is concerned with how consumers behave or react to the current or contemplated programs of business firms and protective agencies.[32]

A research approach to consumerism provides an alternative to normative authoritarianism. There is a consistent ideological conflict reflected in the literature of consumerism concerning the issue of what consumers *want* versus what they *ought* to want, and what they *know* about products versus what they *need to know.*

[32]Consumer research can be used, however, to determine what consumers believe sellers or government should do about problems. See Gregory M. Gazda and David R. Gourley, "Attitudes of Businessmen, Consumers, and Consumerists toward Consumerism," *Journal of Consumer Affairs* (Winter 1975), 176-186; and Roger D. Blackwell and W. Wayne Talarzyk, *Consumer Attitudes toward Health Care and Medical Malpractice* (Columbus, Ohio: Grid Publishing, 1977), ch. 6.

Most research seems to indicate discrepancies between what consumer advocates believe, what executives believe, and what consumers believe.[33] Empirical research, conducted under scientific methods, offers the potential for resolving these conflicting views of reality. The differences between executives and consumer advocates concerning what consumers need to know is illustrated in the research of Moran, who observes:

This difference appeared almost without exception when I asked marketers and critics a question of the sort, "What do consumers *need* to know when deciding among the competing brands and models of product?" The critic was never fazed by the question and could easily speak at this normative level. The marketer in most cases would respond not to the question that had been asked but rather to the quite different question, "What do consumers want to know . . .?" Only with prodding and a subsequent feeling of uneasiness and meaninglessness of reply would marketers get out into what they considered to be a "big-brother" way of looking at the consumer.[34]

Consumer research increasingly offers the potential of test marketing proposed protective policies just as it is used in other areas of marketing practice. Such research is more difficult in situations where new alternatives are proposed than in situations in which consumers are asked only to choose from existing alternatives, but progress is continually occurring in methodologies facilitating the evaluation of new alternatives.

In a society where normative authoritarianism prevails, the groups that will specify the rules for consumers are those that have the most power. The basis for power may vary through time and across consumption choices. The countervailing force that provides a more democratic alternative, however, is rigorous research into the *actual* behavior of consumers rather than reliance on normative statements about how consumers *should* behave.[35]

Experimental research is appropriate and emerging in usefulness for consumerism policies. In many instances, policies will have to be evaluated with more sophisticated, quasiexperimental designs compared to other forms of consumer research.[36] Public agencies such as the FTC are increasingly introducing consumer research into their deliberations,

---

[33]Gazda and Gourley, "Attitudes of Businessmen;" F. Kelly Shuptrine, Henry O. Pruden, and Douglas S. Longman, "Business Executives' and Consumers' Attitudes toward Consumer Activism and Involvement," *Journal of Consumer Affairs* (Summer 1975), 90-95; Thomas Stanley and Larry Robinson, "Opinions on Consumer Issues: A Preview of Recent Studies of Executives and Consumers," *Journal of Consumer Affairs* (Summer 1980), 217-220.

[34]Robert Moran, "Formulating Public Policy on Consumer Issues: Some Preliminary Findings" (working paper P-57, Boston: Marketing Science Institute, September 1971), 31. Reprinted by permission of Marketing Science Institute.

[35]A framework for evaluating effects of regulation is presented in Claude Colantoni, Otto Davis and Malati Swaminuthan, "Imperfect Consumers and Welfare Comparisons of Policies Concerning Information and Regulation," *Bell Journal of Economics*, vol. 7 (Autumn 1976), 602-615.

[36]Lynn Phillips and Bobby Calder, "Evaluating Consumer Protection Laws: Promising Methods," *Journal of Consumer Affairs* (Summer 1980), 9-36.

however. Recently, for example, the FTC proposed that television (and other) ads for over-the-counter drug products such as *Alka-Seltzer* and *Rolaids* contain specific warnings about contraindications, rather than the "use as directed" statements carried voluntarily by drug advertisers. Would such a brief insertion in television ads be remembered by consumers? Houston and Rothschild, in a carefully designed and executed laboratory study found that consumers who were exposed to the longer, specific warning had significantly higher recall of the warning than the present policy elicits.[37] In the behavioral measures of this experiment, however, consumers for whom the product was contraindicated did not reduce their purchases of the contraindicated brand. In this low-level situation, it may be unreasonable to expect learning to occur with only a few exposures or perhaps selective processing is occurring and the contraindication words ("sodium-restricted diets") serve to attract the attention of persons on sodium-restricted diets and therefore make the advertisement a more effective learning situation.

On broader issues, consumer research is proving useful in understanding how to segment family nutrition behavior for the solution of social problems[38] and for issues such as audience behavior in order to evaluate relationships between advertising and consumption behavior.[39]

Product Safety   In the development of consumerism in this century, the problem of health and safety has been a prominent issue. The issue goes beyond the problem of adequate inspection and regulation of the food and drug industries. Defective, hazardous, or unsafe consumer products such as automobiles, electrical appliances, toys, and others have often been the focus of the issue in recent years. Additionally, the issue involves the problem of safety in highway and air travel.

The right to safety has been made very specific in the United States under the Consumer Product Safety Act, which established the Consumer Product Safety Commission (CPSC), which has the responsibility to protect consumers against unreasonable risk to injuries that may be caused by hazardous household products.[40] Manufacturers previously were liable for safety problems of their products under common law but the intent of the CPSC is to shift the responsibility for safety from postsale (and postinjury) remedies to *preventive safety.* In other words, more responsibility is required in the *design of the product* to achieve safety.

Consumer research has two major roles in this environment of increased attention to consumers' rights to safety. The first role is in understanding the usage patterns of the product, especially those which

---

[37]Michael Houston and Michael Rothschild, "Policy-Related Experiments on Information Provision: A Normative Model and Explication," *Journal of Marketing Research* (November 1980), 432-449.

[38]Seymour Fine, "Toward a Theory of Segmentation by Objectives in Social Marketing," *Journal of Consumer Research* (June 1980), 1-13.

[39]Robert Jacobson and Franco Nicosia, "Advertising and Public Policy: The Macroeconomic Effects of Advertising," *Journal of Marketing Research* (February 1981), 29-38.

[40]Walter Jensen, Jr., Edward M. Mazze, and Duke N. Stern, "The Consumer Product Safety Act: A Special Case in Consumerism," *Journal of Marketing* (October 1973), 68-71; Warren G. Magnuson and Edward B. Cohen, "The Role of the Consumer under the Consumer Product Safety Act," *Journal of Contemporary Business* (Winter 1975), 21-37.

may cause unexpected safety hazards. The second role is in establishing the level of safety or probability of injuries which may yield liability costs that must be considered in decisions concerning the product.

Consumer Usage Patterns

Consumer research can make a substantial contribution to improvements of product safety and performance by in-depth studies of consumer usage patterns of products. The reason many products perform poorly or unsafely is because they are used incorrectly by some segments of the market. Laundry equipment frequently provides poor performance because consumers overload the machine with clothes, soap or both. Usage studies should be able to determine segments of the consumer population most likely to cause such problems and thereby provide an input to tactics that may prevent some of the occurrences.

Consumer research can aid manufacturers in the problems they face due to the "doctrine of foreseeability." This is a legal doctrine which holds that manufacturers are best able to evaluate the risks inherent in their products and figure out ways to avoid them. This implies not only technical knowledge of the product but in-depth knowledge of how the product is likely to be used by varying segments of the market. A noted consumerist lawyer notes that the courts "should protect not just the unwitting consumer from the consequences of a manufacturer's error, but also the 'witless boobs' who misuse a product in ways that can be anticipated."[41] A Kentucky Court of Appeals held, for example, that a manufacturer was liable for damages that occurred when one of its vacuum cleaners was plugged into a 220-volt circuit and blew up. The label on the product stated that it was to be used in 115-volt outlets but did not warn about the serious consequences that would occur with improper usage.

Another example of the contribution of consumer research on usage patterns is in the area of defining what types of safety features a product should have. Controversy surrounds the usage of seat belts and air bags on automobiles, for example. The problems due to consumer usage patterns of seat belts may cause the government to require producers to supply (and, therefore, consumers to buy) a very expensive air bag (which may have its own defects). After describing the air bag it was pointed out that, "although lap and shoulder harnesses give similar protection, officials brandish the inescapable facts that not even 40 percent of all car occupants wear lap belts and fewer than 5 percent bother with shoulder belts."[42]

The importance of consumer research in understanding normal usage as well as misuse can be observed in the *Ex-cis-or* case.[43] This is a product sold as a cleaning agent for ovens that had been tested extensively in the laboratory by specialists in a variety of household

[41]"Business Responds to Consumerism," *Business Week,* (September 6, 1969), 108.

[42]"The Air Bag Faces a Showdown Fight," *Business Week* (August 14, 1971), 74-75.

[43]This example is extracted from Lawrence A. Bennigson and Arnold I. Bennigson, "Product Liability: Manufacturers Beware!" *Harvard Business Review* (May-June 1974), 122-132.

ovens and found to be an effective and "safe" product. When it was introduced to the market, the company received some rumors about consumer problems with burns from the product but apparently failed to investigate them thoroughly. Finally, a law suit was filed against the company for $2 million by a young homemaker with four children who had been badly burned and blinded while cleaning the kitchen stove. Evidence later revealed that the consumer had used the product on an outside element of the stove (rather than the oven), that the product had been of extra strength due to an abnormality in the production process, and that the user had mixed detergent with the product and applied it to a heated element of the range. Although there was technical abnormality in the product, the engineers were amazed that the customer would use *Ex-cis-or* mixed with a detergent on a heated element. The point is that the previous research of the firm was conducted in the laboratory by specialists who would use the product correctly. Consumer research, however, must be expected to look at the total usage pattern of consumers and, in addition, consider the potential problems that may arise when "normal" consumers use the product abnormally. This concept applies not only to manufacturers but to wholesalers and distributors also.[44]

Levels of Safety

Consumer research can help in the development of specifications of safety and performance levels. Given the assumption that perfect safety is as impossible as zero defects in most other processes, some definition must be made of acceptable levels of safety or nonsafety. While this is partly a question of technical research, it is also a question of consumer research. For example, assume that a manufacturer of automobiles could install as standard equipment an improved braking system that would decrease injuries, but that the cost of the improved system would be $1,000. Or suppose that a manufacturer now averages one defect in the steering mechanism per 800,000 cars. Improved inspection systems and employee incentive compensation, it might be shown, could cut these defects to one in 1 million cars, but at an additional cost per car of $40. Consumer research should be able to provide inputs helpful in making such decisions. For example, a safer computerized braking system is standard equipment on luxury automobiles. If *all* automobiles were required to have this system, would society be better off or not? This is a segmentation question, and consumer research should be able to supply the number of low-income customers who would be denied the ability to purchase a car because of the increased safety standards. Are consumers better or worse served by laws which require high levels of safety and performance but at the same time reduce the possibility of purchasing the product by low-income consumers? Similar questions could be raised in many other industries.

[44]Robert Larsen and Louis Marchese, *Product Liability* (Washington: National Association of Wholesaler-Distributors, 1979).

Table 21.2	Rank	Product Description
The Ten Most Hazardous Products (Based on Reports from Emergency Rooms; Compiled by the Consumer Product Safety Commission)	1	Bicycles and bicycle equipment
	2	Stairs, ramps, landings (indoors and outdoors)
	3	Doors, other than glass doors
	4	Cleaning agents
	5	Tables, nonglass
	6	Bed (including springs and frames)
	7	Football, activity-related equipment and apparel
	8	Swings, slides, seesaws, playground climbing equipment
	9	Liquid fuels, kindling
	10	Architectural glass

Source: Paul Busch, "A Review and Critical Evaluation of the Consumer Product Safety Commission: Marketing Management Implications," *Journal of Marketing*, vol. 40 (October 1976), 42. Reprinted from the *Journal of Marketing* published by the American Marketing Association.

The problem of the right level of safety has a solution; it is called cost-benefit analysis. Dardis explains:

Recognition that zero risk is neither feasible nor attainable (due to resource complaints) has led to a reformulation of the problem of consumer protection, namely, who should protect the consumer and how much protection should be provided. Underlying both these questions are concerns for the consumer's freedom of choice and efficiency. Is the consumer the most efficient risk reducer or should risk reduction be left to the regulatory authority? Given resource constraints, what is the optimal degree of protection? . . . Research demonstrates the role of cost-benefit analysis in evaluating and comparing mandatory safety standards for consumer products.[45]

The Consumer Product Safety Commission has begun to collect information about the relative hazards of products and, using various forms of research, constructs the Product Hazard Index as a guide in policy decisions. A result of this process is shown in Table 21.2, which lists the ten most hazardous products. The process of collecting this research is called the National Electronic Injury Surveillance System (NEISS) and involves a computer-based system for monitoring injuries reported in hospital emergency rooms across the country. The results from this research can then be used for establishing priorities in product standards.

Remember, though, that the research does not create the policies. The research is only an *input* to policy decisions that must be promulgated by thoughtful individuals considering the data. This process was explained by the CPSC's first chairman:

. . . It is important to realize that a high ranking on the Commission's Hazard Index does not mean a product will be banned or be the subject of a product safety rule. It simply means that the product is more likely to receive early attention. A coin, for example, is easily swallowed and can act as a damper and cause suffocation.

[45]Rachel Dardis, "Economic Analysis of Current Issues in Consumer Product Safety: Fabric Flammability," *Journal of Consumer Affairs* (Summer 1980), 109-121.

(This perhaps explains why *Life Savers* have holes in their centers.) But the fact that coins rank high among the Index's "Top 25" does not mean that the CPSC will ban them.[46]

Consumer Information

The right to be informed, enunciated by President Kennedy, was described as the right of the consumer, "to be protected against fraudulent, deceitful, or grossly misleading information, advertising, labeling, or other practices and to be given the facts he needs to make an informed choice." The contributions of consumer research can therefore be of two forms. The first form is in the area of *consumer deception,* while the second form of research is directed toward relevance to *informed choices.*

Consumer Deception

Consumers have the right to obtain information that is not misleading and that does not claim too much. They also have the right to product packaging and labeling that is not deceptive. The theoretical basis for such information is based upon the premise that such information will aid consumers in the proper allocation of their economic resources to maximize benefits and pleasure. Additionally, consumers are believed to have the right to clearly written statements of warranties and credit provisions as well as procedures for the quick and effective handling of complaints.

In most cultures of the world, it is illegal to lie in advertisements. Some might ask then why consumer research is necessary to understand whether or not an advertisement contains a lie. Why is it not possible merely to examine an advertisement and determine whether or not it contains false statements and abstain from making the statement if it is untrue? The research issues in such a situation would be legal and physical. (Does the product contain the attribute stated in the advertisement? Does it have more of the attribute than competitive brands?)

A subjective definition of deception is beginning to be more accepted in the regulation of marketing communications than an objective definition. An objective definition of deception is one in which an objectively ascertainable material fact is presented falsely, is ambiguous, or is misleading. A subjective definition of deception, however, focuses upon the *consumer's perception* of the advertisement. Gardner, after reviewing the contributions of other consumer researchers on this topic, formulated the following definition of deception:

If an advertisement (or advertising campaign) leaves the consumer with an impression(s) and/or belief(s) different from what would normally be expected if the consumer had reasonable knowledge, and that impression(s) and/or belief(s) is factually untrue or potentially misleading, then deception is said to exist.[47]

---

[46]Quoted in Paul Busch, "A Review and Critical Evaluation of the Consumer Product Safety Commission: Marketing Management Implications," *Journal of Marketing* (October 1976), 41-49.

[47]David M. Gardner, "Deception in Advertising: A Conceptual Approach," *Journal of Marketing* (January 1975), 40-46.

With this definition of deception, Gardner suggests three types of deception exist. One form of deception is the *unconscionable lie*, or claim that is completely false even using an objective definition of deception. The second form of deception is the *claim-fact discrepancy* or a claimed benefit that must be qualified (but is not, in the advertisement) for it to be properly understood and evaluated. The third form of deceptive communication is the *claim-belief interaction*, in which the communication interacts with the accumulated attitudes and beliefs of the consumer in such a manner as to leave a deceptive belief or attitude about the product in the communication.[48]

Claim-belief interaction may result from many possible causes. One possible cause would be the use of *color* in the automobile exhaust fumes of competitive gasolines but the absence of color in the exhaust from a car using the gasoline advertised. Although the advertising does not directly make such a claim, a consumer might easily conclude that the advertised brand was more pollution-free than competitive brands. *Symbols* such as *Hi-C* on fruit juice may cause consumers to conclude that the brand contains high amounts of vitamin C even though the product does not directly make that claim. *Endorsements* may cause a consumer to attribute more trustworthiness, credibility or prestige to a product than is objectively true. Similarly, an actor who plays a well-known doctor may also deliver advertisements for a medical product and consumers may conclude that the product is recommended by physicians. It is possible that if the actor mentions that he is not a doctor, the consumer may selectively distort the message and remember only the word "doctor" and attribute *more* credibility than if the actor did not make the disclosure.[49] Consumer research can be used—in fact, is essential—in understanding the ways that such communications may be misleading and the proportions of the population that are misled[50] and it appears that regulatory agencies are beginning to incorporate such behavioral concepts of deception into their policies.[51]

Deception may be more common—perhaps more needed—for low-involvement products than high. High-involvement products are more likely to give "factual" information in ads; information that can be determined objectively as to deception. Low-involvement products, however, are more likely to use "evaluative" claims as substitutes for factual claims in order to create attention and impact beliefs when few, if any, significant differences exist in the physical attributes of competing prod-

[48]Gardner, "Deception in Advertising." For a discussion of some of the research issues involved in these forms of deception see David M. Gardner, "Deception in Advertising: A Receiver Oriented Approach to Understanding," *Journal of Advertising Research* (Fall 1976), 5-11 +; and Jerry Olson and Philip Dover, "Cognitive Effects of Deceptive Advertising," *Journal of Marketing Research* (February 1978), 29-38; and Gary Armstrong, Metin Gurol and Frederick Russ, "Detecting and Correcting Deceptive Advertising," *Journal of Consumer Research* (December 1979), 237-246.

[49]Dorothy Cohen, "Surrogate Indicators and Deception in Advertising," *Journal of Marketing* (July 1972), 10-15. Another good review of these problems is found in John A. Howard and James Hulbert, "Advertising and the Public Interest," *Journal of Advertising Research* (December 1974), 33-39.

[50]Jacob Jacoby and Constance Small, "The FDA Approach to Defining Misleading Advertising," *Journal of Marketing* (October 1975), 65-73.

[51]Ivan L. Preston, "A Comment on 'Defining Misleading Advertising' and 'Deception in Advertising,'" *Journal of Marketing* (July 1976), 54-60.

ucts. This analysis was suggested by Shimp and Preston, who indicate that for "deceptive" advertising to apply, the following conditions must exist:

1. The claim is *attended* to by the consumer.

2. The claim (or implication therefrom) *affects beliefs.*

3. The claim (or implication therefrom) is *important.*

4. The important claim (or implication therefrom) becomes represented in *long-term memory.*

5. The claim (or implication therefrom) is objectively *false.*

6. *Behavior* is influenced as a result of either the deceptive claim or the implication derived from the claim.[52]

Informed Choices

Consumer research has a major function in defining the information required by consumers and its method of presentation to guarantee that consumers have the opportunity to make informed choices. The specific information relevant to a consumer's evaluative criteria varies greatly by the type of product involved, the purchase environment, and the target segment of the population. Thus, a research approach is required to understand the choice process. Such research must include the importance and complexity of the product in the mind of the consumer, the features that are important to each market segment, the accessibility of information, and the processability of information.

The most fundamental question to be answered by consumer research involves what constitutes relevant information to the consumer. In advertising, the attributes about which information is disclosed often involve *psychological association* whereas consumer advocates believe that what is needed is *performance information,* and that the withholding of such factual information by the seller is a deceptive practice.[53] Useful consumer research must define the evaluative criteria of consumers and the weights consumers place on those attributes rather than relying upon subjective interpretation or normative conclusions about what information is relevant to consumers.

Empirical research concerning the amount of information in television advertising indicates that less than one-half of advertisements are deemed informative in terms of price, quality, performance, availability, and ten other evaluative criteria.[54] A recent hypothesis that has been developed is that large-scale media advertising does not need to contain specific product information because consumers understand that the cost

[52]Terence A. Shimp and Ivan L. Preston, "Deceptive and Nondeceptive Consequences of Evaluative Advertising," *Journal of Marketing* (Winter 1981), 22-32.

[53]George S. Day, "Full Disclosure of Comparative Performance Information to Consumers: Problems and Prospects," *Journal of Contemporary Business* (Winter 1975), 53-68.

[54]Alan Resnik and Bruce L. Stern, "An Analysis of Information Content in Television Advertising," *Journal of Marketing* (January 1977), 50-53.

of such advertising campaigns and the prior market testing is so great that only products that are basically effective or fit the purpose for which they were advertised will be seen in national advertising campaigns.

Another possibility is that *too much information* can be communicated, causing consumers to make worse decisions than they make with less information. Jacoby and his associates have advanced the theory based upon their laboratory experiments that *information overload* can occur causing consumers to make poorer purchase decisions while feeling more satisfied and certain regarding their choice.[55] This might occur also if a seller provides many pieces of detailed information about credit costs, itemized prices, detailed product availability, (colors, sizes, etc.) and so forth. Some segments of the market (perhaps highly educated and affluent professional persons) may assimilate and find this information relevant, but other (less sophisticated) market segments may be overwhelmed or confused to the point that they make decisions based upon trivial (but not fully disclosed) criteria rather than more important and basic satisfactions desired from the product.

A number of policies and marketing practices have been adopted in an attempt to provide more relevant or greater amounts of information. One policy that has been voluntarily adopted by many firms and regulated as a policy in other situations is *unit pricing*, or the expression of the price of a good in terms of the cost per unit of measure (ounce, gram, etc.) in addition to its total price. While some research has indicated little effect of unit pricing on consumer choices,[56] most studies conclude that consumers tend to shift their purchases toward lower unit price goods, at least in some product categories.[57] This may vary by market segment, of course, and Houston points out that it may be the "value-conscious" market segment that uses the information contained in unit pricing.[58] To make the issue more complex, Carman reviewed a number of studies on the *costs* of implementing and maintaining unit pricing and concluded that if *all* stores converted, the already low margins of retailers would be under even greater pressure.[59] Consequently, consumers might

[55]Jacob Jacoby, Donald E. Speller, and Carol A. Kohn, "Brand Choice Behavior as a Function of Information Load," *Journal of Marketing Research* (February 1974), 63-69; Jacob Jacoby, "Consumer Reaction to Information Displays: Packaging and Advertising," in Sal Divita (ed.), *Advertising and the Public Interest* (Chicago: American Marketing Association, 1975). Also see Debra Scammon, "Information Load and Consumers," *Journal of Consumer Research* (September 1977), 148-155.

[56]Carl Block, Robert Schooler, and David Erickson, "Consumer Reaction to Unit Pricing: An Empirical Study," *Mississippi Valley Journal of Business and Economics* (Winter 1971-1972), 36-46; David McVullough and Daniel I. Padbert, "Unit Pricing in Supermarkets," *Search: Agriculture* (January 1971), 1-22.

[57]Clive W. Granger and Andrew Billson, "Consumers' Attitudes toward Package Size and Price," *Journal of Marketing Research* (August 1972), 239-248; Hans R. Isakson and Alex R. Maurizi, "The Consumer Economics of Unit Pricing," *Journal of Marketing Research* (August 1973), 277-285; J. Edward Russo, Gene Kreiser, and Sally Miyashita, "An Effective Display of Unit Price Information," *Journal of Marketing* (April 1975), 11-19; Kent B. Monroe and Peter J. LaPlaca, "What Are the Benefits of Unit Pricing?" *Journal of Marketing* (July 1972), 16-22. A nationwide survey indicated 81 percent in favor of unit pricing, reported in "Consumer Attitude Study," *Supermarketing* (April 1972), 38-43.

[58]Michael J. Houston, "The Effect of Unit-Pricing on Choices of Brand and Size in Economic Shopping," *Journal of Marketing* (July 1972), 51-69.

[59]James M. Carman, "A Summary of Empirical Research on Unit Pricing in Supermarkets," *Journal of Retailing* (Winter 1972-1973), 63-71.

be paying more overall, even though receiving greater information. A related practice of providing greater information is *open dating*, or printing of a date clearly understandable by the consumer after which a product (especially perishable products) cannot be sold for consumption without a high risk of spoilage or loss in value. After reviewing the major empirical studies on this topic, Nayak and Rosenberg concluded that open dating was a low priority among marketing practices, but that it generally provided more product information and quality-assured foods.[60]

Improved consumer information may also be attained through more detailed labeling and packaging information, especially *nutritional labeling*. In 1975, rules promulgated by the Food and Drug Administration became effective that substantially increased the amount of information that must be given on some food labels.[61] An example of this type of information is shown in Figure 21.3, and an example of the type which is *not* required is shown in Figure 21.4. Lenehan found that consumers exhibit a clear preference for nutritional labels, but that in supermarkets only about one-fourth of consumers were aware of nutritional labeling, about 15 percent understood them and less than 10 percent used them.[62]

In another study, detailed nutritional labels were used by some consumers, but labels with the promotional information "Succulent and sweet" (as a description of canned peas) were comparable to nutritional labels in providing consumers with a feeling of quality assurance.[63] There is a need for much more research and creativity in understanding how to present relevant nutritional information. In other countries, such as the Netherlands, creative approaches are resulting in new, symbolic approaches to communicating nutritional qualities to consumers in standardized formats. One form of standardized product information, however—beef grading—has been found to provide little relevant information to consumers.[64]

One of the major efforts in recent years to provide additional information to consumers with which to make more informed choices is in the area of credit information, specifically Truth In Lending (TIL). Many research studies have been conducted concerning this topic, and these are thoroughly reviewed by Day and Brandt.[65] By using a comprehensive model of consumer behavior similar to the one in this book, Day and Brandt isolated a major reason why TIL has been generally ineffective. They

[60]Prabhaker Nayak and Larry J. Rosenberg, "Does Open Dating of Food Products Benefit the Consumer?" *Journal of Retailing* (Summer 1975), 10-20.

[61]Warren A. French and Hiram C. Barksdale, "Food Labeling Regulations: Efforts toward Full Disclosure," *Journal of Marketing* (July 1974), 14-19; J. Boyd, "Food Labeling and the Marketing of Nutrition," *Journal of Home Economics* (May 1973), 20-24.

[62]R. J. Lenehan et al., "Consumer Reaction to Nutritional Labels on Food Products," *Journal of Consumer Affairs* (Summer 1973), 1-12.

[63]Edward H. Asam and Louis P. Bucklin, "Nutrition Labeling for Canned Goods: A Study of Consumer Response," *Journal of Marketing* (April 1973), 32-37.

[64]John A. Miller, David G. Topel, and Robert E. Rust, "USDA Beef Grading: A Failure in Consumer Information?" *Journal of Marketing* (January 1976), 25-31.

[65]George S. Day and William K. Brandt, "Consumer Research and the Evaluation of Information Disclosure Requirements: The Case of Truth in Lending," *Journal of Consumer Research* (June 1974), 21-31.

**Figure 21.3
Example of
Nutritional
Labeling**

Source: POST and GRAPE-NUTS are registered trademarks of General Foods Corporation. Package reproduction with the consent of General Foods Corporation.

discovered that, although TIL has increased awareness and knowledge of interest rates, credit information is brought to the attention of the buyer *after* the purchase decision is made and that TIL had relatively little effect on credit search and usage behavior. They concluded:

What is clear, however, is that it is not enough to simply provide consumers with more information. That is simply the first step in a major educational task of getting consumers to understand the in-

**Figure 21.4
Example of
*Non*required
Labeling**

Source: From *The Wall Street Journal* (May 18, 1977), 22—Ray Morin. Reprinted by permission.

formation, and persuading them to use it. Consumer researchers can make a significant contribution to both these tasks.[66]

Where should a consumer researcher begin in determining the kind of information that will improve consumer choices? This question faces researchers in business and in regulatory agencies. A very useful summary of the answers to this question was developed by Day. From Day's report on the topic, the following questions are suggested as the basis for research on consumer information:

1. What information is relevant?

2. Is the information assessable?

3. Can the information be comprehended?

4. How do information requirements vary among segments?

5. What changes occur over time in the effects of information?

6. How is the information of one member of the channel modified (positively or negatively) by other members of the channel?[67]

The proper type of information, the research of Sproles, Geistfeld, and Badenhop indicates, depends on type of product (high-involvement or low-involvement) and other factors. When buying blankets, for example, efficiency of buying is increased with information such as fiber content

[66]Day and Brandt, "Consumer Research," 31.

[67]George S. Day, "Assessing the Effects of Information Disclosure Requirements," *Journal of Marketing* (April 1976), 42-52.

and durability ratings, but for slow cookers, specific product information was not as helpful.[68]

Consumer Choice

The consumer is entitled to spend his or her money on any legal goods and services for satisfying the consumer's needs and wants. For this right to have meaning, however, goods and services should be at competitive prices from a number of alternative offerings.

A basic premise underlying the American, Canadian, and many other economies, is that consumer choice is at a maximum in a competitive market economy. In traditional *laissez faire* economics, the consumer is best served by choosing from business firms freely competing, with individual choice from those firms constrained only by the consumer's own economic and physical resources. But what should the government— "the people"—do when business firms no longer freely compete? What should be done when firms use unfair forms of competition or competition is severely restricted? Even more difficult to answer is the question, "Should consumers be allowed to choose freely when they are choosing unwisely?"

Regulated Choice

An implicit assumption exists among many consumerists that consumers ought to be forced to do what is best for them. Thus consumerism has resulted in laws that force consumers to purchase seat belts rather than allow consumers to make the choice themselves. Laws have been passed in some states that require motorcyclists to purchase and wear helmets for their own protection. Attempts have been made to keep children away from harmful advertising rather than place that responsibility with parents.

At a more basic level, consumerists raise the issue of whether the consumers are spending their resources on the right products. In Moran's study of consumerism and public policy, he quotes a consumerist view on this subject:

What does a contemporary consumer do, faced with the bewildering array of new products, new materials, new processes, compounded by the brand explosion? How does he choose? He is influenced by the sweet purrings of an attractive salesman (or woman) often less informed about product differences than the customer and also biased by push money, spiffs, and other manufacturer bribes. He is beguiled by style at the expense of safety and stamina, by gleam instead of guts, by features and gimmicks in place of performance and economy.[69]

---

[68]George Sproles, Loren Geistfeld, and Suzanne Badenhop, "Types and Amounts of Information Used by Efficient Consumers," *Journal of Consumer Affairs* (Summer 1980), 37-48.

[69]Moran, "Formulating Public Policy on Consumer Issues," 35. Reprinted by permission.

This view is also related to earlier opinions of Galbraith, Packard, and others that the consumer should be prevented from spending money on luxuries and should instead spend them on better schools, highways, health care, and basic needs.

Adaptionists believe that the control of consumer choice can be achieved by *educating* consumers to make better decisions. More radical positions indicate the need for government *intervention* and regulation to ensure that choices are made for products that are good for the consumer and the society.

Consumer research cannot solve these basic policy and philosophical issues, but it can contribute information helpful in their resolution. It is interesting to think through what the meaning of consumer choice is for maintaining competition. One view leads to the conclusion that when marketers provide more and more choice (product differentiations rather than a commodity approach), the ultimate effect is to transform competitive industries into noncompetitive industries. The remedy for such a situation might be to restrict the offering of diverse forms of products. The FTC might place a moratorium on style changes in the auto industry, for example, in order to obtain *more* competition.[70]

Consumer Education

An approach popular in the 1980s is the position that enough regulation of choice already exists—or there is even too much of it. What is needed, perhaps, is not more regulation but more intelligence on the part of the consumers.[71] In an investigation of ten consumerism topics about which regulations exist, one study found that as few as one-third of consumers possessed knowledge of the consumerism law. Furthermore, a sample of attorneys had only a little higher knowledge than consumers.[72] The starting place might well be additional education about consumer rights before additional regulation is enacted.

The conclusion of Sheth and Mammana is that child-rearing practices and secondary school education should be changed to teach new generations to cope with the complex choice processes of mass consumption society. Specifically, they recommend that such education should contain the following elements:

1. Formal knowledge about the criteria with which to evaluate complex technical products and services and choose rationally among them.

2. Managerial and decision-making skills as consumers that are comparable to the type of skills we inculcate in people to become professional workers in industry or government.

[70]H. Paul Root, "Should Product Differentiation Be Restricted?" *Journal of Marketing* (July 1972), 3-9.

[71]James T. Rothe and Lissa Benson, "Intelligent Consumption: An Attractive Alternative to the Marketing Concept," MSU *Business Topics* (Winter 1974), 29-34.

[72]William H. Cunningham and Isabella C. M. Cunningham, "Consumer Protection: More Information or More Regulation?" *Journal of Marketing* (April 1976), 63-68.

3. Increased consumer knowledge of the workings of business, government, and the marketplace.

4. Values and consciousness that will encourage respect and concern for other consumers in their pursuit of collective consumption.[73]

A deregulated or market-regulated economy probably requires more consumer information and education—by both business and government. More responsibility for consumer information flows to the individual consumer and to consumer organizations as well. Research can be helpful in sorting out this balance of responsibility, however. Mazis and his colleagues described an approach for evaluating when consumer information regulation is helpful.[74] This framework is shown in Figure 21.5. Government intervention has both benefits and costs, and the purpose of consumer research is to determine each of those *before* regulations are enacted or promulgated. The major benefit categories include *improved decision making* by consumers, *enhanced product quality,* and *reduced prices.* Not only do firms have *compliance costs* and government organizations have *enforcement costs,* but government intervention also may have many *unintended side effects.* For example, if the FTC enacts higher standards for comparative advertising—normally considered an advantage to consumers—the effect may be to cause firms to abandon comparative advertising. Thus a rule intended to provide more information to consumers may have the unintended effect of causing consumers to receive less information.

The basic philosophy of consumer information systems (CIS) is this: Information has a significant effect on increasing consumers' efficiency of choice and, in the process, assists the consumer. It also develops loyalty and profitability for firms that are effective in flows of consumer information.[75] Hans Thorelli states it this way: "Informed consumers are protected consumers—more than that, they are liberated consumers."[76]

Consumer Redress

The consumer has the right to expect sellers and other organizations to provide a rapid, convenient means for registering dissatisfactions and for assurance that complaints will be heard by competent management and evaluated objectively. Furthermore, consumers have the right to expect a reasonable and satisfactory resolution of the complaint.

---

[73]Jagdish N. Sheth and Nicholas J. Mammana, "Recent Failures in Consumer Protection," *California Management Review* (Spring 1974), 71. Also see Richard Saelin, "The Effects of Consumer Education on Consumer Product Safety Behavior," *Journal of Consumer Research* (June 1978), 30-39; Jack Hamilton, Steven Jung, and Jeanette Wheeler, "Improving Consumer Protection in Postsecondary Education," *Journal of Consumer Affairs* (Summer 1978), 135-139.

[74]Michael Mazis, Richard Staelin, Howard Beales, and Steven Salop, "A Framework for Evaluating Consumer Information Regulation," *Journal of Marketing* (Winter 1981), 11-21.

[75]George B. Sporles, Loren V. Geistfeld, and Suzanne B. Badenhop, "Informational Inputs as Influences on Efficient Consumer Decision-Making," *Journal of Consumer Affairs* (Summer 1978), 88-114; Douglas Webbink, "Automobile Repair: Does Regulation or Consumer Information Matter" *Journal of Consumer Research* (December 1978), 206-209.

[76]Hans Thorelli, "The Future for Consumer Information Systems," Jerry Olson (ed.), *Advances in Consumer Research,* (Ann Arbor, Mich.: Association for Consumer Research, 1980), 222-232.

**Figure 21.5
A Framework for
Evaluating
Consumer
Information
Regulation**

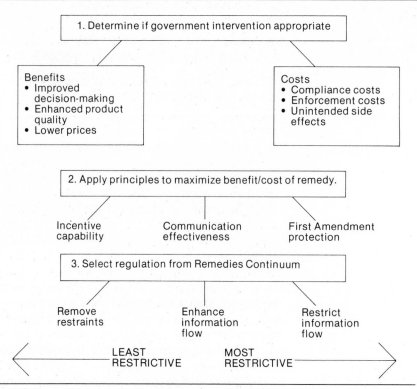

Source: Reprinted by permission from Michael Mazis, Richard Staelin, Howard Beales, and Steven Salop, "A Framework for Evaluating Consumer Information Regulation," *Journal of Marketing* (Winter 1981), 12, published by the American Marketing Association.

Consumer redress can be achieved in at least three ways.[77] The first method is *prevention.* Stated alternatively, one way to solve the problem of redress is for consumers to be heard *before the problem develops.* A second way for consumers to be heard and bring about change in the offering of the offending seller is through *restitution.* Many of these relate to advertising practices, and they include affirmative disclosures and corrective advertising as well as repayment of funds and limitations on contracts.

One limitation on consumer contracts is the imposition of a cooling-off period, which gives the consumer the right to rescind the contract within a specified period.[78] A third form of redress is by *punishment* of the erring seller through fines, incarceration, class action suits, and other legal processes. The Federal Trade Commission can now fine violators of trade practices rules up to $10,000 per day per violation, certainly an incentive to listen to the consumer. See Table 21.3.

[77]Dorothy Cohen, "Remedies for Consumer Protection: Prevention, Restitution, or Punishment," *Journal of Marketing* (October 1975), 24-31.

[78]Dennis H. Tottelian, "Potential Impact of 'Cooling-Off' Laws on Direct-to-Home Selling," *Journal of Retailing* (Spring 1975), 61-70; Orville C. Walker, Jr., and Neil M. Ford, "Can 'Cooling-Off Laws' Really Protect the Consumer?" *Journal of Marketing* (April 1970), 53-58.

Table 21.3	**Prevention**	**Restitution**	**Punishment**
Remedies for			
Consumer	Codes of conduct	Affirmative disclosure	Fines and incarceration
Protection			
	Disclosure of information requirements	Corrective advertising	Loss of profits
	Substantiation of claims	Refunds	Class action suits
		Limitations on contracts	
		Arbitration	

Source: Dorothy Cohen, "Remedies for Consumer Protection: Prevention, Restitution, or Punishment," *Journal of Marketing* vol. 39 (October 1975), 25. Reprinted from the *Journal of Marketing* published by the American Marketing Association.

An important process in obtaining the right of the consumer to be heard is the *warranty.* In 1975, Congress passed the Magnuson-Moss Warranty–Federal Trade Commission Improvement Act, which had improving consumer product warranty practices[79] as a major purpose. This was not just a legal reform but a major effort to understand the needs of the consumer in this area and to meet those needs better. Specifically, the FTC has the power to examine warranties to determine whether, even if objectively accurate, they have the probable effect of producing *misleading* representations. Procedures are also examined to insure *ease of access* for the consumer to obtain warranty service. Finally, an attempt is now made to prevent *obscurity of terms.* The objective by which the warranty should be evaluated (with the assistance of consumer research) is whether the average consumer can understand the warranty.

Many of the provisions that have been enacted to protect consumers' rights to be heard are not new. They may have existed under previous law. However, the average consumer may have experienced so much difficulty or cost in obtaining them, that the rights were essentially inoperative. Many of these new provisions are an attempt to help the little guy, who, as Figure 21.6 shows, needs help.

The right to be heard is not achieved just with force or regulatory policies. Many far-sighted companies have recognized that voluntary action in this area provides a significant opportunity for improved customer relations and loyalty.[80] An outstanding example is the Whirlpool Corporation, which started a Cool-Line program in 1967, which provides a personal and easily accessible communications link between customers and a trained staff of product and service experts. The company receives

[79]Laurence P. Feldman, "New Legislation and the Prospects for Real Warranty Reform," *Journal of Marketing* (July 1976), 41-47; F. K. Shuptrine and Ellen Moore, "Even After the Magnuson-Moss Act of 1975, Warranties Are Not Easy to Understand," *Journal of Consumer Affairs* (Winter 1980), 394-404.

[80]C. L. Kendall and Frederick A. Russ, "Warranty and Complaint Policies: An Opportunity for Marketing Management," *Journal of Marketing* (April 1975), 36-43.

**Figure 21.6
Consumer
Protection by the
Government Is
Sometimes
Misjudged**

*"SURE IT'S UNFAIR TO THE LITTLE GUY – HE'S THE
EASIEST ONE TO BE UNFAIR WITH."*

Source: *The Wall Street Journal* (May 19, 1977), 20. Reprinted by permission of The Wall Street Journal and Bob Zahn.

over 150,000 calls per year and finds that over 90 percent can be resolved during the intital telephone call. Thus, possible sources of major complaints and formal redress are often resolved satisfactorily before the problem gets out of hand.[81]

Environmental Responsibility

Large numbers of people with large amounts of money in a technologically advanced society produce large amounts of energy consumption, pollution, and other stresses on the society. An increased need for research and analytical thinking about consumption is the result of the increased interdependency of consumer decisions described by Feldman:

One reason . . . is that marketing decisions have been made which expanded the range of consumer product choice but disregarded their environmental impact. There has been a failure to recognize that these products, which are marketing outputs designed for in-

[81]"Whirlpool Corporation," in Blackwell, Engel, and Talarzyk, *Contemporary Cases in Consumer Behavior,* 309-318. For another excellent program see "Eaton's Department Store," in this same source, 46-51.

dividual satisfaction, are simultaneously inputs to a large environmental system and as such may affect the well-being of society.[82]

The first task of consumer research is to aid in the definition of what might be acceptable environmental goals. Assuming that perfection is impossible, consumer research should aid in determining what levels of pollution (air, water, and so forth) are really required to coincide with consumers' desired use of time for leisure, physical products, food preferences, location preferences, and so forth. One of the few researchers to approach the issue of environmental goals analytically is Feinberg. He observes:

Given the wide variety of environments existing in the world, each inhabited by people who are reasonably content with it, I have the impression that a person's idea of a good environment is usually the one he grew up in, and that not much thought has really been given to the general question of what makes an environment good.

It is conceivable that most people would prefer the whole world to be like Polynesia with respect to climate and easy availability of food, and that we could actually engineer the world into such a form. If so, it would be good to know this preference so that we could set about working to satisfy it.[83]

Feinberg continues that from the point of view of basic science, no aspect of the natural environment is really essential to human life. Rather, protection or creation of any specified type of environment must be viewed in terms of offsetting aspects of the environment that must be forfeited:

I believe that eventually we will be forced into making many choices of this type, where doing one thing precludes doing something else which otherwise might be desirable. We must ask ourselves whether preserving the environment is to be the controlling factor in making all such choices, or if not, what other principles can be brought to bear. To me, the answer is clearly that preserving the environment is only one of several factors in making any decision, and that we would do well to clarify these other factors.[84]

Identifying consumers who are oriented to protection of the environment and methods of attracting other consumers to be more concerned is currently a major thrust in consumer research. Much of this research is oriented to solving problems of a conserver society in which "more is less." Sometimes firms must employ a strategy called "demarketing" in which purposeful attempts are made to induce consumers to buy less of

---

[82]Laurence P. Feldman, "Societal Adaptation: A New Challenge for Marketing," *Journal of Marketing* (July 1971), 54-60.

[83]Reprinted by permission from Gerald Feinberg, "Long-Range Goals and the Environment," *The Futurist* (December 1971), 244, published by the World Future Society, 4916 St. Elmo Avenue, Washington, DC 29914.

[84]Feinberg, "Long-Range Goals," 245.

a product in an environment where the firm could sell more. The consumer research literature about energy and ecology is much too great to describe in detail here, but it promises to provide significant inputs into strategic decisions in the future concerning the environment.[85]

Responsibility to Minorities and the Poor

Consumer research makes three major contributions to relieving the problems of minorities and of the poor. The first is research directed toward the question of how to stretch or *allocate more efficiently the limited resources* of the those who have been subject to discrimination. These studies require two outputs. First, they need to compare consumption problems of the minorities with consumption problems of the majorities to determine if the basis exists for separate strategies. Is there a unique set of problems among minorities and the poor to which special efforts in regulation, marketing information, or education should be directed? Elderly consumers frequently express fewer concerns than young consumers,[86] but this may be based on their naïveté or a lack of awareness of their problems.[87] Second, studies directed toward stretching the resources of the poor need to determine the feasibility of possible changes in marketing activities.

A second contribution of consumer research in this area is in the *improvement of marketing efficiency* among firms and organizations that serve minorities and the poor. For example, in a study of black store managers, it was found that one of the major problems deterring success was the reluctance of the black community to buy in black-run stores.[88] Sturdivant conducted considerable research on ghetto retailers and concluded that investment guarantees and enlarged investment tax credits

---

[85]Harold Kassarjian, "Incorporating Ecology into Marketing Strategy; The Case for Air Pollution," *Journal of Marketing* (July 1971), 61-65; Thomas Anderson, Jr., Louis Sharpe, and Robert Boewadt, "The Environmental Role for Marketing," *MSU Business Topics* (Summer 1972), 66-72; Thomas Kinnear, James R. Taylor, and Sadrudin Ahmed, "Ecologically Concerned Consumers: Who Are They?" *Journal of Marketing* (April 1974), 20-24; Nessim Hanna, A. H. Kizibash, and Albert Smart, "Marketing Strategy Under Conditions of Economic Scarcity," *Journal of Marketing* (January 1975), 63-67; Alan S. Manne, "What Happens When Our Oil and Gas Run Out," *Harvard Business Review* (July-August 1975), 123-137; Andrew Gross and Warren Ware, "Energy Prospects to 1990," *Business Horizons* (June 1975), 5-18; Sherman Hanna, "Evaluation of Energy Saving Investments," *Journal of Consumer Affairs* (Summer 1978), 63-74; James Bowman, "Business and the Environment: Corporate Attitudes, Actions and Energy-Rich States," *MSU Business Topics* (Winter 1977), 37-49; Stephen W. Brown, Zohran Demirdjian, and Sandra McKay, "The Consumer in an Era of Shortages," *MSU Business Topics,* (Spring 1977), 50-53; Gene Laczniak, Robert Lusch, and Jon Udell, "Marketing in 1985: A View from the Ivory Tower," *Journal of Marketing* (October 1977), 47-56; Stanley Shapiro, "Marketing in a Conserver Society," *Business Horizons* (April 1978), 3-13; Stanley Hollander, "Merchandise Shortages and Retail Policies," *MSU Business Topics* (Summer 1978), 28-33; Malcom Getz and Yuhching Huang, "Consumer Revealed Preference for Environmental Goods," *Review of Economics and Statistics* (August 1978), 449-457; Carter Henderson, "The Economics of Less," *Business Horizons* (April 1979), 25-28; Lewis R. Tucker, Jr., "Identifying the Environmentally Responsible Consumer: The Role of Internal-External Control of Reinforcements," *Journal of Consumer Affairs* (Winter 1980), 326-339.

[86]John Burton and Charles Hennon, "Consumer Concerns of Senior Citizen Center Participants," *Journal of Consumer Affairs* (Winter 1980), 366-382.

[87]Zarrel Lambert, "Elderly Consumers' Knowledge Related to Medigap Protection Needs," *Journal of Consumer Affairs* (Winter 1980), 434-451.

[88]Dan H. Fenn, Jr., "NAFC Probes Three Major Issues of the 70s: Economy, Technology, Consumerism," *Chain Store Age* (December 1970), 31-34.

are needed to stimulate adequate retail facilities to serve the consumers of the ghetto.[89]

A third contribution of consumer research is through *studies of the majority segments* to determine the degree to which they contribute to the consumer problems of the minority. Housing is a major problem among black consumers, for example, and a thorough study by Sanoff and colleagues discloses many relationships between nonwhite housing availability and white movements.[90] This study shows that whites often move out when blacks move in, partially because of the fear that whites have of property values declining, a fear that is largely unfounded.

The responsibility to minorities and the poor is connected to broader issues about urban areas as a whole. Business in general and consumer researchers specifically clearly will want and probably will be required to play a vital role in determining the kind of urban environment that should be built for future consumers and the ways that acceptance will be achieved.

Consumer research has investigated the problems of disadvantaged consumers, but Sturdivant and Deutscher observe that this research mainly focused on questions such as: "Do minorities face discrimination in the marketplace? Do the poor pay more? Where do the poor shop?" Very little was done to construct a theoretical frame within which the findings from these studies could be analyzed and applied.[91] After thoroughly reviewing the research, Sturdivant and Deutscher concluded that the areas of highest priority for research on the purchasing behavior of disadvantaged consumers were the following. First, attention should be directed to the cognitive dimensions of individual factors rather than nose-counting surveys of previous research. This would include concepts such as cognitive effects of communications, quality perception as related to price, cognitive dissonance, and other topics which are well-used in research with majority consumers but seldom used at all in research concerned with disadvantaged consumers. A second field of promise for research on low-income consumers is decision making within the household. A third area of unusual opportunity identified by Sturdivant and Deutscher is the investigation of reference groups and their influence on the disadvantaged consumer. This is of special interest be-

---

[89]Frederick D. Sturdivant, "Better Deal for Ghetto Shoppers," *Harvard Business Review* (March-April 1968), 130-139. For additional solutions to these problems, see Allan T. Demaree, "Business Picks up the Urban Challenge," *Fortune* (April 1969), 102-104+; Richard F. America, Jr., "What Do You People Want," *Harvard Business Review* (March-April 1969), 103-112.

[90]Henry Sanoff et al., "Changing Residential Racial Patterns," *Urban and Social Change Review* (Spring 1971), 68-71.

[91]Frederick D. Sturdivant and Terry Deutscher, "Disadvantaged Consumers: Research Dimensions," (working paper series 76-44, Columbus, Ohio: Ohio State University, July 1976). Also see Henry O. Pruden and Douglas S. Longman, "Race, Alienation and Consumerism," *Journal of Marketing* (July 1972), 58-70. For practical suggestions on helping low-income consumers, see Robin T. Peterson, "Low Income Consumer Education by Business—A Neglected Activity," *Marquette Business Review* (Summer 1976), 74-79; Alan Andreasen and Gregory Upah, "Regulation and the Disadvantaged: The Case of the Creditors' Remedies Rule," *Journal of Marketing* (Spring 1979), 75-83; and Jean Bowers and Kristen Crosby, "Changes in the Credit Repayment Performance of Low Income Consumers," *Journal of Consumer Affairs* (Summer 1980), 96-108.

cause of the effect of reference groups on the aspirations, attitudes, and behavior of disadvantaged consumers.

Marketing of Social Products

Consumer research can also be directed to the problem of when consumers *fail* to buy products beneficial to themselves or to the human community. This is almost the converse of demarketing. Broadening the concept of marketing to include nonbusiness products, services, and ideas, and people is sometimes called "social marketing."[92] It frightens some to think that the techniques of consumer research and tools of marketing can be applied to ideas such as planned parenthood, politics, religion, and so forth,[93] but it is clear that in the United States we are well along the road to doing so.[94]

The applications of consumer research to social marketing are diverse. The marketing of birth control and planned parenthood is a thoroughly researched topic[95] and increasingly so are education,[96] religion,[97] health care,[98] and the arts.[99] Consumer research is increasingly used in political campaigns, both for the marketing of political candidates and for political issues.[100]

Wildlife Conservation

A case example concludes this chapter and demonstrates how social marketing was applied to a wildlife issue, "State Question 2." This issue would have prohibited leghold traps for wildlife. Six weeks before the election, survey research indicated that 70 percent of the voters approved the new law.

Shelly Berman Communicators accepted an assignment to change public opinion on the issue. The agency turned to the diffusion literature

---

[92]Philip Kotler and Sidney Levy, "Broadening the Concept of Marketing," *Journal of Marketing* (January 1969), 10-15.

[93]Gene R. Laczniak, Robert Lusch and Patrick Murphy, "Social Marketing: Its Ethical Dimensions," *Journal of Marketing* (Spring 1979), 29-36. Also by the same authors, "The Ethics of Social Ideas Versus the Ethics of Marketing Social Ideas," *Journal of Consumer Affairs* (Summer 1980), 156-163.

[94]Karen Fox and Philip Kotler, "The Marketing of Social Causes: The First 10 Years," *Journal of Marketing* (Fall 1980), 24-33.

[95]Julian L. Simon, "A Huge Marketing Research Task—Birth Control," *Journal of Marketing Research* (February 1968), 21-27.

[96]H. Lee Mathews and Roger Blackwell, "Implementing Marketing Planning in Higher Education," Leonard Berry and William Kehoe, "Problems and Guidelines in University Marketing," and Karen Fox and William Ihlanfeldt, "Determining the Market Potential in Higher Education," all in Richard Bagozzi (ed.), *Marketing in the 80s*, (Chicago: American Marketing Association, 1980), 1-13.

[97]James Engel, *Contemporary Christian Communications* (Nashville: Thomas Nelson Publishers, 1979).

[98]Katherine Alexander and James McCullough, "Cultural Differences in Preventive Health Care Choice," Raymond Smead and John Burnett, "Understanding the Blood Donor Problem," Jacob Hornik and Mary Jane Schlinger, "Dimensions of Health Maintenance Activities and Opinions," all in Jerry Olson, (ed.), *Advances in Consumer Research* (Ann Arbor, Mich.: Association for Consumer Research, 1980), 617-632. An extensive bibliography on this subject is found in Roger Blackwell and Wayne Talarzyk, *Consumer Attitudes Toward Health Care and Medical Malpractice* (Columbus, Ohio: Grid Publishing, Inc., 1977).

[99]Adrian Ryans and Charles Weinberg, "Consumer Dynamics in Nonprofit Organizations," *Journal of Consumer Research* (September 1978), 89-95.

[100]Michael Rothschild, "Political Advertising: A Neglected Policy Issue in Marketing," *Journal of Marketing Research* (February 1978), 58-71; Sadrudin Ahmed and Douglas Jackson, "Psychographics for Social Policy Decisions: Welfare Assistance," *Journal of Consumer Research* (March 1979), 229-239.

and public opinion literature. Just another clever set of commercials would not be enough; the supporters of the issue were already using an effective advertising campaign. A fear appeal was determined to be risky but possibly very effective in achieving rapid learning. This would be persuasive, the diffusion literature indicated, only with endorsements from highly credible sources. The state commissioner of public health, a physician, well-known and respected personally throughout the state, and other experts from the state forestry department were filmed endorsing the issue. The storyboards for this television ad campaign are shown in Figure 21.7.

Audio copy for the advertisements included items such as the following, "On a Saturday night in October, Matt Winkler, then age 6, was bitten by a rabid animal. Despite rabies shots, Matt Winkler contracted the dread disease. Miraculously, he survived—the first child ever to survive rabies. You can help to control rabies for Matt, and your children. Vote no on State Question 2." Gregg Pruit of the Cleveland Browns appeared on some of the TV ads saying, "There's no good alternative to leghold traps. If State Question 2 passes, it means more animals with distemper and rabies in parks and playgrounds. It may also mean no more trapping rats . . . I say vote no on 2."

In spite of the massive support for the issue six weeks prior, on election day State Question 2 was defeated.

Summary

The consumer has the right to safety, the right to be informed, the right to choose from an adequate selection of products, and the right to be heard. These rights have been reaffirmed by decree and administrative action since John F. Kennedy declared them in 1962. Yet, there is ample evidence to show that these rights are violated constantly, creating a rising interest in consumerism programs.

Historical antecedents of consumerism resulted in legislation such as the Pure Food and Drug Act, just as the outcries of consumers have resulted in contemporary protective legislation. Increased pressures for social responsibility led by educated and affluent segments of the market have been an important impetus for protection of consumer rights.

A research approach to consumerism is provided by the discipline of consumer behavior. This research approach has the potential of becoming a boundary-spanning agent between conflicting interests of business, government, and consumer advocacy groups.

This chapter discussed some of the research, mostly from empirical studies, that is directed to understanding consumer rights and needs. These areas of inquiry include consumer safety, consumer information, consumer choice, the right to be heard (redress), environmental protection, responsibilities to minorities and the poor, and social marketing.

This chapter focused upon objective analysis of consumer behavior as it relates to consumerism issues. The action implications for business firms and consumer protection agencies are described in Chapter 22 along with some perspectives on the ethics of consumer influences.

State Question 2 and our Park System

1. "You may see signs like this in our parks if trapping is banned in Ohio."

2. "These animals are abundant. Trapping helps keep their numbers down, so all of the animals stay healthy."

3. "Without essential trapping, the animal population explodes."

4. "Diseases like rabies break out..."

5. "diseases that threaten our pets and our families."

6. "Only you can prevent it and help to keep our parks safe and open."

**VOTE NO
on
State Question 2**

Disclaimer

7. "Go to the Polls November 8th. Vote No on 2."

Advertising Agency: Shelly Berman Communicators

Source: Courtesy of Shelly Berman Communicators

**Figure 21.7
(Continued)**

Dr. Ackerman on State Question 2

DR. ACKERMAN
Director, Ohio Department of Health

1. "You may not want to vote this year, but if you don't vote, your family may face the spread of rabies."

2. State Question 2 can result in a population explosion among rabies carriers.

3. "Hungry, diseased animals may move into your parks and playgrounds."

4. "If you want more facts about State Question 2 and the threat of rabies, talk to your doctor or any wildlife expert."

5. "For the sake of your family, go to the polls on November 8 and Vote No."

VOTE NO
on
State Question 2

Disclaimer

6. "Vote No on 2."

Source: Courtesy of Shelly Berman Communicators

Review and Discussion Questions

1. Is the consumerism of recent years fundamentally similar to or different from that of previous eras?

2. Provide a definition of consumerism that will be adequate for research purposes in consumer behavior.

3. If you were asked to prepare a list of the most pressing problems in a country, how could it be done? Specify the research design that you would use.

4. Describe the issue of consumer information and analyze the role of market segmentation in understanding this issue.

5. How can the concept of "satisfaction" be measured for a consumer product?

6. Why don't firms design safe products for consumers? In what ways might consumer research be helpful to the engineering and design of new products?

7. Can consumers receive too much information? Explain.

8. What is meant by the concept of deception?

9. What is social marketing? What should be the role of consumer research in social marketing?

10. Analyze the issues raised in this chapter concerning responsibility to minorities and the poor. Develop a proposal for consumer research that might be helpful in solving some of these problems.

"Give Your Baby Love and Lactogen" was the advertising slogan of the Swiss food company, Nestlé. As a promotional theme for Nestlé's infant baby formula, this slogan has been translated into more than 70 languages (even Swahili) and played throughout the world. With urbanization and a growing number of women in the work force throughout the world, hospital procedures that discourage lactation and commercial promotion of artificial milk products for infant feeding process, the market is growing. Suppose, however, that you are a consumer researcher attempting to find growing markets for a company such as Ross Labs, Borden or Nestlé. In highly industrialized economies, the fertility rates are generally falling and the current penetration for infant baby formula is already high. Thus, you might be attracted by the high rates of fertility and nonsaturation of the product in lesser developed countries (LDCs). Would you as a consumer researcher or marketing executive recommend entry and aggressive promotion in the LDCs?

If you had made that recommendation as a consumer researcher for Nestlé, you would have encountered some problems, such as the backlash from a pamphlet published in Great Britain entitled *The Baby Killer.* Social critics charged that intensive advertising efforts in LDCs were leading mothers who could ill-afford to purchase artificial food to abandon the healthier practice of breastfeeding. Through the use of posters and pictures portraying healthy, well-fed, and happy babies in the arms of bottle-feeding mothers, LDC families were seduced into a decision that became irreversible after several days of nonlactation. Additionally, powdered formulas—the usual form in tropical nations—are often mixed with contaminated water, and because formula is so expensive, a poor mother may be tempted to stretch her supply of formula by adding excessive amounts of water.

What should be done? Your answer might be for the company to quit selling the product. Would you, if you were the stockholder, want that to be done? And remember, the product satisfies a legitimate need for many mothers who cannot produce milk. Some children would die without a substitute for mother's milk so it would be difficult to justify outlawing the product. Should it be available only on prescription? Remember that many women as a personal choice prefer this product. Would you deny women in LDCs easy access to a product considered to be liberating in many urban environments? Perhaps you would try to get the government to prohibit advertising of the product, although not actually prohibiting sales. That will greatly benefit the products marketed by pharmaceutical firms (Abbott, Bristol-Myers, American Home Products) because of their historical ties to hospitals and pediatricians and severely restrict food firms (Nestlé, Borden, Carnation) which traditionally have relied on mass advertising. You might recommend such a policy but it would be highly discriminatory against the food firms compared to pharmaceutical firms. Do you want to discriminate against some firms?

Perhaps you would recommend voluntary action by the manufacturers of infant formula. Perhaps they would agree (but be careful about collusion, which is illegal in many countries) to demarket the product. (Demarketing refers to organizational decisions to reduce or stop efforts to sell a product because of risks to the health, safety or welfare of users.) The practice of demarketing, or limiting sales of products in the marketplace for reasons that are not profit-related, has been called an "unnatural act."[1]

So what do you do as a consumer analyst working for one of the interested businesses? Or for a hospital where the product is used? Or for the government? Or for a consumer advocacy organization? Or for an advertising agency? Or simply as a concerned and informed citizen?

THE LIMITS OF POWER: WHERE ARE THEY?

This final chapter adds the last step in the analysis of consumer behavior. Until now the focus has been on understanding how consumers make decisions and how organizations can have power through knowledge to influence those decisions. The emphasis has been upon what *can* or *might* be done by an organization intending to influence consumers or modify their behavior. At some point, however, every consumer analyst must face the additional question of what *should* be done.

Three basic types of consumer policies are possible to help consumers attain the rights described in the preceding chapter. These policies involve *education, information,* and *protection.* The policy makers or power centers include consumer organizations and other citizen groups, business, government, educational institutions, and the mass media. Thorelli, in Table 22.1, indicates the activities that fit into each category of consumer policy.[2] In Table 22.1, Thorelli also indicates a very important principle; namely, *consumer rights can only be achieved when ac-*

---

[1]James E. Post and Edward Baer, "Demarketing Infant Formula: Consumer Products in the Developing World," *Journal of Contemporary Business,* vol. 7 (Autumn 1978) 17-37. The infant formula scenario is developed from this source and S. Prakash Seth and James Post, "Public Consequences of Private Action," *California Management Review* (Summer 1979), 35-48.

[2]Hans Thorelli, "Consumer Rights and Consumer Policy: Setting the Stage," *Journal of Contemporary Business,* vol. 7 (Autumn 1978), 3-16.

Table 22.1
Consumer Policy and Consumer Rights and Responsibilities

Consumer Policy	Consumer Rights			
	1. Choose Freely	2. Be Informed	3. Be heard	4. Be safe
A Education	Decision-making budgeting; nature of market economy, rights and responsibilities	Generic product and materials data, information sources	How to assert consumer rights	Importance of health and safety, user manuals and training
B Information	Buying criteria, buying advice	Models and brands data, independent consumer info programs	Market research, two-way market dialogue	Safety certification, care and maintenance data
C Protection	Maintain open markets, antitrust, stop high pressure and deceptive tactics	Truly informative advertising product claims substantiation	Complaints handling machinery	Minimize health and accident risks
	Choose Wisely	Keep informed	Sound off	Safety first
	Consumer responsibilities			

A third dimension of the matrix would show the makers of consumer policy. These policy makers include consumer organizations, other citizen groups, business, government, educational institutions, and the mass media.

Source: Hans Thorelli, "Consumer Rights and Consumer Policy: Setting the Stage," *Journal of Contemporary Business,* vol. 7 (Autumn 1978), 6.

companied by consumer responsibilities. Thus, while the consumer has the right to choose freely, he or she also has the responsibility to choose wisely.

The limits on the power to influence the consumer reside most visibly in *government* and *business firms* and we will examine the policies of both institutions in this chapter. *Individuals* also play an essential role and we want to think at least briefly about the ability of consumers to influence their own destiny and that of institutions relating to consumers. Are there some activities of consumer influence that an individual employed by an organization ought not to do even though asked to do so by the employer? If so, how does one make such individual decisions? These are the topics for our final chapter in the study of consumer behavior.

The Basis for Regulation of Consumer Influence

The basis for regulating or controlling consumer influence and other business decisions rests upon three primary considerations: (1) legal regulations; (2) self-interest and voluntary codes; and (3) personal convictions or ethics.[3]

Legal regulations are forms of compulsion enacted to force compliance with community or national norms of behavior. Legal regulations may occur at the level of the local community, the state or province, or

[3]Adapted from Robert Bartels, "A Model for Ethics in Marketing," *Journal of Marketing* (January 1976), 26.

at the national level and may include both laws enacted by legislators and rules which have the effect of law promulgated by various regulatory agencies. Generally, laws regulating the ability to influence consumers have arisen because of abuses of those attempting to influence consumers.

Self-interest and voluntary codes are based upon the premise that behavior that influences consumers positively is in the firm's own self-interest, at least in the long run. Belief in the *laissez faire* economic system or modifications of it leads to the conclusion that competition is the best protector of improper competition. While a company may abuse a consumer initially, continuance of such a practice will lead to the demise of that firm and its replacement by one more precisely attuned to the needs of the consumer. Sometimes, the recognition occurs within a group of competitors that some competitors have differing opinions about consumer influence and abuse, and the competitors, usually working through a trade association, prepare a voluntary code for the industry. Such codes may have a positive influence on those firms that have a basic long-term commitment to the marketplace, but usually they are ineffective against deviant members of the industry who do not choose to comply.

Personal *convictions* about ethics arise from an integrated sense of personal and social values. Ethics is concerned with right and wrong. In some instances, the ethical standards of an organization relating to consumer influence may be those of an individual, because that individual has power through ownership to control the ethics of the firm or because of the persuasiveness of that individual in obtaining adherence to those ethical standards by other employees and stockholders of the firm.

Decisions about programs and policies of consumer influence are usually based on a combination of all three bases for controlling consumer influence. Each is discussed in additional detail later in the chapter.

THE REGULATION OF CONSUMER INFLUENCE

Regulation of activities designed to influence consumers has generally arisen because of clear-cut abuses. Historically, at least, this has been true although recently some attention of regulatory agencies is being directed toward the topic of preventing abuses before they have the opportunity of becoming prevalent. Many types of laws and regulatory actions have developed to combat the abuses. Some of those most likely to affect the conduct of consumer research and the development of consumer influence programs (such as advertising, personal selling, and so forth) are described in the following section. Many other laws, such as the Robinson-Patman Act, are important influences on business practices generally and at times may have some direct influence on consumer programs, but the discussion below omits those more general laws and concentrates on those regulations most directly concerned with consumer influence.[4]

The Laws that Regulate Consumer Influence

The laws that protect consumers are based upon a historical foundation of laws that were enacted *to protect competition.* The basic premise of such laws are consumerist in theory even though their enactment was often more closely associated with pressures from small businesses seeking protection from larger predatory business and business practices. Laws designed to promote competition are consumerist in the sense that they are based upon the premise that consumers can achieve the highest average standard of living when the economy is organized on a competitive basis rather than a controlled basis. When monopolies or other aberrations in free competition developed, laws were justified that were designed to prevent such monopolies and restraints on competition.

Sherman Act

The foundation for the most important consumer protection laws is the Sherman Act, passed by Congress in 1890. The Sherman Act was passed after a public clamor over the treatment of consumers and small businesses by huge monopolies or trusts that controlled supplies of sugar, ice, petroleum, and other products. The greatest clamor arose from farmers who were being bullied by the railroads into paying excessive prices and meeting unreasonable conditions for shipping. Congress finally responded, after decades of these abuses, by passing the Sherman Act, which forbids "every contract or combination, in the form of trust, or otherwise, or conspiracy in the restraint of trade or commerce among the several states or with foreign nations."

Although the Sherman Act laid the basis for later legislation, it was generally ineffective, first because of some court rulings that exempted most businesses from the act and later because it was so general in its prohibitions. More specific legislation was passed in 1914 in the form of the Clayton Act which forbids specific practices relating to business organization and practices and in the form of the Federal Trade Commission Act.[5]

The FTC Act

The Federal Trade Commission Act, passed in 1914, was an amendment to the Sherman Act and established the Federal Trade Commission, the

[4]For discussion of broader legal and public policy issues in marketing, see Louis W. Stern and John R. Grabner, Jr., *Competition in the Marketplace* (Glenview, Ill.: Scott, Foresman and Company, 1970). Also, see Theodore Beckman, William R. Davidson, and Wayne Talarzyk, *Marketing* (New York: Ronald Press, 1971); Ben M. Enis, *Marketing Principles* (Santa Monica, Calif.: Goodyear Publishing Company, Inc., 1977), ch. 4; David J. Schwartz, *Marketing Today* (New York: Harcourt Brace Javonovich, 1977), ch. 28; Maurice Mandell and Larry J. Rosenberg, *Marketing* (Englewood Cliffs: Prentice-Hall, 1981), chs. 3 and 4; and John Udell and Gene Laczniak, *Marketing in an Age of Change* (New York: John Wiley & Sons, 1980), ch. 2.

[5]For details of these and other important laws relating to marketing practices, such as the Robinson-Patman Act, see footnote 4 above.

federal agency regulating the greatest number of marketing practices. In its original form, the FTC had power only to police methods of unfair competition—that is, activities that unfairly injured other firms. For example, in the Raladam case (1931) the Supreme Court ruled that the FTC did not have authority to prevent a firm from misrepresenting an obesity cure because the firm's action did not injure competition. To overcome this problem, Congress passed the Wheeler-Lea Act (1938), which was an amendment to Section 5 of the FTC Act (which, it will be remembered, was an amendment to the Sherman Act). The Wheeler-Lea Act made the FTC the watchdog for the consumer by making unlawful those acts unfair and deceptive whether or not they injure competition. Wheeler-Lea (which is sometimes called the "advertising act") also gave the FTC additional enforcement powers and specifically prohibited false advertising of food, drugs, therapeutic devices, and cosmetics.

The Federal Trade Commission is an agency consisting of several thousand staff members, mostly attorneys, economists, and support staff, headed by five commissioners who are appointed by the president of the United States and confirmed by the Senate. The commissioners are normally attorneys appointed on a nonpartisan basis for seven-year, staggered terms. The staff takes the initiative in deciding when business activities are unlawful, based upon consumer and other complaints or their own investigations, and presents its findings to the commissioners, who make the final decisions about whether or not a practice is unlawful. Their decisions, however, can be appealed through the courts and frequently are—meaning that implementation of a decision can take years.

FTC Activities

When a consumer or an organization makes a complaint to an office of the Federal Trade Commission, a staff member investigates the complaint to determine whether it concerns a matter of broad interest to the public welfare. Three possible actions are available to the FTC. First, the complaint may be determined to have no validity or not be of broad interest to the public and the case be closed. Second, the FTC may inform the company of the complaint and obtain voluntary agreement to stop the violative activities. (This occurs about 75 percent of the time.) Third, the FTC may seek to obtain a formal cease-and-desist order.

If a formal complaint is filed by the FTC and the company disagrees with the allegation of the FTC, a formal hearing is scheduled in which the attorneys for the firm and attorneys for the FTC present their evidence before another member of the FTC staff, a hearing examiner, who draws conclusions and proposes an order to remedy the problem. The proposed order can be appealed to the five commissioners who make the final decision. Their decision can be appealed to the US Court of Appeals and eventually to the US Supreme Court in unusual cases. This process takes a considerable amount of time and it might be argued that consumers' rights would be more expeditiously achieved without the extended legal process. However, if the FTC made many complaints later found to be unjustified and without due process within the legal system, the rights of sellers as well as buyers would not be protected. Because the process is so expensive—both for the seller and for the government (paid by taxpayers, of course)—there is incentive to work out voluntary compliance with proposed orders and settle the problem out of court, rather than complete the entire legal process.

The FTC also has other functions and powers. One of these is to investigate an industry and promulgate industry-wide rules that will govern the behavior of all firms in that industry. This reduces the need for a case-by-case approach, which is expensive and often ineffective. Two types of industry rules are possible. The first is *voluntary guidelines* in which the FTC, in cooperation with members of the industry and consumers, adopts a set of standards that will apply to the conduct of business activities in that industry. This may clean up the industry for the most part because most firms will probably comply, but it is ineffective in controlling the activities of those members who refuse to comply.

A second and stronger approach is a *trade practice rule.* In this approach, the staff proposes a detailed set of rules regulating practices of an industry. This might include advertising practices, how price information is to be disclosed, a necessity of informing consumers of the products of competitors, merchandising techniques and methods of sales presentations, and so forth. Public hearings are then conducted concerning the proposed rules in which consumers, consumer advocacy groups, businesses, the FTC, and others are encouraged to present their opinions about the proposed rule. The FTC will give financial aid to organizations that will support the FTC's position in order to hire lawyers and expert witnesses and conduct research to present in the hearings. Businesses also hire expert witnesses, lawyers, and so forth, and frequently consumer researchers are employed by both sides to conduct and present evidence in hearings. A "hearings officer" examines and cross-examines the witnesses and then prepares a conclusion—much like a judge renders a decision—about the proposed rules. The hearings officer's conclusions are then presented to the commissioners for a final decision, appealable through the courts, which may then have the effect of law in that industry. If businesses violate any provision of the trade regulation rule (TRR), they are subject to a fine of $10,000 per violation per day. It appears at the present time that the use of trade practice rules is increasing and thus is likely to be a major factor affecting marketing practices in many industries.

The FTC also conducts some educational activities. Conferences are occasionally held to educate business firms on legal and proper methods of influencing consumers. The FTC has issued some booklets designed to help consumers make better decisions. Generally, these activities have been minimal and largely ineffective compared to the legal actions undertaken by the FTC. One of the problems faced by the FTC is that most of their programs have been developed by lawyers and economists who have little formal training in consumer behavior. Consequently most of the programs of the FTC have been based upon concepts of legal and/or normative economics—or how consumers *ought* to behave according to classical economic models—with little attention to the actual concerns and buying patterns of consumers. Recently, the FTC has attempted to bring some persons with formal training and experience in consumer research into the staff, so possibly the scope and effectiveness of consumer orientation may increase in the future.

A consumer researcher or marketing strategist must understand the effects of the FTC on programs of consumer influence. The marketing management and legal counsel of an organization might on occasions be affected by FTC complaints against specific practices. But much more pervasive effects result from the cumulative law that arises from previous cases establishing the precedents that control marketing practices. Commerce Clearing House monitors these cases (through various appeals that are likely to occur) and prepares summaries of the decisions that affect various methods of consumer influence and other business practices. A consumer analyst can also keep aware of some of the most important decisions by reading the legal abstracts section in each issue of the *Journal of Marketing.*

Federal Consumer Protection Laws

Many other consumer protection laws have been enacted in an attempt to protect the consumer from various abuses. It is not possible to describe all of them here, but a selected list of some of the more important ones is presented in Table 22.2.

State and Local Regulations

All states and provinces have laws that directly affect consumer influence programs. Some are general in that they regulate untruthful communications about credit terms, use of unfair (below cost) prices to obtain customers, bait-and-switch advertising, and so forth. Others are specific in that they relate to specific industries such as banking, insurance (controls over salespersons' presentations, for example), liquor, utilities, professional services (prohibitions against certain forms of advertising for physicians, lawyers, funeral directors, dentists, and so forth), and many others. The attorney general's office of most states encourages consumer complaints, often through a consumer fraud office. Some states have policies that such complaints will not be investigated unless a certain quantity of complaints is received against a particular company. Some states have also established a special agency to represent the interests of consumers.

Some cities and other political entities have established offices to regulate trade practices and assist consumers with complaints. In Dade County, Florida, for example, the consumer protection division has the power to enforce consumer protection laws of the city, county and state. In many cities, such agencies monitor the weights and scales of food

**Table 22.2
Selected Federal
Consumer
Protection Laws**

Act	Purposes
Pure Food and Drug Act (1906)	Prohibits adulteration and misbranding of foods and drugs sold in interstate commerce
Food, Drug, and Cosmetic Act (1938)	Prohibits the adulteration and sale of foods, drugs, cosmetics, or therapeutic devices that may endanger public health; allows the Food and Drug Administration to set minimum standards and to establish guides for food products
Wool Products Labeling Act (1940)	Protects producers, manufacturers, distributors, and consumers from undisclosed substitutes and mixtures in all types of manufactured wool products
Fur Products Labeling Act (1951)	Protects consumers and others against misbranding, false advertising, and false invoicing of furs and fur products
Flammable Fabrics Act (1953)	Prohibits interstate transportation of dangerously flammable wearing apparel and fabrics
Automobile Information Disclosure Act (1958)	Requires automobile manufacturers to post suggested retail prices on all new passenger vehicles
Textile Fiber Products Identification Act (1958)	Guards producers and consumers against misbranding and false advertising of fiber content of textile fiber products
Cigarette Labeling Act (1965)	Requires cigarette manufacturers to label cigarettes as hazardous to health
Fair Packaging and Labeling Act (1966)	Declares unfair or deceptive packaging or labeling of certain consumer commodities illegal
Child Protection Act (1966)	Excludes from sale potentially harmful toys; allows the FDA to remove dangerous products from the market
Truth–in–Lending Act (1968)	Requires full disclosure of all finance charges on consumer credit agreements and in advertisements of credit plans to allow consumers to be better informed regarding their credit purchases
Child Protection and Toy Safety Act (1969)	Protects children from toys and other products that contain thermal, electrical or mechanical hazards
Fair Credit Reporting Act (1970)	Ensures that a consumer's credit report will contain only accurate, relevant, and recent information and will be confidential unless requested for an appropriate reason by a proper party
Consumer Product Safety Act (1972)	Created an independent agency to protect consumers from unreasonable risk of injury arising from consumer products; agency is empowered to set safety standards
Magnuson–Moss Warranty–Federal Trade Commission Improvement Act (1975)	Provides for minimum disclosure standards for written consumer product warranties; defines minimum content standards for written warranties; allows the FTC to prescribe interpretive rules and policy statements regarding unfair or deceptive practices

Source: William M. Pride and O. C. Ferrell, *Marketing: Basic Concepts and Decisions*, 520-521 Copyright © 1981 by Houghton Mifflin Company. Reprinted by permission of the publisher.

markets, register door-to-door sales organizations ("Green River" ordinances) and other activities that are more effectively regulated at the local or state level where immediate and personal attention can be given to individual complaints in a way that probably would never be possible at the national level of a regulatory agency.

Local and state regulations are usually directed toward the most blatant forms of consumer deception and fraud rather than the more sophisticated deceptions investigated by the FTC. Local agencies are important, however, because of the ability of local officials to give quick attention to claims that would be too small to involve the remote, highly expensive legal processes of Washington.

CONSUMER RESEARCH AND PUBLIC POLICY

Consumer research has the potential of providing valuable inputs in the formulation of public policy designed to regulate programs of consumer influence. When something occurs that harms the consumer, the frequent response is, "There ought to be a law." The laws have, for the most part, brought about improvements in the buying environment of consumers.

In some instances, however, the laws did not bring about the anticipated improvements, had related negative effects, or had costs that outweigh the benefits. Consumer research has the potential for understanding the causes of such undesired results and providing inputs for improvements in present and potential regulations.

The contributions of research to public policy, especially the FTC, have been reported by two leading researchers, Wilkie and Gardner, both former consultants to the FTC.[6] They suggest three broad areas of FTC decisions that might benefit from increased consumer research. These decision points include establishing program priorities, fact-finding (including investigation and substantiation), and remedy and compliance. Research needs of each of these areas are described in the following sections.

Establishing Program Priorities

What are the most pressing problems of consumers, as perceived by consumers? What kinds of deceptive or unfair marketing activities are most feasible to regulate? Which segments of the population are most affected or least able to defend against consumer abuses? These are critical information needs in the formulation of public policy, and they are needs to which consumer research can be meaningfully directed.

---

[6]William L. Wilkie and David M. Gardner, "The Role of Marketing Research in Public Policy Decision Making," *Journal of Marketing* (January 1974), 38-47.

Research directed toward establishing program priorities should provide accurate descriptions of the consumer environment, models for resource allocation, measurements of social cost compared to benefits and comparison of potential benefits of structural or trade practice remedies.[7]

The use of research in establishing priorities might help government agencies overcome the problem that results from establishing priorities on the basis of what lawyers believe has the highest probability of success—even if small, insignificant cases are the only ones tried—rather than attacking the most serious consumer abuses. Kangun and Moyer describe this problem:

Most staff lawyers are guided chiefly by their trained habits to find a case that the commissioners "will buy" and that can be made to stick with the available evidence and under prevailing judicial opinions. Any attempt to ascertain the true worth (in terms of consumer protection) of a particular investigation or litigative activity is normally ignored.[8]

To be useful, Dyer and Shimp conclude, the research must be submitted early in the decisions of the FTC and should have wide dissemination outside the FTC in order to achieve more consideration by policymakers.[9]

Research that examines the degree of consumer acceptance of various products, or conversely, the level of dissatisfaction, is presented in Figure 22.1. This study was based upon a sample of 10,000 households and was repeated on an annual basis. Very simple measures are used, but clearly disclosed problem areas for consumers are gasoline (the great increase in price of gasoline occurred in the year of the reported survey), automobile repairs, appliance repairs, home repairs, credit charges, and children's clothing. These results are similar to studies on this topic using other methodologies that were discussed in Chapter 21. By monitoring consumer problems on an annual basis,[10] regulatory agencies could determine trends which would provide useful inputs in establishing priorities for consumer programs.

Consumer research can also be used to guide the allocation of resources in the products, programs, and services furnished by the government. These decisions may be described as *functional* public policy rather than *regulatory* public policy, and they may require evaluations of user satisfaction levels with government services, priorities for government services (such as recreation and medical care), cultural activities

---

[7]Wilkie and Gardner, "Role of Marketing Research," 44.

[8]Norman Kangun and R. Charles Moyer, "The Failings of Regulation," *MSU Business Topics,* (Spring 1976), 10.

[9]Robert F. Dyer and Terence A. Shimp, "Enhancing the Role of Marketing Research in Public Policy Decision Making," *Journal of Marketing* (January 1977), 63-67.

[10]Fabian Linden, "The Consumer's View of Value Received—1974," *The Conference Board Record* (November 1974), 48-53. A simple method for measuring satisfaction is described in Robert Westbrook, "A Rating Scale for Measuring Product/Service Satisfaction," *Journal of Marketing* (Fall 1980), 68-72.

Figure 22.1
The Degree of
Consumer
Acceptance of
Selected Products

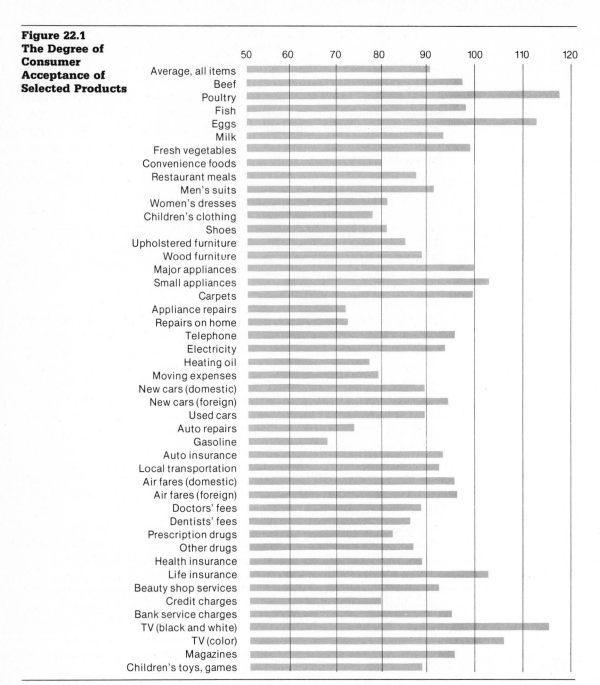

Source: Fabian Linden, "The Consumer's View of Value Received—1974." *The Conference Board Record* (November 1974), 50. Reprinted by permission.

desired by the population, information needs of the population, and so forth.[11]

Fact-Finding

A second type of contribution that consumer research can make in the development of public policy is providing facts for decisions that the FTC (or other agencies) must make. Consumer studies can and have been important in providing *substantiation* about the meaning of advertisements.[12] This is particularly important when deception is defined subjectively in terms of meaning to the *receiver* rather than objective meaning of the words in the advertisement.[13]

Consumer analysts employed by advertising agencies and marketing organizations probably will find their efforts devoted more and more to providing *substantiation for advertising claims.* The FTC now requires that a "reasonable basis" exist for any claims made by any advertising. Where no reasonable basis exists, making such claims is deemed to be deceptive and unfair (whether or not the claim is actually true).[14] In asserting this policy, the FTC argues that consumers may infer when seeing performance claims in an advertisement that supporting tests have been made to back up the claims.

Much of the substantiation research deals with technical or physical properties of the product but consumer researchers may be involved because of the need to understand the meaning of words to consumers as descriptions of technical properties of the product. For example, the FTC has charged that names such as *Accu-Color, Insta-Matic,* and *Total Automatic Color* are trade-invented names to describe essentially the same features but which leave the false impression of uniqueness.[15]

Facts obtained by consumer research may be important in understanding the *differential effects of regulations among market segments.* For example, low-income consumers appear to be attitudinally and cognitively less ready to use a cooling off law than consumers in middle- or high-income areas and may need special education programs to permit such laws to be effective.[16] In rules by the FTC concerning the funeral

---

[11]J. Brent Ritchie and Roger J. LaBreque, "Marketing Research and Public Policy: A Functional Perspective," *Journal of Marketing* (July 1975), 12-19.

[12]J. Thomas Rosch, "Marketing Research and the Legal Requirements of Advertising," *Journal of Marketing* (July 1975), 69-79; and Dorothy Cohen, "The FTC's Advertising Substantiation Program," *Journal of Marketing* (Winter 1980), 26-35.

[13]David M. Gardner, "Deception in Advertising: A Conceptual Approach," *Journal of Marketing* (January 1975), 40-46; David M. Gardner, "Deception in Advertising: A Receiver-Oriented Approach to Understanding," Journal of Advertising (Fall 1976), 5-11+; Terence Shimp, "Social Psychological (Mis)Representations in Television Advertising," *The Journal of Consumer Affairs* (Summer 1974), 28-40.

[14]Robert E. Wilkes and James B. Wilcox, "Recent FTC Actions: Implications for the Advertising Strategist," *Journal of Marketing* (January 1974), 55-61.

[15]Wilkes and Wilcox, "Recent FTC Actions."

[16]Dennis H. Tootelian, "Attitudinal and Cognitive Readiness: Key Dimensions for Consumer Legislation," *Journal of Marketing* (July 1975), 61-64. Also see Alan Andreasen and Gregory Upah, "Regulation and the Disadvantaged: The Case of the Creditors' Remedies Rules," *Journal of Marketing* (Spring 1979), 75-83; Kenneth McNeil et al., "Market Discrimination Against the Poor and the Impact of Consumer Disclosure Laws: The Used Car Industry," *Law and Society Review* (Spring 1979), 695-720.

industry, a portion of the rules would have mandated how prices were to be quoted to consumers. Evidence presented in FTC hearings indicated that the effect of such rules would be to lower the prices paid by some market segments but to raise the price paid by other segments. The segments paying lower prices were those who were usually affluent and well-educated but the consumers who would pay higher prices were most likely to be those from low-income and low-education segments, especially those with cultural values found most often in the black population. Labarbera and Lazer found, however, that minority consumers and less educated, lower-income consumers are underrepresented in the FTC rule-making process.[17]

Market segmentation research by consumer analysts is also needed to provide facts concerning different interpretations that may be made by reasonable consumers as opposed to ignorant consumers. The question facing regulators is whether the standard of deception in advertising should refer to interpretations of the average or reasonable person or to the unreasonable or ignorant consumer—who perhaps is not capable of understanding the difference between a factual claim and puffery of a product. After thoroughly reviewing cases about this topic, Preston concluded:

The FTC holds no longer to the strict ignorant man standard by which it would protect everyone from everything which may deceive them . . . Perhaps we may call the new stance a modified ignorant man standard which protects only those cases of foolishness which are committed by significant numbers of people.[18]

A special group of "ignorant" consumers the FTC has shown special interest in protecting is children, who when very young presumably have not developed some of the defenses against advertising that are developed in later years. A great deal of consumer research by Ward, Robertson, Heslop, and others has investigated this topic.[19]

Consumer researchers have an important role to play in providing substantiation and other facts concerning advertising, sales presentations, and other programs of consumer influence, and it is clear that this role is likely to expand in the future.[20] An example of what might have

[17]Priscilla Labarbera and William Lazer, "Characteristics of Consumer Participants in Federal Trade Commission Rule Making," *Journal of Consumer Affairs* (Winter 1980), 405-417.

[18]Ivan L. Preston, *Great American Blow-up* (Madison: University of Wisconsin Press, 1975), ch. 10.

[19]Daniel Wackman, Ellen Wartella, and Scott Ward, "Learning to Be Consumers: The Role of the Family," *Journal of Communications* (Winter 1977), 138-151; Scott Ward, "Children's Reactions to Commercials," *Journal of Advertising Research* (April 1972); T. S. Robertson and J. R. Rossiter, "Children and Commercial Persuasion: An Attribution Analysis," *Journal of Consumer Research* (June 1974), 13-20; Gilbert Churchill, Jr., and George Moschis, "Television and Interpersonal Influences on Adolescent Consumer Learning," *Journal of Consumer Research* (June 1979), 23-35; George Moschis and Roy Moore, "Decision Making Among the Young: A Socialization Perspective," *Journal of Consumer Research* (September 1979), 101-112; Louis Heslop and Adrian Ryans, "A Second Look at Children and the Advertising of Premiums," *Journal of Consumer Research* (March 1980), 414-420. An excellent bibliography is available in Laurene Merigoff, *Children and Advertising* (New York: Council of Better Business Bureaus, Inc., 1980).

[20]Michael Rothschild, "The Emerging Role of Consumer Research at the Federal Trade Commission: Views of the Players," in Jerry Olson (ed.), *Advances in Consumer Research* (Ann Arbor, Mich.: Association for Consumer Research, 1980), 101-103.

been required if the present environment existed in 1776 in substantiation of claims contained in the Declaration of Independence is shown in Figure 22.2.

Compliance and Remedies

A third area of input by consumer research into policy making is in the area of investigating the effects of various forms of remedies and methods for obtaining compliance. It is important to understand the effects and effectiveness of remedies, both proposed and implemented, to both business and government. It is also in the consumers' interest, Walker and his associates report, because if regulations are implemented that have serious adverse effects or are not cost-effective in their results, the long-run effect will be to injure the ability to obtain *effective* regulation needed by consumers.[21]

A remedy for deceptive advertising used by the FTC in recent years is *corrective advertising,* which may be any advertising designed to correct past deception. The first case in which this remedy was approved by the FTC involved Continental Baking Company, which had claimed that consumers could lose weight by eating *Profile* bread. The bread, however, had the primary characteristics of being *thinner* than other bread slices rather than any unique calorie characteristics. The FTC approved a plan in which *Profile* was required to run 25 percent of its advertising containing corrective statements such as the following (featuring the actress Julia Meade):

I'd like to clear up any misunderstandings you may have about *Profile* bread from its advertising or even its name. Does *Profile* have fewer calories than other breads? No, *Profile* has about the same per ounce as other breads. To be exact, *Profile* has 7 fewer calories per slice. That's because it's sliced thinner. But eating *Profile* will not cause you to lose weight. A reduction of 7 calories is insignificant . . .[22]

Corrective advertising is intuitively an appealing concept. Rather than merely punishing a firm with a fine or ordering them to cease and desist a deceptive practice, why not make the firm correct the perceptions or attitudes that consumers have developed from the firm's deceptive advertising? While some research indicates that corrective advertising has been partially effective, the issue is very complex because advertising effectiveness is based upon interactions between message, source, and consumer characteristics, which may make the effects of corrective advertising difficult to predict.[23] One possibility is that corrective advertising

[21]Orville C. Walker, Jr., Richard F. Sauter, and Neil M. Ford, "The Potential Secondary Effects of Consumer Legislation: A Conceptual Framework," *Journal of Consumer Affairs* (Winter 1974), 144-155.

[22]"Mea Culpa, Sort Of," *Newsweek* (September 27, 1971), 89.

[23]Robert F. Dyer and Philip G. Kuehl, "The Corrective Advertising Remedy of the FTC: An Experimental Evaluation," *Journal of Marketing,* (January 1974), 48-54; William L. Wilkie, "Research on Counter and Corrective Advertising" (paper presented to Advertising and the Public Interest Conference of the American Marketing Association, Washington, D.C.: May 9-11, 1973); James R. Taylor and Thomas C. Kinnear, "Corrective Advertising: An Empirical Tracking of Residual Effects," in Richard Bagozzi (ed.), *Marketing in the 80s* (Chicago: American Marketing Association, 1980), 416-419.

Figure 22.2
The Declaration of Independence, Modified to Meet Regulatory Requirements

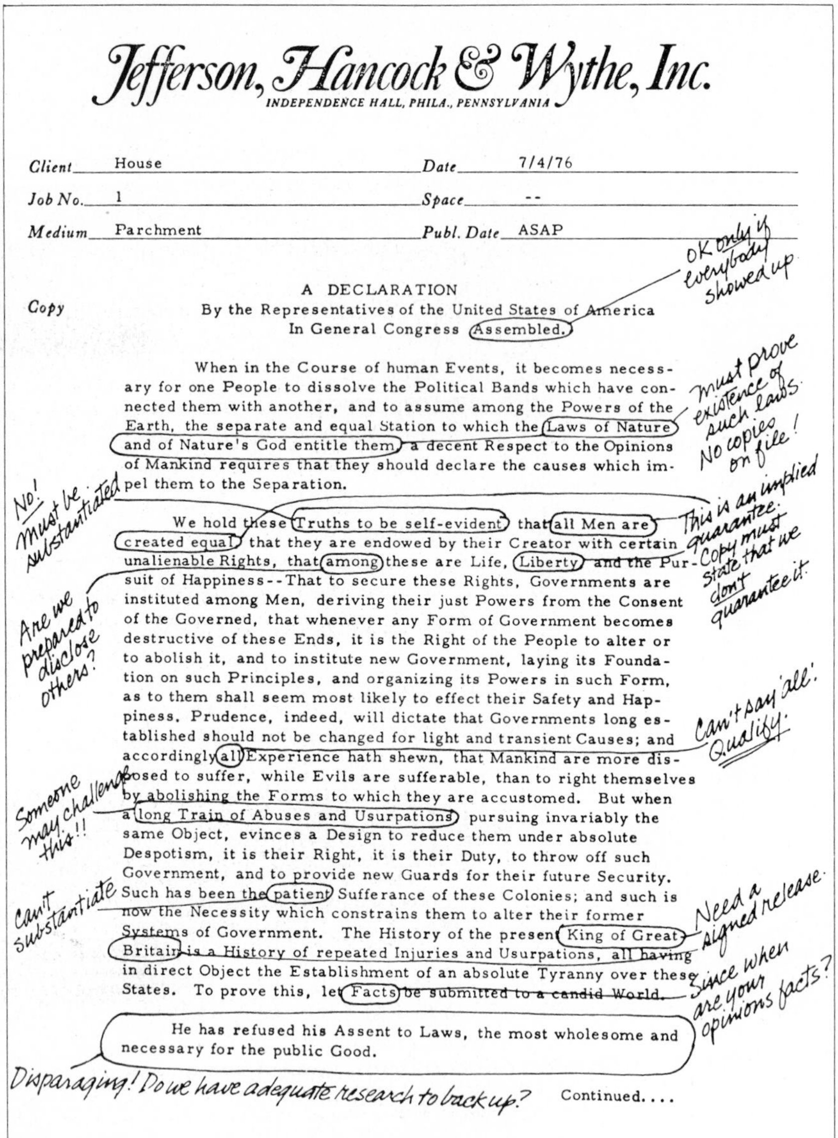

Jefferson, Hancock & Wythe, Inc.
INDEPENDENCE HALL, PHILA., PENNSYLVANIA

Client___House_____ Date_____7/4/76_____

Job No.___1_____ Space_____--_____

Medium___Parchment_____ Publ. Date___ASAP_____

OK only if everybody showed up

Copy

A DECLARATION
By the Representatives of the United States of America
In General Congress Assembled.

must prove existence of such laws. No copies on file!

When in the Course of human Events, it becomes necessary for one People to dissolve the Political Bands which have connected them with another, and to assume among the Powers of the Earth, the separate and equal Station to which the Laws of Nature and of Nature's God entitle them, a decent Respect to the Opinions of Mankind requires that they should declare the causes which impel them to the Separation.

No! Must be substantiated

This is an implied guarantee - Copy must state that we don't guarantee it.

We hold these Truths to be self-evident, that all Men are created equal, that they are endowed by their Creator with certain unalienable Rights, that among these are Life, Liberty and the Pursuit of Happiness--That to secure these Rights, Governments are instituted among Men, deriving their just Powers from the Consent of the Governed, that whenever any Form of Government becomes destructive of these Ends, it is the Right of the People to alter or to abolish it, and to institute new Government, laying its Foundation on such Principles, and organizing its Powers in such Form, as to them shall seem most likely to effect their Safety and Happiness. Prudence, indeed, will dictate that Governments long established should not be changed for light and transient Causes; and accordingly all Experience hath shewn, that Mankind are more disposed to suffer, while Evils are sufferable, than to right themselves by abolishing the Forms to which they are accustomed. But when a long Train of Abuses and Usurpations pursuing invariably the same Object, evinces a Design to reduce them under absolute Despotism, it is their Right, it is their Duty, to throw off such Government, and to provide new Guards for their future Security. Such has been the patient Sufferance of these Colonies; and such is now the Necessity which constrains them to alter their former Systems of Government. The History of the present King of Great Britain is a History of repeated Injuries and Usurpations, all having in direct Object the Establishment of an absolute Tyranny over these States. To prove this, let Facts be submitted to a candid World.

Are we prepared to disclose others?

Can't say 'all'. Qualify!

Someone may challenge this!!

Can't substantiate

Need a signed release.

Since when are your opinions facts?

He has refused his Assent to Laws, the most wholesome and necessary for the public Good.

Disparaging! Do we have adequate research to back up?   Continued....

Source: Created by Edward A. McCabe, vice-president of Scali, McCabe and Sloves. Reprinted from *Advertising Age* (December 9, 1974), 17.

may actually *increase credibility* because of reference to the Federal Trade Commission giving the impression that the firm, by doing corrective advertising, is honestly and sincerely attempting to correct any false impressions that might have occurred as a result of previous advertising, thereby enhancing the firm's overall reputation. Research by Hunt also indicates that even when the FTC mandates the specific copy to be used in corrective advertising, a clever advertising strategist might be able to achieve "refutational innoculation" by other advertising or statements preceding the corrective advertisements.[24]

Criticality of Decision Process Approach to Consumerism Research

A critical need exists for conducting consumerism research and analysis of consumerism programs using integrated, decision process models of consumer behavior. Many of the problems of using research in public policy decisions can be traced to the use of fragmented, limited-paradigm research approaches that fail to consider many relevant dimensions of consumer behavior that affect the implementation and efficacy of public policy.

The most comprehensive analysis of the need for using models of consumer behavior in public policy research is contained in a staff report to the Federal Trade Commission known as the Howard and Hulbert report.[25] After analyzing the testimony of many experts concerning advertising (and some other forms of consumer influence) and public policy, Howard and Hulbert describe the requirements for using a consumer behavior model in conducting public policy research:

First, a model for public policy should avoid the specialization inherent in some of the industry models. It should be general and comprehensive, dealing with the whole process of decision-making. In addition, the model must be fairly detailed. . . . The model should also be disaggregative, dealing with the choice process of the individual. While aggregative models may often be sufficient for industry purposes, public policy needs require a model of individual consumer behavior. Aggregative information can always be obtained from an individual model, but the reverse is not true. Wherever possible, the model should be consistent with theory and empirical evidence, both in the behavioral sciences and in marketing and advertising research. Most desirable, of course, would be a comprehensive model that was itself empirically tested.[26]

The use of comprehensive models of consumer behavior would help in establishing the *relevant evaluative criteria* of consumers so that the FTC might require affirmative disclosure on the proper attributes. A model might help understand how information processing occurs in order that regulatory agencies could more effectively determine what constitutes deceptive advertising and how to correct it. Models can help us understand how behavior differs among consumer segments, a most pressing need in public policy research and one that has generally been ignored by policy makers. The market segmentation problem is particularly troublesome because it implies that some regulations may benefit some con-

---

[24]H. Keith Hunt, "Effects of Corrective Advertising," *Journal of Advertising Research* (October 1973), 15-24.

[25]John A. Howard and James Hulbert, *Advertising and the Public Interest* (Chicago: Crain Communications, Inc., 1976).

[26]Howard and Hulbert, *Advertising and the Public Interest*, 36.

sumers while harming others and that possibly varying laws would be required to protect the entire population. These are difficult policy issues but ones that can better be solved by comprehensive models of consumer behavior such as the Howard-Sheth model and the model in this book than with the fragmented, limited-paradigm approaches that have characterized much previous public policy research.[27]

An integrated approach to public policy is found in Canada in a more advanced form than in the United States. An overall consumer protection agency in Canada was established by Parliament in 1967, bringing together in one department a number of existing consumer protection laws and also providing the rationale, resources, and authority for new programs. The Consumer Affairs Bureau, organized as shown in Figure 22.3, with a staff of about 1,100 employees and a budget of about $25 million in 1977, assumes responsibility for major regulatory activities concerning consumers. A major division of the bureau is the Consumer Research Branch, which has shown a willingness to use comprehensive models of consumer behavior for collecting and analyzing consumer research. The research branch conducts research on *consumer choice,* which it defines as, "a full understanding of the consumption process, the way in which consumers make purchase decisions, how suppliers respond to perceived demand, and how consumers and suppliers interact with each other in the marketplace." The research branch also prepares research on *consumer protection* including information about, "the choice of legal tools available, the economic and social effects of the proposed legislation on consumers and suppliers, and the effective implementation and operation of the law." This branch also conducts research in a third area, *financial transactions,* which is concerned with research on credit, saving, insurance, pensions, and related matters that may be a source of confusion and difficulty, and more specific but developing areas such as electronic payments systems, which transfer funds from debtor to creditor.

In addition to specific marketing practices that require consumer research, important macro-issues exist concerning the role of consumer influence programs. Do the benefits of such programs outweigh the costs? Are consumer influence programs required to stimulate new product development and a healthy economy? Does advertising and other consumer influence positively or negatively affect the taste and life-styles of a society? Does advertising stimulate consumers to buy things they don't need? Does consumer influence unfairly represent minority or women's groups? These important questions are not discussed further here because of space requirements and because they are thoroughly analyzed in other sources[28] but this section on public policy could not be finished without reminding the reader of these critical issues that affect the environment of consumer influence programs.

[27]Howard and Hulbert, *Advertising and the Public Interest,* 36.

[28]James F. Engel, Hugh G. Wales, and Martin R. Warshaw, *Promotional Strategy* (Homewood, Ill.: Richard D. Irwin, 1979), ch. 23. Also, see Jules Backman, *Advertising and Competition* (New York: New York University Press, 1967).

Figure 22.3
Organizational Structure, Canadian Bureau of Consumer Affairs

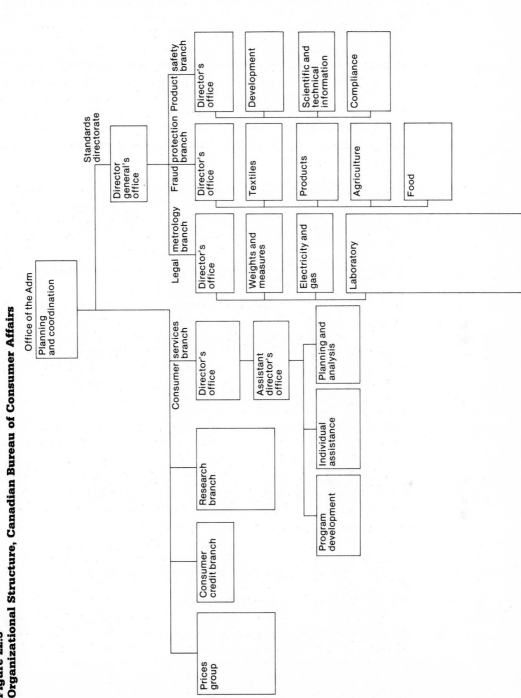

Source: "An Introduction to the Bureau of Consumer Affairs," Ottawa/Hull: Canadian Bureau of Consumer Affairs, March, 1977. Reprinted by permission.

ORGANIZATIONAL RESPONSES TO REGULATORY AND CONSUMERISM FORCES

Contemporary organizations—business as well as nonbusiness—are faced with changing realities in the regulatory and consumer environment. Taking the ostrich—with its head in the sand—approach is a strategy designed to invite litigation and consumer complaint and, in the long-run at least, the demise of economic viability. Organizations need *preventive* approaches to consumerism and regulatory forces rather than *reactive* marketing programs. The solution to this changing regulatory environment requires a carefully designed program implemented both by *individual firms* and by *voluntary associations of firms*.

The failure of business organizations to monitor and understand the nature of consumer concerns and complaints is illustrated by the following selected scenarios:

1. If anyone can expect cooperation from retailers on a test marketing project, it is probably General Mills. Yet when this firm tried out its "Mr. Wonderfull Surprize" cereal in Buffalo, it ran into everything from stern questions to one outright refusal to stock "the only cereal with a creamy vanilla filling." The reason proved to be letters received by food store managers from the Center for Science in the Public Interest (CSPI) calling the product (30 percent sugar, 14 percent saturated fat) a "nutritional disaster" and demanding that they lock it out. Since then, the consumer watchdogs have attacked the cereal in each new city and CSPI director Michael Jacobson dramatically illustrated his point by dashing onstage at the Institute of Food Technologists' convention, seizing the microphone, and presenting General Mills an award of a garbage can for "destroying the American people's concept of good nutrition."

2. Senior citizens, crusading through a group called the Gray Panthers, have overturned three state laws barring retail prescription drug price advertising. The Gray Panthers are now pushing model state legislation to regulate hearing-aid salespersons.

3. Consumer groups are campaigning for the right to use free broadcasting time for counter-advertising as a public service. In the case of aspirin, they have requested broadcasters to run a short message narrated by Burt Lancaster to state plainly the makeup of aspirin. This is intended to counter the Bayer aspirin commercials consumer advocates feel lead consumers into buying a more expensive product than they need.

Business organizations can respond to consumerism forces with a minimum obligatory response—just enough to meet legal requirements—or a firm can respond creatively with a major commitment of corporate resources to develop appropriate programs based on consumerism issues. There is some research to indicate that managers see consumerism as an opportunity for creative response and are optimistic about its effects on the marketplace.[29] Very substantial literature describes the impact of

[29]Stephen A. Greyser and Steven L. Diamond, "Business is Adapting to Consumerism," *Harvard Business Review* (September–October 1974), 38–55.

consumerism on business strategies and the programs needed to respond to consumerism.[30] In the case of product safety and liability, it is
clear that far-reaching changes are necessary in the design and delivery
of products and dire economic consequences will result for a firm if it
fails to make such changes. The methods of handling such complaints
by major appliance firms is described in Exhibit 22.2.

Consumerism Management System

How should business respond to consumerism pressures? Hensel describes a consumerism management system consisting of six major components:

1. Understanding the consumer's world.

2. Redressing grievances and responding to injuries.

3. Creating credibility.

4. Improving customer contact.

5. Providing consumer information.

6. Organizing for responsive action.[31]

Understanding the consumer's world refers to programs designed to insure that top management is acquainted with the reality of the consumer's shopping and consumption world—including the inflationary
consumption pressures, negative attitudes toward business, and inferior
retail outlets, which may not be a part of the highly paid manager's world.

Redressing grievances and responding to inquiries requires responsive approaches to processing and responding to consumer complaints
and inquiries. It recognizes the opportunity for an enhanced information
feedback system and creation of long-term customers through more effective management of postpurchase communications.

Activities to create credibility include programs to satisfy the consumer's need for a trusted, expert and personal buying agent. They
might include merchandising activities designed to provide a soft sell,
institutional advertising, and meaningful involvement in societal or community problems.

Improving customer contact may include programs that affect the
entire distribution channel in an attempt to improve the quality of the
consumer/retail store contact. This necessitates management's concern
about the importance of a quality consumer experience in retail stores,

---

[30]David A. Aaker and George S. Day, "Corporate Responses to Consumerism Pressures," *Harvard Business Review* (November-December 1972), 114-124; Leonard L. Berry, "Marketing Challenges in the Age of the People," *MSU Business Topics* (Winter 1972), 7-13; Stephen A. Greyser, "Marketing and Responsiveness to Consumerism," *Journal of Contemporary Business* (Autumn 1973), 81-93; S. Prakesh Sethi, "Business and the Consumer: Wither Goes the Confrontation," *California Management Review* (Winter 1974), 82-87; Norman Kangun et al., "Consumerism and Marketing Management," *Journal of Marketing* (April 1975), 3-10; Larry J. Rosenberg, "Retailers' Responses to Consumerism," *Business Horizons* (October 1975), 37-44; G. R. Foxall, "Forecasting Developments in Consumerism and Consumer Protection," *Long Range Planning* (Fall 1980), 3-5.

[31]James S. Hensel, *Stategies for Adapting to the Consumerism Movement* (Columbus, Ohio: Management Horizons, Inc., 1974). This section is summarized from Hensel.

Exhibit 22.2 Policies for Handling Complaints

Question 1 The Consumer: What type of policy do you have for handling complaints? Do you have a consumer complaint department? Is there a consumer advocate in-house? Do you have an educational program or participate in educational programs for consumers?

Frigidaire: There is a well-organized consumer relations activity within the National Service Department. A woman supervisor has broad responsibility for handling complaints. She can deal with the consumer or through the national service organization. There is no in-house advocate.

GE: Every consumer complaint is handled promptly and fairly, with appropriate action taken. The consumer complaint structure is complex. It is desired that a complaint be processed at the first step, the nearest GE major appliance office or product service center. There is a vice-president who acts as an in-house consumer advocate. Most consumer education programs are the responsibility of the Consumer Institute, but individual areas provide literature.

Tappan: Most consumer complaints are received by mail or via the toll-free Sentinel Line. Complaints are processed promptly, usually by the division responsible for the product. Complaints go to the consumer relations department, which has a manager, nine consultants, and two clerk-typists. The corporate director of customer relations is the in-house consumer advocate. Educational programs, demonstrations, guides, and trade associations are supported.

Whirlpool: The main complaint resolution system is Cool-Line. Complaints needing field follow-up go to local managers. Cool-Line is under the control of the manager of customer relations. There is no in-house consumer advocate, but there is a vice-president of consumer and public affairs. Educational programs range from a series of newspaper features on how to buy, use, and care for appliances to a booklet on energy savings.

Zenith: Many complaints are processed locally; complaints received centrally are sent to the appropriate area. The complaint organization reports to a vice-president of consumer affairs and managers of customer communications and warranty claims. The consumer affairs vice-president is the in-house consumer advocate. Educational programs consist of public relations material and product information.

Source: Keven Dembinski, "Consumerism and the Appliance Industry," in Joel Evans, *Consumerism in the United States* (New York: Praeger, 1980), 34. Reprinted by permission of Holt, Rinehart, and Winston.

educational programs to insure that retail personnel are competent and motivated to assist consumers, manufacturer or distributor sponsored educational programs for consumers, improved point-of-sale materials, and so forth.

Providing consumer information is a commitment to provide and join with other responsible parties (members of the distribution channel, consumer advocacy groups, educational institutions, government agencies) to increase the buying intelligence of the consumer through relevant information and educatonal programs to increase use of the information. This may include nutritional labeling, care labeling, greater clarity in instructions that accompany the product, honest and relevant advertising, and so forth.

Organizing for responsive action requires a firm to make the organizational and management system changes necessary to undertake and encourage all elements of the organization to involve themselves with appropriate consumer programs. To be successful, consumerism response must be made legitimate by top management and might include a written consumer rights policy, establishing an advisory committee of consumers who have a real voice in company decisions, adequate funding for testing of product claims and safety, and the creation of a high-level consumer affairs executive with sufficient authority to represent effectively the consumer's interest in company decisions.[32]

Giant Foods—a Consumerism-Oriented Firm

An example of a firm with an outstanding reputation for a consumerism orientation is Giant Foods in Washington, D.C. Top management made a commitment to orient the firm toward consumerism by hiring Esther Peterson, formerly the President's Special Assistant for Consumer Affairs. They also work to install unit pricing, develop new programs of testing to insure product safety, insist on full disclosure of ingredients and their nutritional content, provide honest point-of-sale promotion and many other activities.[33] When monitoring the consumer environment, Giant found that some ten percent of the wheelchair-bound consumers in America live in the Washington area. In response to the firm's desire to satisfy all market segments, the company altered its stores to include specially marked parking spaces, a ramp connecting the parking lot to the store walk, widened checkout aisle for wheel chairs, changed restrooms, and other modifications. The cost for changes amounts to about $1,000 per store and reportedly the changes are well-received by the community.[34]

Many other firms have implemented major consumerism programs. These include a buyer protection plan of the American Motors Company, a Cool-Line program for consumer information feedback and redress by Whirlpool, and a consumer advisory committee and major organization modifications by T. Eaton, the major department store group in Canada.[35]

[32]See also Milton L. Blum, John B. Stewart, and Edward W. Wheatley, "Consumer Affairs: Viability of the Corporate Response," *Journal of Marketing* (April 1974), 13-19.

[33]Esther Peterson, "Consumerism as Retailer's Asset," *Harvard Business Review* (May-June 1974), 92-101.

[34]"Handicap Check-out," *Chain Store Age* (April 1977), 18.

[35]These cases are described in Roger D. Blackwell, James F. Engel, and W. Wayne Talarzyk, *Contemporary Cases in Consumer Behavior* (Hinsdale, Ill.: Dryden Press, 1977).

**Figure 22.4
Reactions to
Voluntary Self-
Regulation**

"Personally, I'd feel better with more
police protection."

Source: *The Wall Street Journal* (October 6, 1980). Reprinted by permission of Cartoon Features Syndicate.

**Voluntary Self-
Regulation**

Firms may cooperate with other firms and organizations in an attempt to provide self-regulation rather than legal regulation.[36] Voluntary self-regulation has several advantages, the most important being that it can be more responsive to changing conditions than laws usually are. It also may be less expensive to establish and implement. The problem with voluntary, cooperative groups is that they lack power to enforce responsible behavior by firms that are not members of the group (usually trade associations) or that choose not to comply with the group's rules. The problem is very similar to the feelings of the two gentlemen in Figure 22.4. Furthermore, if a group does not have the means to sanction a firm by withholding valuable services of the association, boycotts, or other actions; those attempts to obtain compliance are likely to be considered restraint of trade and be found illegal under antitrust, no matter how noble the motives of the industry group may be. In spite of the enforcement problems, voluntary self-regulation is growing as more and more groups attempt to establish standards of responsible or ethical behavior. An example of a voluntary code is presented in Table 22.3, adopted by several organizations involved in advertising.

[36]Barry Keating, "Industry Standards and Consumer Welfare," *Journal of Consumer Affairs* (Winter 1980), 471-482.

Table 22.3
The Advertising
Code of American
Business

1. **Truth.** Advertising shall tell the truth, and shall reveal significant facts, the concealment of which would mislead the public.
2. **Responsibility.** Advertising agencies and advertisers shall be willing to provide substantiation of claims made.
3. **Taste and decency.** Advertising shall be free of statements, illustrations, or implications which are offensive to good taste or public decency.
4. **Disparagement.** Advertising shall offer merchandise or service on its merits, and refrain from attacking competitors unfairly or disparaging their products, services, or methods of doing business.
5. **Bait advertising.** Advertising shall offer only merchandise or services which are readily available for purchase at the advertised price.
6. **Guarantees and warranties.** Advertising of guarantees and warranties shall be explicit. Advertising of any guarantee or warranty shall clearly and conspicuously disclose its nature and extent, the manner in which the guarantor or warrantor will perform and the identity of the guarantor or warrantor.
7. **Price claims.** Advertising shall avoid price or savings claims which are false or misleading, or which do not offer provable bargains or savings.
8. **Unprovable claims.** Advertising shall avoid the use of exaggerated or unprovable claims.
9. **Testimonials.** Advertising containing testimonials shall be limited to those of competent witnesses who are reflecting a real and honest choice.

Note: This code was part of a program of industry self-regulation pertaining to national consumer advertising announced jointly on September 18, 1971, by the American Advertising Federation, the American Association of Advertising Agencies, the Association of National Advertisers, and the Council of Better Business Bureaus, Inc.

In summary, it is clear that organizations—both business and non-business—must develop comprehensive, responsible programs for responding to new forces of consumerism and regulatory activity. Consumer analysts and researchers have an important role to play in providing inputs with which management can provide consumerism programs that are relevant, effective and cost-efficient.

Ethical
Standards and
Personal Values

After spending considerable time and thought on how businesses can abuse consumers and the regulatory efforts to control such abuses, this thought might occur to some readers: "If people would merely act in responsible ways—simply do what is *right*—there would be no need for government regulations."

There are two problems with a belief that people will do what is right. The first problem is that no historical evidence exists of a society in which people organize themselves to protect the interests of others when those interests conflict with their own. In other words, societies may vary somewhat in their feelings of responsibility to others, but to assume that people will not protect or maximize their self-interests is an unrealistic understanding of human behavior. The second problem is that two well-meaning parties may disagree on what is right behavior. How then can a consumer analyst make decisions that are responsible or ethical and consistent with the organizational environment in which he or she normally operates?

Responsibility
and Ethics

Executives of firms are increasingly involved in the search for decency and responsibility in the midst of a rapidly evolving and often confusing set of environmental forces. Marketing, because it is the primary interface between business and society, is often more directly confronted by the quest for social and ethical responsibility than other functions of business.

Two types of responsibility impinge upon the planning of marketing strategy. The first is *social responsibility,* defined simply as accepting an obligation for the proper functioning of the society in which the firm operates. It involves accountability for the activities through which the firm can reasonably contribute to the society. *Ethical responsibility,* the second type, is more fundamental than social responsibility. Ethical responsibility is concerned with the determination of *how* things should be, human pursuit of the right course of action, and the individual's doing what is morally right.

Actions alone determine social responsibility, and a firm can be socially responsible even when doing so under coercion. For example, the government may enact rules that *force* firms to be socially responsible in matters of the environment, deception, and so forth. Also, consumers, through their power to repeat or withhold purchasing, may *force* marketers to provide honest and relevant information, fair prices, and so forth. To be ethically responsible, on the other hand, it is not sufficient to act correctly; ethical intent is also necessary.

**Business
Responsibility**

Some persons might question the phrase *business responsibility* and ask if the terms are not contradictory. This negative image may be due to the explicit value in a market economy that a firm should maximize profit. Thus, many conclude that maximizing profits probably includes taking advantage of consumers or any others who are exploitable. That is a simplistic and unrealistic view of the concept of profit.

In any society, the economic resources of land, labor, and capital must be allocated to some organizations for the purpose of maximizing the society's ability to satisfy its own needs. The resources could be given to an organization owned by the state—a planned economy or socialism; or they may be given to nongovernment organizations—a market economy or capitalism. The reason a society permits market controlled organizations to operate and to obtain scarce resources is the belief that such organizations will be more efficient in meeting society's needs than would government owned organizations.

The specific mechanism for determining which organizations are allocated the scarce resources of land, labor, and capital is *profitability* or return on the investment of those resources. Thus, to obtain labor working in a firm, that organization must pay a fair salary; to obtain land, the organization must pay a fair rent; and to obtain capital, the firm must pay a fair return on capital—either through yield on equity or interest on debt. A fair return on any of the factors—even capital—is a cost of operating.

A fair return on equity capital in the United States currently might be considered about 15 percent. Above that, economic profit is said to exist but a fair return on investment is just another cost of the firm in its attempt to satisfy the society's needs. If a firm does not pay a fair return on capital, it will cease to exist (and therefore cease to meet society's needs) in the same way it would if it did not pay a high enough salary to attract workers. In a sense, profit or return-on-investment may be regarded as the salary of capital.

From the above discussion, it can be concluded that a society has the right to impose costs on firms to meet society's needs since the firm exists in the first place because the society allows it to do so as an efficient system for accomplishing the society's objectives. At the same time, members of the society must realize that if those costs cause a firm to yield less than the fair return on capital that could be obtained from meeting other portions of society's needs (i.e., investment in other firms) prices to the consumer must increase or the firm must cease to exist in the economy.

A number of implications or guidelines about social responsibility can be developed from the basic understanding of the market system discussed above. Five such implications for the conduct of contemporary firms have been developed by Davis and are listed below.[37]

1. Social responsibility arises from social power. (Because business now has so much power, it is expected to be a wise trustee for society.)

2. Business shall operate as a two-way system with open receipt of inputs from society and open disclosure of its operations to the public. (Just as business must know what is going on in society, society has a right to a *social audit*[38] of the activities of its largest holder of resources.)

3. Social costs as well as benefits of an activity, product, or service shall be thoroughly calculated and considered in order to decide whether to proceed with it. (Long-run costs must be included and may require social impact statements comparable with today's environmental impact statements.)

4. Social costs of each activity, product, or service shall be prices into it so that the consumer (user) pays for the effects of his or her consumption on society.

5. Beyond social costs, business institutions as citizens have responsibilities for social involvement in areas of their competence where major social needs exist.

From this list of guidelines and other analyses,[39] it is apparent that a new environment is forming concerning the expectations of society concerning social responsibility of the firms that expect to exist in that environ-

---

[37]Keith Davis, "Five Propositions for Social Responsibility," *Business Horizons* (June 1975), 19-24.

[38]Raymond A. Bauer and Dan H. Fenn, Jr., *The Corporate Social Audit* (New York: The Russell Sage Foundation, 1972); John J. Carson and George A. Steiner, *Measuring Business's Social Performance: The Corporate Social Audit* (New York: Committee for Economic Development, 1975).

[39]S. Prakesh Sethi, "Dimensions of Corporate Social Performance: An Analytical Framework," *California Management Review* (Spring 1975), 58-64; Steven Brenner and Earl Molander, "Is the Ethics of Business Changing?" *Harvard Business Review* (January-February 1977), 57-71; James Ownes, "Business Ethics: Age-Old Ideal, Now Real," *Business Horizons* (February 1978), 26-30; Dennis Beresford and Scott Cowen, "Surveying Social Responsibility Disclosure in Annual Reports," *Business* (March-April 1979), 15-20.

ment. These issues, which formerly might have been reserved for discussion in college courses, are increasingly an important part of the day-to-day considerations of persons who have the responsibility of developing marketing strategy and programs.

Business Ethics

Ultimately, the question that faces a consumer analyst participating in the design of consumer-influence programs goes beyond the question of what is effective, what is legal, or what is profitable. Eventually, most consumer analysts must ask the question, "Is it *right*?" That is a question of ethics or judgments about morality. Ethics is sometimes defined as the study of the *morality of human actions* or the determination of the standards for these actions.[40]

Some increase in concern about business ethics may be occurring in the United States, possibly starting with the public scandals associated with political ethics in the Watergate era of the United States. Business leaders are calling for a return to moral considerations in business strategy[41] and the development of business leaders who can speak to the broader issues of a society.[42]

The Basis for Ethics

Two fundamental approaches to philosophy establish the basis for ethics and ethical behavior. The first approach is *speculative philosophy,* and the second approach to ethics is *moral revelation.*[43]

Speculative Philosophy

Speculative philosophy or its derivative, situation ethics, is probably the dominant approach to ethics. Many variations exist but the essential characteristic of speculative philosophy or situation ethics is the severance of ethics from fixed values and standards. Naturalism, idealism, and existentialism are some of the major forms of this approach to ethics, and each of these major forms has variants—such as hedonistic naturalism, political naturalism, humanism, pragmatism, logical positivism, and so forth.

The essential attribute of speculative philosophies is that they are *subjective* or *relative* in their determination of the basis for standards. These philosophies represent the universe as a closed system. Thus, any basis for ethics that exists must have its source of validity in the mind of humans. Any appeal to a principle or existence outside the system (as in an open system) violates the logic of such philosophies. The basis for ethical standards must therefore be the approval of other relevant humans. This is rather important for consumer researchers because the ultimate standard for right or wrong becomes results or the effects on

---

[40]Raymond Baumhart, *Ethics in Business* (New York: Holt, Rinehart and Winston, 1968), 15.

[41]W. M. Blumenthal, "Business Ethics: A Call for a Moral Approach," *Financial Executive* (January 1976), 32-34.

[42]H. Justin Davidson, "The Top of the World is Flat," *Harvard Business Review* (March-April 1977), 89-99.

[43]Carl F. H. Henry, *Christian Personal Ethics* (Grand Rapids, Mich.: Baker Book House, 1957).

humans. Consumer researchers can determine right or wrong in such philosophies by measuring the quantities of people who will be affected in one way or another. An advertisement that was objectively false but that benefited the majority of people in some way could not be declared wrong or unethical by appeal to some standard or set of principles (because that would imply something more than the mind of man).

A currently popular approach to subjective or relative ethics is *existentialism.* Sartre, Camus, and Marcel are leading contributors to this philosophy that, in its purest form, indicates that everything is permitted, but that no reason exists for choices of anything. Evans, who wrote a very understandable book on existentialism, explains:

Man is free, *doomed* to be free, sentenced to total freedom. Man is alone, but worse than alone, he is totally unnecessary. His existence is superfluous, gratuitous in a world in which there is no *reason* for anything. There is no *reason* why a man should choose to marry, rather than remain celibate, no *reason* why a man should love, rather than hate, no *reason* why a man should choose to feed and care for a child, rather than snuff out that child's existence, no *reason* why a man should choose to go on living instead of killing himself. Ultimately, there is no *reason* for any action, for any decision.[44]

Where existentialism provides the philosophical framework for a society, a certain dilemma faces anyone attempting to evaluate the actions of a business firm or formulate business policy. While many contemporary consumers may attempt to apply this philosophy to their personal lives, its application to public policy is a disaster and would result in anarchy and chaos.

Most people probably believe there is some basis for right and wrong and, therefore, a basis for judging the morality of consumer influence programs. The dilemma occurs, however, if one attempts to deify some human principle such as truth, concern, or any other concept in which individuals are stating that they will live their lives by that principle—or that a firm should organize its marketing strategies by that principle. Others may simply state they do not accept your principle and thus moral action becomes a nose-counting matter in which morality is whatever the consensus may be—or whatever the consensus may be among those who hold the power (through force, wealth, education, persuasiveness, etc.) in a society. Under that philosophy, a consumer researcher may indeed be the best source of morality because the researcher's skills in empiricism are useful in establishing the consensus. What happens, though, when the consensus decides to allow the extermination of 3 million persons in Europe; or when the consensus decides that rape or incest are moral because they agree with community preferences; or when the consensus agrees with practice of denying black consumers equal education, or when the consensus of *those in power* is to pollute

[44]C. Stephen Evans, *Despair: A Moment or a Way of Life?* (Downers Grove, Ill.: Inter-Varsity Press, 1975), 16-17.

the environment, discriminate against women or deceive consumers? Is there some basis for calling these practices unethical rather than the consensus of some group of people?

Moral Revelation

Moral revelation is an approach to ethics based upon an open system or one that has the potential for revelation of morality that transcends the human mind and experience.[45] While ethical standards with this approach may be adaptive in application and may require differing interpretations to apply to specific situations, they have as their ultimate criteria for application the existence of fixed, permanent standards of right and wrong.

The Judaic-Christian value system is an example of moral revelation. Biblical revelation, such as in the Mosaic Ten Commandments, presents God's value system, and the choice of humans is to accept it or reject it in the conduct of human affairs. Scholars, judges, and others have the responsibility for applying God's values in specific situations. That may leave room for considerable controversy, but the underlying values are not controvertible. If a national leader is doing wrong, a basis exists for judging the leader's actions regardless of how much power the leader may possess. Similarly, if a business firm is involved in wrong behavior, a basis exists for making that determination.

Personal Values

A consumer analyst or business strategist is ultimately confronted with decisions not only about whether or not the firm's behavior is ethical. An individual must also evaluate whether or not his or her behavior is unethical in the conduct of consumer influence programs (as well as other areas of activity). Situations may arise in which the firm asks or orders the individuals to do things that conflict with the individual's personal values. Carroll found that almost 65 percent of managers find themselves under pressure to compromise their personal standards for their organizations.[46] (See Figure 22.5.)

One of the major pressures reported by some junior assistants in the Watergate scandals was the compliance pressure exerted by others. It was not so much that the junior assistants could not extricate themselves from the desires of their superiors, but rather that they felt tremendous personal pressure to go along with the behavior of others. Lacking any clear personal values upon which deviance from the consensus can be based, such behavior is understandable. In bringing this chapter—and this book—to a close, however, the authors are compelled to state their belief that a basis does exist for personal values.

As a student, it is important that you also think through your personal values and relationships before entering the consumer research profes-

---

[45]Francis Schaeffer, *How Should We Then Live?* (Old Tappan, N. J.: Fleming R. Revell, 1976).
[46]Archie B. Carroll, "Managerial Ethics: a Post-Watergate View," *Business Horizons* (April 1975), 75-80.

**Figure 22.5
The Pressures to
Conform**

"You're a disgrace to all lemmings!"

"Well, heck! If all you smart cookies agree, who am I to dissent?"

Source: Top cartoon: Drawing by Chas. Addams; 1974 *The New Yorker* Magazine, Inc. Bottom cartoon: Drawing by Handelsman; © 1972 *The New Yorker* Magazine, Inc..

sion or organizations making decisions concerning marketing strategies designed to influence consumers.[47]

[47]Consumer researchers have some specific problems with which to deal when conducting research. Discussion of these issues is found in Alice M. Tybout and Gerald Zaltman, "Ethics in Marketing Research: Their Practical Relevance," *Journal of Marketing Research* (November 1974), 357-368; Robert L. Day, "A Comment on 'Ethics in Marketing Research'," *Journal of Marketing Research* (May 1975), 232-233; George S. Day, "The Threats to Marketing Research," *Journal of Marketing Research* (November 1975), 462-467; Donald P. Warwick, "Social Scientists Ought to Stop Lying," *Psychology Today* (February 1975), 38-40+; Robert Bezilla, Joel B. Naynes, and Clifford Elliott, "Ethics in Marketing Research," *Business Horizons* (April 1976), 83-86.

Summary

This chapter discusses questions about what *ought* to be done when using knowledge about consumer behavior to influence consumers rather than what can be done and what might be done.

The question of control over consumer influence involves government agencies, business firms, and individuals. Thus, bases for control over consumer influence may be described as *legal regulations, self-interests and voluntary codes,* and *personal convictions about ethical standards.*

Principal laws that regulate consumer influence include the Sherman Act, which serves as a foundation for many other laws in the United States, the Federal Trade Commission Act, numerous specific laws such as the Food and Drug Act, and various state and local laws. The FTC brings complaints against firms for activities it believes are unlawful, establishes voluntary guidelines for industry standards, promulgates trade practice rules that require compliance, and conducts some educational activities among business firms and consumers.

Consumer research is important in determining public policy in the area of establishing program priorities, fact-finding about specific practices and consumer behavior, and investigating compliance. A number of problems have limited the use of consumer research in FTC actions in the past, however. The use of comprehensive, decision-process models of consumer behavior would be helpful in conducting and analyzing consumer research for public policy decisions.

Business firms and other organizations need a well-developed system for monitoring consumerism forces and designing consumer programs that are responsive to these forces. Hensel suggested using a consumerism management system consisting of six steps: understanding the consumer's world, redressing grievances and responding to inquiries, creating credibility, improving customer contact, providing consumer information, and organizing for responsive action. A number of firms, such as Giant Foods, are responding to consumerism with creative and effective programs.

Consumer influence programs are also affected by ethical standards and personal values. Social responsibility is defined as accepting an obligation for the proper functioning of the society in which the firm operates. Ethical responsibility is more fundamental and is concerned with the determination of *how* things should be, the human pursuit of the right course of action, and the individual's doing what is morally right.

Review and Discussion Questions

1. What are the major regulatory forces influencing the design and implementation of consumer influence programs? How do they appear to be changing in contemporary societies such as the United States?

2. What is the purpose of the Sherman Act? Why is it important in understanding consumer protection laws?

3. Explain the powers and activities of the Federal Trade Commission (FTC).

4. What is a trade practice rule as promulgated by the FTC?

5. Examine the list of federal consumer protection laws in Table 22.2. Prepare a report on one of these, explaining the conditions under which it was enacted, the types of marketing activities affected by the law, major activities to which it has been applied since enactment, and your analysis of the future enforcement or modification of this law.

6. "All consumer protection laws should be at the federal level because of the superior quality of enforcement of federal agencies compared to local and state agencies." Analyze this statement.

7. Assume that you are given the responsibility for establishing the priorities of the FTC for the protection of consumers. Prepare an outline of the research or other activities you would recommend to carry out this responsibility.

8. Assume you are employed as a consumer analyst for one of the infant formulas described at the beginning of the chapter. What factors would influence your decisions about how (or whether) to market the product?

9. Select a firm with which you are familiar or can obtain information. Analyze its program for response to consumerism forces.

10. Prepare a statement of your personal values that will guide you in decisions about consumer influence.

MODELS OF CONSUMER BEHAVIOR:
FORMALIZATION AND QUANTIFICATION

Once consumer behavior began to achieve a measure of sophistication as a discipline around the middle 1960s, some of the pioneering writings on this subject were built upon models of consumer behavior. This book, first published in 1968, was one that took this approach, and models still find widespread use today. It is the purpose of this appendix to elaborate on the nature and significance of behavioral models and then to describe in formal terms three conceptualizations that have proved to be most influential in terms of frequency of citation in published research: (1) the Howard-Sheth model; (2) the revised Howard model; and (3) the model used in this book, typically referred to as the EKB model (reflecting the initials of the three authors of the first three editions).

A model is a replica of the phenomena it is intended to designate; that is, it specifies the elements and represents the nature of relationships among them. As such, it provides a testable "map of reality," and its utility lies in the extent to which successful description and/or prediction of behavior and its underlying influences is made possible. In more detail, here are some of the advantages which are offered:

1. *Explanatory variables are specified.* Everyone has a model of consumer behavior in mind, whether implicit or explicit. In other words, each person has some concept of those factors that shape motivation and behavior. Explanation and prediction are impossible otherwise. The distinction, or course, enters with respect to the comprehensiveness of competing models and the accuracy with which predictions can be made.

2. *Research findings can be integrated into a meaningful whole.* Most analysts of consumer behavior have some familiarity with the underlying behavioral sciences. Delving into this literature can be a highly frustrating experience, however. Of what use is research on the "prisoner's dilemma game," "psychological reactance," "cognitive dissonance," "signal detection theory," "attribution theory," and so on? Possession of a well-formulated model makes it possible to differentiate the relevant from the irrelevant. Otherwise, the literature is little more than a bewildering maze.

3. *Explanations are provided for performance of the system.* Description of variables in laundry list fashion is of little value unless functional relationships between them are specified. This is part and parcel of a good model, and the result is ability to make behavioral predictions with some degree of accuracy.

4. *Avenues for fruitful research are revealed.* Researchable hypotheses readily flow from a carefully designed model. Gaps in knowledge quickly become evident, and the nature of researchable hypotheses is determined by the variables themselves and the linkages between them.

Decision-process models encompassing many variables cannot explain the details of consumer behavior in every specific situation. Rather, a workable model should delineate (1) the variables associated with consumer decision processes; (2) the general relations that exist among variables; and (3) the general principles that express the model's ingression in particular purchase occasions.

The value of a model to guide research cannot be overemphasized. Without a model specifying the range of appropriate variables, the researcher may be lured into looking at a problem from an unduly narrow perspective. A famous story by Sir Arthur Eddington illustrates this danger.[1] It seems that an ichthyologist wished to make some generalizations concerning the size of fish. He took a fishnet of two-inch mesh into the sea. It was dropped into the water and he collected a large number of fish. After meticulous measurement, it was concluded that "All fish are two inches long or more." Unfortunately, this also happens in consumer research. In spite of the rigor of the research design, the facts collected are only partially accurate because only a partial theory has guided the collection.

Inadequate data collection can occur in other ways. The story of Procrustes, the giant who obliged weary travelers to spend the night with him, further illustrates the problem.[2] Procrustes required travelers to sleep in his bed and always trimmed them to fit, stretching the shorter ones on the rack and lopping pieces of the longer ones until their corpses were exactly the right length. With or without a theory, the consumer analyst is often a Procrustes and empirical data are the travelers. Making data fit a model involves exactly the same process.

THE HOWARD-SHETH MODEL

One of the major contributions to the literature of consumer behavior was publication of *The Theory of Buyer Behavior* by John A. Howard and Jagdish N. Sheth in 1969.[3] It has evolved somewhat over the

---

[1]Quoted in Stephen E. Toulmin, *The Philosophy of Science* (New York: Harper & Row, 1960), 124-29.
[2]Toulmin, *Philosophy of Science.*
[3]John A. Howard and Jagdish N. Sheth, *The Theory of Buyer Behavior* (New York: John Wiley & Sons, 1969).

years,[4] culminating in Howard's own model discussed in the next section. The version described here appeared in 1974,[5] and its pictorial representation in simplified form is found in Figure A.1.

There are 12 primary functional relationships specified in this model. These are described below in the form of testable equations. For the most part these equations also can be traced in Figure A.1 simply by locating the variable in question and noting the other variables related to it through direct arrows or dotted arrows indicating a feedback or indirect relationship.

Here is the formal statement of the 1974 version of the Howard-Sheth model:

$$
\begin{aligned}
1.\ & P_x && = f(I_x) \\
2.\ & I_x && = f(F_x^C, A_x, C_x, \underline{C^u}, \underline{S^C}, \underline{S^{OS}}, \underline{T^P}, \underline{F^S}) \\
3.\ & A_x && = f(B_x^C, S_x, F_x^C, \underline{C^u}, \underline{S^C}, \underline{S^{OS}}, \underline{P^T}) \\
4.\ & C_x && = f(B_x^C, S_x, F_x^C, \underline{P^T}) \\
5.\ & B_x^C && = f(F_x^C, \underline{C^u}, \underline{S^C}, \underline{S^{OS}}, \underline{I^P}, \underline{P^T}) \\
6.\ & S_x && = f(P_x) \\
7.\ & F_x^C && = f(F_x^E, A_x^n, P_x^B) \\
8.\ & F_x^E && = f(O_x^S, F_x^A, \underline{M^H}) \\
9.\ & A_x^n, O_x^S && = f(M^a, \underline{I^P}, \underline{P^T}, \underline{T^P}) \\
10.\ & M^a && = f(S_x^A, C_x, F_x^C, \underline{F^S}) \\
11.\ & S_x^A && = f(F_x^E) \\
12.\ & C^C && = f(F_x^C, M^a, \underline{M^c})
\end{aligned}
$$

where symbols are defined as follows, with all terms referring to brand x (the underlined variables are defined as being *exogenous* or factors which exist independently and whose changes are not explained in the model).[6]

P_x = purchase of brand (the overt act of buying)

I_x = intention to purchase the brand (a verbally stated expectation, made in cognizance of possible extenuating factors, that brand x will be purchased the next time this action is necessary)

F_x^C = facts coded regarding brand (recalled information that brand x exists, that it has certain specific characteristics, both favorable and unfavorable)

A_x = attitude toward the brand (a verbal evaluation of the potential of brand x to satisfy motives)

C_x = confidence in brand evaluation (confidence in ability to evaluate brand x)

C^u = culture

S^C = social class

---

[4]See John A. Howard and Lyman E. Ostlund, *Buyer Behavior: Theoretical and Empirical Foundations* (New York: Knopf, 1973), 3-32; and John U. Farley, John A. Howard, and L. Winston Ring, *Consumer Behavior Theory and Application* (Boston: Allyn and Bacon, 1974).

[5]Farley, Howard, and Ring, *Consumer Behavior Theory.*

[6]Where possible, definitions are drawn from Farley, Howard, and Ring. There is some ambiguity, however, necessitating the use at some points of the definitions in Howard and Sheth.

**Figure A.1
The Howard-Sheth
Model, 1974
Version**

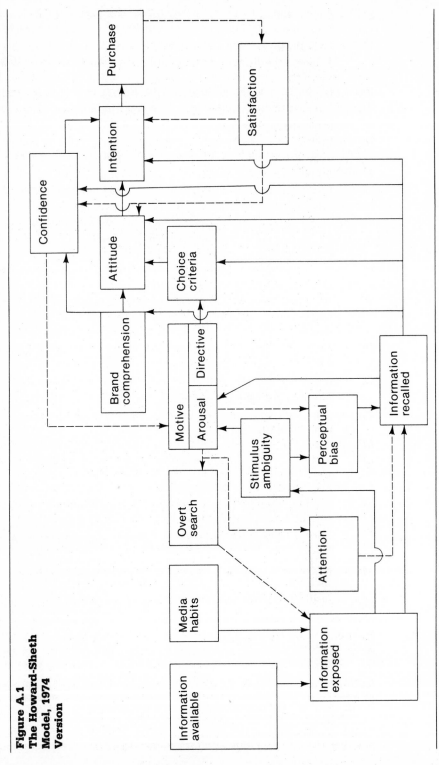

Source: Reproduced by special permission from John U. Farley, John A. Howard, and L. Winston Ring, *Consumer Behavior Theory and Application* (Boston: Allyn and Bacon, 1974), 11.

S^{OS} = social and organizational setting (comparative or normative reference groups)

T^P = time pressure (the inverse of the amount of time the buyer has available both for purchase and consumption as well as information seeking)

F^s = financial status (quantity of funds available or expected to be available to spend on goods and services during some specified time period)

B_x^C = brand comprehension (buyer understanding of brand features)

S_x = satisfaction with brand (satisfaction received from brand use)

P^T = personality traits (enduring dispositions or qualities accounting for relative consistency in emotional, temperamental, and social behavior, which explain differences among buyers)

I^P = importance of purchase (a measure of the relative intensity of motives governing buyer activities relating to the given product class relative to others)

F_x^E = facts exposed regarding the brand (information about the brand to which the buyer was exposed)

A_x^n = attention to brand information (buyer receptivity to information, regulating the quantity of information that reaches the nervous system)

P_x^B = perceptual bias of brand information (the tendency to distort information during its processing)

O_x^S = overt search for brand information (effort expended by the buyer to obtain brand information)

F_x^A = facts available regarding the brand (information available from the environment)

M^H = media habits toward vehicles containing brand information

M^a = motive arousal (the arousing of energizing aspect of motives—the intensity of motives satisfied by the product class of which x is a member)

S_x^A = stimulus ambiguity (perceived uncertainty and lack of meaningful information received from the environment)

C^C = choice criteria (an ordered set of motives relevant to the product class)

M^c = direct motives (motives directly related to choice criteria)

Many readers will be unfamiliar with this way of stating relationships. The alternative is a detailed written explanation, which space will not allow. Furthermore, the model is stated in such a way that it may be tested empirically. The best suggestion is to state each equation verbally, paying careful attention to the manner in which variables are defined. For example, equation one states that the purchase of brand x is a function of intentions to buy that brand on the next occasion, and so on.

The ultimate test of any theory is whether or not it predicts the phenomena under consideration. There have been a series of tests of the Howard model focusing on its 12 basic equations. The methodologies used have varied widely and have included multiple regression (the most common method), cross-lagged correlation, simulation, and longitudinal analysis.[7] In synthesizing these results, Holbrook came to the following conclusions:[8]

1. Most of the studies under consideration dealt only with a very small part of the total 12 equation system.

2. Support for the Howard model is fragmentary at best, based mostly on bivariate relationships (i.e., only two variables), even though the hypotheses called for multiple variables.

3. No single link in the model receives consistent support over those studies that focus explicitly on it.

4. None of the studies can claim on R^2 (the percentage of variance explained) consistently above 10 percent. This is particularly discouraging.

While these findings provide no clear support for the theory, much has been learned:

1. The model is more recursive than was originally thought. This means that some variables that occur only at initial stages in the system (such as attention) should be included in later relationships as well (intention is an example) rather than being assumed to feed through such intervening variables as attitudes.

2. There is substantial measurement error, which introduces a high level of "noise."[9] Many of the measurements used have low reliability (correlations of about .7), which means that different answers are given at varying points in time. Therefore, predictability is substantially weakened for this reason alone.

3. The distinction between endogenous and exogenous variables is not sharp, and it may prove necessary to treat more variables as endogenous for more precise measurement and manipulation.

4. Some variables are difficult to define operationally, and others are difficult to measure. In addition, there have been some wide discrepancies between the theoretical definition of a variable, such as perceptual bias, and the operational specification. This makes some of the tests of the theory to date, especially those undertaken by Farley and Ring, quite debatable.[10]

5. The model implies a definite causal priority among constructs. It has

[7]Farley, Howard, and Ring, *Consumer Behavior Theory*.

[8]Morris B. Holbrook, "A Synthesis of the Empirical Studies," in Farley, Howard, and Ring, *Consumer Behavior Theory*, 250.

[9]John U. Farley and Donald R. Lehman, "An Overview of Empirical Applications of Buyer Behavior System Models," in William D. Perreault (ed.), *Advances in Consumer Research*, vol. 4 (Atlanta: Association for Consumer Research, 1977), 340.

[10]See James Taylor and Jonathan Gutman, "A Reinterpretation of Farley and Ring's Test of the Howard-Sheth Model of Buyer Behavior," in Scott Ward and Peter Wright (eds.), *Advances in Consumer Research*, vol. 1 (Urbana, Ill.: Association for Consumer Research, 1974), 436-446.

proved to be nearly impossible to design experiments that control all exogenous factors and allow for causal priority to emerge.

6. Some of the relationships between variables may be nonlinear rather than linear as hypothesized, but there are real difficulties in assessing nonlinearity.

THE HOWARD MODEL

John Howard has revised the original Howard-Sheth model even further in an influential volume published in 1977 entitled *Consumer Behavior: Application of Theory*.[11] Really he has three different models ranging from his conceptualization of extended problem-solving to be examined here down to routinized buying behavior. His thinking tacitly reflects a high-involvement orientation, however, in that cognitive processes always are assumed to precede behavior rather than follow it as low-involvement theory explicitly postulates. In that sense, all of the consumer behavior models appearing in the literature to date[12] (including the first three versions of the EKB) model have a distinct commonality which means that they do not account for a large proportion of behavior which does not have an explicit decision process.[13] This was remedied, of course, in this book.

It has been difficult for the authors to find a complete statement of a model in Howard's 1977 volume, and he has not stated it in quantifiable terms *per se*. Therefore, the pictorial description in Figure A.2 is somewhat incomplete but does, nevertheless, represent the essence of Howard's current thinking.

The dotted lines in Figure A.2 are designated as feedback, meaning that a variable appearing later in the process "feeds back" and affects an earlier variable in a functional way. In that sense Figures A.1 and A.2 are very much alike.

These functional relationships can be deduced from Figure A.2:

1. $P_y = f(I_y)$
2. $I_y = f(C_y, A_y, I^k)$
3. $A_y = f(I^k)$
4. $C_y = f(LTM, I^k)$
5. $I^k = f(LTM)$
6. $S_y = f(P_y)$
7. $F_y^E = f(O_y^s)$

[11]John A. Howard, *Consumer Behavior: Application of Theory* (New York: McGraw-Hill, 1977).

[12]Frequent reference has been made to James R. Bettman throughout this book, and he includes a simplified flow chart model in his text entitled *An Information Processing Theory of Consumer Choice* (Reading, Mass.: Addison-Wesley, 1979). Also see Francesco M. Nicosia, *Consumer Decision Processes: Marketing and Advertising Implications* (Englewood Cliffs, N. J.: Prentice-Hall, 1966); and Alan R. Andreason, "Attitudes and Customer Behavior: A Decision Model," in Lee E. Preston (ed.), *New Research in Marketing* (Berkeley, Calif.: Institute of Business and Economic Research, University of California, 1965), 1-16.

[13]For a clear perspective on this point see Richard W. Olshavsky and Donald H. Granbois, "Consumer Decision-Making—Fact or Fiction?" *Journal of Consumer Research*, vol. 6 (September 1979), 93-100.

Figure A.2
The Howard Model

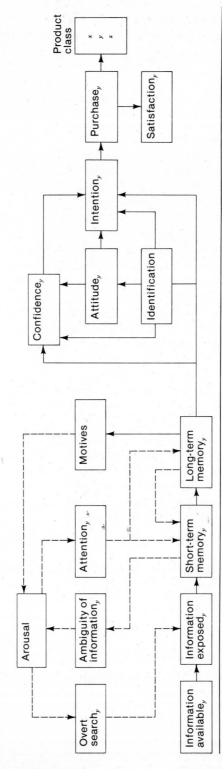

Source: Reproduced by special permission from John A. Howard, *Consumer Behavior: Application of Theory* (New York: McGraw-Hill, 1977), 133. It has been modified slightly to introduce a few linkages between variables appearing elsewhere in his volume.

$$8. \ A_y^n, O_y^s \ = f\,(A^M)$$
$$9. \ A^M \ = f\,(M, I_y^A)$$
$$10. \ PC \ = f\,(P_y)$$
$$11. \ M \ = f\,(LTM)$$

where the symbols are defined as follows, all terms referring this time to brand y:[14]

P_y = (purchase the point at which the consumer has paid for a product or made a financial commitment to do so)

I_y = intention (a cognitive state reflecting the consumer's plan to buy a specified number of units of a particular product or brand in a specified time period)

A_y = attitude (a cognitive state reflecting on a number of dimensions the extent to which the buyer expects the brand or product to yield satisfaction if purchased)

C_y = confidence (the degree of certainty that a consumer subjectively experiences with respect to satisfaction expected if a brand is purchased)

I^k = identification (a cognitive state of the consumer reflecting the extent to which the consumer has sufficient knowledge to exhibit well-defined criteria for recognizing, not evaluating, a particular brand)

S_y = satisfaction (the consumer's mental state of being adequately or inadequately rewarded for sacrifice in product purchase)

F_Y^E = information exposed (external information with which the consumer's sense organs have come into contact)

A_y^n = attention (the active selection of and emphasis on a particular component of a complex experience)

O_y^n = overt search (movement of the body to bring sense organs into contact with some aspect of the environment)

A^M = arousal (the consumer's readiness to respond, manifesting an internal state of tension)

PC = product class (the subjective meaning of a class of similar brands)

M = motive (a long-term disposition of the buyer to act)

LTM = long-term memory (permanent storage of events)

I_y^A = ambiguity of information (lack of clarity with which the content and form dimensions of environmental events are communicated)

Howard has not explicitly tested this version but does describe in useful detail how this might be done through various forms of modeling.[15]

---

[14]These terms are taken from the glossary on pp. 305-306 in Howard, *Consumer Behavior: Application.* Reprinted by permission.

[15]See Howard, *Consumer Behavior: Application,* chs. 12-15.

THE EKB MODEL

The 1968 version of this book was the first real text in consumer behavior. The authors first began to work together in 1965 at Ohio State University, and one of the initial joint assignments was to offer a course in this subject area. There were few guidelines to use, and the available literature was meager indeed. In fact, the basic text was a standard work in social psychology, augmented by various readings. The need for a text in the field was quite obvious, and this was our first major joint activity as colleagues.

When the book was revised for the first time, the authors had the benefit of the Nicosia model (which had just been published prior to the first edition), the Howard-Sheth model, and the benefits from the growing body of published research in this field. Therefore, the model was reshaped to bring about greater consistency with the changes in the state of the art. The primary purpose still was pedagogical, with the result that there was no explicit attempt made to specify quantifiable functional relationships. Although these could have been easily derived from the text itself, it never was our expectation that the model would be tested in the same manner as the Columbia group has done with the Howard model.

The present version is familiar to the reader by now, but it is depicted once again in Figure A.3 for ease of reference. This fourth revision had several distinct purposes:

1. To highlight more clearly the interrelationship between stages in the decision process and the various endogenous and exogenous variables.

2. To clarify the relationship between attitudes and behavior to reflect the contributions of the Fishbein extended model. Beliefs and intentions were introduced as explicit variables for the first time as was normative compliance.

3. To define the variables with greater precision and to specify functional relationships to permit empirical testing.

Formal Statement of the Model

To permit comparison with the two previously discussed models, a series of equations and variable definitions are presented, following where possible similar notational styles. The formal statement is as follows:

1. $C_x = f(I_x, \underline{UC})$
2. $I_x = f(A_x, NC_x)$
3. $A_x = f(B_x)$
4. $NC_x = f(\underline{L}, \underline{SI_x})$
5. $B_x = f(LTM, EC, S_x)$
6. $EC = f(LTM, M_o)$
7. $M_o = f(L)$
8. $E_x = f(S_x^{PC}, St_x, \underline{MU})$
9. $At_x = f(E_x, LTM, PR)$
10. $C_x^o = f(At_x, LTM)$
11. $YA_x = f(C_x^o, LTM)$

Figure A.3
The EKB Model

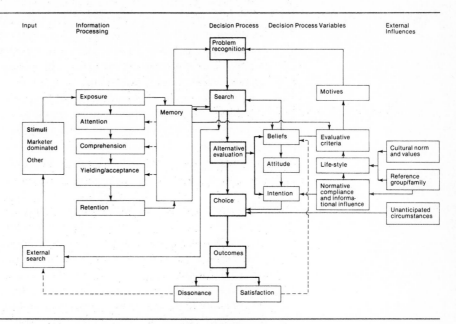

12. $R_x = f(YA_x)$
13. $S_x^{PC} = f(PR, B_x)$
14. $PR = f(LTM, M_o)$
15. $D_x, S_x = f(C_x)$
16. $S_x^{POC} = f(D_x)$

where the terms are defined as follows, all referring to brand x (underlined variables are considered to be *exogenous*):

C_x = choice (selection and purchase of an alternative)

I_x = intention (the subjective probability that a specified alternative will be chosen)

$\underline{UC}$ = unanticipated circumstances (an unexpected change in status of income levels, available alternatives, time pressure, social and organizational setting, and other environmental influences at the time of choice)

A_x = attitude toward the act of purchasing the brand (a learned predisposition to respond consistently in a favorable or unfavorable manner with respect to purchase and use of a given alternative)

NC_x = normative compliance (the outcome of the existence of perceived social influence on the choice of alternative plus a motivation to comply with that influence)

B_x = belief regarding the brand (stored information, which links a given alternative to specified evaluative criteria)

L = personality and life style (the pattern of enduring traits, activities, interests, and opinions that determine general behavior and thereby make an individual distinctive in comparison with others)

$\underline{SI_x}$ = social influence (the outcome of any interacting aggregation of people exerting an influence on an individual's selection and choice of a given alternative)

EC = evaluative criteria (desired outcomes from choice or use of an alternative expressed in the form of the attributes or specifications used to compare various alternatives)

LTM = long term memory (information and experience stored in memory with respect to the product class and a given alternative)

R_x = retention (storage of a stimulus input in long term memory)

YA_x = yielding/acceptance (acceptance of a stimulus input into long term memory, often accompanied by a change in beliefs, attitudes, or intentions)

C_x^o = comprehension (the outcome of information processing whereby the stimulus as admitted into memory conveys the same information as the stimulus itself viewed externally and objectively)

At_x = attention (the active processing of exposed information stimuli with respect to a given alternative such that a conscious impression is made)

M_o = motive (an enduring predisposition to strive to attain specified goals, containing both an arousing and a directing dimension)

E_x = exposure (physical proximity to stimulus inputs with respect to a given alternative such that the individual has direct opportunity for one or more senses to be activated)

S_x^{POC} = postchoice search (a search for information following purchase to confirm the wisdom of the choice)

PR = problem recognition (a perceived difference between the ideal state of affairs and the actual situation sufficient to arouse and activate the decision process)

ST_x = stimuli (information available with respect to a given alternative)

MU = media usage (the individual's habits and preferences with respect to media usage)

S_x = satisfaction (an evaluation that the chosen alternative is consistent with prior beliefs with respect to that alternative)

D_x = dissonance (postchoice doubt motivated by awareness that one alternative was chosen and the existence of beliefs that unchosen alternatives also have desirable attributes)

S_x^{POC} = postchoice search (a search for information following purchase to confirm the wisdom of the choice)

Comparison of the Models

Space does not permit comparison of these three models, variable by variable and equation by equation. But a few general comments are in order.

First, the EKB model is unique in highlighting the decision process and explicitly including the proven relationships of the Fishbein behavioral intentions model under alternative evaluation. Neither of the other options includes normative compliance, for example, and the relationships between evaluative criteria, beliefs, attitudes, intention, and behavior are not as focused. There are many similarities, however, in that all three hypothesize a hierarchy of effects in which a change in attitude leads to corresponding changes in intention and behavior, all things being equal.

EKB and Howard share a general agreement on the functioning of memory. EKB, however, goes into far more detail on specifying the steps which occur between the stages of exposure and retention. This is consistent with the current focus in consumer behavior on information processing.

Stimulus ambiguity is a term not used in the EKB model. It is defined as perceived uncertainty and lack of meaningful information received from the environment. Its definition in the empirical studies undertaken by the Columbia group is a curious one indeed: "confidence in radio and television as sources of information about the product."[16] These are two *very* different phenomena. In fact, the present authors do not think that stimulus ambiguity can be operationalized in any meaningful way and thus have concluded that it adds little to the understanding of decision processes.

Finally, confidence in ability to judge the product has not been included in the EKB formulation. The reason is that we do not feel it has received empirical confirmation in studies to date, although this fact could be argued.[17] Whatever one's evaluation might be at this stage, further research is needed to resolve the issue.

A CONCLUDING WORD

Let's refer to the original justification for model building—to encompass relevant variables, specify relationships, and attempt to explain a process. Models are an absolute necessity, and the lack of definitive empirical verification does not invalidate them if the constructs and hypotheses, taken by themselves, are consistent with present knowledge of the behavior process. The heuristic value, in itself, warrants the whole effort.

It is fallacious to ask which of the models reviewed in this chapter is *best.* Probably the most rigorous test is provided by the *law of parsimony,* which requires an explanation of a phenomenon of human behavior with a minimum of assumptions and a maximum of conceptual precision. Any model will fall short of this standard given present knowledge of the subject and the problems encountered in conceptualization and measurement. Certainly the height of absurdity would be to claim that anyone presently has or will have *the* model of consumer behavior. A

[16]Donald R. Lehmann, et al., "Some Empirical Contributions to Buyer Behavior Theory," *Journal of Consumer Research,* vol. 1 (December 1974), 44.

[17]Certainly the correlations tend to be quite low. See, for example, Lehmann et al., "Some Empirical Contributions." Howard, however, argues differently. See John A. Howard, "Confidence as a Validated Construct," in Jagdish N. Sheth (ed.), *Models of Buyer Behavior: Conceptual, Quantitative & Empirical* (New York: Harper & Row, 1974), 160-168.

model to be useful will change as knowledge changes. Therefore, one should expect fairly substantial modifications over time.

So, which model should the serious scholar use? This answer, in the final analysis, probably is more a matter of individual taste and preference than anything else given the high degree of similarity between the leading contenders.

NAME INDEX

Wynne, Lyman C., 250 n.26

Yaltch, Richard F., 557
Young, F. W., 426 n.59
Young, Shirley, 433 n.83

Yovovich, B. G., 321 n.2

Zajonc, R., 484, 549
Zaltman, Gerald, 15, 17 n.20, 49 n.3, 382, 674 n.47

Zimbardo, P., 468 n.10
Zimmer, Al, 289 n.96
Zimmerman, Ekkaut, 124 n.47
Zins, Michael A., 192 n.9, 423 nn.44, 49; 424 n.51

Zoerner, Cyril E., Jr., 90 n.34
Zuckerman, M., 344 n.116
Zybtniewski, Jo-Anne, 343 n.106; 524 n.45; 526 nn.62, 64; 529 nn.78, 79; 531 n.91; 532 n.96

SUBJECT INDEX